WOLVERHAMPTON WARRIORS

The Town's Battalions in the Great War

This book is dedicated to the men of the 1/6th and 2/6th Battalions The South Staffordshire Regiment who fought in the Great War 1914 – 1919.

A Bright Pen Book

Copyright © Roy C. Evans 2010

Cover design by Roy C. Evans ©

All rights reserved. No part of this publication may be reproduced, stored in a retrieval system, or transmitted in any form or by any means, electronic, mechanical, photocopy, recording or otherwise, without prior written permission of the copyright owner. Nor can it be circulated in any form of binding or cover other than that in which it is published and without similar condition including this condition being imposed on a subsequent purchaser.

British Library Cataloguing in Publication Data.
A catalogue record for this book is available from the British Library.

ISBN 978-07552-1284-2

Authors OnLine Ltd
19 The Cinques
Gamlingay, Sandy
Bedfordshire SG19 3NU
England

This book is also available in e-book format, details of which are available at www.authorsonline.co.uk

Contents	Page No.
Notes by the Author	6
1914	7
1915	25
1916	71
1917	99
1918	113
The Fallen	134

Maps	Page No.
Trench Lines - Christmas 1914	15
Ypres – Wulverghen sector	45
British Trenches at Hill 60 in 1915	46
Area around Loos	52
Loos Battlefield 1915	54
Dublin 1916	76
Somme Battlefield 1916	82
Attack on Gommecourt	83
The Kaiserschlacht	120
Cambrai – St. Quentin Area	123

NOTES BY THE AUTHOR

This is not a book written for the expert in military history although I trust that they will find it of interest, my primary objective in writing this book is to bring to the general public an awareness of the part played by the battalions raised initially from men of the (then) town of Wolverhampton in the Great War of 1914 – 1919.

The 1924 history was written by a committee of officers who served with the Battalions in the war and as with so many similar works, it appears to have been written by those who were there for others who were also there, and assumes a certain amount of 'inside' knowledge on the part of the reader. In writing this book I have endeavoured to redress this issue, to give an insight into the lives of the men both in and out of the trenches, and to describe the major battles in which they fought. I have tried to put their actions into context by outlining events taking place around them and on the occasions of major battles, have contrasted events taking place on the front line with an event back home.

The information contained within these pages comes from a variety of primary and secondary sources. The principle sources of primary information have been the war diaries of the two battalions and these have been supplemented by records taken from the Divisional and Battalion histories, as well as from various other sources. I have not intended this to be an academic volume and so have chosen not to fully reference information, only the sources of direct quotations are given. The spellings of place names used in the book are those in use during the war, in cases where these have subsequently been changed from French to Flemish the modern spelling is shown in brackets.

My thanks go to Express and Star Ltd. for permission to reproduce material from their newspapers of the time, to the staff of the Staffordshire Regiment Museum for making their archive material available for my research and for permission to reproduce photographs from their collection, and to Stuart Briscoe, Doug Lewis and John Pearson for their help and encouragement during the writing of this book.

<u>1914</u>

"We are beginning to collaborate with the English, they are real gentlemen, here as everywhere, and I think that we shall be able to do a good job with them and be home by Christmas"
(General Maxime Weygand, French Army).

THE EARLY DAYS

The men who marched away from Wolverhampton so many years ago to play their part in the Great War were almost a different breed from their counterparts of today, the society in which they lived was far removed from that which we now experience and both have now gone forever. The average man of those days would have received a basic education but little more and would be far more used to manual labour and hardship than most men of today, society then was far more class conscious, people 'knew their place' and were deferential to their 'superiors'. Religion played a much greater role in life in those far off days; patriotism and loyalty to King and Country were rarely doubted. Private cars were then only for the well-to-do, most people had to rely on public transport, hence travelling more than a few miles was a major event; few of the working classes had ever been abroad. Such was the world inhabited by the men who went to war in 1914.

One of those men was my maternal grandfather Christopher Warner who although not a member of the 1/6th Battalion the South Staffordshire Regiment (he initially joined the 2nd Battalion before being transferred to the 7th Battalion Norfolk Regiment) would have experienced the same terrible conditions, the same horrors and the same traumas as any other man involved in that war. I remember him as a gentle, caring person who although able to quote chapter and verse from the bible, which presumably meant that he had a strong Christian upbringing, never as I recall attended church during the fifteen years that I knew him, something which I later attributed to things that he had seen and done when fighting for King and Country, things so unspeakable that I never once heard him mention the war. Today we would recognise this condition as post-traumatic stress disorder but in those far off days it was just accepted.

The 1/6th Battalion of the South Staffordshire Regiment existed before the war as the 3rd Volunteer Battalion, part of the Territorial Force formed in 1908 for the defence of the realm, each man had a contract limiting him to 'home' defence. As 'part-time' soldiers they were called upon to undertake regular military training and in August 1914 were taking part in a two-week annual camp at St. Asaph, but scarcely had the Battalion arrived there before they were ordered to return to Wolverhampton, the Great War had begun.

The Battalion Headquarters in Stafford Street, Wolverhampton
(Private Collection)

The men of the 1/6th South Staffords would have much training to do before they could play their part, but elsewhere their destiny was being shaped by others.

THE SCENE IS SET
On Monday 3rd August 1914 the invasion of Belgium began when 53 Divisions, three-quarters of the German army at that time, were

engaged in the assault and at first everything went well for the attackers, by the middle of August the Belgian stronghold of Liege had fallen, they were sweeping all before them, bearing down on Brussels. The Kaiser had said that they would be home before the leaves fall. Then they came up against the British.

Historically wars had been characterised by movement, cavalry charges forcing their way into the enemy ranks and infantry following up to consolidate positions gained, and so it was when the Germans forced their way through Belgium in August 1914. The Germans were following a plan conceived years before by Graf Alfred von Schliefen who had been Chief of the Imperial German General Staff from 1891 to 1906. Following the rapid recovery of the French army after the Franco-Prussian war the 'Schliefen' plan was intended to sweep like a scythe through Belgium and across northern France, bypassing the French system of fortresses, and to capture Paris from the north. The British Expeditionary Force (BEF) that left England in August 1914 numbered around 100,000 men, some 30,000 regular soldiers and 70,000 Reservists; they were professional soldiers led by Sir John French who wanted to adopt a cautious approach until he would be able to link-up with the French army.

THE FIRST CASUALTY
Private John Parr of the 4th Battalion, the Middlesex Regiment was the first British man killed in action in the Great War. Private Parr's Battalion, had shipped to France at the start of the war and had taken up positions near the Belgian village of Bettignies, on the Mons canal. Parr was a reconnaissance cyclist - riding ahead to uncover information and then returning with all possible speed to update his commanding officer.

Born in 1898 in Church End, North Finchley, Parr lived most of his life at 52, Lodge Lane as the youngest son of Edward and Alice Parr. After leaving school he took a job as a golf caddie but like many other young men of the time he was attracted to the army as potentially a better way of life and one where he would at least get two square meals a day and a chance to see the world. When he joined up with the Middlesex Regiment he almost certainly overstated his age in order to meet the minimum age requirement.

On August 21st, Parr and another cyclist were sent to the village of Obourg just north east of Mons, with a mission to locate the enemy. It is believed that they encountered a cavalry patrol from the German First Army, and that Parr remained to hold off the enemy whilst his companion returned to report. Private Parr was killed in the ensuing rifle fire and was buried in St. Symphorian Military Cemetery, Mons. He was just 16 years old.

The grave of Private John Parr
(Private Collection)

CONFRONTATION
On the following day French deployed his men across a 25 mile front near to Mons where he gave orders that they should make a stand by the canal there. The BEF was heavily outnumbered, the Germans having twice as many men and artillery pieces in that area, although French was not yet to know of this but neither for that matter did the Germans under their Commander Kluck know of the presence of the British in numbers until they engaged them that day.

Such was the accuracy and speed of fire from the British infantry with their Lee-Enfield rifles (up to 15 rounds per minute) that the Germans were convinced they were facing British machine-guns. Unable to stem the German tide for more than a day the British continued to fall-back but although the BEF may have been referred to by the Kaiser as "a contemptible little army", Kluck, when writing in his memoirs of his experiences of the BEF at the Battle of Mons, described them as "an incomparable army".

THE ANGELS OF MONS
Back in England rumours began to spread that a miracle had happened during the B.E.F's first engagement with the German army. The theme of the story was how through some miracle the outnumbered British Expeditionary Force was rescued when fighting at Mons. The story went that the troops were rescued from the oncoming German army by "a heavenly host of Agincourt Bowmen led by St. George, who confronted the Germans and sent them fleeing in terror."

The 'miracle' which became known as the Angels of Mons allegedly began its existence in a book entitled "The Bowmen". This was a totally fictional story written by an American Arthur Madchen and which appeared in London's Evening Standard. The story may have remained just that - a story, but soon afterwards newspapers were full of reports of British soldiers eager to corroborate the story by stating that the incident actually happened. The author subsequently attempted to convince the men that it was in fact only a story.

Eventually the reports were dismissed as pure fantasy, although the publicity surrounding the book 'The Bowmen' helped it on its way to becoming a best seller. 'The Angels of Mons' affair was soon discounted but in 1990 in the booklet 'Bowmen and Angels' Kevin McClure revealed that there was more evidence worthy of investigation. Further examination of the material revealed two distinct camps, with those stories about Bowmen which could be linked to the book, and those about angels which distinctly preceded it. McClure also discovered reports from French soldiers who claimed that Joan of Arc and St. Michael materialized before them thus aiding their escape from German troops. Both British and French troops spoke of a mysterious figure dubbed 'the comrade in white'. This figure believed by some to be Jesus was said to be shielding the men from close range bullets and healing the wounded. The conclusion drawn by McClure was that the affair was after all a genuine mystery.

THE RETREAT CONTINUES
After Mons both the Allied and German troops were moving at impressive speeds with some units marching more than twenty miles in a day. The next confrontation took place around the small French town of Le Cateau, lying in the valley of the River Selle and surrounded on all sides by open, cultivated countryside. Here on 26th August the BEF was again forced to stand and fight against German troops who were now hard on their heels.

The British front line ran along the road between Le Câteau and Cambrai. During the morning the British were able to hold their own, as at Mons their fast and accurate rifle fire inflicted heavy losses on the advancing Germans, but when German reinforcements joined the battle the British came very close to being outflanked at both ends of their line, and yet more Germans were approaching from the direction of Cambrai.

The BEF was close to defeat at this time but the threatened envelopment was prevented by the arrival of General Sordet's French Cavalry on the British left. During the night of the 26th the BEF was able to slip away, continuing their retreat south towards Paris and the River Marne. The British had suffered more casualties at Le Cateau than in any battle since Waterloo – 8,077 men and 38 guns. The fighting at Le Cateau was to be the last of the old style 'one day' battles.

Although the Battles of Mons and Le Cateau had been small conflicts in view of what was to come, indeed smaller than some of the engagements in the Boer War, there is no doubt that the early reverses had begun to cause concern. The heavy losses at Le Cateau and at Mons had seriously demoralised Field-Marshal Sir John French who for most of the period between Le Cateau and the first battle of the Marne was convinced that the BEF would need to be withdrawn from the line to recover, but this had been forbidden by Field Marshall Lord Kitchener who ordered that the BEF should not separate itself from the French army.

As the German advance took them ever closer to Paris, the capital got itself ready for a siege and the French government decamped for the safety of Bordeaux. The French army had now been on the retreat for almost two weeks and had reached a position south of the River Marne; here there were doubts about their continued ability to resist the advancing Germans for much longer.

THE BATTLE OF THE MARNE
Joffre decided that the best form of defence was attack and on 6th September 150,000 French soldiers attacked the right flank of the German army in what was to be the first major battle of the Western Front. The Germans had to counter this attack and in consequence a significant split, a gap of about 27 miles, was opened between the main German attack against Paris and their flank that could not advance past the French attack.
This gap was quickly exploited by the British and French armies but even so the allies still faced probable defeat by the greater force of Germans until some 6,000 French reservists were transported out of the capital and onto the battlefields in commandeered taxi cabs!

A severe disadvantage caused to the Germans by having such a major distance between their attacking forces was that communication between the two factions became almost impossible. The German Chief of Staff, von Moltke, feared that the

Allies, rather than simply driving a gap between two of his armies, were in a position whereby they could not only halt the German advance but defeat the German armies involved in the attack on Paris. Because of this communication breakdown, on September 9th von Moltke ordered his armies to retreat and they withdrew to an area near the River Aisne where they halted and began to dig trenches.

The Schlieffen Plan had been a plan of attack that did not cater for retreat; therefore the German High Command had not planned for anything like what might happen if the French fought back. Hence, when the German army had retreated forty miles from the Marne, it had no other plan than to dig in and wait for the advancing Allied army.

If the Battle of the Marne was very costly in terms of casualties, in fact, it was merely a precursor of what was to come. Some 250,000 French soldiers were lost and the Germans suffered about the same casualties. The B.E.F. lost just fewer than 13,000 men. Paris was saved and the German's expected outcome of the Schlieffen Plan had faltered; now years of near static trench warfare were to dominate the Western Front.

TRENCH WARFARE
Each side began trying to outflank the other, only to be thwarted time and again until eventually there was no more opportunity for further outflanking manoeuvres, the trenches had reached the coast near the Belgian town of Neiuport to the north and the Swiss border to the south. The trenches now ran for a distance of 400 miles.

Realising that their plan to capture Paris could go no further for the time-being the Germans made the decision to consolidate their gains on what would become known as 'the Western Front' and to concentrate their efforts into beating the Russians in the east and then having achieved victory there, would concentrate all their forces on the Western Front. To this end they took the view that "What we have we hold, if you want it back, come and take it" and strategically withdrew to higher ground where they constructed substantial trenches fronted by masses of barbed wire entanglements, often hundreds of yards deep in front of them. In some cases the second and third lines of defence were up to three miles behind the front-line, making it almost impossible for the allies to break through with a single attack.

The Allied powers, having repelled the invasion were now on the offensive and were trying to reclaim the territory lost to the invaders, so there was little point in them creating such semi-permanent structures, they expected soon be moving forwards and capturing the enemy positions and would have no further use for their own trenches. That at least was the theory, the practise was tragically different. The strategy for the war had now been set by both sides; the war of movement had become a static war.

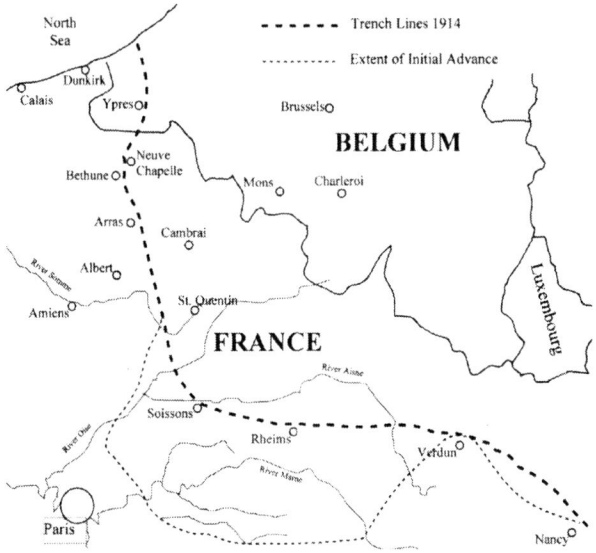

The Position of the Trench Lines - Christmas 1914

The early Allied trenches such as those occupied by the South Staffords at Wulverghem, were little more than unconnected, modified shell holes; later ones, when the Allies realised that there would be no quick victory, were rather more sophisticated affairs with communication systems and substantial defences but still much less substantial than were the German ones.

A NEW TYPE OF WARFARE
Two late 19th century American inventions, barbed wire and the machine-gun, were to change the way in which wars were fought. Joseph Glidden had patented his version of barbed wire in November 1874; his design incorporated a method of locking the barbs in place by trapping them between two twisted strands of wire and had invented the machinery to mass-produce the barbed wire. Originally intended for use as a cheap means of fencing on cattle ranches, it was adopted and modified by both sides in the Great War. The barbed wire used by both sides was much more substantial than the domestic type available today, that used by the Germans especially so. Barbed wire entanglements eventually spanned the whole of the Western Front presenting not only an impenetrable barrier for horses but greatly hindering attacking forces.

Hiram Maxim had invented the machine-gun in 1883 and by 1914 had already made a fortune selling them to armies around the world. The British army used models manufactured by Vickers and Lewis and whereas a skilled man with a rifle could fire up to 15 rounds a minute, at the start of the war a machine gun could fire 450. The proliferation of machine-guns, mortars and artillery made many soldiers little more than the servants of machinery in the age of industrialised war.

TRAINING FOR WAR
We have already seen that many of the original men of the 1/6th South Staffs were members of the pre-war territorial army but such was the degree of patriotic fervour that men flocked in their hundreds of thousands to enlist and 'do their bit'. The popular conception that the war would be over by Christmas encouraged men across Britain, not wanting to miss the chance to play their patriotic part, to enlist at their earliest opportunity and by the end of 1914 over a million men had signed-up for service. In fact four Christmases were to pass before peace would breakout once more.

THE JOURNEY BEGINS
The 5th day of August 1914 was gloriously fine and warm as the men of the 1/6th Battalion, South Staffordshire Regiment were paraded on the market square in Wolverhampton before leaving on

the 11th in full marching order amidst scenes of great enthusiasm but mixed emotions.

The 1/6th South Staffordshire Regiment parade in the Market Square, Wolverhampton in 1914.
(Private Collection)

On the 8th of the month the Mayor of Wolverhampton received the following letter:-

Penn Hall
8th November 1914

Dear Mr Mayor,
24 hours leave from my duties – and possibly my last visit home before we leave – gives me the opportunity to send my sincerest congratulations to you on again being elected as Mayor of Wolverhampton. In so doing I know that I express the feelings of all of the 1125 officers and men of the Regiment which I have the honour to command, so many of whom belong to the Town and immediate district. We know the immense interest you have always taken in the Territorial Force, and the support and help in all directions which you have given them – and with our departure abroad on active service, we are confident that your work and interest will only increase.

> *I wish also to express publicly through you, my most grateful thanks to the countless friends – far too numerous for me to write to personally – who have been so generous to the various units of the Force.*
> *It will be our endeavour, in this the greatest trial the Territorial Force will ever experience, to worthily follow the example of 'French's contemptible little army.'*
>
> *I know too that you will use every effort to bring home to all classes in your district, the fact that we are engaged in a struggle for our very existence as a Nation and an Empire. The imperative need of the hour is more men – and there is no time to be lost. If the Nation really understands the situation, we can easily raise and train a force far in excess of what has already been done, and I confidently hope that a new and great Force may soon arise.*
>   *Yours sincerely*
>   *T.F. Waterhouse*
>   *Lt-Col Commanding 6th South Staffs. Regt.*

Their march was to take them for 18 miles across country and then after an overnight stop, a further 13 miles to Burton on Trent where they were billeted in the buildings of Allsop's brewery.

It was there that the men had to undergo the transition from their peacetime freedom to the rigours of martial law and here also whilst on parade where they were asked if they were prepared to volunteer for active service abroad. It was reported that, "every man who could possibly serve abroad slowly and deliberately and in the full realisation of what it may cost rather than in a moment of blind excitement, slowly and deliberately 'fell in' for foreign service."

It was at this time that the Battalion was re-organised from the existing eight company system to a four company system designated A, B, C, and D. Each company would at full strength be comprised of 227 'Other Ranks' commanded by a Major or Captain with a Captain being second-in-command. Each company was sub-divided into four Platoons, each commanded by a Lieutenant or 2nd Lieutenant and each platoon further divided into four sections consisting of 12 Privates and a Non-Commissioned Officer. In addition to these there would be a number of men filling specialist roles, Signallers, Pioneers, Drivers, Stretcher-bearers, etc.

In 1914 the British Army had a highly organised structure of which a Battalion was then the smallest tactical unit. Six Battalions would operate as a Brigade and three Brigades would operate as a Division. The 1/6th Battalion South Staffordshire Regiment would become part of the Staffordshire Brigade which in turn was a part of the North Midland Division.

A recruiting poster from September 1914
(Reproduced courtesy Express and Star Ltd.)

DIVISIONAL TRAINING

Three days after arriving at Burton the battalion was ordered to assemble with other members of the North Midland Division and to this end entrained at Burton station en route for Chilton Green near Luton. It was during their time at Luton that the each man tore-up his 'Territorial' contract and signed to agree to Foreign Service. The new structure saw Lieutenant-Colonel; T.F. Waterhouse as the commanding officer, his second in command being Major T. E. Lowe.

The Battalion also had two Chaplains at this time, Rev A. Penney MA Chaplain (3rd Class) carrying a rank similar to that of Major and the Rev A. Pratt MA Chaplain (4th Class) with the equivalent rank of Captain.

As has already been written, the 1/6th South Staffords were part of the Staffordshire Brigade, the other battalions in the Brigade were 1/5th South Staffs. (raised in Walsall), 1/5th North Staffs. (raised in Hanley) and 1/6th North Staffs. (raised in Burton-on-Trent), all of them being former Territorial Force Units. At this time therefore a Brigade would be made up of more than 4,000 men.

The Staffordshire Brigade was in turn joined by the Lincolnshire and Leicestershire Brigade and the Sherwood Forester Brigade to form the North Midland Division. There were also a number of ancillary troops attached to the Division in the form of Royal Engineers, Royal Army Medical Corps, Royal Field Artillery, Machine Gun Corps, etc, but these are beyond the scope of this book.

On 10th November, after three months of training, the battalion set off for an undisclosed destination, rumours were rife that due to some sudden emergency they were bound for Belgium but in practice after marching 20 miles to Hertford where they spent the night billeted in local schools, the following day saw them marching once again, this time to their previously secret destination of a training camp at Bishop's Stortford. After three weeks at this venue they were once more on the move, this time to Saffron Walden and it was there that their training would be completed.

Bayonet Training
(Photograph courtesy of Staffordshire Regiment Museum)

A SECOND BATTALION IS FORMED

When the men of the original Territorial Force had been asked to volunteer for service overseas there were some who were unable to do so, either because they were medically unfit for Active Service or for various other reasons. These 200 men formed the nucleus of a 2nd Line or Reserve Battalion and would help to recruit and train men to feed the senior unit with the help of two ex-regular N.C.O.s, Regimental Sergeant-Major Allen and Sergeant-Major Leek. The grounds of Himley Hall, some six miles out of the town, were used for training the new detachment and by the start of November 1914 some 600 men were on the strength of the new Battalion, now known as the 2/6th Battalion The South Staffordshire Regiment, commanded by Major H. Twentyman,

During this period, some time had been spent working on the defences of London, initially at Braintree and subsequently at Epping.

A very youthful looking Officer, of the 2/6th Battalion
(Private Collection)

CHRISTMAS FESTIVITIES

Explicit written orders were received on October 13th that the 1/6th Battalion was to sail "forthwith" and as many of the men as possible were given special 48 hour leave passes and once again enjoyed the comforts of civilian life, returning to camp only to find that the order had been countermanded. Several more such home leaves were granted over the next few weeks but still the men remained in England.

An amusing incident occurred whilst preparations were being made for the men's Christmas dinner, when promised turkeys sent from Wolverhampton failed to be delivered at the appointed time. Near panic ensured in the cookhouse and the Quartermaster was despatched to Smithfield market to obtain replacements, only to be met when his train arrived back at Saffron Waldon by the Wolverhampton birds, which had arrived late.

The men dined really well that Christmas, a Christmas that for far too many of them would prove to be their last.

1915

"... and I shall watch the future career of the 6th South Staffords with the greatest interest and sympathy. Where's my car?"
(The conclusion of a farewell address by a very senior Staff Officer prior to the 1/6th South Staffords leaving Hill 60)

THE 2/6th IN TRAINING

Although the recruits were fired with an initial enthusiastic patriotism, their equipment and uniforms were slow to arrive and both drill and exercises on nearby Highgate Common were carried out by substituting broomsticks for guns. On the 2nd of February 1915 the 2/6th Battalion of the South Staffordshire Regiment were assembled at Harpenden as a part of the 176th Brigade, 59th Division.

THE 1/6th OFF TO WAR

When in mid-February 1915 the entire 46th Division assembled at Hallingbury Park to be inspected by H.M. King George, it was generally taken as a sign that they would soon be sent overseas. The men's suspicions were deepened on the 25th of the same month when they were issued with new equipment, including the latest pattern rifles and it came as no surprise when on Monday 1st March 1915 they entrained at Audley End station for Southampton where on arrival, half of the battalion were billeted in the town whilst the other half marched to a rest camp nearby.

3.30pm on Tuesday 2nd March saw half of the battalion board the S.S. Jupiter and four and a half hours later set off for Le Harve where they would arrive early the following morning, to be joined two days later by the second half of the battalion. After being issued with warm clothing in the form of rather foul smelling goatskin coats, they found themselves at five the next morning making preparations to board a train of cattle trucks, bound for the village of Noordpeene via Rouen and Calais.

The trip was not comfortable one, thirty-seven men occupied each truck with only two bales of straw for seating. Two days after arriving at Noordpeene they marched the fifteen miles to Borre and the following day another fifteen miles to Sailly where they were billeted at Rue de la Lys. The next nine days were a mixture of training and marching, their route taking them through Steent-Je, and Fletre before they arrived at Armentieres on Saturday 20th March.

The 1/6th South Staffordshire Regiment soon after arriving in France.
(Photograph courtesy of Staffordshire Regiment Museum)

An unknown Private wrote of the trip;

> "We, our portion of the 6th, reached Southampton on Monday morning and marched straight off to 'The Common' where we were encamped for the night, and after several spells of 'leave' which enabled us to have a good look round the town, etc., we went on board our ship on Tuesday afternoon. It was not an ocean-going liner as I had expected to find it, but simply a swift Cross-Channel steamer. We left the docks at about eight in the evening, and, after spending about half an hour on deck, just to have a look at 'Old England' most of us went down below. For myself, I went off to sleep, and did not wake till we got to our destination, so you see that fears of submarines or of any damage the Germans could do to us when going across did not affect us in the least, and only a very few were sea-sick.
> On landing we were taken to an enormous store house, as big as the Drill Hall in Wolverhampton, where our company had biscuits – hard as bricks – and tinned beef, served out. Each man also received a fur coat, which gave us the appearance of a lot of motor-drivers. We were then marched to the railway station and entrained in what looked like cattle trucks, but were really troop trains, about 35 men in each 'compartment'. We had a good supply of clean straw and the trucks had a covering to them, so with our fur coats and overcoats we kept fairly warm. One inconvenience was that in order to view the scenery as we went along we had to stand up, as there were no seats, and so gaze through the iron bars at the 'windows'. Our journey altogether, including several long waits, lasted 24 hours so we were not sorry to see the last of the train. As this was my first view of 'Foreign Parts' I stood up until I was too tired to stand any longer, and though it was all new to me, it cannot be said that after all it was worth the trouble.
> But this is the wrong time of year; in summer it is, no doubt, a very pleasant country."

It must have been during these marches that the men began to get an idea of the realities of the theatre of war, as they approached the areas immediately behind the battle zone they became involved in the general melee that ensued from thousands of men, horses, and motor vehicles all trying to reach their different destinations, they could hear the noise and see the muzzle flashes from the large calibre guns of both sides, they passed shelled buildings and saw the graves of allied soldiers, none of which would have instilled them with confidence.

One of the officers wrote;

> *"We have moved twenty miles further since my last letter and are now only two miles behind the trenches. We started to march at 11 o'clock yesterday morning and did not get here until 9.30. The roads are very narrow and frightfully muddy and altogether particularly bad for marching. Some of my men were very done. When we got to our destination we found we had no billets, as a Division which was supposed to be moving had not done so. Nearly everybody slept out of doors.*
> *I saw a church today, and it was absolutely gutted by German shell fire, no roof and not a vestige of glass. All the country around here has been fought over and there is no chance of mistaking it.*
> *The Allies have been doing awfully well lately. At least it seems to be the general idea around here. Any number of prisoners, including a German General. We move on again tomorrow somewhere I believe and have reveille at 4.30 so, as it is now nearly 9.30 p.m. I had better get to bed. It has all been quite amusing so far, but I may have quite a different tale next time I write.*
> *The Division had an officer killed in the Leicesters on Wednesday last. He was in a trench which was a bit too shallow, and got picked off by a sniper."*

Doubtless the Church Parade held that Sunday would have been well attended because the following day two of the four Companies of the 1/6th South Staffords went into the trenches for the first time.

The Wolverhampton battalion had entered the Great War, the first complete former Territorial battalion to do so.

LIFE AT THE FRONT

The two companies ('A' and 'B') of the 1/6th South Staffords that entered the trenches for the first time on 22nd of March 1915 stayed for only one day before returning to camp, having been replaced by 'C' Company. 'D' Company, were withheld due to a Scarlet Fever scare. These visits were merely training exercises intended to familiarise the men with conditions in the front line and to get them used to the idea of being under fire, but what was life like for the men in the trenches, how did they fill their time? Whatever the preconceptions of war that the men had when they enlisted, none could have imagined the reality of the situation.

TRENCH WARFARE

Wherever possible trenches were deep enough for a man to stand up straight without being seen by the enemy, this was fine in chalky soil such as that found in the Somme area but further north in Flanders much of the land had been reclaimed from the sea. There the water table was not far below the surface and trenches could quickly fill with water so sandbags would be used to build up a defensive wall on the front edge of the trench. Such walls were known as 'Breastworks'.

The Allied frontline trenches were formed in zigzags, rather than straight lines to prevent attackers from shooting straight down the trench, and to help to reduce the effects of blasts from shells. It also meant that it was more difficult for the trench to be captured as the enemy had to fight round each corner to capture more and more of the trench.

Another method of slowing down the process of the enemy capturing the trench, were trench blocks or barbed wire doors, situated at intervals along a trench, they fitted into gaps in the sides of the trench and which when they were closed, presented almost impenetrable barriers, the attackers having to fight off the defenders whilst at the same time trying to remove the obstacles to their progress.

Common features in some trenches were 'funk-holes' recesses cut into the sides of the trench walls where possible. Usually only large enough for one or two men they did at least afford some protection from the ever present threat from shrapnel or shell fragments which frequently rained down from above.

Although their time spent in the trenches could vary widely according to the prevailing situation, typically at this time a battalion would spend four days in the frontline trenches which faced directly towards the enemy, usually between 200-800 yards away but distances of as short as 25 yards have been recorded. The space in between the front lines was known as "No Man's Land".

Behind the front line were the 'reserve trenches', also known as the 'second line' or 'support trenches', these were the second line of defence and they were used if the front line was captured by the enemy. Following a spell in the frontline a further four nights would be spent in the support line before being given a period of rest away from the lines. Often the rest periods were anything but restful, granted the men were away from immediate danger but they were frequently engaged in working on the repairing of roads, route marching and general training.

The frontline trenches were joined to the support line and beyond by a system of linking trenches known as 'communication trenches' and they ran over 1000 yards back to safety. All things going up to the frontline, such as fresh troops, water, food, mail, ammunition, etc, had to use these lines, whilst wounded soldiers went in the other direction to hospitals Casualty Clearing Stations.

THE DAILY ROUTINE
In the trenches each day was much the same as the last, nothing really changed, unless there was a raid on the enemy trenches or a major battle. Each day in both the Allied and German frontline trenches began an hour before dawn with 'Stand to' when the men would fix bayonets to their rifles and mount the fire step to guard against the possibility of a dawn attack. As a further precaution, often both sides would fire at random into the half-light of dawn to make doubly sure that they were safe. When in the trenches life,

especially during the daylight hours could become tedious in the extreme. At first light, the order "Stand down" was given and knowing that the threat of a night raid was over, the sentries could relax.

Breakfast for the troops usually consisted of, if not bacon, at least a cup of tea. The cooking in the trenches was done on small fires made of scraps of wood found usually in local ruins. The troops were rarely hungry, unless due to shell damage, the communication trenches were damaged and the ferrying of food up and down the line was temporarily prevented. Although there was usually enough food to go round, the choice was rarely varied. With breakfast over there would be inspection of the men and their equipment, especially their rifles and bayonets by either the Company or Platoon Commander. Every soldier possessed a Lee Enfield rifle and it was his duty to keep this thoroughly clean to prevent it from jamming at a vital moment.

Once this had been completed NCOs would assign daily chores to each man (except those who had been excused duty for a variety of reasons) and by mid-morning most of the troops would be at work. The routine day-to-day work consisted of repairing damage to the trench, filling sandbags, carrying supplies, repairing duckboards and trench walls, running errands, etc.

RATIONS
For their main meal the usual selection was tinned 'bully beef', a loaf of bread to be shared amongst up to 10 men, and jam, which was usually Tickler's plum and apple flavour, of which the men soon became tired. Occasionally there was an abundance of cheese, but this caused constipation and the men thought that it was a deliberate attempt to ease the problem of trench toilets. In case of an emergency there was always a supply of hard biscuits, but these were like cement and caused immense problems to men with false teeth – they had to soak the biscuits in water!

Snipers on both sides were a constant threat to those unwary enough to show their heads above the trench walls, those men coming into the line for the first time were cautioned to resist their natural inclination to peer over into No-Man's-Land. Because of this threat, daylight movement was restricted until night fell so that once the men had concluded their assigned tasks they were free to attend to more personal matters, such as the reading and writing of letters home.

THROUGH THE NIGHT
With the onset of dusk the morning ritual of stand to was repeated, again to guard against a surprise attack launched as night fell, this over, the trenches became a hive of activity, some men would be assigned sentry duty on the fire step. During the hours of darkness one in every four men of the Company would be on sentry duty at any given time as opposed to one in ten during the daylight hours. Generally men would be expected to provide sentry duty for up to two hours, any longer and there was a real risk of men falling asleep on duty - for which the penalty, at least theoretically, was death by firing squad. No member of either the $1/6^{th}$ or $2/6^{th}$ South Staffords suffered this fate.

Supply and maintenance activities would be undertaken during the night, although danger invariably accompanied these as the enemy would be alert for such movement. Men would be sent to the rear lines to fetch rations and water. In the trenches water was usually brought to the front line in petrol cans, and chloride of lime was added to kill off bacteria. The chloride of lime however, gave the water an awful taste. In winter, water was less of a problem because snow and ice could be melted, but occasionally however bodies were found frozen in the ice, and this could cause the soldiers distress.

IN AND OUT OF THE LINE
A Company would move into or out of the Front-line or Reserve trenches under the cloak of darkness, a process that could take several hours and this was considered to be a prime time for the enemy to shell the trenches since potentially there would be twice as many men in the target area. Incoming men, coming down through the communication trenches, would be weighed down with a variety of equipment which would be used during their time of

occupation, (such as shovels, picks, corrugated iron, duckboards, etc.).

Other activities that could only safely be undertaken at night were trench raids, when attempts would be made to capture one or more of the enemy in order to obtain information, and the repairing or adding to of barbed wire defences. It was quite common for patrols of each side to stumble across each other and hand-to-hand fighting would often ensue.

LICE
Every soldier was crawling with lice – in their hair, on their body, in their clothes. Lice were one of the banes of a soldier's life, breeding in the seams of their dirty clothing and causing them to itch unceasingly, even when clothing was periodically washed and deloused, lice eggs invariably remained hidden in the seams; within a few hours of the clothes being re-worn the body heat generated would cause the eggs to hatch. A regular occupation for the men in the trenches was to quickly run lighted matches along the seams of their clothing in order to drive out the lice before cracking them between finger and thumb.

It was not until 1918 that it was identified that lice caused Trench Fever, a particularly painful disease that began suddenly with severe pain, followed by high fever. Recovery - away from the trenches – could often take upto twelve weeks.

RATS
The trenches were over-run by rats, a problem that would remain for the duration of the war. Soldiers detested rats almost as much as anything else that they encountered in the trenches. Scavenging on almost anything edible, including corpses, the beasts could grow to the size of a large cat and so brazen were they that they would run over the faces of sleeping men. Men, exasperated and afraid of these rats, would attempt to rid the trenches of them by various means; shooting, bayoneting, and even by clubbing them to death.

SMELLS
After the first months of the war, in many cases the thing that a man entering the trenches for the first time would notice was the smell.

The most nauseous stench would be that of rotting flesh, men's bodies buried in shallow graves or just lying in water filled shell holes. Many of the South Stafford's casualties at Gommecourt in 1916, (of which we will read later) had to be left hanging on the barbed wire upon which they had become entangled, until the Germans withdrew from the area in 1917. Living conditions were very basic and extremely unhygienic; the latrines used in the trenches were very rudimentary, frequently being only buckets which often overflowed.

Men who had not been afforded the luxury of a bath in weeks or months would exude the pervading odour of dried sweat, the feet were generally accepted as giving off the worst odour. Trenches would also smell of creosol or chloride of lime, used to stave off the constant threat of disease and infection, added to this was the smell of cordite, the lingering odour of poison gas, rotting sandbags, stagnant mud, cigarette smoke and cooking food, yet seasoned men grew used to it although it could thoroughly overwhelm first-time visitors to the front.

Death was a constant companion to those serving in the line, even when no raid or attack was launched or defended against, in busy sectors the frequent shellfire directed by the enemy brought random death, whether their victims were lounging in a trench or lying in a dugout (many men were buried as a consequence of such large shell-bursts). It has been estimated that up to one third of Allied casualties on the Western Front were actually sustained inside rather than in front of the trenches.

RECRUITMENT CONTINUES
As early as August 1914, the War Secretary, Lord Kitchener had warned that the war could last up to four years and that a large expeditionary force would be needed to secure victory. Although an initial patriotic fervour had ensured that recruiting offices were full to overflowing in the first months of the war, over a million men were under arms by the end of 1914, at the start of 1915 fewer and fewer men were volunteering.

A common tactic to encourage recruitment was to show how patriotic some families had been. The picture below, was printed in a local newspaper was headed "SIX SONS SERVING WITH THE COLOURS" and showed the six sons of Mrs. Isaac Morgan of 48, Castle Street, Roseville, Coseley, all of whom were serving in the army.

(Reproduced courtesy Express and Star Ltd.)

Abraham was serving with the 6th South Staffords, John with the 3rd South Staffords and Harry also with the South Staffordshire Regiment but his battalion was not stated. George was serving with the Royal Field Artillery, William with the Royal Garrison Artillery whilst Isaac, who it was said had a wife and two children was reported to be "in France".

Isaac Morgan was to die of wounds on the 17th April 1916 and would be buried in the new churchyard at Christ Church, Coseley; Abraham Morgan would die on the 8th October 1918 and would be buried in Tourgeville Military Cemetery, France. The fate of the other brothers is not known.

Recruits getting 'Kitted out'
(Private Collection)

By the early spring of 1915 enlistments settled down to around 100,000 men per month but as the realities of war became apparent, numbers began to fall. In May 1915 the upper age limit for recruits was raised from 38 to 40 but still numbers were inadequate. The Recruits Committee Minute Book of the 21st April 1915 records a list of recruiting suggestions:-

1. <u>SHOP WINDOW CAMPAIGN</u>
   a. Every Tradesman to be invited to put posters in prominent places in shop window simultaneously at 10 o'clock Monday morning and throughout the week.
   b. Posters to be obtained (free) from Parliamentary Recruiting Committee.

2. SIGN POSTERS
   Small sign posters on every lamp pointing to Territorial Recruiting Office.

3. TRAMS
   The trams to be well posted inside and out and particularly on upper part of two deckers.

4. ROUTE MARCHES
   Route marches of men in khaki, VDF and VR Club, Boy Scouts, Brigades &c., Torch Lights &c.
   Wolverhampton, Heath Town & Wednesfield, Willenhall and Short Heath, Bilston & Sedgley, Darlaston, Brierley Hill.

5. 'CATCH-MY-PAL' RECRUITING
   Khaki men, three or four, to be stationed in the following thoroughfares each evening (Sunday included) from 6 to 9.30 and to persuade likely recruits.

   Darlington Street, Victoria Street, Dudley Street, Lichfield Street, Queen Square, Worcester Street, Snow Hill, Five Ways, Willenhall Market Place, Bilston Market Place, Brierley Hill Market Place.

6. OPEN AIR MEETINGS
   Meetings to be arranged by the secretaries if speakers available from the Parliamentary Recruiting Committee.

7. PICTURE PALACES AND ENTERTAINMENT HOUSES
   'The Army Film' to be obtained from Headquarters, and shown, by permission, at picture palaces; and short addresses to be given by speakers.

8. MOTOR CAR SERVICE
   Cars required for conveyance of speakers to districts where meetings are held.

9. ROLL OF HONOUR CARDS
   Cards to be displayed in houses where husbands or sons have already enlisted.

10. THE REGULAR ARMY
    Some scheme of co-operation with Regular Army Recruiting Sergeants in outlying districts is necessary or Territorials will not benefit by effort outside the Borough.

11. PLACES OF WORSHIP
    The Mayor to ask Clergy and Ministers of all denominations to mention the need for recruits from pulpits next Sunday.

12. SWEARING IN RECRUITS
    Arrangements to be made if possible for the Territorials and Regulars to provide Recruiting Officers to swear in men in the districts where they reside.

13. SPECIAL LEAFLETS OR POSTERS
    Leaflets or Posters of History and Battle Honours of the South Staffordshire Regiment to be circulated.

14. PRIZES
    Prizes to be offered to those bringing in the largest number of men who are accepted as Recruits.

On the 15th July 1915 the British government passed the National Registration Act and all men in the age range of 15 and 65 not already in military service were required to register and to give details of their employment.

The results of this registration showed that of the five million men that had registered, around one and a half million were in 'starred' (reserved) occupations, leaving three and a half million men of military age who had not volunteered. On the 16th October that year the 'Derby Scheme' was introduced by Lord Derby, the Director General of Recruiting. Under this scheme men of 18 to 40 years of age were still encouraged to enlist as before or they could attest that they would enlist if they were called upon to do so.

A famous recruiting poster from the Great War

THE WHITE FEATHER CAMPAIGN

Many people are aware of the white feather campaign, originally founded as the Order of the White Feather, in which women would try to shame men into enlisting for service. The idea for the campaign came from a man, Admiral Charles Fitzgerald R.N. (Retired) who organised some 30 women in Folkestone to hand out white feathers to any men that they saw not in uniform. This was reported in the press and quickly picked up by women across the country, soon any apparently able-bodied man not in uniform was likely to be presented with a white feather, a symbol of cowardice.

The Government used propaganda posters to encourage women to persuade their men-folk to volunteer. Some groups, such as the Suffragettes who had been in conflict with the Government prior to the war, now played an active part in encouraging recruitment by making a number of speeches in support of the war, outlining what men and women could do to help.

Not in every case was the presentation of a white feather necessarily appropriate however; so prevalent did the practice become that men who were engaged in civilian forms of war work or who had been wounded and sent home to convalesce had to be issued with badges which would prevent them being approached. One man, having been given a feather whilst riding on a tram, promptly began cleaning his pipe with it saying that pipe cleaners had been hard to come by when he was serving in the trenches.

Eventually things got out of hand, there were even claims that women and girls were using the tactic to rid themselves of unwanted boyfriends, and the scheme was abandoned. How many under-aged boys who looked big for their years were coerced into enlisting before their time?

By December 1915 the Derby Scheme had been abandoned, having only managed to recruit around 350,000 additional troops. On the evening of 27 December, Lloyd George wrote to the Prime Minister Herbert Asquith emphatically announcing his intention to resign unless the Prime Minister immediately introduced conscription for unmarried men. Asquith capitulated and on 6 January 1916 the Military Service (Compulsion for Unmarried Men) Act received its first reading in the House of Commons. Compulsory conscription was introduced with The Military Service Act of 27 January 1916.

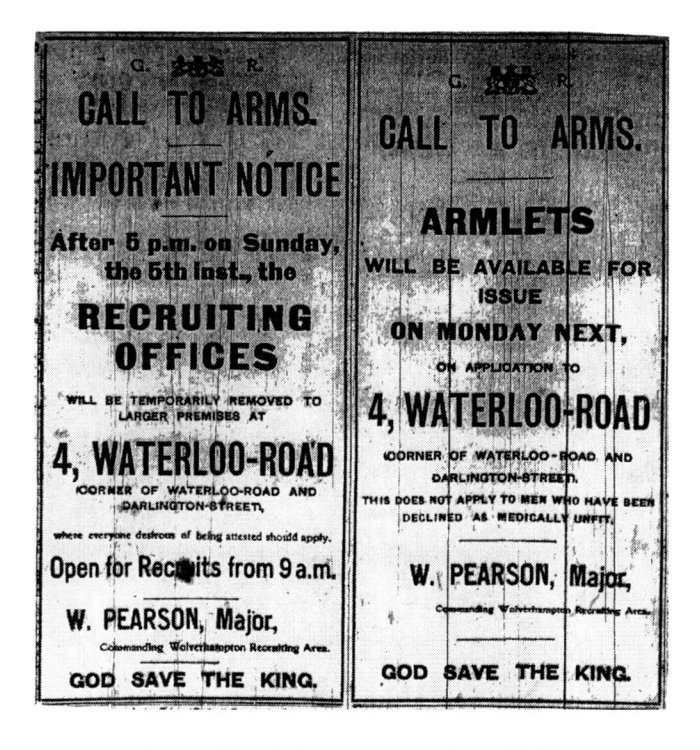

Recruiting Advertisements from 1915
(Reproduced courtesy Express and Star Ltd.)

On the 12th May 1915 the Staffordshire Brigade was re-titled the 137th (Staffordshire) Infantry Brigade and the North Midland Division became the 46th (North Midland) Division.

THE YPRES* SALIENT
The two weeks after their introduction to trench warfare were spent in training before the men once again entered the trenches, this time near the Belgian village of Wulverghem (Wulvergem), 8 miles south of Ypres (Ieper). The British position here was on a low ridge in front of the village and was considered to be a relatively quiet section of the line where inexperienced Battalions could become

acclimatised to life at the front. The trenches at this early stage of the war were relatively unsophisticated affairs, a single line of unconnected breastworks that as yet had neither second line defences nor communication trenches.

The prevailing weather conditions were hardly conducive to the well being of the men, high winds and heavy rain conspired to soak the trenches with water and mud. The South Staffords held the southern-most flank of the 2000 yard long Divisional line immediately north of the Wulverghem – Messines (Mesen) Road.

It was here on the 7th April 1915 that the first of their comrades lost his life. Private George Butler, a native of Somerset but latterly living with his parents at Britannia House, Old Heath, Heath Town, Wolverhampton, was just 20 years old when he died and was buried in Wulverghem churchyard. The Battalion war diary describes this tour of duty as "Situation quiet" even though they had encountered their first fatalities, five men died here and another seven were wounded.

The memorial to Private George Butler, Wulverghem Churchyard
(Private Collection)

Even in death George Butler could find no rest, both the church and the churchyard were destroyed by shelling during later stages of the war and his grave was obliterated. The church was rebuilt in 1925 and George is now commemorated on a special memorial in the churchyard. When the Commonwealth War Graves Commission began erecting stone grave markers, relatives of casualties could have an additional inscription added at the cost of 4d per letter. George Butler's family chose to have the following inscription; "A NOBLE AND BRAVE SON WHO DIED THAT WE MIGHT LIVE"

Private Ewart Barratt was the youngest soldier from the battalion to die during their tour of duty in the Wulverghem sector. He had joined the 6th South Staffords at Wolverhampton shortly before the outbreak of the war. The son of George and Sarah Barratt, of 91, Napier Road, Blakenhall, Wolverhampton, Ewart Barratt was reported to have been killed in action by a bullet hitting him in his side and passing through his heart. He died aged 16 on the 27th May 1915 and is buried in St Quentin Cabaret cemetery, near Wulverghem. (Photograph courtesy Express and Star Ltd.)

Private Stephen Lounds, serving with 'B' Company, was bothered that his friends and relatives were concerned about his welfare and on the 6th May 1915 wrote a letter:-

> *"Dear Lily,*
> *Just a line in answer to your most welcome letter and Woodbines. Lily, I have just heard off Albert that your mother is worrying herself to death over us but tell her it goes hard with us when we are here that they am put so much about but try and cheer her up as you know that someone has got to come and save there country and it was in our heart to join for true so tell her from me she has got two good lads who are fighting for there country and that they are in good health and hearty so I think I have said all this time.*

From your ever loving friend Stephen so don't forget to write back and tell me she is in good health and not worried about us so good night and god bless you all. Stephen x"

Private Stephen William Lounds would be killed in action in the Battle of Loos on 13th October 1915.

At Wulverghem also, 2nd Lieutenant Hugh William Bostock became the first officer of the 6th South Staffords to die in the trenches. The son of J.H. and C.S. Bostock, he had lived in Wolverhampton in his youth but later moved to London where he worked in the offices of the London and North-Western Railway. A fine chorister, he had sung with the choir of St. George's for the Diamond Jubilee of Queen Victoria. When war broke out he was superintendent of the outdoor goods department at Euston but decided that he wanted to serve with those he knew in Wolverhampton and so returned to enlist there. He was found dead by his batman after apparently being hit by a shell when in the act of entering a dug-out. 28 year old Second Lieutenant Bostock also lies in St. Quentin Cabaret cemetery where he was buried at 6.00 p.m. on the 12th June 1915. 2nd Lieutenant Bostock's family chose the inscription "PEACE PERFECT PEACE". (Photograph courtesy Express and Star Ltd.)

HILL 60

When the track of the Ypres – Comines railway was laid in the 1800's it required a cutting to be dug some three miles south-east of Ypres, the spoil from the cutting formed a mound to the side of the railway. This mound, some 260 yards long, later appeared on maps with a contour line at 60 metres, hence its wartime name of 'Hill 60'. There were two other such hills nearby, "The Caterpillar" and "The Dump".

The Germans captured Hill 60 on the 10th December 1914 and in so doing gained a vantage point that gave them excellent views across miles of countryside, particularly towards Ypres and Zillebeke, a matter of considerable military advantage. On 17th April 1915 it was recaptured by the British after they exploded five mines beneath it but they could hold it only until the 5th May of that year. Hill 60 then remained in German hands until the Battle of Messines on 7th June 1917.

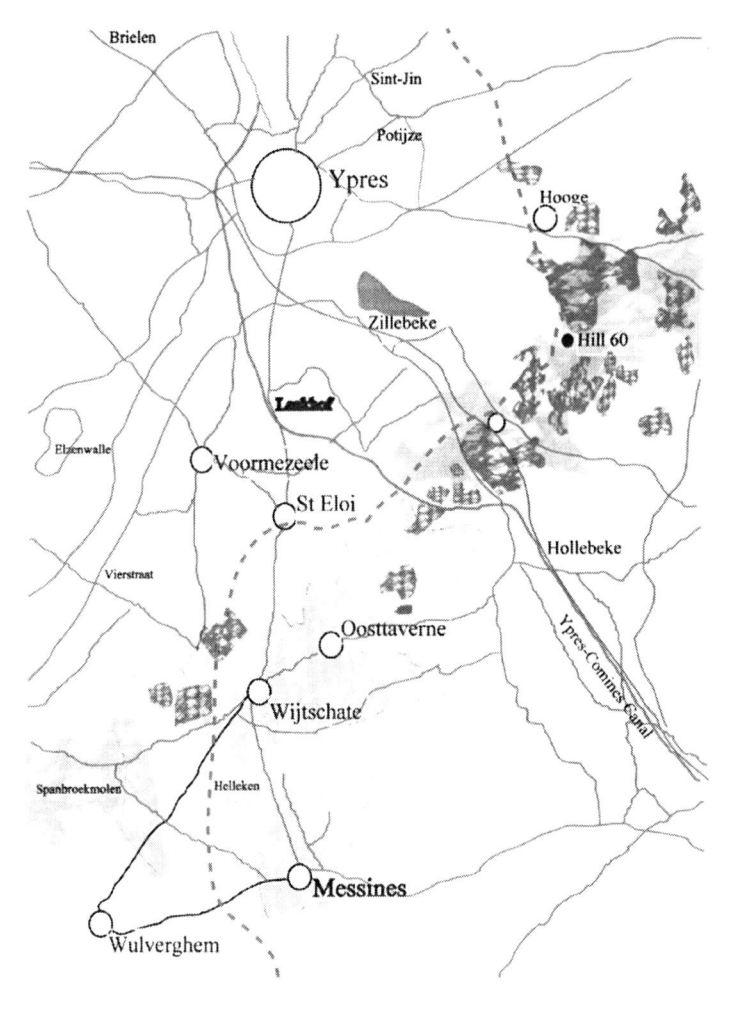

Ypres - Wulverghem Sector 1915

The German Spring Offensive of 1918 would lead to it changing hands yet again before finally finishing in the hands of the allies on 28th September of that year.

The 1/6th South Staffords had moved from Wulverghem on 23rd June 1915 and made their way via Bulford Camp, Neuve Englise and Ouerdom to arrive at Hill 60 where they went into the trenches on Sunday the 18th of July. These trenches were less than ideal, constantly having to be rebuilt after being destroyed by shell fire and due to the heavy rains, permanently flooded. The trenches that the 1/6th South Staffords occupied were some seventy yards from Hill 60, effectively at the bottom of the slope with the Germans above them at the top, a position selected from necessity rather than choice.

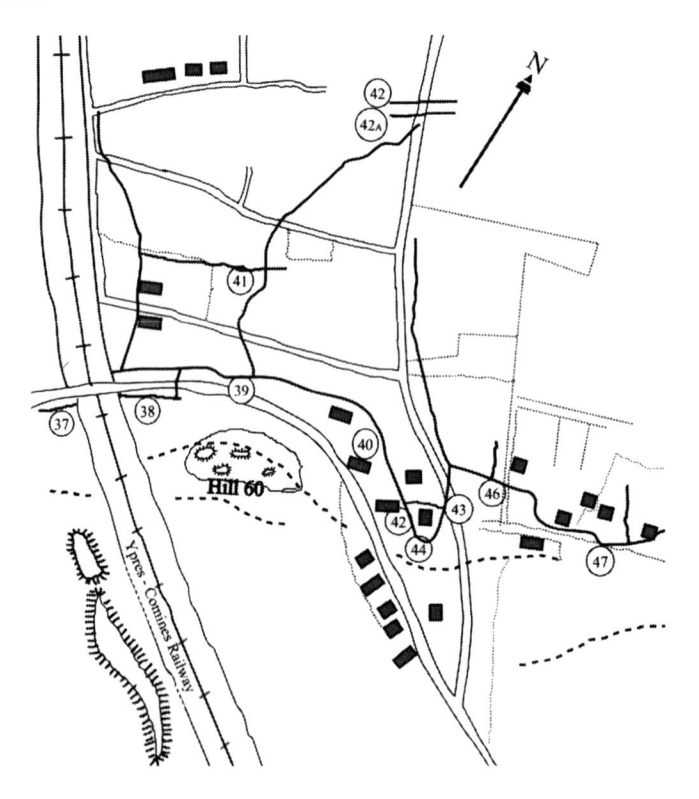

British Trenches at Hill 60 in 1915

Still the heavy rains continued to make the men's lives uncomfortable and so to did a revised system of reliefs, the men would now spend six days in the front line trenches, six in support, another six days in the front line and six days 'resting'.

One officer wrote home:-

> "I did not put anything about our new place in my other letters as I wanted to give it a letter to itself. How many men, I wonder, have written their first impression of Ypres? The first thing to strike you is the enormous number of troops around you. Here, if anywhere, you feel that the war is really being fought in England. In neighbouring fields are battalions of three or four different Divisions. All around are boards pointing to every sort of headquarters, Corps, Division, R.E., Artillery supplies, and bivouacs of well known line regiments that one has thought long cut up – the same name indeed but probably hardly a man there who came over last August. In every bivouac there are shelter trenches for although we are many miles behind the line here, if ever a hostile aeroplane were to spot our 'bivvy' we should be shelled right away.
> This happened in a field nearby, while we were last up the line, and the tale runs that our cobbler and tailor (who of course remain with the transport and stores) did not eat bread nor drink wine until a substantial dug-out had been built next to their 'Shops'.
> The march to the trenches is far different to our night walk at the last place. We have ten miles to go, with full pack and tomorrow's rations. Many of the men carry the contents of their last parcels. We start after tea, following a broad sandy track – a road that is marked on no map, but cutting straight through the cornfields. The place is full of these tracks, for which a map is no guide. The enemy gunners have long ago made the roads too unsafe for bodies of troops. We rest in a field a few miles behind and wait for darkness. Then on over the canal, passing by carefully masked guns in every hedge. Every now and then a shell falls away over Ypres, followed by a clatter of tiles.

We are in Indian file now, constantly 'concertinaing' and always tripping over telephone wires. Another far-off bang, a long-drawn whistle, and a whiz-bang thuds into the ground a yard or two off. It is only another dud fortunately. A great many German shells are duds now; sad for the Belgian farmer after the war!

About a mile behind the firing line we get into a communication trench, and then the trouble begins. First your feet get mixed up with one telephone wire; then another knocks your cap off; next someone gets his rifle mixed up in one; then another catches him across the back. Wires and wires everywhere. As fast as a wire is poled up, or pegged down, it gets loose again. We take about one and a half hours to cover the three-quarters of a mile, as another battalion is sticking in front of us; and then we get mixed up with a battalion just relieved and coming down. The trench stops and we come into a wood. Mysterious figures meet us. 'Is that the 6th South Staffs? 'Is the O.C. there? 'This way sir; we had to move our headquarters this evening; crumped out of Sanctuary Wood. Colonel's dug-out blown up just after he left. We had to take the new dressing station dug-out in Maple Copse for Headquarters for the present.'

Guides from the Battalion are relieving to take off each Company as it arrives, up to the firing line and supports. The last party to come up is taken to log-and-mud dugouts in the Copse. This party is in 'reserve' and has to do all the carrying for the remainder in the trenches. No man is ever allowed to go back on an errand from the trenches, or we should never be certain of the strength of our garrisons.

Then the work of the night begins. Some eighty petrol tins of water have to be taken up, together with the various stores, indented for the following day; also 2,000 sandbags, planks and quartering, nails, ammunition, corrugated iron, barbed wire, staples, stakes, star lights, canvas and the hundred other things that our trenches swallow up nightly, as sand drinks water.

All these things are dropped by the transport every night at the 'dump' a spot by a track some thousand yards or more behind the line. Tomorrow night there will be rations for 800 men in addition, making a full night's work.

Then there are the wounded to evacuate. A low log hut in one of the little woods is the battalion M. O's 'dressing station.' Here all the wounded are first brought, and their wounds made fast by the light of a couple of candles.

These must serve, unless the case is a bad one, until the patient reaches a base hospital, or perhaps England. The light cases go down on the transport limbers, the more serious are carried some distance to where the motor or horse ambulance has come up.

The stretcher-bearers are busy tonight, with so many men on the move; two or three have been hit by stray bullets. Also the enemy are still sending an occasional 'crump' into one of the little woods, though most of them are harmless, and only the bits come whistling through the trees. Those of us near a dug-out quickly bob inside while they pass. At last morning comes, and the reserve Company settles down to sleep until breakfast, after their journeys up to the front line with the stores.

Both we and the Germans have dropped all thoughts of a quiet life in these parts. When we first came out, artillery fired between the hours of 12 and 1 p.m. and 4 and 5 p.m. and then retired to lunch and tea respectively. Now odd whiz-bangs, crumps, etc. arrive at odd hours, in ones, twos, threes, and fours. At 5.20 a.m. four crumps arrive in quick succession; at 5.50 another four; at 6.20 another four again. Now we know where we are. Our friends have returned for once to their old habit, and with true German precision they continue their time-table throughout the day. After an hour or so's careful observation we find the four guns of this battery seem to be pointing at the same four places. In each salvo of four we find one comes into the field outside, one on, or near our path to the trenches, one by the telephone hut, and one by the mess hut. We make the necessary arrangements, change our position a little, and pass the day with no casualties, except for one shell, which drops short and lands at the door of our stretcher bearers' dug-out. Two of them are asleep and merely have their feet and legs a bit cut about. The doctor's place is close by, so there is no trouble. I am writing about 'The Moated Grange Strong Point' in Sanctuary Wood.

Here is a sight I saw from an artillery observation station, which I struck while following a telephone wire.

A bend in the lines gave a telescope view of the back of the German trenches – a couple of Boches with pick and shovel, and in our trenches, fifteen yards off, a man peacefully examining his shirt for the 'enemy'.

My chief impressions of the Ypres line are woods full of shell-scratched trees, long huts, rotting sandbags, smells, flies, old rifles and equipment tins, the smell of chloride of lime, very deep fire trenches, the tired whisper of spent crumps, everywhere the great untidiness and wastefulness of the Army, the fearsome echoing of a bombardment in the woods, little 'grocery-box' crosses to French and English, countless telephone wires, innumerable fallen-in dug-outs, and above all that feeling which one used sometimes to have in the old buildings and quads at the 'Varsity', of being on the scene of 'Great Days done'".

One of the more poignant casualties of this time was Captain Sydney John Sankey, the son of John and Elizabeth Sankey of Hunley Lodge, Penn Fields, Wolverhampton. In civilian life he was a Director in the family firm of Joseph Sankey and Sons of Bilston and had joined the battalion some four years earlier. In the absence of his senior officer he was in command of his Company when he sent out a patrol commanded by an inexperienced officer, when they had not returned by the expected time, he peered over the trench parapet in an effort to see them. In doing so he was spotted by an enemy sniper and shot through the head. Captain Sankey died at 4.30 a.m. on the 25th of September 1915, just days after he had applied for a special ten-day leave pass so that he could return home to get married. He was buried that afternoon in Larch Wood

(Railway Cutting) cemetery, some 2½ miles south-east of Ypres. Captain Sankey was 25 years old, his family requested the following additional inscription on his headstone; "GRANT HIM O LORD ETERNAL REST AND LET LIGHT PERPETUAL SHINE UPON HIM." (Photograph courtesy Staffordshire Regiment Museum).

As summer turned into autumn, the lives of the men became routine, periods spent in the trenches being interspersed with time spent in training, perhaps they would even have become accustomed to death. Another 54 men were killed over these months, but what was to happen on 13th October of that year was to be far worse than anything that they had yet experienced, over 90 more of their number would die that day and many more would be wounded.

LOOS en GOHELLE
In the autumn of 1915 an Allied offensive was conceived in order to distract the German effort from their Eastern front where they were achieving significant success against the Russians and causing real fear amongst the British and French commands that the Russians might sue for peace, thus releasing more German troops for the Western front. The plan for this new offensive was that the French would attack in the region of Champagne, the British at Loos.

The small coal-mining town of Loos-en-Gohelle is situated between Lens and La Bassee and lies north of the town of Arras in the Pas de Calais. The French pronounce it as 'Loss' but the British still use the war-time pronunciation of 'Looz'. Marshall Joffre, the Commander-in-Chief of the French armies on the Western Front, convinced his British counterpart Lord Kitchener that an attack by the French armies in the Lens – Arras area and by the British in the region of Loos – La Bassee would result in a breakthrough and lead to a rapid end of the war.

There were however some reservations held by some of Kitcheners subordinates. Of Joffre's contention that the British would find the ground between Loos and La Bassee particularly favourable, the British General Rawlinson passed comment that

> *"My new front at Loos is as flat as the palm of my hand. Hardly any cover anywhere. Easy enough to hold defensively, but very difficult to attack. It will cost us dearly and we will not get very far."*

Prophetic words indeed. In fact in the mining area around Loos the otherwise flat ground was covered with slag heaps, abandoned mines and destroyed villages. It was ideal defensive territory, the villages particularly posing formidable obstacles and the slag heaps providing excellent observation posts for the German observers.

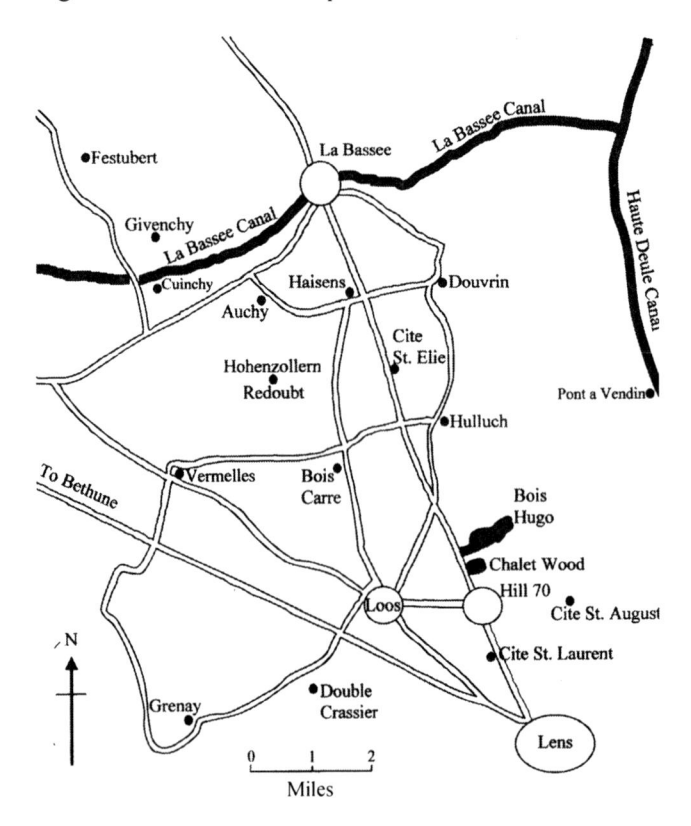

The Area Around Loos en Gohelle

THE BATTLE OF LOOS

Whilst the 1/6th South Staffords were being eased into their new lives at the front, the Battle of Loos had started without them. On Saturday 25th September the French attacked along a 15 mile front and initially made early gains, including the well defended position at La Courtine. The British covered a six-and-a-half mile front but although they had numerical superiority, the open nature of the ground over which they attacked meant that they were vulnerable to raking machine gun fire from the German positions.

A number of the British troops deployed in the battle of Loos were members of the so called 'Kitchener's Army', men who had responded to the recruiting campaign initiated by Lord Kitchener and this was their first experience of battle, indeed many of them had been in France for only two weeks. At this stage of the war the British army still had many lessons to learn, all too often their tactics were simply to use their numerical superiority to make frontal assaults across open ground against heavily defended enemy positions, invariably enfiladed by machine gun fire, and so it proved in this case, with disastrous consequences.

On the British front the battle began at 5.50 a.m. when they opened the first of 5,500 cylinders of chlorine gas, allowing the gas to drift towards the enemy lines. Gas had first been used by the Germans near Ypres some 6 months earlier but this was the first occasion that it would be used by the British. The use of chlorine gas was intended not only to cause casualties and alarm amongst the Germans but it also had the effect of causing rifles and artillery pieces to rapidly rust, thus rendering them useless. Unfortunately the wind was not constant and in some cases blew back towards the British lines causing casualties amongst their own men.

Past experience had shown that the standard 18 pounder guns and 4½" howitzers were incapable of causing serious damage either to the German defensive positions or to their barbed-wire. In consequence, every heavy gun that could be spared from elsewhere on the Western front was brought into the area in an attempt to redress the situation.

The Loos Battlefield – October 1915

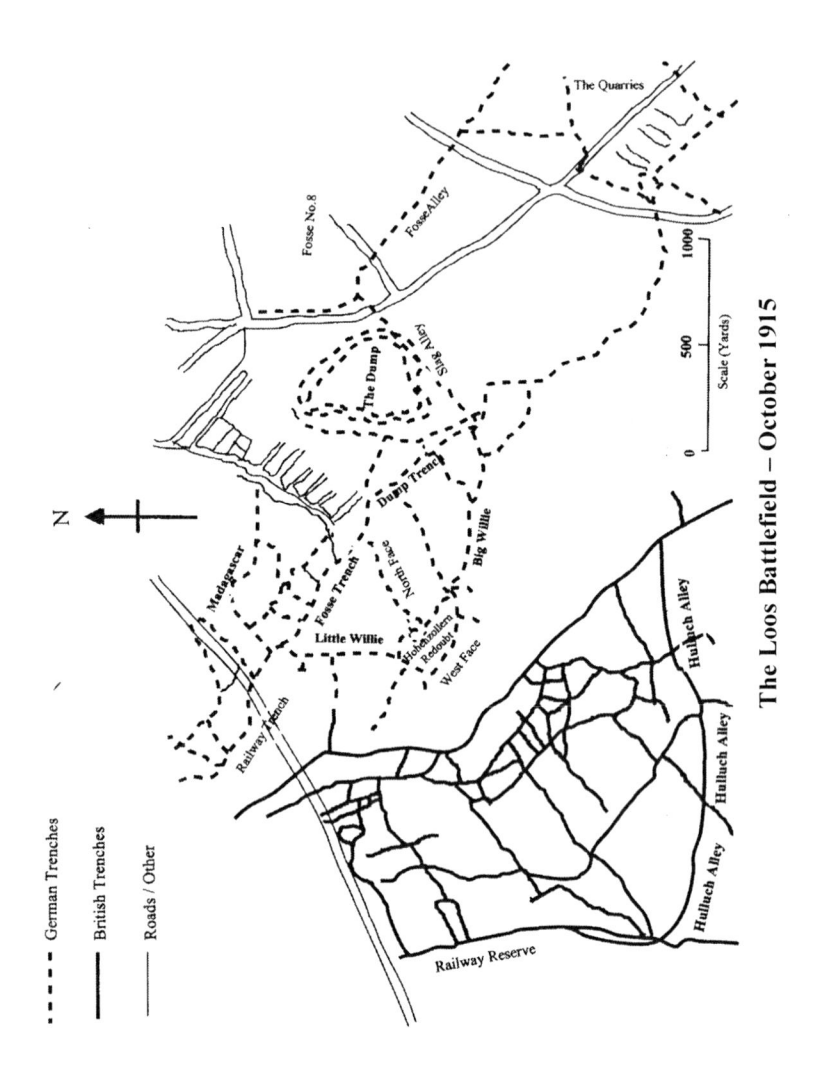

A preliminary bombardment had begun on the 21st September 1915 and continued both day and night until the morning of the attack, the 25th September. The heavy guns were allocated 90 rounds per 24 hours, the smaller field guns 150 rounds each, a mixture of both high explosive and shrapnel shells. In practice little damage was done to the German positions and their casualties were disappointingly few since they were able to shelter in dugouts set at fifty yard intervals along their trenches, dugouts which were up to 25 feet deep in the chalky soil and were thus impervious to shell-fire.

THE ATTACK
At 6.30 a.m. the artillery lifted from the front-line trenches and moved to shell the German communication trenches so as to prevent either the defenders retreating or reinforcements being brought-up. Simultaneously the British troops climbed out of their trenches and followed the gas and smoke across No-Man's-Land.

The 9th (Scottish) Division was to attack on a 1,500 yard line between the strongest points in the German lines, a fortified hillock known as The Hohenzollern Redoubt, the pit-head known as Fosse 8, 'The Dump' which was a 20ft high slag-heap affording the enemy excellent views across the battlefield, and the two trenches that linked these three features, known to the British as 'Big Willie' and Little Willie'.

The 7th Battalion Seaforth Highlanders and the 5th Battalion Cameron Highlanders led the attack and having passed through the smokescreen found the wire entanglements well cut by the artillery but advancing into intense machine-gun fire suffered heavy casualties. They succeeded in capturing the Hohenzollern Redoubt and by 7.00 a.m. had bombed their way through it and into 'Fosse Trench', once the German front-line. From Fosse Trench they pushed forward over open ground to Fosse 8 and The Dump but met with minimal resistance as the Germans retired towards Auchy. Their attack finally halted when they reached Corons Trench where their orders were to convert the trench into a fire trench to cover Fosse 8.

By the end of the first day the Allies had made substantial gains and had established a clear break in the German lines but now their lack of reserves presented them with problems. The men who had done so much fighting and had lost so many comrades on the 25th were now exhausted and able to contribute little to the fighting of the 26th.

THE SECOND DAY
That task fell to the men of the 21st and 24th Divisions, recently arrived in France and concentrated to the west of St. Omer. They had begun to march towards Loos on the 20th September but were under orders only to move between 6.00 p.m. and 5.00 a.m. so as to avoid being spotted by enemy aircraft. A single Division marching in closed formation would stretch for 15 miles along the road and would take a considerable time to pass a given point, nevertheless they covered over 20 miles on each of the first two nights and arrived at in the area of Lillers at the end of the 3rd night's march. The following night (the 24th) the two Divisions began to march the final 8 or so miles to the reserve areas.

From the outset the march was fraught with difficulties. Whilst the troops were marching up to the front, horses and motor vehicles were travelling in the opposite direction, all this on roads that were not much wider than were required for traffic going in one direction only and that had deep ditches on either side. In addition, further problems arose each time that they came to a crossroads or to one of the many level crossings where they often had to halt to allow trains to pass. It was not until 6.00 a.m. on the 25th that the last parties arrived at their allotted areas and were able to lie down in the fields to rest although how much rest they would get with the noise of battle ringing in their ears is questionable.

On that part of the front which the 1/6th South Staffords would inherit some 18 days later, the remaining troops of the 26th Brigade were relieved by those of the 73rd Brigade, (24th Division) comprising of Battalions of the Royal Sussex, Royal Fusiliers and Northampton Regiments.

Although the attack on the 25th September had surprised the Germans, any withdrawals that they made were orderly; they were still in relatively good shape and had been able to take most of their artillery with them. When the men of the 73rd Brigade began their attack at 11.00 a.m. on the 26th, it was against the German second line which had been largely unaffected by the four-day bombardment, the barbed wire entanglements were mostly intact. The British advanced to the wire but sustained so many casualties that they were forced to retreat, such was the scale of the British casualties that many of the Germans stopped firing on the retreating Tommies. This part of the battleground, the part which the South Staffords would later inherit became known as 'The corpse ground of Loos."

The early gains, won at such a horrific loss of life, had needed to be capitalized on quickly but the reserves (mostly inexperienced New Army Divisions) had been brought into action too slowly. The Germans counter-attacked and by the 27th September the offensive was breaking down, the Germans retook the Hohenzollern Redoubt and Fosse 8 on 1st October.

Even before the South Staffords went into battle things began to go awry for them, on the 8th October their C.O. Lt. Col. T.F. Waterhouse was badly wounded by a shell fragment, and then when on the night of 12th to 13th October they were to relieve the Guards Division in the front line trench known as 'Big Willie' (named after Kaiser Wilhelm) and the original British frontline trenches behind it, they found their way obstructed by congestion in the communication trenches and were compelled to climb out of them and make their way above ground. The relief was not completed until 6.00 a.m.

THE 46th DIVISION ATTACK

The 46th Division was to ordered to attack the same ground as had the 9th Division several days before; The Hohenzollern Redoubt, Fosse 8, 'The Dump', and the two trenches Big Willie and Little Willie. The Redoubt was a maze of trenches and machine gun posts, and stood out from the German front line by some 500 yards, fronted by heavy barbed wiring and lying water between the British and German lines. Fosse 8 was a slag heap around 600 yards behind the German lines and like the Hohenzollern Redoubt was also a maze of trenches and strengthened machine gun emplacements.

Selected parts of the 46th Division Operation Orders read:-

> 1) Right Attack
> The 137th Brigade from the old British front trench between G.10.b.98 and G.4.d.26 and assembly trenches in rear will assault at 2.00 p.m. with their left directed at the north-west corner of the Dump.
>
> 1st Objective: Track crossing Fosse Alley at G.5.b.68 – G.5.b.39 and A.29.d.22 to Pentagon Redoubt at A.29.c.53 (inclusive). The assault will pass on without pause to the far side of the Dump. Bombing parties will be told off by the commander, Right Attack to bomb along the following trenches as they are successfully reached by assault;
> (i) South Face
> (ii) Fosse Alley to join up with the left of 12th Division about the track at G.5.b.68.
> (iii) Trench running towards Three Cabarets from A.29.d.22.
>
> > Bombing parties will be organised to deal with Dump Trench and Slag Alley and with machine gun emplacements and other defences found in the Dump and clear them of the enemy. Dugouts must be cleared by bombing, and the greatest care taken that none are left unsearched
> >
> > Allotment of Communication Trenches
> >
> > 137th Brigade
> > Gordon Alley to junction with Hulluch Alley – Hulluch Alley to G.10.b.89

Wednesday the 13th October 1915 was a bright autumnal day but at 12 noon the air was rent by the start of a two-hour artillery bombardment against the enemy positions from 54 heavy howitzers, 86 field howitzers, 286 field guns and 19 counter-battery guns. This bombardment was later found to have been largely ineffective, the German positions in Big Willie and Little Willie being almost untouched. At 1.00 p.m. the British opened the taps on their gas cylinders and although on this occasion the wind was in their favour, it had little effect on the Germans, most of it settling into shell craters and old trenches now in No-Man's-Land. In practice it merely served to alert the Germans that an attack was imminent.

Waiting in their collecting trenches, the 46th Division men were subjected to a very heavy German barrage, causing Lieutenant-Colonel Law to report to the Divisional Head Quarters that the effectiveness of the German fire would render any forward movement futile. The warning was ignored and the attack ordered to proceed as planned.

It was probably whilst waiting nervously in the collecting trenches that 20 year old Private Frederick Cliff wrote this letter to his parents Francis and Alice at 136 Gorsebrook Road, Wolverhampton:-

> *"We are about to go into action at ----------, and I hope to come out of it safely, but in case I should not, I have given this letter to my pal. I want you to have a good heart and to remember that you are British and that if I go down it will be doing my bit for King and country."*

The letter was duly delivered; Private Cliff died that day and is commemorated on the Loos Memorial to the Missing.

Even before the attack began the Germans had been raking the jumping-off trenches with machine gun fire from positions at the Dump, Dump Trench, and Little Willie and when at 2.05 p.m. the first wave of the attack was led on the left flank by the 1/5th North Staffords they lost 20 officers, including their Commanding Officer Lieut-Colonel J.H. Knight, and almost 500 other ranks in the first few yards. On the right flank, led by half of the 1/5th South

Staffords, things went no better and every officer and man who left the jumping off trench was either killed or wounded.

In front of the 1/6th South Staffords the second wave fared little better, 'A' and 'C' Companies of the 1/6th South Staffords formed the third attacking wave alongside two Companies of the 1/6th North Staffords and were to follow the second wave at a distance of some 200 paces. The men made their way in 'fighting order' i.e. without packs but with haversacks slung over their backs. Each man carried 200 rounds of small arms ammunition, 3 empty sandbags, iron rations including an extra cheese ration and in addition to their own kit also had to carry equipment for use by the Royal Engineers.

At the sound of a whistle the men clambered out of the trenches and lay down until they were all ready to move off. During the initial rush of 20 yards or more, many men were struck by machine gun bullets before they got to their first objective, so too in their second rush. During the charge Captain Edwin Collison was hit and would die an hour later. His last words were reported to be "Are the boys alright?" Lieutenant Thomas Dann was hit whilst running, the bullet going into his thigh and out through his foot. Although having been taken back to the Stafford's line, he died an hour later through loss of blood.

Part of the War Diary entry for the 13th October reads:-

> *"Enemy machine guns were heard ranging on our assembly trenches at 1-30 p.m. and 1-45 p.m., which was notified to Headquarters. Having received no message that our front line had not been able to advance, and not being able to see their position for smoke, the two Companies forming the third line followed the second line and suffered very heavy casualties. The fourth line then advanced and also suffered from machine gun fire from the direction of South Face. All that remained of the 3rd line reached our fire trench between point 87 and point 89 to assist the 5th South Staffs Regt. to hold that portion of the line until this Battalion was ordered to retire at noon on the 14th."*

Acting Sergeant Frederick Watson had been born and bred in Wolverhampton and before enlisting was living with his parents Wallace and Hannah at 299 Hordern Road. During the fighting he took his party of 50 men from 'C' company to intercept Germans advancing towards them along a communication trench, but so heavy was the enemy fire that only 20 men reached the trench. Watson kept the enemy at bay for five hours by means of hand-grenades with which his men kept him supplied until they too were hit. When he finally ran-out of grenades he then held off the Germans by sniping them with rifle-fire until he was killed. (Photograph courtesy Express and Star Ltd.)

One of Watson's men later described him as "The bravest and most daring fellow I ever knew." Another of his comrades remarked "Watson won the Victoria Cross that day if any man did." Fredrick Watson was just 20 years old when he died and has no known grave but is commemorated on The Loos Memorial to the Missing.

Lieut.-Colonel Law later reported that at about 3.00 p.m. he had observed signalling from the Dump for more bombs and ammunition, and later for reinforcements. At the time he took the signals to come from the advanced bombing line although he had convinced himself that it could not have got so far.

Private T. Persall of the 1/6th South Staffords wrote to his parents at 179 Owen Road, Wolverhampton:-

> *"No doubt that you will be rather anxious to know what has become of me when you see the account of the charge we made recently. I might tell you that I am quite whole and alright.*
> *It was without a doubt a gallant charge, but at a cost. At 12 o'clock on Wednesday 13th October our artillery bombarded the German position for an hour until one o'clock, and then we sent over gas until two o'clock. At 2*

p.m. our lads mounted the parapet only to be swept down by machine gun and shell fire. Our supports, second, third and fourth lines had to advance across the open to reach our first line of the trenches because the communication trenches were blocked with dead and wounded. That is where we lost a lot of the boys.

I was very fortunate in that I was one of the reserve telephone sections to go over the parapet as the first section could not get into communication. We were rushing up the communication trench to the first trench to see if we were needed when we met our signal officer who had just been wounded through the wrist. He ordered us back to the second line to await orders. Fortunately communication kept good and we were not needed to go over to the advanced point.

All day the Germans kept up very heavy fire. We were helping with the wounded and getting them in from the open which was not a very pleasant job as the Germans kept the machine guns playing across the open but one could not stay in the trench when there were wounded crying out for help within fifteen or twenty yards of the parapet.

Two of our good fellows got killed when endeavouring to bring men in and another who went out with me got wounded in the arm. Everyone who escaped ought to thank God. I know I do. Of course many of the other battalions who took part in the charge (in our division) came out worse.

You ought to have seen the way the lads went out without a waver – as some of them fell others went on. Of course it was, as you might know, a very difficult thing to do in daylight across a stretch of open ground without any cover and a distance of some five or six hundred yards before they reached the redoubt and a trench. Braver lads never put foot on a battlefield, but it made my heart ache to see the few that answered the roll call.

The Colonel of the Grenadier Guards said it was the most orderly charge made since the war started. The fellows acted as if they were on the parade ground."

That night the 1/6th South Staffords were relieved in the trenches by the Guards Division and retired to their billets in Sailly le Bourse. The Battalion war diary has the following casualty returns for the month of October 1915:-

Officers Killed	*5*
Officers Wounded	*14*
Other Ranks Killed	*35*
Other Ranks Died of Wounds	*5*
Other Ranks Wounded	*239*
Other Ranks Missing	*105*

The roll call taken by Regimental Sergeant Major A. Burgoyne on the morning of October 14th recorded;

Company	*Officers*	*Sergeants*	*Other Ranks*
A	*1*	*2*	*27*
B	*5*	*5*	*71*
C	*0*	*5*	*63*
D	*1*	*4*	*69*
CO	*1*	*0*	*0*
Total	*4*	*16*	*230*
Deficit	*18*	*9*	*447*

Private Leonard Lawson, 1/6th Battalion, South Staffordshire Regiment, the son of Mrs Lawson of the Briars, Merridale Road, Wolverhampton was born on September 5th 1896, and had attended the Wolverhampton Grammar School, representing them in the 1st IX football team. He enlisted when war was declared and went to France with the battalion in March 1915. Private Lawson was one of those originally reported missing after the attack on the Hohenzollern Redoubt, later confirmed as having been killed. Leonard Lawson has no known grave and is commemorated on the Loos Memorial to the Missing. (Photograph courtesy Express and Star Ltd.)

Many of those initially recorded as missing would later be confirmed as having died and the official total of those men of the 1/6th South Staffs who died on 13th – 14th October is 91, only 6 of whom were able to be identified for burial, the others having no known graves.

In the Battle of Loos the B.E.F. lost 2,013 officers and 48,367 other ranks, of whom around 800 officers and some 15,000 men fell in the fighting of the 13th – 16th October, fighting that did nothing to improve the position in any way but only resulted in futile slaughter, any ground won was later lost once more.

Dud Corner Cemetery and the Loos Memorial to the Missing
(Private Collection)

Although the 46th Division played only a small part in the Battle of Loos the total losses from 13th-15th October were 180 officers and 3,583 other ranks killed, wounded or missing. The 137th Brigade had failed to capture any of their initial objectives; their casualties alone amounted to 68 officers and 1,478 other ranks. From the Allies perspective, the battle of Loos, in common with all of the battles of autumn 1915 all ended in failure and resulted in heavy losses.

As with the other Territorial Force battalions, the losses incurred by the 1/6th South Staffords meant that the pre-war local character of the battalion would be changed forever, although new troops were quickly drafted in, few of the new men would have any connection with the battalion's home town.

Meanwhile, back in Wolverhampton;

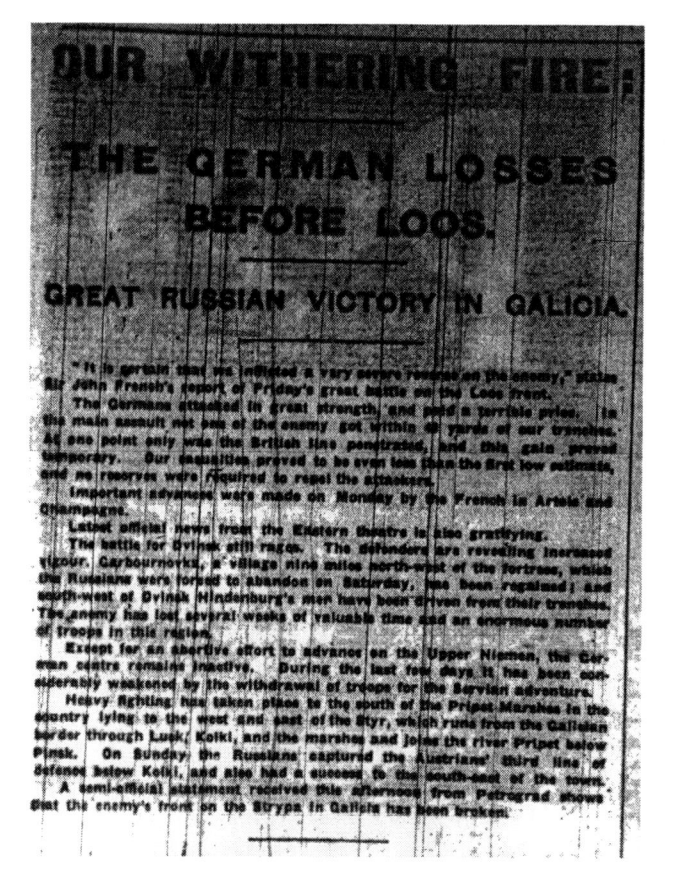

OUR WITHERING FIRE:

THE GERMAN LOSSES BEFORE LOOS.

GREAT RUSSIAN VICTORY IN GALICIA.

(Reproduced courtesy Express and Star Ltd.)

Three weeks after the fighting the Commanding Officer of the 1/6th South Staffords sent the following letter to the editor of the Wolverhampton 'Express and Star' newspaper:-

> "Sir,
> I shall be glad if you would express through the columns of the Express and Star my deepest sympathy with all the relatives of the officers, non-commissioned officers and men of the 1/6th Battalion of the South Staffordshire Regiment who have fallen in the recent attack on the Hohenzollern redoubt.
> It is impossible for me to write to everyone as my time is fully occupied but a more courageous and gallant attack could not possibly have been made.
> The whole line went forward in perfect order as if carrying out an ordinary parade and although the enemy machine-guns ploughed our leading line, this fact made no difference.
> On came the next in the same steady order and one was filled with pride to see such coolness displayed under such heavy fire.
> Both the Corps Commander and the General Officer commanding the Division have visited the Battalion and have expressed their admiration for the manner in which the attack was made.
> I feel sure that the relatives of those who met such a glorious end will accept some consolation in the sympathy extended to them by the comrades of all those who have fallen, and also in the manner in which the Battalion acquitted itself when called upon to undertake a task requiring such qualities of endurance and determination.
> Yours
> F.W. Laws"

Private Harold Segar who before the war had lived at 'The Elms' Ettingshall Road, Wolverhampton was badly wounded in the attack on the Hohenzollern Redoubt. He would have been carried to the nearest Regimental Aid Post, often located very close to the front-line; in the support trenches, or slightly further back in the reserve trenches, where his wounds would have firstly been assessed by the medical staff but they would have been able to do little for him before being passing him on to an Advanced Dressing Station manned by members of the Royal Army Medical Corps. It is probable that due to the large volume of casualties that day, he would have had to lie on a stretcher in the open for a considerable time but once there he would be tagged with a label showing his name, rank and number and the nature of his wounds but would receive only limited medical treatment for his wounds, although they would be able to carry out emergency operations when necessary, before moving him once again, this time to a Casualty Clearing Station a few miles behind the line where at last there were facilities akin to many hospitals in England.

The Casualty Clearing Stations in this area were probably housed in numerous tents and would be capable of treating something like 1,000 casualties at any one time and of performing major operations such as amputations. Often a number of Casualty Clearing Stations would be grouped together close to a railway line but even so, following a major battle they would struggle to cope. Having made it as far as Casualty Clearing Station a man's chances of survival would be much improved although many of the larger Commonwealth War Graves Commission cemeteries on the Western-Front are based near to the sites of Casualty Clearing Stations and contain the bodies of those that could not be saved.

From the Casualty Clearing Station he was passed back to one of several Base Hospitals located near to the Army's main depots on the French coast where his condition would have been further assessed and the decision made that he should be shipped back to England for further treatment. Harold was duly sent back home but on the 5th December 1915 he died of the wounds he had received some seven weeks earlier. Whilst Sgt. Frederick Watson, Private Cliff and Private Lawson have no known graves but are commemorated on the Loos Memorial near to where they fell, Private Harold Segar was accorded a full military funeral in the packed Wesleyan Chapel in Ettingshall. So many wreaths were presented that the large hearse was unable to accommodate all of them. Harold was buried in the family plot in Bilston Municipal cemetery and a volley of rifle-fire was fired above his grave. He was 23 years old.

46th Division Memorial erected near Vermelles
This picture, taken by Doug Lewis, shows it now in a sorry state.

REFITTING

In the weeks after their chastening experience at Loos, reinforcements had been supplied to bring the battalion back to near full strength and still at this stage of the war the new men would all have been volunteers. Whereas in the early days a man may have had some say in regard to which unit he joined, now men where sent where they were most needed and the 1/6th South Staffords certainly needed them, during the month of October the recorded casualty count of dead, wounded, and missing was Officers 19, Other ranks 384.

Much effort was expended in acclimatising the new men to life at the front and the days to the 13th November were spent in instruction in bayonet fighting, bomb throwing, rapid loading and musketry as well as the men's usual fitness regimes of route marching and gymnastic exercise. On the 13th the battalion was back in the trenches, this time to the south of Neuve Chapelle. At the end of November 1915 this area was relatively quiet and in the three visits into the trenches made during that month only two men were killed and one wounded, a contrast indeed to the previous month.

If the soldiers felt rather safer here, they certainly did not feel comfortable. The trenches here were almost completely waterlogged and had only a three and a half foot high parapet. Trench Foot, a fungal infection of the feet brought on by prolonged exposure to damp, cold conditions allied to poor environmental hygiene was an incessant problem, patients sometimes had to have toes amputated (following gangrene) such were the effects of the condition.

In November 1915 large drafts of officers and men joined the Battalion and on 6th December they were lectured on 'Duties on board ship', later learning that they would be embarking on Christmas Day for an undisclosed destination. Hasty preparations were made for a premature Christmas celebration and in the absence of turkeys or geese, local roast pork, accompanied by plum puddings from home ensured that the festivities were celebrated in style.

1916

"The Staffords relieve the battalion on June 30th. Gommecourt is attacked on July 1st. The attack fails……….. the Staffords and Sherwoods lose heavily. The taps of the Somme blood bath are full on."
(Extract from the war diary of the 4th Leicester's)

AN EGYPTIAN EXCURSION

Christmas Day 1915 had seen the 1/6th entrain for a two day journey to Marseilles where they enjoyed a week of light duties and sea bathing before embarking on H.M.S. Transylvania, still unaware of their intended destination. On the 8th January 1916 they docked at Alexandria. Rumour had it that this was only a break in the journey but on the following day they disembarked and at 11.00 p.m. that night boarded a train bound for Shalufa on the Suez Canal. Once there, with no idea as to their intended purpose, they discovered that they were to assume command of a fort on the opposite side of the canal.

If duties during the first fortnight were light, largely comprising of lectures and practical exercises, the food left something to be desired, bully beef and weevil infested biscuits being all that was initially available. Long hot days, light duties and the fighting far behind them meant that the men were at last able to relax to a degree thought impossible just a few weeks before.

On the 26th January the 1/6th South Staffords, together with half a battalion of North Staffords, a troop of Indian Cavalry, a company of Royal Engineers and 100 camels made their way for 6 ½ miles into the desert in order to create 'No. 3 Post'. Compared to the digging of trenches in France, digging here was much easier and the men hoped that that their Egyptian sojourn would be an extended one but it was not to be.

Four days later they were bound once again for Alexandria where many officers and N.C.O.s were given forty-eight hour leave passes to visit Cairo before, on the 5th February they embarked once again on board ship, this time their transport was H.M.S. Magnificent, a first-class cruise liner which afforded rather more in the way of home comforts than had the Transylvania.

Returning to France aboard H.M.S. Magnificent
(Photograph courtesy Staffordshire Regiment Museum)

February 1916 found the Allied armies in a state of transition, accommodating many extra troops, the 1/6th South Staffords were undergoing various forms of training at this time and seemed to change location with alarming frequency.

1/6th at NEUVILLE St. VAAST

After a further period if training, at midnight on the 13th March they once again returned to the trenches, this time relieving French troops at Neuville St. Vaast, a once prosperous town just north of Arras, but now in ruins. The trenches here had been occupied by the Germans until they had been driven out by the French just a few days previously and were distinctly battle-scared. The Germans, still smarting from their loss were making strenuous efforts to reclaim that part of the line, to the extent that the French had suffered eighty casualties on the night before being relieved.

The South Stafford's first tour of duty in this sector was relatively quiet but on the 29th of the month the entry on the war diary read:-

"*Enemy shelled our trenches heavily from 2 p.m. to 2.20 p.m. using Howitzers and H.E. ...... Our Artillery barrage operated very quickly. At 6.50 p.m. last night we sprang a mine which formed a crater .... The whole was occupied and partly consolidated. Our Artillery support followed prompt upon the explosion, and was excellent in effect. Intermittent artillery fire continued till 8.00 p.m. and from that time the situation was quiet, and the work of consolidating and repairing pressed on.*"

One of the casualties of this fighting was Lieutenant Gerald Howard-Smith who died aged 36 on 29th March 1916. Lieutenant Smith was the son of Judge Howard-Smith and the grandson of William Smith, D.C.L. LL.D. He had been educated at Eton, where he was Cadet Lance-Sergeant in the Officer Training Corps, and Trinity College, Cambridge and had played in the Eton cricket XI's of 1898 and 1899 and that of Cambridge in 1903, the year in which he was elected president of the Cambridge University Cricket Club. A fine all-round sportsman, he had won the high-jump in the sports against Oxford in 1901, 1902 and 1903 and had twice competed in the hurdle race. Back home he became captain of the Wolverhampton Cricket Club, excelling as both batsman and bowler.

For some time before the war he had been a junior partner in the practice of Messer's Underhill, Thorneycroft and Smith, solicitors and was commissioned as 2nd Lieutenant on the 10th October 1914.
Having been wounded on two previous occasions, the wounds that he received on the third occasion developed complications and subsequently proved fatal, he was buried in Aubigny Communal Cemetery extension, some 9 miles north-west of Arras, France. His family commissioned the following inscription; "LOVE IS CROWNED BY SACRIFICE." (Photograph courtesy Staffordshire Regiment Museum)

His father sent a letter to the editor of the Express and Star which was published on the 3rd May 1916.

> "Sir,
> I desire with your permission to put on record in your columns the substance of a conversation I had with my late son Lieutenant Gerald Howard Smith last November when he was at home recovering from a wound that he had received in the attack on the Hohenzollern Redoubt last October.
> Speaking of his platoon, which I believe was mainly comprised of men from Bilston and the surrounding district thereabouts, he told me – and I think the remarks applied to the whole of the South Staffordshire Regiment – that though some of them were rough and their language not always refined, he had learned to love them for their patriotism, courage, and loyalty; that he would do anything and go anywhere with them; and that they would do anything and go anywhere with him.
> This testimony from one who was the soul of truth and honour I venture to think will be gratefully received by the relatives and friends of all those brave soldiers, especially of those who have fallen in the good fight and set such a magnificent example to others.
> May I take this opportunity, Sir, of expressing my thanks to the many kind friends who have sympathised with me on the loss of my son?
> Faithfully yours
> Howard Smith, The Ford House, near Wolverhampton."

On the 4th May Mr R.E. Ivens of 15, Allen Road, Wolverhampton replied;

> "Sirs,
> Seeing the letter in tonight's paper from his Honour Judge Howard Smith respecting his son's praise for the 6th South Staffords, I think it only right to say that his men thought equally well of their late officer.
> My son who is in the machine-gun section of this regiment, when writing home telling us of this affair said how much

they deplored his loss and added "he was one of the finest and bravest men who ever wore khaki" and that when Lieutenant Smith was being carried away on a stretcher he coolly whistled 'Tipperary'.

Since then my son, who has been home on leave, amplified this and expressed the regret of the regiment at his loss. This may perhaps be of some little comfort to the sorrowing parents in their great loss."

Mr Ivens was to lose his own son Richard on the 2nd July the following year, dying of wounds received.

Another casualty of the fighting at Neuville St. Vaast was Sergeant Walter Neville Court of the 1/6th Battalion, the, third son of William Henry Court, a Wolverhampton solicitor and his wife Mary. Born on March 10th 1895, he subsequently attended grammar school before going to Denstone College where he was a member of the Officers Training Corps in which he served for three years. On April 2nd 1916 when aged 20, he was killed while leading a bombing party ten yards from the German trench. On a number of occasions he had refused to be recommended for a commission, as he said that he preferred to stay with his men. His officer is reported to have said, "He always showed a very keen interest in his work and rapidly earned promotion. His work was of great value. He was always ready for any duty, however dangerous or difficult, and set a splendid example by his courage and devotion. Not only by his considerable military attainments, but by his personal qualities, he endeared himself to all ranks." Sergeant Court is buried in Ecoivers Military Extension, Mont-St.-Eloi, France. (Photograph courtesy Express and Star Ltd.)

THE 2/6th IN IRELAND

The 2/6th South Staffords had moved to St. Albans in July 1915 and there they remained for some ten months until late in the evening on Easter Monday 24th April 1916 orders were received to move to action and speculation was rife as to where they were going and why. Early next morning 'A' and 'B' Companies together with the Battalion H.Q. marched the 12 miles to Berkhampstead, to be followed an hour later by 'C' and 'D' Companies and the Battalion Transport.

Despite having already supplied two drafts of men to the 1/6th Battalion, the 2/6th were again at fighting strength and eager to play their part on the Western Front. It was not until they arrived at the train station to find that their port of embarkation was to be Liverpool rather than Southampton that they realized that their destination was to be Ireland and their enemy was to be the newly formed Irish Citizen Army (ICA).

The ICA planned to control the city of Dublin by establishing a defensive crescent of strong-points on each side of the city and the General Post Office on O'Connell Street was to be their H. Q. Rapidly they took control of a number of major buildings including Boland's Mills on the Grand Canal, the Jacob's Factory in Bishop Street, The Four Courts, the South Dublin Union Workhouse, the Mendicity Institution, the area around Mount Street Bridge over the Grand Canal, Carisbrook House (now the Israeli Embassy in Ballsbridge), St. Stephen's Green and the College of Surgeons.

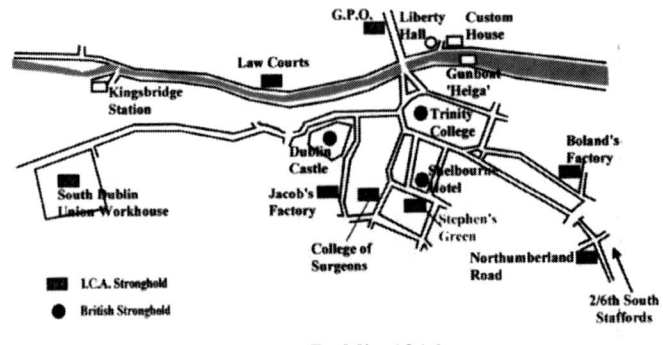

Dublin 1916

Amongst other buildings controlled were City Hall, a Wireless School on the south corner of Lower Abbey Street, Hopkins and Hopkins, on the corner of O'Connell Street & Eden Quay, J and T Davy's Public House on Portobello Bridge, the Metropole Hotel on O'Connell Street, Westland Row railway station, and Broadstone Railway Terminus.

After travelling from Liverpool on two regular cruise ships escorted by destroyers to counter the German submarine threat, the 2/6th South Staffords landed at Kingstown just after dawn on Wednesday the 26th and there they remained throughout the day before taking billets that evening in a large unoccupied hotel nearby.

Soon after 8.30 p.m. that evening orders were received to move to Dublin to support the 2/7th and 2/8th Battalions of the Notts and Derbys Regiment (the Sherwood Foresters) who had gone before them. Having passed through Black Rock, just before reaching Ballsbridge the men were ordered to load their rifles as intelligence had it that they could encounter opposition at the cross-roads there but this did not materialise. The 2/6th South Staffords eventually reached Beggars Bush Barracks soon after midnight and were at last able to rest.

Their rest was to be short-lived as at 2.15 a.m. they were ordered to move forward to relieve the Sherwood Foresters who had taken heavy casualties after engaging the enemy at the corner of Northumberland Road and Haddington Road. The Foresters had met with stiff resistance but by a series of bombing raids had driven the rebels backwards and were now in positions occupying houses in Northumberland Road, Warrington Place, Percy Place, Mount Street and Herbert Place.

The relief took place just before dawn, 'A' and 'B' Companies taking the advanced positions, with 'C' and 'D' Companies behind. When daylight broke the reality of their situation became clear. Training back in England had been concentrated on trench warfare whereas here they were hemmed-in by buildings, some of which were ablaze, snipers were very active and a direct attack was out of the question.

It was in Dublin that the 2/6th were to suffer their first casualty of the fighting when 19 year old Private Harold Barratt of 'A' Company was killed and several others, including 2nd Lieutenant Halliwell were wounded. Private Barratt had lived with his parents George and Elizabeth at 31, Harrow Street, Whitmore Reans in Wolverhampton. Several other men became casualties during the course of the day, Sergeant Joseph Henry Fletcher of 'C' Company was the only other to lose his life.

The grave of Private Harold Barratt, the first 2/6th South Staffs man to be killed in fighting during the Easter Uprising.
(Private collection)

In the early morning of Friday 28th April the 2/6th were relieved in their positions by the 2/6th North Staffords and together with the 2/5th South Staffords fought their way to Trinity College which they gained at about midday. After a short break during which they dined on oranges, these being the only food available, they were again on the move, this time via Lower Gardiner Street and Great Britain Street before halting on the corner of Chapel Street. The area between here and North King Street was a congested maze of alleyways and small terraced houses, and the rebels were using the situation to their best advantage.

Such streets were easy to defend by constructing make-shift barricades which could be supported by sniper fire from the upper floors of nearby houses and 'C' Company suffered heavily in unsuccessfully attempting to storm the first of these between Coleraine Street and Linenhall Street. It was apparent that other tactics would need to be developed and one of the more ingenious of these was to make use of a boiler belonging the Guinness brewery located on the banks of the River Liffey.

It was established that twenty men could be accommodated inside the tank and the Guinness employees readily adapted the boiler by cutting rifle slots into its sides and mounting it onto a motor lorry. The 2/6th South Staffords now had an armoured car!

The 2/6th Battalion defending a barricade in Nelson Street, Dublin
(Private Collection)

Another tactic employed to avoid frontal attacks on the rebel positions was to enter houses on either side of the street and to make progress along the street by breaking down the adjoining party walls and by means of these two methods of attack the whole of the lower part of North King Street had been cleared by 11.00 a.m. on the morning of Saturday 29th.

It now fell to 'C' Company to regain the remaining buildings in the street and in so doing they sustained many casualties before being relieved by 'D' Company who finally cleared the rebels from a barricade in Upper Church Street and joined-up with the 2/5th South Staffords to complete a cordon which now completely surrounded the rebel forces. The end of the fighting was in sight and at 3.30 p.m. the surrender was signed.

Even then there remained small pockets of resistance and the next ten days were spent in the search and clearance of the area, the men being under constant threat from isolated snipers. One particularly troublesome group of rebels occupied a house with a commanding position in North King Street until a local priest negotiated their surrender. During their first tour of duty the 2/6th South Staffords had eleven men killed, four officers and thirty one men wounded.

In mid-May the Battalion transferred some seventeen miles south-west to billets under canvas in the village of Staffan on the banks of the picturesque River Liffey where they were joined by a draft of 120 men, mostly from the Leicestershire area. Here they resumed their training and made much use of the excellent rifle-range nearby. In July 1916 the 2/6th rejoined the rest of the 176th Brigade and later moved back to England.

GOMMECOURT
Two battles fought in the Great War possibly stand to show the futility of the whole madness, 'The Somme' and 'Passendaele'. Gommecourt, a village some 8 miles north of the French town of Albert, saw the 1/6th South Staffords involvement in the blood-bath that was the Somme and shows the sheer waste of human life incurred.

On the 6th December 1915 initial plans had been made for a major offensive to be led by the French, with the British in support. There had been strong debate between the allies, Joffre for the French argued for the offensive to take place in the Somme area, General Sir Douglas Haig who had recently succeeded Sir John French as Commander-in-Chief of the British, wanted the attacks to take place in Flanders. In the event Joffre held sway and in February 1916 the Somme plan was adopted.

The plan would involve some 40 French and 13 British Divisions but only days after the plan was adopted it was thrown into disarray when the Germans launched an offensive of their own towards Verdun. The French had no alternative but to send more and more troops to reinforce the defences around Verdun, eventually leaving only 5 Divisions to take part in the Somme offensive. Now the brunt of the responsibility for the actions on the Somme fell upon the British. Joffre was insistent that the offensive went ahead in order to relieve some of the pressure against his own troops.

Part of the Fourth Army Operation Orders dated 5th June 1916 read:-

1. *The Fourth Army will take part in a general offensive with a view to breaking up the enemy's defensive system and of exploiting to the full all opportunities opened up for defeating his forces within reach.*
2. *The Third, First and Second Armies are undertaking offensive operations at various points along their fronts in conformity with the attack of the Forth army.*
3. *The French will assume the offensive on both banks of the Somme. The XX French Corps, in close touch with the right of the Forth army, is attacking at the same hour north of the Somme.*
4. *The three successive tasks of the Forth Army are:-*
   a) *To capture the enemy's defences on the line Montauban – Poziers – Serre, forming a strong defensive flank on the Grandcourt – Serre Ridge.*
   b) *To extend the defensive flank from Grancourt to Martinpuch, and, at the same time, advance our line eastward to the line Montauban – Martinpuch.*
   c) *To attack eastward from the line Montaban – Martinpuch and secure the Bazentin le Grand – Ginchy Plateau.*

As we have seen, the Germans had attacked Verdun some two weeks earlier, forcing the French to concentrate their forces there, so the British were now almost on their own.

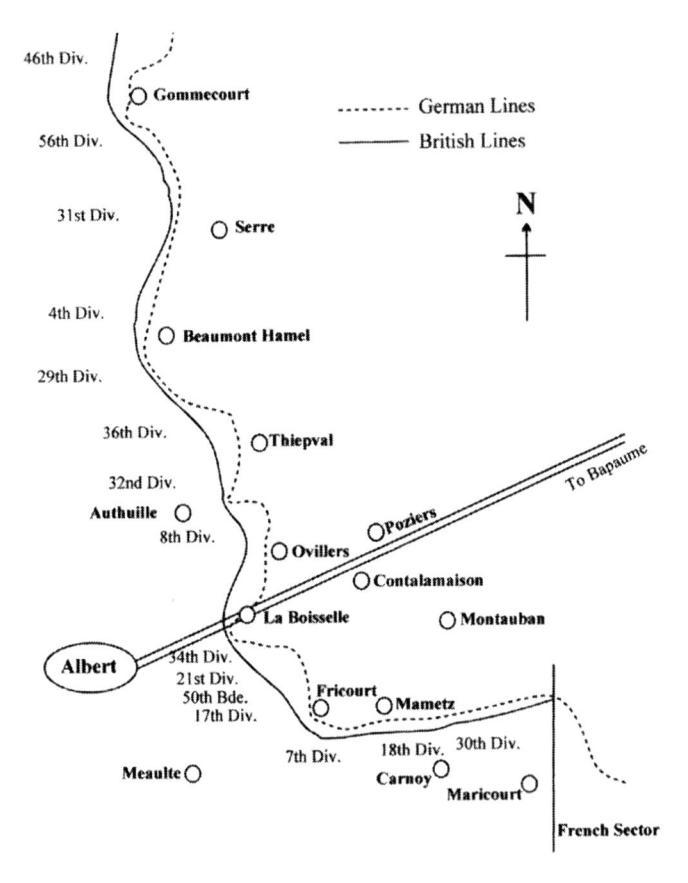

The Somme Battlefield 1st July 1916

The village of Gommecourt was the western-most part of the German lines and occupied a salient around which the 46th Division were to circle to the left and the 56th (London) Division to the right, meeting behind the village and thus bypassing and isolating it. Partially because of its strategic position and partially because the French had previously made several attempts to capture it, the Germans had heavily fortified what was already a naturally strongly defensive position and had turned it into an almost impregnable one.

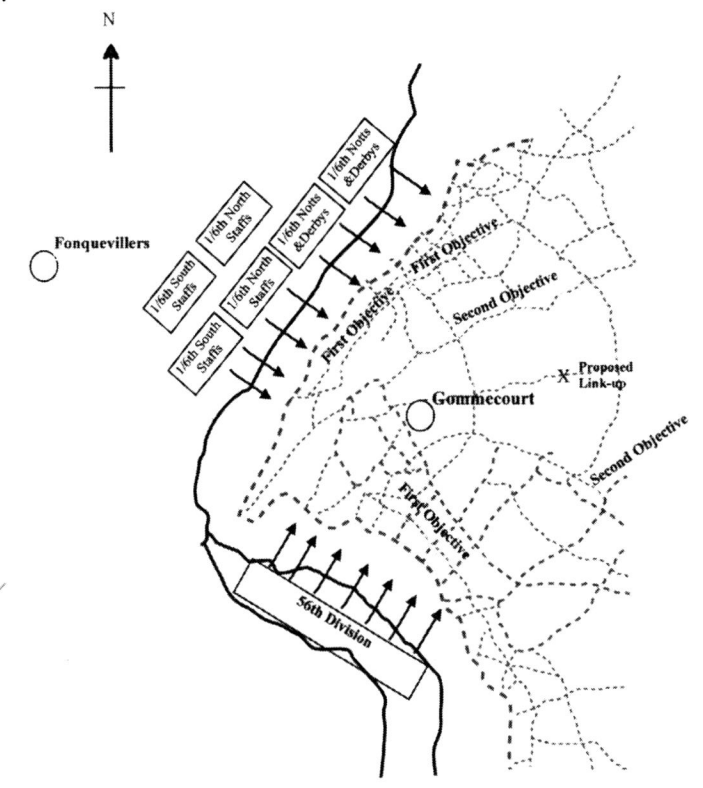

Map of the attack of the 46th Division 1st July 1916

Many of the dugouts were over forty feet deep, connected by reinforced communication tunnels, serviced by electricity and with most of the comforts of home. To add to the problems of the attackers, the enemy had recently received reinforcements in the form of two fresh Divisions, doubtless a result of the high profile preparations of the 46th Division of which no attempt was made to disguise.

Gommecourt was at the extreme northern end of the line in the Somme area and was not considered to be an essential target; rather, the purpose of the action here was to draw German troops and equipment from the area between Serre and Montauban to the south where the major Anglo-French breakthrough was planned. The 'Official History of the Great War' states; "..... assist in the operation of the Fourth Army by diverting against itself the fire of artillery and infantry which might otherwise be directed against the left flank of the main attack near Serre." With this in mind (but unknown to the rank and file) nothing was done to disguise the preparations from the enemy. In this they were successful, causing the Germans to bring up yet more troops from the south.

On 6th May 1916 the 1/6th moved to Fonquevillers (known to the troops as 'Funky villas'), a village which was just behind the British front lines in the 1916 battles and after a period in Brigade Reserve they relieved the 1/5th North Staffords in trenches in front of Gommecourt. A single line entry in the Battalion War Diary for the 26th May 1916 reads "Battalion practiced The Attack", an entry which would be repeated another five times before 22nd June when the Battalion moved to billets at Souastre.

It had been decided at Brigade Headquarters that an advance front line should be dug in front of the trenches occupied by the South Staffords in order to straighten out the Divisional line. The engineers had taped out the new line and from the 23rd to the 28th the 1/6th South Staffords were engaged in digging those same trenches, hardly the ideal preparation for their part in the coming attack, an attack that had originally been planned for the 29th June but which heavy rain caused to be postponed for two days.

OPERATION ORDERS
Part of the operation orders for the attack read:-

> *"Company Commanders will dispose their men in the available trenches on their respective fronts in such a manner that the succeeding waves can follow one another at not more than one minute intervals.*
> *All ranks will push forward to the final objective without delay, when the assault is commenced, with the exception of one Platoon of 'A' Company and one Platoon of 'D' Company who will consolidate Strong Points Nos. 1 and 2.*

The left flank will keep in touch with the 1/6th North Staffs. Regt. throughout the forward movement.

Artillery lifts opposite the front of the 137th Infantry Brigade from zero hour of attack will be as follows:-

	Minutes.
Off the enemy's front line	*Zero*
Off the enemy's second line	*3*
Off the enemy's third line	*8*
Off the East edge of the Wood	*15*
Off the Sunken Road	*20*
Off Oxus Trench	*25*
Off Fill Trench	*30*

The time of 'zero' (hour of attack) will be issued to all concerned.

The four Lewis Guns detailed to advance with the second and third waves, will protect the advance on the right flank and establish themselves in positions north of the Gommecourt Road. They will remain in such positions until the arrival of the troops specially allocated for the defence of this flank, after which they will rejoin their Companies.

The trained bombers will remain with their Companies and will advance with the assaulting waves, but will be so dispersed that they may be readily formed into bombing parties to deal with the enemy's C.T.'s in case the general advance is delayed. They will carry a supply of bombs but will be equipped as other ranks with the exception of Small Arms Ammunition.

All Company runners will make themselves acquainted with the position of Battalion Headquarters both before and after the advance.

Four scouts per Company will be detailed to advance at 'zero' minus five minutes in order to locate the best routes through the enemy's wire, where they will remain until the arrival of the fourth wave.

The scouts will be warned of the actions of our artillery, trench mortars and machine guns.
The Battalion will parade in Fighting Order at an hour to be notified tomorrow.

All ranks are reminded that it is of the utmost importance to keep in touch with the troops on their right and left, and to render mutual support whenever circumstances require it."

Waiting nervously in their trenches the men had been fed on thick bacon sandwiches and were given the traditional tot of rum before going 'over the top'. At 6.25 am the field guns began a 65 minute bombardment of 11,660 rounds of high explosive and shrapnel shells and the howitzers and heavy guns 7,000 shells. Half an hour later the Germans replied by shelling the 137th Division's assembly trenches causing heavy casualties.

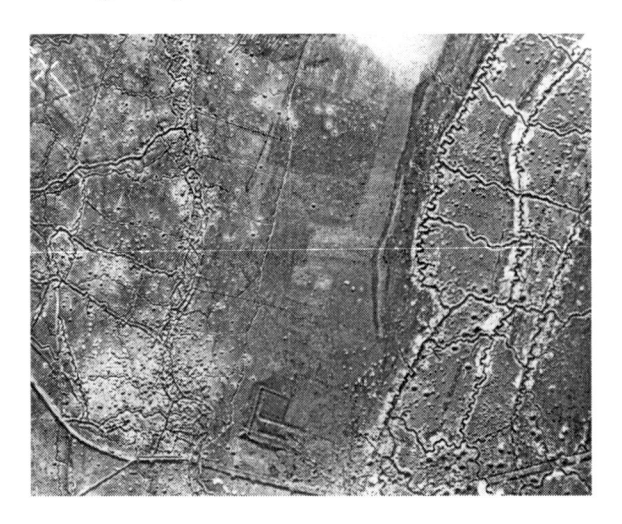

An aerial view of the trenches in front of Gommecourt
The Allied trenches are on the left of the picture and the more substantial German ones on the right. The Fonquevillers to Gommecourt Road is in the lower left corner. (Photograph courtesy Staffordshire Regiment Museum)

The South Staffords had taken up their position immediately to the left of the Fonquevillers – Gommecourt road in order of Company

D, B, A, C, with C Company being alongside the road. Each company had a frontage of 75 yards and they were to advance in four waves, each 80 yards apart.

All along the line the Tommies had been told that preliminary bombardment would destroy the German defences and barbed wire entanglements, but in practice the high explosives merely lifted the wire only for it to fall back unbroken whilst the lead shrapnel balls were almost totally ineffective against the steel wires. When the bombardment was lifted just before the attack, the Germans had time to climb out of their dugouts and man their machine guns.

THE ATTACK
The attack when it came was nothing short of carnage. Weighed down by their 66 lbs of equipment, the thick glutinous mud made even the act of climbing out of the jumping-off trenches a laborious one, and once out the men were confronted with crossing a maze of old French trenches that had been destroyed by shell fire, by the remnants of the old French wire entanglements, by a thick smoke screen laid down by the men in the front line throwing smoke grenades into No-Man's-Land and by smoke from bombs laid down by Special Brigade, Royal Engineers.

The wind, instead of blowing the smoke towards the German lines was blowing across No-Man's-Land from right to left and was much thicker than any that had been encountered during the training exercises. In the event, the smoke screen was so thick that that many of the men lost their direction completely, all this even before they reached the German wire.

Less than 50 yards in front of the trenches occupied by C Company were the ruins of a small sucerie (sugar factory) which was occupied by a small party of Germans who caused many casualties. Beyond this and running across the whole width of the front attacked by the South Staffords the ground dropped away and here the concentration of German wire was at its thickest.

After around half an hour the wind dissipated the smokescreen and the full horror of what was happening could be clearly seen. One man later reported

> "I was in the first wave. My first impression was the sight of hundreds of unexploded mortar bombs. As large and round, as big footballs. I thought how like oranges they looked, they were bright orange-yellow. They were supposed to cut the German wire which was almost untouched. I doubt if even one had exploded. The German entanglements which should have been cut by the six days of shelling were almost intact and many men had become stuck on the wires, many more had made scarcely and progress before being mown down by hails of machine gun bullets which raked No-Mans-Land and dead and wounded men were everywhere".

Effectively the attack was already over; the battalion had suffered 239 casualties out of a fighting strength of 523 men.

2nd Lieutenant Reginald Page of the 1/6th Battalion, the youngest son of Charles and Mary Page of 3, Westland Road, Wolverhampton was killed in action on July 1st 1916, Born on St. Valentine's Day 1893, after leaving school in Wolverhampton he went to work in Canada, but enlisted for service following the declaration of war, and arrived in England in October 1914. Having spent his early war in the ranks he received a commission. Reginald Page was killed while leading his platoon in a charge at Gommecourt. His mother subsequently received a letter from his commanding officer saying: "I shall miss your boy exceedingly, for his past experience was most useful to me. He looked after his men so well, inspiring them with confidence and showing a splendid example in leadership."

23 year old 2nd Lieutenant Page has no known grave and is commemorated on the Thiepval Memorial to the Missing, Thiepval, France. (Photograph courtesy Express and Star Ltd.)

The Aftermath of Battle
(Photograph courtesy Staffordshire Regiment Museum)

Part of the War diary recorded that day:-

> *"During the course of this bombardment the enemy replied vigorously with howitzers and field guns upon our front line and communication trenches and at intervals he directed short bursts of machine gun fire on our parapet and exits from the direction of our front and right front.*
> *At 7.30 a.m. the four platoons of the leading wave having moved out to the new front line, under cover of the smoke advanced to assault the enemy's position and were followed by the succeeding waves. The fourth wave was delayed for about five minutes by the casualties that blocked the communication trenches leading to the front line and by the heavy loads which they were carrying......*
> *........ the only Company which was able to penetrate the enemy's line in any strength was 'D' Company on the left, who found that the wire was well cut on their frontage; three platoons of this Company obtained a footing in the front line and some men are said to have gone further but they were outnumbered and accounted for by the enemy.*

The remaining three Companies on the right were held up by the enemy's wire which had not been so well cut, and although small parties were able to enter the enemy's line they could not obtain a permanent footing there.

Eighty men returned within an hour to our front line where they remained until noon, when they were ordered to occupy our supports, and they were subsequently withdrawn from the trenches."

Given that the primary aim of the 137th Brigade was to attract attention to their activities in order to draw enemy forces away from the main area of attack further south, and that the heavily fortified village of Gommecourt was not a primary objective, it is difficult to understand why their attack was not broken off earlier. The total number of casualties suffered by the Allied armies that day was approximately 19,000 killed and 40,000 wounded.

Meanwhile, back in Wolverhampton:-

SPLENDID NEWS FROM THE BRITISH FRONT

THE LONG-EXPECTED IS HAPPENING.

There is Great News from the British Lines. It reached London to-day from our Special Correspondent at the Front.

TO-MORROW'S Lloyd's News will give you the Fullest and Latest Account of how the **"GREAT PUSH" IS GOING.**

(Reproduced courtesy Express and Star Ltd.)

The day after the attack, Sir Thomas Snow, General Officer Commanding VII Corps, reported that "I regret to have to report that the 46th Division in yesterday's operations showed a lack of offensive spirit." The reality of the matter is that the 46th Division had been given an impossible task. The Chief of Staff of VII Corps, Brigadier-General Francis Lyons, later admitted that the capture of the Gommecourt salient was unnecessary to the purpose of the diversion. The Battle of the Somme finally ended on 18th November 1916.

ANATOMY OF A RAID
During quieter times in the trenches, raids would often be carried out against enemy trenches by a small party of men, perhaps consisting of a single officer and twenty five men, but a raid on a much larger scale was ordered to take place on the 25th of October. The Officer Commanding 'B' company, Captain H. V. Mander, was to lead and on the 18th October the party was withdrawn from the trenches for a short period of intense training.

As always, raids were planned in meticulous detail and this one was no exception as can be seen below.

    1.   *REFERENCE:- Trench Map RANSART, 1/10,000*
    2.   *OBJECT.*
          a. *To secure identification by taking prisoners.*
          b. *To kill Germans.*
          c. *To inflict damage.*
    3.   *COMPOSITION OF PARTIES*
    'A' Party. 2nd Lieut. S. McGowan in command, 2nd Lieut. J.A. Sheddon second in command.
    (1) Cpl. Partridge and 4 other ranks.
    (2) Sgt. Fryer and 4 other ranks
    (3) L./Cpl. Fallon and 4 other ranks.
    (4) Sgt. Greatrix and 9 other ranks.
    'B' Party, 2nd Lieut. J.M. Frew in command, 2nd Lieut. J.L.C.S. Wallace second in command.
    (1) Sgt. Ford and 6 other ranks.
    (2) Sgt. Southall and 6 other ranks.
    (3) Sgt. Washington and 2 other ranks.

'C' Party, 2nd Lieut. T. Walker in command.
(1) Sgt. Pennington and 9 other ranks.
'D' Party, 2nd Lieut. J.P. Woods in command.
(1) Sgt. Hooland and 3 other ranks.
(2) L/Cpl. Shields and 10 other ranks.
(3) 'E' Party, 2nd Lieut. W.K.C. Adams in command.
(1) 1 Lewis gun and team and 5 other ranks under L-Cpl. Sullivan.
(2) 1 Lewis gun and team and 5 other ranks under command of Sgt. Whittall.
RESERVE PARTY. 2nd Lieut. J.G. Brady and 8 other ranks
4. ASSEMBLY. These parties will assemble as per Battalion Operation Orders.
5. RUNNERS. Each officer will detail 2 men to act as runners.

At 6.30 p.m. 2nd Lieut. Sheddon led a reconnaissance patrol to lay tapes from the front-line trench to the gap in the enemy wire and happened upon a German working party working to repair the very same gap. Artillery fire was called-up and the working party was sent hurrying back to their trenches. The tapes were duly laid and the party returned at 8.45 p.m. to report that although the gap in the German wire was of a good size, it was not completely cut.

A BANGALORE TORPEDO

To rectify the situation it was determined to use a Bangalore Torpedo. Bangalore torpedoes were primarily used for clearing barbed wire before an attack and could be used from a protected position in a trench. The torpedo was standardised to consist of a number of externally identical five foot (1.5 metre) lengths of threaded pipe, one of which contained the explosive charge. The pipes would be screwed together using connecting sleeves to make a longer pipe of the required length, somewhat like a chimney brush or drain clearing rod. A smooth nose cone would be screwed on the end to prevent snagging on the ground and it would then be pushed forward from the protected position and detonated to clear a gap through the barbed wire. At 9.45 p.m. the raiders left their trenches and made their way stealthily to the German wire where they placed the torpedo and lit the fuse at a pre-arranged time. The artillery barrage designed to cover the explosion of the device opened on time and the remaining twenty feet of wire was cut.

The raiding party now quickly passed through the gap and into the enemy trenches, taking prisoners and killing as they went. By 10.45 p.m. the party were back in their own trenches with the spoils of their efforts, six prisoners, many documents and having gained an inside knowledge of the enemy lines. Over twenty Germans had been killed as against just four of the South Staffs men being wounded.

2nd Lieutenant McGowan wrote in his report:-

"........*My party entered the German trench. Immediately on our right as we got in we found a dug-out, and on searching it found three prisoners who were despatched at once to our trenches. No papers or information were to be found. The dug-out was in good repair, with beds for 24 men. There were food and cooking utensils on shelves in the wall, and a large brazier heated the place. When we left the dug-out we found that the right blocking party under Sgt. Fryer was being pushed back by bombers, so all our time was devoted to holding that block. We had no casualties, but have no doubt that we inflicted some, as after the explosion of some of our bombs, cries were heard"*

2nd Lieutenant Frew reported:-

"........ *Last night 'B' party entered the German trenches and secured three prisoners. We entered close to the enemy sentry post of three men. One was captured and the other two killed. At this point I amalgamated my party with 2nd Lieut. Walker's and took command of both.*

We proceeded northwards along the trench until we reached a Communication Trench to the south and an enemy dug-out with two entrances under the parapet.

2nd Lieut. Walker proceeded along the main fire trench to form a block.

Sgt. Washington and five men remained behind to hold the two exits from the dug-out, while the remainder of the party proceeded down the C.T. About 50 yards down, the trench (which bore traces of heavy shelling) became impassable for a distance of about 8 yards. I therefore left three men to form a fighting head there, should the enemy attempt to come up the trench. On returning to the front line I found Sgt. Washington and two other ranks had investigated the dug-out after bombing it. There were two dead Germans in it and no occupants.

2nd Lieut. Walker now returned and reported. Having driven off an enemy bombing group, who appeared to suffer casualties. He secured two prisoners.

Our barrage was about 20 yards on the other side of the artificial block, and he had found a small party who were willing to rush through the barrage and endeavour to capture a machine gun in the long sap. This I refused to permit.

2nd Lieut. Wood, who was in charge of the parapet party, then personally passed the order to withdraw, but until I had ordered the men out myself none of them showed the slightest intention of going back.

The German trenches were deep, dry and well revetted. They had been considerably knocked about by the artillery. There were no traverses but the zigzag method of trench was employed. The firing step was very broad and quite high. From the firing step to the parapet there were spars of square timber, which fulfilled the double purpose of revetting and a ladder by which to climb out.

The dug-outs were deep and unharmed by our artillery. They were clean and tidy, with accommodation for about ten men.

A noticeable feature was the absence of gas-masks, both upon the prisoners and in the dug-outs. One of my party who spoke German asked for a telephone, but was informed that there were none in the vicinity.

The behaviour of the men was excellent, and their coolness at certain awkward moments excited my highest admiration."

Lieutenant-Colonel F.J. Trump saw fit to request immediate recognition for a number of officers and men after the raid:-

> 2nd Lieutenant J.A. Shelton *"Who when in charge of one of the reconnoitring patrols which was twice checked by hostile patrols and wiring parties, succeeded in locating a gap which he successfully explored to within ten yards of the enemy parapet under the very nose of a sentry group whose presence he had detected. After reporting the presence of a gap to the O.C. Raid he again accompanied the advance party, took forward the R.E.'s with an Ammonal torpedo which was exploded whilst our bombardment was at its height only a few yards away. The success of the operation depended upon his being able to complete the partial gap."*
> 2nd Lieutenant Shelton was awarded a Military Cross.
>
> 2nd Lieutenant T. Walker *"When in the German Trench he found that an artificial obstacle prevented the progress of his party. The parapet being blocked with Chevaux-de-frise, he took a party on the parados beyond the block, killed seven and captured two Germans. He then attempted to lead on his party to capture a Machine Gun, but was prevented by our barrage. This is the second time he has commanded a party in a successful raid."*
> 2nd Lieutenant Walker also received a Military Cross.

Six men received the Military Medal:-

> No. 2129 Sgt. Washington W.J. *"Who during the reconnaissance of the gap and the attack on the German Trenches behaved with conspicuous gallantry, fearlessly entered dugouts and when his party was being hard pressed formed up a blocking party which effectually kept back a hostile bombing attack."*
>
> No. 3184 Cpl. Hale E. *"Who was recommended by me for his conduct in the raid on 2nd September, showed utter fearlessness in entering dugouts and clearing them out, He*

also volunteered to go for a Machine Gun on the other side of our barrage."

No. 5558 Pte (L/Cpl.) Palmer C. *"With his knowledge of German he was able to warn his party officer of an impending bombing attack by a party beyond an artificial block. He took part in the defeat of this party and protected with his bayonet his officer who had dropped his revolver in the struggle."*

No. 2619 Sgt. Greatrix R.G. *"Against considerable opposition he handled his party admirably. It was largely due to his courage and energy that the hostile bombing attack was effectively countered."*

No. 5601 L/Cpl. Hipkins W. *"Personally accounted for two Germans. Behaved admirably throughout the operation".*

No. 5601 Pte. Lane E. *"Showed great coolness during the time the right block was hard pressed and helped greatly to hold the trench whilst the dugouts were being cleared."*

The final man to be recommended for an award was Captain H.V. Mander MC, *"Who earned the Military Cross at Messines, has twice commanded successful raids by this Regiment, on September 2nd and October 25th. His careful training and management of Officers and men resulted on each occasion in complete success. His attitude on both occasions inspired Officers and men with confidence of success."*
Captain Howard Vivian Mander was the son of Benjamin and Lillian Mander of Trysull Manor, members of the locally prominent printing ink manufacturing family 'Mander Brothers'. Captain Mander, who had been a pupil at Wellington College, where he was a member of the Officer Training Corps, had

received his commission to Second Lieutenant on the 10th October 1914. He was granted ten days home leave for his part in these raids. (Photograph courtesy Staffordshire Regiment Museum)

After a spell in Divisional Reserve the 1/6th Battalion were given a month's rest before in November 1916 being engaged in Battalion training and were at last able to bathe, the only casualties for the month had been two men accidentally wounded.

December saw them back in the trenches on three occasions, each time taking over from the 1/5th South Staffords. Here, between Bienvillers and Monchy au Bois, conditions were worse than any previously experienced; water so deep that the 'C' Company Lewis Gun post could only be supplied with rations and ammunition by having a Private swim out to it!

Christmas Day 1916 was spent in Brigade Reserve and now at least the 1/6th was able to do justice to the festival.

1917

"Of the six or seven hundred men who marched into
Bourlon Wood, fewer than one hundred marched out"
(Extract from the original 1924 history)

For the 1/6th Battalion, January 1917 began rather quieter if no drier. The trenches now held so much water that it was almost impossible to move down supplies and changes to duty patterns were made from necessity.

In the latter days of February the Germans began their controlled withdrawal to the Hindenberg Line, although not yet those directly opposite the 1/6th South Staffords, so this gave cause for the raising of a large number of night patrols to constantly monitor the situation. Even given the increasing number of patrols, the casualty roll for the first three months of 1917 was relatively low; killed 7, wounded 22, gassed 2.

THE 2/6th GO TO FRANCE
On the 24th of February 1917 the 2/6th South Staffords received orders to proceed to Southampton and the following day saw 31 officers and 653 other ranks entrained at Codford station where, after arriving at the port at 11.30 a.m. they eventually embarked on H.M.T. Viper at 4.00 p.m. en route for France.

On arrival at Le Havre at 7.00 a.m. on the 26th, the troops proceeded to No. 5 Rest Camp before at 4.00 p.m. in bitterly cold weather they once again boarded a train, this time bound for Saleux, near Amiens, where they arrived at 2.30 p.m. the next afternoon and from there went into billets in Dury. From the 2nd of March the Battalion spent five days training at Mericourt sur Somme before marching to the ruined village of Foucaucourt where they became Battalion in Brigade Reserve.

On the 9th March two officers and one platoon from each Company went to the front-line and were attached to the 2/5th North Staffords for instruction before the following day saw the Battalion takeover from the North Staffords in the front-line just south of Genermont. The 2/6th South Staffords had joined their senior comrades in The Great War.

Their first real experience of trench life was not a comforting one, a severe frost that chilled them to their very bones and made the roads difficult to use, shortages of water and of supplies together with increased activity from the German artillery all conspired towards a miserable existence. Damaged trenches which were repaired at night, quickly became damaged again the next morning and soon became almost untenable, both the front-line and communication trenches were very wet and muddy, in some places the mud being knee deep.

Owing to the exhausted condition of the men and the number of sick, the Battalion were relieved by the 2/6th Sherwood Foresters. The relief when they finally came were late and the change over was not completed until 3.30 a.m. on the morning of the 16th of March, the men arriving back at their billets in Foucaucourt an hour later. It was here on the same date that Major J. Stuart-Wortley assumed command from Lieutenant-Colonel Spier.

GOMMECOURT REVISITED
Two days after the 2/6th went into the trenches for the first time, the 1/6th moved to Bayencourt, a village four miles from Gommecourt, the stronghold against which they had made their futile attack on the 1st July the previous year.

Sergeant Bridgewater took the opportunity to visit the old battlefield and what he saw caused him to record;

> *"I went over our old No Man's Land in front of Fonquevillers, and I shall never forget the sight I saw of our boys who had done their part here in July 1916. Little remained save their skeletons and tattered clothing; it appeared to me that they had not got further than 200 yards or so when they had met their death. It was much the same on the right, close to Gommecourt Park, where the London*

Scottish (56th Division) had attacked. Little was left but kilts and skeletons."

Many of these men now lie in Gommecourt Wood New Cemetery.

A CHANGE OF TACTICS
The 1917 Allied Spring Offensives had seen a radical change in the tactics adopted by the allies. One of the reasons for the failures of earlier attacks was that tactics had been determined at Brigade level and disseminated down through Battalion HQ to the officers on the ground who were expected to follow them to the letter, whilst the Other Ranks had each been trained to play one specific role and only that role. The Canadian General Sir Julian Byng determined that not only should every officer be able to make decisions in accordance with prevailing conditions, but that every soldier should have knowledge of the general plan.

THE 2/6th ON THE MOVE
Towards the end of April 1917 the 2/6th had been engaged in repairing roads and generally making good the damage left by the retreating Germans. Entering the deserted German trench lines at Fresnes they found that the Germans had left behind them a trench system that the Staffords could only envy. The deep and substantial trenches and dugouts were fitted with electric lighting (a feature not yet common in many houses back in England), tables, chairs and wire beds, and the Officers' Mess quarters were even found to be furnished with upholstered chairs.

From Fresnes their journey took them on to Mazancourt, Misery, Mons-en-Chaussee and Bouvincourt, where they had a brief respite from marching, but only to be engaged in road-mending. In freezing conditions, Good Friday (6th March) found them reaching their intended destination – Montigney Farm near the village of Le Verguier and here they erected shelters and made preparations to attack the village itself.

When the attack came, it was found that the preliminary shelling with 4" howitzers had failed to cut the dense thickets of barbed wire so perhaps it was as well that the enemy had already vacated Le Verguier.

APRIL 1917

Mid-April 1917 saw the 2/6th leaving Le Verguier for the quieter village of Hamelet and the 1/6th spending a few pleasant days in Bethune from where on the 18th of that month they moved to Lievin in accordance with Operation Orders No. 4:-

Operation Orders No.4
By
Major R. Evans
Commanding 1/6th Battalion South Staffordshire Regiment
Wednesday, 18th April 1917

1. <u>Move.</u>
    The Battalion will move today to Lievin.
2. <u>Parade</u>
    The Battalion will Parade in the road outside the Tobacco Factory, head of Column facing S.E. at 4.15 p.m.
    Order of March:- 'D' – 'A' – 'B' – 'C'.
3. <u>Route</u>
    Via Beuvry – Sailly la Bourse and thence south to Grenay where Guides will meet the Battalion at 7.30 p.m. From Sailly la Bourse movement will be by Companies and from (map reference) by Platoons.
4. <u>Watches</u>
    Watches will be synchronized at Orderly Room at 3.00 p.m. and halts observed independently.
    After dark connecting files will be maintained between units, and care must be taken not to lose touch at the halts.
5. <u>Valises & Blankets, Mess Kits.</u>
    Officers' valises will be delivered to the Q.M. Stores by 2.00 p.m.
    Officers' Mess Kits will be at the Q.M. stores at 3.15 p.m. Blankets will be neatly rolled in bundles

of tens and taken to the Cook's Shed, in Barrack Yard, at 12.30 p.m.
6. *Tea.*
Tea will be served at 3.00 p.m.
7. *Transport*
Transport will accompany the Battalion.
8. *Certificates & Cleaning of Billets.*
Officers Commanding companies will render to Orderly Room at 3.00 p.m. certificates re damage to Billets. They will see that Billets etc. are left clean. O. C. 'D' Company will detail a party to pay special attention to the cleanliness of the Barrack Yard.
9. *Stores*
Care must be exercised in taking over all stores, especially regarding Pack saddlery and Gum Boots. Transport Officer will see that all Pack Saddlery is complete.
10. *Acknowledge at Once*

Signed H. Hanford
Captain,
Adjutant, 1/6th Battalion, South Staffordshire Regiment

Issued at 11.05 a.m.

Copy No. 1 issued to Commanding Officer
Copy No. 2 issued to O.C. 'A' Company.
Copy No. 3 issued to O.C. 'B' Company
Copy No. 4 issued to O.C. 'C' Company
Copy No. 5 issued to O.C. 'D' Company
Copy No. 6 issued to Transport Officer
Copy No. 7 issued to Quartermaster.
Copy No. 8 issued to Orderly Room.
Copy No. 9 issued to War Diary

On the 19th April the 1/6th relieved the 1st Battalion of the Royal Fusiliers in trenches in front of Lievin and the following day were holding the line with two Companies in outposts amongst the ruined houses whilst the other two were in well constructed trenches in which were sited two strong points. On the afternoon of the 22nd they were told that the Notts and Derbys would be attacking 'Hill 65' a commanding position that was well wired and entrenched.

In the expectation that the Germans would abandon their positions in front of Lens if the attack succeeded, the South Staffords were to send out patrols to monitor the situation and to occupy the deserted trenches if possible but when the attack failed they were heavily fired upon and had to withdraw, suffering several casualties in the process. In contrast to the first three months of 1917, the 1/6th sustained more men killed and wounded in April of that year than for those three months combined.

UNDER ATTACK
In May the 1/6th found themselves once again taking positions in the line between Lens and Loos where on the 25th May they were support battalion for the 1/6th North Staffords in an attack on Nash Alley.

2nd Lieutenant P.R. Teeton, O.C. 'C' Company 1/6th South Staffords entered his report as follows:-

> *"I received orders from Lieut-Col Trump, commanding 1/6th Btn. South Staffordshire Regt., that my company was to support the 1/6th Btn. North Staffs. Regt. and that I was under the direct orders of Lieut.-Col. Stoney, commanding 1/6th North Staffs. Regt. I received orders to take two platoons to saps in Bugs Walk and two platoons to dig in at M.6.c.65.80, in existing trench, with my Company Headquarters at N.1.c.15.90.*
>
> *My Company was in position at 4.45 p.m. on the 24th inst. At 12.10 a.m. Captain Sheddon, M.C. 1/6th Btn. North Staffs. Regt., asked me to send him a platoon to support him in Netley trench in case of a counter-attack, as he was unable to collect enough men of his own Company. This platoon returned at 4 a.m. At 7.30 a.m. on the 25th I received orders to send two platoons to report to Major*

Macnamara at M.6.a.90.45.., and to move my other two platoons up to Bugs Walk. I sent Lieut. R. N. Bullock with Nos. 11 and 12 Platoons to Major Macnamara who, later, ordered him to take one platoon up to Nash Alley to 2nd Lieut. Edge.

2nd Lieut. Bullock posted the Lewis-gun team in a good position midway between the two Flank Bombing Posts. The Left Bombing Post was ordered to push their Post up to O.G.1 Trench and two of my sergeants were included in this party; a shell-burst wounded both sergeants. Shortly after the enemy was seen massing troops on the right, and 2nd Lieut. Edge sent word by one of my Corporals to Major Macnamara.

2nd Lieut. Bullock returned to Major Macnamara after posting the platoon as per instructions, and was ordered to stand by with the other platoon in the dug-out at N.1.a.5.8. My Lewis-gun team saw the enemy advancing, and fired twenty-two magazines, causing heavy casualties to the enemy; then the gun was thrown out of action. The team were then ordered by Major Macnamara to take up bombs and slowly withdraw over the top to O.G.1 Trench at N.1.a.5.8. The Bombing Section posted to the Right Bombing Post was heavily pressed from Netley Trench on both sides of Nash Alley, and were told to withdraw; and as they withdrew, they took up firing positions in a sap running west from Nash Alley. At least ten of the enemy were killed by rifle fire before the party withdrew over the top to O.G.1.

The party on the Left Bombing Post withdrew with the 1/6th North Staffs. Regt. down O.G.1. Trench.
Four of my men were wounded, and seven are missing. During the heavy bombardment from 11.30 a.m. to 1.15 p.m. I had the remainder of my Company all ready to move, and also I had previously arranged firing positions in Bugs Walk in case the enemy should attempt to break through."

QUIET DAYS ON THE WESTERN FRONT

Whilst the 1/6th were still engaging the enemy, the 2/6th had life somewhat easier, euphemistically referred to by the original history as "Quiet days on the Western Front", the days were far from easy, strenuous days and nights were spent strengthening wire entanglements and generally improving defences, though enemy artillery caused a number of casualties.

There was a lighter side to their stay when they were relieved in the trenches by troopers of the cavalry. Since from the very early days of the war, barbed wire entanglements had made cavalry charges impossible, now the cavalrymen were used in the same manner as the infantry. Not to let their standards slip entirely however, they still attempted to live like gentlemen, changing for dinner and dining off tablecloths.

On one occasion a Frenchman visited the area to present an official pass and permit authorising him to reclaim the contents of his father's wine cellar. There was no shortage of volunteers to help him with the excavations but just how much of the contents were actually returned to the owner and how much was diverted elsewhere is not recorded.

CONTRAST

For the 2/6th South Staffords life continued in much the same vein until August 1917 but for the 1/6th the fighting continued as before. In June the 1/6th were withdrawn from the line, supposedly to rest, but in reality they found themselves practising over tapes before on the 21st of that month they moved near to Lievin before going into an assembly area by Fosse 8 two days later. From here they launched an attack on 'Hill 65', A and D Companies led the assault with C Company in support and B Company in reserve.

The attack was a complete success, but a follow-up attack made on the 1st July, a date which must have filled many with a sense of foreboding, was another matter. The 1/6th South Staffords were in close support of the 1/5th North Staffords and, having started the assault at 2.47 a.m., by 6.30 a.m. all objectives had been taken.

Even before the newly taken trenches could be secured, the Germans launched a ferocious counter-attack and despite valiant efforts, the Staffords were gradually forced to retire. At 6.00 p.m. orders were received for the 1/6th South Staffords to withdraw to Lievin where they finally reached their billets some 9 hours later. 2 officers had been killed and 8 wounded in the action, 57 Other Ranks were dead, 25 were missing and 261 had been wounded.

CAMBRAI

The town of Cambrai is most associated with the battle of that name in November 1917, the British offensive which brought the successful use of large numbers of tanks into modern warfare for the first time - nearly 400 were employed. The attack gained considerable ground initially although the Germans then counter-attacked and recovered a great deal of the land, even pushing the British further back than their original starting point in places. The battle lasted officially until 6th December and the furthest advance by the British encompassed Bourlon Wood which lies on a ridge dominating the relatively flat countryside to the west of Cambrai.

November 1917 had started well for the men of the 2/6th South Staffords when several of their numbers were presented with gallantry awards for their conduct in the Ypres sector during the previous months. Now back in France, during the remainder of that month they were engaged in the usual routine of time spent in the trenches, route marches, working parties, and training until on the 28th they relieved the 2nd Battalion Coldstream Guards in trenches at Bourlon Wood.

BOURLON WOOD

The wood that had existed before the war was now almost unrecognisable, the ground pock-marked with shell craters, any trees still standing were shattered and limbless whilst many others had been felled by the ferocity of the shell fire. When the South Staffords got into the woods they found it already teeming with Allied troops, Guards, Cavalry, London and Northern battalions all present. It was here on 30th November the 2/6th who were in the support trenches were to suffer terribly by being subjected to a continuous heavy bombardment with both gas and explosive shells.

The gas presented them with their worst problem since with no wind to disperse the poisonous clouds; gas masks had to be worn constantly, eating or drinking was impossible without removing the masks and to do so resulted in dire consequences.

The Royal Army Medical Corps were overwhelmed by the constant stream of casualties being brought out of the wood, strings of blinded men each with his hand on the shoulder of the man in front and led by one man who could still see. Stretcher cases had to be carried over half a mile over arduous terrain.

Captain Bernard Stewart Atkinson, the eldest son of Herbert and Etheldred Atkinson of 'Weardale', Newbridge, Wolverhampton, had been educated at Cranmore House School and Denstone College before joining Walsall solicitors Wilkinson and Co. as an articled pupil in September 1909. He passed his final exams in November 1914 and after joining the Inns of Court Officers Training Corps he was appointed adjutant to the 'School of Musketry' at Berkhampstead, and was promoted to the rank of Captain in March 1916 before seeing active service with the 2/6th South Staffords in February 1917. Having returned from leave on the eve of the 30th of November he declined to avail himself of the usual practise of staying in the transport lines overnight and returned to the front to be with his men. Captain Atkinson died that day and is buried in Orival Wood Cemetery, Flesquiers, he was 24 years old. The inscription chosen by his family was; "MINE HONOUR IS MY LIFE, IN THAT I LIVE AND FOR THAT I DIE. SHAKESPEARE." (Photograph courtesy Express and Star Ltd.)

Colonel Sir T. G. Cope, Bart. Of the 176th Infantry Brigade, later recalled;

"We stayed in this area till November 17th, when we were relieved by the 3rd Canadian Brigade, and moved South to be in reserve for the Cambrai battle, which commenced on November 20th. On November 23rd we arrived at Heudicourt in reserve to the South portion of the salient we were now holding in front of Welsh ridge. I went up to see the 6th Buffs of the 12th Division, and was shocked to see how thin the whole line was. The men had been in the line since carrying out the first attack, and had suffered 50 per cent. of casualties, and the O.C. told me all the Brigades of the Division were in like plight. This so impressed me that I determined to practice for a counter attack on Gouzeaucourt. On the supposition that the enemy had broken through, I held a tactical scheme for officers on November 26th, and on November 27th we were to have done it with the whole Brigade, but unfortunately the morning dawned wet, so we stood by. At 10 a.m. we were told to march across the base of the salient to Flesquieres to relieve the Guards, who had one Brigade roughly handled at Bourlon Wood. The Brigade billeted that night round Ribecourt, and on November 28th took over from the 2nd Guards Brigade in the Bourlon Wood and Fontaine sectors. The 2/5th Leicesters were attached to the Brigade, and were put to the right support.

2/5th South Staffs. On right.
2/5th North Staffs. In centre.
2/6th North Staffs. Bourlon Wood.
2/6th South Staffs. Support in Bourlon Wood.

I at once realised that no sane man would attempt to attack through Bourlon Wood, which at that time was so knocked about that it was almost impossible to get through, and I asked General Romer if I might hold the wood with two Companies and move the remainder back to a more healthy position, where they could be used if required to counter attac, as it seemed quite obvious that in case of a Hun attack, the enemy would fill the wood with gas and attack on each side. General Romer quite agreed, and orders for *this had actually gone out when a wire arrived to say that Corps did not approve as they considered Bourlon Wood a most important tactical feature, and the minimum garrison must be two Battalions. I could have cried as I knew what was coming, and if my Battalions broke on the Fontaine Sector (they were stretched like a bow-string), I had no reserves. On 30th November the storm broke, but miraculously the bow string held, but all the while gas was being pumped into Bourlon Wood. The Hun broke through the 55th Division front and captured Gouzeaucourt, threatening our rear. If only we had still been at Heudicourt we should have had the unique experience of actually carrying out in reality what we had practiced in a field day, and I have always regretted that this experience was denied us. Certainly no one could have done the job better than the Guards did without any rehearsal at all, but I could not help smiling to myself when I remembered the unholy glee with which the Guards handed over to us, and departed to their well-earned rest, only to be hauled back again. On December 1st the poor 2/6th South and 2/6th North were in a very bad state suffering from gas; the whole wood smelt like a laboratory, and these Battalions had now had 36 hours of it, so that it was almost impossible to avoid taking off your gas mask, if only to put some food in. The result, of course, was that these Battalions, with the T.M. Battery, had to be sent back to Rue on the sea coast to recover. They left on December 10th, and did not rejoin the Brigade until the end of January; practically all those who had been in the wood had to be evacuated and took no further part in the War."*

Between five hundred and six hundred men of the Battalion had marched into Bourlon Wood on the night of the 28th November, yet fewer than one hundred were left unscathed when they were relieved by the 2/4th Leicesters on the 1st December.

Meanwhile, back in Wolverhampton:-

```
POST OFFICE AS A NEWSPAPER
                Amusements.
GRAND THEATRE, WOLVERHAMPTON.
To-night.         Once Nightly              7.30
RETURN VISIT OF WALTER HOWARD'S BEAUTIFUL PLAY,
        "SEVEN DAYS' LEAVE,"
   U-BOAT, BRITISH DESTROYERS, GALLANT SOLDIERS, AND PLUCKY
   ENGLISH GIRLS.   SPECIAL MATINEE ON SATURDAY at 2.0.
  BOXES 5s. 6d., STALLS 3s.  Box Office open 10 to 4, 6 to 10, and all day Saturday.  Tel. 134.
  MONDAY NEXT: The "Full-of-Smiles" Play, "DADDY LONG-LEGS."

EMPIRE.        TWICE NIGHTLY.       6.50 and 9.0
           THIS WEEK.          First House ten minutes earlier
                                   on Mondays and Saturdays.
  MOSS EMPIRES LTD. Present ALBERT DE COURVILLE'S PRODUCTION, with
        HARRY TATE in a New Revue:
               "GOOD-BY-EE."
  EDDIE VINCENT, CONNIE BROWNING, KITTY SINCLARIS, HARRY DALVA, KENNETH
       SEYMOUR, JIMMIE HOOPER, BEAUTY CHORUS OF FIFTY.

THEATRE ROYAL, WOLVERHAMPTON.
6.50            Twice Nightly                9.0
      MR. AND MRS. F. G. KIMBERLEY'S COMPANY, IN THE ROMANTIC PLAY,
  "THE WILD GIRL OF THE FOREST," BY MRS. F. G.
                                              KIMBERLEY.
  MRS. F. G. KIMBERLEY will play "The Wild Girl" (First Houses only) by special request
  FRIDAY NIGHT (First House only) the entire proceeds will be given to BLUE CROSS FUND.
  Seats may be booked at Theatre Box Office in Bilston-street, 11 to 4 p.m., or by 'Phone 515.

        COLISEUM, DUDLEY-ROAD
  COMMENCING DECEMBER 3rd, for Six Days only, J. W. GRIFFITHS' MIGHTY SPECTACLE,
       "THE BIRTH OF A NATION."
    The Most Stupendous and Fascinating Motion Picture Drama ever created.
     MATINEES DAILY at 2.30.   EVENING PERFORMANCE 7 O'CLOCK.

HER MAJESTY'S THEATRE, WALSALL.
         TWICE NIGHTLY              Tenders.
```

(Reprinted courtesy Express and Star Ltd.)

1918

"…. And what appeared well nigh impossible has been carried right through to a great victory. The story of the storming of the St. Quentin Canal, the capture of Bellenglise and the subsequent advance will make one of the most glorious stories of the whole war".
(Major-General G.F.B. Boyd, Divisional Commander 46th Division)

THE FINAL YEAR

The 1/6th South Staffords spent New Year's Eve in trenches near Hulluch and on New Year's Day found themselves successfully fighting off a trench raid before being relieved and going into Brigade Reserve at Mazingarbe.

For the 2/6th Battalion the New Year began with a Route March followed by kit inspection and a bath. At this time they were billeted at Rue, near Abbeville and there they stayed until on the 8th February they marched to Pommier and on the 9th to Mory. The 10th saw them take-over trenches at Noreuil from the 14th Battalion Argyll and Sutherland Highlanders and the situation is recorded as 'Quiet' until on the 14th they were on the receiving end of a barrage of high explosive and gas shells, 2nd Lieut. Proud and fifty Other Ranks were gassed, twelve of whom died. From this time until late March the 2/6th were engaged in the usual routine of time in and out of the trenches.

THE GERMAN SPRING OFFENSIVE

In November 1917 the Russian economy was close to collapsing under the strain of their war effort and following the rise of the Bolshevik government the Russians began talks with the Germans to sue for an end to the war. Although it was not until the Treaty of Brest – Litovsk in March 1918 that the Russian war officially came to an end, at the start of 1918 the Germans began to move their troops and weaponry to the western front in an attempt to defeat the Allies before the massive influx of American forces could be deployed, something like 10,000 American soldiers a week were landing in France. In reality the psychological impact of the

American intervention would prove to have a greater effect on the Germans than would their physical presence.

THE KAISERSCHLACHT
On the 21st March 1918, what was to prove to be the last great battle of the First World War began when the Germans struck a blow against the weakened divisions of the British Third and Fifth Armies. It was an offensive that the Germans called 'The Kaiserschlacht' (Kaiser's battle) and was intended to break the deadlock on the Western Front before the Americans could bring to bear their massive resources of men and equipment.

We have seen that the early days the war began dramatically with sweeping advances by the Germans through Belgium and France en route for Paris until a stalemate brought about a statistic war in the trenches. Now, in the spring of 1918 the war once again became one of rapid movement.

Both sides had learned lessons from the Battle of the Somme, the Germans had developed Storm-trooper tactics by which they would bypass enemy strong-points wherever possible, leaving them to be attacked by follow-up waves of infantry. The Storm-troopers' objective was to attack and disrupt enemy headquarters, artillery units and supply depots in the rear areas, as well as to rapidly occupy territory. The Allies in turn had developed their defences in depth, reducing the number of troops in their front line and moving reserves and supply dumps back beyond German artillery range.

The 1/6th were holding the line at Annequinn when they were subjected to a tremendous bombardment on 21st March and immediately believed that the long awaited German assault had begun. Despite manning the defences in a state of readiness the expected attack did not materialize, for the 2/6th Battalion however, things were rather different.

2/6th AT MONCHY le PREUX
Late on Tuesday 19th March 1918 'A', 'B' and 'D' Companies of the 2/6th South Staffords had taken over forward defensive positions between the Hirondelle valley and the west of Bullecourt, on the

promontory that was Monchy le Preux, 'C' Company went into the reserve trenches.

Early on 21st March 1918 the men were doing their best to get some rest when between 2.00 and 3.00 a.m. the Germans began shelling the rear areas of their position and an hour later began to bombard the Front and Support lines with high explosive and gas shells, Operation Michael had begun along 50 miles of front line.

Private R.T. Smith of the 2/6th South Staffords recalled;

> *"I was on sentry duty about 1 o'clock in the morning of the 21st. As I stood on the fire-step I could hear sounds coming from the German lines; they were of the movement of the wheels of transport wagons and occasionally I heard voices. When the platoon officer came round at about 3 a.m. I reported these facts to him. He seemed rather concerned and said that other posts along the line were making similar reports.*
>
> *By the way, the visit of the platoon officer was the only contact we had with anyone after stand down the previous morning and no one came up with the rations."*

Several thousand German guns blazed away to a predetermined plan which lasted for five hours, firing a mixture of shrapnel shells which exploded in mid-air and rained down shell fragments and hundreds of balls of lead, high explosive shells that detonated on impact and three types of gas shells, one containing chlorine with its familiar distinctive smell, another contained phosgene which apparently "smelt like rotten fish or corpses", the third type contained an early form of tear gas.

Lance Corporal T. Fletch wrote:-

> *"We kept up rapid fire as they advanced but there were so many of them and we seemed so pitifully few. In the heat of the attack I was nearly shot by my comrade on the left. He suddenly saw a party of Germans bombing their way from the right, swung his rifle round and fired, the bullet burned my ear as it passed. But now we could do no more. A lot of our chaps put up their hands and surrendered but we*

> *decided to fall back to our reserve positions, a decision which I'm afraid cost many of our men their lives because we were under shell and machine-gun fire as we fell back.*
>
> *I particularly remember, as I passed one shell hole, seeing one of our lads, who was small of stature but was always most cheerful, lying there with both his legs shot through. Our sergeant, a tall Irishman, dropped into the shell hole beside him but I do not think he would have been able to do much for him. It is a tragedy to be badly wounded in a retreat because, naturally, the enemy attend to their own wounded first. Then I came across a lad of my own section. He had taken a burst of shrapnel in his legs and could not walk. With the help of another lad, we carried him out of the action. He wrote to me afterwards from a hospital in Liverpool thanking us for saving him. As he put it, he would never have got away and would have fallen into enemy hands. He had nineteen wounds in his legs."*

An urgent message was sent to the garrison at Ecoust that reserves were needed and two companies of the 2/6th North Staffords were dispatched to help but before they were able to get to the aid of their compatriots they were themselves attacked. The position of the South Staffords became desperate and they were eventually overpowered.

THE 2/6th OVERWHELMED
At 12.35 p.m. an un-named officer is known to have sent a final message from the Battalion headquarters in the reserve line trenches to the effect that he was now alone, that the enemy was at the top of the dug-out steps, that he had burnt all papers and was smashing the instruments. The 2/6th Battalion of the South Staffordshire Regiment had been all but obliterated.

Extracts from the Battalion war diary read as follows;

21st March   *23 Officers and about 600 Other Ranks are 'Missing', including Lt. Col. J. Stuart-Wortley Capt. C.E.L. Whitehouse (Adjutant), Capt. W.A. Adam, Capt. W.A. Jordan, Capt. T.L. Astbury and Capt. W.S. Lynes, (Company Commanders), The following Officers are missing:- Lieut. W.T. Butler, Lieut. R.G. Boycott, Lieut. L.J. Shelton, 2/Lieut. H.P. Bunn, 2/Lieut. H.E. Shipton, 2/Lieut. H.W. Gregory, 2/Lieut. J.A. Geyton, 2/Lieut. R. Baxter, 2/Lieut. F.W. Spibey, 2/Lieut. C. Haworth, 2/Lieut. J.H. Hickman, 2/Lieut. T.A. Gough, 2/Lieut. C.A. Yates, 2/Lieut. J. Bonshor, 2/Lieut. J. Rigby, 2/Lieut. H.E. Jones, and Capt. W.M. Christie.*

When the roll was called after the fighting just six officers and eighty other ranks, mainly Bandsmen, were all that remained of 2/6th South Staffords. Of the officers listed as missing, Lieutenant-Colonel Stuart-Wortley, Captain Astbury and 2nd Lieutenants Jones and Rigby were dead, as were 106 other ranks, the remainder having been taken as prisoners of war.

Meanwhile, back in Wolverhampton:-

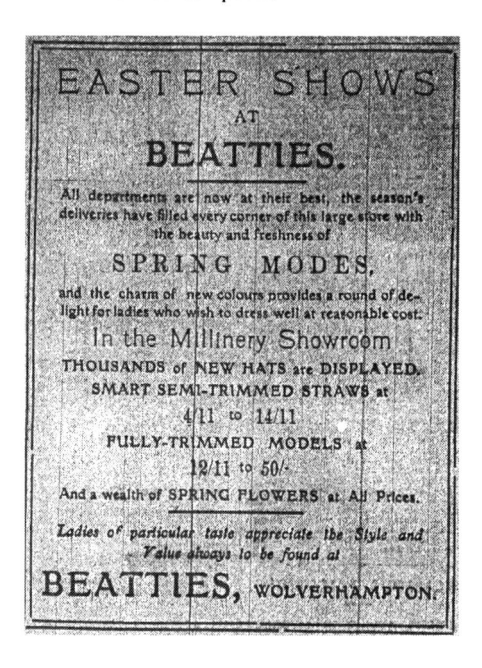

EASTER SHOWS AT BEATTIES.

All departments are now at their best, the season's deliveries have filled every corner of this large store with the beauty and freshness of

SPRING MODES,

and the charm of new colours provides a round of delight for ladies who wish to dress well at reasonable cost.

In the Millinery Showroom
THOUSANDS of NEW HATS are DISPLAYED.
SMART SEMI-TRIMMED STRAWS at
4/11 to 14/11
FULLY-TRIMMED MODELS at
19/11 to 50/-
And a wealth of SPRING FLOWERS at All Prices.

Ladies of particular taste appreciate the Style and Value always to be found at

BEATTIES, WOLVERHAMPTON.

(Reproduced courtesy Express and Star Ltd.)

Private John Alfred Hinton, 2/6th Battalion, was the eldest son of Mr A J Hinton of Wolverhampton and after leaving school took a position in his father's business, but when he reached the age of 18 he made a number of attempts to enter the army before becoming successful and gaining a place in the 2/6th Battalion. After initial training at Lincoln, Salisbury and Mablethorpe he travelled with the battalion to Ireland in 1916 but an attack of spotted fever prevented his going to France in 1917. On the 1st January 1918 he was drafted out to rejoin his unit. On March 21st he was attached to the Headquarters signalling platoon and was severely wounded and taken prisoner. John Hinton was transferred to a Prisoner of War camp in Hameln near Hanover, and died there aged 20 on September 17th 1918. (Photograph courtesy Express and Star Ltd.)

Despite the Battalion being almost wiped-out on the 21st, the 22nd found them back in action when the senior surviving officer, Major Curtis, led a party and took up position about 500 yards north-east of Mory and in spite of heavy shelling and enemy attacks managed to hold that position until an hour after midnight when, due to their flanks being exposed, they withdrew some 300 yards. Sometime later they found themselves in an isolated position once again and withdrew to dig-in on a ridge above Ervillers, a position that they held until relieved by the Suffolks.

When Ludendorff called off Operation Michael on March 25, by the standards of the previous fighting there had been a substantial gain in territory. It was, however, of little value - a pyrrhic victory, as Amiens, an important rail centre, still remained in Allied hands, and the newly-won territory would be difficult to hold against Allied counterattacks.

Captain Frank Pitchford Silvers, 1/6th Battalion, was the youngest Son of Frederick and Sarah Silvers, of the Talbot Hotel, King Street, Wolverhampton. He had attended the Wolverhampton Grammar School and played football for the 1st XI of 1909-1910, later becoming captain of Penn Fields FC., as well as being a keen tennis player. He had been articled to Mr. R. H. Johnston, Accountant, but enlisted as a Private in the South Staffordshire Regiment at the start of the war. He rose through the non-commissioned ranks before being commissioned as Lieutenant in 1915, and being promoted to Captain in 1917. He was awarded the Military Cross in 1918; the citation read *"This officer has done very good work since the Division came to France. As Battalion Lewis Gun Officer he did valuable work in training and instructing Lewis Gunners. He is now commanding a Company in a most efficient manner. During the successful attack on the 24th June 1917, his company captured and consolidated Fosse 3, de Lievn, and Admiral Trench".*

Captain Silvers died on May 27th 1918, as the result of severe wounds to the head received during a bombardment; he was 25 years old and was buried at Pernes British Cemetery. His family added the inscription "HE DIED THAT WE MIGHT LIVE." (Photograph courtesy Express and Star Ltd.)

THE BEGINNING OF THE END
By the 5th of April the Kaiserschlacht had run out of steam, the Germans had been unable to convert their tactical successes into a strategic victory and their offensive had lost its momentum due to lack of supplies. The stalemate on the Western Front had been broken, desperate as the fighting had been, Franco-British forces had finally blunted the assault, during the battles of March-April, Haig's army of 59 Divisions had met 109 German Divisions in the field and had fought them to a standstill once more.

The Germans had pushed back the Allies by up to forty miles but had failed to achieve their main objective, which had been to separate the British from the French and to capture the channel ports, thus cutting off the British supply chain. In so doing, even with the reinforcements from their Eastern Front, much of the strength had been drained out of the German army. Although the Allies lost nearly 255,000 men (British, British Empire, French and American.) as well as 1300 artillery pieces and 200 tanks, all of this could be replaced in the field, either from British factories or from American manpower. German troop losses were 239,000 men, largely specialist shock troops (*Stosstruppen*) who were irreplaceable at the front. Ludendorff ultimately achieved little more than saddling his own army with an extended front line, and vastly diminished resources with which to hold it.

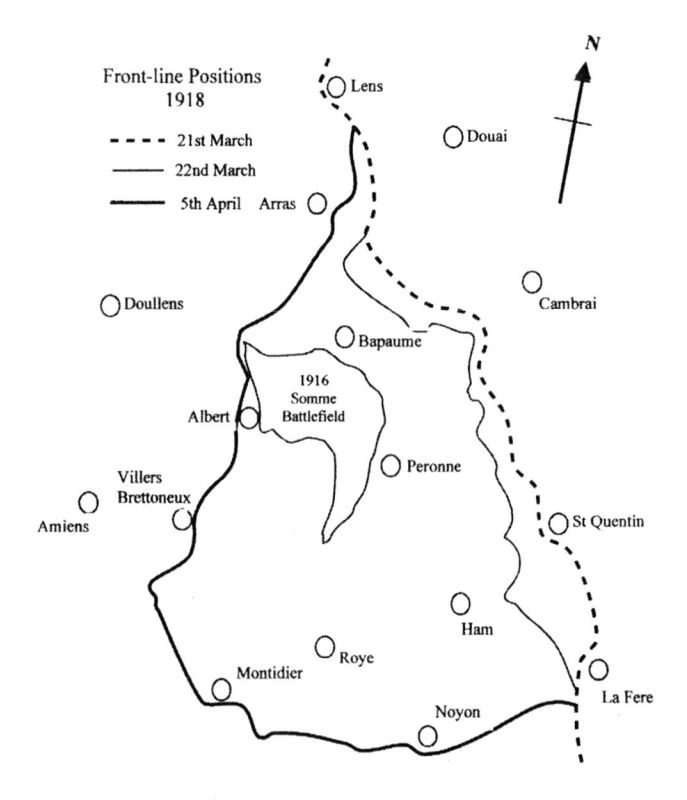

Map of German gains during the Kaiserschlacht

THE 2/6th REBORN
When a battalion went into the front-line a cadre of officers and men remained behind so that in the event of the main force being overwhelmed, the battalion would still have a nucleus on which to rebuild. Thus it was that despite their losses on 21st March, the 2/6th was reborn. A Draft of 150 Other Ranks was received on the 1st April, 173 on the 2nd, 127 on the 3rd, 97 on the 4th and a further 157 on the 6th April. On the 10th of that month the revived Battalion left their camp at Watou and marched to Poperinghe to entrain for Ypres where they arrived at 2.30 p.m. before continuing by road to Brandhoek.

THE 2/6th DISBANDED
Despite having been rebuilt to almost full strength, the 2/6th South Staffords would enter the front-line trenches just twice more, on 11th April they relieved the Kings Royal Rifle Corps at Passendaele, a tour of duty described in the war diary as "Quiet" and on the 15th of that month they were south-east of Bailluel where they repulsed a strong German attack, losing one officer and 90 other ranks in the process.

The end of April found the 2/6th in Reserve at Renighelst and there they stayed until 5th May. On 9th May, the Battalion paraded before the General Officer Commanding 59th Division who addressed the men and distributed a number of decorations. Following this parade, 18 officers and 746 men entrained to return to Base, the 2/6th had now been reduced to a Training Cadre and would play no further part in the fighting of the war.

ADVANCE TO VICTORY
The technical advantages held by the Allies were now to prove their value, better communications, use of aircraft, and improved artillery support were all advances over British operations earlier in the war. More significant however, was the sheer weight of material now filling the ranks of the Allies. Equally critical to success was the improved organization of the British Army. The officer corps was much stronger by 1918, reflecting the benefits of a seasoned group of officers who had survived years of conflict.

While the German offensive had not brought them victory, the Allies were equally unable to achieve immediate success. At the same time as the German army had run out of steam, the appointment of the French Marshall Foch as Commander in Chief of all Allied Armies on the Western Front brought a new impetus to the allies. Acceding to the priorities of the coalition chief Foch, Haig's pursuit of grand victories was abandoned in favour of smaller more persistent actions.

THE FINAL HUNDRED DAYS
The fighting of 'The Hundred Days' (18 July-11 November 1918) would prove to be the final allied offensive on the Western Front and began with a French counter attack that pushed the Germans back to the River Aisne.

The first phase of Foch's plan was to eliminate the salient created when the Germans had overrun the old Somme battlefield of 1916 and which extended almost to Amiens. The Battle of Amiens began on Thursday 8th August when a surprise attack by the British drove back the Germans by over nine miles in one day, a day described by Ludendorf as "The black day of the German Army".

The follow-up Battle of Bapaume forced the Germans back across the River Somme and then to the Hindenburg Line from where they had started the Kaiserschlact six months earlier. The Americans made their presence felt when they fought their first major battle when clearing the final salient south of Verdun, capturing thirteen thousand German prisoners in the process.

THE SECOND PHASE
Foch now planned the next assault, an attack on three fronts and which began towards the end of September. The Americans, having proved themselves at Verdun, would attack in the south from the Meuse River to the Argonne Forest, the French from the Argonne Forest eastwards towards Reimes, a joint force of Belgian, French and British troops under King Albert of Belgium would attack through Flanders, whilst in the centre of the attack Haig would lead British and French assaults on the Hindenburg Line between St. Quentin and Cambrai.

The southern attack began on Thursday 26th September when the French advanced nine miles, whilst at their side the Americans, facing difficult fighting through the Argonne Forest, made two miles there and five miles along the Meuse river. By the middle of October they had breached the main German defences and by the end of that month had cleared the forest. By this time the French had advanced twenty miles to reach the River Aisne and had hastened the end of the war by cutting the Metz – Sedan railway line, one of Germany's main supply routes.

In the centre the forty British divisions, supported by the American II Corps were opposed by fifty seven German Divisions. If the quality of the German divisions was questionable after the heavy losses endured during the Kaiserschlact, the defences of the Hindenburg Line were as formidable as ever. It was into this area that the 1/6th South Staffords moved from Bethune on 12th September and passed into G.H.Q. Reserve where they took part in a few days of rest and training.

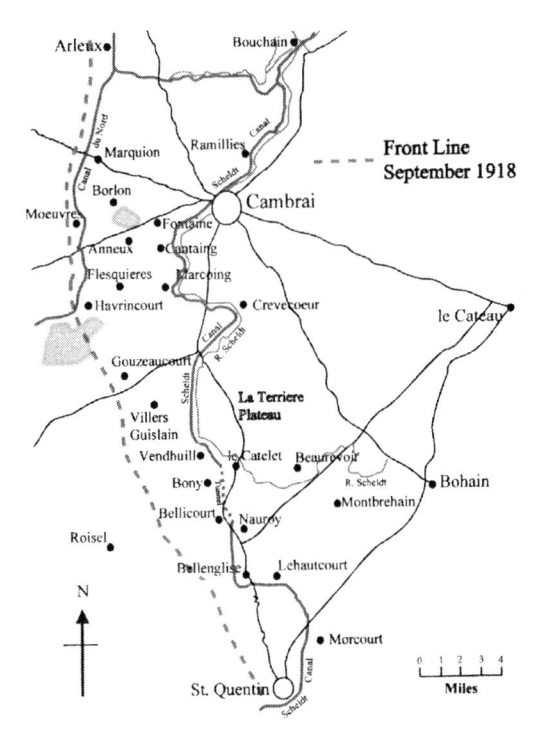

Cambrai – St. Quentin Area

Haig began his attack against the Canal du Nord on 27th September and two days later the 46th Division joined in battle against the defences of the St. Quentin Canal. The 46th Division took over a 2,500 to 3,000 yard stretch of the front line which consisted of old German trenches, now modified to afford defensive positions from the opposite direction. In front of these trenches the ground sloped gently downwards towards the new German positions, affording the Allies clear views of the enemy activity in front of them.

THE STAFFORDS GO IN

Three Staffordshire Battalions were to lead the attack on the German positions along the canal with the 1/6th North Staffords on the left, the 1/5th South Staffords in the centre and the 1/6th South Staffords on the right of the Divisional front, to the north-west of Bellenglise. During the night the men moved into their assembly areas, some in the front line trenches, others in shell holes in No Man's Land and yet others in the shelter of various sunken roads.

Here the men stayed, in an atmosphere eerily still and quiet until a few minutes before 'zero' hour (5.50 a.m.) the air was rent with the indescribable noise of the artillery barrage and the clatter of machine guns trained upon the enemy trenches. Successive waves of the 1/6th South Staffords, on a four hundred yard front and with gaps of around three yards between each man, began a slow walk across the undulating ground, each hundred yards of the advance taking some five minutes, and all the time the bullets from their own machine-guns were whistling past just feet above their heads.

The Germans began to retaliate when the attackers were half way to the canal and laid down an intense bombardment, but due to the ever thickening fog were unable to properly range their fire. Before the Staffords reached the canal they encountered a number of enemy outposts but these were lightly manned and presented little resistance. Passing through these defences and on over the crown of the hill they came to the west bank of the canal and there they regrouped.

What lay before them, still only half seen through the fog was a steep slope of perhaps fifty feet down to the wall of the canal and then a further drop of five or ten feet to the water itself. Each man was under orders to make his own way across the canal.

The Germans were defending their positions with machine-guns and bombs, but such had been the intensity of the preliminary Allied barrage and the rapidity of the following infantry attacks that the attackers were upon the Germans before they were able to fully emerge from their shelters to man the defences.

The St. Quentin Canal 1918
(Photograph courtesy The Staffordshire Regiment Museum.)

Once across, the attackers regrouped once more and now in a single line moved up the eastern bank and after passing lines of unoccupied trenches came upon their next objective, a second line of trenches, substantial barriers in the form of heavily fortified concrete defences and machine gun emplacements. Still enshrouded by the fog the Staffords were able to work their way almost up to the German trenches before rushing in to bayonet the defenders. In the face of such tactics many of the defenders made use of the fog to make good their escape although many more were made prisoner.

The Staffords pressed on with their attack towards the next lines of defence which they overcame with equal determination and there at between 9.30 and 10.00 a.m. they halted and allowed the 138th and 139th Brigades to pass through in accordance with operation orders.

Major Edwin Lewis died of wounds received in this attack. The only son of Mr Rowland Lewis J.P. of Penn, Wolverhampton, after being educated at Repton he had joined the Territorial battalion some ten years earlier. He embarked upon active service with them when they first went to France in 1915, subsequently being promoted to the rank of Major. In civilian life Edwin Lewis had been running his family firm of Edwin Lewis and Sons Ltd., of Ettingshall. Having previously been severely wounded whilst acting second in command in 1917, Major Lewis died aged 36 on the 30th September 1918 and is buried in Brie British Cemetery, France. (Photograph courtesy Express and Star Ltd.)

BELLENGLISE

After a brief pause for reorganization, two companies of the 1/6th South Staffords continued the forward advance whilst the other two companies now turned to their right to enter Bellenglise. Such was the devastation caused to the village by the heavy shelling, that the

Staffords met with little resistance and had little more to do than mop-up the remaining Germans and in this they paid special attention to the entrance to the Bellenglise canal tunnel, a previously impregnable part of the Hindenburg Line, and from where they captured almost a thousand prisoners.

Following the success of the attack, the Divisional Commander received a letter from General H. S. Rawlinson in which he said "The forcing of the Hindenburg Line on the canal, and the capture of Bellenglise ranks as one of the finest and most dashing exploits of the war.", stark contrast to the disparaging remarks made by Sir Thomas Snow after the debacle of Gommecourt.

The canal tunnel at Bellenglise 1918
(Photograph courtesy Paul Reed)

The South Staffords left Bellenglise at 2.00 a.m. on 3rd October and three hours later were in a position outside of Sequehart to began their attack at 6.05 a.m. with 'C' and 'D' Companies in the first line of attack, 'A' and 'B' Companies in the second wave. They encountered little resistance until they approached the crest of a hill just south of Chataignies Wood where they had to overcome considerable resistance, especially from the enemy machine guns which were protected by concrete emplacements. The only means of overcoming this resistance proved to be by rushing the positions and using bayonets against the gun crews. Not surprisingly the Staffords lost heavily during this stage of the fighting.

Outposts were then pushed forwards towards the final objective, the slopes of Mannequin Hill, but the Germans were holding this position in numbers and heavy enfilading machine-gun fire forced the Staffords to withdraw. The South Staffords had to fight off German counter-attacks during the rest of the day and were subject to heavy shelling and machine-gun fire, attacks which intensified during the following day before they were relieved in the front-line by the 1st Battalion of the Gloucestershire Regiment.

THE FINAL ACTS

On October 3rd the Kaiser appointed Prince Max of Baden, a political moderate, as Chancellor of Germany. It had been decided that the only way to gain a good peace was to transform Germany into a democracy. There was also an increasing amount of unrest on the home front, where the Allied blockade was being felt, sacrifices that were acceptable while the German armies were advancing were not tolerable now they were in retreat.

German hopes were based on President Woodrow Wilson's fourteen point peace terms which had been announced on 8 January 1918 in a speech to Congress, and were seen as the basis for an honourable peace. That speech had been made before the massive battles of 1918, and the eventual armistice terms would be rather less generous.

Prince Max had the sense to get Hindenburg to admit in writing that there was no further chance of forcing a peace on the enemy, this was fortunate, as towards the end of October Ludendorff had recovered his nerve. The German army was still in retreat but it was now a fighting retreat. On 24 October Ludendorff issued and then withdrew a proclamation denouncing Prince Max. One copy was leaked, and on 27 October Ludendorff was ordered to resign.

As the British prepared for their attack on the Sambre, the Kaiser left Berlin and moved to the military headquarters at Spa (29th October) and there he soon lost all contact with reality, beginning to plan to use the army to restore order in Germany.

A KEY DAY

The 30th day of October 1918 was a key day. On that day Turkey surrendered and then Germany's only remaining ally, the Austro-Hungarian Empire, was in the process of dissolving. With defeat clearly imminent the German High Seas Fleet was ordered to sea to seek a final suicidal battle with the British Grand Fleet. Not surprisingly the fleet mutinied, and refused to sail. On 4th November the Kaiser's brother, Prince Henry of Prussia, the commander at Kiel, was forced to flee, on the previous day the Austro-Hungarian cease fire had come into effect.

THE STAFFORD'S LAST SHOTS

For the 1/6th South Staffords the final fighting of the Great War began at 7.30 a.m. on the 6th of November 1918 when they advanced from Le Sart and pursued the Germans through Prisches and on to Cartignies which they reached around mid-day.

Just after 5 o'clock on the cold and dull morning of 11th November 1918, (the 1,568th day of the war), British, French and German officials had met in a railway carriage to the north of Paris and signed the armistice to end the war. That cease fire would not come into effect until 11am and in those final hours of war hundreds more men would die. In the strangest of coincidences the end of the war found units of the British Army fighting close to the same ground as they had actively begun operations in August 1914, the familiar drab mining and industrial district around the Belgian town of Mons.

The news that the armistice had been signed quickly spread along the frontline. That same morning Private George Edwin Ellison had every reason to think he had been one of the lucky ones. Born in York in 1892, at the start of the war he was a regular soldier serving with the 5th (Royal Irish) Lancers and after surviving four years of the greatest war in history, at 9.30 a.m. found himself as part of a scouting party investigating the reported sighting of German troops in a nearby wood. Doubtless he would be looking forwards to returning home to his terraced house at 49, Edmund Street, Leeds, to his wife Hannah, his son James and to his pre-war job in the local coalmine. Private George Ellison was shot in the head by a sniper just an hour and a half before the fighting stopped.

By a quirk of fate, George Ellison the last British man to die in the war is buried in **St Symphorian Military Cemetery, Mons,** just yards from Private John Parr, the first to die. George Ellison was 26 years old.

The Grave of Private George Ellison
(Private Collection)

Meanwhile, back in Wolverhampton;

> **WAR ENDED.**
> **ARMISTICE SIGNED**
> **AND**
> **FIGHTING OVER.**
>
> The war has ended. This great news was conveyed to the people this morning in these words:—
> The Prime Minister makes the following announcement:
> The armistice was signed at 5 a.m. this morning, and hostilities are to cease on all fronts at 11 a.m. to-day.

(Reproduced courtesy Express and Star Ltd.)

If the men of the 1/6th South Staffords were looking forward to an early return home they were to be disappointed. Although the Armistice was signed on the 11th November, it did not in itself necessarily mean the end of the war, had the Germans not complied with the stringent terms imposed upon them by the Allies, hostilities would have resumed.

For the 1/6th South Staffords the remainder of 1918 was spent in a mixture of general military training, physical exercise, salvage work, education and recreation. Christmas Day, although celebrated in the traditional way in comfortable billets, must have been a day of mixed emotions, the knowledge that they had survived the greatest war in history, knowing that they would be returning home to their loved ones, but also knowing that they would be leaving behind comrades who could never do so.

The final entry in the war diary of the 1/6th Battalion the South Staffordshire Regiment reads;

> *"May 1st – 31st 1919 Cadre Establishment of this Battalion awaiting instructions to entrain."*

IN MEMORANDUM

Located in Little's Lane, this is the last remaining street shrine in Wolverhampton
(Private collection)

ROLL OF HONOUR – THOSE WHO FELL

ABBOTT	John	Private
ADAMS	Alfred	Private
ADAMS	Edwin	Private
ADAMS	George Norman	Captain
ADAMS	John Thomas	Private
ADEY	Cyril Archibald	Private
AFFRON	William Reuben	Private
ALLAWAY	William John	L/Corporal
ALLCOCK	Seth	Private
ALLEN	Albert	Private
ALLEN	Henry Oliver	Private
ALLEN	Herbert Abram	Private
ALLEN	James Alfred	Private
ALLEN	John Arthur	L/Sergeant
ALLETT	Bertie Harold	Private
ALLGOOD	Reginald	Private
ALLMARK	Joseph	Private
AMBLER	George Frederick	Private
ANDERSON	Albert	Private
ANDERSON	Edward	Private
ANDREWS	Thomas Richard	Private
ANSLOW	Harry	Private
ANSLOW	Horace Charles	Private
ARKINSTALL	Harry	Private
ARKINSTALL	Joseph	Private
ASH	Frederick George	Private
ASH	John	Private
ASHLEY	Thomas	Private
ASPREA	David William	Private
ASTBURY	Thomas Leslie	Captain
ASTLE	William Leslie	L/Sergeant
ASTON	John	Sergeant
ATKINS	Harry	Private
ATKINSON	Bernard Stewart	Captain
BACON	William George	Private
BADDELEY	Arthur Howard	Private
BAGLEY	John	Private
BAGNALL	Thomas	Private
BAGSHAW	Leonard	Private
BAILEY	Albert	Private
BAILEY	Arthur Eric	Sergeant

BAILEY	Samuel	Private
BAKER	Alfred	Private
BAKER	Francis George	Private
BAKER	George	Private
BAKER	James	Private
BAKER	John	Private
BAKER	Thomas Samuel	L/Sergeant
BAKER	William	Private
BAKER	William Bernard	Private
BALL	John	Private
BANKS	Arthur	Private
BANKS	Frank Cecil	Private
BANKS	George William	Private
BANTING	Frederick Charles	Private
BARBER	Arthur	Private
BARKER	Ernest	Private
BARKER	J	Private
BARKER	Percival Sidney	Private
BARNES	Frederick	Private
BARNES	Stephen	Private
BARNSLEY	Joseph	Corporal
BARNWELL	George Thomas	L/Corporal
BARRACLOUGH	Amos	Private
BARRATT	Arthur	Private
BARRATT	Ewart	Private
BARRATT	Harold	Private
BARRATT	John	Corporal
BARRATT	William Thomas	Corporal
BARRY	Francis Joseph Fry	Corporal
BARTHOLOMEW	Charles	Private
BARTLE	Harry	Private
BATES	Herbert Bertram	Private
BATES	John Thomas	Corporal
BATEY	Arthur	Private
BAYLEY	Edward Vincent	2nd Lieutenant
BAYLEY	Joseph Francis	Private
BAYLISS	John	Private
BEAN	Charles Reginald	2nd Lieutenant
BECKETT	Alfred	Private
BEDDOWS	Sydney Samuel	Private
BEECH	Arthur Henry	Corporal
BEESTON	Walter	Private
BEILBY	Samuel Augustus	Private

BELL	Edgar Allan	Private
BELL	Ernest John	Private
BELL	George Herbert	Private
BELLAMY	Thomas	Private
BENNETT	Henry	Private
BENNETT	Sidney	Private
BENNETT	William	L/Corporal
BENNETT	William Edward	Private
BENTLEY	Harry	Private
BENWELL	Percy William	Private
BICKNELL	Frederick Richard	C.Q.M.S.
BIDDLE	William	Private
BILLINGTON	Edward	Private
BINDON	Herbert Henry Josiah	Private
BIRCH	Thomas	Private
BISHOP	James	Private
BISHTON	Edward Henry	A/Sgt
BLACK	John	Private
BLACKBURN	Herbert	L/Corporal
BLACKBURN	Joseph	Private
BLACKHAM	Clarence	Private
BLACKWELL	Leonard	Private
BLAKEMAN	Leonard	Private
BLAKEMORE	Cecil	Private
BLEWITT	Thomas	Private
BLEWS	A	Private
BLEWS	Albert	Private
BLISS	Sidney	Private
BLOOM	Herbert	Private
BLOOMER	Charles Harry	Sergeant
BLUNDELL	William Edward	Private
BLUNT	William Henry	Private
BLUNT	William Henry	Private
BLYTHE	Walter Holtby	Private
BOND	William	Private
BONE	Harry Whittenburg	2nd Lieutenant
BONSHOR	John	2nd Lieutenant
BOOTH	Hector	Private
BOSTOCK	Hugh William	2nd Lieutenant
BOSTOCK	William Henry	Private
BOTT	Joseph	Private
BOTT	Joseph Henry	Private
BOTTEN	Charles	Private

BOUCKLEY	Richard	Drummer
BOULTON	Vernon	Private
BOURNE	Harold	Private
BOWCOTT	John	Private
BOWDLER	David	Private
BOWEN	Granville	Private
BOWEN	Walter Holtby	Private
BOWERS	Douglas Phillips	Private
BOYCE	Horace	Private
BOYDEN	Charles Fred	Private
BRADBURY	Henry	Private
BRADBURY	Joseph William	Private
BRADDOCK	Arthur Harold	L/Corporal
BRADLEY	Albert	Private
BRADLEY	Arthur	Private
BRADLEY	Patrick	Private
BRADSHAW	Charles	Private
BRADSHAW	Robert Sydney	Private
BRAILSFORD	John	Private
BRASIER	William	Private
BRAZIER	Don	Private
BREADNEY	John	Private
BREAKWELL	William Thomas	Private
BREVITT	James Bertie	Private
BREWERTON	Arthur Robert	Sergeant
BREWSTER	S G	Private
BREWSTER	Sidney George	Private
BRIDGEWATER	William	Private
BRIDSON	Herbert	Private
BRIGHTON	George	Private
BRINDLEY	John	Private
BRITTAIN	William Henry	Private
BROAD	Albert	Private
BROCKBANK	William John	Private
BROWN	Hugh Reginald	L/Corporal
BROWN	Thomas	Private
BROWN	Thomas	Private
BROWN	Wilfred	Private
BROWNING	John	Private
BRUCE	Robert James	2nd Lieutenant
BULLOCK	Abner	Private
BULLOCK	W.	Private
BUNT	Thomas Avery	C.Q.M.S.

BURCH	Robert Alban	Private
BURGOYNE	Joseph	L/Corporal
BURKE	Edward	Private
BURKE	Edward	Private
BURKE	Henry Joseph	Lieutenant
BURMAN	Charles Henry	Private
BURROWSON	B W	
BURTON	Thomas Henry	Private
BURTON	William Samuel	Private
BURWOOD	Archibald Frank	Private
BUSSLEY	Alfred John	Private
BUTCHER	J	Private
BUTLER	Bernard Walter	Private
BUTLER	George Frederick	L/Corporal
BUTLER	Sydney Melville	L/Corporal
BUTTERWORTH	Tom	Private
CADBY	Clarence or Charles	Private
CADDICK	Harold	Private
CADDICK	Samuel Frederick	L/Sergeant
CALLIS	Arnold	Private
CAMP	John Henry	L/Sergeant
CARELESS	Lyons William	Private
CARNELL	Archie	Private
CARPENTER	Joseph	Private
CARR	Thomas William	Private
CARSON	Walter	L/Sergeant
CARTER	Charles Henry	Private
CARTER	James	Private
CARTER	Thomas William	Sergeant
CARTWRIGHT	Harry	Private
CARTWRIGHT	John	Private
CARVER	Thomas	Private
CASTREE	Frank	Drummer
CATTELL	Edwin James	L/Sergeant
CAYTOR	E	
CHAMBERLAIN	Arthur Edward	Private
CHARLTON	Robert	Private
CHEETHAM	Arthur William	Private
CHEETHAM	Walter Ernest	Private
CHESSMAN	Alfred	Private
CHESTER	Bert	Private
CHEVINS	Joseph	Corporal
CHICK	James	Private

CHILDE	Herbert	Private
CHINN	G.A.	Private
CLARK	William	Private
CLARKE	Everard Bernard	Private
CLARKE	Sidney	Private
CLARKSON	William Henry	Private
CLAY	J T	Private
CLAYTON	Frederick Nicholson	Private
CLAYTON	Walter Leslie	Private
CLEE	Samuel	Private
CLEVERSLEY	Sydney Wilson	Private
CLIFF	Frederick Percy	Private
CLIFFORD	William Alfred	Private
CLIFT	Mark	Private
COAPE-ARNOLD	R De N	Lieutenant
COCKERILL	Alfred John	Private
COLBOURNE	Alfred Leslie	Private
COLEY	David	Private
COLLETT	Ronald Frederick	Private
COLLEY	Joseph	Private
COLLIER	Henry	L/Corporal
COLLINS	Alfred Colin Campbell	Private
COLLINS	Horace Alexander	Lieutenant
COLLINS	Thomas Albert	Private
COLLISSON	Edwin Read	Captain
COLLYER	Horace Goodwin	Private
CONLEY	William Cockayne	Lieutenant
CONSTABLE	Albert	Private
CONSTABLE	William	Private
CONWAY	Alfred	L/Corporal
COOKE	Henry Elliott	Private
COOMES	Arthur	Private
COOPER	A.	Private
COOPER	Charles Sidney	Private
COOPER	Ernest Arthur	Private
COOPER	Jack	Corporal
COOPER	John	Private
COOPER	John Thomas	Private
COPE	George	Private
COPE	Herbert Sydney	Private
COPE	James	Private
COPE	Walter Raymond	Private
COPLAND	James Hay	Private

CORFIELD	Geoffrey Howard	Private
CORFIELD	Geoffrey Howard	Private
CORFIELD	William Frederick	CSM
COTTRELL	Levi	Private
COULSON	William	Private
COURT	Walter Neville	Sergeant
COUSENS	Sydney Francis	Private
COX	Alfred Sidney	Private
COX	Francis Harry	Private
COX	George William	Private
COX	Thomas	Private
COX	Walter	Private
COX	William James	Private
COYNE	Frank	Private
CRADDOCK	Horace Edward	Private
CRADDOCK	Joseph	Private
CRAGG	Charles Gibson	Private
CRANSTAUN BROWN	A	2nd Lieutenant
CRESSWELL	Edward Arthur	Captain
CROFT	Aguila Sidney	Private
CROFT	Bert	L/Corporal
CROSS	Bert	Private
CROSS	Sampson	Private
CROSSLEY	William	Private
CROUSAZ	Cecil Francis	Lieutenant
CROXHALL	J	
CRUDGINGTON	Thomas	Private
CULLEN	Bernard	Private
DAINTY	John	Private
DANDY	William	L/Corporal
DANIELS	Harry	Private
DANN	Tom Vincent	2nd Lieutenant
DARBY	Henry	Private
DARBY	Joseph	Private
DARBY	Levi Joseph	Sergeant
DARWICK	Norman	Private
DAVENPORT	John Thomas	Private
DAVEY	Charles George	Private
DAVIES	Alfred	Private
DAVIES	Arthur	Private
DAVIES	E W	
DAVIES	Isaac	Private
DAVIES	Joseph H	Private

DAVIES	Joseph James	Private
DAVIES	Kenneth	Lieutenant
DAVIES	Robert	Private
DAVIES	Robert	Private
DAVIES	Samuel	Private
DAVIS	Denis	Private
DAVIS	George Albert Edward	Private
DAVIS	Roland	Sergeant
DAWSON	Albert Sydney	Private
DEAN	Charles	Private
DEGG	Joseph	Private
DENHAM	Frederick Richard	Private
DICKENS	Harry	Private
DICKENSON	George	Private
DICKINSON	John Henry	Private
DICKINSON	Thomas Arthur	2nd Lieutenant
DILKES	Harold Poole	L/Corporal
DIXEY	Albert	Private
DODD	Ernest Samuel	Private
DOMAN	George William	Private
DORRELL	Henry James	Private
DOWNES	David Valentine	L/Sergeant
DUDLEY	Albert Vincent	Private
DUDLEY	Charles	Private
DUDWELL	James	Private
DUNN	George Harold	Private
DUNN	Herbert Gladstone	Corporal
DUNN	William Sidney	L/Corporal
DUNVILLE	Fred	Private
DUROSE	John	Private
EASTHAM	Herbert	Private
EATON	George Frederick	Private
EATWELL	William George Arthur	L/Corporal
EDGE	Alfred	Private
EDLIN	Arthur Harold	Private
EDWARDS	Alfred Samuel	Private
EDWARDS	Hubert	Private
EDWARDS	John	Private
EDWARDS	Jonathan	Private
EDWARDS	Lancelot	Private
EGAN	William	L/Corporal
ELKS	William	Private
ELLIS	Charles	Private

ELSMORE	William Reginald	Private
ELVIDGE	John George Henry	Private
ELWELL	John Thomas	Private
EMBREY	Cyril Stewart	2nd Lieutenant
EMMERSON	Stephen	Private
ENNIS	Percy	Private
EVANS	Charles Wilmot	Captain
EVANS	George	2nd Lieutenant
EVANS	Isaac	Private
EVANS	James	Private
EVANS	John	Private
EVANS	John George Henry	
EVANS	Joseph	Private
EVANS	Joshua	Private
EVANS	Samuel	Private
EVANS	Sidney Charles	Private
EVESON	Arthur Henry	Private
FACER	William Arthur	Private
FALKENER	J	
FARMER	Walter Harry	Private
FARR	Arthur	Private
FARRANCE	Frank	Private
FAULKNER	George	Private
FAVILL	Arnold Wilfred	L/Corporal
FELLOWS	James	Private
FELLOWS	John Thomas	Private
FENDELL	Ernest Henry	Private
FENNELL	Cecil Francis	Private
FERRIN	William	Private
FEWTRILL	Alfred James	Private
FIELD	Edward Arthur	Private
FIRTH	Willie	Private
FITCH	Alfred George	Private
FLANAGAN	George	Private
FLAVELL	Arthur	Corporal
FLAVELL	Sidney	Private
FLAXMAN	Alfred Edward	2nd Lieutenant
FLEET	George	Corporal
FLETCHER	Joseph Henry	Sergeant
FLETCHER	W H	Private
FLETCHER	William	Private
FLETCHER	William Henry	Private
FORD	W H	

FORDHAM	Thomas Clement	Private
FORRESTER	Henry Albert	Private
FORRESTER	John	CSM
FORRESTER	Samuel	L/Corporal
FOSTER	Bertie David	Private
FOSTER	Roger	Private
FOSTER	Samuel James	Private
FOSTER	Wilfrid Ernest	Private
FOSTER	William Augustus P.	Lieutenant
FOTHERGILL	Sidney	L/Corporal
FOWLER	Alfred Alexander	Private
FOX	Ernest	Private
FRANCIS	Robert William	CQMS
FREAKLEY	Henry	Private
FREEMAN	Herbert Henry	Private
FREEMAN	W H	
FREESTON	Horace Edward	Private
GALLEAR	W	
GAME	Frank Ernest	Private
GARNER	Frank	Private
GARNER	John Ratcliffe	Private
GARNER	Robert Norman	L/Corporal
GARNER	Thomas Montague	Sergeant
GATES	Benjamin Walpole	Private
GEDEN	Harry	Private
GERRARD	Percy	Sergeant
GETHING	William Gordon	2nd Lieutenant
GILBERT	William David	Private
GILL	J T	
GILL	John William	Private
GILL	W	
GIRT	George Alfred	Private
GLASBY	George Henry	Private
GLEDSTONE	William Arthur	Private
GLOVER	William	Private
GOBOURN	George Alfred	Private
GODSON	Henry	Private
GOOD	John Robert	Private
GOODE	Joseph Emmanuel	Private
GOODERIDGE	Harry	Private
GOODEY	Arthur Thomas	CSM
GOODRICK	John	Sergeant
GOODRIDGE	Alfred Thomas	Private

GORDON	Douglas Neave	2nd Lieutenant
GORDON	Horace Edwin	L/Corporal
GORICK	James	L/Corporal
GOUGH	Edward William Taylor	Private
GRACE	George Horace	Private
GRAHAM	Anthony	Private
GRAHAM	Robert Joseph	Private
GRAIL	Stanley James	Private
GRANT	Frank	Private
GRANT	Joseph	Drummer
GRANT	Joseph	Drummer
GRANT	Robert	Private
GRANT	William	Private
GREEN	Alfred Edward	Private
GREEN	George Thomas	Corporal
GREEN	Henry	Corporal
GREEN	John Thomas	Private
GREEN	Joseph Edward	Private
GREEN	Thomas	Sergeant
GREEN	William	Private
GREENWOOD	John	Private
GREGORY	Arthur	Private
GREGORY	Ernest	L/Corporal
GREGORY	Ezra	Private
GRIBBEN	James Grenfell	2nd Lieutenant
GRICE	William	CSM
GRIFFITHS	Arthur	Private
GRIFFITHS	John George	Private
GRIFFITHS	Rowland	Private
GRIFFITHS	Thomas	L/Sergeant
GRIMSLEY	Stanley	L/Corporal
GROVES	Samuel	Private
GROVES	William Norman	L/Corporal
GUEST	Samuel Joseph	Private
GUNN	Sidney	Private
GUTTERIDGE	Edward	Private
GUY	Joseph	Private
GWYTHER	Edwin Thomas	2nd Lieutenant
HADDOCK	Samuel	Private
HADEN	John Emmanuel	Private
HADLEY	Cecil	Private
HALE	William	Private
HALL	Bruce	Lieutenant

HALLETT	Albert Victor	Sergeant
HAMMOND	Albert	L/Corporal
HANSTOCK	Thomas	Private
HARDING	Charles	Private
HARDY	George Ernest	Private
HARDY	W J B	Private
HARGREAVES	Rudolph	Private
HARLEY	Arthur Darent	Captain
HARMAN	Bernard	Private
HARPER	John Henry	Private
HARPER	Leonard Alfred	L/Corporal
HARPIN	John	CQMS
HARRIS	Edward	Sergeant
HARRIS	Enoch Benjamin	Private
HARRIS	Jack St Clair Gainez	2nd Lieutenant
HARRIS	Noah	Private
HARRIS	Warren	Private
HARRIS	William	Corporal
HARRISON	Arthur	Private
HARRISON	Charles	Private
HARRISON	Phillip	Private
HARRISON	Samuel George	Private
HARRISON	Thomas	Corporal
HART	William Henry	L/Corporal
HARTILL	A	
HARTILL	James Sidney	Private
HARTILL	Joseph	L/Corporal
HARVEY	Alfred Anthony	Private
HATHWAY	Laurence George	Private
HAWKINS	Charles James	Private
HAWKINS	George	Private
HAWKINS	George Henry	Private
HAWKINS	Walter	L/Corporal
HAWKINS	William	Private
HAWKSWOOD	Charles Percival	Private
HAYES	George Thomas	L/Corporal
HAYNES	Joseph	Private
HAYWARD	Arthur	Private
HAZELDINE	William	Private
HEATH	Charles	Private
HEATH	Charles Gray	Private
HEATH	Frederick	Private
HEATH	William Henry	Private

HEATON	Charles	Private
HEENAN	Charles Stuart	Private
HELYAR	Samuel Ebenezer	L/Corporal
HENSON	Albert	Private
HEWITSON	Basil Victor	Private
HEWITT	T.	Corporal
HICKMAN	A	
HICKMAN	Philip Gregory	2nd Lieutenant
HICKSON	Harold Charles Vivian	Private
HICKTON	Ronald Arthur	Private
HIGGINS	Stafford	Private
HIGGINSON	Fred	Private
HIGGS	Albert	Private
HIGSON	Alfred	Private
HILDITCH	Joseph William	L/Corporal
HILL	Arthur	Private
HILL	Arthur Walter	Private
HILL	Henry	L/Corporal
HILL	Henry	Private
HILL	Horace	Private
HILL	Samuel	Private
HILL	Thomas	Private
HILL	W	Private
HILL	W	
HILL	W. N.	Private
HILL	W. N.	Private
HILL	William Isiah	Private
HILL	William James	Private
HILTON	John	Private
HINSLEY	Charles Henry	Private
HINTON	John	Private
HITCHCOCK	William Richards	Private
HITCHMAN	Ernest	Private
HOBSON	Albert	L/Corporal
HODGES	Frank	Private
HODSON	Harold	Sergeant
HOLDER	James	Private
HOLDOM	Edward	Private
HOLLIS	Albert	Private
HOLLOWAY	Samuel	CSM
HOLMES	Francis Lennox	Lieutenant
HOMER	Jason	Private
HOMER	Thomas	Private

HOPKINS	Lambert Gray	Private
HOPTON	John Edward	L/Corporal
HORTON	Thomas St. Clair	Private
HORTON	Walter	Private
HORTON	Walter Cyril	Private
HOUGH	John	Private
HOWARD	William Henry	Private
HOWELL	Harry	Sergeant
HOWELL	Thomas	Private
HUGHES	Charles	Sergeant
HUGHES	John	Private
HUGHES	Joseph	Private
HUGHES	Thomas	Sergeant
HULME	William	Private
HUME	Charles Geoffrey	Lieutenant
HUMPHRIES	William Henry	Private
HUNT	Charles	L/Corporal
HUNT	Charles	A/Corporal
HUNT	Frederick William	Private
HUSSELBEE	William Palmer	Private
HUTCHINSON	Cecil Dunbar	Lieutenant
HUTTON	Matthew	L/Sergeant
ILIFF	Frederick John	2nd Lieutenant
INCHES	Robert James Hay	L/Corporal
IND	Joseph Henry	Private
IVENS	Richard Thomas	L/Corporal
JACKSON	Joseph	Private
JACKSON	Walter	L/Corporal
JAMES	Amos	Private
JAMES	Edwin Thomas	Corporal
JAMES	George Frederick	Private
JAQUES	Ernest Henry	Private
JASPER	Thomas	Sergeant
JEFFCOCK	Robert Salisbury	2nd Lieutenant
JENKINS	Charles	Private
JENNINGS	Charles Joseph Bayliss	Private
JEPHSON	Howard	2nd Lieutenant
JERVIS	Thomas Alfred	Private
JOBBER	Frank	Private
JOHNS	Herbert	Private
JOHNSON	William Roland	2nd Lieutenant
JOHNSON	Albert	Private
JONES	Horace Edwin	2nd Lieutenant

JONES	Kenneth James D.	T/LT (A/CAPT)
JONES	Albert	Private
JONES	Arthur	Corporal
JONES	Arthur Henry	Private
JONES	Charles	Private
JONES	David Albert	Private
JONES	George Arthur	Private
JONES	Horace Harry	Private
JONES	Horace Samuel	Private
JONES	John	CSM
JONES	John	Private
JONES	Joseph	A/Corporal
JONES	Joseph Herbert	Private
JONES	Walter	Private
JONES	Wilfrid Ray	Private
JONES	William	Private
JONES	William Henry	Private
JONES	William Joseph	Private
JONES	William Weldon	Private
JOYNSON	Leonard Charles	Lieutenant
JUDSON	John	L/Corporal
KELLY	Alfred	Private
KELLY	Anthony	Private
KELLY	John	Sergeant
KELLY	William	Private
KENDRICK	Bertie Samuel	Private
KENDRICK	John	L/Corporal
KENNARD	Percy Douglas	Private
KENNINGS	Arthur	Private
KENTFIELD	Harold Arthur	Private
KILBY	J W	Private
KIMBERLEY	Horace Thomas	Private
KING	Arthur Charles	Private
KIRK	Harold	Private
KIRK	J.	Private
KNIGHT	Harold Norman	Private
KNIGHT	William Herbert	Private
KNOWLES	Haydn	L/Corporal
KNOWLES	Hubert	L/Corporal
KNOWLES	John William	Private
LACEY	Frederick	Private
LAFFEY	J.	Private
LAMBERT	Frederick	Private

LAMBERT	Frederick	Private
LANDER	Arthur Holland	Private
LANGFORD	Edwin	Private
LANHAM	Walter James	2nd Lieutenant
LATON	J C	Private
LAW	Thomas	Private
LAWFORD	Richard Roland	Private
LAWLEY	Frank	Private
LAWSON	Leonard	Private
LAWTON	Joseph Thomas	Private
LAXSON	Thomas John	Private
LEACH	Percival	Private
LEE	Albert	Private
LEE	Arthur	Private
LEES	J	Private
LEIGHTON	Ernest	Private
LEIGHTON	Thomas Henry	L/Corporal
LEWIS	Edward Rutter	Private
LEWIS	Edwin	Major
LEWIS	John William	Private
LEWIS	Thomas	Private
LITTLE	William	Private
LLOYD	Frederick	Private
LLOYD	Jeremiah	Private
LLOYD	John Edward	Private
LOCKLEY	Frederick	L/Corporal
LOCKLEY	Frederick	Private
LODER-SYMONDS	John Frederick	Major
LOTE	George William	Private
LOUNDS	Stephen William	Private
LOVATT	John Price	Private
LOWE	James Harold	Private
LOWE	Thomas	Private
LOYDEN	Samuel	Private
LUND	William	Private
LUNN	Thomas	Private
LYCETT	George	L/Sergeant
LYGO	Alfred	Private
MACDONALD	Archibald	Private
MACKMAN	Gapp Campbell	Private
MADELEY	Herbert John	L/Corporal
MALPAS	Samuel	Private
MALUGANI	Edward	Private

MANBY	William Henry	Private
MANDLIN	Charles	Private
MANSFIELD	Bernard James	Private
MARKLEW	Samuel	Private
MARR	Archibald	Private
MARRION	James	A/S.M.
MARSDEN	Sam	Private
MARSHALL	Samuel Edward	Private
MARSHALL	Thomas	Private
MARSHALL	William	Private
MARTIN	Fred	Private
MARTIN	Henry	Private
MARTIN	Joseph	Private
MASON	Arthur	Private
MASON	Bertie	Private
MASON	Edward	L/Corporal
MASON	Ernest Argyle	Private
MASON	Frank	Private
MASON	James William	Private
MASON	William	Private
MATKIN	John	Private
MATTHEWS	Jack	Private
MAYES	Frederick	Private
MAYES	John Edward	Private
MAYO	Thomas	Private
MAYO	William	Private
MCHALE	James	L/Corporal
MCNALLY	Michael	Private
MEASDAY	Walter	Private
MEEK	George Alfred	Private
MEEK	William Henry	Private
MERRICK	Arthur Frank	CQMS
METHERINGHAM	Robert Edward	Private
MIDDLETON	Percy	Private
MILLER	Charles Davy	Private
MILLS	Frederick	Private
MILLWARD	Sidney Chamberlain	Private
MILLWARD	Thomas	Private
MILLWARD	William Richard	Private
MITCHELL	Herbert Walter	Private
MOORE	Jack	Private
MOORE	William Hector	Private
MORGAN	Abraham	L/Sergeant

MORGAN	Basil William	Private
MORGAN	Frederick George	L/Corporal
MORGAN	Leonard Wood	Private
MORGAN	William Charles	Private
MORLEY	Richard	Private
MORRIS	Harold	Corporal
MOSELEY	John Thomas	Private
MOUSLEY	Samuel Charles	Private
MOZLEY	Bertram William	Private
MUGGERIDGE	John	Private
MUNDELL	John William	Private
MURFIN	Harold Herbert	Private
MURLEY	C	
MURRAY	Thomas	Private
MYNETT	Leonard Samuel	L/Corporal
NAVEN	John E.	Private
NELLIST	Mark	Private
NELSON	Walter	2nd Lieutenant
NEVILLE	George	Private
NEVILLE	George Henry	Private
NEWBURY	Frank	Private
NEWELL	Patrick	Private
NEWING	Edward	Private
NEWMAN	James	Private
NICHOLLS	Bernard Lockley	Private
NICHOLLS	Frank Arnold	L/Corporal
NICHOLLS	Harry Carl	Private
NICHOLLS	Joseph Henry	L/Corporal
NICHOLLS	Thomas	Private
NICKLIN	Alfred	A/C. S. M
NOBLE	John William	Private
NOKES	William Herbert	2nd Lieutenant
NOLAN	Harry	Private
NOLAN	Patrick	Private
NORTHALL	Charles Stewart	Corporal
NORTHWOOD	Richard	Private
NORTON	John James	Private
NUTTING	Henry Thomas	Private
OAKLEY	John	Private
OATES	George Leslie	L/Corporal
OGDEN	George James	Private
OLIVER	William John	Private
ONION	Charles	Private

ORGAN	James Bert	Private
OWEN	E.	Private
OWENS	Ernest Greenwood	Sergeant
PAGE	Joseph William	Private
PAGE	Raymond Charles	2nd Lieutenant
PAGE	Reginald	2nd Lieutenant
PAINTER	Clarence	L/Sergeant
PALMER	Thomas Sinclair	Private
PARKER	E J	Private
PARR	Charles Frederick	L/Corporal
PARRY	Arthur	Private
PARSONS	Sidney James	Private
PARTRIDGE	George	Private
PATCHING	John Frederick A.	Private
PATTERSON	Robert	L/Corporal
PAYTON	William	Private
PAYTON	William	Private
PEACOCK	Benjamin	Private
PEARSON	Charles Hugh	2nd Lieutenant
PEARSON	Frederick Phillips	Corporal
PENTELOW	George Norman E.	CSM
PERKINS	Horace Victor	L/Corporal
PERKS	Arthur Leslie	Private
PERRIN	Gilbert Dennis	Lieutenant
PERRY	Arthur Stafford	Private
PERRY	Charles	Private
PERRY	Edgar	Private
PERRY	Frank Percy	Private
PERRY	John William	Private
PERRY	William	Private
PHILLIPS	Jesse	Private
PHILPOT	Albert George	Private
PICKERILL	Fred	Private
PICKERING	Enoch T	Private
PICKIN	George Edwin	Private
PIPER	Alex James	Private
PIPER	Arthur Whateley	Private
PIPER	Reginald C	Captain
PITT	Alfred	L/Corporal
PITT	John	Private
PLANT	Arthur Alfred	Private
PLANT	Walter William	Private
PLATT	H	

PLUMB	Charles Henry	Private
POLLARD	Henry George	Private
PONDER	Alexander Charles	Private
POOLE	William	Private
POPE	Walter Charles	A/Sgt.
PORTMAN	Joseph James	Private
POTTER	Henry Samuel	L/Sergeant
POTTS	John William	Private
POTTS	Samuel	Private
POULTON	Samuel	Private
POUNTNEY	Thomas Henry	Private
POWELL	Harry Wilfrid	Private
POWELL	Horace Walter	Private
POWELL	John	Private
POWIS	Percy Hartland	L/Corporal
PRATT	Arthur (Ma)	Reverend
PRESTON	Charles Henry	Corporal
PRICE	Frederick Charles	Private
PRICE	Howard Kitteringham	Private
PRICE	Issac Norman	L/Corporal
PRICE	John	Private
PRICE	Thomas	L/Corporal
PRIESTLEY	Harold Aaron	Private
PRINCE	Laurence	Private
PRITCHARD	Charles	Private
PRITCHARD	Frederick	Sergeant
PUGH	Samuel Henry	Private
PULLEN	Leonard	Private
PYMM	F L	Private
PYMM	John Thomas	Sergeant
QUINCEY	Albert Henry	Private
RAMM	John Twell	Private
RAMSAY	Walter	Private
RANSFORD	Clement Gascoyen	Captain
RAWLIN	John	Private
RAWLINGS	Arthur Sidney	Private
RAY	Aubrey	Private
REDDLE	Thomas	Private
REECE	William	Private
REED	Arthur	Private
REEVE	Arthur Edward	L/Corporal
REEVES	George	Private
REYNARD	Henry Corner	2nd Lieutenant

RICHARDS	Harold	Private
RICHARDS	William Charles	Private
RICHARDSON	George	Private
RICKETTS	Godfrey	Private
RIGBY	John	2nd Lieutenant
RILEY	C	
RILEY	Ernest	2nd Lieutenant
RILEY	John	Private
RIMMINGTON	Reginald Alfred	Corporal
RISPIN	John	Private
ROBERTS	Arthur	Private
ROBERTS	Harold	Captain
ROBERTS	Thomas	Private
ROBINSON	Edward George	Private
ROBINSON	George	Private
ROBSON	John Flockart Erskine	Private
ROCHELLE	Horace Arthur	Private
ROGERS	Cyril Eric	Private
ROGERS	Jack	Private
ROLFE	James	Private
ROSE	Frederick Job	Private
ROSS	George Walter	Private
ROUND	Alfred	Sergeant
ROUND	Daniel Barnett	Private
RUGG	Stanley Theodore	Private
RYDER	Ernest	Private
RYDER	John	A/Sgt.
SADLER	Charles Bernard R.	Private
SADLER	James	L/Sergeant
SANDERS	Charles	Private
SANKEY	Sydney John	Captain
SATCHELL	Edward Edgar	Private
SAUL	Henry	Private
SCOTHERN	Samuel	Private
SCOTT	John Edward	Private
SCOTT	Richard	Sergeant
SCRAGG	Arthur John	Private
SCREEN	Thomas	Private
SEAGER	Robert Thomas	Private
SEGAR	Harold	Private
SELLARS	Arthur	Private
SENIOR	Harold	CQMS
SHAKESPEAR	William Thomas	Sergeant

SHAW	Fred	Private
SHAW	Frederick William	Private
SHAW	Harry	Private
SHELDON	Sidney	Private
SHENTON	Francis	Private
SHEPHERD	John Herbert	Sergeant
SHERWOOD	John Henry	Private
SHINTON	Henry	Private
SHIPSIDES	Joseph	Private
SHONE	Geoffrey Beville	Lieutenant
SHOTTON	Walter Albert	Sergeant
SHREWSBURY	Harry	Private
SIDAWAY	Simeon	Private
SIDDALL	Frederick William	Corporal
SIER	J. F.	Private
SILVERS	Frank Pitchford	Captain
SILVESTER	Bertram	Private
SIMMONS	Albert James	Private
SIMMONS	Leonard Maurice	Private
SIMNER	William	Private
SIMPSON	Leonard	Private
SINDERSON	Richard	Private
SKIDMORE	John	Private
SLATER	Francis Ewart	Private
SLATER	Harry	Lieutenant
SLATER	Richard	Private
SMART	Cyril Henry Arthur	Private
SMITH	Albert	Private
SMITH	Cornelius	Private
SMITH	Frank	Private
SMITH	Frederick Leonard	Sergeant
SMITH	Frederick Ridgway	Corporal
SMITH	George	Private
SMITH	Gerald Howard	Lieutenant
SMITH	John	Private
SMITH	John or James	Private
SMITH	John William	Private
SMITH	Joseph	2nd Lieutenant
SMITH	Matthew	Private
SMITH	Norman Frederick	Private
SMITH	Samuel	Private
SNAPE	Harold George	Private
SNAPE	John	Private

SOMERFIELD	Arthur	Private
SOMERFIELD	J P	
SOUTHALL	Clifford	L/Corporal
SOUTHALL	Cyril	Private
SPARKES	Walter John	Private
SPEED	Bert	Private
SPRUCE	William Joseph	Private
STAFFORD	Frank	Private
STANFORD	Ernest	Private
STANILAND	Christopher	Private
STANLEY	Ernest	Private
STANLEY	Stephen Law	Private
STATTERS	George Henry	Private
STEVENS	John	Private
STEVENTON	Alfred	Private
STOCKTON	George James	L/Corporal
STOKES	William	Private
STUART-WORTLEY	John	Lieut. Col.
STUBBS	James	Private
STYLES	George	Private
SUGDEN	William Clarke	Private
SWAIN	Frederick Richard	Private
SWIFT	Andrew	Private
SYKES	Leslie Hindle	2nd Lieutenant
SYLVESTER	Charles Percival H.	2nd Lieutenant
TANDY	Arthur	Private
TANDY	Bernard Joseph	Private
TANKARD	Samuel	Private
TAYLOR	Alfred William	Private
TAYLOR	Charles Cyril	Private
TAYLOR	Christopher George	CSM
TAYLOR	Frederick Thomas	L/Corporal
TAYLOR	George James	Private
TAYLOR	Herbert	Private
TAYLOR	John	Private
TAYLOR	John James	Private
TAYLOR	Joseph	Private
TAYLOR	Joshua John	Private
TAYLOR	William	Private
TEETON	Percy Randolph	Captain
TEMPEST	David Percival	CQMS
TETLEY	George Ernest	L/Corporal
THACKER	Herbert	Private

THEOBALD	Reginald John	Private
THOMAS	James	Private
THOMASON	Allan	Corporal
THOMPSON	Harry	Private
THOMPSON	John Moore	Private
THORNEYCROFT	George Benjamin	Private
THORNHILL	Frank	Private
THRIPPLETON	Joseph Webster	Private
TILL	Arthur William	Private
TIMMINS	William Benjamin	2nd Lieutenant
TITLEY	William	Private
TITLEY	William Fred	Private
TOMKINSON	William	Private
TOMLINSON	Ferdinand Roger John	2nd Lieutenant
TONKS	Reginald	L/Corporal
TONKS	Roland	Private
TORDOFF	William Henry	Private
TOTNEY	Edward William	Private
TOTTY	Charles Thomas	Sergeant
TOWLER	Herbert	L/Corporal
TRANTER	Frank	Corporal
TRANTER	John Thomas	Private
TRANTER	Lewis John	Private
TREADLE	John	Private
TUDOR	James Herbert	Private
TUFT	John Lyttleton	Private
TURGOOSE	Herbert	Private
TURNER	Edward Thomas	Private
TURNER	Harold Edwin	Private
TURNER	Richard Arthur	Private
TURNER	Simeon	Private
TURNER	William	Private
TURTON	Thomas William	Private
UPSALL	Horace	Private
VAILL	John William	Private
VEASEY	Frank	Private
VITTY	Laurence	Private
WAGER	Ernest Charles	Private
WAGHORN	Stanley	Private
WALKER	Albert John	Private
WALKER	Herbert Newton	2nd Lieutenant
WALKER	James	Private
WALKER	William	Private

WALL	A	
WALL	Arthur	Private
WALL	Ronald Addison	Private
WALLES	Henry Stephen	Private
WALTERS	Harry	Private
WALTERS	John	Private
WALTERS	Sidney	2nd Lieutenant
WALTERS	Tom Henry	Private
WALTON	Samuel	Private
WANNOP	Alfred	Private
WARBOYS	Archibald George	Sergeant
WARBURTON	Harry	Private
WARD	Eric	Private
WARD	James	Private
WARD	John	Private
WARD	Joseph Edward	Corporal
WARD	Seth	Private
WARDLE	George Henry	Private
WARDLE	Robert Claughan	Private
WARRIOR	Cecil	L/Corporal
WATERHOUSE	Charles	Private
WATERS	William Albert	Private
WATSON	Daniel	Private
WATSON	Frederick Wallace	A/Sgt.
WATTS	Joseph	Private
WEAVER	Charles Henry	Private
WEBB	B.	L/Corporal
WEDGE	Alfred	Private
WEDGE	William Henry	L/Corporal
WELCH	Albert	Private
WELLFARE	Edwin Thomas	Private
WESTWOOD	William	Private
WHEELER	Ernest	Sergeant
WHEELER	Harold	Private
WHITE	Arthur	Private
WHITE	Hubert	L/Corporal
WHITE	Joseph	Private
WHITEHOUSE	Edward	Private
WHITEHOUSE	Frederick William	Private
WHITEHURST	Ernest	Private
WHITEMAN	John Ernest	Private
WHITTINGHAM	William Henry	Private
WHITTLE	William Steen	Private

WHITWICK	Ernest Frederick	Private
WICKES	Sidney William	Private
WILDBOAR	Samuel	Private
WILES	John Thomas	Private
WILFORD	Lionel Russel	Lieutenant
WILKES	Richard	Private
WILKINSON	J	Private
WILLIAMS	Alfred	Private
WILLIAMS	Alfred James	Private
WILLIAMS	David Marmaduke	Lieutenant
WILLIAMS	Edmund Theodore	Private
WILLIAMS	Ernest	Corporal
WILLIAMS	Evan	Private
WILLIAMS	G. E.	Private
WILLIAMS	George	Private
WILLIAMS	James	L/Corporal
WILLIAMS	James	Private
WILLIAMS	James Griffiths	Private
WILLIS	Samuel	Private
WILLNER	John	Captain
WILLS	Gordon	Private
WILSON	Arthur	Private
WILSON	Gamble	Private
WILSON	John	Private
WILTSHIRE	Thomas	Private
WISE	Frank Howard	Private
WISHART	Robert Henry	L/Corporal
WITHERS	Alfred	Private
WITTON	Benjamin	Private
WITTS	Vincent Royden	Private
WOOD	Albert	Private
WOOD	Arthur William	Private
WOOD	Cornelius	Private
WOODFIELD	John	Private
WOOLDRIDGE	Benjamin	Private
WOOTTON	F	
WORTHINGTON	S	
WORTHINGTON	William Henry	Private
WORTON	Ernest James	Private
WRIGHT	Frank	Private
WRIGHT	Harold Walter	Sergeant
WRIGHT	William Thomas	L/Sergeant
WRIGHT	William Thomas Percy	Private

WYLDE	George Henry	Private
WYNN	Ernest	Private
YATES	Harry	Private
YEO	Leslie Farquhar	Lieutenant
YOUNG	Robert Warton	Private
ZELLY	Ernest Albert	Private

Dulce et decorum est Pro Patria mori?

THE RUPERT RATIO UNIT SINGLE MANUAL

VOLUME 2:
EVERYTHING BUT THE ENGINE

BSA C15 B25 B40 B44 B50 &
TRIUMPH TR25w

Panther Publishing

Published by Panther Publishing Ltd in 2014

Panther Publishing Ltd
10 Lime Avenue
High Wycombe
Buckinghamshire HP11 1DP

www.panther-publishing.com
info@panther-publishing.com

© Rupert Ratio 2014
The rights of the authors have been asserted in accordance with the Copyright Designs and Patents Act 1988

The Rupert Ratio Unit Single Manual

The Rupert Ratio Unit Single Manual Volume 1: The Engine ISBN 9781909213166
The Rupert Ratio Unit Single Manual Volume 2: Everything But The Engine ISBN 9781909213142
The Rupert Ratio Unit Single Manual Volume 3: Lesser Known Models ISBN 9781909213173
The Rupert Ration Unit Single Manual (Three Volume Set) ISBN 9781909213180)

All rights reserved, no part of this publication may be reproduced, stored in a retrieval system or transmitted, in any form or by any means, electronic or mechanical, including photocopying, digital copying, and recording without the prior permission of the publisher and/or the copyright owner.

ISBN 978-1-909213-14-2

CONTENTS

Chapter		Page
	Foreword	v
1.	Identification	1
2.	Frames	10
3.	Shock Absorbers	42
4.	Front Forks	50
5.	Brakes, Hubs and Wheels	97
6.	Chains and Sprockets	134
7.	Exhaust Systems	144
8.	Stands	160
9.	Controls	165
10.	Seats	189
11.	Petrol Tanks	201
12.	Oil Tanks and Lubrication	219
13.	Side Panels, Central Tinware and Air Filters	229
14.	Mudguards	240
15.	Paints, Finishes and Transfers	255
16.	Nuts and Bolts	276
17.	Electrics	282
18.	Instrumentation	316
19.	Tools	329
20.	Index	336

Works prototype lightweight oil-bearing frame of 1971. One of a small number of experimental projects under way in the BSA 'comp-shop' when closure brought a premature end to developments there in September '71. This design was originally intended for Enduro use with a B25 or B50 engine although this specific frame received a Bantam engine! Yet another 'Might Have Been'

FOREWORD

Since writing Rupert's first book dealing with the BSA Unit Single Engine, the obvious question has been 'what about the rest of the bike?' By necessity, this resulting work has to be of much greater scope than a relatively simple engine manual, to adequately cover the wide range of Unit Single models, variants, updates and modifications which occurred during the fifteen or so years during which they were produced. Indeed, the range of Unit Single motorcycles numbers at least as many variants as any other type of BSA motorcycle, and sometimes to a bewildering degree.

As with Rupert's engine manual (Originally *The Rupert Ratio Unit Single Engine Manual* and now *The Rupert Ratio Unit Single Manual Volume 1 The Engine*), this volume is intended to help the Unit Single owner be 'hands on' in maintaining their machine, to repair and restore it where necessary, and to get the best out of it on the road or track. The more greasy thumb-prints collected by your copy, the happier I will be!

Due to the extensive range of Unit Single models covered by this volume, a slightly different approach is required whereby the first step in putting your bike together properly is to make sure that all the bits are correct for your particular model. This book will help you to identify the parts you need to complete your restoration jig-saw and thus shorten the search for them.

Extensive use of original BSA part numbers has not been made here. If these are needed in dealings with the few surviving spares dealers who continue to operate by the BSA part numbering system then use of an original BSA parts book is recommended.

The information and advice contained here is offered in good faith, having been continually gathered over a period of thirty-some years of restoring and using a wide range of these machines. As such, I have tried to avoid simply regurgitating existing information from the many excellent BSA manuals which are already easily available. Such 'common knowledge' must be a component of any fully inclusive manual but additionally I have tried to 'fill in the gaps' by detailing my own methods and experiences and by including original BSA data which is less well known or previously unpublished.

Illustrations included in this book intentionally show Unit Single parts which are not in excellent restored condition, rather they show typical original and unrestored parts, now up to 50 years old in the conditions in which they are usually obtained for restoration. This will hopefully reassure the potential restorer that this is 'the norm', this is what we are all up against in returning our machine to its former glory and that it is all do-able.

I am a firm believer in the saying that 'knowledge is power'. Therefore do also obtain the correct parts book, hand book and BSA manual for the Unit Single which is of interest to you, and any number of publications with illustrations of these machines to act as a guide. These days, the internet is a rich source of information and inspiration for the owner of these machines. Hopefully you will find that this book offers to increase your knowledge and as a result, your power to make the most of your BSA Unit Single.

I wish that I could say that this is the end of the process but it cannot be: tomorrow we shall know more. With this in mind I can only apologise for omissions and as yet unknown errors which this book is bound somewhere to contain despite my best efforts; it having been written nearly forty years after these machines were last produced and when no one person who knows the whole Unit Single story is alive to ask - if ever such a person existed.

With Thanks To

Amassing the knowledge contained in Rupert's two books has been made possible by the nature of the British bike movement in the UK. The machines and parts are out there in significant quantities awaiting only the next willing owner, and the first-hand knowledge of how to make them go is still available to be tapped, if often unpublicised by those in the know. For this I owe thanks to these other 'keepers of the true faith' who have shared their nuggets of British bike wisdom with me and have helped me to develop my knowledge and interest.

Dave Simpson	Andy Peachey
Lee Mitchell	Chris Burrell
Steve Foden	Matt Colling
Neil Jenkins	The BSA Owners Club of Great Britain

Additionally, thanks for their specialised expertise are due to –

Prestige Electro Plating, Mexborough
GP Brake Relines, Bloxham
Auto Colour Match, Banbury

And to Rollo Turner at Panther Publishing for his unflagging encouragement and guidance.

Additional illustrations for this book provided by:

Chris Burrell
Johnathan Lodge
Ashley Briggs
The BSA Owners Club of Great Britain

Using This Book

Production year
Frequent references in this book are made to years with regard to Unit Single model details, eg B25 '70. In all such cases, the year refers to the BSA production year, which at BSA began in August of the preceding year. In terms of the calendar, the example quoted above would be August 1970.

Model names
Throughout this book the general terms 'road models', 'off-road models' and 'competition models' are used. This is to avoid excessive repetition of lists of specific models.

Road Models	C15, B40 Star and SS models, B25 Starfire, B44 Victor Roadster and Shooting Star, and OIF Gold Star models
Off-road Models	Covers two distinct groups.
Competition	C15 Trials and Scrambles, B44GP AND B50MX
Trail oriented	C15 Trials Pastoral, B40 Enduro Star, B44VE and VS. TR25w and OIF Victor Trail.
	B40 Military is similarly a dual purpose machine but is frequently referred to separately due to its different lineage.

Abbreviations
Some abbreviations are used throughout the book:-

o/s	off side is the right hand side of the vehicle when seated upon it, also known as the timing side.
n/s	near side is the left hand side of the vehicle when seated upon it, also known as the drive side
o/d	outside diameter
i/d	inside diameter

1. IDENTIFICATION

The BSA Part Numbering System

Pieces of your Unit Single which are made by casting eg brake shoes, brake pedal, side and centre stands and many other items can often be found to have a number moulded in or stamped onto them. This number can aid identification of the part and the model it is intended for, if it is found to fit the format of the BSA part numbering system.

From early days, BSA employed a system of six digit part numbers wherein the first two related to a particular model or range; the last four specifying the individual part. The first two model-related numbers range from 00 to 99 and were allocated across the whole range of BSA manufacturing, not just to their motorcycles. An example of a complete number would read 12-3456, the first two digits link this part to the specific model to which it was first fitted. Some therefore are specific to the Unit singles as these made use of many new parts and are as follows:

40	C15 and B25 prior to '68
41	B40 and B44
47	B40 military

As usual with BSA the picture is more complex than it may at first seem.

1. Many parts from earlier and other contemporary BSA models found a new home on the Unit Singles, hence their part numbers frequently appear, eg 65-9111 is the C15 competition speedo bracket originally used on the pre-unit Gold Star. '90' parts are borrowed from Bantams and '68' are borrowed from the Unit Twins.

2. From 1968 BSA and Triumph introduced a new system for parts introduced wherein the first two digits related to specific areas of the machine irrespective of model: '37' for example related to the wheels. This system did not replace the numbers already in use from the previous system but was additional to it

3. In 1973 BSA and Triumph introduced their 'part number rationalisation' whereby parts from the old model-related numbering system which were still in current production (either as a high demand spare or as fitment on a current model) were given a new number to conform to the later system. Many pre-'68 Unit Single parts therefore have both their original number and also their 'change number' as it is known. This can help should you be dealing with a spares supplier who still 'keeps the faith' with BSA.

Regardless of the above complexities, it is useful to see the number on a particular part and recognise it as the one you need. It should be borne in mind that the exact number visible on a part may be one or two digits out from that given in the parts book; the number in the metal may refer to the raw casting or component and not the finished part. For example, the C15 frame headstock often has its '40' number cast into it; this is the number for this cast component only, it is not the number of the complete frame nor is it the frame/chassis number of the motorcycle (a frequently made mistake).

Identifying Your BSA Unit Single Model And Its 'Date Of Birth'.

A few points to bear in mind:

> Engine and frame numbers did not usually match until 1967. Prior to this only B44 machines had matching numbers.
>
> New production model numbering usually began at 101. Numbers 1 to 100 were available for pre-production and prototype machines if required.
>
> Frame (and latterly matching engine) numbers did not automatically start afresh at 101 for each new production year. A new start other than for a new model did not occur each year until '70 and thence did so each year after. Prior to this, the numbering of continuing models ran consecutively from one year to the next, albeit sometimes with a small gap and a new start at a round number eg 5001 for a new season.
>
> It should also be noted that production of any particular model did not necessarily begin at the start of a given year, due to lack of production capacity at BSA as well as planned mid or late-season introductions. Similarly, termination of a particular model did not necessarily happen at the exact end of a production year eg the supposedly '67 only C25 Barracuda continued until the start of '68 B25 production began in November '67.
>
> Should you be lucky enough to own a BSA with a frame stamped 'CDF' and not fitting the usual numbering sequence you may have an ex-works machine - Competition Department Frame - as this was one of their means of identification; 'CDE' similarly translates as a 'comp-shop' engine. However, don't be confused by normal frame numbers including the date letters 'CD' (3/'70) and 'ED' (5/'70), they *do not* indicate competition department or experimental department.

Basically it is all rather confusing, muddled and typically British with exceptions to the rule seemingly being the norm!

Although the letters and numbers of engines and frames may be the same on the post '67 models, the actual stampings may not, with different punches clearly having been used. From that time complete engines with their number already stamped were fitted to the frame during assembly and the frame would subsequently be stamped to match*. For earlier machines with non-matching numbers both engine and frame would be fully stamped separately before the machine was assembled.

Frame number location

Finding your frame number to identify your Unit Single should be simple enough. See photos opposite.

> Pre '67   Most models prior to '67, n/s top of the front down tube on the headstock casting or gusset plate.
>
> 67 to '70   On the n/s of the front engine lug. Variations in the clarity of each digit depend on BSA's man with the hammer: errors are not uncommon
>
> 71 on   OIF models, initially on the side stand mounting plate (not exactly prominent) and from mid '71 on, the n/s of the headstock.

This procedure resulted in the paint finish of the frame being damaged in the area of the stamping leading to localised corrosion problems. Remedies to this were discussed at length by BSA but none were adopted.

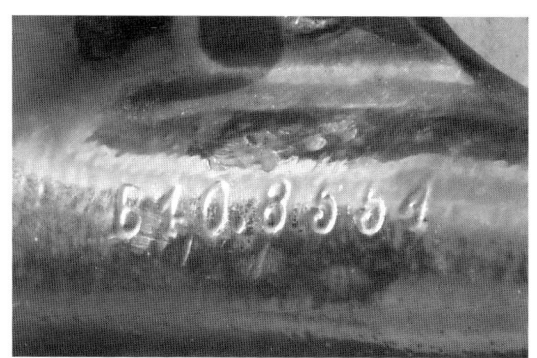

Fig 1.1. Pre '67 frame no is on the top n/s down tube as on this B40 Star.

Fig 1.2. '67 to '70 on the n/s of the front engine lug reads: Frame no. DC15597 B44VS. This '69 onward style of numbering incorporates the year and month code letters and demonstrates just how indistinct these can be.

Fig 1.3. '71 on OIF models, number stamped on the side stand mounting plate before the number was moved to the headstock from 5/'71.

Fig 1.4. The original stamping by BSA - here seen as B40M 189 is often faint and indistinct; especially in comparison with numbers added later by owners; in this case the Jordanian military. Their additional stamping 21164 is typical of the additional numbers often found on ex-military machines.

Model identification

For the uninitiated, a basic summary of the Unit Single models:

C15	250cc built in various guises from 1958 to 1967.
B40	350cc built in various guises from 1960 to 1970
B25	250cc built in two main formats, 1967 to 1970 and 'OIF' for 1971 and '72
TR25w/T25	Triumph equivalent of the B25, built from 1968 to 1971
B44	441cc built in road and off-road formats from 1965 to 1970
B50	500cc OIF built in road and off-road formats from 1971 to 1973
TR5MX	Triumph equivalent of the BSA B50MX, built 1973, correctly called the 'Avenger'.

Fig 1.5. The BSA factory despatch books give a fascinating insight into the methods and practices employed there; a typical page of the thousands produced is shown above covering some of the 1965 C15 production – sorry, no prize if your bike is shown here!

Fig 1.6. B40GB brass ID plate, pop riveted to the n/s headstock of a B40 Military Mk1. This provides an additional source of information (see p5)

The frame number will contain the model code (shown in bold in the tables on the following pages) which will identify exactly what sort of Unit Single you are dealing with. Prior to 1969 these are usually found as a prefix to the number, from 1969 usually as a suffix. 1968 models are a bit of both! Notably, the later B40 military models generally kept the earlier prefix format. Gaps in the sequence of frame numbers are apparent in the BSA despatch books *(see fig 1.5)* notably towards the end of production for any given model. Also in the tables below it is not possible to account for the small numbers of machines built as exceptions to the usual production sequences.

From 1969 the frame (and matching engine) numbering sequence was common to all of the Unit Single models being produced in any given year. For example in 1969, B25S, B25FS, B44SS, B44VS and TR25w were all built in batches; the frame numbering simply carrying on consecutively from one model to the next without interruption.

Date codes 1969 on

The move to the suffix position for the model code for most machines from 1969 corresponded with the addition of the new date code prefix eg 'HC19226B25S' The HC at the start of the above number are the month and year code letters employed by BSA and Triumph from 1967 onward (it does not stand for 'high compression'). In the case of BSA the A and B year letters for '67 and '68 respectively were inconsistently applied, the system being generally adopted in 1969 on all models except B40 military. The Month and Year codes used from 1969 are:

Code	Month	Code	Month
A	January	B	February
C	March	D	April
E	May	G	June
H	July	J	August
K	September	N	October
P	November	X	December

Code	Year	Code	Year
A	1967	B	1968
C	1969	D	1970
E	1971	G	1972
H	1973	J	1974
K	1975	N	1976
P	1977	X	1978

Military B40 dating

B40 Military Mk1 models for the British army carry a Brass identification plate on the n/s of the headstock (fig 1.8). This plate will carry a month/year date stamp. This is not the date of manufacture for the bike in question but the date of the army contract for which the bike was manufactured. The actual manufacture date could be months or years after the contract date. Each different contract number usually entailed a slightly different build spec.

The serial number stamped on the plate is entered in the despatch books next to the frame number; thus there is a direct traceable relationship between this serial number and the actual frame number stamped on the engine mount. The contract number – 'C.T.' on the brass plate is traceable through army records and specifies the quantity and build state for this batch of machines.

Production numbers

The data below should not be used to calculate production totals. But, just for the sake of it, very approximate production totals for each model, including all variants are shown below.

Model	Approx Prod. Qty.	Model	Approx Prod. Qty.
C15	58,000	B40	18,000
B25/T25	33,000	B44	20,000
B50	9,000		

Unit Single Year and Frame Numbers

Each production year/season commenced in August following the annual factory holiday. Machines produced late in the previous season would continue to be dispatched well into the new season.

Model	Prod. Year	Description & commencing frame number
C15		Star, Sports Star ('66 Sportsman) and police models '59 to '66 (production start 9/58).
	'59	C15 101
	'60	C15 11101
	'61	C15 22001
	'62	C15 32001 (no clear break in production to denote new season)
	'63	C15 38030 (no clear break in production to denote new season)
	'64	overlap between first '64 model (with 'C15D' engine) at frame C15 41811 and last '63 model at frame C15 42306
	'65	overlap between first '65 model (with 'C15F' engine) at frame C15 44658 and last '64 model at frame C15 45508
	'66	overlap between first '66 model at frame C15 48915 and last '65 model at frame C15 49234. Last despatch 7/'67 at frame 51178
C15G	'67	Star - 6/'66 to 2/'68, frame number C15G 101 to C15G 2407, all being '67 models.
C15SG	'67	Sportsman, uses C15G frame number sequence as above.
C15PG	'67	Police, uses C15G frame number sequence as above. Earlier C15 Police models engine numbers DP and FP, used the standard C15 frame code.
C15S		Trials, Scrambles and USA Starfire competition models '59 -'63 with four digit number (production start 4/'59)
	'59	C15S 104
	'60	C15S 501
	'61	C15S 2731
	'62	C15S 3558 last despatch 1/'63 at frame C15S 4056
C15S	'62 only	Trials or Scrambles 'Special' with five digit number between C15S 10001 and C15S 10051, 5/'62 to 10/'62
C15A		Trials Pastoral '62 to '63 (production start 7/'62)
	'62	C15A 101
	'63	C15A 122 last despatch 2/'64 at frame C15A 228
C15C		Trials, Scrambles, USA Starfire competition models and B40 Enduro Star '63 to '65 (B40 Enduro Star introduced '64) Production start 2/'63 last despatch 8/'65 except for two B44VE 11/65
	'63	C15C 101
	'64	C15C 801 (no clear break in production to denote new season)
	'65	C15C 1531 up to C15C 3134
C15E		Trials Pastoral 7/'64 to 3/'65, frame number C15E 101 to C15E 242
C15AA	'64	Australian Military prototype 2/'64 to 3/'64, frame number C15AA 105 to C15AA 131

C15CA	'65	Military prototype 2/'65 to 4/'65, frame number C15CA 101 to C15CA 135
C15CB	'63	Military prototype 2/'63 to 3/'64, frame number C15CB 101 to C15CB 105
B40		Star, Sports Star (All markets) and Sportsman (USA) '61 to '66. Production start 7/'60
	'61	B40 101
	'62	B40 3511
	'63	B40 5043 (no clear break in production to denote new season)
	'64	B40 6664 (no clear break in production to denote new season)
	'65	overlap between first '65 model frame B40 6912 and last '64 model frame B40 7902
	'66	B40 9883 (no clear break in production to denote new season) last despatch 12/'66 and frame B40 10184
B40G		Star '67 - 6/'66 to 7/'66, frame B40G 103 to B40G 470 (plus 497)
B40 GA		Military Mk1 Australian Army, 1/'67 to 2/'67, frame B40GA 101 to B40GA 562
B40 GB		Military Mk1 British army '67 to '70. Additionally, small numbers of machines with frame numbers outside those given below supplied to other buyers.
	'67	6/'67 to 3/'68 frame B40GB 101 to B40GB 2103
	'69	1/'69 to 6/'69 frame B40GB 3001 to B40GB 3453
	'70	12/69 to 7/70 frame B40GB 4001 to B40GB 5266
B40GD		Military Mk1 Danish Army '67 to '70
	'67	7/'67 to 3/'68, frame B40GD 101 to B40GD 716
	'69	12/'68, frame B40GD 750 to B40GD 959
	'70	12/'69 to 1/'70, frame B40GD 1001 to B40GD 1202
B40GR		Military Mk1 Royal Air Force '69 to '70
	'69	3/'69 to 4/'69 frame B40GR 201 to B40GR 231
	'70	3/'70, frame B40GR 300 to B40GR 340, 6/70 frame B40GR 401 to B40GR 414
B40GN		Military Mk1 Royal Navy '69 to '70,
	'69	2/'69, frame B40GN 101 to B40GN 116
	'70	12/'69 to 1/'70 frame B40GN 301 to B40GN 310
B40M		Military Mk2 '68 to '69
	'68	11/'67 to 4/'68, frame B40M 101 to B40M 378
	'69	1/'69 to 3/'69, frame B40M 402 to B40M 460
HCB40M		Roughrider: 7/'69 to 10/'69, frame HCB40 461M to HCB40 577M
C25		Barracuda, USA Starfire
	'67	3/'67 to 7/'67, frame C25 101 to C25 2627
	'68	8/'67 to 9/'67, frame C25 2648 to C25 3014
B25S		Starfire '68 to '70, Woodsman '70 ('68 models initially stamped 'B25B----'. Suffix 'S' or 'FS' introduced mid-season to differentiate between these two models after Fleetstar introduced)
	'68	11/'67 to 10/'68, frame B25B101 to B25B6300S
	'69	9/68 to 10/68 (prior to new numbering system frame B25C6002 to B25C6300
		10/'68 to 8/'69, frame KC6301B25S to HC19949B25S
	'70	9/'69 to 10/'70, frame HD00101B25S to JD14218B25S
B25FS		Fleetstar '68 to '70 see B25S above, same frame number sequence used ('68 models stamped 'B25B----FS'). '72 OIF Fleetstar uses 1972 frame numbering sequence detailed below.

TR25w '68 to '70
  '68   2/'68 to 7/'68, frame TR25W104 to TR25W4616
  '69   7/'68 to 9/'68, frame TR25WC 5001 toTR25WC 6061, then 10/68 to 7/'69, frame NC7300TR25W to HC19912TR25W (using numbering sequence common to B25 and B44)
  '70   9/'69 to 10/'70, frame JD01259TR25W to JD14107TR25W (using numbering sequence common to B25 and B44 models).

B44   Grand Prix '66 to '67. Huge gaps in numbering sequence, total production approximately 500 machines.
  '66   9/'65 to 7/'66, frame B44 101 to B44 2646 (some machines in this range built for '67 season)
  '67   9/'66 to 7/'67, frame B44 2647 to B44 2775

B44E   Victor Enduro, USA Victor Special
  '66   2/'66 to 7/'66, frame B44E 101 to B44E 2619
  '67   9/'66 to 11/'66, frame B44E 2645 to B44E 2695

B44EA '67   Victor Special '67, 9/'66 to 7/'67, frame B44EA 101 to B44EA 3344
B44VS   Victor Special '68 to '70 ('68 models stamped 'B44B----VS' or 'B44BVS----', first batch for '69 built to '68 spec stamped B44C----VS)
  '68   11/'67 to 5/'68, frame B44B1374VS to B44B4718VS
  '69   first batch (B44C) 9/'68 to 10/'68, frame B44C5001VS to B44C 5512VS, then 11/'68 to 5/'69, frame PC7751B44VS to EC15930B44VS
  '70   7/'69 to 9/'70, frame HD00101B44VS to JD14102B44VS

B44R   Victor Roadster/USA Shooting Star '67 – '68
  '67   2/'67 to 8/'67, frame B44R 104 to B44R 2611
  '68   first production built to '67 spec. stamped 'B44RB ----' up to 9/'67 at frame B44RB 2816

B44SS Shooting Star '68 to '70
  '68   9/'67 to 2/'68, frame B44B101SS to B44B3729SS
  '69   11/'68 to 7/'69, frame PC07751B44SS to HC19363B44SS
  '70   8/'69 to 7/'70, frame JD01075B44SS to HD13944B44SS

1971 models
All 1971 models share the same frame numbering sequence, generally being built in batches, the numbering continuing consecutively from one model to the next. The numbering began at JE00101 (8/70 - although production and despatch was delayed until 12/'70) and ended at JE15761. 250cc production effectively ended at EE11243 whereupon B50 quantity production began. B50 frame and engine numbers followed their own format with both model and date codes as prefix, often separated by a forward slash, eg B50T/HE14935.

From '71 to combat tampering, the background to the engine number is machined and has 'BSA' lightly and repeatedly stamped:

Model codes for '71 models

B25SS	Gold Star SS
T25SS	Blazer
B25T	Victor Trail
T25T	Trail Blazer
B50SS	Gold Star SS
B50T	Victor Trail
B50MX	Motocross

1972 models

All 1972 models share the same frame numbering sequence, generally being built in batches, the numbering simply continuing consecutively from one model to the next. Approximately 60 initial machines were carried over from the end of the '71 season and hence have date codes GE/JE whilst using the '72 number sequence. '72 numbering began at JG00101 and ended at DG2971

B25FS	Fleetstar (production from NG2765 onward).
B50SS	Gold Star and Gold Star SS
B50T	Victor Trail
B50MX	Motocross

1973 models

At the time of writing, the whereabouts of the factory despatch record for 1973 production is not known. The information below therefore results from 'train-spotting' of '73 models from several sources and whilst being acceptable as a general guide it cannot be considered as definitive - particularly in view of the conditions under which production occurred at that time.

B50MX	Three batches AH00350 to DH01250 HH01400 to JH01450 JH0301 to JH03150
TR5MX	began at DH75101 ended at HH75632

B.S.A. MOTOR CYCLE DIVISION
SMALL HEATH,
BIRMINGHAM,
ENGLAND.

THE QUEEN'S AWARD TO
INDUSTRY
1967 1968

BSA
PASSED BY
QUALITY
CONTROL

QUALITY CONTROL DEPARTMENT

1.7. An example of the quality control ticket attached to machines being despatched. The BSA Queens Award to Industry badge is occasionally found as a tank top transfer on '67-'68 models.

2. FRAMES

Identification of Unit Single Frame Types

There are three basic designs of Unit Single frame as used from 1958 to 1973, commonly known as:

Swan Neck	'59 to '67
Welded/Duplex	'63 to '70
Oil-In-Frame (OIF)	'71 to '73

Each of these basic types was produced in a range of sub-types featuring detail differences. Additionally the '66 to '67 B44GP frame is a fourth, but rare frame type fitted only to that model. This frame is included in the notes below for the contemporary Welded/Duplex frame to which it is most closely related.

Swan Neck frame ('59-'67)

Fig 2.1 shows a B40 Swan Neck frame headstock design. Well, it's probably as good a name for it as any, and is borrowed from the preceding Triumph Tiger Cub frame design. All of these frames comprise a front loop which is of single tubing except for the 'duplex cradle' of two tubes under the engine. Onto the front loop is bolted the subframe at the swinging arm pivots and saddle nose, and in effect comprises the rear half of the complete frame.

Differentiating between Swan Neck frame sub-types

Quick identification features for this frame are the headstock design and the bolt-on subframe. Four versions of this were produced:

> The standard C15 roadster frame used for all C15 Star and Sport Star/Sportsman models from '59 to '67 *(fig 2.6)*.

> The C15S competition frame used by C15 trials and Scrambler models (and off road USA C15 Starfire derivatives) from '59 to '63 *(figs 2.5)* identified by the level and parallel duplex tubes under the engine *(fig 2.2 - 2.3)*.

> The B40 roadster frame used for all B40 Star and Sport Star models from '60 to '67 (fig 2.7). Here the normally brazed-on pressed steel saddle for the front tank mounting is replaced by an assembly bolted to a small lug either side of the headstock . The thicker $1^{3}/_{8}$" diameter top tube is harder to spot. (Fig 2.1 lug A)

> The C15A Trials Pastoral frame of '62/'63, which is an otherwise standard B40 frame with minor differences. Don't expect to find a C15A frame unless you live in Australia; it is to all intents and purposes a B40 frame but without any brazed-on lugs for the central tinware, these being clamped on instead.

Frames 11

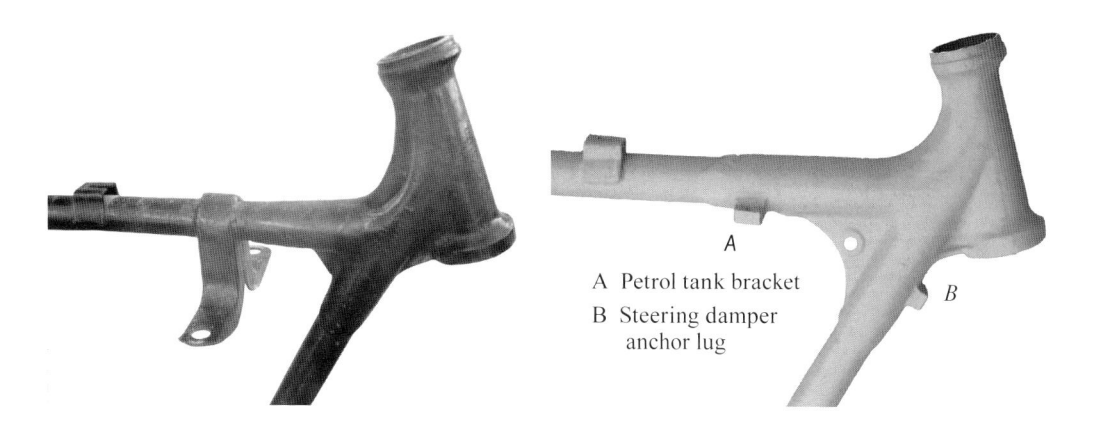

A Petrol tank bracket
B Steering damper anchor lug

Fig 2.1. Swan Neck frame headstocks.

Left, C15 for all road models and C15S frames.

Right, B40 headstock. This arrangement of headstock casting into which the top and down tubes are brazed is the definitive feature of the Swan Neck frames. This particular example is identifiable by the hole and lugs 'A' and 'B' as B40 rather than C15.

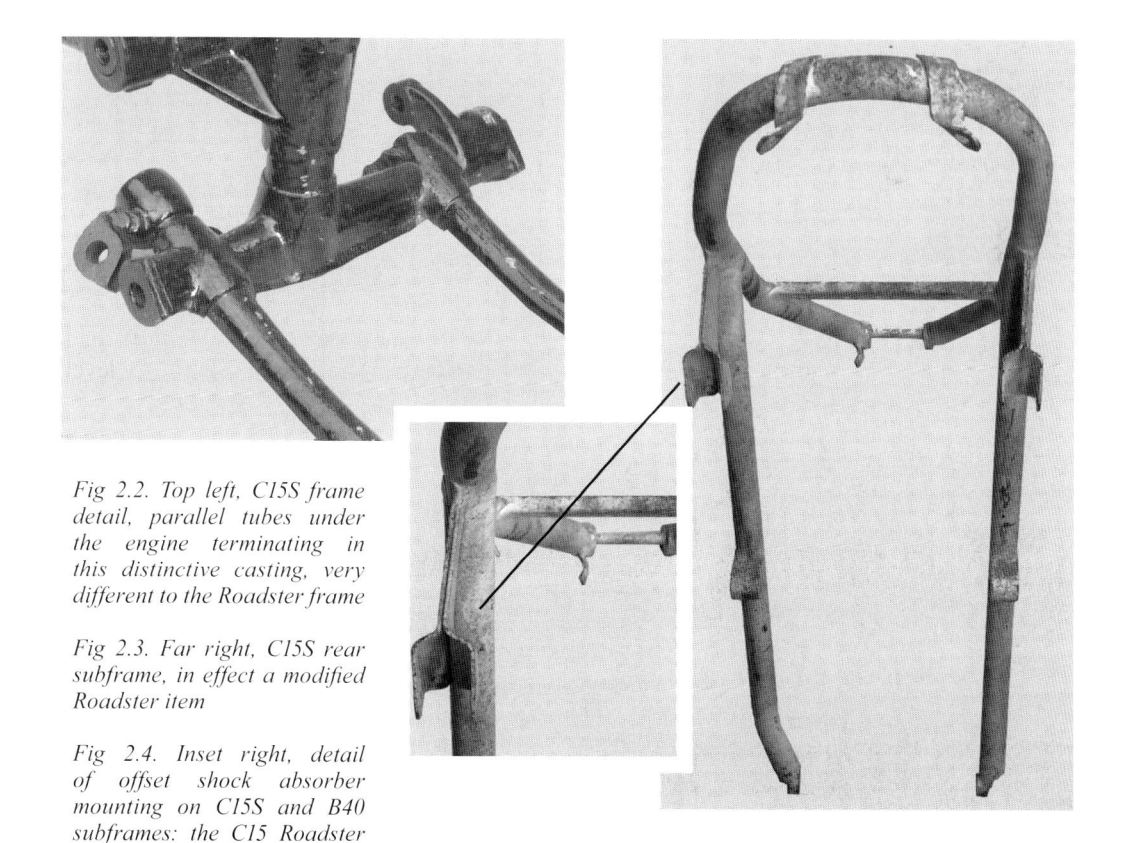

Fig 2.2. Top left, C15S frame detail, parallel tubes under the engine terminating in this distinctive casting, very different to the Roadster frame

Fig 2.3. Far right, C15S rear subframe, in effect a modified Roadster item

Fig 2.4. Inset right, detail of offset shock absorber mounting on C15S and B40 subframes: the C15 Roadster version is vertical

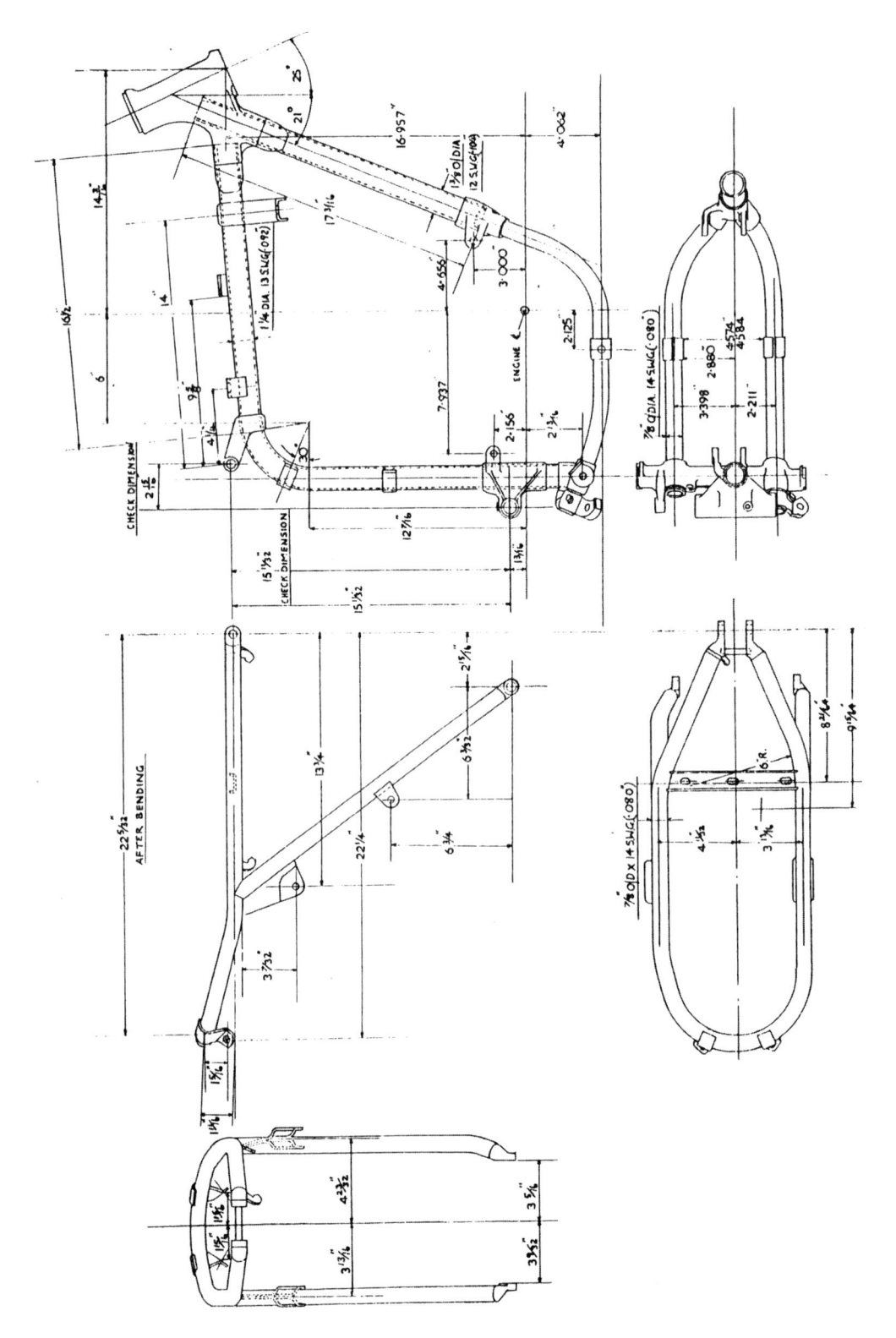

Fig 2.5. C15S Swan Neck frame for C15 Trials and C15 Scrambles '59 -'62

Frames

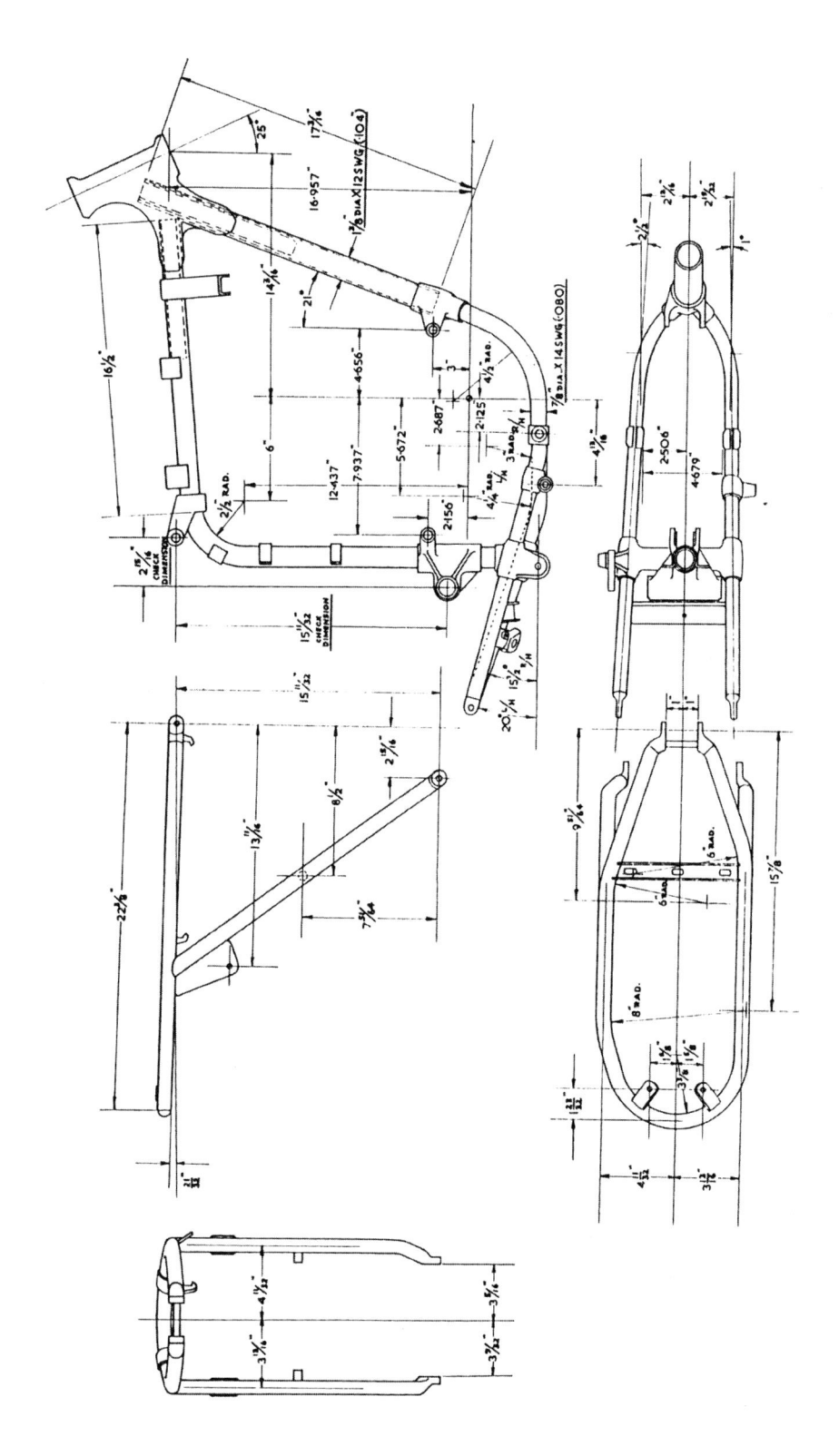

Fig 2.6. Swan Neck Frame for C15 Star and C15 Sports Star (road models)

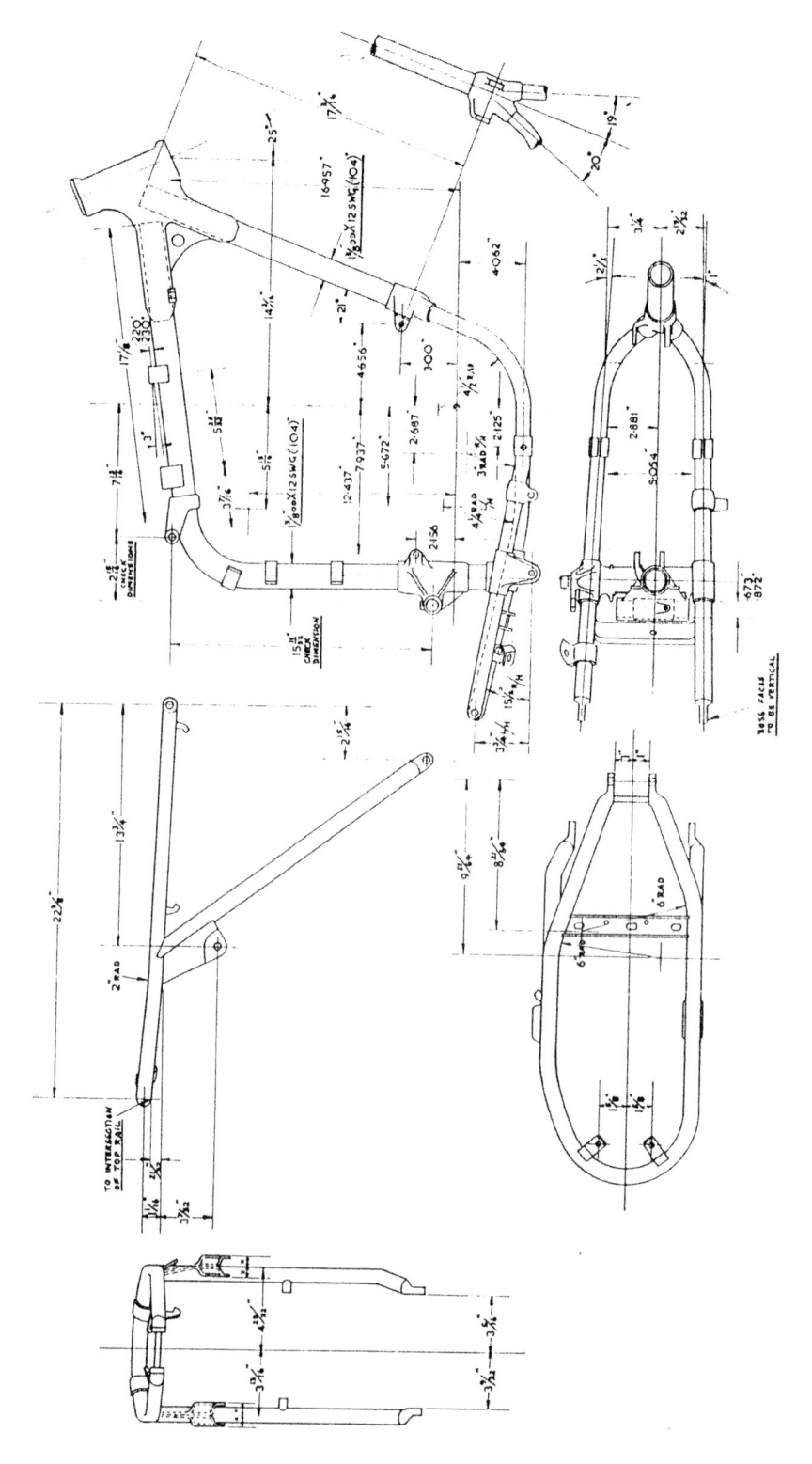

Fig 2.7. B40 frame '60 - '67 road models. (Also used on C15A Trials Pastoral '62 - '63 with minor changes, see p10)

Swan Neck subframe

Three slightly different versions of the subframe were produced and these are fully interchangeable;

>The standard item to go with the C15 roadster frame,

>The standard B40 subframe which differs from the C15 item only by having the nearside shock mounting point set outboard by $^3/_8$" to suit this 'wide chain line' model.

>The competition subframe fitted to C15S and C15A frames. This has the same $^3/_8$" offset of the shock mount and also the rear end of the frame loop is kicked upward rather than being straight and level. The two rear mudguard brackets are positioned outside the sub-frame tubing rather than inside as on the roadsters.

Fig 2.4 shows the offset n/s shock absorber top mounting as on the C15S and B40 sub-frame. The subframes are mostly of welded construction and therefore differ from the main loops which employ the traditional construction method of malleable steel castings for the various lugs which are brazed to the connecting tubes.

Swan Neck frame problems

The 'Swan Neck' label for all of these frames relates to the design of the headstock of the main loop with the attached top tube and front down tube and was borrowed from the Triumph Tiger Cub (along with the design of the forks and engine). Like the borrowed engine design it was a cheap and simple way of doing the job but it had inherent weaknesses: if the frame suffers a head-on bump the two tubes linked to the headstock - top and down - will bend next to it. If the bike is dropped the headstock is liable to twist on the frame loop. For drawings of the C15 and B40 Swan Neck frames, see *figs 2.5-2.7*.

Attachment of the subframe to the main loop is at three points. Two are securely achieved at the ends of the swinging arm spindle by substantial bolts. The upper fixing point to the front loop is somewhat suspect by comparison and relies on the ½" o/d dowel tube, which runs through the front loop and subframe lugs, being a tight fit. Additionally the $^3/_8$" cycle bolt which passes through the hole needs to be done up fully tight if the 'hinge in the middle' effect is to be avoided. The dowel should only be removable by drifting or pressing if it is of the requisite tightness. This may result in unavoidable damage. Any doubt, obtain a new dowel.

In addition to the above mentioned propensity to accident damage, one or two areas can be prone to wear and tear but overall the Swan Neck frames stand up to normal use quite well. Chief culprits for damage are the projecting tubes which support the sidestand and the pillion pegs; these will bend or fracture if the bike is habitually started on the side-stand, and preventing the pillion rider standing on the pegs will help keep them straight and true. Favourite brackets to fail due to vibration are those for the rear guard on the subframe loop and those for the central tinware on the main loop.

Unusually for BSA, the centre stand mounting points on the frame are very robust, being part of a substantial steel casting rather than the usual welded-on lugs. The stand itself and its pivot pins are much more prone to wear.

The method of swinging arm attachment to the main frame means that the fit of the swinging arm pin in the frame lug will deteriorate if the pin has been removed and replaced a number of times. It should be tight and require a press to persuade it to move. A loose pin is one which can be moved easily just by tapping its end and means reject the frame or affect a repair (see p33)

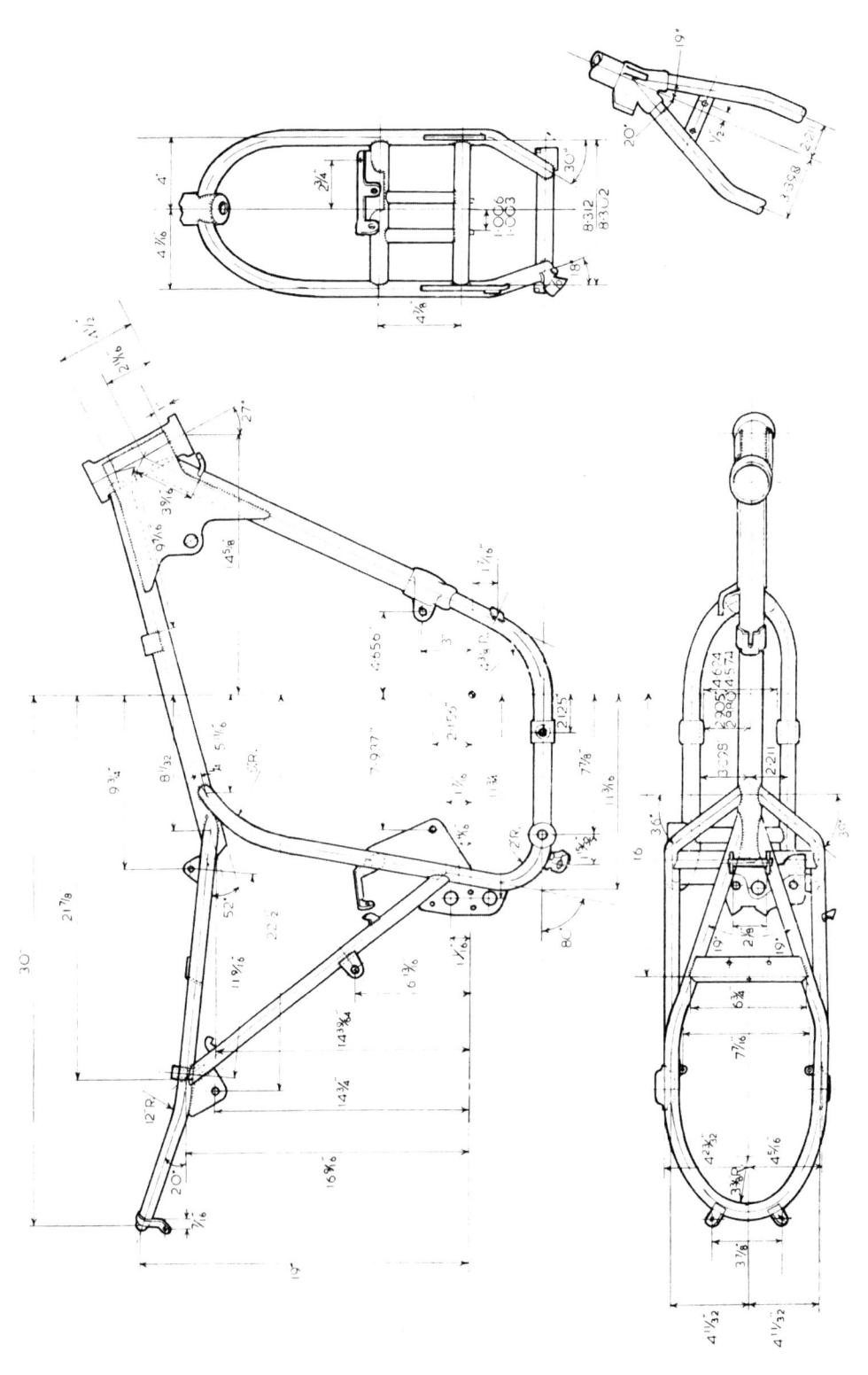

Fig 2.8. Welded/Duplex frame, here the '67 B44 Victor Enduro, which is the same as the C15C frame used on the off-road models from '63

The Welded/Duplex frame ('63 -'70)

This title covers the range of frames used on several models spanning the years '63 to '70 *(fig 2.8)*. The term 'Welded/Duplex' is almost accurate; the brazed lug method of assembly, as used throughout the C15 frame production run, is still applied to the front and lower engine mounts, the rest of the frame joints being electric welded – and to a standard high enough to shame the Japanese bike frames by comparison, long after the demise of BSA! The Duplex label refers to the duplex engine cradle extending up and behind the engine to terminate on the top tube at the seat nose.

With one exception - the B44 Victor GP frame (*fig 2.10*) - the Welded/Duplex frames all share the same geometry, dimensions and tubing and differ only in the minor brackets and mounting lugs necessary for the different parts fitted for each model. These will be considered in more detail later. None of these variations affect the interchangeability of engines in these frames or between the Welded/Duplex and the Swan Neck frames.

Identification of sub-types of the Welded/Duplex frame

Identification of a Welded/Duplex frame is easiest by reading the frame number stamping on either the nearside top of the front down tube (early models) or nearside of the front engine mount ('67 on).

However, some useful clarification of which frame was fitted to which model is given below.

    C15C   Developed as a result of the BSA competition shop scrambling efforts (C for 'Competition'). Used on C15 Trials, Scrambles and export derivatives of these from '63 to '65 ie Starfire Roadster, Starfire Scrambler, Trials Cat and B40 Enduro Star.

Fig 2.9 BSA publicity showing the first production Welded/Duplex C15C frame, here on the '63 C15 Scrambler

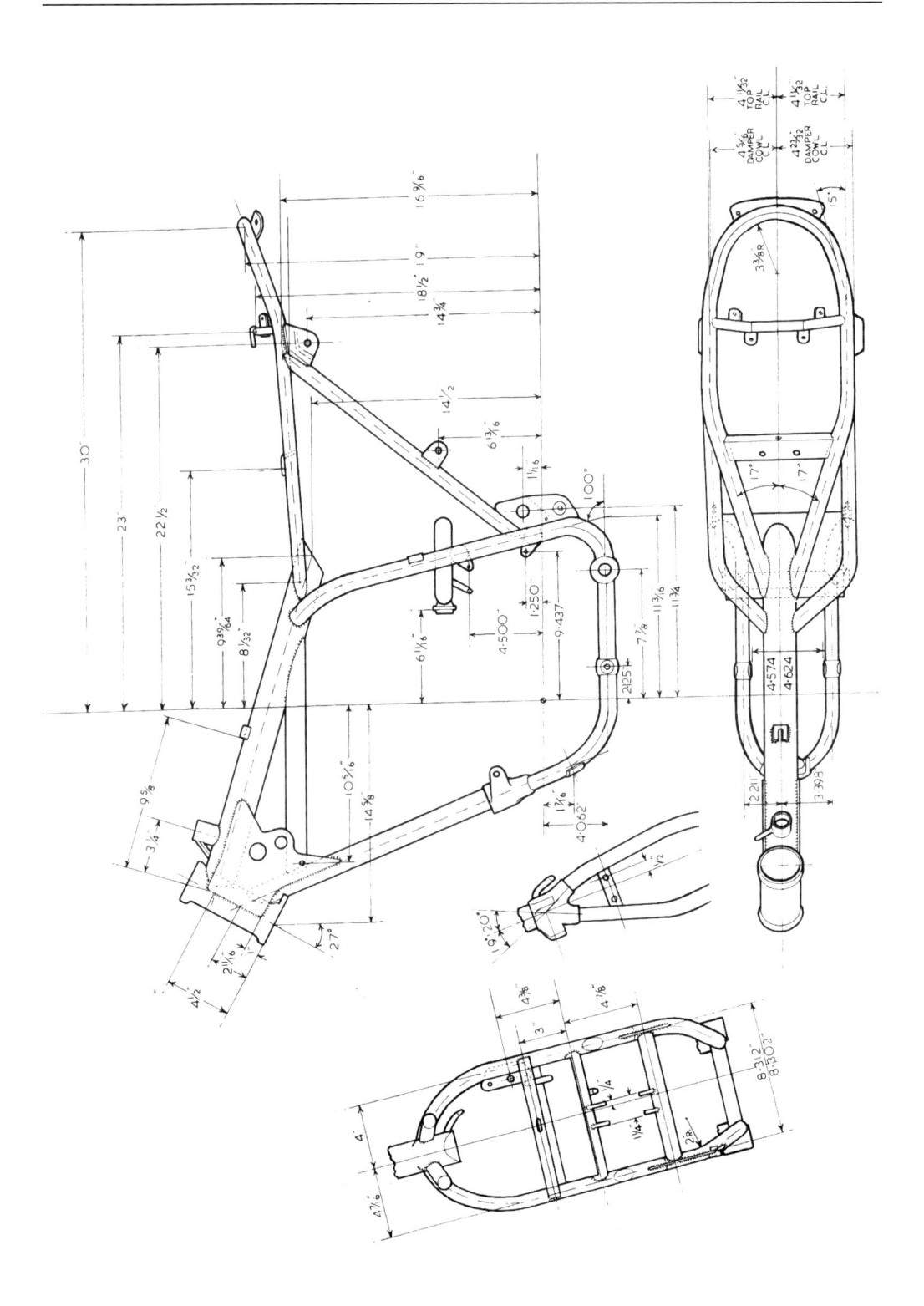

Fig 2.10. B44 Victor Grand Prix frame. Based on the Welded/Duplex item but much modified to carry the oil.

Figs 2.11 and 2.12 (right). The B44GP engine oil header tank which is brazed onto the frame tubing, houses the oil filter and takes oil from both the front down-tube and the frame top-tube

Alongside the C15C production, detail bracketry changes for new models resulted in:

C15CB   First military prototype '63

C15CA   Used on competition bikes for the army to special order eg the Royal Artillery display team and B40 Military prototypes in '64/'65.

C15AA   As above but used for the initial batch of Australian Military machines.

C15E   Used for the '64/'65 Trials Pastoral for Australia.

B44 production, beginning in late '65 for the '66 season, comprised two models which adopted the Welded/Duplex frame. The B44 Victor GP *(fig 2.10)* and the Victor Enduro/Special.

B44 Victor GP.
The 'over the counter' copy of Jeff Smith's world championship scrambler, known as the B44 Victor GP, which used a new frame. It was physically similar to the existing Welded/Duplex versions but modified to carry the engine oil within the tubing and thus dispense with the separate oil tank (other than a small header tank behind the engine which housed the filter see *fig 2.11*). This frame is specific to the B44GP and is not to be confused with that used on the 'Oil-In-Frame' models produced from '71 onward. GP frame production also differed by being of a higher standard - high tensile tubing (Reynolds 531) connected by Bronze welding. *Fig 2.10* shows the B44GP frame based on the Welded/Duplex item, but much-modified to carry the oil.

B44 Victor Enduro/Special
For trail use. The 'Enduro' name was initially used for home and general export machines and 'Special' for the USA market. As the vast majority of sales were to the USA the Enduro label was soon dropped and the Victor Special label was applied to all B44 trail machines regardless of where they were sold. The '66 Victor Enduro/Special adopted the existing C15C

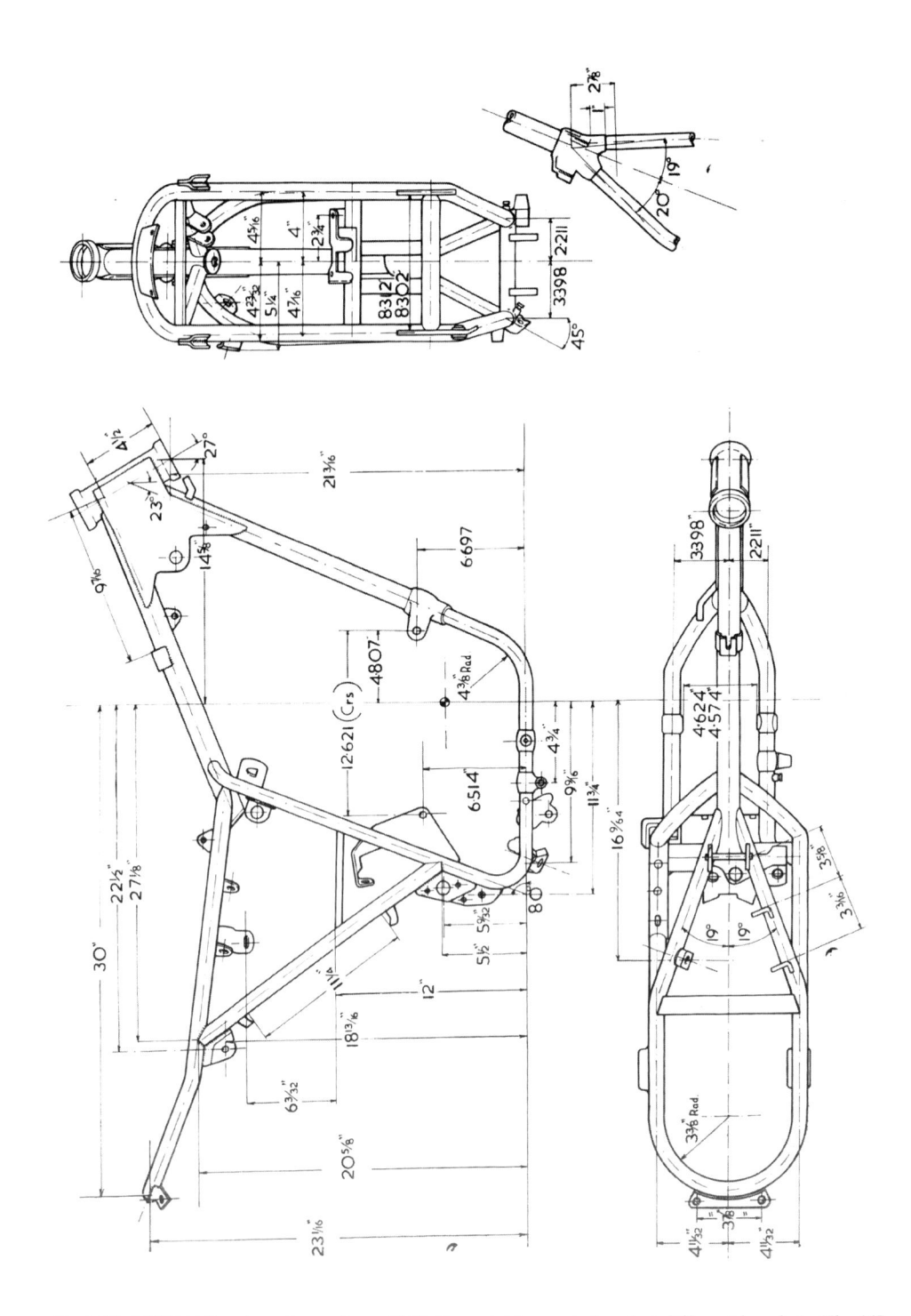

Fig 2.13. B25/B44 Roadster frame from 1968. Same tubing as before but different brackets. The '67 version of this frame is identical other than:

The subframe cross bar (under the seat) is tubular rather than channel section

The subframe to the rear mudguard mounting plate was previously two separate lugs

frame and after C15 off road production ceased at the end of '65 this same frame type was stamped B44E ('66) and B44EA ('67) to match the engine now fitted.

Roadster
The first roadsters to use the Welded/Duplex frame were the '67 C25 Barracuda (UK), B25 Starfire (USA) and B44 Victor Roadster (UK) and Shooting Star (USA) *(fig 2.13)*. Frame tubing and geometry continued as before but many details were changed to suit the new roadster bits being bolted on, namely changes involving oil tank, footpegs, centre stand, side panels, battery tray, ignition switch and ignition coil.

All Welded/Duplex frames from this time onward were strengthened by the addition of a second tube within the seat and engine support tubing (don't be tempted to saw your frame into bits to check it is there, I've already done it for you as shown in *fig 2.14*).

The '68 B25/B44 roadster frame used the same '67 frame with minor changes to the subframe *(see fig 2.13)*

B40 Military Mk1
1967 also saw production begin of the B40 Military Mk1 which likewise used the Welded/Duplex frame *(fig 2.16)* with a new mix of brackets and lugs. Identification of the military frame is often simplified by its' colour – green (various shades used), and the model is commonly known as the 'War Department B40' (correctly called B40 Military) regardless of original customer as differentiated by the frame number stamping – GB, GD, GA, GR etc.

Victor Special
By '68 the 'Enduro' name was dropped, but the Victor Special had more significant changes for '68 as it adopted the roadster type frame arrangement for the footpeg mounts, oil tank and battery tray (not previously fitted). In effect it adopted the roadster frame minus the centre stand lugs; plus the bash-plate front bracket. The TR25w was introduced for '68 and shared the B44VS frame through to '70.

Fig 2.14 Frame sawn throgh to reveal the inner tube within the seat and engine support tubing

Fig 2.15 Footpeg boss of the C15C and B44E frame. B44GP is similar but with the flat angled forwards

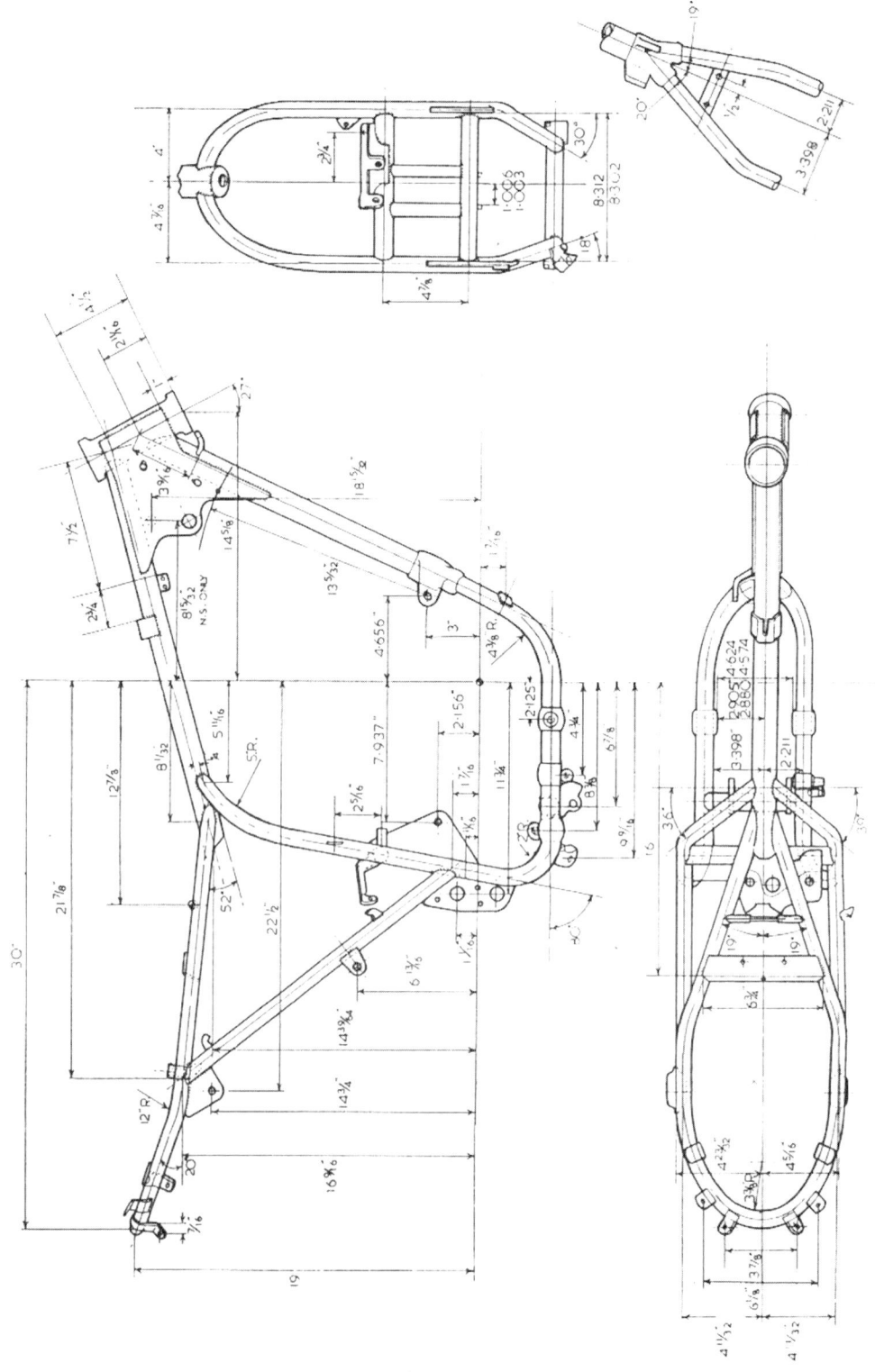

Fig 2.16 The Welded Duplex frame: '67 B40 Military version shown. Geometry and tubing were as the contemporary Roadster frame. Differences relate to the various brackets

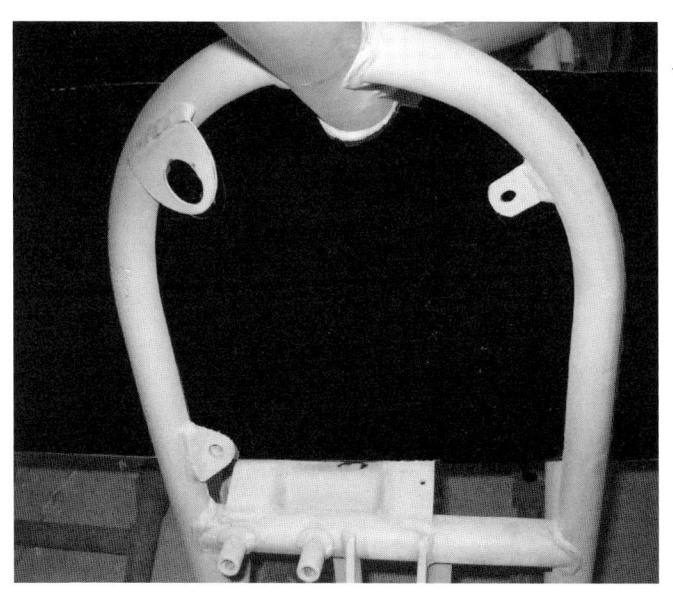

Fig 2.17. '68 - '69 B40 Military Mk2 frame showing brackets peculiar to this model. This frame also lacks the oil filter bracket of the B40 Military Mk1 which is instead mounted from the o/s rear engine plate

The change to the roadster type of footpegs was a retrograde step for the off-roaders, this being a weaker arrangement than the previous competition frame design of a substantial boss with the footpegs located on a machined flat as shown in *fig 2.15.*.

Anyone contemplating building a 'green laner' or similar machine around a Welded/Duplex frame, which would be subjected to frequent standing on the pegs, would be wise to start with one of the '63 to '67 off-road frames. The problem being that the taper fit footpeg lugs which are brazed around the frame tubes can come loose and rotate around the tube after the pegs have received heavy use. Often this distorts the frame tube in the process.

This is a particular problem with the B40 Military frame which combined weak footpegs with arduous use. Rather than attempting to cure this on the drawing board, BSA treated the symptom by supplying military customers with 'Repair kit, footpeg, B40' consisting of a ¼" Allen bolt and nut to be fitted as a cotter pin through boss and frame tube after drilling through both to suit.

The frame shown in *fig 2.16* is the Welded/Duplex frame in '67 B40 military guise. Geometry and tubing were the same for the contemporary roadster; detail differences relate to the various brackets only.

1968 also saw the introduction of the B25 Fleetstar which at all times used the current home market Starfire frame.

1969 saw the frames for the roadsters and the trail models modified under the engine (B40 Military variants deferred until '70) where the space between the frame tubes was widened. This was done to prevent contact between the nearside tube and crankcase, a common problem, and necessitated wider bottom engine mount bosses to compensate so as to leave engine interchangeability unaffected. Fairing mounting tubes were also added to the headstock at this time (except B40 Military).

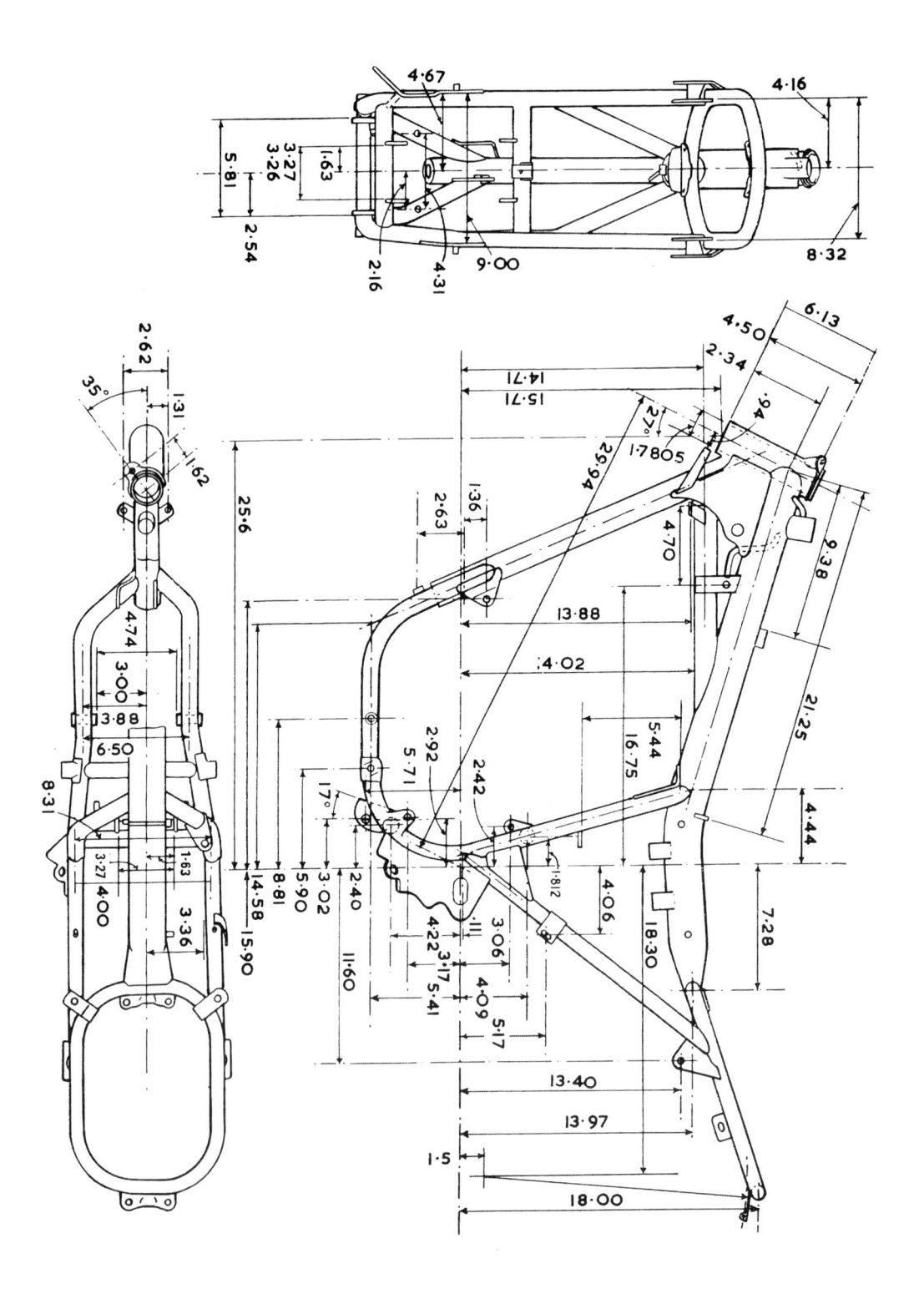

Fig 2.18. The Oil-In-Frame frame for the B25 and B50 '71 - '73

Introduction of the B40 Military Mk.2 and Roughrider during '68 necessitated minor changes to the Mk.1 frame (which continued in production) by the addition under the saddle nose of brackets for ignition switch and rectifier, and the deletion of the oil filter bracket. These are shown in *fig 2.17*.

All '70 B25, B44 and TR25w models gained a small mounting lug for a 2MC capacitor on the subframe. TR25w and USA B25 now shared a common frame to accept the l/h hi-level exhaust system and no centre stand. However, the USA B25 regained this feature in November '70 when, nearing the end of the line for these models – with Oil-In-Frame production imminent – one common frame was introduced for all B25 models and B44 Shooting Star permitting fitment of bash-plate, centre stand and l/h hi-level exhaust.

Welded/Duplex frame problems
Common defects across the range of Welded/Duplex frames are as previously mentioned and relate to side stand lug bent/worn; taper fit foot peg bosses bent or loose on the tubing; centre stand mounts bent and holes worn oval; rear guard top mounting lugs to '67 and additionally the oil tank bottom mounting point - a bit of tube - often departs from the post '67 Roadster frames. The top-tube and front down-tube will not resist the sideways force generated if the bike is dropped heavily resulting in the headstock being pushed to one side - always check for this and the equally common bent top and down tubes resulting from a front-shunt.

Oil-In-Frame (OIF) '71-'73

This frame (with minor differences for the MX models) was used on '71 to '73 B25T, SS and FS, B50T, SS and MX, and also '73 Triumph TR5MX. Easy visual identification of these frames centres on the rectangular loop of tubing under the seat along with the large diameter top tube. A longer look will show that everything about this frame is different from its predecessor.

Two types were produced, one for B50MX/TR5MX and one for all other B25/T25/B50 (see *fig 2.18*) road and trail models. Both frames are of the same design and differ only in the lack of minor brackets on the MX version. One minor addition to all frames early in '71 was the strengthening gusset plate welded across the frame tubes above the swinging arm pivot on both nearside and offside.

OIF frame problems
Weaknesses which apply to these frames are few. This is a robust and durable design partially due to the larger diameter tubing and fully welded construction. The shortcomings apply to

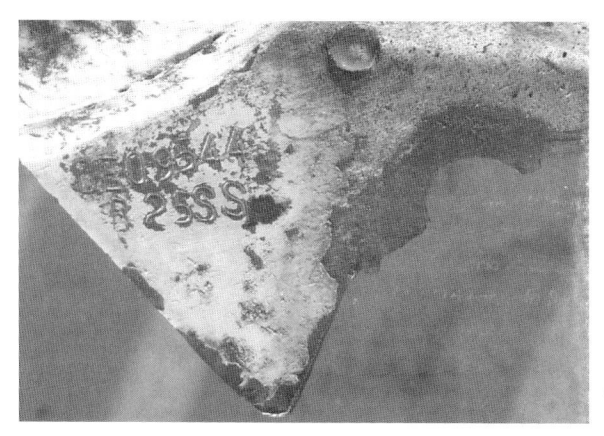

Fig 2.19 Damaged sidestand mounting plate. A common problem with the OIF design is side stand lug fracture

some of the welded-on pressed steel brackets which were not sufficiently well engineered to cope with normal levels of day to day stress. First to fall off the OIF frame is the front lower silencer bracket. This was twice improved by BSA as it was simply not up to the job of coping with vibration and weight of the large lozenge silencer. The final version (from '72 onward) of $3/16$" thick steel which wraps around the frame tubing seems adequate. Similarly the silencer top mount was beefed up for '73 to take the heavier load generated by the twin-silencer system. Next to go will be the side stand mounting plate which usually snaps off half way up across the pivot hole *(fig 2.19)*

Also susceptible is the pressed steel steering stop on the front down tube. Any dents made on the front of the tank by the fork stanchions tell that the steering stop is no longer stopping the forks when it should!

Welded repairs to all of these problems are straightforward but for the silencer bracket some slightly thicker steel would help. For the side stand bracket replace the original two layer effort with one single piece of the correct thickness. Centre stand mountings will also deteriorate commensurate with use and weight placed upon them if this optional extra is fitted.

In view of the frequently found damage of bent and broken side and centre stands and associated lugs and frame tubes on all Unit Singles I really do feel it should be writ large across the top of every petrol tank **take the bike off the stand before operating the kick start!**

Checking for Frame Damage and Wear - All Frame Types

All frames - *is it straight?* Much can be done to ascertain the answer to this with the Mk.1 human eyeball. It is best to assume that every used Unit Single frame, now approaching at least 35 years old, is bent to some degree. Next is to decide whether or not the amount of bend is minor enough to see it fit for further service. This can be done simply by having a good look at it, without resorting to the surface plates and vernier gauges as shown in the 'works' method (*see fig 2.20 and 2.21*).

Of the three types of Unit Single frame the Swan Neck frame is the weakest and therefore the type most likely to now be displaying signs of being bent. The upside is that it is the one most easily straightened in the shed due to its' simpler design and construction. The OIF frame is easily the strongest due to its design and larger diameter tubing but rectification of a bent frame of this type is rarely possible at home. The Welded/Duplex frame falls between its relatives in regard to both resistance to damage and repair possibilities at home.

With any frame the first thing to do is to have a good look at it from astern. Get the eyeball close to the end of the seat loop and look towards the headstock. This is to ascertain whether the top tube aligns directly with the centre of the loop. Do this by lining up the left side of the front down tube with the top tube and mark the rear loop where they point to. Do the same with the right hand side of the tubes and the centre point between the two resulting marks should be smack in the middle of the loop – central between the mudguard mounting points.

If it isn't the question is how much misalignment can be tolerated? I cannot really answer this for you; it depends on the extent to which you like riding a bike with crab-like tendencies. For myself; $1/8$" out at this point is OK, and I would probably go with it. Any more than this, get it straightened or find a better frame. The more the frame is 'out' in this manner; the harder it will be to achieve correct wheel alignment. This is a likely cause of handlebars not being

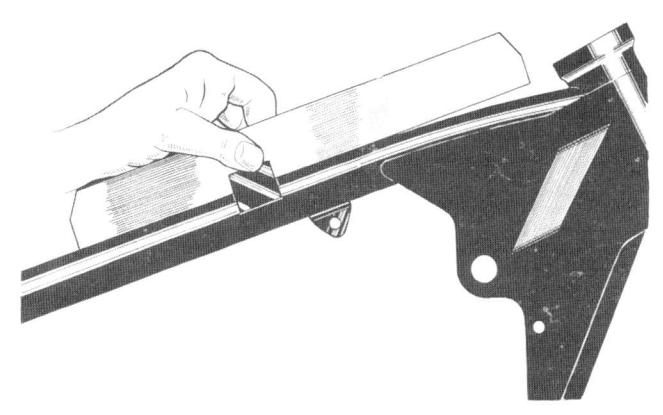

Fig 2.20. Checking the frame top-tube with a straight edge; the same needs to be done with the down-tube. The Swan Neck frames cannot be checked like this but for these it is visually easy to see any kink in these tubes where they join the headstock lug.

straight and level when riding straight ahead and rear wheel adjustment not being equal on both sides when alignment is achieved.

Misalignment of this sort is likely to have been caused by side force applied to the headstock – dropping the bike heavily for example. This will tend to knock the headstock sideways; the most obvious deformation being where the top tube meets the sub-frame. It is also likely that damage of this nature will be replicated in the front down tube, but here it is usually more gradual and less easy to spot without a straight edge placed against the tube side.

Similarly, side impact on the sub-frame will push this whole area over and will be indicated by the support tubes no longer being vertical when viewed from the front or rear.

Thinking beyond the simple test above implies that any misalignment which is apparent is unlikely to be limited to this one area, and this throws doubt on how straight the rest of the frame is likely to be.

Swan Neck frames are easier to check for the type of damage resulting from a sideways knock to the headstock which will have the effect of causing the front frame loop to twist. By eye it is easy to line up the vertical saddle tube behind the engine which should be spot-on parallel with the front down tube when seen from ahead or astern.

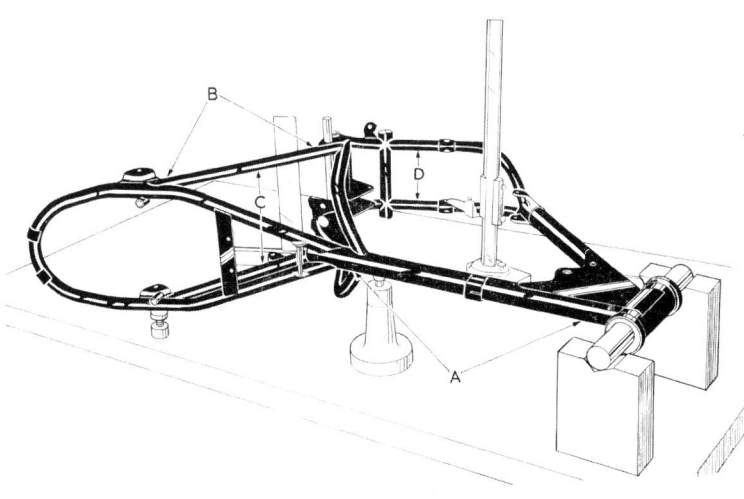

Fig 2.21. Checking the frame for straightness; the 'works' method on a surface table. Any decent flat surface will do if attempting this - the kitchen worktop, for example, but don't tell her I said that!

With a bare frame, any twist of the headstock will show up more clearly if a snug fitting metal bar or straight piece of wood is passed through the headstock and viewed from dead ahead or astern in comparison to the vertical aspect of the rest of the frame. It helps to position the frame perfectly vertical when doing this check by passing a bar through the lower engine mounting holes and supporting the ends on blocks or similar. The 'works' version of this aid is to produce a 'checking mandrel', machined to mount on the steering head bearings just as the yokes do, so that it will exactly show trueness – or not - of the headstock.

Next check is from the side. The top tube and front down tube should each be dead straight. A front impact will bend them adjacent to the headstock. Any doubt thrown up by the eyeball method can be checked with a straight edge as shown in *fig 2.20*.

To sum up all of the above, what you are trying to decide is whether the frame is 'out' to a small enough degree to render it fit for further service as it is. In doing this the above checks are the first and obvious ones to carry out but also look for anything else about the frame which looks wonky, lopsided or uneven, particularly around the subframe whose two straight tubes from the swinging arm spindle to the shock absorber top should be parallel, as should the horizontal seat loop tubes.

The point is that any damage to a frame may only be easily visible in one place, but the frame may at the same time have been knocked out of line in several other less obvious ways and places. Therefore the approach to take is to assume that the frame which displays some misalignment by the eyeball method is actually worse than it looks.

So, in general, does its appearance lack wonkiness? Are all the tubes which should be straight actually straight? Is it straight front to rear, or within the ⅛" tolerance as explained above? If the answer to any of these is no, then either straighten it or find a better one. Going to the trouble of checking how much the frame is 'out' by the works method is perhaps a waste of time as the person straightening the frame (if this option is chosen) will be doing these checks anyway.

Note that any front impact severe enough to bend tubing next to the headstock may also have elongated the headstock bottom bearing housing. This will result in a loose bottom bearing cup which will exhibit itself as play at the steering head exactly as would insufficiently adjusted steering head bearings. The elongated housing in itself is easy to fix by setting the bottom bearing cup in epoxy resin in its' housing and assembling the complete set of bearings and yokes to ensure that the loose cup is held in the correct position while the resin sets.

Other reasons to reject a frame are localised damage to tubing from impact or weakening from serious corrosion. Breaks in the tubing obviously mean it isn't fit for use but this problem is the easiest to fix, by welding. Similarly, damage to brackets and lugs is of relatively minor importance and usually easy to repair.

The rank order of likely areas of damage to frames by normal wear and tear is:

    Side stand mounting lug – worn working surfaces and elongated pivot hole, broken off (OIF models), bent or broken frame tube on which it mounts (earlier models);
    Minor brackets broken off and missing for the rear mudguard, central tinware etc.
    Footpeg mounts loose and bent and adjacent frame tubing distorted or broken (roadster frames to '70).
    Mounting points - expect to see some wear to engine mounting points, centre stand mounts and pivot holes, the tank centre fixing point, and shock absorber top mounts.

All of the above can be reshaped and have missing metal replaced with welding equipment and a modicum of metalworking skill.

Engine bottom mounting point - all frames to '68

Another common distortion is nipping-in of the two tubes under the engine at the lower engine mounting point lugs. This is because most road models (check your parts book) fit a $1/8$" spacer between crankcase and o/s lower mounting lug. Omitting this spacer will bend the tube inwards until it hits the crankcase when the lower bolt is tightened. Remedy this with an 8" or so length of $3/8$" or 10mm threaded rod and two nuts to match. Fit the rod through the bottom frame lugs screwing the two nuts onto it *between* the frame tubes as you go. With the threaded rod through both lugs the nuts can be screwed outward to jack the tubes apart.

Frame straightening - at home and professionally

Straightening a frame has as its main aim the correct alignment of the points at which other things connect, the swinging arm and headstock primarily. So long as this is achieved, what the connecting tubes do between these points is to some extent irrelevant, so a straightened frame may not necessarily look exactly as it did when it left the factory whilst still managing to travel in a straight line. This may sound odd but the main job of the frame is to hold the wheels in correct relative position whilst allowing them to move with steering and road shocks. Everything else attached to the frame is secondary to this.

Rectification of slight problems such as a slight bend in the middle of a frame or a slight kink in the central part of an otherwise straight tube, is about as much as can be attempted at home with basic equipment. What is required is a bottle jack and beam of stronger steel than the offending bent fame tubing and a means of attaching the ends of the beam to the relevant areas of frame by chains and pegs, bolts and hooks or shackles. Once the beam is attached to the frame at its extremities the jack can be applied to push the tubing back to where it was.

This sounds crude and indeed may well be so, but as with any tool the skill lies in its application by the user. To attempt this method you will definitely need several hands to hold everything in place and operate the jack. Use a piece of hard wood between the jack and the frame to avoid localised damage to the tube being pushed. When applying pressure, you will need to push the tube significantly beyond where it should be as it will spring back when pressure is released. Repeat the process of applying pressure and releasing it with a bit more pressure added each time until the tube springs back to where it should be. Sounds like fun? Possibly the easier suggestion and certainly the only one for more severe 'bent frame' problems is to seek expert help of which there are several to choose from in the bike papers.

The traditional method of heat and pressure to persuade metal back to where it started is well suited to British bikes. A small number of exponents of this art are currently in business, applying the same skills and methods as were used by BSA in frame manufacture and repair. Alternatively the modern method is to employ a 'Motoliner Jig' to hold, check and hydraulically push the frame back into shape. This is clearly more scientific than the blowtorch and block and tackle method of old, or the beam and jack method above but as previously mentioned the outcome always depends on the skill of the tool operator.

Swinging Arm

The three distinct designs of Unit Single swinging arm are specific to the frame type, Swan Neck, Welded/Duplex or OIF, with which they are intended to fit. As with the frames there is a basic design for each of the three types of swinging arm with some variations within each type.

The main differentiating feature which identifies each of the three types of swinging arm is the bearing arrangement upon which it pivots. This is the feature which prevents interchangeability between the three types.

> **Swan Neck** swinging arms use bronze bushes pressed into the swinging arm, running on a steel pin pressed into the frame.
>
> **Welded/Duplex** swinging arms use bonded rubber 'silentbloc' rubber/steel bushes pressed into the swinging arm.
>
> **OIF** uses needle roller bearings pressed into the swinging arm, rotating on a spindle mounted on the frame.

The B44GP swinging arm is special to this model but it is closely related to the standard Welded/Duplex swinging arm and is actually interchangeable with these due to common bearings and swinging arm spindle used.

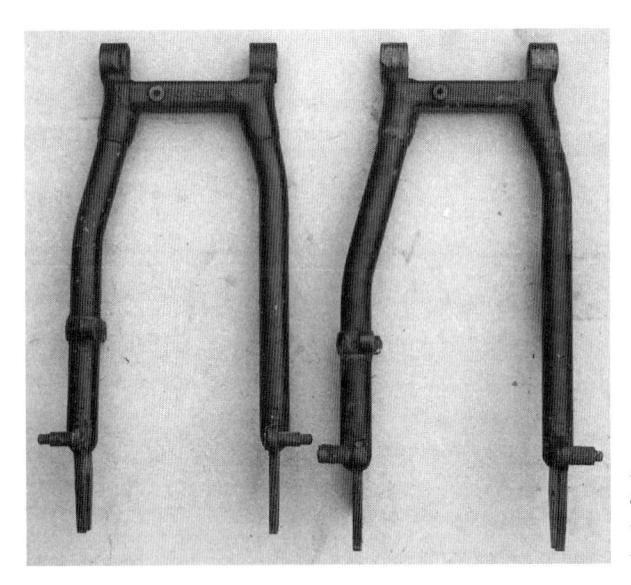

Fig 2.22 For the Swan Neck frames - standard swinging arm (left) and the wide chain line swinging arm (right) (C15S and B40)

Fig 2.23 The 'Works' method for checking the swinging arm for straightness. A quick visual check from the side will show if the tubes are not parallel. Additionally, checking the squareness of each arm to the spindle requires a straight piece of bar through the spindle hole and a large tri-square positioned outside each arm (see fig 2.32)

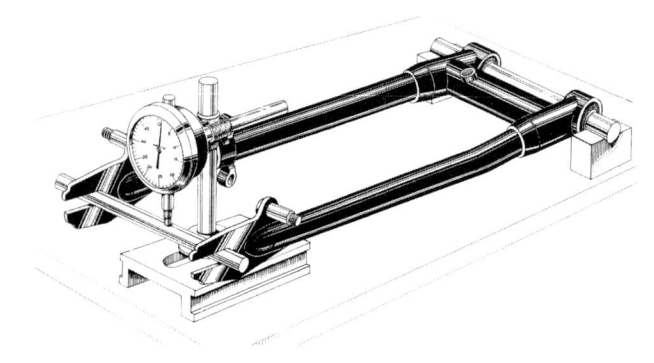

Frames 31

AUGUST 1961

BSA SERVICE SHEET
No. 0. 18.
MODELS D7, C15 AND B40
SWINGING ARM PIVOT

A new method of greasing the swinging arm pivot bearing has been adopted on these models, the central grease nipple being replaced by two nipples, one in each of the pivot end bolts.

New parts are fitted to all machines after the following frame numbers:
- D7—24727
- C15—29841
- B40—3182

In the interests of standardisation the new parts will be supplied against all future orders.

When fitting new parts to earlier models the centre grease nipple hole must be blanked off with bolt No.10715—0645.

Part numbers are as follows:—

Model	Old No.	Description	New no.
All	11115-5290	Grease nipple	40764-0092 (2)
D7	13490-4312	Pivot spindle	93490-4317
D7	10990-4298 (2)	Bolt	90990-4318 (2)
C15, B40	14240-4211	Pivot spindle	14240-4215
C15	10940-4070 (2)	Bolt	10940-4216 (2)
B40	10841-4037	Bolt (N/S)	10941-4067
B40	10940	Bolt (O/S)	10940-4216

Fig 2.24 Swinging arm pivot maintenance. Regardless of grease nipple position, neglect of greasing will lead to rapid wear

As usual, each type of swinging arm exhibits its own foibles but for all the starting point is to check for the two sides being straight and parallel.

Checking the swinging arm for twist is done by the method shown in *fig 2.23*. It is most important that in use the swinging arm spindle and rear wheel spindle are held parallel to each other by the swinging arm.

Swinging arms for Swan Neck frames

Two versions of this were produced; the standard item used on all C15 roadsters and the 'wide chain line' swinging arm used on B40 and all C15 off-road bikes with frames C15S or C15A *(fig 2.22)*. The difference is in both width and length. Width differs across the fork end plates by $^3/_8$" this giving $7^1/_4$" for the C15 roadster arm between the outside surfaces of the fork ends, and $7^5/_8$" between the outsides of these plates for the 'wide chain line' swinging arm. Comparison between the two types shows that the extra width is achieved by the nearside (chain side) tubing being angled outward over a longer distance before bent straight toward the fork end. Length differs in overall from front to back; $17^1/_4$" for C15 roadster and $17^7/_8$" for 'wide chain line'.

Swan Neck frame swinging arm, damage and defects

The most obvious thing to look for is the two arms being twisted. They should be parallel when seen from the side. The fork ends are often bent, twisted and the fork slots for the wheel spindle no longer parallel sided (splayed) or parallel with each other when viewed from the side or above. These defects can usually be rectified with a bit of heat and persuasion; as can a fork end plate which has come loose from the tube end where it was originally brazed. If so, re-braze after locating in the correct position.

Of the two arms, an unwanted bend is most likely to occur at the nearside lug where the rear brake plate stay attaches. Again, heat, and persuade it straight.

On the nearside tube there will often be a big dent on its underside where the foot of the side stand bashes against it! If so fill with weld or braze and smooth off. Consider adding a blob of weld on the side stand lug to prevent it folding up too far again.

The front casting of the swinging arm into which the two tubes are brazed rarely gives trouble.

Swan Neck frame replacing swinging arm bushes and spindle.

Expect the two bronze swinging arm bushes in the above casting to require replacing along with the swinging arm spindle. All are prone to wear – often due to corrosion caused by ingress of moisture and lack of lubrication.

The biggest headache with the Swan Neck frames and their swinging arm results from the swinging arm pin being a tight fit in the central frame lug. It will need a press to push it out – do not be tempted to resort to any other (invariably more brutal) method for the reasons below (*see* 'Re-fitting the spindle' *p33*).

Bush removal

To remove the old ones one at a time, have a look in your set of socket spanners and select one which has an open end big enough to sit on the flat steel surface around the outside of the bush and also big enough internally for the bush to fit loosely into. A second one is needed of exactly the right outer diameter to push the bush out of the steel housing without itself binding in the housing. Offer up the swinging arm with the two sockets correctly positioned to a vice and simply squeeze, (the same principle as shown in *fig 3.6)*.

Fitting new bushes is easiest with the same vice and no sockets to simply squeeze them into the housings one at a time. Do use a vice for this and resist the temptation to reach for your favourite knocking stick, the latter will never insert them squarely – note that the bushes are split and will go askew if this is tried - and will cause damage to the end of the bush. Before fitting the new bushes have a look inside at the lubrication grooves which are purposefully positioned. Prior to fitting it is preferable to rotate the bush so that the widest possible area of bearing surface between these grooves is facing toward the rear wheel. Arguably this is the place where heaviest loading will occur as the bike is pushed along by the rear wheel. The pattern of the grooves will also offer an optimum position for distribution of grease via the spindle ie where the grooves cross. Before finally pressing in the swinging arm spindle (see below) similarly rotate this so the grease hole lines up with a groove crossover point. These minor points should contribute to longer bush life.

After fitting the bushes do not expect the swinging arm spindle to slide through them nicely, they will need to be reamed out to a size which allows the spindle to push through without any perceptible clearance – a close sliding fit. An expanding reamer is required for this and it must be used with a pilot and mandrel to ensure both holes line up *(fig 2.25)*. Don't be tempted to open up the bushes by any other way - files, rotary

Fig 2.25. Line reaming the bushes of the Swan Neck frame swinging arm. The expanding reamer on left is piloted in the opposite bush

wheels etc. If you haven't got the required kit, take the swinging arm to someone who has. Incidentally, the bushes and reaming procedure are exactly the same on BSA Bantam models D7 onward.

Fitting the swinging arm to the Swan Neck frame
Before thinking about inserting the spindle offer the swinging arm up to the frame. Insert the thrust washer part no. 40-4213 on the *offside* between swinging arm and frame lug. With this washer in place, side to side play of the swinging arm on the frame lug should be hardly perceptible – as it was when new. More than about 0.015" clearance here necessitates a thicker washer to be made and fitted instead of the original. Loads of play between frame lug and swinging arm will be the result of cumulative wear on both sides and should ideally be cured by fitting a thrust washer on both sides, the one on the offside being thicker than the nearside by $1/32$" – the thickness of the original BSA washer. Try to avoid using lots of thin shims in this role as they will disintegrate in use.

Re-fitting the spindle
Pushing the spindle through the frame lug to fit or remove the swinging arm should require a hydraulic press as it should be a tight fit. Do find someone with a press and don't resort to the favourite knocking stick. Hammering the ends of the spindle will splay them - guaranteed - and the ends will then be too big to go through the nicely reamed bushes. The spindle is not hardened all the way through, being merely case hardened, hence its susceptibility to the hammer.

If the spindle isn't tight and can be tapped through easily with a mallet then the hole in the frame lug has worn (usually by repeated fitting and removal of spindles) and a remedy is needed. The standard answer for any too-loose fit of good ol' Loctite would do nicely – if it could be introduced to the central portion of spindle and lug without contaminating the bushes. Hence, coating the spindle with Loctite and simply pushing it through isn't going to work – it will set in the bushes. Solution: drill a ¼" hole near each end of the central lug on its rearward side. Degrease the spindle and interior of the lug. Fit the spindle, swinging arm and washer(s) and introduce Loctite into the two holes (through which the sides of the spindle can now be seen).With a reservoir of Loctite in each hole insert a bolt into the end of the spindle and tighten this until the whole spindle rotates, thus smearing Loctite all around its circumference. With the Loctite hardened the bolt can then be unscrewed from the now fixed spindle. When correctly fitted the chamfered spindle ends should both stand proud of the swinging arm by a small amount, equally on either side.

A spindle which is so loose in the lug that play can be felt requires a more drastic remedy –

> bore the lug true and have a one-off oversize pin made to suit.
> bore the lug and sleeve it back to standard diameter.

Or, if you don't have access to a machine shop: find a replacement frame, definitely the easiest solution for the common C15 road frame.

Swinging arms for Welded/Duplex frames and B44GP
Four varieties can be found and are all interchangeable on all versions of the above frames. All use identical bonded rubber 'silentbloc' bushes and a $13/16$" diameter swinging arm spindle. Of the four varieties, the B44GP swinging arm stands alone by being longer and by being made from heavier gauge and diameter Reynolds 531 tubing. The two arm-to-crosstube joints are bronze welded as per the GP frame itself.

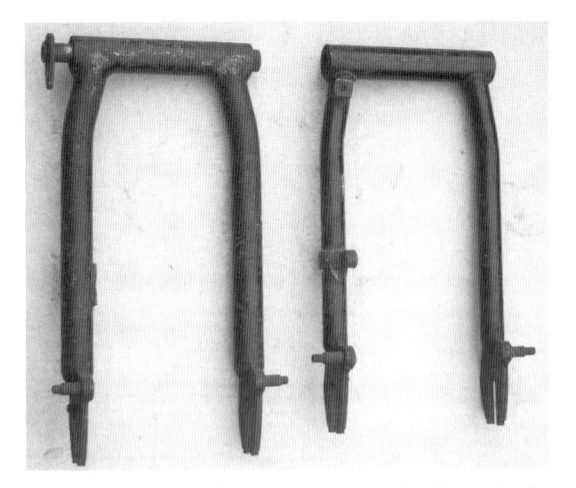

Fig 2.26 Left, B44GP swinging arm. On the right the standard item for Welded/Duplex frames '63 to '68

Fig 2.27 Seemingly standard fitment on later production B44GP models was an even longer swinging arm with the earlier GP item shown below for comparison. This itself being longer than the standard s/arm for the Welded/Duplex frames

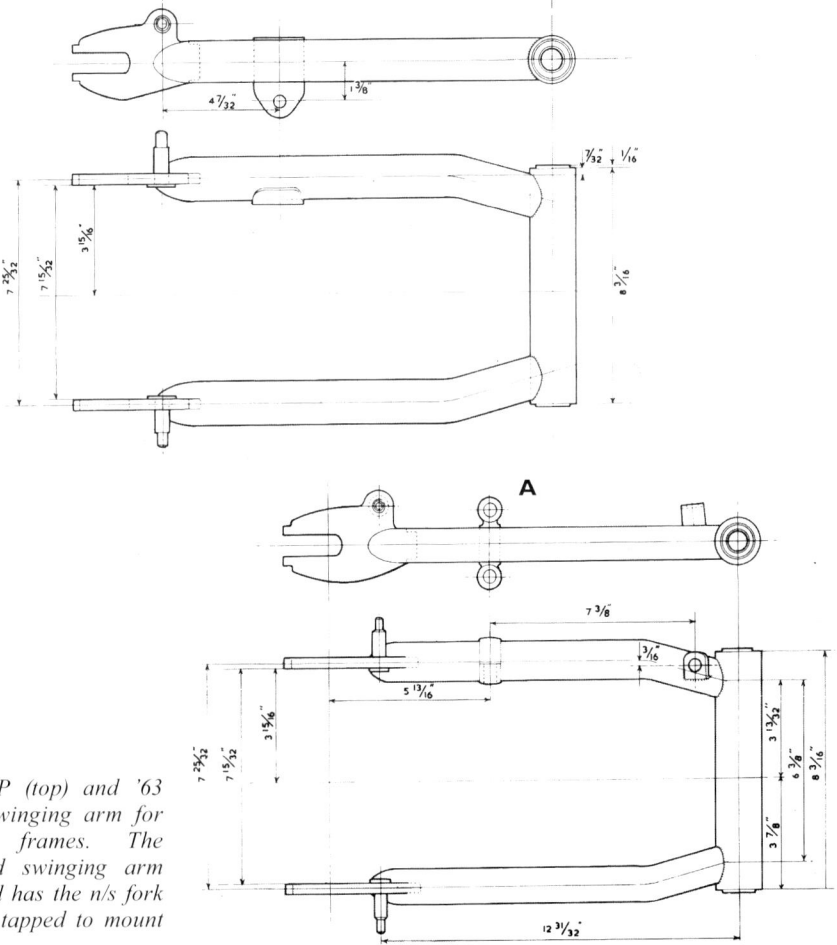

Fig 2.28. B44GP (top) and '63 -'68 standard swinging arm for Welded/Duplex frames. The '69/'70 standard swinging arm lacks lug 'A' and has the n/s fork end drilled and tapped to mount the chainguard

Leaving aside the distinctive B44GP swinging arm, the remaining three variants for the Welded/Duplex frame are dimensionally identical and differ only in detail. These are:

> The '63 - '68 item shown in *fig 2.28*,
> The '69/'70 version which has a revised chain guard rear mounting point,
> The B40 Military Mk.1 item has a revised front chain guard mounting.

All are identical with regard to geometry and tubing. The only differences concern alterations to the chain guard fixing points. The original type used from '63 to '68 has the chain guard mounting point on the same lug as the rear brake anchor strap. Subsequently for '69 to '70 (for B25 and B44) the guard was mounted by a strap to the nearside fork end plate which gained two tapped holes for this. All B40 Military Mk.1's had their own arrangement of welded-on brackets to suit their fully enclosed chain guard.

Confusion has arisen regarding these swinging arms as the various Unit Single parts books for '63 to '68 models using the Welded/Duplex frame clearly show the swinging arm as being of the type fitted to the Swan Neck frames: this is incorrect.

Welded/Duplex swinging arm - damage and defects
This is a reasonably robust design of swinging arm (especially the GP item) but it can still exhibit the usual twists, bends and distortion of end plates and tubing as a result of hard use/abuse. However, normal usage should not result in any of these problems.

One minor but common problem is the front chain guard mounting point (not GP, it doesn't have a chain guard). This has a habit of falling off due to vibration as it is weak and simply butt-welded on. If it is missing it is relatively easy to fashion an equally feeble bit of steel strip and crudely weld it on as originally done to affect a repair! However, any repair processes to the Welded/Duplex swinging arm which involves serious levels of heat should be carried out with care due to the risk of damage to the rubber silentbloc bushes. Check for straightness using the procedure previously described and illustrated in *fig 2.23* and *fig 2.32*

Silentbloc swinging arm bushes (Welded/Duplex frames only)
The silentbloc bushes (*fig 2.29*) each consist of two lengths of steel tube, one inside the other, with rubber filling the annular gap between them. The rubber is bonded to the steel tubes and fitting the swinging arm to the frame involves clamping the inner silentbloc steel tube to the frame plates by tightening the swinging arm spindle nut. Thus the inner steel tubes of the bushes do not rotate with the swinging arm as it moves up and down, and the spindle nut must be fully tightened to achieve this. The outer steel tube is fixed firmly into the swinging arm and so moves with it. When the swinging arm moves up and down the rubber is forced to twist. This is known as rubber in torsion and is widely used where limited relative movement without free play is required.

As well as allowing the swinging arm to swing, the design of the rubber bush allows a small amount of lateral movement – sideways flex – of the back wheel. Thus this cheap, simple, low tech method of allowing swinging arm rotation may be OK for road use but may be regarded as being too imprecise for rear wheel alignment if racing antics are planned.

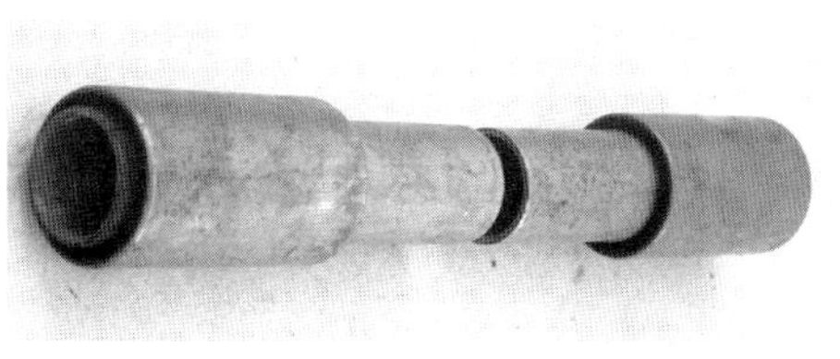

If the swinging arm spindle nut isn't done up tight enough the inner tube will rotate with the

Fig 2.29. Silentbloc swinging arm bushes used on all Welded/Duplex frame swinging arms '63 - '70. Correct fitting pulls the inner sleeves into contact

swinging arm and the ends of the inner tubes will wear away against and with the inside of the frame plates. Inner tube ends which are worn away in this manner, and no longer square and flat, need remedial work for further service; or alternatively replacement of the whole bush may be easier. Another option is to cut back the protruding ends of the inner tubes level with the swinging arm and fit spacing washers of the correct thickness to make up for the missing tube ends. After trimming the inner tube ends the required thickness of washer is that which will restore the swinging arm to a tight push-fit between the plates. The inner diameter is $^{13}/_{16}$", the o/d is not critical. Stainless steel washers in this role would be best. The silentbloc bushes never 'wear' out. What sometimes happens is the rubber separates from the steel it is bonded to at the outer ends of the tubes. If you see such a gap under the rubber, slide something thin into it to see how far it penetrates. Anything over half an inch would suggest replacement is needed.

Removing silentbloc bushes is not a pleasant job. Heat a thin steel strip – an old hacksaw blade is ideal – so one end is red hot and plunge it end-on into the rubber between the tubes. Reheat and plunge repeatedly until the rubber has been cut through all around the inner tube and this can be extracted. Cutting through the rubber in this way, like a hot knife through butter, will give off lots of smelly smoke – not nice to inhale, so outdoors with a blowtorch is preferable. Avoid doing it in the kitchen on the gas hob as domestic harmony will be impaired. Removing the inner steel tube in this manner allows easier access to the outer tube with (another) hacksaw blade so it can be slotted, collapsed inward and withdrawn. Alternatively it should be possible from the inside to saw a slot through both complete bushes to loosen them.

Fitting new silentblocs is best done by pulling them into the swinging arm with a length of threaded rod of at least ½" diameter, two nuts to suit, two washers to suit and additionally two thick washers, 1" i/d, and of big enough o/d to ensure the pressure is applied only to the ends of the outer tubes when the rod is threaded through and the nuts tightened. Check the inner surface of the tube which will house the bushes - it should be smooth to allow easy fitment and a smear of grease will help. Before fitting the above and starting the process, put the two bushes together end-to-end and measure the total length of inner tube: this figure will be required later. With all of the above in place pull the bushes into the swinging arm by tightening the nuts until the outer steel tube is flush with the swinging arm. At this point measure the overall length of the inner tubes again. It may be found that this is longer than the previous measurement which indicates that the bushes need to be pulled further into the swinging arm until the inner tubes touch. Achieve this by halving the difference between the two measurements and fit a shim of exactly this thickness on each side under the thick washer. It is necessary for these shims to be of the correct o/d to bear on the ends of the outer tubes. All of this is a bit of a palaver but is necessary to ensure that:-

> The bushes are both pulled in by an equal and correct amount to guarantee centrality of the swinging arm.
>
> The bushes are not damaged in any way. The knocking stick is again not the recommended tool to help persuade these bushes into place.

Note that the swinging arm with its bushes, when offered up to the frame, should be a light interference fit between the frame plates and may need to be gently tapped in with a mallet until the holes line up. Damage to paint on the inside of the frame plates is to be expected!

The swinging arm spindle should be a sliding fit through the inner tubes of the bushes. Grease or anti-seize compound such as 'copperslip' is recommended on this spindle, not for lubrication (remember the bushes do not rotate on the spindle), but to make future dismantling easier. A stuck swinging arm spindle of this type is a somewhat irksome thing; try removing the nut but don't unbolt the fixing plate on the nearside end of the spindle. Then work the swinging arm up and down. If it travels further than the normal springiness of the rubber would allow then let joy be unbounded; you will be able to work the spindle out. If not then soak copiously with penetrating oil, wait and try again. How long you persevere with this method without resorting to the final bottom-line cure described below is up to you. Unfortunately for the rash and impatient this is another instance when the knocking stick must stay in its box and not be applied to the threaded end of the spindle; or this will simply spread and then not go through the holes in frame plates or bushes.

The final, desperate, bottom line remedies for a seized spindle depend on your equipment. If you have access to large drilling tools, bore into the ends of the hollow swinging arm spindle with a $^{13}/_{16}$" drill below the thickness of the frame plates to free the swinging arm. Alternatively, slip a hacksaw blade into the thin gap between swinging arm and mounting plate and cut through the end of the protruding inner tube and the spindle on both sides. Both of these methods junk the bushes and spindle.

Final fitting of the swinging arm and spindle to the frame requires the spindle nut to be fully tightened (with its shakeproof washer fitted under the nut). Before tightening the nut, rotate the spindle end plate on the nearside into correct position and secure it with its $^{5}/_{16}$" fixing bolt. Next fit one of the shock absorbers to correctly position the swinging arm in its 'at rest' position then tighten the nut. This will ensure that the bushes are not unduly pre-loaded in normal use.

OIF swinging arm

This design pivots on needle roller bearings. In engineering terms this is a better, but more complex set-up. Correctly assembled and greased, this arrangement can cope with load more rigidly than the previous silentbloc bushes which permit a little flexure (being made of rubber), and last longer than the original C15 bronze bushes. But grease and effective seals are vital. Water penetration means rust, followed by a speedy demise.

Fig 2.30 Right, the OIF swinging arm

Fig 2.31 Below. Swinging arm assembly details

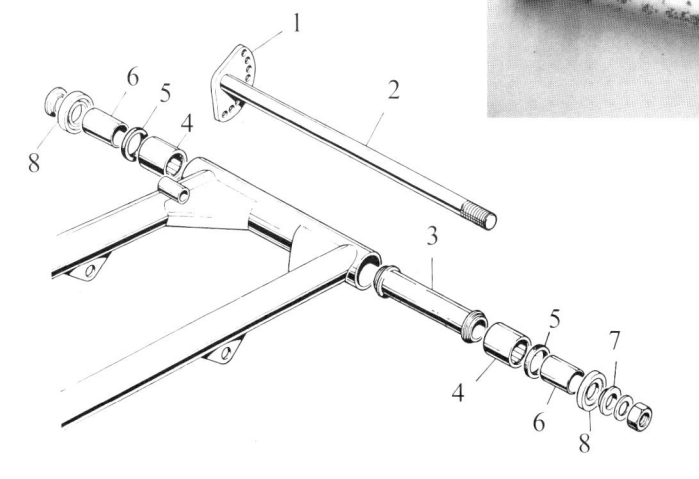

1. Adjuster cam
2. Swing arm spindle
3. Spacer tube
4. Needle roller bearing
5. Oil seal
6. Bearing sleeve
7. Thrust washer
8. Dust excluder

The swinging arm itself *(fig 2.30-2.33)* is a robust item with no obvious shortcomings. Only the pillion foot peg mounts are likely to bend in use if your passenger applies their full weight to them, and to combat this BSA strengthened them for 1972

Removal of the swinging arm from the frame is much as the Welded/Duplex item, ie remove the nut and withdraw the spindle. This latter may require a hammer and soft drift (aluminium or brass) if any seizure has occurred between the spindle and bearing components. The swinging arm assembly can be then removed from the frame, note the position of the loose spacer and cover on either side including the steel bushes within the needle bearings, these can be extracted with pliers. The external surface of the steel bushes on which the bearings run must be smooth, unmarked and unworn otherwise replacement is required.

Fig 2.32. Using a large tri-square, or in this case a builder's square to check that each side of the swinging arm is 'true': this one looks OK

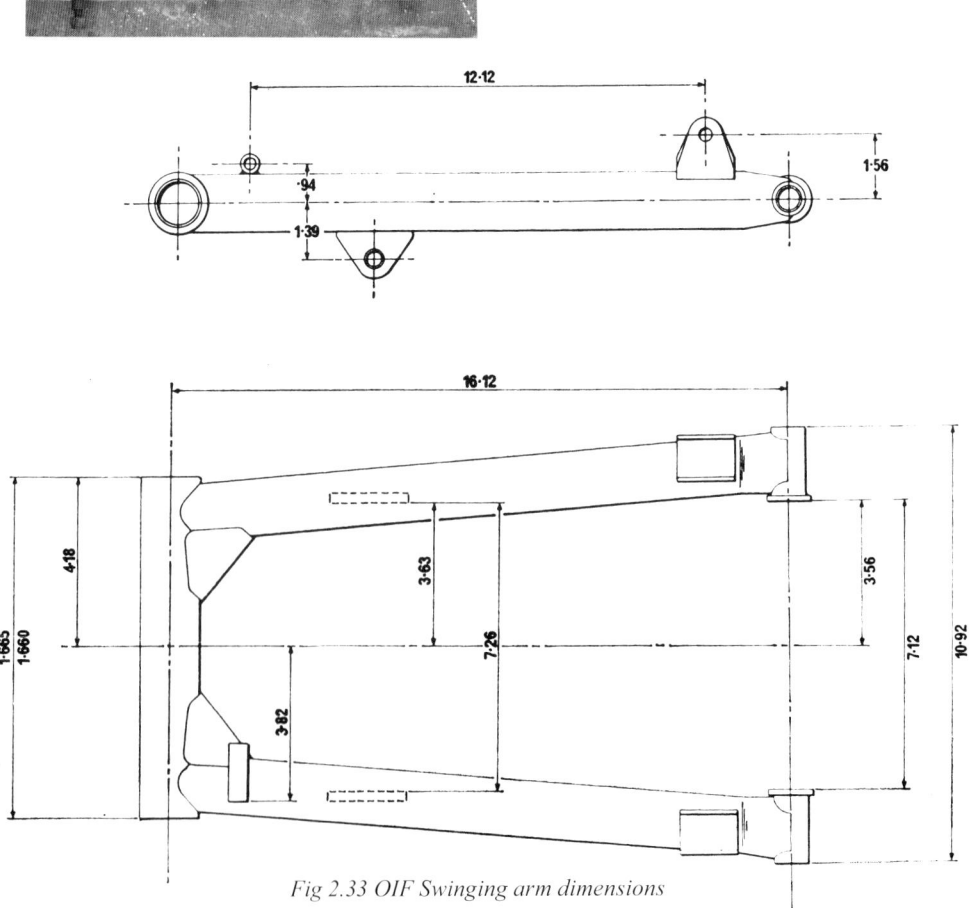

Fig 2.33 OIF Swinging arm dimensions

Each needle roller can be drifted out from the opposite side, the first by applying the hammer and a soft drift to the end of the central spacing tube between the bearings. This may however, not have the end flanges as shown above and be found to pass through the bearings. In which case apply the drift to the inner end of the needle roller bearing. This may well cause damage to the bearings so don't attempt removal of them unless you intend to fit new replacements. Unless they have been previously prized out, this will also push out the oil seals.

Re-fitting the bearings
If at all possible press or squeeze the new needle bearings into position. Do not hammer which risks damage. If hammering is the only possible way then use a flat steel plate between hammer and bearing followed by a socket spanner or a tubular spacer to see them fully home against the shoulders inside the swinging arm. Don't forget to fit the tubular spacer between them.

In use it is necessary to disturb the swinging arm spindle each time the rear chain tension is adjusted by slackening the spindle nut sufficiently to free the adjuster plates from the frame anchor pegs. Any stiffness in the movement of the swinging arm spindle when this is done would prompt removal, cleaning and re-greasing to keep seizure at bay. Do check that you have carried out this adjustment with the holes on the adjuster plates being positioned identically on both sides.

A Bit on the Side for the Unit Single frame

Whilst never being highly thought of as a sidecar tug, such marriages are certainly known to have happened. Particularly notable are the many successes of B44 machines when attached to a Trials chair. To some extent, this relatively unexplored territory of Unit Single plus sidecar in everyday use was due to the lack of power of the smaller machines and the late arrival of the larger ones, when sidecars were already 'old hat'. The bottom line though is that for road use, a Unit Single is not the best machine in terms of power characteristics for towing a chair; certainly not a Busmar double-adult with the usual handful of kids.

Realistic options did exist in the '60's in terms of small, light chairs, such as the Watsonian 'Avonette' and' Bambini'. These were often marketed to provide a way around the 250cc learner restriction in the UK: buy big bike, fit chair and 'L' plates, pass test and remove chair. A UK quirk where a 3-wheel test covered two-wheelers as well. This idea actually continued until relatively recently with the 'Sidewinder' attachment.

Thus the optimum time for Unit Singles to be considered in terms of sidecars was early in their saga and the best on offer at this time, the B40, and also the C15, did receive a small measure of publicity - for example magazine articles featuring of these machines in this role - and the specification changes needed for this were listed by BSA.

Exactly how many customers resulted from this speculative thinking is anybody's guess, after being geared down sufficiently to pull a small chair the C15 would struggle to exceed the mid 40's: the B40 maybe the mid 50's, the latter being a more realistic proposition.
Although no specific sidecar attachment parts were produced by BSA for the B40, this model was the only one to have provision built-in for a steering damper: necessary with a chair. You can see this as a rectangular lump on the bottom end of the headstock casting just above the front down-tube. This is the anchor point for the plain plate of the optional steering damper assembly, components for this being shown in the early B40 parts books. Additional specification changes for this role require the spring ratings of the forks and shock absorbers to be increased and the overall gear ratio to be lowered.

Suitable attachment points for anyone contemplating such an endeavour follow standard practise: attachments to the top of the shock absorber, another as high on the front down-tube as possible and one from the area of the swinging arm spindle. This last area is likely to be most problematic; the centre stand lugs possibly offer most scope as this feature would no longer be needed. The only remaining issue being which side to put the chair on.

Frame Related Components

Bashplate (Sumpguard)

Unless it is new from the dealer's shelf don't expect this item to be straight. It is regarded as sacrificial in nature, to take punishment instead of the bottom of the engine and adjacent frame tubes. But, being simply a steel plate with a couple of up-stands to act as cushions so impacts are not transmitted directly to the frame tubes, it requires only straightforward tin-bashing to put it right. Shown below *(fig 2.34)* are most of the variants to suit the different frames/models of the various Unit Singles.

The B40 military item is made of thicker steel than all others and hooks around the centre stand spacer tube at its rear end. The plates which are mounted on the frame by 'U' bolts will distort if the fixing nuts are over-tightened. A 'P' clip to the frame cross-tube is the alternative rear end fixing method if a single mounting hole is provided there in the bashplate.

Fig 2.34. Sump guards (bash plates). Top row, left to right, C15S framed models, C15C framed models and B44 '66, C15E Trials Pastoral ('64 to '65), B44GP and B44VE/VS '67. Bottom row, TR25w/ B44VS '68 to '70, B40 Military (still encrusted with the desert sands), '71 onward OIF.

Cylinder Head Steady

The various head steady tubes and brackets are shown in *figs 2.35-2.36*. C15 Swan Neck frames have a clamp arrangement to the top tube. B40 has a tubular stay to the hole provided in the headstock. Welded/Duplex frames bolt their tubular stay to the lower n/s headstock gusset. OIF head steadies bolt to the bracket on the top tube. Ensure all head steady components are fully tight in use.

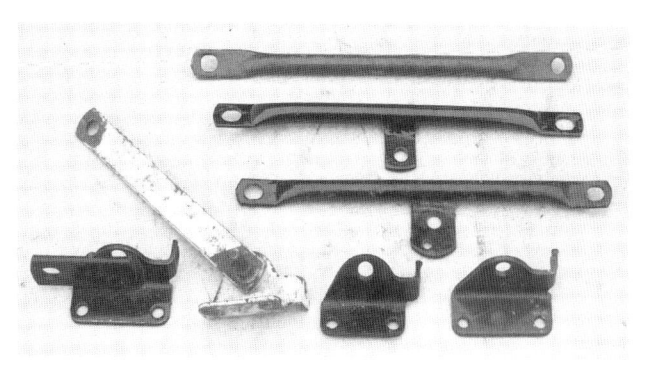

Fig 2.36. Head steady brackets: top, tubular tie-strap for B40 military 10$^{1}/_{4}$" between centres, B25 etc '67 to '69 9$^{1}/_{2}$" between centres with elongated holes - variations of this tube relate to the lug for the horn. Lower left B50 bracket and OIF B25 with strap. Lower right brackets for B25 (stud holes 1$^{5}/_{8}$" between centres) and B40 military/B44 (2" between centres).

Fig 2.35. C15 competition head steady arrangement to '62. The flat tie strap is 1$^{1}/_{4}$" between centres. C15 roadsters have a longer tie-strap

Tyre Inflator

The tyre inflator *(fig 2.37 - 2.38)* is usually missing but an acceptable replacement can be borrowed from the wife's bicycle. The original is steel-bodied and of 11$^{1}/_{2}$" free length (not including the connector). In practical terms it is of limited capability but it should be able to put enough air in your tyre to get you to the nearest garage.

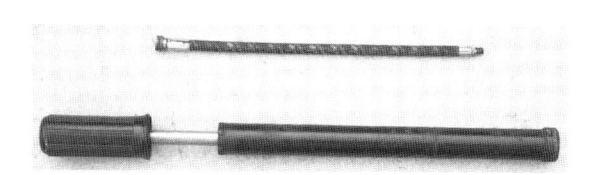

Fig 2.37. Above, the tyre inflator

Fig 2.38. Opposite, tyre inflator in position on the frame: the lugs provided for this vary in location depending on the model

3. SHOCK ABSORBERS

Originally supplied to BSA by Messrs Girling, you may convince yourself that your original 50 year old shockers are OK because they still compress and extend. In practice, expect to replace them and be pleasantly surprised by the improvement in ride quality.

Removal

Removal from the frame should be straightforward: top mounting bolt out first, remove the bottom nut (or bolt for OIF), rotate the top end out of the yoke on the frame and pull the lower end off the swinging arm. Likely problems in this procedure are mounting bolts seized to the steel sleeves inside the mounting rubbers.

Seized top bolts can be ground off level with the outsides of the mounting yoke. The lower edges of the yoke can then be prised apart enough to let the damper slip out. They should straighten again easily should this have been necessary. If you don't fancy bending the sides of the yoke drill centrally into the ends of the bolt with a 3/8" bit until enough of the bolt is removed to free the unit.

Up to '70 the lower end of the unit fits onto a ½" stud on the swinging arm. If seizure has occurred here pull the unit away leaving the rubber on the stud. The rubber can then be cut away to expose the steel sleeve stuck on the stud. This can be gripped with mole grips to twist it off or ground through to free it.

Your BSA Unit Single originally fitted conventional oil-filled units *(Fig 3.1)* in the following lengths taken between the mounting-hole centres when fully extended:-

    C15 Roadster (Swan Neck frame) 10.5"
    B40 Roadster and C15 competition models with Swan Neck frame 11.3"
    All models with Welded/Duplex frame and OIF 12.9"

All of the above comprise two main parts:-

    The spring, which allows the upper end (with bike attached) to move up and down in a supported and cushioned way.

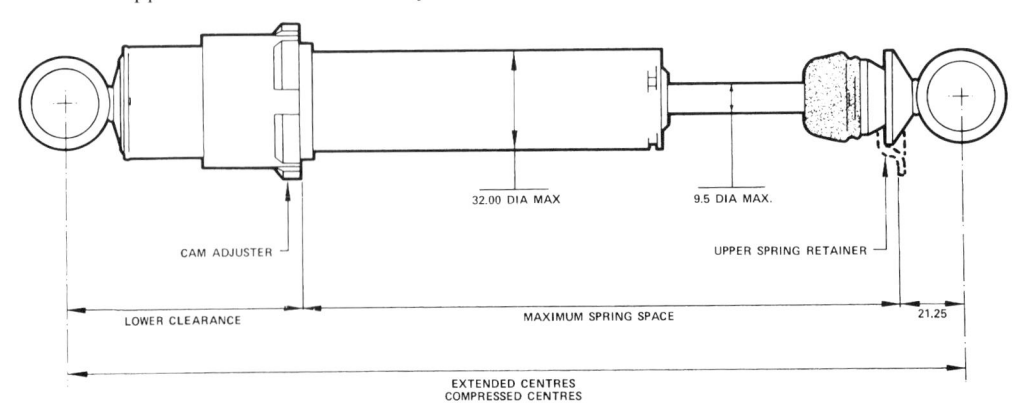

Fig 3.1 The Unit Single rear damper, all dimensions in mm. Welded/Duplex, OIF design is shown here, but the shock absorbers for the Swan Neck frames, whilst visually different, are of similar internal design

The damping mechanism: a cylinder (attached to the swinging arm at its lower end) which is filled with oil, with a piston (attached to the sprung part of the bike by a rod) moving within it.

The latter, also known as a 'dash pot', allows easy travel of the piston into the cylinder through the oil within it, but restricted movement outwards by means of a valve on the piston through which the damping oil must flow. This then prevents bounce, allowing the spring (with bike) to compress easily but not bounce smartly back. The net result should be a smoother ride.

In principle this is the same action as is produced in the double damped fork legs - the Rod Damper, Heavyweight BSA, Triumph and OIF types. All of these have rebound damping as well as oil cushioning when compressing *(see Chapter 4 Front Forks)*.

Dismantling and checking - spring removal

Before you can really inspect the shock absorbers they need to be dismantled. All these types of original shocks and their modern classic replacements have springs retained by collets, usually two, with a one piece collet sometimes found on the 12.9" items. Further to this there are two main designs for Unit Singles:-

Original type C15/B40. 10.5" and 11.3" have two large chromed collets below the spring.

All 12.9" shock absorbers have two (but sometimes one) collets above the spring.

The two piece shrouds, if fitted to the 12.9" items, are removed with the spring inside them, this assembly can then be separated. All types require the spring to be compressed independent of the damper to free and remove the collets and then the spring.

Fig 3.2 Right, the C15/B40 shock absober dismantling tool

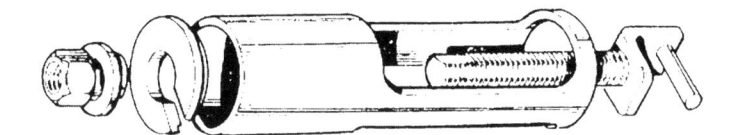

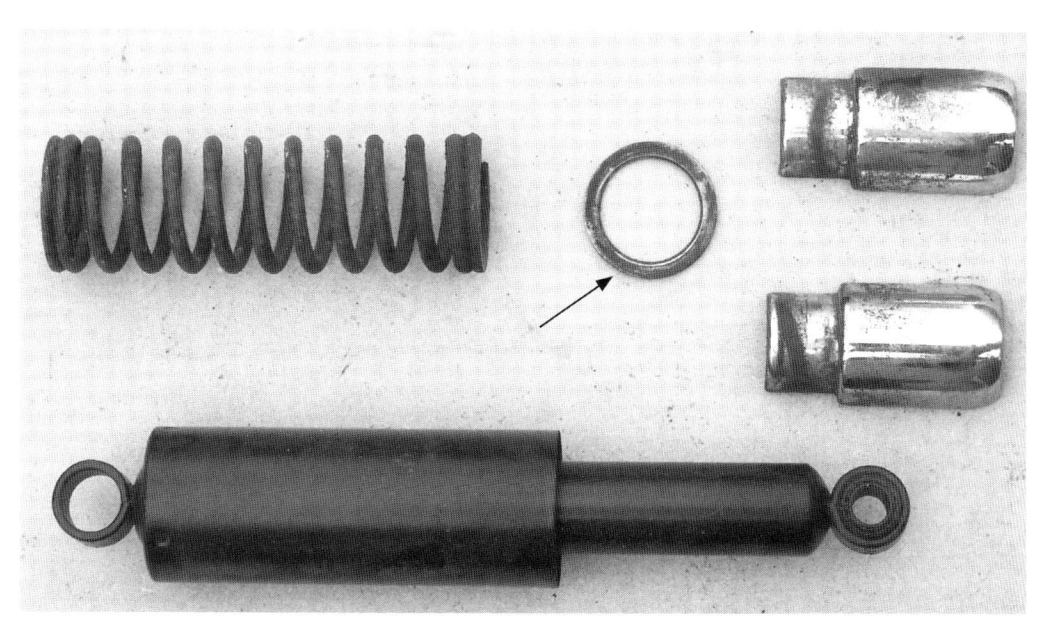

Fig 3.3 Dismantled C15/B40 Shock absorber; note the spring support ring (arrowed) is chamfered internally - fit this towards the collets

C15/B40 units.
Sorry, these need a special, and hard to obtain tool *(see fig 3.2)* to compress the spring up inside the fixed shroud. I haven't found a simple way around this yet and, as you can see, making one is a bit involved. With the tool in use and the spring compressed the collets can be withdrawn through the windows in the side of the cylinder. Take this rare opportunity to get them re-chromed if necessary. *Fig 3.3* shows a dismantled C15/B40 shock absorber.

Dismantling the 12.9" units
There is a special tool for this *(fig 3.5)* but a bit of brute force will do instead. Obtain a firm wall (outdoors so you don't damage the décor). With both hands grip around the top half of the spring or shroud and push the unit horizontally against the wall. Pressing hard enough will allow the collets to slip out from beneath the collar under the top mount and fall to the ground. A selection of the collets used is shown in *fig 3.4*

Reassembly

In both cases reassembly requires the spring again to be compressed to insert the collets. Note that there is a steel ring beneath the spring of the C15/B40 Swan Neck frame shock absorbers *(see fig 3.3)*. The internal chamfer on this goes towards the collets. The correct tool is again needed for this type to permit reassembly.

Reassembly of the 12.9" items is best done by pressing the spring (with shroud if fitted) as before but this time downwards onto the floor, with the damper rod fully extended. You then need your beautiful assistant to slip the collets into place. Explain this process thoroughly before attempting it; otherwise trapped finger ends (hers) are likely which will result in considerable domestic disharmony.

While the units are stripped to the bare essentials other refurbishments should be carried out as required. This basically boils down to repainting and changing the rubber bushes in the mounting holes.

If you plan to use abrasive blasting for the units prior to repainting, take pains to protect the chrome damper rods and the area around where the rod enters the cylinder. Otherwise, ingress of blasting grit will lead to rapid wear.

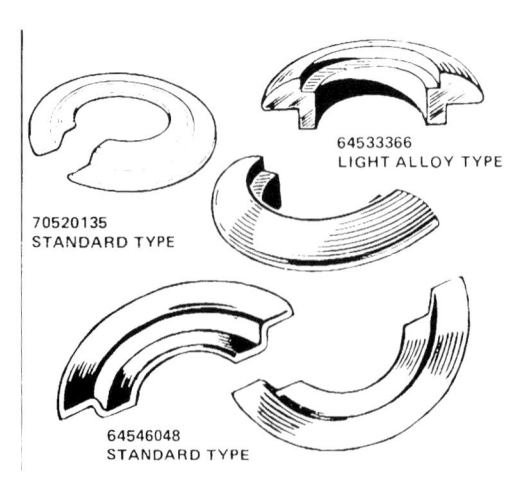

Fig 3.4, Collets used to retain the springs

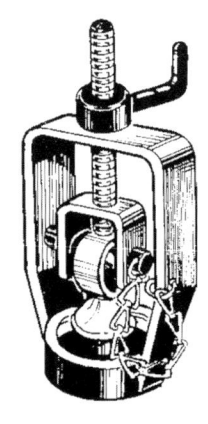

Fig 3.5 Dismantling tool for the 12.9" units

The original paint finish applied by Messrs. Girling was bargain basement with no primer used, The colour used was black for all years except '71 which used Dove Grey. No doubt you will be able to improve on this, but be wary about doing too good a job on the 12.9" Units, or on any others of similar design. The problem here is with the lower spring collar fitted to these units. This needs to be able to rotate around the cylinder to provide the three positions of pre-load for the spring. Too much paint on the cylinder means the collar won't go on, let alone rotate. The only answer being to remove your nice new thick coat of paint and to replicate the original thin coat of cellulose.

Checking for Correct Operation (after Spring Removal)

Visual inspection

The main part to see is the chromed damper rod which should be smooth and shiny. Any signs of pitting or scoring, or loss of the chrome is a worry. This is mostly caused by road filth getting in the works. Additionally, rust and the pitting it causes can be a problem if the bike has been left standing for a long time. Fitting shrouds over the springs will drastically extend shock absorber life.

All of this accumulated roughness on the damper rod spells eventual death for the oil seal through which the rod passes in the upper end of the cylinder. This then allows the damping oil to escape (an MOT failure) and the damping action is lost. However, a damper unit displaying the above symptoms may well continue to give good service for as long as sufficient oil remains inside the cylinder.

Refilling the cylinder with oil to restore damping is easy to do by drilling and tapping a small hole on the lower end. After refilling with engine oil or similar the hole is stopped with a short screw and sealing washer. OK, where did the old oil go? Out past the seal, soon to be followed by the new oil, so this is a short-term measure, and probably a waste of time. Further repairs to a damper unit in this sort of condition are not really worth the bother, they were not designed to be stripped and refurbished. New replacements are recommended.

A bent damper rod is also easy to spot and straighten. With the spring removed compress the damper until the rod jams (where the bend is) and with the cylinder protected from, and held in a vice, simple hand pressure on the upper end will pull the rod straight. Check visually, and by operating the damper, that the rod is straight and does not bind when moving in and out of the cylinder.

Testing the damper is simple. Free of the spring it should:-

    Compress easily (pushing the ends together) without binding or jerkiness.

    Extend smoothly (pulling the ends apart) but with noticeably more force required than when compressing, again without jerkiness or any suspiciously easy patches in the movement.

Do this test with the shock absorber in its normal working position, ie upright. It may not work so well upside down if it has lost some oil.

Mounting bushes

The original mounting rubbers had a steel sleeve bonded inside them. Try to find this type if replacements are required rather than ones which are entirely rubber or with a loose steel sleeve. These alternatives are generally found to have too much 'give' in them.

Removing and replacing the mounting rubbers from the ends of the units is easy to do with a vice and a couple of sockets from your socket spanner set. Select one socket which is just small enough to pass inside the mounting "eye" for the rubber. Select another which is just big enough for the rubber to fit inside (*fig 3.6*). Arrange these in the vice as shown and squeeze. Fitting the replacement bushes is done in the same way with some help from lubrication, WD40 or soap, on the rubber or in the eye. Squeeze the new rubber into place so that the steel tube protrudes equally on either side.

When fitting the new or refurbished unit to the bike put a smear of grease or anti-seize compound on the mounting bolts. Fit the lower end to the swinging arm first then rotate the unit to bring the top end up into the yoke on the frame. All mounting bolts for the shock absorbers should be done up tight to grip on the steel sleeves inside the rubbers and not allow any rotation on the mounting bolt itself. On models to '70, a cupped washer is normally fitted under the lower shock absorber mounting nut to protect the rubber bush.

Maintenance

Looking after the shock absorbers in use amounts to keeping them clean and keeping an eye out for oil leaks and deterioration of the rubber bushes.

Adjusting the pre-load on the 12.9" units is done by rotating the spring support ring which has three positions. This really needs the correct C-spanner to hook into the castellations or hole provided. Gripping the ring in any other way ie with your favourite pipe-wrench to turn it will only cause damage and loss of self-esteem. Girling data for the 12.9" shock absorbers is shown in *fig 3.7*.

Replacing the springs.

Finding any of these original new Girling springs is not likely and in any case, the manufacturers original choice of spring rating was always something of a compromise: significant variables such as usage, and the load carried lying outside their control. New,

Fig 3.6. Using sockets and a vice to extract the mounting bush

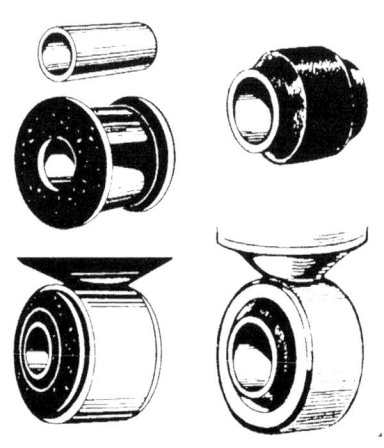

Fig 3.7 Mounting bushes Top right, the bonded rubber/steel bushes as originally fitted. For Unit Single applications the top bush has a 3/8" diameter bore, the lower bush a ½" diameter bore except for OIF models which use a 3/8" bush in both positions.

replacement shock absorbers will be listed by your vendor as being suitable for any particular machine you own. In reality, be prepared to return these for harder or softer springs to better suit your own personal requirements. Springs rated at about 100lb/in seem to be a good starting point for road use on Unit Singles.

Girling shock absorber application list for the later BSA models is shown in *fig 3.9*, the spring reference numbers can be found in the list in *fig 3.10*. Earlier Unit Single models (C15T/S, B25, B40 military and B44) which fit the 12.9" shock absorber use the same rate springs as listed for later models.

The information in *fig 3.9* clearly indicates that the internal damping mechanism of the shock absorber can vary even if they look the same from the outside. Original Girling dampers usually had their part number stamped on them near the bottom end; in view of the possibly unknown internals a matched pair of part numbers would be a good idea.

Modern replacement 'classic' shocks vary from cheap and cheerful to expensive and sophisticated. Yes, there is a difference in ride quality between the two and basically you pays your money and takes your choice, so don't expect miracles if you haven't paid for them. However, for most normal road use to which Unit Singles are now put, spending huge amounts on replacement shocks isn't really warranted.

Spring Shrouds

All of the C15 and B40 shock absorbers fitted to the Swan-Neck frame models (10.5" or 11.3" length) are shrouded; these generally incorporate the single painted upper shroud which is welded to the upper end of the shock absorber.

The only exceptions to this are the 3-position shock absorbers which are found on the '62 C15 Trials and Scrambles Special models. These follow the design of the later 12.9" shock absorbers with separate, removable upper and lower shrouds.

The 12.9" shock absorbers usually each carried a pair of shrouds with a black upper and chrome lower shroud from '63 to '65. From '66 to '68 they fitted only the Chrome shroud, now in the top position to give a sporty look to the road models. From '69 onward no shrouds were fitted with the predictable shortening of shock absorber life-span. As function was more important than style to the various military customers, the B40 military models kept the fully shrouded shock absorbers.

DECEMBER 1971
No. 45/71

BSA

SERVICE SHEET

B50 MX
REAR SUSPENSION

Under certain conditions it may be desirable to stiffen the rear suspension on the B50MX machine. This may be done by exchanging the existing damper units for those employed on B50SS machines, part no. 19-7474, but the original MX damper springs should be retained

Fig 3.8 Internal damping mechanisms vary, as indicated by this BSA Service sheet

Year	Application	cc	Shock	Spring Absorber	Complete Unit
1970-on	B25T Victor	250			
1970-on	B50T Victor	500			
1970-on	B25 SS Gold Star	250			
1970-on	B50 SS Gold Star	500	6066	64543708	6217
1970-on	B25 R Gold Star	250			
1970-on	B50 R Gold Star	500			
1970-72	P34 Street Scrambler	250			
1970-72	P34 Street Scrambler	500			
1970-72	E35 R Fury	350	6075	64543708	6218
1970-72	E35 SS Fury	350			
1970-71	A50 RS Royal Star	500			
1970-71	A65T Thunderbolt	650			
1970-71	A65L Lightning	650	6075	64545350	6219
1970-71	A65 SS Firebird Scram.	650			
1970-71	A70L Lightning	750			
1970-72	B40 NATO Forces	350	6066	64541530	6212
1970-72	B40 R.A.F.	350			
1970-71	Rocket Three	750	6081	64544235	6214
1970-72	A50R Burma Army	500			
1970-72	B12 V Police	350	6075	64543708	6218
1971-72	A65P Police Special	650	6075	64543820	6220

Fig 3.9 Girling shock absorber application list. The spring reference numbers can be found in fig 3.10 Earlier Unit Single models (C15T/S, B25, B40 military and B44) which fit the 12.9" shock absorber use the same rate springs as listed above (64543708)

Shock Absorbers

Spring Part No.	Colour Code	Rate lb/in.	Free Length	Minimum Working Length	Solid Length	Normal fitted Length	Normal fitted Load	Spring Code
9054-53	Green/Blue	100	7.70	3.60	3.21	7.4	30	100GB74
9054-58	Green/Yellow	90	8.30	3.60	3.53	8.0	27	90GY80
9054-59	Yellow/White	88	8.71	3.60	3.59	8.4	28	88YW84
9054-63	Red/Yellow	126	8.80	4.00	3.97	8.4	50	126RY84
9054-64	White/Blue	45	8.78	3.60	3.18	8.0	35	45WB80
9054-66	Yellow/Green	78	9.69	4.00	3.97	9.4	23	78YG94
9054-88	Red/White	110	9.65	4.50	4.48	9.4	28	110RW94
9054-90	Yellow/Blue	54	9.77	4.00	3.83	9.4	20	54YB94
9054-94	Green/White	90	9.70	4.50	4.42	9.4	27	90GW94
9054-103	Yellow/Red	80	7.80	3.60	3.42	7.5	23	80YR75
9054-165	Blue/Green	160	7.20	3.60	3.48	7.0	42	160BG70
9054-277	Red/Red	110	8.32	3.60	3.57	8.0	35	110RR80
9054-280	Green/Green	100	8.68	4.00	3.96	8.4	28	100GG84
9054-312	Red/Pink	110	8.03	4.00	3.83	7.8	25	110RP78
9054-317	Yellow/Yellow	75	8.53	4.20	4.12	8.0	40	75YY80
64532786	Red/Blue	110	8.21	4.40	4.32	8.4	45	110RB84
64539002	White/Yellow	42	9.63	4.00	3.60	9.4	18	42WY94
64539963	Red/Orange	132	8.47	4.30	—	8.0	62	132RO80
64540471	Blue/White	195	9.58	5.83	—	9.4	35	195BW94
64541530*	Green/Pink	70-100	9.10	4.70	4.70	8.4	70	100GP84
64541653	Blue/Orange	210	8.97	5.40	4.68	8.8	35	210BO88
64541788*	Green/Purple	60-90	8.66	4.25	4.13	8.0	60	90GP80
64541820*	Green/Orange	60-90	9.20	4.09	4.13	8.1	100	90GO81
64543626*†	Green/Pink	70-100	9.10	4.70	4.70	8.4	70	100GP84
6454370 8†	Green/Green	100	8.68	4.00	3.96	8.4	28	100GG84
64543735†	Green/White	90	9.70	4.50	4.42	9.4	27	90GW94
64543764†	Red/Orange	132	8.47	4.30	4.17	8.0	62	132RO80
64543817	Red/Green	120	8.03	4.70	4.14	7.5	63	120RG75
64543818	Blue/Yellow	145	8.19	4.20	4.11	8.0	28	145BY80
64543819	Green/Red	96	8.38	3.60	3.59	8.1	27	96GR81
64543820	Blue/Pink	150	8.88	4.85	4.85	8.4	73	150BP84
64542234†	Blue/Yellow	145	8.19	4.20	4.11	8.0	28	145BY80
64544235†	Red/White	110	9.65	4.50	4.48	9.4	28	110RW94
64546621†	Red/Yellow	126	8.80	4.00	3.97	8.4	60	126RY84
64544754†	Red/Blue	110	8.81	4.40	4.32	8.4	45	110RB84
64545134†	Yellow/Yellow	75	8.53	4.20	4.12	8.0	49	75YY80
64545350†	Yellow/Orange	88	9.49	5.62	5.52	8.4	96	88YO84

Suspension Springs in order of Spring Rate

Rate lb/in.	Spring Part No.	Colour Code	Free Length	Minimum Working Length	Solid Length	Normal fitted Length	Normal fitted Load	Spring Code
42	64539002	White/Yellow	9.83	4.00	3.50	9.4	18	42WY94
45	9054-64	White/Blue	8.78	3.60	3.18	8.0	35	45WB80
54	9054-90	Yellow/Blue	9.77	4.00	3.83	9.4	20	54YB94
60-90	64541820*	Green/Orange	9.20	4.09	4.13	8.1	100	90GO81
60-90	64541788*	Green/Purple	8.66	4.25	4.13	8.0	60	90GP80
70-100	64541530*	Green/Pink	9.10	4.70	4.70	8.4	70	100GP84
70-100	64543626*†	Green/Pink	9.10	4.70	4.70	8.4	70	100GP84
75	9054-317	Yellow/Yellow	9.53	4.20	4.12	8.0	40	75YY80
75	64545134†	Yellow/Yellow	8.53	4.20	4.12	8.0	40	75YY80
78	9054-66	Yellow/Green	9.69	4.00	3.97	9.4	23	78YG94
80	9054-103	Yellow/Red	7.80	3.60	3.42	7.5	23	80YR75
88	9054-59	Yellow/White	8.71	3.60	3.59	8.4	28	88YW84
88	64545350†	Yellow/Orange	9.49	5.62	5.52	8.4	96	88YO84
90	9054-94	Green/White	9.70	4.50	4.42	9.4	27	90GW84
90	64543735†	Green/White	9.70	4.50	4.42	9.4	27	90GW94
90	9054-58	Green/Yellow	8.30	3.60	3.53	8.0	27	90GY80
96	64543819	Green/Red	8.38	3.60	3.59	8.1	27	96GR81
100	9054-280	Green/Green	8.68	4.00	3.96	8.4	28	100GG84
100	64543708†	Green/Green	8.68	4.00	3.96	8.4	28	100GG84
100	9054-53	Green/Blue	7.70	3.60	3.21	7.4	30	100GB74
110	9054-312	Red/Pink	8.03	4.00	3.83	7.8	25	110RP78
110	9054-277	Red/Red	8.32	3.60	3.57	8.0	35	110RR80
110	9054-88	Red/White	9.65	4.50	4.48	9.4	28	110RW94
110	64544235†	Red/White	9.65	4.50	4.48	9.4	28	110RW94
110	64532786	Red/Blue	8.81	4.40	4.32	8.4	45	110RB84
110	64544754†	Red/Blue	8.81	4.40	4.32	8.4	45	110RB84
120	64543817	Red/Green	8.03	4.70	4.14	7.5	63	120RG75
126	9054-63	Red/Yellow	8.80	4.00	3.97	8.4	50	126RY84
126	64546621†	Red/Yellow	8.80	4.00	3.97	8.4	50	126RY84
132	64539963	Red/Orange	8.47	4.30	—	8.0	62	132RO80
132	64543764†	Red/Orange	8.47	4.30	4.17	8.0	62	132RO80
145	64543818	Blue/Yellow	8.19	4.20	4.11	8.0	28	145BY80
145	64544234†	Blue/Yellow	8.19	4.20	4.11	8.0	28	145BY80
150	64543820	Blue/Pink	8.88	4.85	4.85	8.4	73	150BP84
160	9054-165	Blue/Green	7.26	3.60	3.48	7.0	42	160BG70
195	64540471	Blue/White	9.59	5.83	—	9.4	35	195BW94
210	64541653	Blue/Orange	8.97	5.40	4.68	8.8	35	210BO88

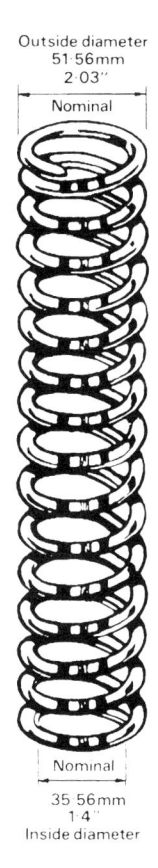

Outside diameter
51·56mm
2·03"
Nominal

35·56mm
1·4"
Inside diameter

A system of colour markings for the identification of suspension springs has been devised, and it consists of three splashes of paint applied to the coils of the springs in the manner shown in the illustration. The colour combination together with the list opposite, provides the key to the part number and spring rate.

The two outer colours are the same and called the 'primary' colour and the inner is the 'secondary' colour.

All the springs listed are for the adjustable unit (B type). Lengths and Loads are at extended centres.

A range of Chrome springs are available in certain sizes and are listed directly under the black equivalent spring and marked thus †

Fig 3.10 Original BSA Spring identification table in part number order for the 12.9" units

4. FRONT FORKS

The Unit Single Forks

Five types were used from '58 to '73 with some exhibiting significant variations. These are:-

C15 forks	All Roadster models; C15 Star, SS80 and Sportsman '58 – '67
Heavyweight forks	All C15 Competition models '59 to '66, all B40 models from '60 to '66, B44 VS '66
Rod-Damper forks	All models (except C15) '67 to'68 also B44VS '69 to '70 and all WDB40 Mk.1 and 2 '67 onward
Shuttle-Valve forks	All B25, TR25w and B44SS '69 to '70. Triumph design
OIF forks	Marzocchi type forks. All B25, T25 and B50 '71-'73

Description and Identification by Slider Type

C15 forks - Roadster models '58-'67

These are scaled down version of the contemporary 1950's Triumph heavyweight fork design and are thus also an enlarged version of the Triumph Tiger Cub and Bantam D7 forks introduced at about the same time as the C15 (*see fig 4.1*). They have internal springs, no rebound damping and minimal oil sealing. Despite these shortcomings they actually work reasonably well! Other than detail improvements to the oil seal arrangement, the C15 Roadster forks are identical for all years from '1959 to '1967. The fork slider which identifies these forks is shown in *fig 4.3*.

Heavyweight forks '59-'66

In terms of their design these Unit Single forks are as per the forks widely used by BSA from 1947 to 1966 on A, B, and pre-unit C-range models and they share several parts: bushes, top and bottom nuts, seals etc. Parts which are specific for the Unit Single application are the yokes, some of the sliders, stanchion lengths and headlamp brackets.

The Heavyweight BSA fork leg components from a B40 are shown in *Fig 4.2* Nothing much to it really, the external fork spring, is not shown here but fits between the chrome fork seal holder and the bottom yoke. Top bush shims may be required to stop this part rattling in use, if so these are fitted between the top bush and the circlip which fits inside the top of the slider.

Whilst being built down to a price, this rudimentary telescopic fork design can work very well, but this will rarely be found to be the case if off-the-shelf parts are fitted ie the stanchions and bushes. The problem with these is the tolerances to which they are made; the clearance between even new parts is often much too generous and is exacerbated by wear inside the fork slider - result, forks which have an imprecise feel and whose action in use can often be described as agricultural. The hard-chrome plated stanchions, nowadays available as replacements, are advantageous in terms of wear but do not address the issue of excessive clearance between themselves and the top bush. Stories of new replacement bushes having more clearance than the worn out originals they were intended to replace are not unknown.

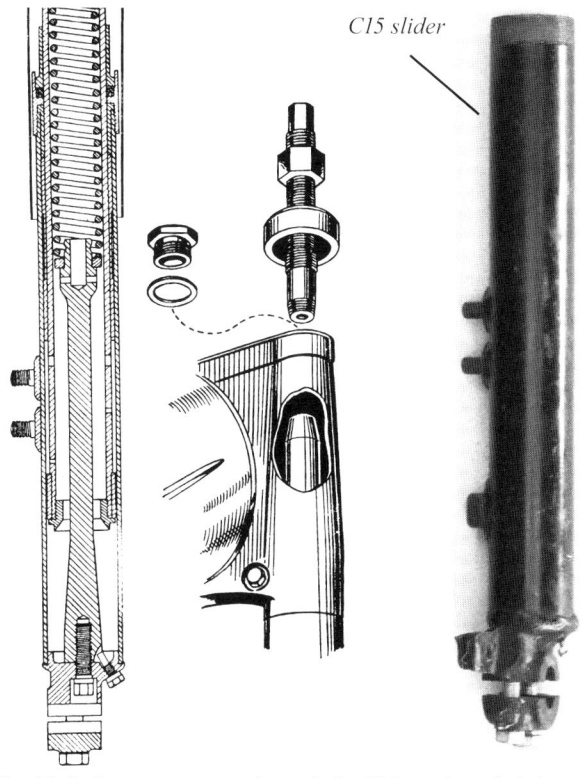

Fig 4.1. Left, cross-section through the C15 roadster fork leg showing the correct stanchion pulling tool for all Unit Single forks prior to '71. Right the C15 slider.

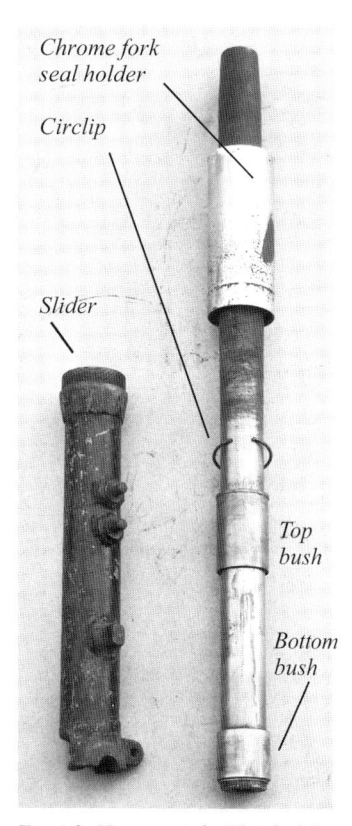

Fig 4.2. Heavyweight BSA fork leg components from a B40 Star

It is possible to produce a set of excellent forks of this type (practically as good as the double-damped designs which replaced them) *if the fork stanchions are hard-chrome plated and ground to a correct clearance-fit size to suit the new bushes*; $1\frac{1}{2}$ thou clearance per inch of diameter is a good rule-of-thumb between stanchion and top bush, but less than this is preferable if it can be achieved. Or alternatively, the top bush can be purpose made to suit the stanchion.

Similarly, the bottom bush may, if necessary, be purpose made and turned to the correct size to obtain minimal ($1\frac{1}{2}$ thou) clearance between it and the inside of the slider. Slider condition is a factor in this; the less it is worn internally the easier it will be to obtain minimum working clearance over the full extent of fork travel; the wear being concentrated at the mid-point of fork travel. A slider could theoretically be bored out and sleeved; realistically it is probably easier to find a replacement in better condition, if new bottom bushes are not found to restore a close sliding fit.

The bottom line is that the bushes should be free to slide against the stanchion or slider but with no perceptible clearance. These facts equally apply to the C15 forks and to the Rod-Damper and Shuttle-Valve forks.

Heavyweight fork slider identification
With heavyweight BSA forks, due to the long production period and wide range of models to which they were fitted, the sliders, being otherwise interchangeable, exhibit many model specific detail differences. The variations relate to the wheel spindle fixing method, brake

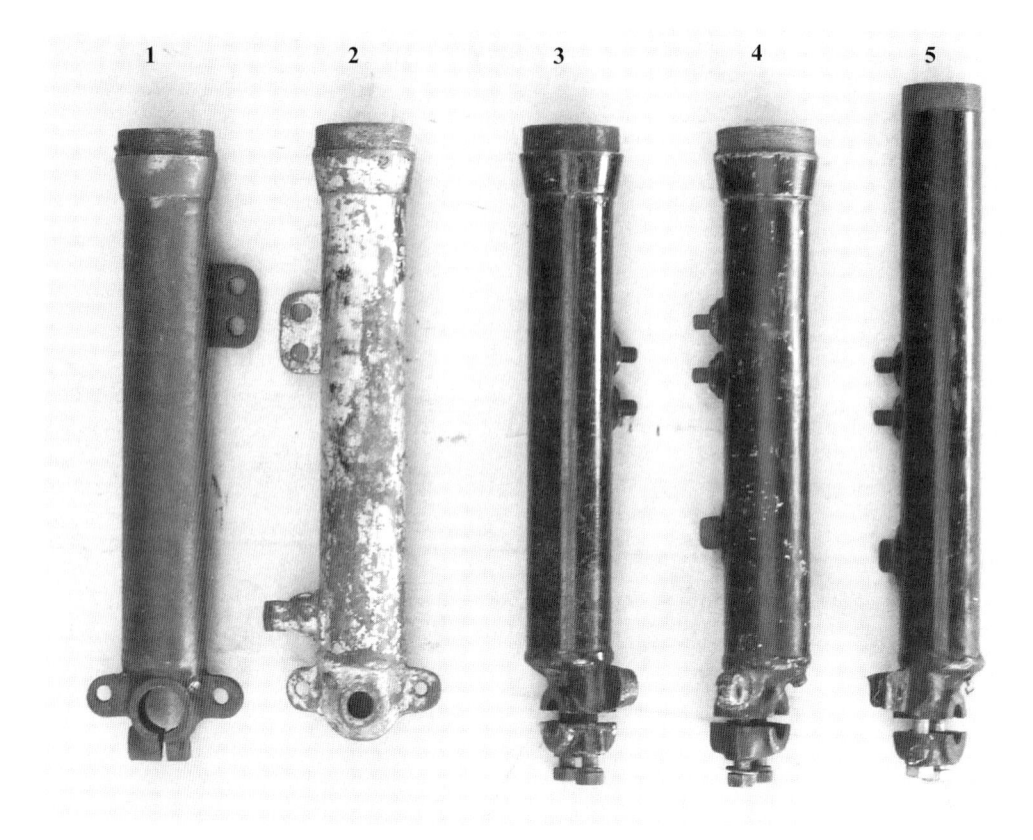

Fig 4.3. 1-4 heavyweight fork sliders, 5 C15 fork slider

plate anchorage and mudguard mounting method. Specific permutations of these variables produce fork sliders which are particular to the Unit Singles. Fitting sliders from another model opens up a range of alterative front wheel options.

In *fig 4.3*, numbers 1 to 4 are Heavyweight sliders with the C15 slider, 5, shown on the right for comparison. Off side examples of the clamp-up spindle type carry the brake plate anchor peg. Sliders 1 and 2 are n/s and o/s for the screw-in type spindle, but are clearly not a pair due to the different heights of the mudguard bracket lugs. 2 is the correct item for the C15/B40 competition models '62 to '65. Both of these sliders were originally used on the pre-unit models along with many other variants of this part. 3 is the C15 competition item '59 to '62 for the $^9/_{16}$" spindle. The mudguard stay lug by the spindle clamp is left un-drilled. 4 is the B40 slider, '60 to '66. This is the same as that used on the late A10 and early A65. 5 is the C15 slider. Being steel, all of these sliders can be rendered scrap by water damage if this is allowed to penetrate and reside there, thus pitting the working surface on the inside. As can be seen in fig 4.3, a quick tell-tale for a BSA Heavyweight fork slider is the tapered collar at the upper end.

Rod-Damper forks '66-'70

Outwardly these are identical in appearance to the standard BSA heavyweight fork they replaced for '67, but are internally modified to provide two-way damping. As a result, only the yoke assemblies, bushes and seals/holders are interchangeable with the Heavyweight forks. This design, as previously used by Jeff Smith and company in the works scrambles team, was an improvement as regards ride quality but was a rather complex and expensive way of achieving this result. Hence this design, which is the most intricate to overhaul, had a relatively limited production life before being replaced by a simpler design for '69.

Front Forks

Incidentally, the design of the internal damping mechanism follows closely the design used by AMC on their post-war models. BSA's non adoption of this type of rebound damping when the design was available in the 1940's (and henceforth used on BSA 'works' machines) is one way in which BSA managed to undercut the opposition on price.

A quick way to distinguish the double damped Rod-Damper forks from earlier single damped (no rebound damping) BSA heavyweight forks is to look at the bottom end of the fork sliders; Rod-Damper sliders have a central hole up the end of the slider for the Allen screw which holds the damper assembly in place, the earlier heavyweight sliders don't. The Rod-Damper sliders also lack the top bush circlip groove of the heavyweight sliders.

Rod-Damper fork slider identification
The Rod-damper sliders (*see fig 4.4*), at a glance are much the same as the previous heavyweight sliders but all now have the hole in the lower end for the $^5/_{16}$" Allen screw which secures the damper assembly. This assembly is still in place in the last example. All are o/s examples.

In *fig 4.4* left to right – Numbers 1 and 2 are the o/s item for the screw-in spindle (n/s has spindle pinch bolt). The boss on the lower left on both of these is the cable abutment and anchor socket for the 7" half width hub brake plate. The mudguard stay lug differentiates them – forward facing (1) for B25 and B44 road models, rearward facing (2) for B40 military Mk1 and B44VS

Numbers 3 and 4 are the '68 road model type for the full width hub fitted to B25, TR25w and B44SS with or without the redundant front guard stay lug. These are o/s examples and so both carry the brake plate anchor peg. Note the square shape to the casting around the spindle hole rather than the round profile found on earlier clamp-up spindle, Heavyweight sliders. 5 is the '68 to '70 B44VS slider for the screw-in spindle 8" half width hub. The mudguard stay lug here also acts as the anchor point for the brake plate strap and is therefore of the stronger

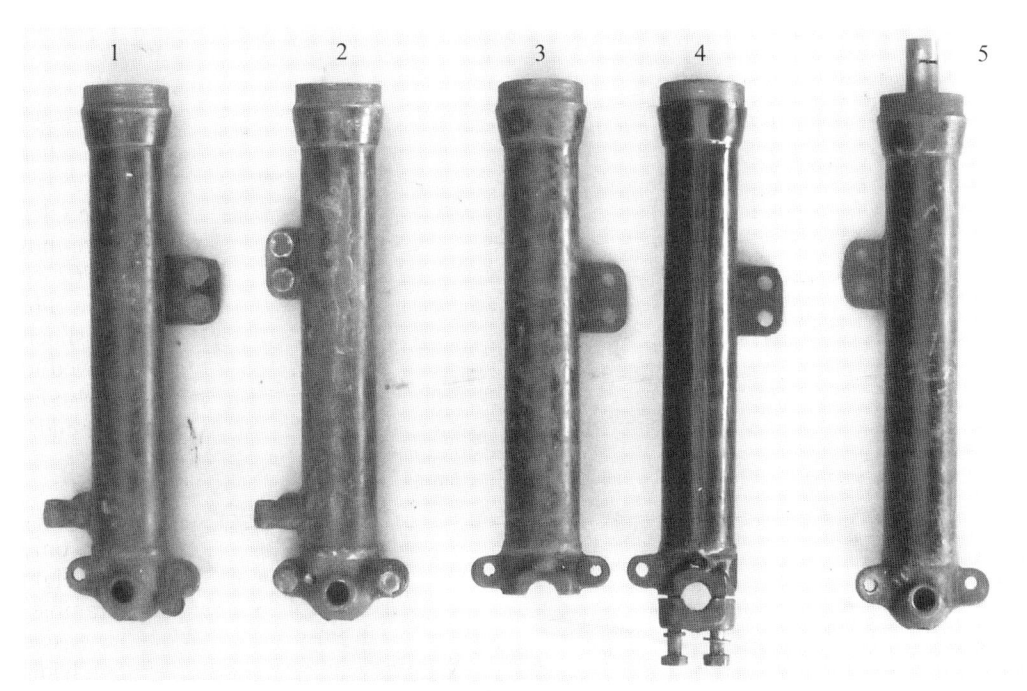

Fig 4.4. Rod-Damper fork sliders

cast and brazed-on type rather than the simpler flat plate of the other examples which do not perform this function (the cast lug is occasionally found on slider 2 fitted to the 7" half width hub). Beware the Gold Star boys offering you large sums of money for this part, also used on mid '60s A65 models. A sectioned view of the Rod-Damper forks is shown in *fig 4.5*.

Whilst all fork sliders for rod-damper forks are interchangeable on the Rod-Damper stanchions, the clamp-up spindle type fitted to B25S and B44SS for '68 are stamped '68' (sometimes faintly) on the outside of the lug by the wheel spindle. Presumably this is to enable identification at a glance and to differentiate them from the many earlier clamp-up spindle sliders used on earlier BSA models. These '68 sliders also feature a squarer shape to the boss around the wheel spindle rather than the circular shape of the earlier sliders, and this feature is replicated on the spindle clamp itself.

Double - Damped Forks '67 -'70

Rod-Damper fork   **Shuttle-Valve fork**

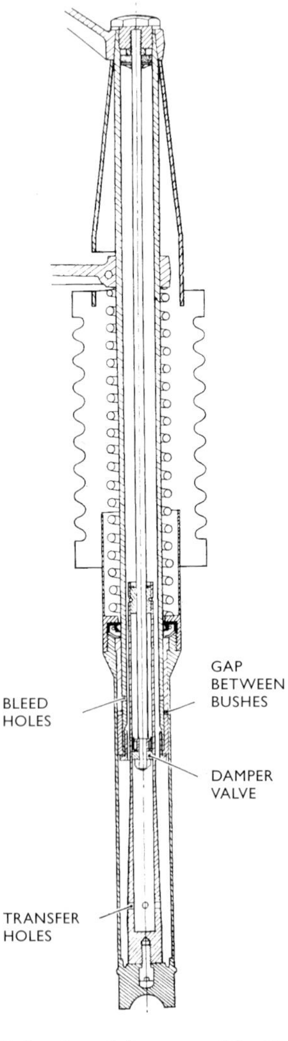

Fig 4.5. Sectioned diagram of the Rod-Damper fork leg used from '67 -'70.

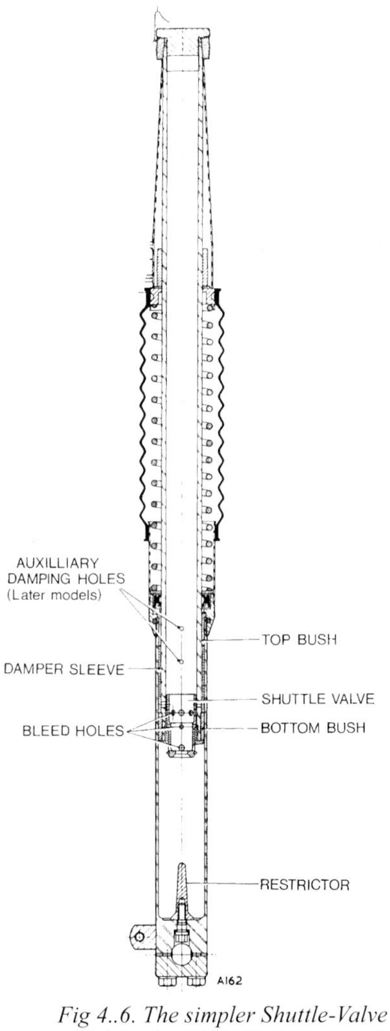

Fig 4..6. The simpler Shuttle-Valve design which replaced the Rod-Damper fork on all but the B44VS for '69 and '70

Front Forks 55

Shuttle-Valve fork '69-'70

These are a Triumph design and applied across the whole BSA range, A, B, (and D in scaled down form) models for '69 and '70. Below the yokes these are as fitted to contemporary and earlier Triumph models. Hence the stanchions are a hybrid design with top halves machined to suit the BSA B25/ B44 'wide yokes' carried over from the previous Rod-Damper design of '68. *Fig 4.6* shows a sectioned view of the Shuttle Valve forks.

The simplicity of this design in achieving two-way damping is a big improvement on the previous BSA Rod-Damper attempt. The only relative weakness of this design stems from the slightly reduced bearing surface because the bushes have a slightly smaller diameter and length which can result in accelerated wear on the heavier models (A65 etc), especially if lubrication is neglected. This situation was tackled by the '70 stanchions for this design being hard-chrome plated on their working surface to extend working life.

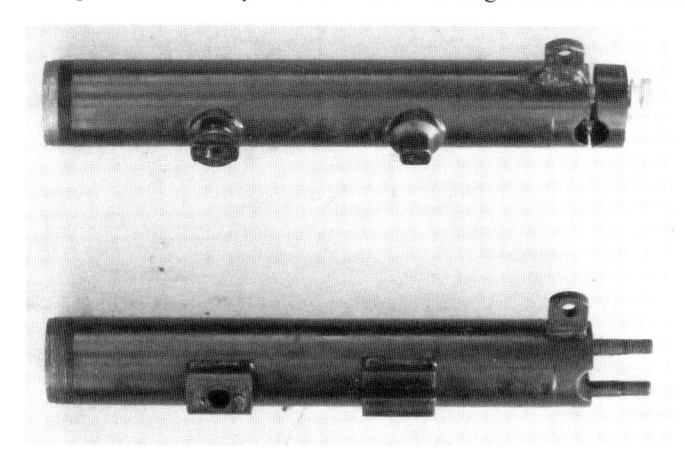

Fig 4.7. Triumph type Shuttle-Valve sliders; '69 above, '70 below, both are o/s and carry the brake plate anchor lug. The differences (mudguard stay boss, brake plate anchor lug and spindle pinch bolts or studs and nuts) do not prevent inter-changeability(see also p55)

Shuttle-valve slider identification (B25, TR25w, B44SS '69 and '70)

The Shuttle-Valve sliders are shown in *fig 4.7*. There were two types, as shown, which are interchangeable. They are parallel sided and lack the tapered collar at the top so should be easy to distinguish from the earlier BSA Heavyweight fork sliders.

OIF forks '71 On

Common fitment across the BSA and Triumph ranges from '71, these forks are based on the Italian Marzocchi design and provide increased travel compared to the earlier Unit Single forks. These are a simple and very effective fork with both two-way damping and greatly enlarged bearing surface area – the whole of the inside of the aluminium slider forms the bearing, riding directly on the hard-chromed stanchion. This results in a very good fork, basically of the same design as fitted to millions of motorcycles since the early '70s by almost every manufacturer. See *fig 4.8* for a sectioned view of the OIF fork

This design therefore brought BSA very much up-to-date in terms of appearance and ride quality. All BSA and contemporary Triumph models from '71 onward of 250cc and over fitted this design of fork with detail differences. The Unit Single version has aluminium yokes rather than the steel items fitted to most of the larger twins. The only other component particular to the singles is the offside slider which has lugs to anchor both 6' and 8' front brakes. The only other model to share these features is the Triumph Adventurer.

OIF fork slider identification
The first thing to note is that they are aluminium and not black painted steel as are all previous types. The '71 fork sliders are identified by being left in a rough-cast finish with a vertical styling rib running from bottom to top on the outer surface (*fig 4.9*). Fork sliders '72 onward lack the styling rib and are fully polished. Similarly the yokes are rough-cast for '71 and polished for '72 The higher brake plate anchor point on OIF fork sliders in *Fig 4.9* identifies these two o/s examples as being suitable for both 6' and 8' front brakes. These are therefore for Unit Single and Triumph Adventurer use. The equivalent o/s slider for twin and triple use has only the lower anchor point for the 8" brake. In all cases, the n/s slider has no brake anchor lugs.

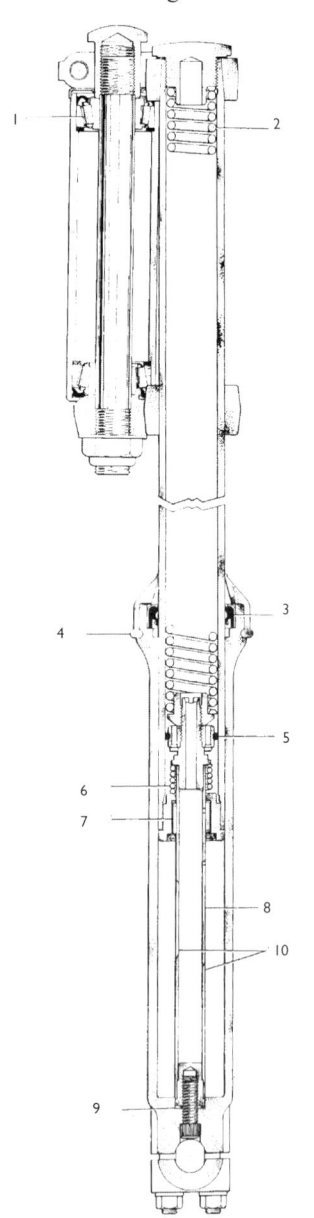

4.8. Left, sectioned diagram of '71 onward fork leg

Head bearing
Main spring
Outer member oil seal
Scraper Sleeve
Damper valve O ring
Recoil spring
Plastic sleeve
Damper tube
Damper tube cap screw
Bleed hole - damper tube

Fig 4.9. Above. OIF fork sliders; '71, bottom, and '72 onward, top

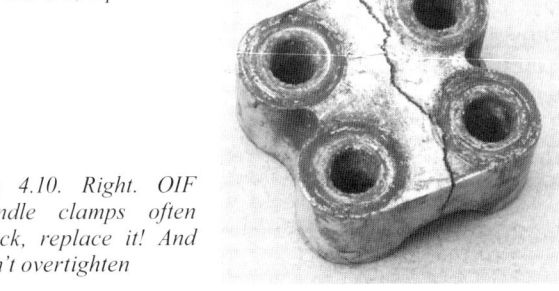

Fig 4.10. Right. OIF spindle clamps often crack, replace it! And don't overtighten

Keep an eye out for broken front wheel spindle clamps: a fairly common problem *(fig 4.10)* which require replacement. The part from the subsequent disc-front end Triumph models can be used after removal of the mudguard stay lug.

Assessing Condition - All Unit Single Forks.

It is thankfully true that the (UK) MOT test is designed to spot any shortcomings that your forks may have which would definitely warrant attention from a safety point of view. Hence excessive - or inadequate - play at bushes and bearings and oil leaks are checked for. However, why be faced with an MOT failure when you can check for, and rectify any such defects yourself?

Basically your forks should turn from side to side and go up and down – nicely. Riding the bike can tell you lots about fork condition. Any feelings of instability, weaving or falling into corners, lack of precision of steering etc must raise suspicions regarding fork condition or adjustment. Likewise would any obvious rattling or knocking from the front end, particularly when the brake is applied. These scenarios should then prompt tests and checks to pinpoint the problem area as follows.

Sit aside the bike, hold the handlebars, apply the front brake and rock the bike back and forth. Forks subjected to this test should be expected to flex a little but not display any movement between parts which can be felt to touch and part as the bike rocks. Obvious play such as this requires attention. Assuming that all fork pinch bolts etc are done up tight (worth checking) this play will be either at the headrace bearings or at the fork bushes between slider and stanchion.

> Play at the headrace can often be seen between the steering head dust cover and headstock top when the above rocking test is carried out. If in doubt a finger tip placed across this joint as the bike is rocked against the front brake will feel any play so long as this isn't confused by accidental rotation of the forks.
>
> Play at the bottom headrace bearing can indicate a bearing cup which is loose in the head stock caused by a previous head-on collision. Such a problem will persist and continue to be felt as play no matter how tight the centre nut is done up.
>
> Play at the bushes will be accentuated and easily felt and seen if the rocking test is carried out with the forks as fully extended as possible.

Beware not to confuse play accompanied by an obvious knocking somewhere at the fork bottom, as play at the bushes. It is most likely to be play between the front brake plate and the anchor lug on the slider, if this method of brake anchorage is used on your bike.

An alternative approach is to put the bike on the centre stand or similarly get the front wheel off the ground and grip the lower end of the fork sliders so the forks can be pushed and pulled back and forth. Again, play will be easily felt if present. Headstock play will result in the whole forks being felt to move; fork bush play should be evident at the slider but if in doubt drop the front wheel out and feel for play in each leg alone. *Remember, some flex is to be expected, obvious play is not!*

The opposite of play is binding. This is shown by a lack of free movement in the suspension movement of the fork legs, or in the rotation at the headstock.

> Binding of the fork legs is likely to be caused externally by the rubbing of fork shrouds, mudguard or similar parts unless incorrect assembly or accident damage has caused

internal tightness between slider and stanchions. Impact on the outside of the fork slider will, if severe, cause a bulge internally thus restricting fork movement. Slight damage of this nature can be removed by careful use of a half round file inside the slider. Severe bulges may require the attention of an expert such as someone who repairs hydraulic cylinders – removal of dents from these is a similar and common exercise. The OIF aluminium sliders may be more problematic in terms of such a repair in which case replacement is the only option.

Binding or lack of free movement at the headstock will be due to over-tightened or damaged headstock bearings.

Fork oil leaks usually fall into two categories – from the lower end of the slider at the drain plug or damper bolt; or from the top of the slider/oil seal holder. The former can be cured locally by minor disassembly and a new sealing washer; the latter requires a fork leg strip and new seals.

Beyond the above checks, for what should be relatively obvious defects, a great deal can be done during assembly to produce a set of forks which work effectively and unobtrusively – no rider really wants to hear and feel them working. This can be achieved by careful and where possible, selective assembly of parts.

Fork Overhaul

Preparation.

You will need special tools! There are some jobs involved in dismantling all types of Unit Single forks which will require tools beyond the normal spanners etc unless of course, you are happy to butcher the offending stubborn part whilst removing it. Luckily, all these special tools can be improvised, made, or in the last resort bought. Hopefully the illustrations below will assist in the making of improvised versions.

However this will require a modicum of forethought and planning to ensure you have what you need in advance, unless you are happy to have your forks in bits for weeks or months. This thinking-ahead will hopefully include consideration of all wearing parts which are due for replacement, stanchions, bushes and seals etc so that new replacements are waiting at the ready.

Lubricants should also be readily available when working on the forks because all internal moving parts should be oiled on assembly. Additionally, on models prior to '71 grease can be applied in a thin layer to the stanchion outer surface above the slider and between the yokes after assembly. This is not to reduce wear but to help keep rust at bay. Do not grease the contact surfaces between yokes and stanchions; these must be assembled dry and clean. Similarly the exposed areas of OIF stanchions should be kept clean with an occasional squirt of WD40 and application of the oily rag.

Other items to be available prior to working on the forks are the usual cleaning materials along with a suitably sized metal rod to poke a rag to the bottom of the sliders to persuade out the accumulated filth which will have collected there. I am repeatedly surprised by the amount of dirt which collects in the bottom of forks which are in effect a sealed system; where does it come from? Regardless of the source of said dirt, it all needs to come out and the slider must be flushed clean, so have the wherewithal to do this at the ready.

Tools for Unit Single forks

The correct BSA tools for working on the various designs of fork are shown in *fig 4.11*; some are currently still available, others will need to be improvised.

BSA were as usual very thorough in making available special tools to ensure that stripping and reassembly of their forks was as painless as possible – until the factory closed that is. Realistically today there are only a few special tools which are readily available from suppliers. These are a must, but do be prepared to make the ones you can't buy; it will work out cheaper in the long run.

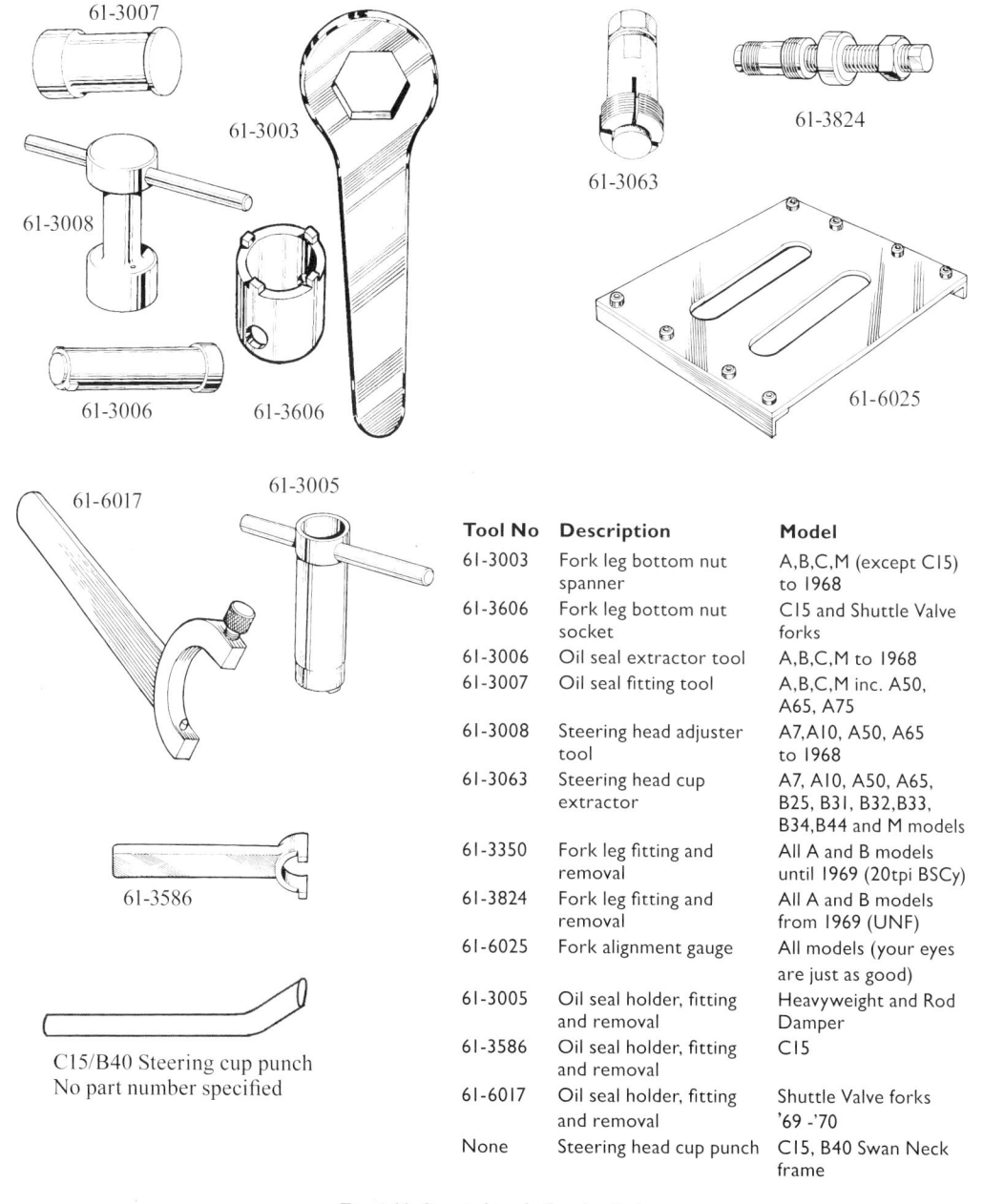

Tool No	Description	Model
61-3003	Fork leg bottom nut spanner	A,B,C,M (except C15) to 1968
61-3606	Fork leg bottom nut socket	C15 and Shuttle Valve forks
61-3006	Oil seal extractor tool	A,B,C,M to 1968
61-3007	Oil seal fitting tool	A,B,C,M inc. A50, A65, A75
61-3008	Steering head adjuster tool	A7, A10, A50, A65 to 1968
61-3063	Steering head cup extractor	A7, A10, A50, A65, B25, B31, B32, B33, B34, B44 and M models
61-3350	Fork leg fitting and removal	All A and B models until 1969 (20tpi BSCy)
61-3824	Fork leg fitting and removal	All A and B models from 1969 (UNF)
61-6025	Fork alignment gauge	All models (your eyes are just as good)
61-3005	Oil seal holder, fitting and removal	Heavyweight and Rod Damper
61-3586	Oil seal holder, fitting and removal	C15
61-6017	Oil seal holder, fitting and removal	Shuttle Valve forks '69 -'70
None	Steering head cup punch	C15, B40 Swan Neck frame

C15/B40 Steering cup punch
No part number specified

Fig 4.11. Special tools for the forks

Must have tools
The following are the must have tools. If you can't buy then make.

Heavyweight forks	oil seal holder fitting/removal tool
	stanchion puller (fork leg fitting and removal tool)
Rod -Damper forks	oil seal holder fitting/removal tool
	stanchion puller (fork leg fitting and removal tool)
Shuttle-Valve forks	oil seal holder fitting/removal tool
	(different design to above), stanchion puller
OIF forks	Long screwdriver (BSA tool not readily available)
C15 forks,	oil seal holder fitting/removal peg spanner, stanchion puller

The stanchion puller is required for dragging the stanchion up through the yokes when you can't grip it directly due to the headlamp shrouds, and/or against spring pressure. To make one, get an old fork stanchion nut and grind/file/turn the corners off the nut so it will drop easily through the stanchion hole in the yoke. Next drill and tap it centrally to allow a 6" length of threaded rod (minimum $^3/_8$" diameter) to screw into it and secure these together with a locknut. File a couple of flats on the top end of the threaded rod so a spanner can be used to turn the whole thing and screw it into the top of the stanchion either before or after this is offered up to the yokes. When ready for pulling, the top end of the threaded rod will protrude up through the top yoke so that the top plate as shown can be placed over the rod to rest on top of the yoke, followed by a nut which, when wound down the rod will drag it and the attached stanchion upwards until the tapers meet. If it is felt that the stanchion is likely to descend again as soon as the tool is removed then temporarily nip it with the bottom yoke pinch bolt until the stanchion top nut can be fitted. Remember to slacken the pinch so the top nut can be tightened.

BSA's version of this tool was a robust lump of steel which, after being screwed into the top of a stanchion stuck in the yokes, could also be used as a drift to persuade a stuck stanchion downward. Early versions had only the 20tpi thread to suit the C15, BSA Heavyweight and Rod-Damper forks. Later versions had both this and the 28tpi Unified thread used on the Shuttle-Valve forks.

For OIF forks the only 'must have' tool is a very long screwdriver to go down the inside of the stanchion and locate in the slot on the top end of the damper tube. This is simply to stop it rotating when the Allen bolt up the bottom end of the slider which attaches it is turned. At 2'6' in length this screwdriver is possibly too long to buy, so fabricate one from a length of steel bar, flattened at one end to form a blade and bent 90 degrees at the other so you can get a grip on it.

To aid long fork life treat all of the fork parts with the same attention to cleanliness as you would the engine internals to avoid contamination with grit and dog hairs etc. With this in mind think about where you will do the fork overhaul and to help keep the road filth on the outside, clean the forks externally before approaching them with the spanners.

Hints, Tips and Mods for Unit Single Forks

The persuaders
From time-to-time, when a bit of extra oomph is needed to separate or bring together fork components for Unit Single forks, always use a mallet, nil by hammer please or damage to appearance and/or wallet is bound to result.

Removing stanchion top nuts
On C15 Roadsters and OIF models. Don't remove both stanchion top nuts at the same time if the front wheel is carrying any of the bikes weight. If you do the forks will instantly collapse as the second nut relinquishes thread engagement and is propelled skyward by the fork spring. Damage to hapless owner (trapped fingers and large hexagonal imprint in facial area) and the bike (when it then falls over) is likely. So, when replenishing fork oil etc remove only one nut at a time if the front wheel is carrying any weight.

The top bush retainer 68-5134
This part (called 'spacer, top bearing' in the parts books) fitted to the Rod-Damper forks can be retro fitted to all earlier BSA heavyweight forks to replace the top bush circlip-and-shim palaver. A top bush not thus retained by one method or the other will rattle noisily – and annoyingly - as you ride along. This retainer is *incorrectly shown* upside down in most BSA parts books. The B40 Military parts book only correctly shows it the right way up; with larger diameter uppermost.

Increasing the suspension travel
The 1950's Ariel and Sunbeam models were equipped with BSA heavyweight forks differing only in detail to suit non-BSA parts attached. Whilst many parts are interchangeable the most interesting feature is the top bush which was sometimes fitted to the Ariel models. These are half the length of the standard BSA top bush and therefore potentially afford an extra inch of suspension travel. This modification can easily be applied to any BSA heavyweight forks (therefore applicable to the Unit Singles which fitted them in original or rod-damper form on some models up to '70) by simply shortening the top bush. But, shortening the top bush in this manner allows the forks to extend further and therefore extra suspension travel must then be achieved by increasing fork spring pressure (spacers or longer springs) to cause the forks to assume a longer than usual at-rest position. All in all this seems a useful mod for off-roaders; the main downside being that the reduced working surface of the top bush will promote wear.

Water-proofing for your forks.
Just as many fork stanchions have to be replaced due to rust pitting caused by water getting in, as by wearing out of the working surface - at least they did when BSA's were ridden in the rain. The metal shrouds often fitted by BSA are quite effective at stopping water getting inside the oil seal holder by the most direct route, ie up under the shroud. The rubber gaiters commonly fitted in later years are a bit better. Neither of these methods alone can prevent water entering via the holes in the fork shrouds/headlamp brackets around the bottom yoke pinch bolt. From here it can run down the stanchion and collect inside the seal holder; there to corrode the stanchion at leisure. BSA tackled this from 1968 onward and the parts then introduced can be retro-fitted. They consist simply of a rubber washer which is a tight fit on both the stanchion and within the lower portion of the fork shroud/headlamp bracket. This rubber washer is supported above and below by plain steel washers, the whole being sandwiched between the fork spring and bottom yoke.

If this seal is fitted along with sealed gaiters, the space between seal holder and bottom yoke is thus rendered air tight and the gaiter will inflate/deflate as the forks compress/extend; good for a laugh with your mates, but not really the done thing. BSA solved this by piercing a small hole in the lower rear of the headlamp shrouds on roadster models to allow air in and out. B40 Military models have an even more waterproof air transfer tube to further prevent ingress of water on the lower front of the headlamp bracket – that's it – the small loop you thought was for tying your luggage onto is actually to allow air to escape from below the bottom yoke. Additionally, some gaiters will be found to have a small hole near the bottom to allow passage of air, if so position the hole to the rear.

Mind the gap!
Between the top of the headlamp bracket (all models to '70 featuring separate headlamp brackets) and the underside of the top yoke, there will often be seen an unsightly gap of up to $1/8$" or so through which can be seen the bare fork stanchion. A good idea here is to cover it with a black cable tie. This looks tidier and helps keep water out if riding in the wet. Rotate the tie so the buckle is hidden under the yoke.

Spanners and chrome nuts

The chrome yoke stem nut
That fitted to many BSA's up to '70 can be awkward but a standard 14mm spark plug spanner fits it. Avoid using an open ended spanner as this will quickly damage the corners and the chrome, always use a ring spanner or a socket, and always be prepared to remove the handlebars prior to adjusting the yoke stem nut.

Stanchion top nuts.
Applying any pressure to these when slackening/tightening and keeping the chrome intact can only be achieved reliably with a ring spanner or socket to spread and thus reduce the load/pressure on each corner. As finding these tools of the correct size may be difficult I have found that the optimum solution is to start with a 'water pump' spanner (thin, flat and soft enough to be nice to the chrome), weld a small piece of steel across it's open end and file it out to fit exactly. The length of the chrome life is directly proportional to how much effort you put into obtaining the most suitable spanner.

Stanchion top nuts on '69/'70 Triumph forks and OIF forks are the same hexagon size as the gearbox sprocket nut, just in case you have already sorted a spanner to suit this.

Stanchion top nuts for the Rod-Damper forks originally had the same shallow hexagon as the previous heavyweight nuts. Damage to these resulting from spanner slip prompted their change to nuts with a deeper hexagon for '67.

Handlebar clamp bolts
The special-to-BSA handlebar clamp bolts also suffer from flaking chrome disease which is why BSA changed the finish to the softer and less flaky Cadmium plate in '69 (it took them long enough!). Again, correctly fitting ring or socket spanners will help the chrome last if you insist on having it. Also necessary to this end are the correct thin washers under the bolt heads.

Screw in spindle repair
The Heavyweight and Rod-damper forks which use a screw-in front wheel spindle are prone to the thread stripping in the o/s slider if the spindle is repeatedly over-tightened. This is the first thing to check when buying a used example of this slider. The most effective repair which I have carried out fix this problem - and cost-effective for the less common sliders - is to drill out the stripped thread to $11/16$" but not fully through; allow the angle of the drill point to leave a ring of undisturbed metal at the inner end of the old thread. This will act as a support for a threaded sleeve once this has been turned and fitted.

The internal thread required in the repair sleeve to suit the original spindle is $9/16$" 20tpi BSCy *left hand thread*. A press-fit of the threaded sleeve in the slider is preferable and its inner end should be turned to match the drill-point angle. Once inserted a ring of weld around its outer end to fix it in place will require minimal tidying to render it indistinguishable."

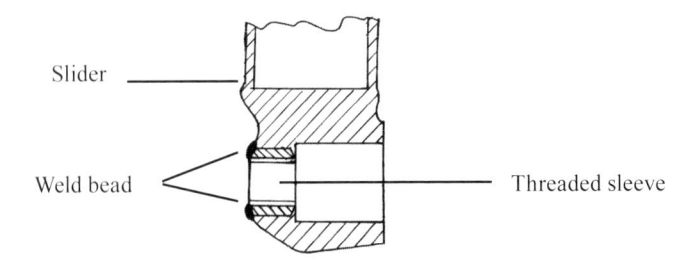

Slider

Weld bead

Threaded sleeve

Forks Removal From The Complete Machine - All Models

Preparation

Put the bike with its centre stand on a 1" thick spacer such as a block of wood, or securely chock it beneath the engine to raise the front wheel off the ground by about 1½". This height will aid front wheel removal later. Drain the fork oil. Disconnect speedo/tacho cables at the instrument. Put a thick cloth or similar over the petrol tank to protect the paintwork from dropped spanners and fork components as work progresses, or even better, remove the tank.

Disconnect the wiring between frame and forks. With a separate headlamp this is easiest by removing the headlamp mounting bolts so that the lamp, still attached can be left behind. Other C15 and B40 models with the fork 'trousers' will require wiring to be disconnected inside the headlamp. Also disconnect wiring from the headlamp to handlebar switches and remove the connections to the Zener diode if fitted to the bottom yoke. Disconnect the control cables – throttle, slacken the twistgrip clamp screws and slide this off intact with cable still attached. Disconnect - the front brake cable at either end or both; clutch cable, at handlebar lever; valve lifter and choke cables if fitted, at handlebar controls.

Fork removal

Before attempting to remove the forks, slacken all nuts and bolts on both top and bottom yokes, these being both stanchion top nuts, top yoke pinch bolt nut, yoke stem nut (don't worry about this one if it is inaccessible beneath the handlebar) and both bottom yoke pinch bolts/nuts. You can now grip the front wheel between your knees and turn the handlebars back and forth to cause the yokes to rotate slightly but not the wheel, thus forcing the yokes to twist. This action will break the stiction between all the mating surfaces which were clamped tight and thus make the forthcoming separation easier.

Next, remove all items bolted to the forks - handlebars, speedo, headlamp, OIF headlamp brackets, mudguard and wheel.

The bare forks, still attached to the frame, can be removed by the standard procedure, which is to remove the top yoke and drop the entire bottom yoke with the fork legs away from the headstock. (Alternatively, for the Shuttle-valve and OIF forks only, fork legs can be dismantled bit by bit where they are, as explained on p71-75)

The stanchions should be a tight fit into the top yoke due to the taper fit. The top yoke may therefore need tapping upward with a mallet to free it. If you are removing just one stanchion out of the yokes, loosely fit an old top nut a few turns and apply the mallet to this to break the taper. If removing the forks intact, chock them to provide support thus preventing them dropping when the top yoke is freed. As they begin to separate from the headstock expect a shower of ball bearings from the bottom of the headstock on all but the OIF forks as these have caged taper rollers. The top bearing and dust cover should remain on the headstock as the forks are lowered.

With the forks minus the top yoke now separated from the frame each complete stanchion should pull down through the bottom yoke. If necessary this can be eased by gently prising open the bottom yoke pinch slot. The '70 and OIF bottom yoke is slotted centrally so unfortunately prising these to free a stuck stanchion is less easy to do. Try penetrating oil and mallet persuasion on '70 forks by refitting the stanchion top nut (or fork puller tool) and tapping downward on this whilst supporting the bottom yoke. The exposed OIF fork stanchions can easily be held in a vice with soft jaws and the bottom yoke worked upward and off one at a time. On models up to '70 with the separate headlamp bracket or shrouds, removal of the stanchion from the bottom yoke frees these parts plus the external spring assemblies and gaiters if fitted.

Fork Leg Dismantling

C15 Roadster fork leg stripdown after removal of the legs from the yokes

Dismantling of a C15 fork leg in-situ with the standard 'trouser' assembly or shrouds fitted is not possible as these prevent access to the oil seal holder and prevent it being unscrewed from the slider. Instead, with the leg on the bench, remove the small hex headed bolt fitted up the bottom end of the fork slider. This releases the internal damper cone/spring support from the slider. (See *fig 4.1* for a diagram of the C15 forks)

Remove the slider from the chrome oil seal holder by unscrewing it. Hmm, easier said than done without the correct tool. First grip the slider spindle boss in a vice. The problem is then to hold the oil seal holder firmly so it can be screwed off, but doing this without damaging the chrome is not easy. The correct BSA tool to achieve this (*see fig 4.11*), locates in the square cutaways provided on the chrome seal holder, is not now available over the counter. Making one is do-able but it needs to be an accurate fit. The optimum solution is to fit a worm drive/ jubilee clip as tightly as possible around the holder. Do not be tempted to now hammer on the side of the buckle to make the clip rotate; thus taking the seal holder with it, but instead fit a large adjustable spanner around the outside of the clip and rotate this so one jaw bears against the buckle. Pressure can now be applied via the spanner and clip to try and unscrew the seal holder. If this does not have the desired result and the clip simply spins around the seal holder; resort to plan 'B'.

Plan B involves fashioning a 'tab' of metal to fit in one of the cutaways in the seal holder which is then locked in place by the worm drive clip. Fit this so that the corner of the buckle locks against the side of the metal tab and thus applies pressure to unscrew the holder when the spanner is again applied to the outside of the clip. Once the holder has started to move on its thread it should spin off easily. The last, undesirable resort is to reach for the Stilsons and buy some new seal holders,

If you didn't do it before 'cos you couldn't see the point of it, now remove the small hexagon bolt recessed into the bottom end of the slider. This connects the internal damper cone/spring support to the slider and failure to remove this bolt now will lead to inconvenience later.

The slider would now be able to pull off the stanchion were it not for the aluminium spacing sleeve which is fitted between the top and bottom bushes and which is usually a tight fit inside the slider. Due to the tight fit of the aluminium spacer in the slider, BSA originally produced a substantial (and now unavailable) puller to draw the slider and stanchion apart, but in practice the two can normally be persuaded to separate by repeatedly pushing the slider up as far as it will go (remove the fork spring) and then sharply pulling it downward so the bushes, with spacer between, jar together and gradually more and more of the top bush will be seen to emerge, followed by the aluminium spacer and bottom bush with the stanchion. If more force is required clamp a snug fitting bar to the end of the slider instead of the wheel spindle and tap on this. Do not be tempted to hammer on the mudguard stay lugs on the slider. Hopefully, *voila*, slider removed with the damper cone loose inside the stanchion and hanging out of the lower end.

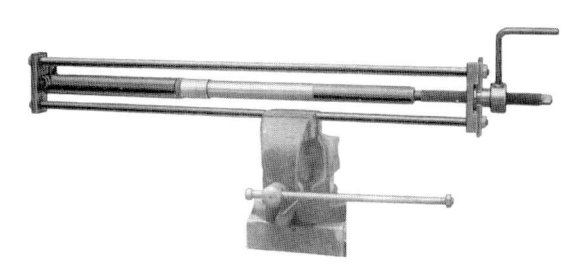

Fig 4.12. The factory tool for stripping and rebuilding the C15 fork leg. Never seen one, never needed one!

The aluminium spacer does not need to be so tight that it makes stripping and rebuilding the C15 forks problematic. If it is, ease off the outside diameter with abrasive paper so that it will just push home in the slider. On the other hand it must not be loose inside the slider as this would allow it to rattle up and down in use.

Removal of the remaining parts from the stanchion just requires the bottom bush retainer to be unscrewed from the end of the stanchion by application of, you guessed it, the special BSA tube spanner. To overcome the absence of this select a large adjustable spanner and fit it so it is snug on the outside of the retainer. Obtain an old Allen key of a size which can permit one end to be ground to a square (from hexagonal) which will fit end-on into one of the cutaways on the retainer. The spanner can trap and apply pressure to the end of the Allen key and thus unscrew the retainer. Holding the retainer in a vice and screwing the stanchion off it is another method.

As is usually the case, the bottom bush should be a tight fit on the end of the stanchion and require tapping off/on with a mallet. All of the other components should slide off/on easily.

During dismantling watch out for:-
The damper cone/spring support which was inside the stanchion can be removed up through the stanchion after removing the retaining bolt in the lower end of the slider. Note the collar which is a press fit on its upper end and on which the lower end of the fork spring rests. If the small retaining bolt recessed in the bottom end of the slider was not removed before the slider was separated from the stanchion, then this collar will have been forced off of the damper cone and now be rattling around inside the slider. Take care not to lose it or forget to refit it to the cone.

C15 fork seal removal and refitting

The seal holder comprises two parts, the upper tube and the lower chrome part. The upper tube is a crude and partially effective attempt to keep road filth away from the seal which is a press fit inside the lower chrome part. This tube has to be removed to get at the seal. Protect, and gently grip the upper tube in a vice with a large snug fitting socket or bar inside the tube so it isn't squashed, and with a soft drift tap the chrome part away. The old seal can then be prised out.

For '66 the design of the upper tube was changed to allow fitment of a second seal at its top end: this seal can be accessed easily when removal is required and separation to change the lower seal is as above. After replacing the lower seal, the upper tube and chrome holder should be squeezed back together in a vice fitted with soft jaws.

The lower seal should be fitted with the lip facing downward. If you are lucky enough to have the later forks with the second upper seal, then fit it with the lip facing upward on the grounds that the lower seal keeps the oil in and the upper the dirt out – much as the '69/'70 Shuttle-Valve forks have a double lipped seal, one facing up, one down.

C15 Roadster fork leg reassembly.

To the bottom of the stanchion slide on the following parts in this order: oil seal holder, top bush, aluminium spacer sleeve, bottom bush (should need tapping on) and finally the retainer ring which needs to be fully tightened (see method for removal above or the tightening can usually be done using a soft aluminium drift and hammer).

The fork slider can then be fitted and the oil seal holder screwed to the slider. If persuasion is needed to make the aluminium spacer and top bush enter the slider try the following: turn the fork leg upside down and rest the oil seal holder on top of the jaws of a vice. Do not tighten the vice on the stanchion and preferably wind PVC tape around this to prevent any damage from the vice jaws. It should then be possible to tap the slider down onto the bushes etc until the thread of the seal holder can engage with the slider and be screwed on to finish the job off.

There is no provision for a seal of any sort between the slider and seal holders to prevent oil seeping down the thread as there is on the BSA heavyweight forks. As such, there is no harm in degreasing the thread on the seal holder and the slider and applying a smear of non-setting gasket goo before fitting them together.

The damper cone now needs to go down inside the stanchion and locate with the spigot on the 2BA drain screw before the fixing bolt is tightened. Note that there is a slot on one side of the bottom end of the damper cone. When re-fitting, this locates on a spigot on the inner end of the 2BA fork drain screw (as per heavyweight forks). This arrangement stops it rotating as the bottom bolt is tightened. This spigot is not very robust and is easily damaged which results in difficulty in engaging it with the slot. Check the fit of these parts while exposed to save tears later, and tidy the spigot with a file if necessary. Rotating the damper cone to locate it correctly on the spigot can be achieved by using a long screwdriver or similar flat blade in the slot on its upper end.

Heavyweight and Rod-Damper forks

These two designs share a common approach to overhaul, the Rod Damper design being a development of the basic Heavyweight design to produce two-way damping. It is theoretically possible to strip these fork legs in-situ on the machine but in reality, the chance of unscrewing the chrome oil seal holder from the outside is slim unless you are prepared to destroy it in the process. In practice it is therefore more straightforward to first remove the complete stanchion from the yokes and strip it on the bench but, for the brave, this is how to do it in situ (good luck!).

Slider and seal holder separation

As stated above this is problematic as it depends on whether the chrome oil seal holder will readily unscrew from the slider. This has to be achieved by external pressure alone as the BSA tool, which fits inside the seal holder to unscrew it, cannot be used as it cannot be fitted over the stanchion while this is still mounted in the yokes. So, the previously suggested jubilee/worm drive clip method is the best bet but it is by no means guaranteed as it is likely to slide around the smooth chrome surface. A strap wrench is another alternative but be prepared to drop the stanchion out of the yokes and remove the seal holder with the specified tool. This is the only guaranteed method unless you are prepared to buy some new seal holders and thus can use 'Stilsons' or similar butcher's tools on the old ones. Any such pressure needs to be applied on the bottom ¾" of the holder as above this the metal is thin and will collapse. Alternatively, filing through to the threads on a small patch of the bottom ½" of the seal holder will invariably allow it to loosen and unscrew.

Front Forks 67

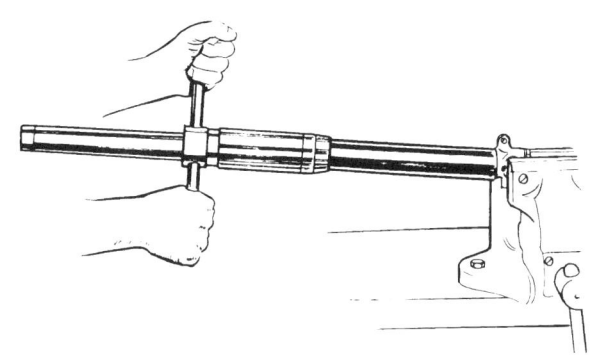

Fig 4.13. Removing the oil seal holder, Heavyweight and Rod-Damper forks

If attempting any of the above, rotate the slider relative to the seal holder by refitting the wheel spindle or similar metal bar between the sliders, or just to the slider you are working on, so it can act as a tommy bar. If your sliders have flat plates welded to them on which the centre mudguard stay mounts, resist the temptation to put an adjustable spanner on these in an attempt to rotate the slider. If you do these plates will bend.

Failure of the seal holder to unscrew at this juncture – butchered or not - means that the complete stanchion/slider assembly needs to be dropped from the yokes for dismantling on the bench as follows.

Seal holder removal - preferred method with fork leg on the bench
With the fork legs removed from the yokes, hold the slider in a vice by the wheel spindle mounting lug. The tool to remove the seal holder can now be fitted so its lugs engage with the cutaways inside the holder (fig 4.13). Much force may be needed to get the seal holder to unscrew so be prepared to exert yourself!

Heavyweight fork leg dismantling
With the seal holder unscrewed and raised clear the BSA heavyweight forks will need the circlip, fitted inside the top of the slider, to be prised out – a fiddly job, requiring something thin, pointed and strong to poke behind it. BSA provided a notch inside the top of the slider to make it easier to get behind this circlip and lever it upwards. This circlip retains the top bush within the slider and between the two may be shim washers (alternative thicknesses were originally available) to stop the bush rattling. The slider will now pull off the stanchion and bushes.

Remove the bottom nut from the stanchion which will free the bottom bush with washer, top bush and seal holder. The bottom stanchion nut for heavyweight forks has a central hole $5/8$" in diameter. A much larger $15/16$" hole in this nut indicates that it is intended for rod-damper forks.

Oil seal removal
With the seal holder now removed from the stanchion, poke the blade of a medium sized screwdriver through the cutaway provided behind the seal in the holder. Angle the screwdriver tip so it bears against the outer metal part of the seal between it and its housing. Hold or trap the seal holder so it can't tip sideways while a firm tap on the screwdriver handle will free the seal.

Seal replacement
New replacement seals are best fitted by being squeezed into place in the chrome seal holder by a vice and a cylindrical spacer to reach down inside the seal holder. This should ensure they are fitted squarely. If you have to resort to the knocking stick to push them home always do this via a spacer or suitable dolly to spread the force of the blows evenly and prevent

localised damage. Similarly, any use of a vice in the above jobs requires soft-jaws to be fitted to avoid damaging the chrome plate.

Fork seals should all be fitted with the lip/spring facing downwards. If the new seals are bare metal on their outer diameter rather than rubber apply a thin smear of gasket goo to the outer surface before fitting, this will prevent leakage between the seal and its housing.

Heavyweight fork leg reassembly

A simple and straightforward reversal of the dismantling process and common to the Rod-Damper forks (see p69-70), excepting the Rod-Damper assembly. The only peculiarity of the Heavyweight forks being to shim the top bush under the circlip to ensure it is firmly fixed in place.

Rod-Damper fork leg dismantling

After unscrewing the seal holder, the Rod-Damper forks differ in that they do not have the large circlip to retain the top bush and instead have a simpler cupped spacer to hold the top bush in place. This is compressed as the oil seal holder is screwed on. This means that after unscrewing the oil seal holder the slider and stanchion can immediately be separated.

Removal of the Rod-Damper assembly from the slider can be done regardless of whether the stanchion and slider have first been separated, but it is wise not to remove the Rod-Damper assembly, just for the sake of doing so. If the stanchion and slider are to remain together, refitting the damper assembly down the inside will be fiddly (see p70).

Removal of the damper assembly is done by unscrewing the single Allen cap screw from its recess in the bottom end of the slider. This Allen screw is the means by which these forks are readily identifiable as Rod-Damper rather than the previous heavyweight design. This Allen screw needs to be fitted with a thin aluminium or copper sealing washer to prevent oil leaks. The main requirement of the washer, is that it should not be thick enough to raise the head of the Allen screw into contact with the wheel spindle.

In this way the Rod-Damper assembly can be removed upwards from the fork leg while still on the bike, with the damper rod still attached to the fork top nut, but, as already stated, re-fitting it to a complete fork leg will be fiddly, so only remove it if you plan to strip the fork completely, and thus it can easily be re-fitted to the bare slider.

The preferred method
With the damper assembly attached inside the slider - first separate the stanchion and slider by unscrewing the oil seal holder (as per normal heavyweight forks). Separating these two parts with the damper assembly fixed in the slider needs the rubber on the top end of the rod to be removed. The purpose of this rubber is to stop the rod disappearing down inside the stanchion when you don't want it to: right now you do want it to.

With the slider (complete with damper assembly) pulled free of the stanchion, the bottom nut, washer and bottom bush can be removed, thus freeing the top bush and seal holder. The stanchion bottom nut for the Rod-Damper forks has a large $^{15}/_{16}$" diameter hole through it. Those fitted mainly to roadster models have a 1" long tubular extension. (*see fig 4.34*)

Damper unit dismantling.

Whether attached to the slider or not, dismantling the Rod-Damper assembly requires the circlip inside the top of the damper tube and the spring clip in the groove on the outside to be removed so that the rod with valve and the steel top bush can be pulled upwards and out. On the bottom end of the rod is the valve assembly and bottom bush, all of which is retained by the nut on the end.

The main part of the Rod-Damper assembly to check and possibly change is the small, scalloped bronze bush on the end of the damper rod. If this is excessively worn it will allow the damper cup to tilt and jam inside the tube thus preventing smooth up and down travel of the damper rod. Otherwise, if there is no obvious damage and the rod nicely slides in and out of the tube then leave it alone.

Check that the damper rod is straight when free from the damper assembly.

Rod-Damper fork leg reassembly: the damper unit

Start with one small job which, if attended to now will prevent high blood pressure later: check that the spigot on the end of the 2BA fork drain screw is straight and tidy and that it fits easily in the slot on the lower end of the damper tube. If necessary, tidy the spigot with a file.

Damper valve

Now start the assembly proper with the damper unit. The valve components present no problems other than ensuring that they are fitted to the end of the damper rod in the correct order as per the diagram (*fig 4.13*). Also fit the spring clip for the rubber washer to the top end of the rod ¼' below the threaded portion.

Fit the rod assembly to the damper tube and push the steel bush in just far enough to line up its groove with the notches near the top of the damper tube. Insert the circlip and top bush clip. Ensure that the free ends of the top bush clip do not foul the inside of the stanchion and will pass through the bottom nut; file or grind these back if necessary.

Fit the damper assembly – complete except for the rubber on the top of the rod – into the slider. Loosely fit the retaining Allen bolt with aluminium sealing washer in the bottom end of the slider so the damper assembly is free to rotate until it can be felt to locate, and drop into position on the drain screw spigot. Tighten the Allen screw.

Fitting the stanchion

Next turn your attention to the stanchion. Slide the oil seal holder, top bush retainer and top bush up on to the stanchion. Fit the bottom bush and bottom nut with washer. Fit the stanchion with bushes to the slider (with damper assembly) but don't yet screw on the seal holder.

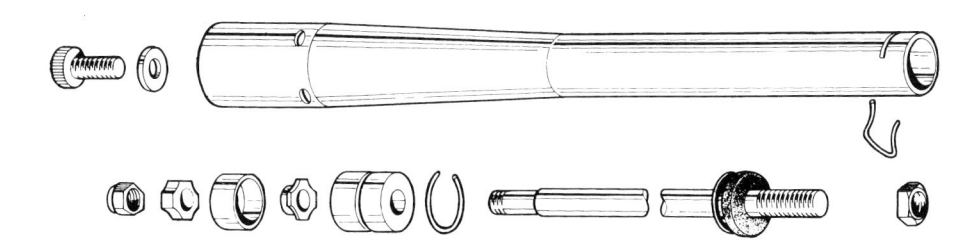

Fig 4.14. The damper valve assembly. All components are common to both narrow and wide yoke forks using this design, the only difference is the length of the damper rod
Narrow yokes 20 $^{15}/_{16}$"
Wide yokes 21 $^{5}/_{8}$"

Turn the whole fork leg upside down and the damper rod should drop and protrude through the stanchion top with its spring clip. If it is reluctant and sticks for any reason inside the stanchion, shaking while upside down may do the trick, otherwise you will need a $5/16$" cycle nut attached to the end of something long to reach down inside the stanchion, screw onto the rod and draw it out. Fit the rubber on the rod against the spring clip and keep it in place by screwing the $5/16$" cycle nut fully onto the thread. The rod cannot now descend inside the stanchion until it is forced home against the resistance of the rubber when the stanchion top nut is finally fitted.

The oil seal holder can now be screwed onto the slider with the time honoured BSA method of twine (string, natural, not synthetic of any sort) used to stop oil leaking down the thread. Clean/degrease the thread on the slider and seal holder and remove any remnants of old twine. Yes, you could use a Concentric carburettor flange 'O' ring here instead. About the twine: coat it with non-setting gasket goo (Welseal or similar), loop it around the bottom of the thread, twist the ends over each other once only and get someone else to pull these tight while you use both hands on the seal holder tool to screw it fully home thus pinching the twine. Trim off the ends of twine with a knife afterwards.

Refitting the damper assembly to the complete fork leg
If for any reason the damper assembly has been released inside a complete fork leg by slackening of the bottom Allen screw, the problem will be to re-engage the damper tube slot on the drain screw spigot. My preferred method is to lower the damper assembly inside the fork leg, fit the Allen screw in the bottom of the slider and engage only the first couple of threads so the damper assembly with Allen screw is free to move up and down by about ½". With the fork leg vertical, next fit the 2BA drain screw (check the spigot is tidy and straight) and as it screws in closely watch the Allen screw to see it rise up into its socket as the spigot on the drain screw pushes up on the damper tube. Raise the Allen screw in this way by $3/16$" or so. Next fit the Allen key to the screw, this will allow you to push upward on the screw thus raising the whole damper assembly. While in this raised position you can fractionally rotate the whole damper assembly by turning the Allen key and screw and then lower it again to see if the spigot has located in the slot – when it does the whole assembly with Allen screw and key will drop by the extra $3/16$" that it was lifted by the spigot. Obviously you may need to repeat this several times until you find the slot or you may be lucky and find that it locates straight away.

Fully tighten both drain screw and Allen screw preferably with new Aluminium sealing washers on each. Next time don't separate the damper assembly from the slider!

Damper rod attachment
The upper end of the damper rod should be firmly fixed to the fork top nut. Screw the $5/16$" cycle nut fully onto the threaded end of the rod above the top rubber. After eventually fitting the fork leg to the top yoke, screw the fork top nut (washer first) fully onto the rod and wind the $5/16$" nut up to the underside of the fork top nut to lock against it. The sealing rubber and its supporting clip should then be pushed up tight against the $5/16$" nut. Thus when subsequently fitting and removing the fork top nut (and its washer) the damper rod should come and go and rotate with it. Fitting the top nut should therefore involve the top sealing rubber being forced down inside the stanchion a short way.

1969/70 Shuttle-Valve fork leg stripdown.

Compared to previous designs of Unit Single fork, these are simplicity itself to work on and can be dismantled with the stanchion still in the yokes or with the whole leg removed to be serviced on the bench. The main problem with the former is to unscrew the chrome seal holders without damaging them. This is best done with a correctly fitting peg spanner to engage with the two holes on the outside of the holder as per the original BSA/Triumph service tool. As these forks are of Triumph design it is also worth trying Triumph spares suppliers for the correct tool. If making such a spanner use ¼" or ⁵⁄₁₆" Allen screws for the adjustable, or fixed pegs as these are hard enough not to bend in use. Grind the threads from around the ends leaving ³⁄₁₆" diameter pegs which will engage with the holes.

Lack of the correct tool may mean an attempt along the following lines. Using grease, hold either two ³⁄₁₆" ball bearings (or if the two holes in the holder are too deep to allow these to protrude sufficiently, two clutch centre rollers) into the two holes on the seal holder. A very large adjustable spanner with jaws set to fit snugly around the seal holder will then bear upon the protruding balls or rollers, allowing rotary pressure to be applied. Definitely better than Stilsons but some risk to the chrome around the holes still exists.

The seal holder in its upper side should be found to contain a thick washer under a cupped washer on which the fork spring seats, and in the underside an 'O' ring and a thin steel ring which bears against the top bush. Remove this steel ring to expose the notch through which the seal can be driven upwards and out with a suitable drift. The 'O' ring is fitted to prevent oil leaking past the threads; change this along with the main seal. Note the main seal is double lipped and should be fitted with the main lip downward.

After unscrewing the seal holder the slider can be pulled off the stanchion. The only other part contained in the slider is the damper cone which is retained by a small hex headed bolt, found in a recess in the bottom end of the slider. Normally this need not be disturbed.

The stanchion will be left with, in descending order: seal holder, top bush, plastic spacer tube, lower bush and lock-ring with Shuttle-Valve. All of these are to be released after removing the lock-ring which, unless the correct 'C' spanner is available, will need to be removed by the same method as the equivalent C15 lock-ring above. The aluminium sleeve which forms the Shuttle-Valve is retained in the lock-ring by the easily visible circlip. This need not be disturbed if the sleeve is free to move up and down. The lower bush may, as usual, need to be tapped with a mallet to free it from the stanchion and everything else should then slide off. The plastic spacer tube will be seen to be internally thicker at one end; this thicker end is fitted uppermost. See *fig 4.15* and *4.16* for the Shuttle-Valve fork assembly.

1969/70 Shuttle-Valve fork leg reassembly

This is done just as the book usually says, ie in reverse order to dismantling, and should be just as straightforward. Take care to persuade the 'O' ring in the lower end of the seal holder to fit over the top bush flange and slider without being torn or nipped; a smear of grease will help.

When fitting new stanchions check and if necessary remove any burrs from the inside of the bleed holes. If present, these can interfere with the free movement of the Shuttle-Valve.

As this design of fork was previously applied to many Triumph models before being applied to the BSA range for '69 and '70 (even the D175 Bantam had a scaled down version at this time) it is worth considering that items which look like fork parts for your B25/B44 may not be.

Fig 4.15. Above. Shuttle-Valve parts in correct order ready to fit to the stanchion. Left (top) to right (bottom) thin washer, rubber washer, thin washer, main spring. cupped spring support (only fitted on BSA versions of this fork), thick washer, oil seal and holder, spacer, 'O' ring, top bush, plastic spacer, bottom bush, and Shuttle-Valve assembly with stanchion bottom nut.

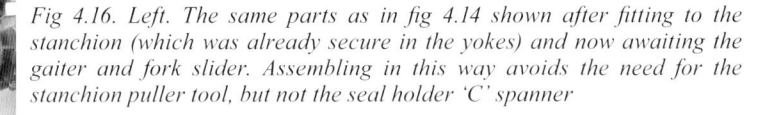

Fig 4.16. Left. The same parts as in fig 4.14 shown after fitting to the stanchion (which was already secure in the yokes) and now awaiting the gaiter and fork slider. Assembling in this way avoids the need for the stanchion puller tool, but not the seal holder 'C' spanner

Whilst there is a large commonality of parts it should be borne in mind that some parts vary from model to model. The cupped fork spring support housed inside the seal holder is not fitted on forks for Triumph use as the main forks springs are of larger diameter and do not require this part to locate their lower end.

The chrome oil seal holder shown is the correct type for these forks when fitted to Unit Singles. Other equivalents are found on the larger Triumph and BSA machines which are interchangeable due to the same thread being used.

The sliders themselves come in two main versions; sliders up to '69 have a circular tapped boss at the front mudguard mounting position and front wheel spindle UNF pinch bolts. The '70 sliders have a rectangular bracket to accept a square nut instead of the circular boss at the mudguard mounting position and UNF studs with nyloc nuts for the front wheel spindle clamp (see p55).

Sliders with a modified wheel spindle position (eg as originally fitted to some twin cylinder models) are identified by a large dot (as would be made by heavy centre-punching) next to the wheel spindle on the slider and on the 'D' shaped spindle clamp. Parts with or without the dot, were produced to both designs of slider ie the design to '69 and the '70 version. Parts for Unit Single use are not marked with this dot and should not be mixed with parts which are marked in this way. The 'D' shaped spindle clamps themselves vary in thickness, initially $^9/_{16}$" thick, and subsequently $^5/_8$" thick; all being interchangeable with a matching pair being desirable.

OIF fork leg strip and rebuild - '71 on

This design is the simplest of all Unit Single forks to work on and as a result there are few foibles relating to them. I can therefore add little to standard procedure for overhauling them; the best version of this which I have found was produced by the USA subsidiary company who handled service and distribution in the US. These instructions are reproduced below. (*fig 4.20 p74*)

Front Forks 73

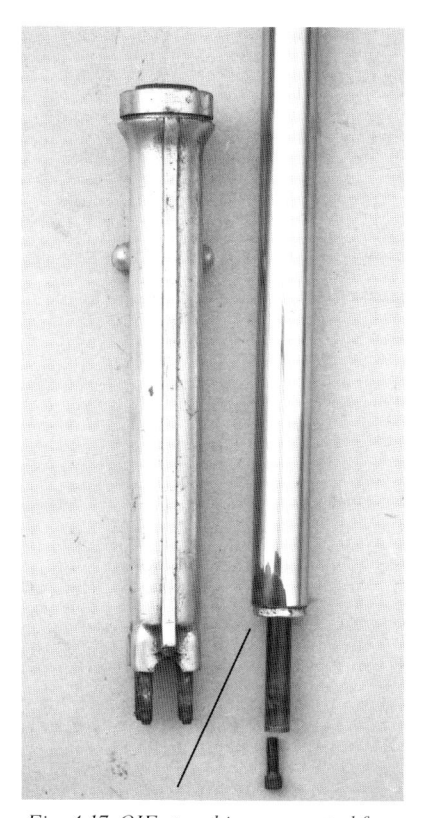

Fig. 4.17. OIF stanchion separated from the slider. Note typical wear pattern at the lower end.

Fig. 4.18. OIF stanchion wear marks 8" or so above the bottom on the opposite side of the stanchion from that shown in fig 4.17.

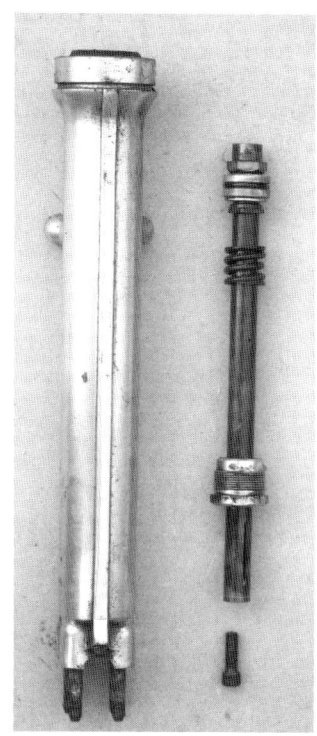

Fig. 4.19. The OIF damper assembly after removal from the stanchion.

Figs *4.17, 4.18* and *4.19* show the OIF stanchion separated from the slider after simple removal of the one Allen screw in the bottom end of the slider. The stanchion exhibits a typical wear pattern; the worn patch at the lower end, and 8" or so above it on the opposite side. The chrome having worn through in this way means that replacement stanchions are needed.

The stanchion bottom nut (shown mid-way up the damper tube) contains an internal plastic sleeve. When new this should slide on the damper tube with a little resistance. Wear of this plastic sleeve means that new bottom nuts are desirable. Similarly, the aluminium collar at the top of the damper tube is fitted with an 'O' ring which should offer some resistance when it slides inside the stanchion. Change this 'O' ring as a matter of course.

OIF fork seal replacement
OIF forks require a different method of seal removal due to their differing fork slider material and design. The general idea is to collapse the seal inward by driving a wedge between the outside of the seal and the aluminium of the top of the slider which surrounds it. This wedge must be made of aluminium or a softer material to avoid damaging the fork slider. New OIF fork seals are easily fitted by turning the slider upside down on a flat surface and then tapping the lower end of a stanchion with a mallet to drive the seal home.

BSA SERVICE BULLETIN

Improved Fork Seal
B25/B50
11/10/71

IMPROVED FORK SEALS

A new, improved fork seal (97-4001), which has eliminated fork oil leak problems, is now being fitted to 1972 models. The new seal is of different design, produced by a different manufacturer than the previous seal. For quick Identification, the new seal is covered with black neoprene (the old seal had no neoprene covering the metal outside diameter)

FIG. I

DISMANTLING FORK LEGS

1. Remove handlebar and fork cap nuts.

2. Remove front axle clamps and wheel assembly,

3. FIG. I - Remove Allen screw from the bottom of the fork outer member, This is accomplished by inserting Special Damper Removal Tool 61-6113 through the top of the fork stanchion and into the slot at the top of the damper assembly. if Special Tool 61-6113 is unavailable a 13/16-inch socket and along extension can be used for holding the damper unit.

4, After the Allen screw is removed, slide the outer member off the fork stanchion.

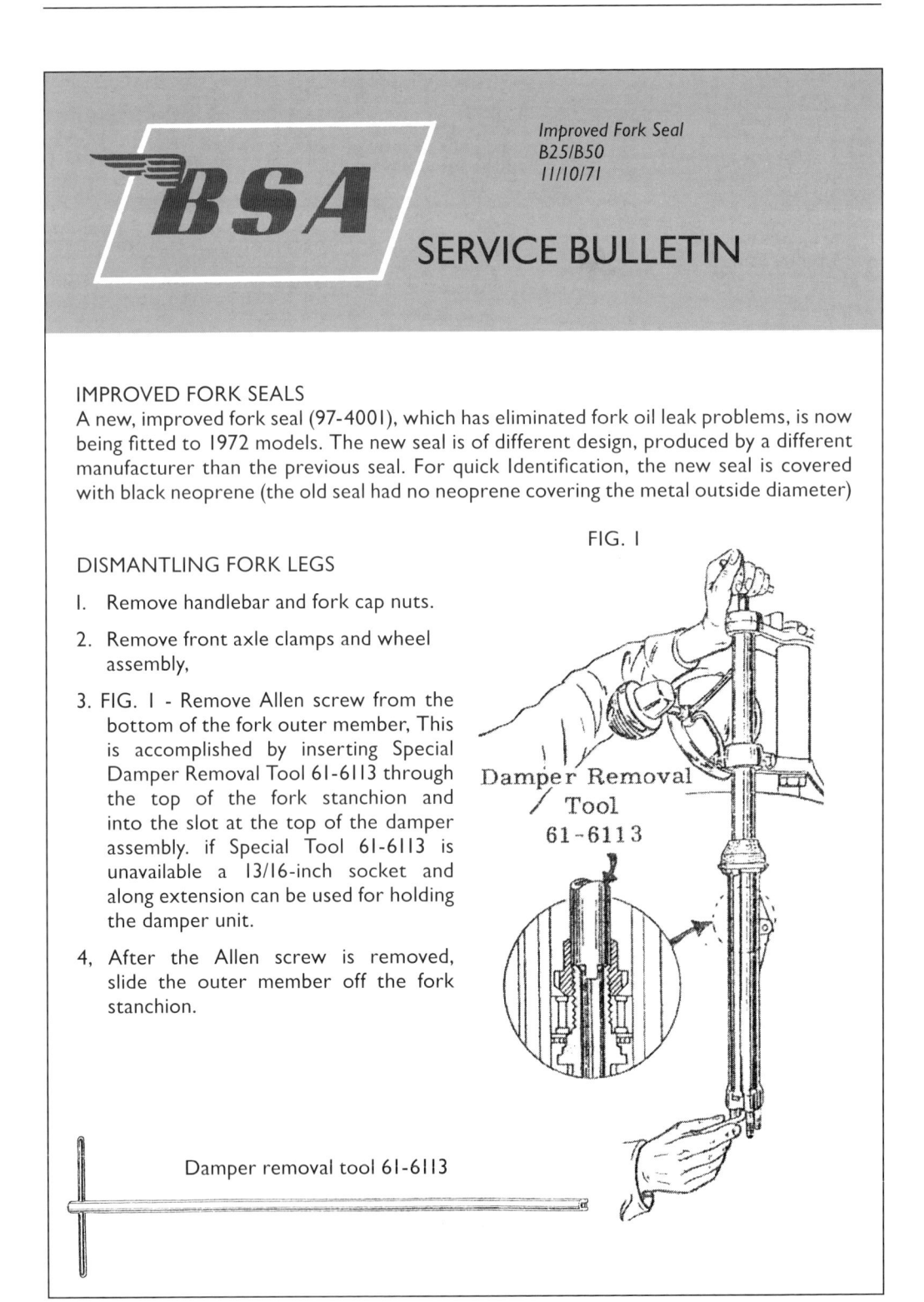

Damper Removal Tool 61-6113

Damper removal tool 61-6113

Fig 4.20. (This page and next) US Service Bulletin explaining how to dismantle and reassemble the OIF forks

Front Forks

SEAL REMOVAL

1. Hold the outer member by the wheel spindle lug in a soft-jawed vise. Remove the scraper seal.

2. FIG. 2 - Using a small chisel and hammers collapse the metal body of the seal inwards. Caution - make certain the chisel is applied to the rim of the seal only - otherwise the fork outer members may be damaged causing an oil leak. Once the seal is partly collapsed, it can be easily removed with the aid of a screwdriver.

FIG. 2   FIG. 3

1.900
1.350

Piloted Drift

FORK LEG (EXPLODED VIEW)

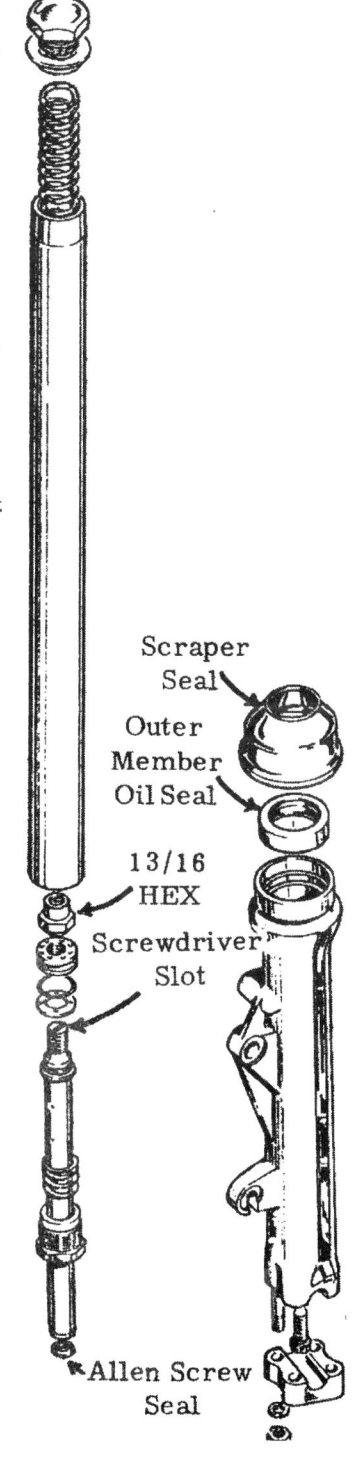

Scraper Seal
Outer Member Oil Seal
13/16 HEX
Screwdriver Slot
Allen Screw Seal

SEAL INSTALLATION

1. FIG. 3 - The use of a piloted drift is preferred for installing seals. This tool can be fabricated from a short length of tubing or a bar slight'y smaller in diameter than the seal. Note - to insure proper seal installation, be sure that the lips of the seal are pointing up toward the crown.

2. When pressing the seal in, be certain it is entering the outer member squarely.

REASSEMBLING FORKS

1. Apply a small amount of oil to the lower end of the stanchions.

2. Make certain that the Allen screw seal is properly positioned in the recess at the bottom of the outer members.

3. Slide outer members onto the stanchions - being careful not to damage the new seals.

4. Hold damper in position with Special Tool 61-6113, or 13/16-inch socket, and tighten the Allen screw.

5. Install front wheel assembly.

6. Fill each fork with 190cc of ATF Fluid 'F'

7. Install top cap nuts and handlebars.

Yokes and Headrace Bearings Removal and Fitting, All Models

If the fork stanchions have already been withdrawn, removal of the yokes from the headstock of the frame simply needs the central yoke stem nut to be fully unscrewed after its pinch bolt and nut have been slackened. Three hands are needed when doing this to hold the spanner you are using, the top yoke and the bottom yoke otherwise the latter will hit the ground or your foot on the way down. Having done this the only other remaining parts are the top bearing cone and its dust cap (integral with the top cone on all C15 and B40 Swan-Neck frame models), and the loose ball bearings on all but OIF models.

Assume that the steering head bearings (like any other bearing when overhauling the bike) will need changing. Always renew the balls and additionally the cups and cones if there is any blemish on the shiny track around them where the balls have rolled. Similarly the OIF taper roller bearings; clean these and reject them if there are obvious signs of rusting or blemishes on the rollers or tracks.

Steering head bearings - removal

The outer parts of the steering head bearings - the 'cups' - should be a tight fit in the headstock and therefore require to be tapped out from behind with a hammer and suitable piece of metal bar to act as a drift. On C15 and B40 Swan Neck frames the drift will need to be angled to reach behind the cup as these are deeply recessed in the headstock *(see fig 4.11)*. Without the shaped drift to remove the bearing cups from the Swan-Neck frames, then a stubborn and worn out cup can be removed by doing a run of weld (with a MIG welder) around the inside of the cup along the bearing track. As the weld cools the cup will contract and fall out.

The lower cone is a tight fit on the yoke on most models and may require careful use of two slim tyre levers or screwdrivers under opposite edges of the cone to free it.

On OIF models the yoke stem can be unscrewed from the bottom yoke after removal of the locknut to facilitate removal of the bottom cone. For this design, the inner race of the taper roller bearings should slide on the yoke stem with no trace of play or wobble.

Yokes Reassembly to the Frame, All Models

Reassembling the yokes, starting with a bare headstock is fairly straightforward.

Fitting steering head bearings

Outer races

Fitting the outer races (the bearing cup) of the steering head bearings should be a straightforward tap into place in the headstock with a mallet. The outer race should be a tight fit in the headstock. Check the housing is clean before fitting it. Any signs of looseness or movement here will be magnified in use and feel like play in the steering bearings. If the bike has had a head-on impact the lower bearing housing may have been stretched thus creating such looseness.

Epoxy resin to fix a loose outer race in the headstock is a possibility but do this with the yokes and bearing assemblies in place to guarantee alignment while the glue cures.

If there is any doubt about the outer race sitting firmly and flat on the shoulder in the headstock (due to the cup being heavily chamfered externally) then in addition to the glue an accurately machined piece of tube with faced-off ends fitted inside the headstock and between the outer races for them to seat against is a good idea.

Inner races (cones) up to '71 - general principles
The lower race should be a tight fit on the bottom yoke and the top race a snug push-fit on the yoke stem. I wouldn't say 'tight' as the top cone invariably isn't, but any play is unwanted as far as the fit of the cones is concerned. The bottom cone is best fitted squarely by using a piece of tube of suitable length and diameter to act as a drift.

Swan Neck headrace bearings
C15 and B40 models with the Swan Neck frame have identical top and bottom cones, the lower being a tight fit on the bottom yoke. The top cone would therefore be a very loose fit on the top of the stem were it not for the dust cover having a protruding sleeve which fits inside the cone and reduces its inner diameter to suit the stem. The top cone should then be a close sliding fit on the upper portion of the stem with no sloppiness evident. C15 headrace bearings are the same as Bantam headrace bearings, D7 onward.

Welded/Duplex headrace bearings
Headrace bearings for all Welded/Duplex frames have differing top and bottom cones. The lower cone is thinner than the upper with a base flange $1/8$" thick, the upper cone being $3/16$" thick in this dimension and having a smaller centre hole to suit the diameter of the yoke stem. The bottom cone has a larger internal diameter to suit the shoulder on the stem where it meets the bottom yoke. The lower cone should be a tight fit on the bottom yoke.

Again, the upper race should be a snug sliding fit on the upper part of the stem but a common problem is wear of the stem where the cone sits at the lower end of the threaded portion. The best solution to this problem is to build up the worn portion around the stem with braze or bronze welding and carefully file this back to the correct diameter. Be careful not to allow the brazed area to spread too far up the threads and interfere with the yoke stem nut. A top cone which is loose on the stem due to this worn portion will exhibit the same behaviour as loose steering-head bearings - behaviour which will persist no matter how much the centre nut is tightened.

OIF taper roller headrace bearings
These should be a snug sliding fit on the yoke stem, both being the same size. (See *fig 4.20*, BSA's Service Sheet on thread changes on the OIF steering head stem and nuts). As the yoke stem unscrews from the bottom yoke on this design it is worth considering removal of this to aid fitment of the lower bearing inner race.

Problems with pattern headrace bearings
The same problem of a top cone which is loose on the yoke stem may be the result of inferior pattern head-race bearings being fitted – unfortunately, a too-common problem. If this is found to be the case by all means return them to the vendor and complain but it is unlikely that an exchange will solve the problem, the entire batch is likely to be just the same. Remedying this situation can be done by shimming or sleeving the top cone internally. Go for shimming if the clearance is small enough to accept a ring of shim steel between the cone and stem, but; the shim must be prevented from dropping through the cone. This can be done using Loctite (to the cone only) or by leaving sufficient shim protruding from the cone to allow its ends to be carefully flared and persuaded over to form a flange top and bottom of the cone. A small knife blade can be used for this to carefully and gradually flare the shim ends.

```
                                         NOVEMBER 1972
                                         No. 23/72

         BSA            SERVICE  SHEET

                        STEERING HEAD BEARING ADJUSTMENT
```

In order to provide a fine adjustment for the steering head bearings, the thread on the stem and the adjusting nut has been revised from 16 tpi to 24 tpi.

It is essential than, if either the nut or the stem is being renewed, a check is made to ensure that the threads on the two components correspond.

Note: Although the 1972 Replacement Parts Lists show the new component numbers, these items have not, in fact, been introduced until the 1973 season. Hence for models built prior to 1973, the components shown below should be specified.

ITEM	TWIN CYL. MODELS	TWIN CYL. MODELS (POLICE ONLY)	SINGLE CYL. MODELS	THREE CYL. MODELS
Bottom Yoke Assembly	97-4082	97-4226	–	97-4138
Steering Stem	–	–	97-4116	–
Steering Stem Nut (without damper)	97-4029	97-4029	97-4029	–
Steering Stem Nut (with damper)	97-4029	97-4029	–	97-4159

Fig 4.21. BSA service sheet about changes to the threads on the steering head stem and nut of the OIF forks

Making a sleeve (on a lathe) is not easy if the thickness required is only a few thou. It is therefore a better proposition to obtain a top cone for an A10 or A65 (these models have a much thicker yoke stem, hence a larger hole in an otherwise identical cone) and turn a thicker sleeve which is a press-fit in the cone and push-fit on the stem.

Fitting the yokes to the frame (except OIF '71 on)

These have loose ball bearings (Swan Neck frames $^3/_{16}$" diameter, Welded/Duplex ¼") and fitting them requires the balls to be stuck into the cups with grease. The books always say fit a full complement of balls (about 25 per race) and then remove one; in practice fit as many as you can so long as a gap of some size remains in the ring of balls. With both sets of ball bearings retained in the cups by grease, proceed with the assembly.

Fit the yoke stem nut to the top yoke and check that its lower end protrudes through the yoke so that it alone and not the underside of the yoke will bear against the top cone/dust cover (when fitted, daylight should be visible between the top yoke and the top cone dust cover).

Place the top cone dust cover and top yoke with stem nut within easy reach and offer up the bottom yoke carefully so the stem comes up through the headstock. Make sure the bottom cone seats properly in its bearing race and maintain upward pressure to keep it there while you fit the top cone/dust cover and screw on the top yoke. See why you placed the top yoke 'in easy reach'? You can't let go of the bottom yoke, and if you do it will drop, disturbing the balls and that means you have to start again. OIF models having caged rollers rather than loose balls, and are therefore more user friendly for this job.

Also in easy reach is a spanner for the centre nut if it needs persuasion; usually at this stage it is easy to spin the top yoke with the centre nut to screw this on. Screw down the yoke stem nut to obtain correct bearing clearance with free movement. This will be indicated by the yokes flopping sideways easily due gravity with no play being evident at the bearings. The difference between play at the bearings and too tight (binding) will be only a few degrees of rotation of the centre-nut, not half a turn. After this align the top yoke with the bottom one but don't fully tighten the centre nut pinch bolt.

Fit the 'trousers and headlamp brackets
Next to fit, on most models to '70, are the fork 'trousers' for C15/B40 road models and headlamp brackets on the other models. The OIF wire headlamp brackets can be fitted at any time.

Fit the forks to the yokes
The fork legs with springs and any associated parts (washers, gaiters etc) can be fitted intact to the yokes if they have been previously rebuilt on the bench. Alternatively (more so the later models as explained previously) the bare stanchion can be fitted to the yokes.

The steel (2 off) and rubber (1 off) washers fitted above the springs on most models '67 to '70 will be forced up into the headlamp bracket as the complete stanchion is fitted or the rubber and upper steel washer can first be fitted alone inside the shroud. It is a good idea to retro-fit these washers to help exclude water on all models using BSA heavyweight forks (C15 competition, B40 etc).

On all models to '70, fitting the complete fork leg to the yokes will be made simple by fitting the stanchion puller tool to the stanchion top and offering this up through the yokes (*see fig 4.1*). When it emerges, fit the collar and nut to the tool; this can then be tightened to draw the stanchion up through the yokes. When fully engaged with the top yoke, tighten the bottom yoke pinch bolt to grip the stanchion so it doesn't drop when the puller is removed. OIF stanchions can simply be gripped by hand and persuaded upward into the yokes; rotating as you go will help. Rod-Damper forks will require the damper rod with its rubber to be pushed down far enough inside the stanchion for the tool to engage. Before doing this ensure that you possess the means to reach inside and pull the rod back up later; some long nosed pliers for example in lieu of a purpose made tool - a length of steel bar, drilled and internally threaded $^5/_{16}$" BSCy at one end. With the stanchion secured in place by the bottom yoke pinch bolt, remove the tool and replace it with the fork top-nut and washer.

With both stanchions thus fitted check for free steering movement, no play at the headstock and parallel stanchions. BSA originally produced a service tool (the 'fork alignment gauge' shown earlier) for checking that the fork legs are parallel but the Mk.1 human eyeball will serve just as well if the sliders are viewed edge-on and lined up by eye.

Check also that daylight can be seen under the top yoke between it and the top bearing dust cover, ie that only the lower end of the centre nut rests on the dust cover. The top yoke can be clamped onto the centre nut at any height; so long as the centre nut protrudes beneath the yoke.

When satisfied slacken the bottom yoke pinch bolts, fully tighten the stanchion top nuts, then the bottom yoke pinch bolts, then the top yoke centre nut pinch bolt/nut. Go over the checks again including correct fork movement from side to side then put the kettle on.

Identification of Fork Components for your Unit Single

Oil Seal holders

The chrome oil seal holders fitted to BSA Heavyweight and Rod-Damper forks originally came in two common lengths; short, approximately 4' in length for use with gaiters, and long at approximately 5' for use under metal shrouds *(fig 4.22)*. Those which you may find available today can be anywhere between these two sizes in length! The short example with the external circlip was used from '68 onward, and suits the later type fork gaiters, as explained below. Note that the Triumph type chrome oil-seal holder *(see figs 4.15 and 4.16)* which was used for '69 and '70 is not interchangeable with the BSA examples shown here.

Fig 4.22. Oil seal holders for C15 (left), Heavyweight and Rod-Damper forks The C15 item is the later type with the facility for fitment of a second upper seal. Retro fit this to earlier single seal holders if you can find them

Gaiters

Two types of rubber gaiter were used; the first, needing external clips to hold them in place suit seal holders and headlamp brackets which terminate in a slight flare. The second type of gaiter used from '68 to '70 has internal grooves to locate on the ridge or circlip on the '68 onward oil seal holders (including Triumph type forks for '69 and '70) and the flange on the lower edge of the headlamp bracket. No external clips are needed on this second type of gaiter.

Fork stanchion identification

All the Unit Single fork types have stanchions of a specific design which differ from each other and can be spotted at a glance when encountered in naked condition *(see Fig 4.25)*.

C15 Star, SS80 and Sportsman.
Parallel sided with a short taper fit for the top yoke. Four $^3/_{16}$" diameter bleed holes around the bottom end with two additional $^1/_{16}$" holes on one side. Bare steel, $20^3/_8$" long.

BSA Heavyweight as fitted to C15 T and S, and B40 to '66
Tapering above and below the bottom yoke at which the stanchion diameter is largest. Two $^1/_{16}$" bleed holes on one side near the bottom. Bare steel finish (except chromed for C15S), deep taper fit for the top yoke. $21^7/_8$" long.

Front Forks 81

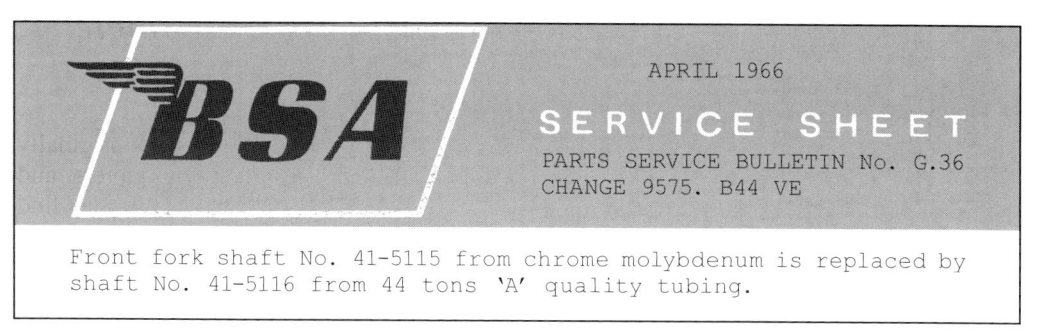

> **APRIL 1966**
> **SERVICE SHEET**
> PARTS SERVICE BULLETIN No. G.36
> CHANGE 9575. B44 VE
>
> Front fork shaft No. 41-5115 from chrome molybdenum is replaced by shaft No. 41-5116 from 44 tons 'A' quality tubing.

Fig 4.23. BSA Service Bulletin showing the material and part number change for the narrow yoke Rod-Damper fork legs. The new part was subsequently used for all models employing this fork

Rod-Damper

As fitted to B25/B44 '66/67 and all B40 Military Mk1 for the Narrow Yoke forks. As per BSA heavyweight fork stanchions except for four $1/8$" bleed holes spaced around the stanchion bottom end and with a knurled grip pattern at the bottom yoke position. Available with a chrome plated finish for the B44GP.

Rod-Damper stanchions, as fitted to 1968 B25/B44, B40 Military Mk.2 and Rough Rider, also B44VS '68 to '70, are for Wide Yoke forks. As Narrow Yoke except no knurled grip pattern at the bottom yoke and $22\frac{1}{2}$" long.

Shuttle-Valve

As fitted to '69/'70 B25 and B44SS. Parallel sided, slightly larger diameter at the bottom yoke, deep taper fit for the top yoke. Eight $3/16$" bleed holes around the bottom end (*fig 4.24*), originally available in bare steel and, in '70, with hard chromed finish over the lower half. These differ from the equivalent stanchions used on Triumph forks at the time only in the differing taper to suit the BSA top yoke. This design is therefore BSA from the bottom yoke upward when fitted to a Unit Single (and twin) and wholly Triumph below this.

OIF

As fitted to all Unit Singles '71 onward. Parallel sided stanchions, slight step down in diameter above the bottom yoke, deep taper fit for the top yoke. No bleed holes, hard chrome finish all over. $25\frac{7}{8}$" long. These are commonly known as 'conical' stanchions due to the front wheel hub design used with them. Similar plated stanchions lacking the taper fit for the top yoke are the 'disc' stanchions fitted to '73 onward Triumph twin models.

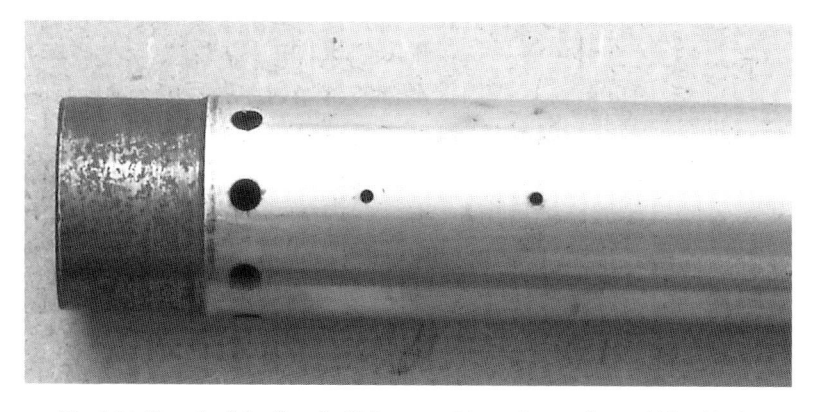

Fig 4.24. Detail of the Shuttle-Valve stanchion oil transfer and bleed holes

Fig 4.25. 1969 to 1970 fork stanchions

The fork stanchions used from 1959 to 1970 are shown in *fig 4.25*. These are, from the top

1   C15 all years. Four $3/16$" and two $1/16$" bleed holes.

2   All C15 competition and B40 to 1966 ($21^7/_8$" long), two $1/16$" bleed holes.

3   The Rod-Damper equivalent, four $5/32$" bleed holes. Note knurled finish at bottom yoke position. For 'narrow yoke' use 1966 to 1970. This and the above stanchion could be obtained with chrome finish for use on competition models with bare stanchions between the yokes.

4   Rod-Damper 'Wide Yoke', 1968 to 1970, $22^1/_2$" long.

5   Triumph type Shuttle-Valve, eight $3/16$" bleed holes, 1969 to 1970. 1970 version shown with two additional $5/64$" bleed holes and hard chrome plated lower half.

Fork stanchion interchangeability

As mentioned above, two versions of the Rod-Damper forks were used on Unit Singles. Fitted to '66/'67 B44, '67 C25/B25, and all '67-on WDB40 (B40 Military Mk1) is the 'narrow yoke' version at $6^1/_8$" between stanchion centres.

The narrow yoke Rod-Damper forks are the same width as the earlier roadster B40 and C15 competition forks. Hence, the complete fork legs are interchangeable in the yokes to enable double damping of the '67 type to be applied to these earlier models. This interchangeability of stanchions opens up a perhaps confusing level of swapping potential for sliders and front hubs. 7" full or half-width and 8' full or half-width hubs can all be fitted to both Heavyweight and Rod-Damper forks if the correct sliders can be found to marry between hub type and stanchions. The C15 and OIF forms, which by dint of their lack of commonality with other Unit Single forks, leave little scope for 'playing'. The main area for non-standard combinations of parts lies with the remaining three fork types..

Front Forks 83

The '68 to '70 'wide yoke' yokes (6¾" between centres) and stanchions are also interchangeable with the narrow yoke types, but due to differences in stanchion length between the yokes the two types should not be mixed. It should be remembered that the same yokes were used in '68 with wide yoke Rod-damper stanchions and in '69 with the Triumph Shuttle-Valve stanchions.

Fork Yokes Identification.

Prior to '71, two widths of forks were fitted on Unit Singles, the 'narrow yokes' and the 'wide yokes'. Variations exist with each width of yoke, particularly the narrow type.

Narrow Yokes

These are illustrated in *figs 4.26 - 4.29*.

C15 Star yokes

Only one set was used for all years. Look for part number 40-5022 under the top yoke. These have no bosses for the speedo mounting. The bottom yoke has steering stop pegs.

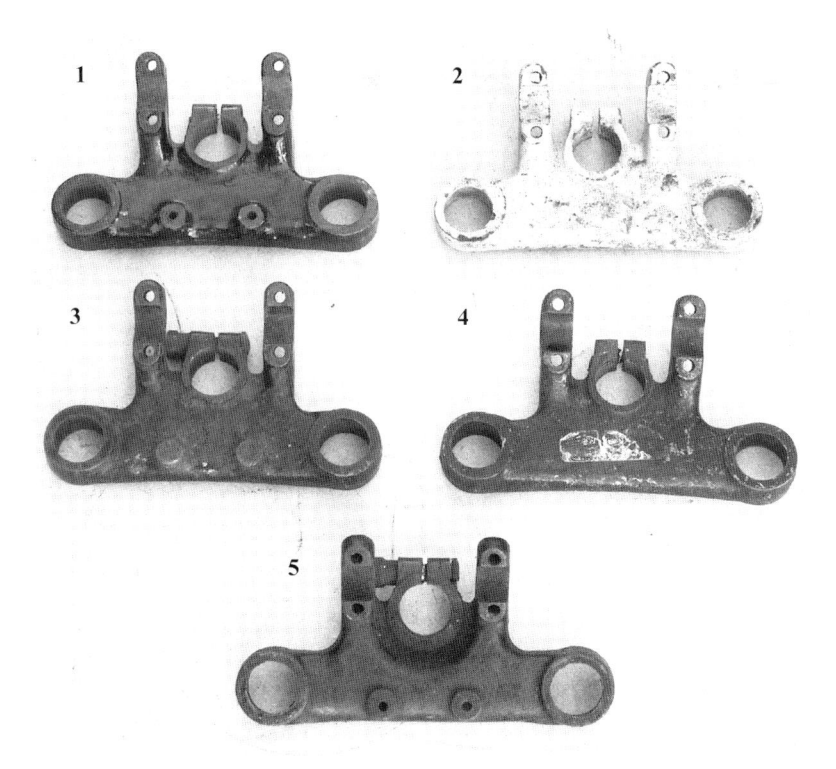

Fig 4.26. Top yokes to '70

Narrow yoke
1. C15/B40/B44 off-road models to '67 and B25/B44 road models '67, marked 40-4094 or more commonly 40-5116
2. C15 roadster (no speedo bosses) marked 40-5022:
3. B40 Military Mk1 marked 40-5116 (speedo bosses not machined),
4. B40 roadster (no speedo bosses) marked 41-5012:

Wide yoke
5. All models '68 to '70 (except B40 Military Mk1) marked 97-2525

¹/₄ inch difference

Fig 4.27. C15 competition top yokes overlaid to show the ¹/₄ inch difference in yoke stem to stanchion distance between the '59 item (marked 40-5094) and the '60 onward item (40-5116) seen here on top. The corresponding bottom yoke for the '59 competition top yoke is essentially the same as the later bottom yoke but with the stanchion bosses machined to suit the slightly steeper fork leg angle.

Narrow yokes: Heavyweight and Rod-Damper forks

'Narrow yoke' yokes were used on both of these fork types and whilst being interchangeable, the yokes display a variety of detail differences.

Top yokes

The top yoke will be marked 40-4094 on its underside for 1959 C15 competition models only (these yokes give a slightly steeper fork angle) and 40-5116 thereafter *(fig 4.27)*. Other variations in the narrow top yokes (regardless of use on Heavyweight or Rod-Damper forks) relate only to the speedo mounting bosses: spot-faced and drilled indicates C15 competition use or B25/B44 to '67. If the speedo bosses are not machined this indicates B40 Military (and also some D10/D14 Bantam models which used a similar fork). A similar top yoke marked 41-5012 and lacking speedo mounting bosses is for B40 roadsters only.

Bottom yokes

The corresponding 'narrow yoke' bottom yoke will have two upstanding stop pegs by the yoke stem if used with a swan-neck frame. These are machined off for use with the '63 Welded/Duplex frame. '67 Roadsters have an additional ⁵/₁₆' hole through this bottom yoke to mount the diode heat sink. The B40 Military bottom yoke has pinch bolt holes enlarged to ³/₈", all previous being ⁵/₁₆".

Wide yokes: Rod-Damper and Triumph forks

The 'wide yoke' fork was fitted to the '68 to '70 B25/B44 and B40 Military Mk2. The wide yokes are visually identified by the centre nut being recessed down into the upper surface of the top yoke. This gives an increased distance between top and bottom yokes compared to the previous narrow yoke design. On the underside the part number 97-2525 will be visible. The corresponding bottom yoke has the usual angled stanchion pinch slots for '68 and '69 and central slots (much as the subsequent OIF yoke) for '70. *(See fig 4.26, no.5 for the recess.)*

Front Forks 85

Fig 4.28. Narrow Yokes. Bottom yokes,

1. *C15 competition '59 to '62 for Swan Neck frame (also found on some prototype B40 Military machines*
2. *Off Road '63 to '67 and B40 Military Mk1*
3. *B25/B44 roadster, '67 with hole for mounting the diode heat sink*

These are all basically the same casting which allows fairly easy modification of one into another

Fig 4.29. The C15 (left) and B40 Roadster (right) bottom yokes - all years.

The projection behind the yoke stems is drilled to allow the owner to insert a padlock as a rudimentary form of steering lock to deter thieves. The small cutaway on the leading edge is to allow the speedo cable an easier route; early examples of these yokes omit this feature. Although the B40 item is clearly more robust than the C15 and with larger diameter stanchion holes, the stanchion distance between centres is the same.

The two vertical steering stop pegs are easily bent out of position but can be persuaded back by localised heating.

OIF yokes

OIF yokes are the same for all models (*fig 4.31*) from '71 onward with only detail changes to the finish as explained above, and also enlarged bottom yoke steering stops for '72 and the addition of spot face and drilling to mount the Zener diode on the bottom yoke on MX Models from '72 *(fig 4.32)*.

Checking yoke condition

The yokes are likely to display twisting after a high mileage This condition can of course be the result of accident damage but normal use will gradually cause twisting due to braking forces being applied mostly to one leg. The easy, and BSA recommended way to check yokes for straightness, is to put a pair of (straight) stanchions in the bottom yoke and view it edge on. Any deviation from straight will be easily spotted by the stanchions not being exactly parallel. This also works for the top yoke. Also check that the handlebar lugs have not been bent, as can happen if the bike has been dropped, by placing a straight edges along both lugs at the same time; the straight edges should of course be seen to be parallel when viewed. The

Fig 4.30. Left. 'Wide yoke' bottom yokes, '70 above, '68 to '69 below. The pinch bolt holes are tapped ³/₈" UNF

Fig 4.31. Below left. OIF aluminium yokes as used on the Unit Single range, in effect, one-size-fits-all

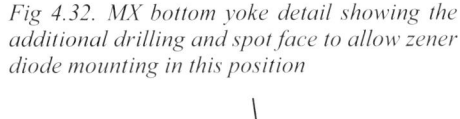

Fig 4.32. MX bottom yoke detail showing the additional drilling and spot face to allow zener diode mounting in this position

upward protruding steering stops on C15 and B40 bottom yokes for the Swan Neck frame are prone to distortion but can be reshaped when red hot.

Correcting distorted yokes requires a welding torch to heat the steel yokes to cherry red adjacent to the stanchion holes so they can be twisted back. Old stanchions clamped in place in the yoke make a good lever for this while the yoke or yoke stem is held in a vice, and if two stanchions are in position you can tell when the yoke has been bent back to shape by their being parallel. Do try to tweak both stanchion bosses in this way to meet the other one 'half way' rather than bending one fully to match the other

The OIF aluminium yokes can be softened prior to applying pressure by smearing household soap over them and heating with a blow torch. The soap will act as an indicator that the correct temperature to soften (anneal) the aluminium has been reached by turning black. Allow the yoke to cool and then apply pressure.

Old stanchions through the offending bent yoke are good for applying pressure while one of them is gripped in a vice.

Fork Springs.

Ride quality depends to a large degree on the properties of the fork springs fitted. Firstly they should be a matched pair. They should produce a ride height for the front end of the bike which when at rest has the forks compressed by about ¼ of the total extent of compression possible. They should possess sufficient compressive strength to resist normal road shocks without allowing the forks to compress excessively and 'bottom out', whilst not being over resistant and thus produce 'topping out' on the rebound when riding over bumps. Several variables affect this performance:-

The fork springs.
Have you got the right ones for your model? Two factors determine spring strength, overall length and wire thickness. C15 road models have no alternatives to the standard springs but a range of alternatives were available and interchangeable for BSA Heavyweight/Rod-Damper/Shuttle-Valve forks (*see fig 4.25)*, and for the OIF machines for which the '70's Triumph twin parts books can be plundered.

Weight of motorcycle.
This in itself is not as simple as it sounds as the real issue is the amount of weight carried by the forks and this varies during use. For example, when braking a large proportion of the motorcycles weight is transferred to the forks and front wheel, much less at other times. The weight distribution can also be markedly affected by rider position and extra weight being carried; luggage or pillion (don't tell her I said that). The weight distribution, for example, is easily affected by changing standard handlebars for clip-on's (more weight forward) or high-rise bars (more weight rearward). The former may result in forks which feel solid and less compliant; the latter may result in forks 'topping out'.

Oil
The way the springs allow movement in the sliders depends on the correct quantity and grade of oil being contained within as this acts as a lubricant, cushioning and damping medium: thicker oil means stiffer forks.

On the whole BSA got it right and a machine in standard condition should ride well on the fork springs specified in the manual. Changes to the machine may produce problems as outlined above and require new springs of different rating to restore ride quality.

```
                    AUGUST 1969
                    No. 230

  BSA        SERVICE SHEET

                    All Models 1968/70
                    FRONT FORK SPRINGS

The model B25 Fork was fitted with springs rated at 34 lbs/in, but, to
provide a more comfortable ride, now has springs rated at 26½ lbs/in.

The springs detailed below, which are all interchangeable with
each other in pairs, include those fitted to all current models

    MODEL              SPRING        RATING         COLOUR CODE
                       No.
    B25      1968/69   89-5036       34 lb/in       Red/Green
    B44SS    1968/69   89-5036       34 lb/in       Red/Green
    B44VS    1968/70   89-5036       34 lb/in       Red/Green
    B25      1969/70   97-3678       26½lb/in       White/Green
    B44SS    1969/70   97-3678       26½lb/in       White/Green
    A50/65   solo      89-5036       34 lb/in       Red/Green
    A50/65   s/car     42-5145       50 lb/in       Yellow
    A50/65   Police    68-5043       37 lb/in       Red/Yellow
    A75      Rocket 3  97-1892       32½lb/in       Yellow/Green
```

Fig 4.33. BSA front fork spring rates, earlier and later models are similarly equipped

In lieu of correct replacement springs, shortening or jacking up your existing ones may make an improvement, but this is not likely to be as satisfactory as correct replacements because these will be different by dint of length *and* wire strength. Try finding springs from a heavier or lighter model as a direct replacement. The internal fork springs for C15 road models and OIF models are similar and easily confused. The C15 springs are 18½" long, OIF 19½" long - both give or take ¼"

Stanchion bottom nut

There are a number of stanchion bottom nut types to retain the bottom bush (*fig 4.34-4.35*).

C15 Star	one type all years
Heavyweight	⅝' diameter centre hole
Rod-Damper	¹⁵/₁₆' diameter centre hole 97-2709 H 2639 41-5130
	¹⁵/₁₆'diameter centre hole with tubular extension 41-5190, generally used on the roadsters thereby resulting in slightly less fork travel. Consult your parts book for original fitment but as these nuts can be swapped, make sure you fit two the same, this being more important than which type you fit.
Triumph	one type only, similar to C15 but with larger central hole to accommodate the Shuttle-Valve assembly.
OIF	One type only with integral plastic damper rod bush (*see fig 4.19*)

Fork stanchion top nuts

Again the different models had different nuts as shown in *fig 4.36*

Front Forks 89

Fig 4.34. Bottom stanchion nuts for the Heavyweight (left), Rod-Damper (centre) and the tubular extension nut (right). All need to be fitted with the correct thick washer shown.

Fig 4.35. Bottom stanchion nuts for, left, Shuttle-Valve forks '69 to '70, and right, C15. Very similar in appearance, both of these forks were of Triumph design.

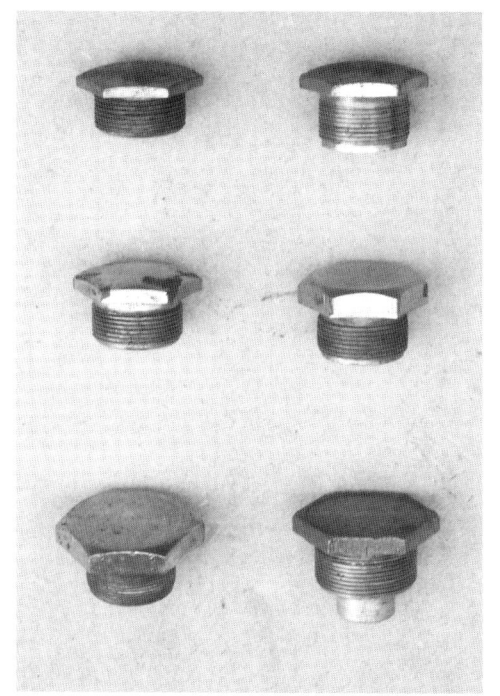

Fig 4.36. Top nuts

Top row
C15 (left) and Heavyweight fork top nut (right). The only difference is the length of thread which is 20tpi Cycle thread.

Middle row
Rod-Damper forks top nuts, '66 (left) and '67 onward (right). These are solid underneath except for the $^5/_{16}$" tapped hole for the damper rod. Still 20tpi Cycle thread.

Bottom row
Shuttle-Valve forks top nut '69-'70 (left) with 28tpi UNF thread. This is a flat-topped nut; alternatives with a slightly raised top were fitted on other models.

OIF fork top nut, '72 version shown (right). The slightly recessed top of the nut is to accept the fork oil capacity sticker. The '71 version of this nut lacks the top recess and sticker for the fork oil and is bright chrome plated. The spigot locates the upper end of the internal fork spring

> **SEPTEMBER 1971**
> **No 33/71**
>
> **BSA SERVICE SHEET**
> SEALING OF FORK TOP CAP NUTS
> ALL MODELS
>
> A sealing compound is being applied to the thread of fork top nuts during assembly to prevent oil seepage.
>
> In the event of these nuts being disturbed the threads must be cleaned thoroughly and treated with Loctite Hydraulic Sealant as recommended by the manufacturers

Fig 4.37. BSA Service Sheet - sealing the fork top nuts

> **SEPTEMBER 1967**
> **No. 162**
>
> **BSA SERVICE SHEET**
> FRONT FORK TOP & BOTTOM YOKES
> ALL MODELS
>
> The machine steering and braking performance can be adversely affected if certain simple precautions are not clearly understood and properly followed when dismantling and re-assembling front forks.
>
> 1. Before re-assembling the steering head and fork legs, a thorough check must be made to ensure that the bores of the bottom yoke and the taper holes in the top yoke, are free from residual paint, dirt or grease.
>
> 2. During assembly, the forks should be pumped up and down several times to ensure alignment.
>
> 3. The wheel spindle can then be tightened up, followed by the two (2) fork top caps, steering stem cap nut, two (2) bottom yoke pinch bolts, steering stem pinch bolt and nut, and lastly the wheel spindle pinch bolt.
>
> 4. Always apply the correct torque load to each nut and bolt when tightening, as detailed in the current workshop Manuals, and Service Sheets.

Fig 4.38. BSA Service Sheet on fork dismantling and reassembly

Front Mudguard Mounting

I haven't yet come across any significant design faults in any of the standard front mudguard mounting arrangements excepting perhaps, the OIF effort (see Chapter 14 Mudguards for OIF front mudguard mounting).

On most models the main enemy of the mudguard is the mounting on the brackets from the fork sliders. These are 'unsprung' meaning they go up and down with the wheel and therefore the mudguard mounting gets shaken about an awful lot and this means it is subject to fatigue cracking. The OIF T and MX models are exempt from this as their 'sprung' mudguard is rubber mounted on a bracket from the bottom yoke.

Basically, most of the various front mudguard support arrangements used to the end of '70 are made of thick enough metal to cope with the vibration. One possible exception is the C15/B40 fully valanced guards which sometimes lose their welded-on tabs. However, their 'Y' brackets from the fork sliders are perfectly adequate. There is a tendency for the $^5/_{16}$" 'Y' bracket mounting studs on the sliders of C15 and B40 models to come adrift. The remedy is to carefully braze a suitable short length of stud back on.

Our American friends, apparently, have a saying that the British approach to engineering is simply to put more metal around anything which breaks. In this way BSA succeeded admirably in keeping front mudguard vibration fractures at bay until they decided to 're-invent the wheel' with the OIF models. The thin steel support rods are welded to the OIF front guard and will often crack around the area of the weld. Two solutions to this were introduced by BSA/Triumph in 1972. One, an improved guard for current models, with an additional central piece of rod welded in on both sides and, two a bolted-on centre stay for retro-fitting to 1971 models. Of the two, the bolted-on solution is more successful as the welded-on version is itself prone to fatigue cracking where it meets the guard.

On most Unit Singles, fitting the correct, standard stays and brackets will result in a pleasingly positioned guard. Doing this with the '69 B25 and B44 Shooting Star models will result in the leading edge of the guard being too close to the tyre; not nice on the eye when you step back and look at it. BSA recognised this and introduced new slider-to-stay brackets during '70. These protrude perpendicular to the sliders rather than angling downward as per the '69 items, thus raising the front of the guard. Fitting these to the 69' forks to raise the guard is an easy swap (*fig 4.39*).

Fig 4.39. New flat mudguard stay mounting bracket intoduced for the '70 season on B25, TR25w and B44SS

Headlamp Brackets.

All models with a separate headlamp have brackets from which the headlamp is supported. On all but OIF models these also shroud the fork legs between and below the yokes, or locate the top end of the gaiters, if fitted. Knowing which version of bracket should be used on each Unit Single can be a problem if yours are missing or wrong. This problem is compounded by confusion with other similar, but different brackets used on the BSA twins and Bantams.

C15/B40 fork trousers

C15 and B40 Star models used a 'trouser' assembly comprising tubular shrouds for the fork legs and which also wraps around the yokes and is bolted to a shortened headlamp shell. The trouser assembly for the C15 has tubular shrouds $1^7/_8$" diameter. That for the B40 has tubes with a $2^1/_4$" diameter and is physically wider to accommodate the more substantial B40 yokes *(see figs 4.40 and 4.42)*. These trouser assemblies should not be confused with the equivalent assembly used at the time for the D7 Bantam, which is smaller, and the A50/A65 which is the same size as the B40 item but differs by having a rounded rather than flat upper edge behind the headlamp shell. '65 B40 USA models used an assembly with the trouser legs cut short and flared to accommodate gaiters, and the USA SS90 version with separate chrome headlamp used separate conventional brackets to accept gaiters, as per the '63 onward C15 competition item *(see fig 4.43)*

The B40 trouser assembly is wider than the equivalent C15 item although the distance between the stanchion centres is the same for both C15 and B40 Heavyweight/Narrow Yoke forks, at $6^1/_8$" between centres. The extra overall width of the B40 'trouser' assembly shown here compared to the C15 item is due to the increased diameter of the trouser legs which is needed to clear the larger diameter oil seal holders of the Heavyweight forks. The top cover for the 'trouser' assembly is therefore found in two widths for Unit Singles; $8^1/_8$" wide for C15 and $8^3/_8$" wide for B40. A Narrower version at $7^1/_4$" wide is for Bantams, and one, as per the B40 item, but additionally featuring a circular steering lock hole, is for pre-unit A and B models.

Fig 4.41. Trouser assembly top yoke cover

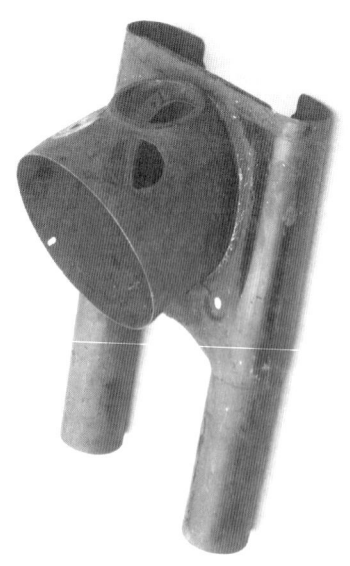

Fig 4.40. B40 fork trouser assembly

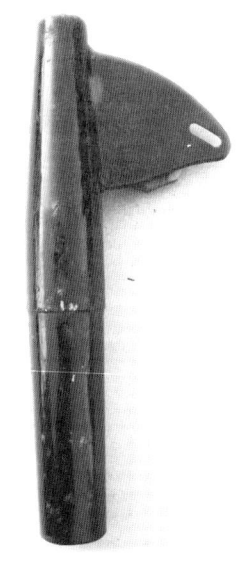

Fig 4.42. C15 Sportsman headlamp bracket

Front Forks 93

C15 Sportsman models of '66 and '67 fitted the MCH56 separate headlamp which necessitated independent mounting brackets with a tubular leg to reach downward over the chrome oil seal holders in usual BSA practice. These brackets have smaller diameter tubes than the similar long brackets/shrouds used on many BSA heavyweight forks. The C15 sportsman item is similar but larger than the equivalent long brackets used on D10/D14 Bantam Sports models at that time.

The C15 Sportsman headlamp bracket (*fig 4.42*) has the lower portion below the join flattened on its inner surface and the top edge of the tubular portion is rounded inward below the top yoke.

Headlamp brackets for Heavyweight and Rod Damper forks
Unit Single headlamp brackets for heavyweight and Rod-Damper forks fall into two camps: those for narrow yoke forks and those for wide yoke forks, the determining factor being the distance between the pinch bolt-hole centre and the top edge. Narrow yoke headlamp brackets are shorter over this distance at $5^{13}/_{16}$" and wide yoke brackets longer at $6^{1}/_{2}$".

Fig 4.43 shows C15 competition headlamp brackets for models with lights. Left, '59 to '62, small ear and short length used with gaiters, mainly fitted to USA models. Centre, small ear and long shroud mostly fitted to UK models. Right the '63 -'65 replacement with large ear which was also available as the long shroud type. The long type shown centre is seemingly the same as fitted to early pre-unit C10 and C11 models.

C15 Scrambler models were built to two main specifications in this area; bare chromed stanchions between the yokes with spring shrouds below the bottom yoke borrowed from the earlier Gold Star models, or a plain tapered shroud minus the headlamp ears between the yokes with gaiters below. The former set-up was standard for the Home and General Export Market, the latter with gaiters being the norm for the USA market. The B44 GP followed Home market Scrambler practice with the spring shrouds below the bottom yoke now being polished aluminium rather than painted steel.

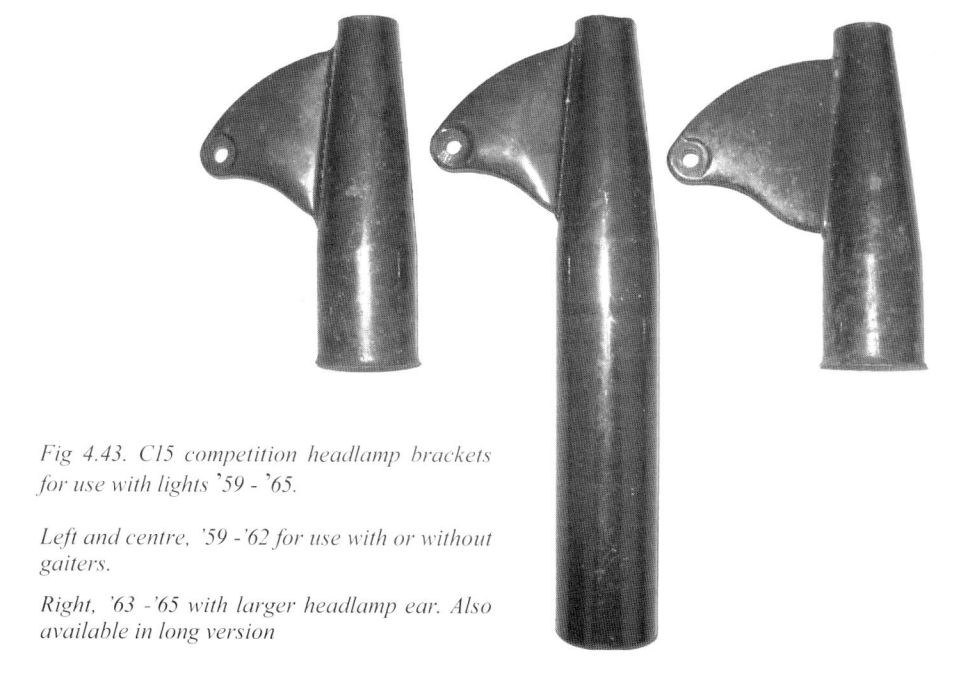

Fig 4.43. C15 competition headlamp brackets for use with lights '59 - '65.

Left and centre, '59 -'62 for use with or without gaiters.

Right, '63 -'65 with larger headlamp ear. Also available in long version

Narrow Yoke '66 -'67 headlamp brackets

The B44VE/VS followed previous C15 competition models practice at this time. The same long or short brackets but with larger, normal sized headlamp ears were used on Victor special models to '67. These now and subsequently, had slotted headlamp bolt holes to permit headlamp direction to be adjusted. '67 B25 and B44 road models used the long version of these shrouds. At a glance these are identical to those used on the '67 B44 Victor Special but have the ears positioned differently; ½" from the top edge of the shroud to the top edge of the ear on the Roadster item and a longer distance of 1" at this position for the VS item. Hence these have different part numbers.

The Narrow Yoke' headlamp brackets (*see fig 4.44*) are: left, '67 B/C25 and B44VR. Centre, '66 to '67 B44VS, and right, the equivalent '66 to '67 B44VS short bracket for use with gaiters as used on USA B44VS models. All 'narrow yoke' brackets are $5^{13}/_{16}$" from the pinch-bolt hole centre to the top.

The short version of the narrow yoke headlamp bracket was further modified for the B40 Military Mk1 (*fig 4.45*) by repositioning the headlamp ear, the addition of the air transfer tube on the front and a reinforcing strip around the position of the pinch bolt holes, now enlarged for $^3/_8$" bolts rather than the previous $^5/_{16}$". All the subsequent wide bottom yokes adopted the $^3/_8$" pinch bolts introduced on the military model.

Wide yoke headlamp brackets

Wide yoke headlamp brackets come in three types all with the same large headlamp ears and slotted headlamp bolt holes:

No dent on the rear surface.	'68 all B25 and B44SS, B40 Military Mk2.
Small dent $2^1/_4$" long on rear.	TR25w and B44VS '68
Large dent $3^1/_2$" long on rear.	All models '69 and '70.

The dents provide clearance with the petrol tank with the forks on full lock, the larger dent being required for the large steel tank fitted on B25 and B44 roadsters for '69 and '70

Left: '67 B25/C25 and B44VR
Centre: '66 to '67 B44VS
Right : '66 to '67 B44VS short bracket

Fig 4.44. Narrow Yoke headlamp brackets

Fig 4.45. B40 Military Mk1 headlamp bracket, usually available in green.

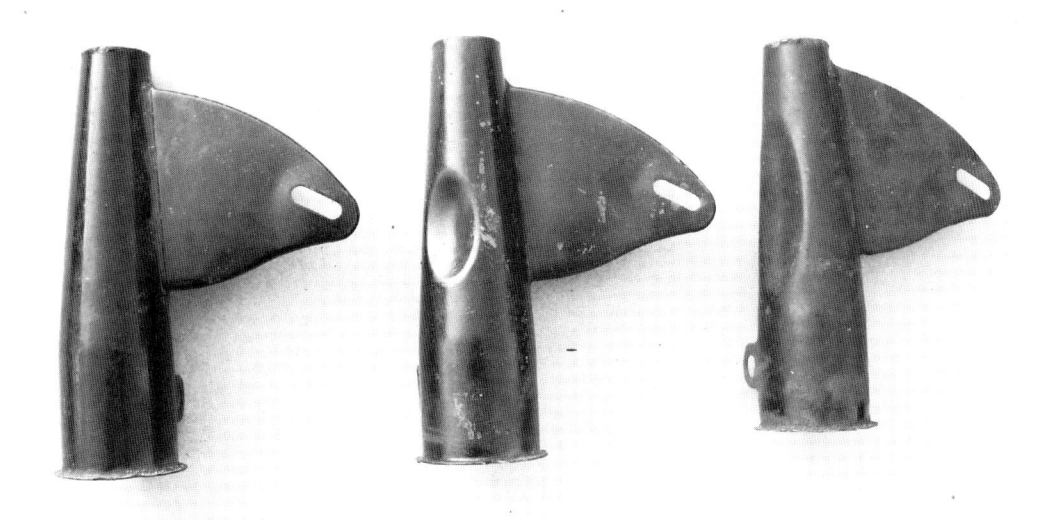

Fig 4.46. Wide Yoke headlamp brackets.
Left: B25S and B44SS '68. Centre: B44VS and TR25w '68. Right: All models '69 to '70.

The three versions of the 'wide yoke' headlamp brackets for Unit Single use were $6\frac{1}{2}$" from the pinch-bolt hole centre to the top (*see fig 4.46*). Left is '68 B25S and B44SS, centre is '68 B44VS and TR25w, right is for all models '69 to '70.

Damage commonly found on the headlamp brackets (understandable as they are quite vulnerable) usually shows as bent ears, splits around the pinch bolt holes, dents to the tubular portion and lower edges worn thin on the long shrouds due to rubbing against the chrome seal holder (they shouldn't do this, position them carefully when fitting). All such damage can be repaired with careful application of welding torch and persuasion.

Headlamp spacers
All headlamp brackets with slotted holes for the headlamp mounting bolts should be used with a spacer between the bracket and the shell which has a slightly domed outer end, the surface of the bracket around the slot should similarly be raised to suit the domed spacer and the thick chromed washer under the headlamp bolt head should be cupped to fit correctly over the domed bracket surface beneath it. All of this should permit easy adjustment of the headlight beam from side to side. The thickness of the headlamp spacers is dependent on the yoke width regardless of the 6" or 7" headlamp size – Narrow Yokes spacers $\frac{1}{8}$" thick, wide yokes $\frac{9}{16}$" thick. C15 sportsman headlamp spacers are an exception being $\frac{1}{2}$" thick. Some of the earlier unslotted competition brackets are found with the $\frac{1}{8}$" washer held captive on the inside of the ear.

Fork Interchangeability

All Unit Single forks can be swapped between models with no apparent shortcomings; ie by 'trading up' and fitting a better set from a later/bigger model onto your machine. The usual significant issues involved in fitting forks from another Unit Single (or other BSA, or indeed from any other model) are the headrace bearings and the steering-stop arrangements.

The basic approach to take with the headrace bearings is to keep to those which go with the frame and if necessary modify them to suit the yoke stem. I have not yet found it necessary to alter any Unit Single yoke stem length to make the yokes fit another Unit Single frame.

The steering-stop issue is a bit more involved when it comes to fitting later forks to a C15 or B40 swan-necked frame as this relies on the vertical stop-pegs on the bottom yoke hitting the headstock. Later bottom yokes do not have these pegs and would require something like them to be welded on (admittedly there are more obtrusive ways of achieving the same end). A fork swap in the other direction simply requires the stop-pegs to be removed from the bottom yoke as BSA originally did when fitting the early C15 competition/B40 bottom yoke to the Welded/Duplex frame (as per narrow yoke forks, until '67).

The steering stops for these and later yokes are now provided by the lower edge of the bottom yoke coming into contact with the steering stop bracket on the frame. All Welded/Duplex and OIF steering-stops line up nicely and therefore fitting OIF forks to a Welded/Duplex frame is not a problem in this regard. The steering head bearings are the main problem in achieving this, the simplest solution being to sleeve the Welded/Duplex bearing cones to suit the thinner OIF yoke stem.

Examining the possibilities of fitting forks from other models and marques is largely beyond the scope of this book. However, fork assemblies from other (larger or earlier) BSA models should not prevent problems beyond the already mentioned head race bearing and steering-stop issues and generally speaking, contemporary forks from Triumph twin models should not pose insurmountable problems. The only question is, why would you want to do it?

Fig 4.47. '59 C15T fitted with the steep forks used only for that year

5. BRAKES, HUBS AND WHEELS

Brake Shoes

As a rule, Unit Single brakes are generally OK and up to the job of stopping the machine in its original, intended role - one or two examples are particularly good at this. All follow the basic format of shoes carrying friction material which expand into contact with the inside of the hub; simple, effective and very much the norm until disc brakes started to become common fitment in the '70's.

This principle, applied to some ten different Unit Single brakes with some featuring detail improvements to the design, means that all are easy to cope with, but, all are also capable of not performing to their best unless looked after; very much in keeping with the whole British Bike ethos.

Most owners neglect their brakes until the performance has deteriorated enough to give them a scare on the road. I'm not expecting to change your habits of a lifetime, but hopefully I can encourage the reader to be more aware of the lump of metal in the middle of each wheel and keep an eye on things. Your life may depend on it.

Most Unit Single brake shoes carry symmetrical linings and are therefore interchangeable in the leading and trailing positions. But there are exceptions to this. The B40 road models and the 1968 B25/TR25w both use the same front hub and brake design which has floating brakes with asymmetrical shoes. *Fig 5.1* is a BSA service sheet from 1961 giving the part numbers for the floating brakes, and showing the position of the asymmetric brake shoes. Notice the different position of the linings for the leading and trailing shoes. Putting the shoes in the wrong way round will noticeably reduce brake performance. This feature of asymmetrical linings was also used on the OIF 6" front and conical rear brake. Pattern shoes for these brakes can be found with symmetrical linings – idiot proof but not so good for the brake. Some BSA/Triumph factory literature unfortunately shows these brake shoes fitted the wrong way round!

In general, simply putting your Unit Single brake together 'by the book' should produce an acceptable stopper. But, as can be seen from the following Service Sheets, braking efficiency was an issue taken seriously by BSA, as it should equally be by today's rider *(figs 5.1-5.4)*. These refer primarily to the post-'71 brakes at which some criticism has been levelled. The existence of these Sheets, which explain how to obtain best performance in a degree of detail hitherto not required, possibly suggests that there is no smoke without fire.

NOVEMBER 1961
No. 65

BSA SERVICE SHEET

FLOATING BRAKE SHOES

It is essential that floating brake shoes now being fitted to both 7" and 8" diameter brakes are correctly assembled. The assembly arrangement is clearly shown in the drawing.

Floating brake shoes can be fitted to all A and B group machines with 7" or 8" brakes, with frame prefix letters FA, GA, FB and B40 respectively. The parts required for conversion are as follows:

7" Diameter Brake
Leading Shoe 68-5515
Trailing Shoe 68-5516
Pivot pad (2) 68-5519

8" Diameter Brake.
Leading Shoe 68-5524
Trailing Shoe 68-5525
Pivot pad (2) 68-5519

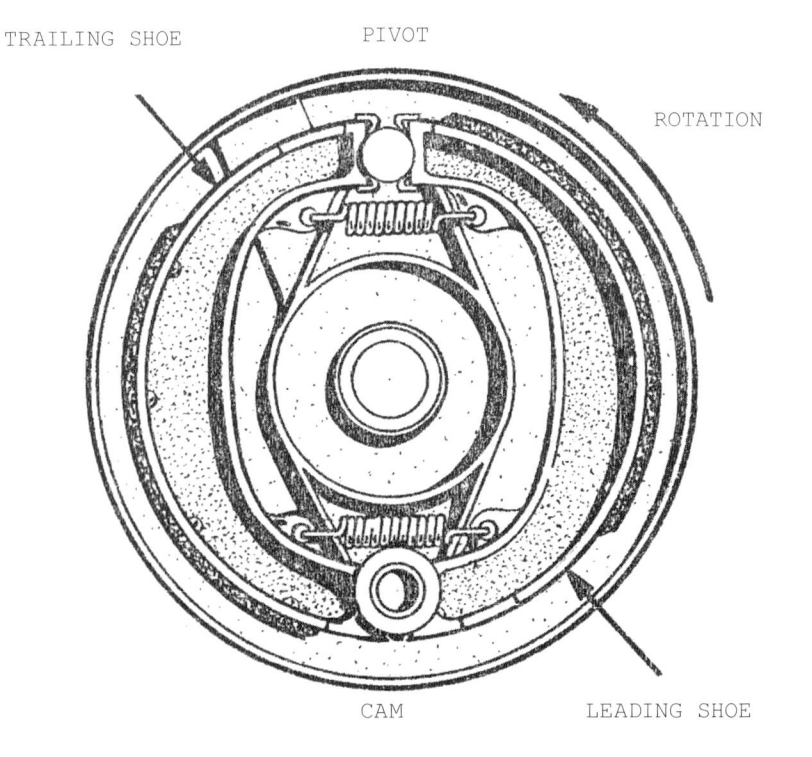

Fig 5.1 BSA Service sheets for the brakes, above and opposite.

Above, floating brakes shoes showing position of leading and trailing shoes.

Brakes, Hubs And Wheels

BSA

FEBRUARY 1971
No. 2/71

SERVICE SHEET

1971 8" FRONT BRAKE

In order to ensure positive pull-off for the front brake shoes, a return spring, part number 37-4014, is fitted between the two brake operating levers on the brake plate, in place of the gaiter, part number 60-3148. To fit the spring, proceed as follows:-

(a) Remove the hand lever from the handlebar by removing its lock nut and pivot pin.
(b) Disconnect the cable from the bush in the forward operating lever on the brake plate.
(C) Slide the bush outwards, noting the two washers which are fitted, one either side of the cable.
(d) Remove the gaiter and fit the spring in its place.

Refitting the cable is a reversal of the above procedure, but care should be taken to ensure that the bush is fitted the right way round, ie with the countersink facing forward, to enable the cable nipple to locate correctly. Make sure the washers are in position on either side of the cable.

BSA

JUNE 1971
No. 16/71

SERVICE SHEET

1971 Model A65, B25, B50 & A75
ADJUSTMENT OF 8" FRONT BRAKE

It is important, when adjusting the 8" front brake, that the following procedure be strictly adhered to.

Before making any adjustment to the shoes, it is necessary to remove the brake control cable from the handlebar lever.

1. Completely slacken the cable adjuster at the handlebar lever.
2. Take out the handlebar lever pivot pin.
3. Release cable nipple from handlebar lever.
4. Slacken cable completely by removing slotted cable adjuster nut and threaded sleeve.
5. Having removed the rubber grommet from the front wheel hub, adjust first one shoe and then the other by turning the adjuster screw clockwise with a screwdriver until the shoe is fully expanded against the brake drum.
6. Now unscrew the adjuster screw a 'click' or two, sufficiently only until the shoe is clear of the drum and the wheel rotates freely.
7. Re-assemble brake cable adjuster parts and refit the handlebar lever.
8. Finally, adjust the front brake cable by means of the adjuster at the handlebar lever. This adjuster is for cable adjustment only - it is not to be used for brake adjustment.

Fig 5.1. cont. Top, return spring advice. Below, adjustment of the 8" brake

```
                                    JUNE 1, 1971
                                    No. [single] 4/7
```

BSA

SERVICE SHEET
B50
FRONT BRAKE ADJUSTMENT

CABLE REMOVAL
Remove front brake cable from handlebar lever before adjusting brakes to ensure that all tension has been removed from the brake shoes.

BRAKE SHOE ADJUSTMENT
1. Rotate cable adjuster until it stops and tension is removed from brake cable.
2. Remove brake lever pivot bolt and separate lever from bracket.
3. Remove brake cable from brake lever.
4. Remove grommet from front wheel hub (see below)
5. Revolve front wheel until adjusting screw is visible through aperture.
6. Rotate adjusting screw in a clockwise direction until brake shoe is expanded against brake drum.
7. Reverse adjusting screw rotation (rotate counter-clockwise) until brake shoe just separates from drum and wheel rotates without drag.
8. Revolve wheel half a revolution and adjust other brake shoe in same manner as described in Steps 1-7 above
9. Install brake cable in handlebar lever and adjust cable for proper operation of brake.

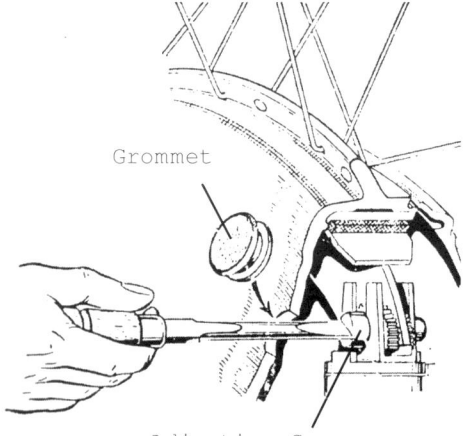

Grommet

Adjusting Screw

NOTE. There is one brake shoe adjusting screw for each of the two front brake shoes.

Fig. 5.2 BSA Service Sheet, front brake adjustment '71 -'72 8" TLS front brake

JUNE 14, 1971
[single] 8/71

SERVICE SHEET

B25T/B25SS
BRAKE BURNISHING

BRAKE BURNISHING PROCEDURE

Brakes should be bedded in progressively during the first 300 miles. This is done by gradually increasing brake lever pressure during the period, and braking from progressively increasing speeds.

For guidance refer to the table below. The deceleration in ft/sec^2 is converted to the equivalent braking time/distance.

Stage	1	2	3
Speed of commencement of stage (mph)	30	50	70
Speed at end of stage (mph)	0	30	30
Deceleration (ft/s^2)	12.5	12.5	12.5
Distance travelled (ft)	77	135	344
Time taken (sec)	3.5	2.3	4.7

Stage 1
A minimum of 20 stops using the front and rear brakes together. Decelerate from 30 mph to rest using the distance travelled or time taken to obtain the required deceleration.

Stage 2
A minimum of 50 decelerations from 50 to 30 mph using front and rear brakes together.

Stage 3
A minimum of 30 decelerations from 70 to 30 mph using front and rear brakes together.

The distance between brake applications should not be less than 1/4 mile in each case. Disengage the clutch when carrying out the procedure to ensure that the brakes receive the full braking load. The use of the above procedure, subject to traffic conditions will ensure that any high spots on the brake linings are not hardened, resulting in reduced brake efficiency. Correct burnishing will give an approximate minimum lining contact area of 50% which qualifies the published brake performance figures.

Fig 5.3 BSA Service Sheet, brake burnishing, similarly applicable to other Unit Single brakes

> **JUNE 1971**
> **No. 18/71**
>
> # SERVICE SHEET
> 1971 A GROUP TWINS
> A75 MODELS AND B GROUP
> REAR WHEEL BRAKE
>
> Efficiency of the 7" rear brake can be improved by fitting a longer lever to the rear brake cam. A new return spring is also introduced. The longer lever is fitted in the inverted position whilst the new return spring, located in the sane anchor plate position, pulls off clockwise, as illustrated below.
>
> | | OLD | NEW |
> |---|---|---|
> | Brake lever | 37-3916 | 37-4034 |
> | Brake lever return spring | 37-3880 | 37-4049 |

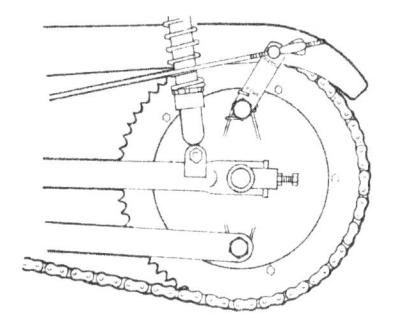

Fig 5.4. BSA Service Sheet showing the longer brake lever. Changing from 'down' to 'up' lever will require new bedding-in of the brake shoes before full braking efficiency is restored

Fig 5.5. OIF rear brake lever: left, long up, and right, short down

Brakes – Assessing Condition

Brake shoe wear is easily checked by looking at the angle of the lever on the brake plate to which the cable attaches. With the brake fully on, this lever should be at an angle to the operating cable or rod of 90° or less. If it goes past this point, it is likely that the brake linings are excessively worn and more importantly, actual leverage (mechanical advantage) to make the shoes grip the hub is reduced.

At the handlebar or left foot, the brake lever should be smooth and light in operation with the biting point as the shoes contact the hub being distinct and firm. The biting point of the front brake should occur way before the lever touches the handgrip; far enough away so your fingers cannot be trapped between the lever and the grip when the brake is fully on.

The rear brake, being foot operated, is less easy to 'feel' in use, so operation by hand is required (with the bike stationary!) to allow the above checks to be carried out. The foot brake pedal should be free in movement and return smartly to its at-rest position. Greasing is required at the pedal pivot and at the connections at each end of the brake rod.

Brake 'feel'

Jerkiness and stiffness of brake operation is a danger to the rider and may be the result of several causes. Chief among these is lack of lubrication of the operating mechanism or cable. In the hub itself this relates to the brake cam spindle and the contact points between the shoes and cam or fulcrum pin which all need to be greased or in some cases oiled. Take particular care to keep lubricant away from the brake linings and their contact area inside the hub and to this effect, application of lubricant to the brake cam with a grease gun (via the external nipple on most models) should not be excessive. As soon as you see grease emerge from the end of the brake cam boss - stop. Outside the hub, lubricate by oiling; inside the cable, the clevis connections to the lever or rod and further away the cable nipple and pivot pin at the handlebar lever or left foot is equally vital.

Cable routing

Also contributing to smooth operation of the front brake is the choice of cable routing. If the owner has the correct standard length of cable and handlebars of more or less normal height and style then the cable run should be obvious and straightforward - from the lever to the offside rear of the top yoke to curve down behind the fork leg. The notable exception to this cable run is the original specification B40 military cable. Being thicker and less flexible than standard, this curves over and then beneath the yokes to meet the offside fork leg by the front mudguard. Any deviation from standard regarding cable and handle bars may result in cable runs which interfere with brake operation. Try to avoid tight bends in the cable run which will increase friction where it isn't wanted.

Brake judder

Juddering of a brake when it is applied may well result from a brake drum which is no longer circular and is out-of-true. The only satisfactory solution to this is to have the drum skimmed to restore circularity. If this is carried out, the brake shoes must be fitted with thicker than standard linings to compensate for the larger diameter drum in which they now have to work. Skimming of the drum should be done to the complete, trued wheel rather than a bare hub as spoke tension can affect the shape of the drum.

An even layer of light surface-rust on the braking surface of a drum should not pose a problem and can be easily removed with glass-paper (this will remove rust but not remove the underlying metal). Unfortunately, rust is not often found to be evenly distributed and will usually be significantly worse in some areas if, for instance, water has collected inside the drum. Damp linings can cause areas of rust on the drum if the bike is left unused for a while. Using the abrasive paper on areas affected in this way will show up how far the rust has penetrated. Deep pitting which would affect brake performance and ruin linings can only be cured by drum skimming. To some extent, areas of light pitting can be tolerated – if they are too severe you will know about it as the effect and feel in use which results will be similar to an oval/out-of-true drum.

An out of true drum will be felt as on-off-on-off ... when the brake is lightly applied at low speeds. Juddering, as stated above, occurs at high speed. Loose steering head bearings can produce a similar effect except that the whole of the forks will be doing the juddering.

Anchoring of the brake plate

A front brake which has a judder accompanied by a knocking noise when the brake is applied is telling you that there is play at the point at which the brake plate is anchored to the forks. This is most commonly found where the front brake plate has a slot which anchors on a peg on the fork slider, rather than those with a bolted-on anchor method as per the Unit Single rear brakes.

To allow easy assembly, this peg is a clearance fit in the slot when new and the clearance will only increase in use as the brake plate, usually made of aluminium, gives way to the steel peg. Another symptom of too much clearance between peg and slot is the brake plate centre nut on the wheel spindle frequently becoming loose in use. Elimination of this knocking noise and a permanently loose spindle nut requires minimal clearance to be restored to the fit of peg and slot. Building up a badly worn brake plate with weld and re-cutting the slot to restore the fit may be necessary, but shimming is also a possibility.

To do this, cut from a 6 thou or so piece of brass shim (or aluminium drink can will do) a ³/₈" wide strip about 2" long. Wind this around the anchor peg and test the fit of the brake plate as you go until the two will just slide into engagement. Trim off excess shim and then rearrange it if necessary on the peg so the exposed end of the shim is facing upward on the slider with its end bent over the top of the peg; this will prevent it unravelling when the brake plate (and wheel) is finally fitted *(fig 5.6)*.

After shimming, but before fitting the wheel, fully tighten the brake plate to spindle fixing nut. Do try to obtain the correct deep socket for this, and resist the temptation to tighten the nut with a hammer and punch. However, over tightening this nut alone to cure brake plate judder is not recommended as the tightening pressure is applied onto a narrow spigot of aluminium on the inside of the brake plate where it abuts the wheel bearing. Excess pressure from the nut will simply squash this spigot. If you can see that the end of this spigot has collapsed in this way where it has contacted the bearing inner race, consider shimming it to restore correct brake plate position.

Brake plate distortion

It is also worth checking that a brake plate has not distorted in use, aluminium plates are prone to this. This

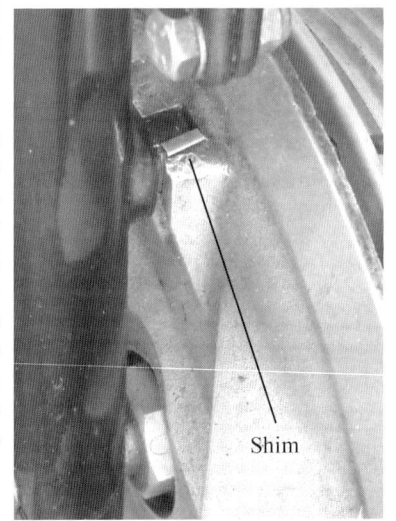

Fig 5.6. Shimming the anchor peg in the brake plate slot to take up clearance and eliminate front brake judder.

is best checked by spinning the plate and spindle on the hub when you should see the edge of the plate run true, give or take $1/16$" of run-out. Excessive up and down wobble at the edge of the plate as it spins indicates distortion centred on the spindle hole. Rectifying the problem can usually be done by the simple application of a mallet to the plate wherever it is high while it is still fixed to the wheel spindle. Spinning it after each application of the mallet to check progress is best.

Examining the plate edge-on should show that the brake cam, fulcrum pin, and wheel spindle are parallel and in line with each other. Braking forces will tend to twist the cam and fulcrum pin and the surrounding areas of brake plate. Untwisting the brake plate at the cam and fulcrum pin holes requires two close fitting steel bars. One to be firmly held in a vice while the fulcrum pin hole is slid onto it, the other to pass through the cam hole to act as a lever and also a checking mandrel. If the brake plate is true the two bars should be parallel. All aluminium plates, particularly so the die-cast examples (eg rear brake on the B25/44/50) will benefit from being annealed before straightening in this manner is carried out. (see annealing in section 'Checking yoke condition p86)

Other reasons for inefficient brakes

If lubrication has been neglected, the brake cam can wear itself and its hole in the brake plate. For a decidedly sloppy fit the easiest remedy is a replacement cam and/or the bushing of the hole in the plate. On some brake plates eg C15 rear, 7" half width front and others, the fulcrum pin hole is enlarged or slotted to allow movement of the pin if its retaining nut is slackened. Correct procedure for setting up brakes with this facility is to slacken the fulcrum pin nut, apply the brake fully and hold it on while the nut is tightened. Those who like to tinker could consider modifications to allow slight movement of the pin with the nut fully tightened; the self-centring of the shoes in the drum which this would allow being a worthwhile step to a better brake.

Sponginess in the feel of the front or rear brake is not desirable. It may be caused by one or more of several components in the mechanism from control lever to hub. Things to check:

> Handlebar lever not securely mounted on the handlebar
> Cable poorly routed (too many bends)
> Damaged cable (outer having been stretched for example or trapped between the steering stops)
> Worn out cable
> Hub brake lever at incorrect angle to cable
> Air gap between linings and shoes
> Partial or insufficient area of contact between linings and drum

Or joyful permutations of any of the above. This list is by no means all-inclusive, so keep an eye out for other maladies.

Brake Linings

Which brings us to the brake linings themselves; BSA originally used a small range of friction materials of different effectiveness for their brake linings, choice of which material to use depended on such thing as the intended use for the machine, the weight and speeds of the machine, front or rear wheel fitment and the design of the brake assembly. A crude way to determine the different original linings is by colour; the bog-standard stuff was originally brown (AM2), with 'stickier' linings being red (MZ41) or more commonly green (MS3).

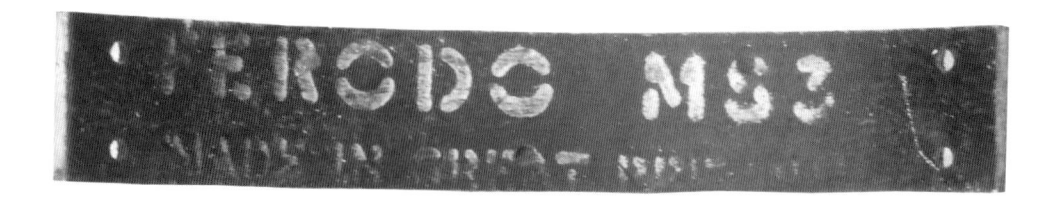

Fig 5.7. Original linings, nice if you can get them.

```
                                           JANUARY 1967
         BSA              SERVICE SHEET


              CHANGE 10075 B44GP AND VE MODELS

       Front brake shoes with MZ41 linings replace shoes with MS3 linings

                  OLD NO    NEW NO      DESCRIPTION
                  65-5401   65-5940     Brake shoe complete
                  19-7716   19-7717     Brake lining
```

Fig 5.8. From a BSA Service Sheet of January '67, this is one of the rare instances of BSA specifying brake lining material

B44GP production line

On the whole, all of this is now irrelevant unless the gods are with you and you happen upon some original new-old-stock Unit Single shoes or more likely the linings alone. If you get lucky in this way, using this original equipment should be a priority as it wasn't selected randomly by BSA.

Replacement pattern shoes these days are invariably shod with ubiquitous asbestos-free grey stuff which hasn't gained much of a reputation for grip since its adoption on the grounds of health and safety. This 'Jack of all trades' material cannot be expected to work as effectively as more specialised linings which can be obtained.

Brake re-lining

A worthwhile alternative is to have your shoes re-lined by one of the small number of specialists in this art. The benefit of this is that these people know what friction material from those currently in production will best suit your application, and which ones equate to the original fitment MS3, AM4 etc which are no longer widely obtainable.

If following this course of action it may be worth considering new linings which are a bit stickier than standard to improve brake performance, but increasing grip in this way has a hidden cost – increased wear. Increased friction destroys the rubbing parts more rapidly: the legendary Ferodo AM4 green racing linings which was the material of choice for front wheel fitment on the race track (originally introduced for use on milk floats!), along with AM3 for the rear, were unlikely to last more than a season when used in anger, and would ruin the drum surface in the process.

Fitting new shoes

Which brings us back to drum skimming and thicker than standard linings to suit. Even with a drum surface in used but good condition, new, off-the-shelf shoes are unlikely to immediately provide full contact with the working surface of the brake drum, so will be unlikely to provide effective stopping and may require careful bedding-in. The burnishing process described in BSA's notes *(fig 5.3)* refers to the shiny appearance of the lining material after it has been in contact with the drum and adopts the profile of the drum surface.

Personal attention to the new shoes can accelerate the bedding-in process if you have the patience. After initial use, the new shoes will exhibit the smooth shiny burnished areas indicating contact with the drum. Careful application of a flat file or abrasive paper to these areas of contact to remove the high-spots, should result in more of the lining contacting the drum, but this must only be attempted with a gradual, trial and error approach - and don't inhale the dust even if it is now supposed to be asbestos-free. You need at least half of the lining surface to show contact with the drum before leaving the rest to bed-in during use. *fig 5.9* shows the brown woven friction material often originally found on the rear brake and which is almost full bedded in..

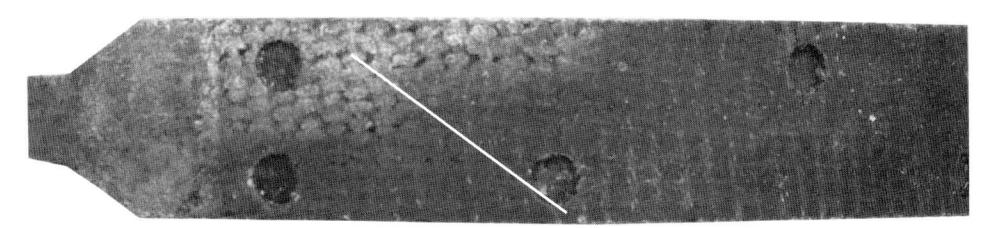

Fig 5.9. Almost fully bedded-in - just a small patch of light coloured, un-burnished lining left to go

New lining

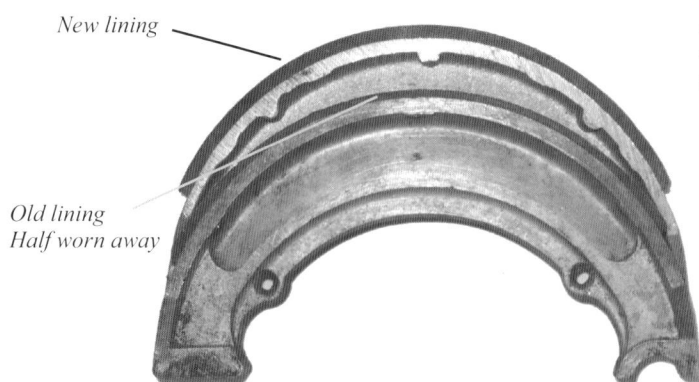

*Old lining
Half worn away*

Fig 5.10 New lining shown above the old, worn lining on the lower brake shoe.

It should go without saying that careful use on the road is vital during the bedding-in period until you feel confident in the effectiveness of the brake.

The above help-with-a-file method is a crude but potentially effective alternative to the preferred method, which is to have the linings skimmed on a lathe to ensure that their profile and working diameter on the brake plate matches the diameter of the drum. Result, minimal bedding-in required. This is do-able at home if you have a (large) lathe but the aforementioned specialist may well be a more time-effective option.

Deciding when to replace your old, nicely bedded-in shoes used to be easy; ie before the lining rivets come into contact with the drum, which amounts to about $^1/_2$ of the lining thickness left. Unfortunately modern bonded (glued) linings don't have the rivets as a guide but $^1/_2$ worn away is still a good rule of thumb for when to replace, which equates to about 2mm of lining thickness left as shown in *fig 5.10*.

This amount of lining wear should already have made itself visibly apparent from the outside of the brake as the operating lever on the brake plate will rotate to an angle with the brake rod or cable of more than 90 degrees when the brake is applied (*fig 5.11*). The lever could of course be causing this by being incorrectly positioned on its splines but don't be tempted to

Fig 5.11. Cable to lever angle looks about 90 degrees here with the brake on. This particular brake still works well but some new shoes or linings will soon be required.

simply reposition the lever without first verifying that the linings aren't significantly worn. As all the old manuals say, putting a substantial chamfer on the leading edge of the linings will reduce their desire to 'grab' and lock the wheel under braking.

All of the above is common practice for many BSA and classic bike drum brakes, the following items relate more specifically to the Unit Single brakes.

Brake improvements

Up-rating the Unit Single brakes in ways other than changing the linings is possible in some instances.

Floating cams

The 7" half-width front brake can be improved by adopting the 'works' floating cam boss idea (*fig 5.12*) as fitted to the factory scramblers and B44GP production model. Finding the original parts necessary for this conversion is asking too much nowadays, so modification of the standard parts would be necessary. This requires removal of the steel cam-boss (by grinding, it's too hard to saw), reducing the larger hole in the back of the brake plate where the cam fits, drilling and tapping the plate $5/16$" BSCy to accept the two fixing bolts (with $3/8$" shoulder) for the cam boss, elongating the cam hole in the plate by $1/16$" in both directions to give $1/8$" of cam movement, fitting a $1/8$" spacer between the cam and the back of the plate, and finally making the boss itself. The original is cast aluminium but a fabricated item would suffice. Its two mounting holes for the bolts to the plate need to be elongated to permit the $1/8$" of cam and boss movement. With the two bolts done-up tight against their shoulder, the boss should be free to move without sloppiness.

Fig 5.12 Floating cams

Twin leading shoes

Front brakes with a 7" full width hub (B40 Star/SS90 and '68 B25/TR25w) can be improved by exchanging the single leading shoe brake plate for the excellent twin leading shoe item originally fitted to '69 to '70 B25/TR25w and B44SS models. This will fit straight in on the '68 B25/TR25w (and a similar swap can be made on the 8" brake of the '68 only B44SS with the 8"TLS plate from larger BSA/Triumph models), but on the B40 the plate may be found to foul the fork slider (due to narrower forks) and require metal removal from the plate to make it fit.

7" twin leading shoe brake - setting up '69 to '70

Correct setting-up of this twin-leader requires synchronisation of the two levers. This involves disconnection of the adjuster end of the tie-rod between the levers so they can both, together (two hands needed) be rotated fully on and held there while your third hand rotates the tie-rod adjuster until the clevis pin holes line up exactly. The aim is make both independent brake shoes contact the drum at exactly the same time.

OIF 8" twin leading shoe front brake set-up

The 8" conical front hub used on OIF models is often criticised for its performance but this is usually found to be caused by incorrect setting-up in some way *(see fig 5.2* regarding this at the start of this chapter). The most legitimate criticism is that the twin brake levers are too short to provide sufficient leverage with normal handlebar lever pressure. This was addressed to some extent by BSA/Triumph as slightly longer alternative levers were produced to effect some improvement – but these seem to have been inconsistently fitted as original equipment. The part numbers for the longer levers, 3" long as opposed to $2^1/_2$" *(fig 5.13)*, are 37-3913/4. In the UK at least, after-market levers of longer than standard length seem to be easily available at the moment.

5.13 OIF 8" twin leading shoe brake levers. Left, the commonly found short lever and right, the longer alternative.

As shown in the BSA literature *(figs 5.4 and 5.5)* at the beginning of this chapter, the OIF conical rear brake has two alternative lengths of lever much as the front 8" conical brake described above. The longer ($3^1/_8$" as opposed to $2^5/_8$") lever, part number 37-4034, will need to be fitted vertically upward rather than in the normal position to avoid fouling the wheel spindle nut.

7" full width front hub

As fitted to B40 road models, this brake has a lever $3^5/_8$" long. In its second incarnation, fitted to '68 B25 and TR25w models, a longer lever $4^1/_2$" overall was used. This longer lever can usefully be fitted to the earlier B40 front brake. The longer lever is identified by having a $^1/_4$" hole half way along it (due to this lever being borrowed from the '68 TLS brake of the twin cylinder machines - the middle hole is for the tie-rod connection).

Rear Wheel Hubs

There are only three types to consider for Unit Single applications:

    Cast iron full width C15 hub

    QD 'crinkle' hub

    OIF conical rear hub

The full range of which hub was fitted to which model in which years is shown in the table below.

Rear Hubs: Types and Years

Model	Full Width	QD Crinkle no speedo drive	QD Crinkle with speedo drive	Conical
C15 Star/SS	59-67			
C15T/ S	59-65			
B40 Star/SS	60-67			
B40E	64-65			
B40 Mil Mk1			67-70	
B40 Mil Mk2			67-70	
C25/B25			67-70	
TR25w			68-70	
B25/T25 SS				71
B25/T25 T				71
B25 FS			68-70	72
B44 GP		66-67		
B44 VE/VS	66		67-70	
B44 VR/SS			67-70	
B50 SS				71-72
B50 T				71-72
B50 MX				71-73
TR5 MX				73

Table 5.1. Rear hub fitment showing the types of hub and years fitted to the Unit Single models

Cast iron full width C15 and B40 rear hub

This was used on most production models to the end of '66. This hub *(fig 5.14)* continued in use on C15 and B40 road models to the end of their production in '67. Exceptions to the fitment of this hub before this date were the B44GP, the B40 AA (Australian Army) of '64/'65 and other small batches of machines made to special order around this time; these all used the crinkle hub instead.

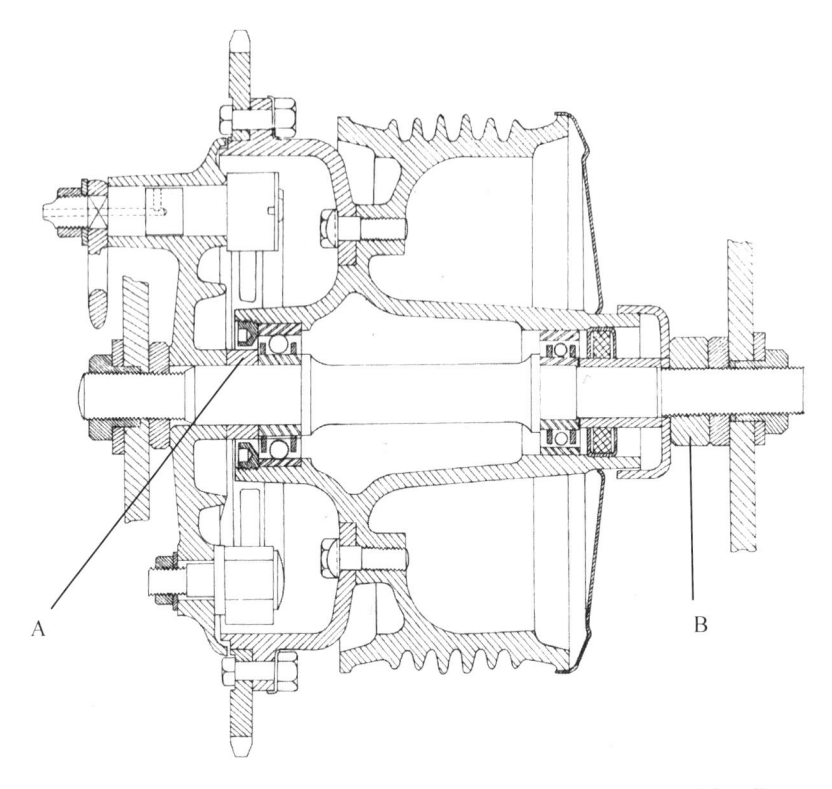

Fig 5.14 The full width cast iron rear hub as applied to C15 and B40 road models (all years) and most competition models prior to '67. The spindle spacers, A and B in this diagram (and in fig 5.15) indicate usage with the Welded/Duplex frame swinging arm

This is the version used from '63 onward with the Welded/Duplex framed C15 etc competition models. It has the longest of the three spindles shown below and therefore the additional spacers on both n/s and o/s.

The cast iron hub with bolted-on brake drum/sprocket followed contemporary BSA practice as on the late pre-unit twins and early A65 models. It is heavy but basically bomb-proof in use. The main problems are to do with butchery in use such as stripping the threads from the tapped holes for the brake drum bolts (repair by thread insert back to $^5/_{16}$" BSCy) and breakage of the speedo drive spigot (repair by filing two new drive notches if the originals are damaged).

The only variations relating to this hub concern those parts normally fitted along with it such as the previously described brake drum being of C15, B40 or C15 competition type, and the spindle length to suit.

Spindle length depends on the swinging arm to which this hub is fitted and the correct length of spindle will be required – three different lengths were produced *(fig 5.14)*. The shortest, for

Brakes, Hubs And Wheels

all C15 road models at 8³/₈" long was increased in length by ³/₈" on the near-side (brake side) for this hub assembly to be used on B40 road and C15 competition models (prior to '63 when the Welded/Duplex frame was introduced for them). These B40 road and C15 competition models with the Swan-Neck frame are said to be 'wide chain-line' models.

Subsequently putting this hub into the Welded/Duplex frame as done from '63 onward on C15 competition, B40 E and B44 VE/VS models to the end of '66, required the spindle to be lengthened by a further ½" on the offside.

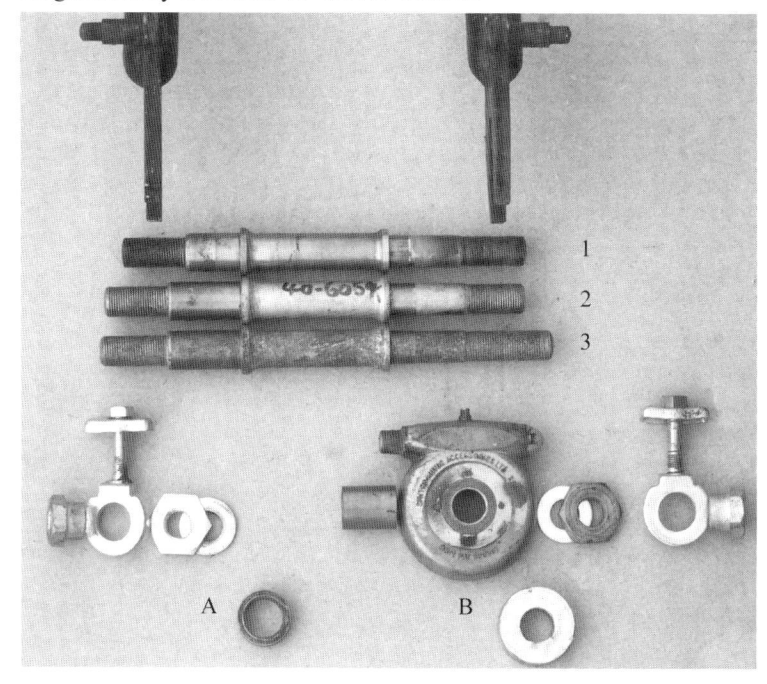

Fig 5.15. The three lengths of C15 full width rear hub spindles and associated components, these being shown in correct order for the spindle.

1. *C15 road*
2. *B40 road and C15 competition '59 - '62*
3. *'62-'66 with Welded/Duplex frame*

The separate spacer A, (³/₈" thick) fits between the brake plate and the n/s bearing on all but C15 road models.

Spacer B, (¹/₂" thick) fits outside the speedo drive under the large nut and washer on the longest spindle only. As used with the Welded/Duplex frame '63 - '66.

The crinkle hub

The famous BSA quickly detachable crinkle hub *(fig 5.16)* is famous because basically it is a good design - it is small and, therefore lightweight, allows the use of straight-pull spokes which are stronger than those with angled heads and, as suggested above, allows quick removal of the wheel alone without disturbing the brake assembly or drive chain.

This type of rear hub was used on all C25, B25, B44, TR25w and B40 military models from '67 to '70 with small numbers of pre-production and special order machines using it prior to this, as well as all B44GP machines. The B44GP used the pre-unit version of the crinkle hub with no provision for a speedo drive. The pre-unit parts - a cover disc and spindle spacer were used here - the spindle head being circular and drilled for a tommy bar rather than hexagonal.

There is very little to go wrong with this hub when it is fitted to the Unit Singles with their relatively low power output. The main weakness, the loosening of the rivets which connect the central spool (which contains the two hub bearings as seen *(fig 5.16)* in the sectioned drawing) to the two crinkled halves tends to be found when this hub is applied to the more powerful models and often with the additional burden of a sidecar. This failure in itself is not a terminal problem if the joint between the two halves is ground or turned away to expose the inner spool so that all three parts can be welded together around the hub centre.

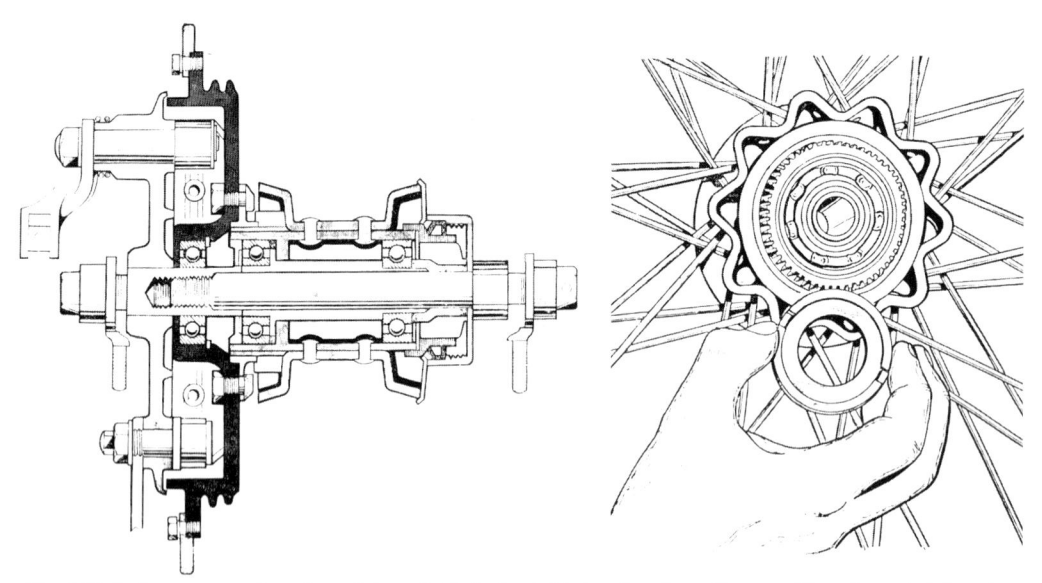

Fig 5.16. Left, cross-section view of the crinkle hub, right showing the splines and bearing retaining ring

The splined end of the spool which mates with the internally splined ring on the back of the brake drum can deteriorate in use if road filth is allowed to contaminate it and act as grinding paste. The rubber seal pressed inside the crinkle next to the splines should prevent this. Wear of these splines will be felt if the back wheel (clear of the ground) can be rotated back and forth with the brake applied. Exactly how much wear at this point constitutes an excessive amount depends on how sensitive you are to this situation; it isn't dangerous in use or likely to dramatically fail but any audible 'knock' would suggest replacement is in order, of both the hub and the drive ring on the rear of the brake drum. Visually, if the splines on the hub have worn to a point, consider replacement.

Having been in production from '47 it would be surprising if this design had not been modified along the way to the end of its production life (late '70). Crinkle hubs for pre-unit models do not have the offside end of the spool threaded to accept the speedo drive-ring; they have a simpler plain cover at this point. Additionally, pre-unit versions have a grease nipple on the centre side of the hub.

When the crinkle hub was first adopted by unit models, ie for the A50/A65 in '66, the new speedo drive-ring thread was applied in the usual direction ie clockwise. Due to the rotation of the wheel, these tended to unscrew in use hence this thread was soon changed to left hand and was applied to all Unit Singles in this form. The centre part of the speedo drive ring should be stamped L/H to indicate the direction of the thread. The outer disc of this cover is simply pressed onto the central portion which sometimes results in them becoming loose. A couple of spot-welds should solve this.

The best way I have found to tighten or remove the speedo drive ring is to put a flat tyre lever. or similar steel bar, horizontally in a vice and protruding upward to provide a raised edge which will fit snugly into the two cutaways. The wheel can then be positioned horizontally and rotated to tighten or free-off the drive ring.

OIF conical hub

The OIF conical rear hub was used on all BSA and Triumph models (250cc and over) from '71 onwards *(fig 5.17)*. Whilst there are no inherent design flaws in this hub; which these days is a rather sought after and expensive item, the fact that it is cast in aluminium renders it more likely to some types of damage. The areas most prone to this, and which should be checked, are the sprocket bolt holes and the bearing housing in the middle. Basically any damage to these hubs usually comes down to careless assembly and neglected maintenance. The bearing housing can easily be scored or broached if a bearing is driven in off-line. The bearing lock-ring, circlip and associated parts can all cause damage to the surrounding aluminium if not fitted and removed with care. Yes, remedial work in the form of welding and/or machining is of course possible but it's better to not go there in the first place by taking more care. It may of course not be possible, but warming the hub before fitting bearings as per engine casings is worthwhile.

To answer the problem of the oft-damaged thread for the bearing lock-ring, '74 onward Triumph models changed to an external thread with screw-on cap for this job. This introduction happened well after the end of BSA production but these later hubs are fully interchangeable with the earlier type.

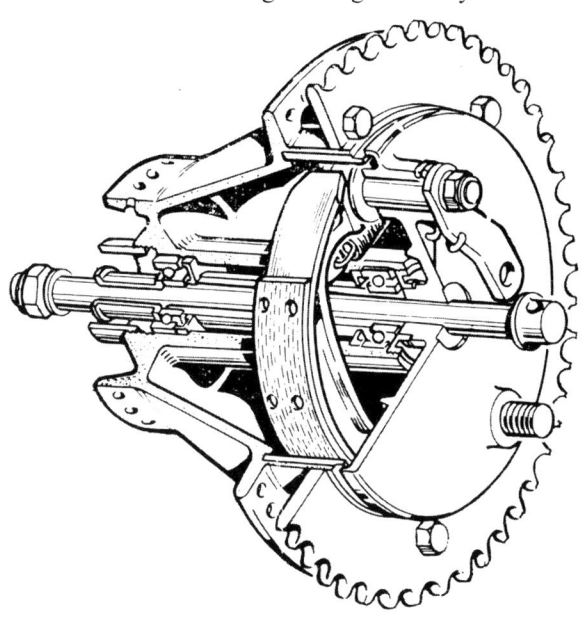

Fig 5.17. The conical rear hub fitted to the OIF models

Rear brake anchor straps

Fig 5.18 shows the anchor straps fitted to all models.

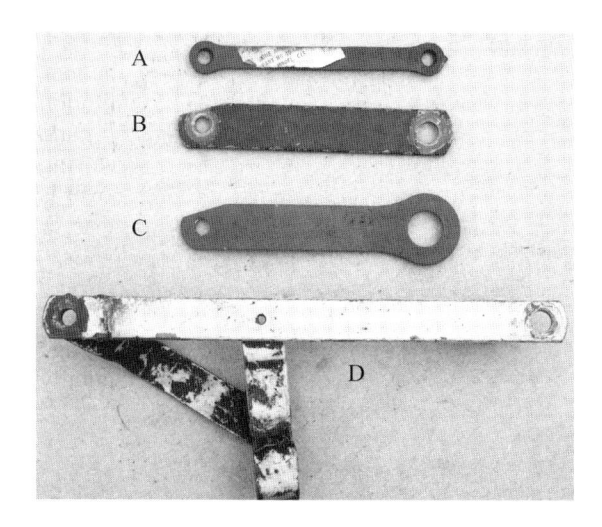

Fig 5.18. Rear brake anchor straps.

A. All models with C15 type full-width rear hub

B. 1967 to '70 all models except B40 Military Mk1 and B44GP. (GP item is longer)

C. B40 Military Mk1; all of the above being 5,11/16" between centres

D. OIF B25/B50 T and MX 11 1/4" between centres, the SS models have the plain strap without the integral chain guide assembly

Front Wheel Hub

The full range of which hub was fitted to which model in which years is shown in the table below.

Front Hubs: Types and Years

Model	6" Full Width	7" Half Width	7" Full Width SLS	7" Full Width TLS	8" Full Width	8" Half Width	6" Conical	8" Conical
C15 Star/SS	59-67							
C15T/ S	59-62	63-65						
B40 Star/SS			60-66					
B40 E		64-65						
B40 Mil Mk1		67-70						
B40 Mil Mk2			68-69					
C25/B25		67	68	69-70				
TR25w			68	69-70				
B25/T25 SS							71 USA	71 Home
B25/T25 T							71	
B25 FS			68	69-70				72
B44 GP		66-67						
B44 VE/VS		66-67				68-70		
B44 VR/SS		67		69-70	68			
B50SS								71-72
B50T							71-72	
B50MX							71-73	
TR5MX							73	

Table 5.2. Front hub fitment showing the types of hub and years fitted to the Unit Single models

6" full width hub

The C15 cast-iron, full-width hub (*fig 5.19*) with 6" brake remained unchanged and was used for all years on C15 road models and on C15 competition models up to '62. Like its counterpart at the rear, this was a scaled-down version of the full width hubs used on the larger BSA models at the time. Similarly it is known as being OK as a stopper but heavy, particularly for competition use.

To digress a little; the reason why BSA persistently fitted their over-the-counter Trials machines with hubs which were (are) too big and heavy to make the machine competitive is basically down to safety. In view of the range of uses to which such a machine may be put – including riding it on the road – BSA rightly felt it necessary to play safe in the braking department.

Brakes, Hubs And Wheels

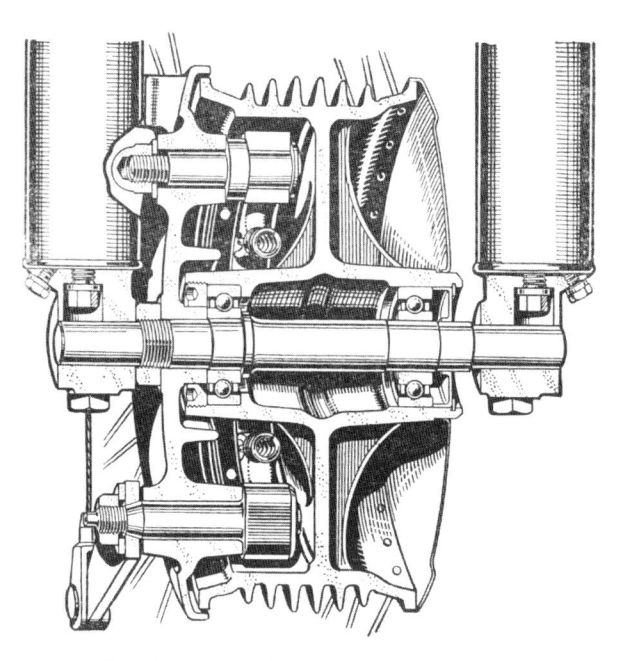

Fig 5.19. Section through the 6" full width hub

For serious competitive trials use, fitting Bantam hubs instead was, and still is the norm. These are fine for trials machine speeds and relatively light in weight.

For Scrambles/Motocross you don't really want to be reducing stopping power, quite the opposite, but the alternatives in BSA's range (no chance whatsoever of BSA fitting hubs from a competitor) were very limited if weight remained a consideration. The best all-round front hub for scrambling was already used by the works team on the pre-unit models in modified form – the 7" half width job with screw-in spindle (also called 7" single-sided). The modifications possible for this brake are dealt with above in the section on brakes (p109).

7" half width front hub

Fig 5.20 shows the 7" half width front hub. The C15 competition models adopted this front hub in standard form from '63 onward. The inset shows the floating cam-boss modification found on the B44GP.

In its original form this hub was introduced to the first post-war models and it remained a regular favourite throughout the 1950's. The version found on most pre-unit models differs in detail from the type used on the unit models. The earlier type has a grease nipple on the centre-side of the hub and the steel brake plate is retained on the threaded spindle sleeve by a nut. The Unit type has no grease nipple and the brake plate simply pushes onto the now plain spindle sleeve, having a central boss where the nut would be to aid location. This version of the brake plate was first introduced on the 7" full width hub of the C12 model (with painted finish which means, should you need one it would just need chrome plating to make it look like the Unit Single part).

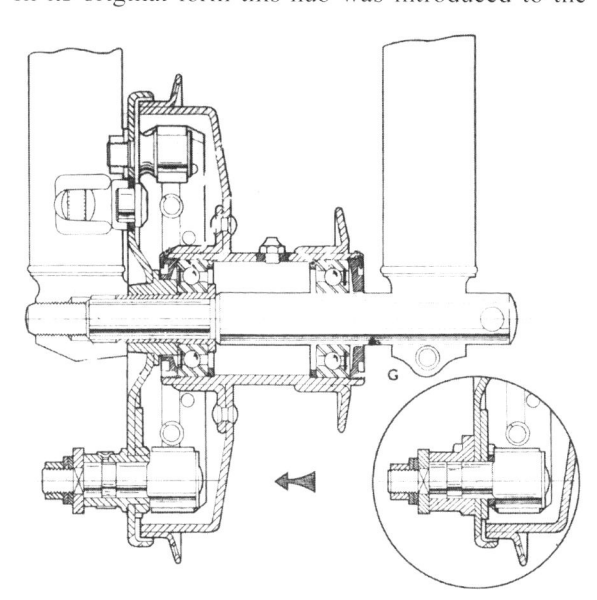

Fig 5.20. Section through the 7" half width front hub. Inset shows the B44GP floating cam boss

Uses for this reliable and adequate brake continued to be found on the Unit Singles: B44GP (in modified form), all other B44 models to 1967, C/B25 1967 and all B40 Military Mk1. The length of the L/H threaded screw-in spindle for this hub is 8½".

7" full width front hub

B40 road models fitted the 7" version of the full width front hub as found on some of the larger BSA models at the time (*see fig 5.21*). Again an adequate but heavy design, this hub subsequently re-appeared as the front stopper on the '68 B25/TR25w (with a lengthened brake lever and new style brake plate) and the B40 military Mk2, as well as on several of the smaller '60s Triumph twins.

In most cases the brake plate for this hub is a simple smooth Aluminium casting; the B40 road models feature a plate with a painted rough-cast centre area and raised, polished rim much as the smaller C15 item. These two types of 7" Aluminium brake plate are interchangeable on this hub.

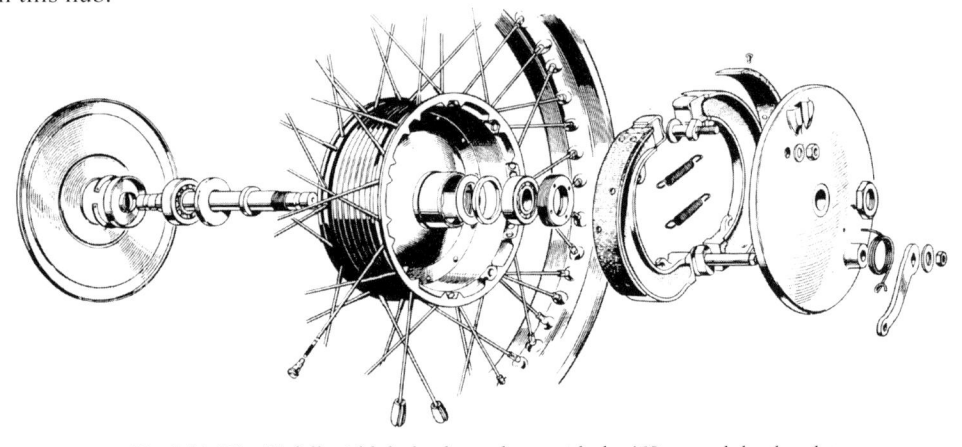

Fig 5.21. The 7" full width hub, shown here with the '68 smooth brake plate.

8" half width hub

The '68 to '70 B44VS used an earlier BSA cast iron design of 8" half width/single sided hub. This hub accepts a l/h threaded screw-in spindle much as the 7" half width hub detailed above. This renders both of these wheels quickly detachable. On the Unit Singles, these hubs are specific to the forks they are fitted to; the 7" item being for the 'narrow yokes' and the 8" being for the 'wide yokes'. The spindle length is therefore also specific; the 7" hub spindle is 8½" long, and the 8" hub spindle is 9".

Again, this design of hub had been used since the early '50s on the largest BSA models and it rightly gained a reputation as a 'good stopper'. As usual, changes to the basic design occurred and the version for Unit Single use has two ribs cast around

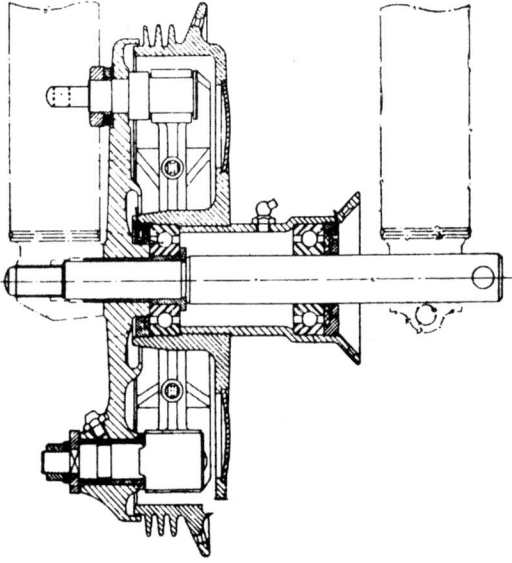

Fig. 5.22. 8" half width hub found on the B44VS from '68 to '70; only used with the "wide yoke" forks.

the brake drum by the edge of the brake plate. This type was first used on the now obsolete Gold Star and subsequently the mid to late '60s Unit Twins, hence it is rather sought after and pricey today. The flat, smooth aluminium brake plate for this hub has a slightly rounded outer edge on the later B44 version rather than the square corner of the pre-unit version.

8" full width front hub

The '68 B44SS alone fitted an 8" full width hub in cast iron. Similar to earlier full width designs used on the larger BSA models, this hub now gained a spoke flange on the brake side and is therefore the same as those fitted with the Twin Leading Shoe brake plate on the BSA/Triumph Unit Twins '68 to '70.

In its Single Leading Shoe form, as on the B44, it was previously the top-of-the-range Triumph front stopper in the mid'60's.

7" full width front hub with twin leading shoe brake

The B25 and B44SS for '69 and '70 fitted the 7" version *(fig 5.23)* of the very good twin leading shoe design as used in 8" diameter on the twins; the hub is similarly full width, cast iron and with a spoke flange on the brake side. This is an excellent brake for your Unit Single to the extent that it is often sought-after and robbed for fitment to pre-unit models with the 7" full width hub.

Fig. 5.23. 7" Twin leading shoe 'stopper' '69 -'70

OIF front hubs, '71 onward

Only two designs of OIF front hub were produced in 6" or 8" diameter, these being the aluminium conical hubs which have aroused mixed feelings ever since they appeared (*fig 5.24*).

The performance of the 8" version can only be described as 'variable' with BSA going to significant trouble to publicise the correct setting-up procedure in an attempt to help all such brakes produce a satisfying effect (see p99). There is nothing fundamentally wrong with the design of this brake and certainly, for Unit Single use, it has the potential to be a powerful stopper when set-up correctly.

Making it work comes down to; use of the correct lining material (don't use Morris Minor front brake shoes – yes they fit but the lining material is wrong for this application), fully bedded-in linings, correct adjustment via the snail cams and where possible the use of the longer types of brake levers.

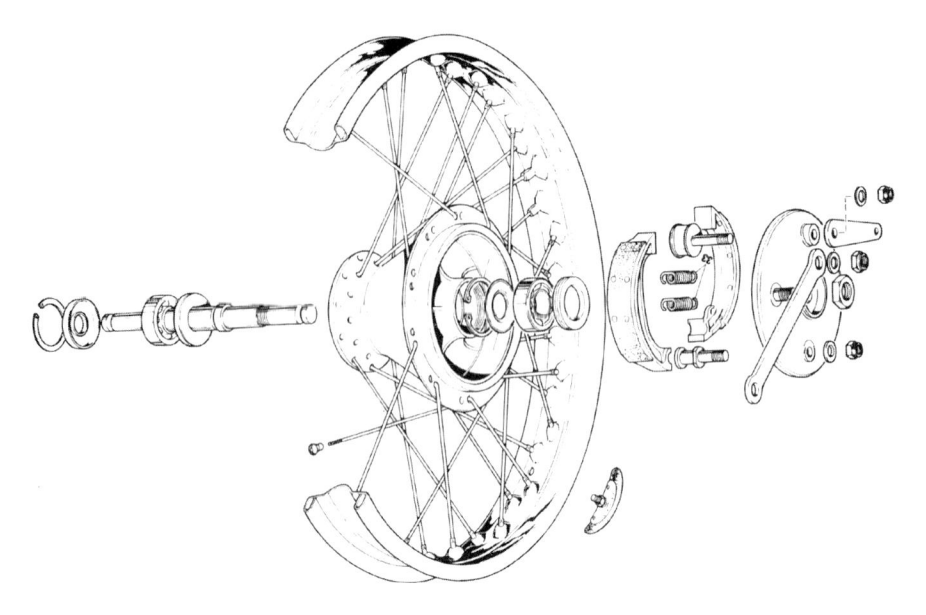

Fig 5.24. The conical hub, here in 6" form

The 6" brake is generally considered to be alright but nothing special. It is after all a close equivalent to a C15 front brake in stopping power and the Umberslade magic wand and asymmetric linings did not disguise this fact. It is therefore adequate for the relatively low off-road speeds of the Trail models to which it is fitted but not really up to coping with the higher road speeds of the B50. It does however, have one small advantage (in common with the conical rear hub) in that the shoes are operated by a floating cam to allow them to centralise in the hub.

It must be admitted that the OIF 'comical 'ubs' are nice on the eye, less heavy than their earlier equivalents and arguably on a par with the contemporary Japanese drum brakes in terms of performance.

Wheel Bearings - Removal and Refitting

The common approach to wheel bearing fitting and removal stems from the fact that most Unit Single hubs have the brake side bearing locked in place in the hub (by the bearing lock-ring) and to the spindle (by the brake plate/spindle nut). The other bearing is permitted to position itself according to the hub or spindle and associated spacers. The exception to this being the front hubs with screw-in spindle which have both bearings retained by a lock-ring - this actually makes life a bit easier. This generally means that the brake side bearing should be the first to be removed and the last to fit. This doesn't have to be the case; it just makes life a bit simpler if it is.

To remove the brake side bearing unscrew the lock-ring which has holes provided in which the correct tool locates - simple unless you don't have the correct tool, if so don't resort to the hammer and punch but find an old clutch push-rod or similar piece of steel bar which will fit snugly in the lock-ring hole. Put the other end of the wheel spindle in a vice and rotate the ring by fitting a tyre lever between the spindle and rod – which you need to hold vertical as pressure is applied to the lever.

When re-fitting this ring the spindle may not be there to lever against, so the method is to position two metal rods upward in a vice (the blunt ends of $3/16$" drills), spaced apart to locate in two opposite lock-ring holes, and to screw the wheel onto the lock-ring. In most instances the lock ring will have a left hand thread and be marked as such.

Driving out the old bearings is easily done in most cases by using the wheel spindle as a drift with the application of a mallet – nil by hammer please. The exceptions to this being the front hubs with screw in spindles and the rear crinkle hub which requires the spindle sleeve, which protrudes through the non-brake-side bearing, to be driven out with the brake side bearing (try using a socket spanner as a drift, pick one with an O/D which will just go through the bearing or turn a spigot on the end of a bar of suitable diameter). For the hubs with screw in spindles, the non-brake-side bearing can be driven out using the spindle as the drift if the spindle sleeve is first fitted.

Refitting the wheel bearings

Fitting the (new) bearings to the hub should be done by applying force to the bearing outer. If you choose to take the easy option, which is to use the spindle as a drift through the bearing inner, this can give problems. The bearings are, or should be a tight fit. So you may need to hit the drift so hard that you may damage the bearing tracks, which will shorten bearing life. If you have caused this type of damage it will be felt as notchiness in the rotation of the bearing, the only cure for which is to buy another bearing.

Applying force to the bearing outer by means of a tubular drift of the correct diameter is the best answer. It needs to be long enough to clear the spindle (if fitted) and be square-ended. Tapping around the bearing outer with a small punch is possible, the difficulty being to keep the bearing going in square until it seats on its abutment ring. A change in the note produced as the bearing is tapped in usually indicates that it is correctly seated. Fitting the 2nd bearing should be done with the same tubular drift until it meets the abutment ring in the hub or the shoulder on the spindle (or spindle sleeve) if this feature is provided.

Front hubs with a clamp-up spindle usually lack a shoulder on the spindle or in the hub which would provide accurate positioning of the non-brake-side bearing. To enable the bearing to be positioned so that it is a snug fit against the dust cover and circlip, fit this bearing first to a depth which will allow the dust cover and circlip to be comfortably fitted. The bearing can then be tapped outwards to take up clearance between the dust cover and circlip. Removal of this dust cover is best done by driving the bearing out with it from behind. Attempts to prize it out alone will result in mangling it.

After fitting the bearings check that the spindle rotates freely; with some designs it is possible to tap the non-brake side bearing in too far and apply pre-loading to the bearings – result, stiff to turn. This is dealt with by tapping the spindle or sleeve from the brake side until free movement returns. The other cause of stiffness in rotation is the bearings being out of alignment if they have not been fitted squarely, resulting in the bearings not being correctly seated on the abutment ring or spindle.

It goes without saying that wheel spindles should be straight and a snug fit inside the bearings. If the bike has suffered impact it will often be the wheel which first makes contact. Following such a misfortune, suspect bent wheel spindles. All spindles are capable of suffering wear if for any reason they are forced to rotate inside the bearing inner. The front screw in spindles seem particularly prone to this. Loctite may offer a temporary cure but the only real solution is a new spindle

Wheel bearings - modern equivalents

Fit rubber sealed bearings if possible! Two bearings per hub except the Crinkle hub rear/brake drum which has three bearings. All bearings in each hub are an identical pair except C15/B40 full width rear hub.

Bearing	Hub
6203	C15 full width front and o/s C15, B40, B44VS '66 full width rear
RLS7	7" half width front, 8" half width front, Crinkle rear
6204	All other hubs and C15, B40 n/s full width rear

Rear Spindle Spacers

After fitting the bearings to the hub, the rear hub is likely to require spacers of various sorts to be fitted onto the wheel spindle as assembly proceeds. In view of the ease with which these sorts of things get lost or mixed up I have listed below their applications and sizes.

Full width rear hub spacers *(see fig 5.25 below and fig 5.15)*

The brake side (n/s) spacer (wide chain line models only) B40/C15 competition (between brake plate and wheel bearing) is $3/8$" thick, $1^1/_8$" o/d, $3/4$" i/d

The o/s spacer between wheel bearing and speedo drive is $1^3/_{32}$" long, $7/_8$" o/d, $11/_{16}$" i/d. The felt seal with its retaining cup and flat washer runs on the outside diameter of this spacer.

Spacer Dimensions

63-66 C15/B40/ B44 with Welded/Duplex frame

Spacer 1			Spacer 2			Washers	Spacer 3		
width	O/D	I/D	width	O/D	I/D	width	width	O/D	I/D
$3/_8$	$1^1/_8$	$3/_8$	$3/_{32}$	$7/_8$	$11/_{16}$	$1/_{16}$	$1/_2$	$1^3/_8$	$11/_{16}$

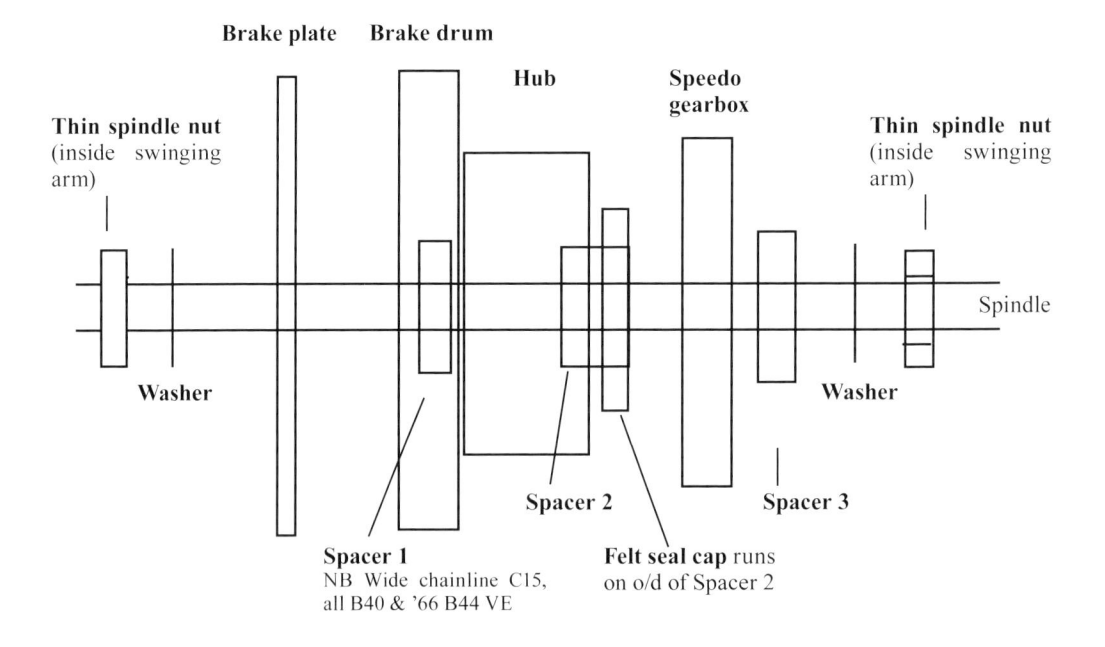

Fig 5.25. Full width rear hub spindle spacers in diagramatic form

Brakes, Hubs And Wheels 123

Outside the speedo drive is a $1/16$" thick washer and thin spindle nut. Models fitting this hub into the Welded/Duplex swinging arm have an additional spacer between the speedo drive and the washer which is $1/2$" thick, $1^3/8$" o/d, $11/16$" i/d.

Crinkle hub spacers

All Welded/Duplex framed models fitted with the crinkle rear hub *(see fig 5.16)* have spacers on the o/s. Between the bearing and speedo drive the spacer is counter-bored to fit over the protruding spindle sleeve, and is stepped on the o/d from $1^1/8$" to $1^1/16$", is $1^1/8$" long, outer end i/d $11/16$" counterbored to $7/8$" i/d at the inner end.

The felt seal runs on the wider portion of this spacer. Ensure that the steel washer either side of the felt seal is correctly fitted, the whole lot being retained by the speedo drive ring.

Outside the speedo drive is a spacer $7/8$" long, $1^1/8$" o/d, $11/16$" i/d. It is this spacer which allows the crinkle rear hub to be 'QD'. After withdrawing the wheel spindle knock this spacer out sideways. This provides the space for the wheel to move to the o/s and disengage the driving splines between it and the brake drum; this does not need to be disturbed to then remove the wheel.

The B40 military is alone in fitting spacers both under and over its rear steel brake plate.

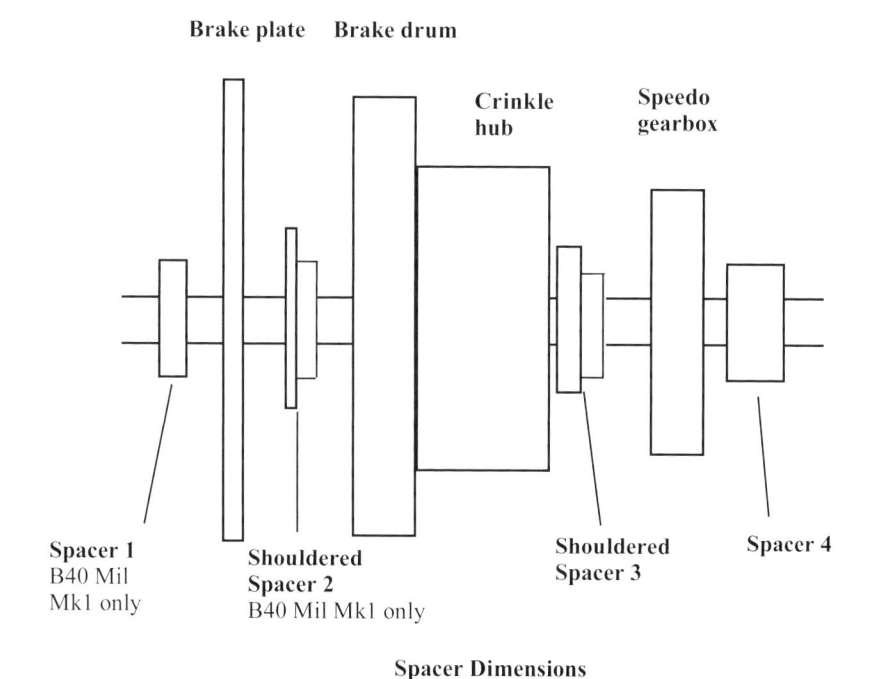

Spacer Dimensions

Spacer 1			Spacer 2			Spacer 3			Spacer 4		
width	O/D	I/D	width	O/D	I/D	width	O/D	I/D	width	O/D	I/D
$3/8$	$1^1/8$	$7/8$	$1/2$	$1^3/4$	$7/8$	$1^1/8$	$1^1/8$	$7/8$	$7/8$	$1^1/8$	$11/16$

Fig 5.26. Crinkle hub spindle spacers

OIF rear spindle spacer

Only one is fitted, on the o/s underneath the speedo drive; this is $1^5/_{16}$" long. On the n/s the brake plate fits directly against the swinging arm. This brake plate for Unit Single use is flat in the centre, the same plate but with a raised boss around the spindle is used on the twin cylinder models.

Brake plates

As an aid to identification the following pictures of Unit Single brake plates may be useful.

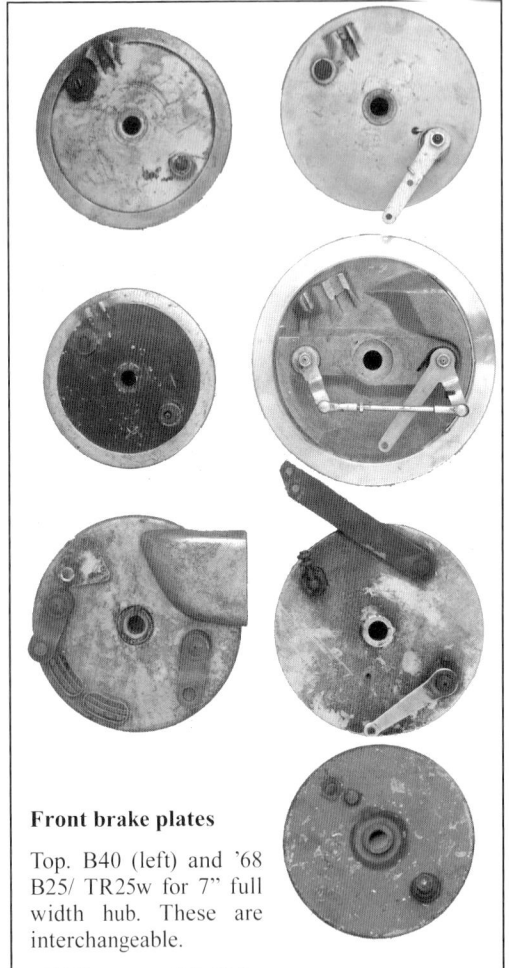

Front brake plates

Top. B40 (left) and '68 B25/ TR25w for 7" full width hub. These are interchangeable.

Middle upper. C15 6" for all road models, left and 7" TLS B25/TR25w/ B44SS '69 -'70

Middle lower. 8" TLS '71 -'72 (left) and 8" half width '68 -'70 B44vS (right)

Bottom. B40 Military Mk1 left front brake plate for the 7" half width hub (also found with chrome finish on competition models) '62 on, and B25/B44 '67.

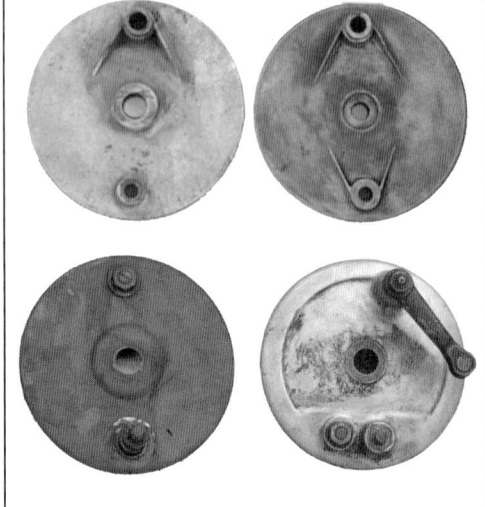

Rear brake plates

Top left. '67 -'70 brake plate for the crinkle hub.

Top right. '71 on for the conical hub. The two are easily confused, the tell-tale is whether they have one or two pairs of stiffening ribs. The '71 onward brake plate with a raised spindle boss is used on the twin cylinder models, the Unit Single item is flat. The B44GP is similar to the example on the left but has a coarser sand cast finish

Below left. B40 Military Mk.1 rear steel brake plate much as previously used on pre-unit models.

Below right. C15/B40 road models, all years, and also competition models to '66.

Fig 5.27 Unit Single brake plates

Wheel Rims

All Unit singles originally fitted steel wheel rims made by Jones and stamped as such. Other details stamped on the rim indicate its size eg WM2.18 (WM2 is the width and 18 the diameter in inches) and its BSA part number along with the obligatory 'Made in England'.

Fig 5.28. Original Jones Rim marked WM 1.20 Jones 40-5544 fitted to a B40 Military Mk1. The '40' is barely visible after the name, 'Jones'.

Fig 5.28 shows an original Jones rim from the front wheel of a B40 Military Mk1. In case you were wondering, the right hand hole is for the tyre security bolt, provision for this or not would necessitate a different part number on otherwise identical rims.

The part number marked on the rim will correspond exactly with the number shown in the parts book for your model. The dimple pattern and angles of the spoke holes are specific to the hub for which the rim is intended; attempting to lace a rim – albeit an original Jones item but with the wrong part number – to the wrong hub will be fraught with problems and should be avoided.

All such Unit Single rims were chrome plated with the exception of the painted finish applied to most of the B40 military machines (not all, one batch of these for escort duties carried chrome rims).

Wheel rim sizes

The rim sizes originally fitted to Unit Singles are as follows:

Model	Front	Rear
C15 road models, all years	WM2 x 17"	WM2 x 17"
C15 competition models		
Trials, and USA market equiv. all years	WM2 x 20"	WM3 x 18"
Scrambles '59 to '62	WM2 x 20"	WM2 x 19"
C15 Starfire Roadster, Trials Pastoral	WM2 x 19"	WM3 x 18".
B40 road models, all years	WM2 x 18"	WM2 x 18"
B40 Enduro Star,	WM2 x 19"	WM3 x 18".
B40 Military Mk1	WM1 x 20	WM3 x 18".
Australian market and Mk2	WM2 x 18"	WM3 x 18
B25 and B44 road models '67 to '70	WM2 x 18"	WM2 x 18
B44 GP, VE/VS, TR25w '66 to '70	WM1 x 20"	WM3 x 18.
B25SS, T25SS and B50SS	WM2 x 18"	WM2 x 18
B25T, T25T and B50T	WM1 x 20"	WM3 x 18"
B50MX 1971/'72	WM1 x 20	WM3 x 18".
B50MX 1973	WM1 x 21	WM3 x 18

Although not catalogued, a WM2 x 19" rim has also been found as original fitment on the 6" conical front hub of OIF machines.

Tyre sizes and options

At present only two of the above rim sizes are questionable in terms of tyre choice in today's market. All of the original tyre sizes to suit the above rims are available, but the 17" and 20" sizes are harder to find and command a premium.

If the opportunity arises, changing your rims to a size which will permit easier tyre selection is simple common sense, unless your main priority is to remain faithful to originality. The 17" rims used on C15 machines can usefully be exchanged for 18" rims; there are no issues with the resulting larger tyres fouling any of the frame parts. To my eyes, this change seems to give the machine a better proportioned appearance and the slight raising of the gearing should not unduly stress an engine which is in good condition. If necessary, this can be compensated for by reducing the size of the gearbox sprocket.

The 20" rim widely used on off road models can usefully be exchanged for a WM1 x 21" item to suit today's commonly available 21" trials/trail tyres. BSA's choice and continued use of the 20" rim was a legacy of that size being more commonly used in the 1950s. There was also the supposed problem of a 21" wheel fouling the front down tube with the forks fully compressed when the machine was fitted with the steep yokes used in '59 only on the C15 competition machines. Why they repeatedly selected this size until '72 is unclear.

The 19" front rim fitted above to Unit Singles, which can generally be termed 'trail' models is also now somewhat questionable in terms of tyre choice and again, the 21" size is worth considering as a replacement for off-road use.

Changes to wheel rim width to allow fitment of wider section tyres should be undertaken with care. Due to the limited space, the sensible approach is to only widen the rear rim to a larger size which was standard fitment on another model with the same swinging arm. In terms of the front wheel there is no advantage in going wider than a WM2 rim on a nominally standard machine .

Wheel restoration

If considering a wheel refurbish/rebuild there are several possibilities to consider, the simplest but most expensive of which is to ship your old wheel to the wheel builder of your choice and leave the rest to them. It depends on how authentic you want your wheels to be.

Modern replacement rims are not always direct replacements for the original Jones items in faithfulness of profile (the WM series), finish and dimple pattern. Yes, they will fit and work if laced to the hub by a competent wheel builder; it all depends on how much trouble you are prepared to go to in having wheels which visibly match the originals.

If you choose the option of new replacement rims then you need to ensure that these are dimpled as per the originals and pierced at the correct angles to suit the original spoke pattern, thus allowing the wheel to be laced up as the original without the spokes fouling each other and with the nipples pointing the right way.

Drilling or piercing a new rim yourself is an absolute nightmare of a job unless you are prepared to go to the extent of making a drilling jig to ensure that the nipple holes pierce the dimples at the correct angle and are in the correct position on the dimple. It's much easier to obtain your replacement rim ready pierced to suit the hub if you fancy building the wheel yourself.

Use of a rim with the wrong dimple pattern may force spokes to contact and distort each other when tensioned. If you don't fancy doing any of the above jobs yourself, provide as much information as possible to the person who is. All of the above is equally relevant should you decide to fit aluminium rims as replacements.

Wheel rim refurbishment

The other option is to do as much of the wheel refurbishing as is reasonably possible yourself. This is quite feasible if your rims are in good enough condition to stand polishing and a re-chroming. Good enough that is, in that the rust hasn't left pits which are too deep to polish out without leaving the rim too thin and unsafe. At least in the UK, there are chrome plating companies who will deal with wheel rims and who know from experience how much metal can be safely removed in the polishing process.

If re-chroming of the original rim (or a better second-hand example if yours is too far gone) isn't possible then a modern replacement is your only choice, but select carefully if the 'look' matters to you.

Any visible flat spots or dents in the original rim mean discard it. On the other hand a slightly buckled rim (lay it on its side on a flat surface and see if it rocks) with no specific areas of damage should pull straight by correct attention to the spokes when truing it.

The other factor in whether or not to re-use an original rim in this way is obvious impact damage which usually tells you not to bother.

Spokes

If you plan to refurbish your wheel yourself then photograph it before dismantling to record the spoke pattern and any other relevant details such as whether a spoke head goes inside or outside of a flange on the hub. Also select one spoke of the intact wheel and centre punch or otherwise mark the rim and hub next to the ends of your chosen spoke. Marking thus will save a lot of head scratching later when it comes to working out which way around the rim should be laced onto the hub.

The spokes number forty in total on all Unit Single wheels and are arranged in patterns of four, this being repeated ten times around the wheel. In terms of length, thickness and angle of the head (the 'pull' of the spoke eg straight pull, 90 degree or 45 degree pull and others all being found on Unit Single wheels), the spokes are specific to their particular position on any wheel and are not normally interchangeable to another wheel/position.

Spoke lengths for Unit Single wheels

The following lengths *(see Table 5.1)* are for the standard size rims listed as fitted to Unit Singles. Spokes for non-standard rim diameters can be determined by adding or subtracting approximately 12.5mm (½") for every 1" difference in rim diameter on the crinkle hub rear wheel and 11mm ($7/_{16}$") on all other wheels. The exact increase/decrease in spoke length will vary from wheel to wheel and may require some experimentation.

The 'degree' given for the spokes in the table below is the angle of the head, also known as the 'pull' of the spoke eg 'straight pull', '90 degree pull' etc.

Model	Rim	Spoke Size Front	Spoke Size Rear	Spoke Pull	No. Spokes
Cast iron C15 full width	17"	10swg x 133mm	10swg x 140mm	straight	40
Cast iron B40 full width (& 7" full width front '68)	18"	8/10swg butted x 143mm	10swg x 151mm	straight	40
7" half width (front)	18"	Long: 10swg x 211mm	—	90°	20
		Short: 10swg x 178mm	—	90°	20
7" half width (front)	20"	Long: 10swg x 235mm	—	90°	20
		Short: 10swg x 203mm	—	90°	20
		(B44GP 8swg)	—		
8" full width (front)	18"	Long: 10swg x 211mm	—	straight	20
		Short: 10swg x 181mm	—	90°	20
8" half width (front)	19"	Long: 10swg x 222mm	—	90°	20
		Short: 10swg x 191mm	—	90°	20
7" full width TLS (front)	18"	Long:8swg x 140mm	—	straight	20
		Short:8swg x 120mm	—	90°	20
Crinkle hub (rear)	18"	—	Long: 10swg x 189mm	straight	20
		—	Short: 10swg x 187mm	straight	20
OIF 6" conical (front)	18"	o/s Outer: 10swg x 163mm	—	100°	10
		o/s Inner: 10swg x 160mm	—	80°	10
		n/s 10swg x 196mm	—	45°	20
OIF 6" conical (front)	20"	o/s Outer: 10swg x 187mm	—	100°	10
		o/s Inner: 10swg x 184mm	—	80°	10
		n/s 10swg x 223mm	—	45°	20
OIF 8" conical	18"	o/s Outer: 10swg x 119mm	—	100°	10
		o/s Inner: 10swg x 115mm	—	80°	10
		n/s 10swg x 176mm,	—	45°	20
OIF 7" conical (rear)	18"	—	n/s Outer: 10swg x 150mm	100°	10
		—	n/s Inner: 10swg x 176mm	80°	10
		—	o/s 10swg x 176mm	45°	20

Table 5.3. Spoke lengths. See Tables 5.1 (p111), Rear hubs, and Table 5.2 (p116), Front hubs, for which models are fitted with which hubs.

If at all possible when dismantling the wheel, remove at least one spoke (of each different size/type if they are not all the same) intact to act as a pattern for the new replacements. It may even be possible to re-use your old spokes if they are in good condition and the nipples screw off without any breakages; likewise the nipples, there's no reason why not if they are in good enough cosmetic condition but usually this isn't the case.

Wheel Building

Firstly support the hub horizontally about 1 foot above the work surface. Fit the spokes to the hub, if any 90 or 45 degree pull spokes are used fit these before the straight pull spokes.

If using the original rim, identify the previous centre-punch mark on the hub and the rim and use these to work out the rim position in relation to the hub and thus the spoke which links together the centre-punch marks. Support the rim at more or less the correct height in relation to the hub and position and loosely fit all of the nipples to the spokes by a few threads. The half width hubs have a keyhole arrangement for the spoke heads on the n/s; the nipples for these may need to be screwed on further to keep the spoke head in place.

Do not fully tighten any nipples in isolation. As an intermediate stage to tensioning the spokes I usually screw on all the nipples until the thread is just hidden.

Take up the remaining slack on each spoke; the general approach to take is to work your way around the wheel from a known start/finish point – the tyre valve hole for example - to ensure you attend to each spoke in turn without missing any. In this way, tighten each spoke one turn at a time until the first few spaced around the wheel just begin to tighten on the spoke. When this happens, take up the slack on all of the other spokes; the rim is then ready for 'truing': to do this you will need a spoke key and patience.

Truing the wheel

Truing needs the wheel to be spun – mount it on its spindle in a vice, horizontally or vertically – in a position where a pointer or flat surface can be positioned close to the rim edge as an indicator. Don't be alarmed at how much the rim appears to wobble in relation to this indicator when you first spin the wheel!

Concentricity

In truing the rim the first thing to attend to is its concentricity or run-out, the up and down movement with the wheel mounted vertically. Tighten spokes as required no more than ½ turn at a time to gradually pull the rim inwards where it is highest. At this stage it is a case of pulling 'bulges' inward rather than slackening spokes to allow 'hollows' in the rim to move outward; this should only be done as a corrective measure if a hollow remains after all spokes are fully tightened. Try to ignore side to side wobble of the rim at this stage.

When pulling in a bulge find the exact highest point of the rim against the indicator and tighten the group of four or five spokes around this point. Whilst patience and time is required for the truing process you may be surprised to find how easily the rim moves for a small adjustment to a nipple. Your target is to get the rim running concentrically true to within 1/16" before attending to side to side run-out.

If the rim has a slight flat spot as a result of a previous impact it may be best to ignore it for the time being and deal with side to side run-out as explained below. After this a slight flat on the rim can be persuaded to move outward by slackening the spokes inside it and tightening all of the others equally around the wheel.

Side-to-side run out

This second stage of truing the wheel, attending to side to side wobble or run-out requires your fixed indicator to be positioned so it is set at the correct off-set position for the rim. This means that you are not just trying to get the rim to run true but also to get its side to side position correct in relation to the hub. It may need a bit of head-scratching as to how to position the indicator thus, which depends on how you have set your wheel up so it can be spun.

Several methods for checking rim off-set can be devised: checking the rim to find a point which already has the correct off-set gives you a position for your indicator.

Mounting the wheel on the spindle with a straight edge across the wheel diameter and resting on the hub edges will allow easy measurement of the off-set gap between rim and straight-edge. Whichever method you use for the above measuring; try to keep it simple.

Rim off-set

The off-set distances listed below for the various Unit Single wheels are all measured on the brake side of the wheel; either from the edge of the brake drum or the edge of the hub on the brake side. All sizes given are for a WM2 rim, off-set for a WM3 rim requires $1/8$" to be subtracted from this distance; WM1 needs $1/8$" be added to this distance.

Rear wheel	Offset	Notes
C15 full width hub	$1/8$"	
Crinkle hub	$11/16$"	off-set measured from the end of the splines
OIF conical hub	2"	

Front wheel	Offset	
C15 full width hub	$1/8$"	
7" half width hub	$5/8$"	
7" full width hub	$3/16$"	
8" full width hub	$1/4$"	
8" half width hub	$9/16$"	
7" twin leading shoe hub	$1/4$"	
6" conical front hub	$1/2$"	
8" conical front hub	$1/2$"	

With the front hubs, I generally true-up to the offset given above before fitting the wheel to the forks for final checking and adjustment – it needs to be exactly central between the fork legs and finally trued accordingly in situ. This in effect supersedes the offset distances given above for front wheels although these should be found to concur..

Adjustment of the spokes for side to side truing of the rim is done by tightening and loosening the spokes in the area of the rim you are trying to move. Tightening of a spoke from the left will pull it to the left and so on, but whenever you tighten a spoke – and no more than half a turn of the nipple at a time – you need to slacken an adjacent spoke by the same amount to allow the rim to move sideways without effecting concentricity. Usually it will be a case of dealing with a group of four or five spokes at a time to move an area of the rim sideways. Again, aim for an accuracy of $1/16$" in terms of off-set and run-out.

Lastly (if you are happy to persevere and toys are still in the pram), go around all the spokes and check that all are tight enough to produce a note when tapped with a screwdriver blade, or similar, rather than a dull clunk when struck which means further attention is required.

It is often the case that a slight dip will be seen at the join of the rim when the wheel is spun. This can be minimised by careful attention to the spokes but may always persist.

When satisfied with your efforts, check for and remove (use a small grinding head in an electric drill) any spoke ends which poke through the nipple, these would puncture the inner tube if left.

Spoke patterns

The following illustrations show the spoke patterns used on Unit Single wheels. The dimple patterns such as 1 & 1 , 2 & 2 etc refer to the number of dimples on each side of the centre line of the rim. ie a 1 & 1 pattern has one dimple on the left of the centre line, the next on the right, a 2x2 has 2 dimples on the left followed by two on the right.

5.29. C15 - all front and rear full width hubs. 2 & 2 dimple pattern.

Fig 5.30. Crinkle hub rear. All models. 1 & 1 dimple pattern.

Fig 5.31. 7"half width hub, '62 onward competition models, '67 B25/44 and all B40 Military Mk 1 (shown). Note keyhole flange for spokes nearest camera. 2 & 2 dimple pattern.

Fig 5.32. 8" half width brake ('68 to '70 B44VS). 1 & 1 dimple pattern.

Fig 5.33. 7" full width hub, '68 B25 example shown. Also as per B40 road models and Mk 2 Military. Note use of butted spokes. 2 & 2 dimple pattern with close grouping of each set of four.

Fig. 5.34. '69 to '70 7"twin leading shoe front hub. 2 & 2 dimple pattern. Also same pattern for '68 B44 8" full width hub.

Fig 5.35. '71 onward 8" conical front hub. 1 & 1 dimple pattern.

Fig 5.36. '71 onward 6" conical front hub. 1 & 1 dimple pattern.

Fig 5.37. '71 onward conical rear hub. 1 & 1 dimple pattern.

Wheel Alignment

All models to '70 (with adjusters on the rear wheel spindle)

I don't have a problem with the straight edge method of checking rear wheel alignment as shown in all of the BSA manuals, but if a simple procedure is followed the Mk1 human eyeball alone can be just as accurate.

> Carry out the following visual check as high up the wheel as obstructions allow.
>
> The bike is best put on the centre stand but this isn't vital, especially if you haven't got one.
>
> If possible, have an assistant to adjust and hold the handlebars to position the front wheel in exact line with the rear wheel. The exact centre position of the front wheel can easily be seen as part of the visual check shown in *fig 5.38 opposite*. If no assistant is available chock the front wheel centrally.

When viewed as shown, distance 'X' is the width of the rear tyre visible beyond its rear edge as the front tyre disappears behind it. Spot-on wheel alignment means that distance X is equal on both sides when the view is taken on left and right sides of the rear tyre. In practice the distance should be easy to visually memorise from one side to the other if some detail on the tyre surface is used as a reference point on both sides; if none is available use a marker pen.

If, after establishing correct wheel alignment it is found that:

> The rear wheel adjusters are not equally positioned within a couple of turns of the nuts
>
> The handlebars are not straight and level,

Then something is 'OUT' with the frame or forks.

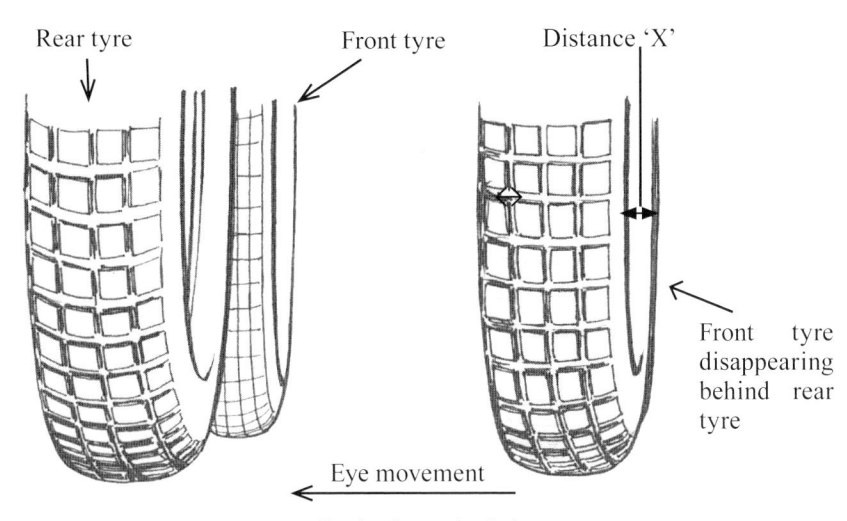

Fig 5.38. Visually checking wheel alignment

TYRES FOR RIMS 18″, 19″, 20″ AND 21″ DIAMETER

Nominal Tyre Section (Inches)	\multicolumn{6}{c}{Inflation Pressures—lb. per sq. in.}
	16	18	20	24	28	32
	\multicolumn{6}{c}{Load per tyre—lb.}
2.25-21 Autocycle	80	100	120	145	170	200
2.25-19	80	100	120	145	170	200
2.375	120	135	150	180	210	240
2.50	120	135	150	180	210	240
2.75	140	160	175	210	245	280
3.00	160	185	210	255	300	350
3.25	200	230	260	320	380	440
3.50	280	310	335	390	450	500
4.00	360	395	430	500	570	640

TYRES FOR RIMS 16″ AND 17″ DIAMETER

Nominal Tyre Section (Inches)	\multicolumn{6}{c}{Inflation Pressures—lb. per sq. in.}
	16	18	20	24	28	32
	\multicolumn{6}{c}{Load per tyre—lb.}
2.50	115	130	140	170	195	220
2.75	135	150	170	195	230	255
3.00	155	175	195	240	280	320
3.25	190	215	245	295	350	400
3.50	265	290	315	360	405	450
4.00	340	370	400	460	520	580
5.00	490	520	545	600	655	710

Fig 5.39 Tyre pressures for tyres in the early sixties

To me these tyre pressures seem a little low; perhaps the compounds are softer these days and require more air to keep them in shape? Personally, I find the bike feels better under way with around 28-32psi and noticeably different with less. But exact air pressures are generally a matter of personal preference.

6. CHAINS AND SPROCKETS

Chains

Sizes and lengths

The final drive chain on your Unit Single will be ½" x ⁵⁄₁₆" (modern 428) on all C15 models, all B40 models (except Military Mk 2), and early B44GP; and ⅝" x ¼" (modern 520) on all B25, B44 (excluding early GP models), B40 military Mk2 and B50.

The length of new chain required depends on the size of gearbox and rear wheel sprockets fitted. In view of the huge numbers of sprocket permutations which can be fitted it is possibly futile to list every chain length required for every possible sprocket combination.

The most realistic approach when buying a new chain is to buy one longer than the length you need and to also buy a chain breaker to cut it to the exact length required. Then simply fit the chain to the sprockets and cut off the excess.

As a starting point, the basic length to aim to exceed (10 extra links to cope with all eventualities if you are totally 'in the dark'), for each category of Unit Single is given below. You could of course count the links on the old chain.

Model	No Links
C15	112
C15T/S	120
B40	114
B40 Mil. MK1	120
B44GP –	126
B25/B44/B50	are all between 100 and 110 links for the standard range of sprockets. Start with 110 unless you are using sprockets larger than the normal range; for example the 19 tooth gearbox sprockets for 520 size chain now available were not included in BSA's original chain length listings.

When fitting a new chain put some clean newspaper on the floor on the n/s from engine to back wheel. At least once during the fitting, the new chain will end up in a heap on the ground where it will pick up all of the grit, fag ash and dog hairs it touches. The neatest way to fit a new chain - but not really an option unless you are taking the dubious step of fitting a new chain to used sprockets - is to attach the end of the new chain to the old one and pull it around.

Chain life

Compared to the many different qualities of chain in these sizes which are available nowadays, the Reynolds chain originally fitted is pretty basic stuff being 'economy' or 'commuter' grade from today's ranges in terms of its power transmission rating. In other ways though, the Reynolds original is better quality than many of today's equivalents by having shouldered rather than plain pins, and utilising better quality steel. Today's chains also tend to have heavier gauge and more substantial side plates than the Reynolds original which, due to the resulting increase in overall width, can cause the chain to foul the insides of chain guards. This is particularly a problem in the B40 Military fully enclosed chaincase where chain clearance is minimal. In reality, the beefed-up side plates of today's plates are unnecessary for most Unit Single applications where risk of stretching the plates is minimal. By comparison, the weedy looking Reynolds plates are perfectly adequate for the task.

With any such simple chain the main issue is wear of the pins and rollers ie between the moving parts of the chain, which is caused by abrasive road-filth getting into the works. As such, all chains are equally susceptible to this unless they are fitted with 'O' rings or similar to keep the muck out and the lubricant in. On all but the most powerful machines a chain due for replacement won't have stretched, it will have worn out. If you are considering covering high mileage on your Unit Single (and hopefully someone out there is) then the extra outlay required for 'O' ring chain may produce a cost saving in the long run.

Prolonging the life of your 'economy' chain comes down to how well you look after it. Firstly, if possible protect it; the more you can cover it up the less the muck can get at it. Only the B40 Military Mk 1 has a fully enclosed chain and longer chain life as a result. Fitment of this four-part assembly to other Unit Singles is only realistic on other Welded/Duplex framed models. These would need the mounting bracket from the military swinging arm to be welded onto the standard item (or a swinging arm swap) and attention to the rear of the primary chaincase to mount the front two chain guard parts.

Chain lubrication

Basically, anything is better than nothing and the more of it you can keep on the chain, the better. The normal motion of the chain flings off all lubricant, so stickier oil is best. A bit of lateral thinking would suggest chain-saw oil being sticky and clingy, as an appropriate choice. Squirting the chain with WD40 or similar is good for penetrating between the moving parts and for flushing dirt off the chain, but it is too thin to provide lasting lubrication in use.

The best way to lubricate your chain is to carry out the following ritual, nay, rite of passage, which every self-respecting 'biker' should undergo at least once in their life. The ensuing 'flak' from mum or subsequent better half for your desecration of the kitchen stove and attendant stench throughout the house only adds to the status of the ordeal. I am of course talking of boiling your chain in grease - a foul procedure.

Two proprietary names from days of yore come to mind in relation to this - Duckhams' Chain guard and Castrol Linklyfe - both being wide circular tins containing hard wax-like grease, blackened by the addition of powdered graphite: the Devil's own chip-pan! The chain first needs to be removed from the bike and washed and rinsed in paraffin or similar to remove dirt before being immersed in the grease which has been liquefied in its tin by being heated on the stove. The chain should be simmered thus for 15 minutes or so with occasional agitation to help the grease penetrate.

It then needs to be hooked out of the grease with a piece of wire or similar and moved onto the tin lid to drain and cool. This is where the desecration of the kitchen stove is likely to occur, if it hasn't already. Don't attempt to move the hot tin of melted grease unless you habitually ask for trouble.

Intermediate lubrication of the chain on the bike comes down to oil or 'chain lube' if you wish to pay a premium.

Chain wear

If the chain shows $1/8$" elongation per ft (3mm per 300mm) then put 'new chain' on your shopping list. $3/16$" per ft - throw it away now. Measuring is done by washing the old chain in petrol or paraffin before stretching it out on a flat surface alongside a ruler with a convenient starting point, eg pin centre or plate edge at the end of the ruler.

Measuring a new and unworn $1/2$" x $5/16$" (modern 428) chain in this way should see it fit exactly - pin to pin - into 1ft (24 links). The $5/8$" x $1/4$" (520) chain won't fit exactly into 1ft the nearest being $11^7/8$" pin to pin (19 links), so if it can be pulled tight to reach 1ft it's worn out.

However, going to this trouble when replacement chain is relatively cheap is a job that can be neglected; if in doubt buy a new chain, and there shouldn't be much doubt as the sprocket teeth will act as an indicator of chain condition. If the sprocket teeth are worn to a point, you need to replace them along with the chain; all should be replaced together. Don't put new chain on partially worn sprockets or vice-versa.

Replacement sprockets with different numbers of teeth to the ones you are replacing may mean that a different length of chain is needed from the standard quoted length (see listings above). Hence, if you are contemplating this there should be a chain splitting tool in your tool kit to enable you to shorten or lengthen your new chain. It is bad practise to add new links into an old worn chain or vice-versa. Also, any added links should be of the same make and grade as the existing chain.

Half-links used to be available to produce a chain with an odd number of links: I have never found these to be needed on any Unit Single rear chains: an even number of links has always been found to fit within the range of chain adjustment available.

Chain adjustment

Always check chain tension with enough weight on the bike to compress the rear suspension to half way along its travel. At about this point the chain is at its tightest with the gearbox sprocket, swinging arm spindle and rear wheel spindle in a straight line. Adjust the tension to obtain $3/4$" up and down play in the middle of the bottom chain run.

Other than OIF models, which have their adjustment at the swinging arm spindle and which cleverly doesn't affect rear wheel alignment, a bit of care is needed to ensure that the rear

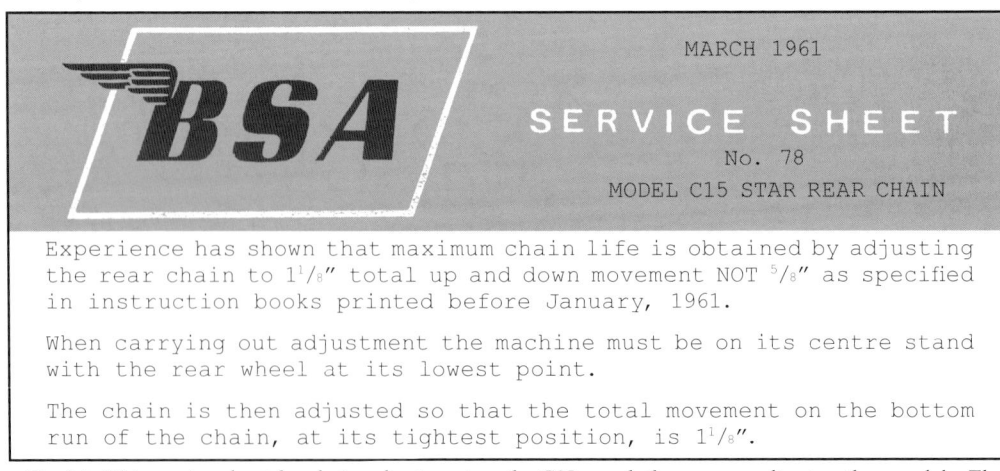

MARCH 1961

BSA SERVICE SHEET
No. 78
MODEL C15 STAR REAR CHAIN

```
Experience has shown that maximum chain life is obtained by adjusting
the rear chain to 1¹/₈" total up and down movement NOT ⁵/₈" as specified
in instruction books printed before January, 1961.

When carrying out adjustment the machine must be on its centre stand
with the rear wheel at its lowest point.

The chain is then adjusted so that the total movement on the bottom
run of the chain, at its tightest position, is 1¹/₈".
```

Fig 6.1. BSA service sheet for chain adjustment on the C15, much the same applies to other models, The quoted $1^1/8$" with the rear wheel at its lowest point equates to $3/4$" at rear wheel mid position

wheel stays pointing in the right direction as adjustment is carried out. Firstly and always slacken both ends of the rear brake anchor strap. When turning the chain adjuster nuts do this by no more than ¼ of a turn at a time, alternating from one side to the other. Judge this ¼ of a turn by observing 90 degrees rotation of the spanner on the nut.

Sprockets

All of the Unit single gearbox sprockets are interchangeable which helps should you wish to fit the stronger ⅝" x ¼" chain to your C15 or B40, however the rear sprocket (as explained below) may pose difficulties.

Fitting a larger gearbox sprocket raises the gearing ie it will give you a higher top speed if your engine can produce enough power to get you there. If your bike is in standard condition, fit the standard size sprocket as quoted by BSA as this should produce optimum performance. It should be possible to increase the gearing by one tooth at the gearbox sprocket without too much suffering being inflicted on the engine but the change will be noticeable. A change of one tooth on the gearbox sprocket is equivalent to two to three teeth on the rear wheel sprocket.

Rear wheel sprocket

The rear wheel sprocket is not widely interchangeable throughout the Unit Single range. The sprockets are specific to the three distinct rear hub types. At the risk of being out of sequence the rear sprocket must be considered in conjunction with the brake drum to which it fits.

Full width hub sprockets and drums

Fig 6.2 shows C15 and B40 sprockets. Top left is the combined brake drum/sprocket as used on C15 and B40 road models. The B40 example is shown which is 1¹³⁄₁₆" in total height. The C15 item is ⅜" less than this to bring the chain line inboard. The C15 and B40 examples are therefore not interchangeable in terms of chain line.

Top right is the 'competition' drum and below is the bolt-on sprocket to be used with it. The sprocket is identifiable by the turned recess in which the eight fixing bolts fit and are thus prevented from rotating. This assembly is interchangeable with the B40 sprocket/drum as it gives the same wide chain line.

Fig 6.2. C15 and B40 sprockets

The C15 and B40 combined sprocket/drums have 45 and 46 teeth respectively. Alternative sizes are not available.

The bolt-on sprocket was originally available with 52, 56 and 60 teeth. Difficulties in obtaining these sprockets may force the owner towards having a suitable replacement specially made. This also gives the option of upgrading to ⅝" x ¼" chain.

Crinkle hub and OIF rear wheel sprockets

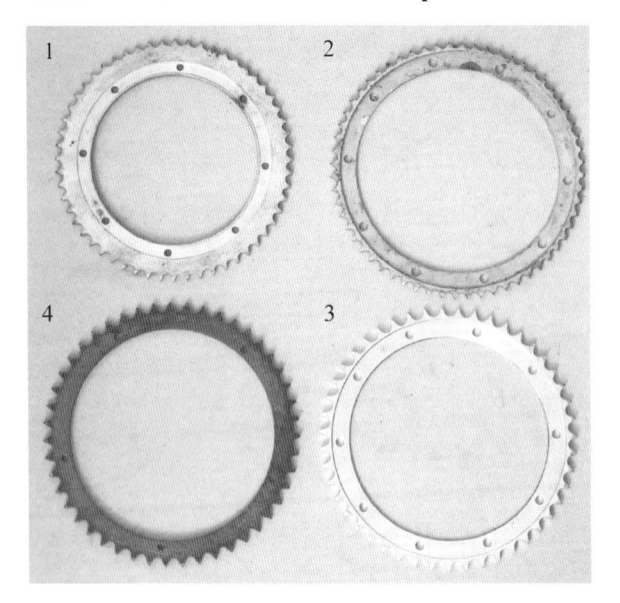

Fig 6.3. Unit Single rear sprocket types for comparison.

1. '59 - '66 competition models ($1/2$" x $5/16$" chain) for full width rear hub. 8 bolts.

2. B44GP ($1/2$" x $5/16$" chain) for crinkle rear hub. 10 bolts.

3. '67 to '70 ($5/8$" x $1/4$" chain) for crinkle rear hub. 10 bolts.

4. OIF '71 onward ($5/8$" x $1/4$" chain) five bolt fixing directly to conical hub.

Note 2 and 3 are deeply recessed. 3 and 4 are also available for the wider $5/8$" x $3/8$" chain for fitment to A65 models and are easily confused.

'67 to '70 B25/TR25w and B44 models using the QD crinkle rear hub fit a sprocket with 10 bolts to fix it outboard of the flange on the brake drum and are toothed to suit $5/8$" x $1/4$" chain. This sprocket is heavily recessed on the back to obtain correct chain alignment and was originally available with 47, 49 or 52 teeth, these teeth numbers were also the standard alternatives for the OIF sprockets which followed.

Crinkle hub brake drum '67 to '70

Fig 6.4 below, shows the 7" rear brake drums '67 to '70 for the crinkle rear hub. On the left is the Unit Single item, on the right the A65 item. As well as the different position for the sprocket flange, the twin item has a larger diameter bearing and stub-axle; it is clearly similar at a glance but avoid it!

All of the brake drums shown below for the QD crinkle hub rear wheel are fully interchangeable and this includes full inter-changeability with the pre-unit BSA crinkle hub - the splines on the hub and driving flange on the drum are the same .

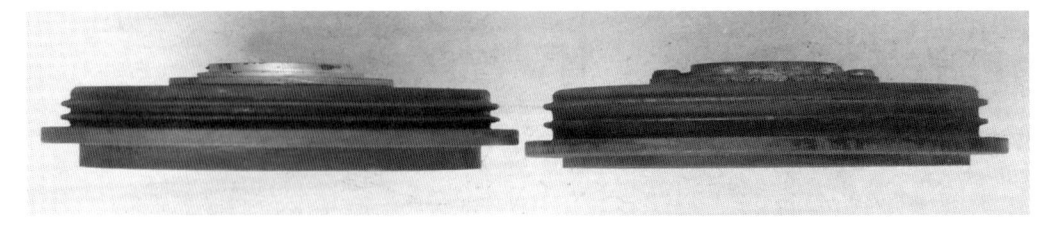

Fig 6.4. 7" rear brake drums for the '67 60 '70 crinkle rear hub

B44GP machines use the same general QD set-up but the brake drum mounts the sprocket on the inside of the flange to allow speedier sprocket changes without disturbing the brake. To suit this, the flange is repositioned and lacks the two external ribs which would get in the way.

Chains And Sprockets 139

Fig 6.5. More brake drums for the crinkle rear hub.

Left, the B40 Military Mk 1 item with integral sprocket.

Centre, the B44GP drum used to mount the sprocket on the rear of the flange. This is the large flange example as originally fitted with the ½" x ⁵/₁₆" sprocket.

Right, the later small flange version to accept the standard B25/B44, ⁵/₈" x ¼" sprockets, again, on the rear of the flange for speedy changing without disturbing the brake..

Fig 6.5 shows more brake drums for the crinkle rear hub fitted to the B40 military Mk1, and the B44GP. I suspect that these types of brake drum may have been used earlier on pre-unit models but have as yet to establish this categorically.

Fig 6.6. Sprocket overlay emphasising the difference between the large and small flange sprockets to suit the two B44GP brake drums shown in fig 6.5. In addition to the example on this page, BSA pre-unit models which used the crinkle rear hub have their own brake drum with integral sprocket. These will fit but may give an incorrect chain line.

The difference between the large and small flange sprockets is not great, see *Fig 6.6*. *Fig 6.7* shows a comparison of the two brake drums B25/B44 rear brake drum on the left (for outside sprocket), B44GP item on the right (for inside sprocket) - both produce the same chain line.

Fig 6.7. The B25/B44 rear brake drum on the left (for outside sprocket) and the B44GP item on the right for the inside sprocket

OIF rear sprocket
OIF models have their own sprocket type to suit the conical rear hub with its five $1/4$" fixing bolts. These sprockets have no grooves or recesses and were originally available in 47, 49 or 52 teeth to suit the $5/8$" x $1/4$" chain.

The common sizes for the three designs of Unit Single rear sprocket are usually frequently re-manufactured and are therefore fairly easy to obtain. For the less common sizes and types the easiest way to obtain the one you want is usually to have one made by the specialists who advertise this service. On second thoughts, while you're at it get two, 'cos as we know, they wear out!

Before throwing away your old one have a good look at it; it may be knackered but it should have worn out evenly. Look for pronounced wear on one side or the other which would indicate problems with the rear wheel alignment.

Chain Guards

The standard chain guards all do a good job of protecting the top chain run with those from the 1966 to '70 B44 B44VS/VE (also the road models for 1967) having an additional plate to protect the bottom chain run from muck cast off the rear tyre. This is a good idea for all of the potentially 'off-road' models and is used in conjunction with a chain guide bracket to which it bolts as a stiffener. Clearance between the chain and plate (which is a spot-welded addition to the standard guard) and between the plate and the tyre is minimal so expect to persuade it and its supporting guide bracket into the best position so nothing fouls the chain or tyre when under way.

As can be seen from the illustrations below there are three basic types of chain guard main pressing which mostly relate to the three frame types; Swan-neck, Welded/Duplex and OIF. Variations are found in the mounting arrangements of chain guards of the first two frame types, for which some interchangeability is also possible.

Both the B40 and C15 chain guards are very similar (*see fig 6.8*). The B40 item is slightly longer, the difference being due to the increase in distance between the two clearly visible mounting points (as per the longer B40 swinging arm). Centre to centre these mounting points are $8^7/_8$" apart on the B40 item and $8^3/_8$" apart on the C15 item. The other obvious difference is the indented portion to clear the rear tyre on the C15 item, the B40 being flat-backed as it clears the tyre by being positioned 3/8" outward to the n/s due to it being on a 'wide chain line' model.

Fig 6.8 Top, B40 and below, the C15 chain guards seen from the off side.

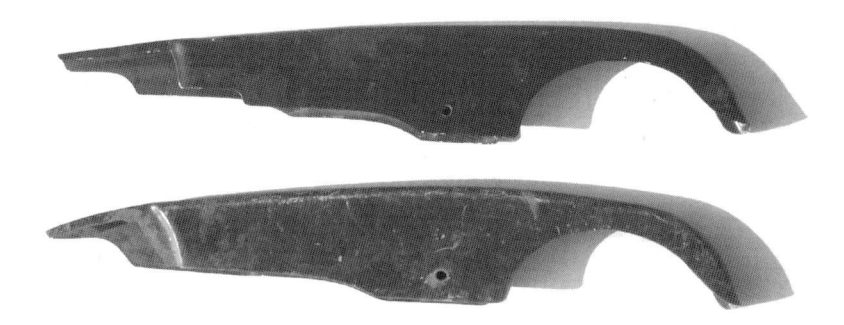

Fig 6.9. Nearside view of the B40 (top) and C15 (bottom) chain guards

The two sides of the chain guards guard are connected by a $^3/_8$" i/d tube at the visible mounting point hole in *Fig 6.9*.

Fig 6.10. C15 competition chain guard and below the chain guard fitted to the Welded/Duplex frames from '63 - '67

Fig 6.10 shows the C15 competition chain guard (top) as fitted to all C15S framed models ('59 to '62).The front mounting bracket is on the o/s as per the roadster chain guard. Below, the chain guard fitted to all Welded/Duplex framed models from '63 and continuing in use on the B44VS for 1968, seen here to show that it uses the same pressings as the earlier competition chain guard. The square panel with indented stiffening ribs is to prevent road filth transferring from tyre to lower chain run. This panel is supported and held in place by the chain guide, which connects to the damaged corner on this example by a 2BA bolt. The front, unsupported corner of this panel needs to be carefully positioned (bend it as necessary) if it is to avoid contact with the side of the tyre and the bottom run of the chain.

From the illustrations above it can be seen that there is only one common pressing used for all of the Welded/Duplex frame chain guards (an invitation to convert the first one you find into the one you need).

Fig 6.11. Top, the late '67 to 68 guard – as per the one shown in fig 6.10 but without the square panel - used on B25, B44SS.
Middle, the '69 to '70 guard with revised rear mounting point, for all models except B44VS
Bottom, '69 -'70 B44VS, TR25w guard which used the same guard with the addition of the square panel.

Most damage to all of the above guards can be repaired by the application of tin-bashing skills and welding torch. Where metal has worn thin it is usually best to cut out the area in question and let-in a new section. All of the typical damage/abuse displayed on the above guards is 'do-able' in this way.

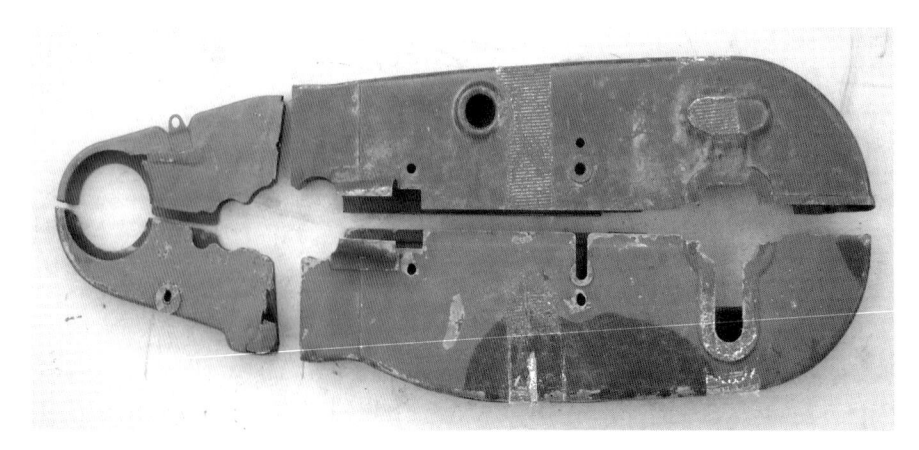

Fig 6.12 B40 Military Mk1 fully enclosed chainguard showing the four main parts

Chains And Sprockets 143

OIF chain guard

Only one design of chain guard was used and fitted to the '71 onward OIF 'T' and 'SS' models; the B50 MX omitted this item. The design comprised two parts; the chain guard itself which bolted in two places to the swinging arm and the 'chain guard extension' which bolted to the rear engine mount to cover the chain run above the gearbox sprocket.

In use, the OIF chain guard itself stands up well to vibration damage, this occurring most frequently at the rear mount. The extension similarly stands up well in use the main issue being its scarcity; many seemingly having been removed permanently by previous owners. As a replacement, something which looks the part is fairly simple to make from sheet steel, and with a bit more care a very good replica can be produced.

Fig 6.12. The OIF chain guard (above), and the extension piece (below).

Fig 6.13. The discrete fitted appearance of the OIF chain guard as seen on a '72 B25 Fleetstar

7. EXHAUST SYSTEMS

Silencers

This chapter begins with a small anecdote to illustrate the effect which the silencer can have on the performance of your Unit Single engine.

> *My first Starfire, a 1969 model, about 15 years old at the time but still in standard condition, including the exhaust system - would normally be happy rattling along at about 55mph on about ³/₈ throttle. It could be wound up quite a bit above this but on country 'A' roads, when in no particular hurry, this speed was the norm.*
>
> *During one particular journey between Lechlade and Highworth the feeling dawned on me that the bike was noticeably 'on-song' and that the improvement was perceptibly happening during this short, five miles or so stretch between these two towns. The improvement added up to an additional five mph or so for the usual amount of throttle, 3/8 or so open, and hence cruising along this stretch of 'A' road at around 60mph was noticeable and prompted my curiosity.*
>
> *When stationary it was apparent that the exhaust note was a bit louder than usual (this wasn't noticed at the time when under way due to the helmet and the fact that I was leaving the noise behind me). So, later on, off with the silencer for a look inside. This showed that the internals were starting to disintegrate due to rusting and that about one third of a circle of daylight could be seen right through the silencer; the last time the silencer had been off and I had performed this check no daylight was visible.*
>
> *I have read several times that fitting a louder silencer does not improve performance, that the increase in noise is simply giving this impression. The manufacturers themselves fostered this belief possibly to deter customers from fitting non-standard, after market silencers (and hence giving their cash to someone else). The above assertion is therefore not strictly true, it is clear that a silencer which allows unrestricted exit for the exhaust gasses will permit better breathing for the engine compared to one which requires the gasses to go through convoluted pathways to aid noise reduction.*

A silencer is at best a good compromise (but nonetheless still a compromise) between noise reduction and power output: if you increase quietness then power output is to some extent reduced.

It is an accepted fact that for best all-round performance a straight-through pipe of correct length is recommended, with the exception of a megaphone for racing use to provide power enhancement at certain rpm. This in itself contradicts the view that the correct, original pattern silencer is always the best one to fit. For those contemplating speed work with a straight through pipe the optimum length (at least as a starting point) is 36" to 40" measured around the outside of the pipe from cylinder head to outlet.

Regarding the above adventure with the Starfire, the silencer in question was of the type introduced for the '69 season to meet tightening USA noise level requirements. In connection with fitment of this silencer, BSA themselves recommended use only of the gauze air filter element rather than the paper one to reduce that restriction on the breathing and resulting power output of the engine.

It would be wrong of me to advocate the use of silencers which do not perform this function to a level acceptable to society. The MOT tester, your neighbours and the local constabulary may well object to this as well. On the other hand the sound our bikes make is very important to us; it is important that it sounds like a British Bike rather than a 'rice burner', and we also want it to perform at its best, don't we? Without accepting any liability in this matter I would therefore suggest that selection of a modern replacement silencer through which some daylight can be seen may well be the optimum choice.

The replacement silencers for your Unit Single which are available today are generally of good quality and serviceability; they generally fit and work well. The main bugbear with modern replacements is that the positioning of the mounting point is sometimes incorrect due to one generic silencer being listed for a range of models. In reality, detail differences exist between silencers for different models, which for reasons of cost have been overlooked by the manufacturers of today's replacements. Where possible when seeking a replacement, compare the new silencer against one which is already known to fit correctly. Otherwise be prepared for disappointment when the replacement is offered up.

Compared to original BSA equipment, replacements can come close but are generally inferior in quality and 'look', noticeably in the quality of the chrome plating. An original BSA silencer will generally rot out from the inside and take a while to do so even in the UK climate; a modern equivalent will generally rust through the chrome from the outside unless kept well protected in use.

Fig 7.1. '59 to '60 C15 Scrambler with straight through pipe - seen here as the USA Starfire Scrambler shown with lights, as standard.

Faithfulness to shape and size also varies but we are at least fortunate in still having a choice and the shortcomings of modern replacements are no worse than can be expected from the low volume batch production by which they are made. It's a good job that someone is actually still making these parts for us to use.

To some extent it is therefore a waste of time to detail all of the different shapes and types of silencer fitted to the Unit Single models, as when it comes to finding this item the choice may well be limited to a small number of available pattern variants. However, for those pursuing originality with regard to the less common exhaust systems I have included details which will allow manufacture from scratch or modification from more common parts. For example, the L/H high level silencers used on the '69 to '70 USA B25 and '70 TR25w are identical to the contemporary low level silencers with the rear let-in to clear the shock absorber and with the addition of threaded pummels to attach the heat shield. Modification from an easy to obtain silencer is therefore straightforward.

Exhaust Pipes

All models use pipes of $1^3/_8$" outside diameter except B50 models which use $1^1/_2$". As with the silencer, it is difficult to find modern-day replacements which can match original BSA quality. Visually the main issue is the lack of a smooth run-out from bends in the pipe, often seen as a perceptible step where the inner curve of a bend terminates. BSA avoided this, and also had access to a wider range of radii to bend their pipes around. Result, original BSA pipes with graceful bends and which fit correctly.

Exhaust Systems

Fig 7.2 shows a typical Unit Single low level exhaust system. The pipe shown is as used on all of the C15 and B40 road machines with the Swan-neck frame as indicated here by the lower portion of the pipe being straight. Fitting these engines into the Welded/Duplex frame requires a 'joggle' (shallow 'S' bend) mid-way along the straight portion as per the pipe for the B40 Military, B25 and B44 '67 to '70.

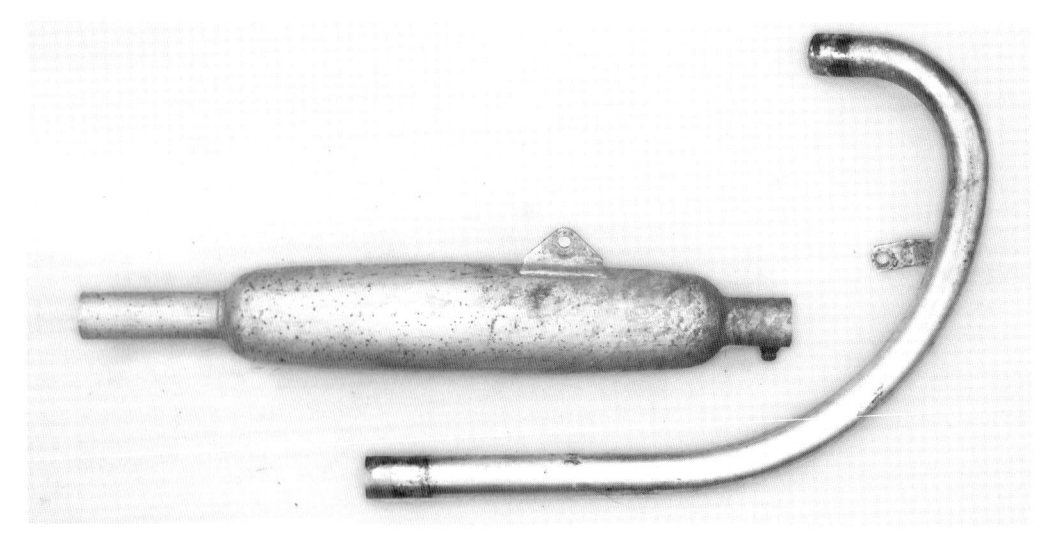

Fig 7.2. Exhaust system for the C15 and B40 models with Swan Neck frame

C15 and B40 pipes of this type are virtually identical but the B40 item is slightly taller. If the lower straight portion is placed on a flat surface with the pipe held upright the C15 item should measure $14\frac{1}{2}$" to the highest point; the B40 item 15".

The silencer shown (*fig. 7.2*) is the 'bargain basement' B40 military item with integral pipe clamp and welded-on bracket. The overall shape is the same for the C15 and B40 Star models for all years. The SS80 and 90 used a silencer which was slightly longer and also parallel sided (as per pre-unit 'C' range models) rather than being slightly wider in the middle as shown here.

From late '61 the silencer gained the familiar slotted mounting lug and separate bracket instead of the welded-on bracket shown and in this form continued on the B25 and B44 road models up to '68.

The next few pages show the different types of pipes and silencers fitted to the Unit Singles. Since it is more or less impossible to give dimensions of bends etc, this section relies on pictures to show the various exhaust systems fitted.

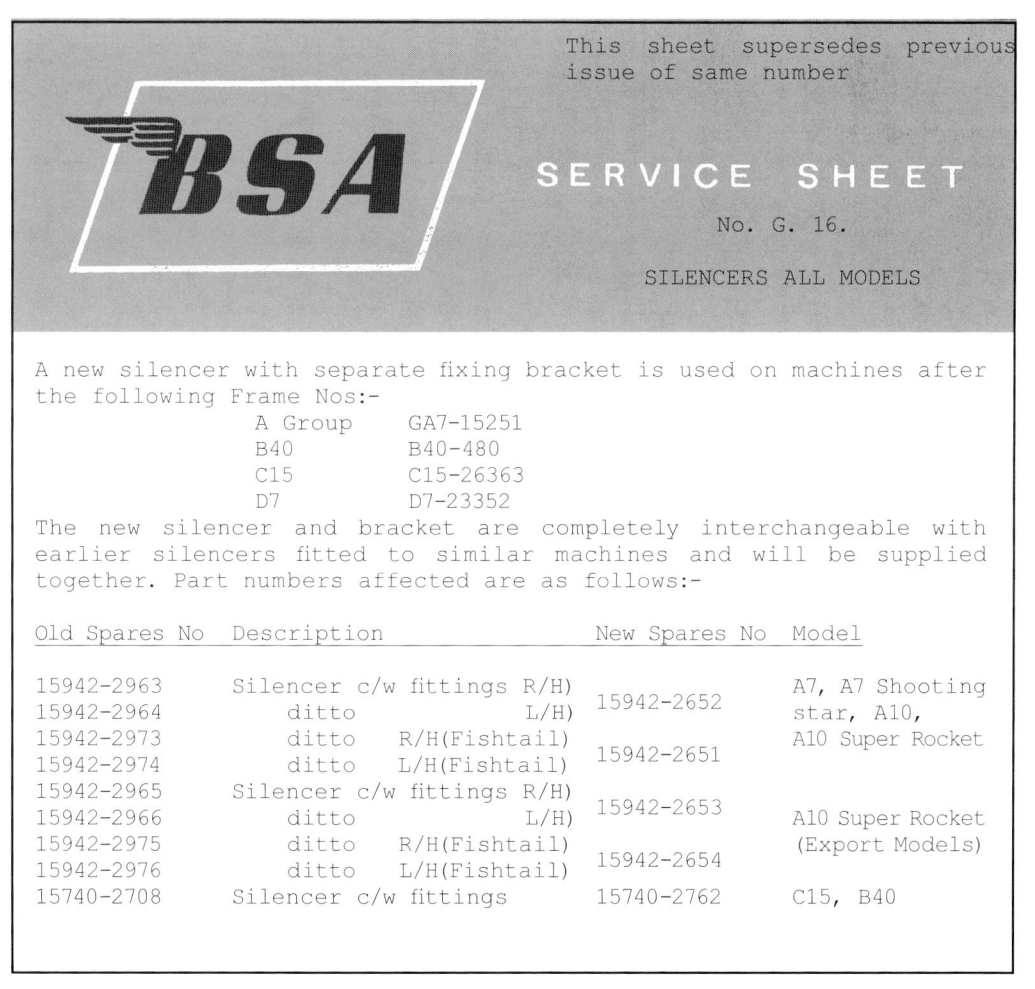

```
                                    This sheet supersedes previous
                                    issue of same number


        BSA                         SERVICE    SHEET

                                         No. G. 16.

                                    SILENCERS ALL MODELS

A new silencer with separate fixing bracket is used on machines after
the following Frame Nos:-
              A Group    GA7-15251
              B40        B40-480
              C15        C15-26363
              D7         D7-23352
The new silencer and bracket are completely interchangeable with
earlier silencers fitted to similar machines and will be supplied
together. Part numbers affected are as follows:-

Old Spares No  Description                  New Spares No   Model

15942-2963     Silencer c/w fittings R/H)                   A7, A7 Shooting
15942-2964         ditto              L/H)   15942-2652     star, A10,
15942-2973         ditto     R/H(Fishtail)                  A10 Super Rocket
15942-2974         ditto     L/H(Fishtail)   15942-2651
15942-2965     Silencer c/w fittings R/H)
15942-2966         ditto              L/H)   15942-2653
15942-2975         ditto     R/H(Fishtail)                  A10 Super Rocket
15942-2976         ditto     L/H(Fishtail)   15942-2654     (Export Models)
15740-2708     Silencer c/w fittings        15740-2762      C15, B40
```

Fig. 7.3. BSA's notification of silencer changes to include a bolted-on bracket.

Fig 7.4. See what I mean about graceful bends? As seen on a '65 C15T with its 'inside frame' system for the Welded/Duplex framed machines. The example shown is an original pipe which has been re-plated.

Fig 7.5. A '62 C15 Trials Special and Scrambles special with the leg-burning outside frame system used on the Swan-Neck framed machines. Works competition machines from this period were occasionally seen with l/h high level systems; these were not found on the production C15T or S.

Fig 7.6. The '59 to early '63 short silencer for Trials and Starfire Roadster models with the C15S Swan-Neck frame. It is $15^{1}/_{2}$" long, 3" o/d.

Exhaust Systems 149

Fig 7.7. The one-piece pipe and reverse-cone mega for the '61 to '62 Scrambler. The mega is of the same dimensions as that used with a separate header pipe on the '63 to '65 C15S and the B44GP and is completely empty. The '59 to '61 C15 Scramblers used a lengthened plain header pipe alone. Both systems produce a 'music to the ears' noise.

Fig 7.8. Graceful bends identify this as an original BSA pipe. This high level example in dull chrome is from a B40 Roughrider, as marked at its outlet end (see fig 7.9) but here also written on the pipe.

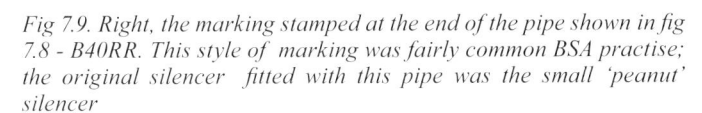

Fig 7.9. Right, the marking stamped at the end of the pipe shown in fig 7.8 - B40RR. This style of marking was fairly common BSA practise; the original silencer fitted with this pipe was the small 'peanut' silencer

The R/H hi-level pipes of the type shown were fitted to several unit single models. Despite appearing similar, detail differences are necessary to suit the various engines and silencers eg the postion of the front mounting bracket and the angle/length of the outlet. 'One size will not fit all' - expect pattern pipes to require 'persuasion'.

Fig 7.10. The weird and wonderful exhaust system to allow wading as seen on the '64 C15AA military prototype for the Australian army.

Introduced purely for reasons of style, '69 -'70 left-hand high level systems with pipes known as the hockey stick, (*see fig 7.13*) carried large bulky silencers which produce a striking appearance but reduced practicality. The '69 pipe carries the wire mesh heat shield, the '70 version the GRP shield finished in silver metal flake. Note that the '70 pipe has an outlet of enlarged diameter; the silencer to suit is the '69 TR25w (right hand fitting) item but with one threaded pummel rather than two.

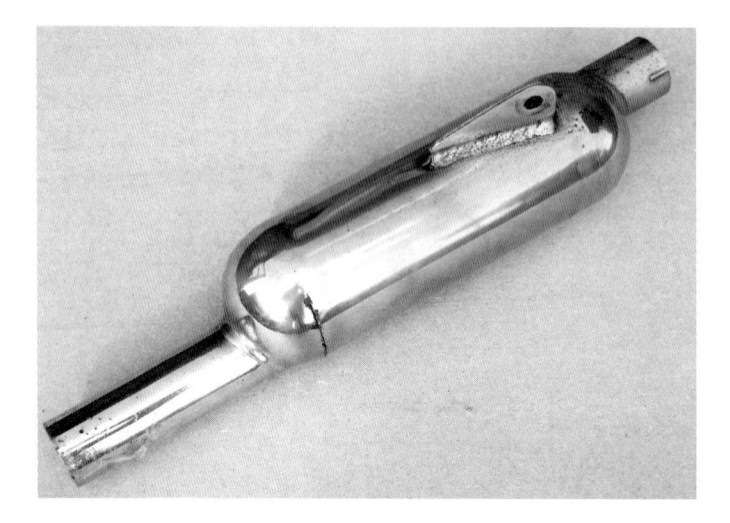

Fig 7.11. The small high level silencer as used on the C15T and Starfire Roadster '63 to '65, and B44VE '66; original example shown but clearly in need of repair.

Fig 7.12. The ever popular 'peanut' silencer which replaced the slightly larger item shown above. The peanut was originally used on the '67 B44VS and '68 TR25w and Roughrider with inside-frame high level pipe; neat, attractive and beautifully noisy.

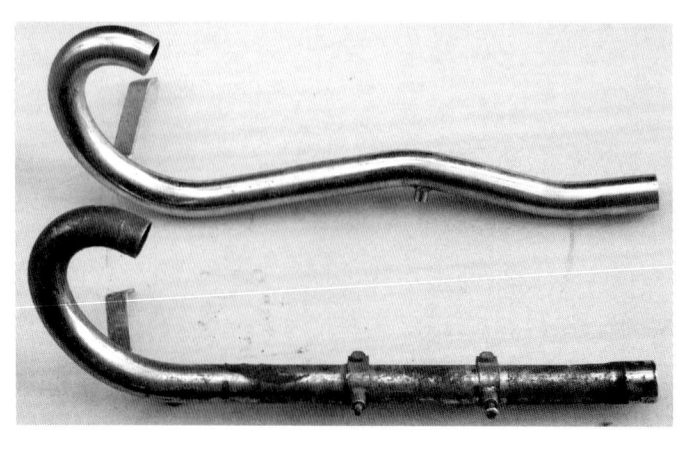

Fig 7.13. USA B25 left hand high level pipes, '69 upper and '70 lower (also '70 TR25w and known as the 'hockey stick')

Have you ever noticed that riding as we do in the UK on the left, the road camber necessitates a slight lean to the right to prevent ending up in the gutter? Under these circumstances, the Unit Single is additionally disadvantaged by the engine being positioned to the left rather than centrally in the frame. This factor adds to the right-leaning tendency necessary to proceed in a straight line. The left-hand, high-level exhaust systems add more weight in this direction leading to an even more imbalanced ride in the UK; assuming that the rider is sensitive enough to notice! Riding on the right, as in most countries, may in this case be a blessing.

Fig 7.14. The l/h high level exhaust as fitted to the '69 USA B25S. The silencer is as per the '69 and early '70 low level item but with the threaded boss for the heat shield and indent on the rear to clear the shock absorber. This is the silencer which restricts performance and was introduced to meet US noise regulations as explained in the service sheet which follows (fig 7.15)

```
                                                    October 1968


                  ┌─────────┐
                  │  BSA    │     S E R V I C E   S H E E T
                  └─────────┘
                                         No. 188
                                   B25 MODELS SILENCING


 The silencing of 1969 model B25 machines has been considerably
 improved by the use of a new silencer. To maintain performance, we
 have changed to a two layer gauze air filter with a 180cc main jet
 in the carburetter.

 Pre 1969 models can be converted to the latest specification by
 using the following parts

        Part No   Description
        60-1053   Air filter complete
        70-9652   Silencer (B25 Home, B25 Fleet Star)
        70-9683   Silencer (B25 USA)
        19-2878   180 Main Jet (Amal 376/100)

 NOTE:  The two layer gauze air filter element CANNOT be used in the
 four layer air filter case
```

Fig 7.15. The service sheet describing the silencer changes to meet US regulations. These changes were also applied to the B44SS (except the main jet size), the effect being similarly restrictive of performance

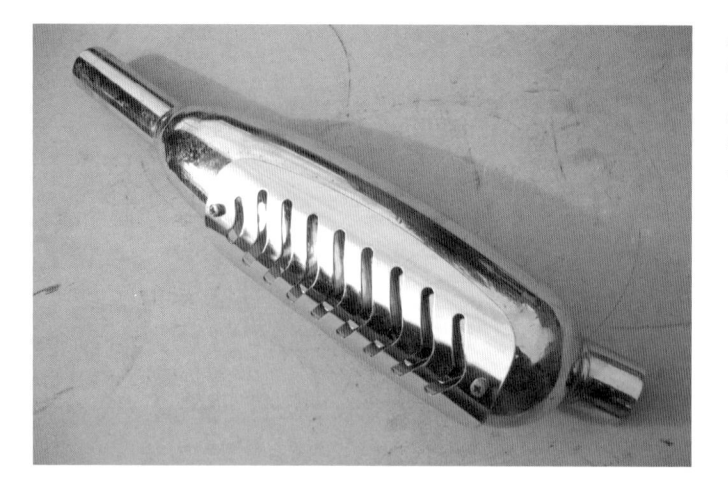

Fig 7.16. The '68 to '70 B44VS r/h high level silencer with its 'chevron' heat-shield; used with the inside-frame high level pipe much as the Roughrider item shown earlier.

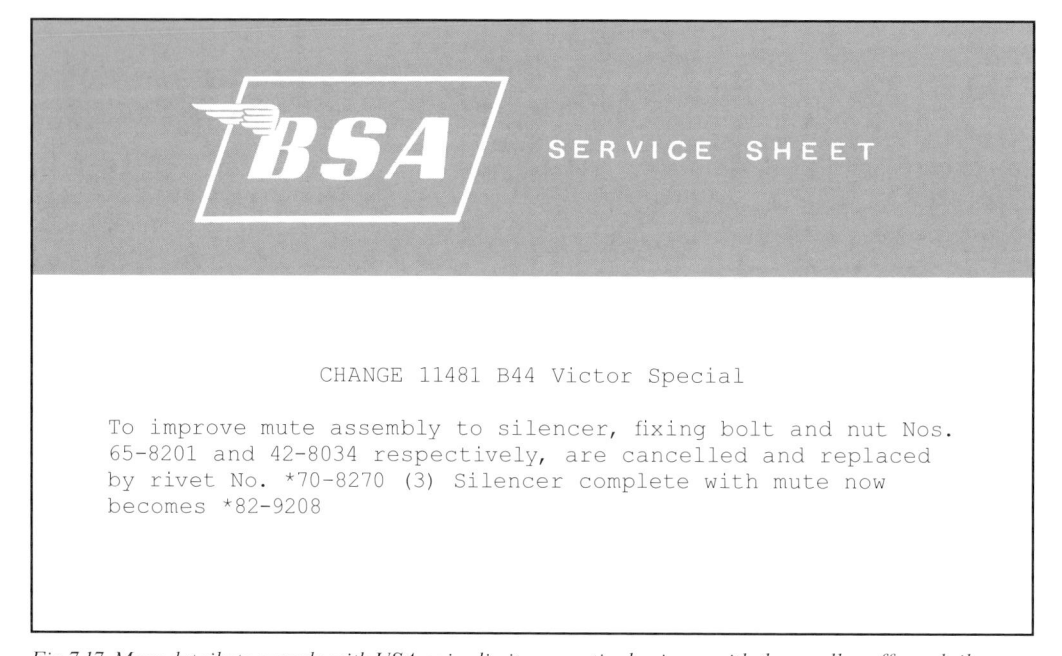

BSA SERVICE SHEET

CHANGE 11481 B44 Victor Special

To improve mute assembly to silencer, fixing bolt and nut Nos. 65-8201 and 42-8034 respectively, are cancelled and replaced by rivet No. *70-8270 (3) Silencer complete with mute now becomes *82-9208

Fig 7.17. More details to comply with USA noise limits, a particular issue with the smaller off-road silencers

Regarding replacement exhaust pipes, as ever we have to take what we can get these days but the bottom line in not replicating BSA quality means not replicating BSA fit; problems in getting a new pipe to line up are not uncommon. Obtaining a pipe with a view to cutting it and welding it to fit before re-plating it is sometimes the only way to solve a difficult plumbing problem. Of the Unit Single pipes the high level ones are the most likely candidates for this, the r/h high level pipes which should pass inside the frame often hit the frame.

Faced with these kinds of problems, a viable solution is to stick with the original BSA pipe (if you have one). After all, it is made of steel and no matter how bad it is, it can be repaired by weld or braze. Rust pits for example can be flooded with braze or silver solder, flatted off, re-polished and chromed, but this obviously involves work, meaning time and/or money.

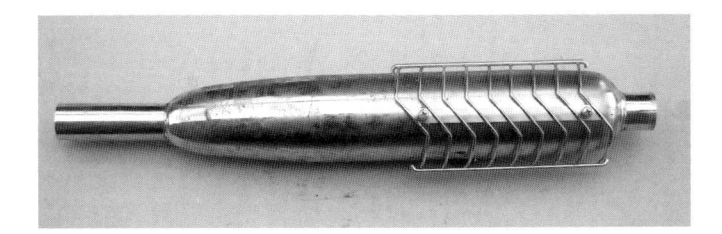

Fig 7.18. (Above) The TR25w '69 right hand high level silencer

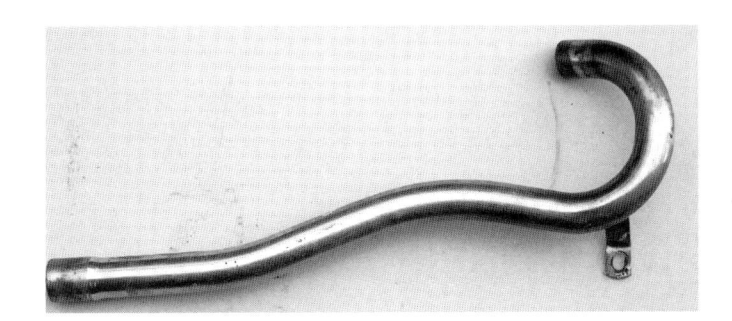

Fig 7.19. The outside-frame, high level pipe to suit the silencer shown in Fig 7.18 above. Note that the outlet of the pipe is enlarged to 1½" to suit this silencer which was borrowed from the A65 Firebird.

Fig. 7.20. The GRP heat shield with silver metal flake finish as fitted to the '70 TR25w and USA B25S. This exhaust system uses the straight 'hockey stick' header pipe with the silencer (minus the front threaded boss) from the '69 TR25w.

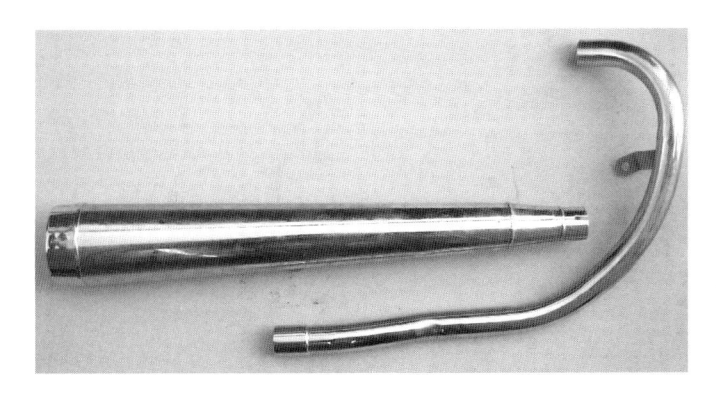

Fig. 7.21. The mid '70 onward B25S/B44SS low level system with megaphone silencer borrowed from the twins with enlarged pipe outlet (to 1,½") to suit. The megaphone silencer (shown in fig 7.21) was subsequently re-used on the '72 B25 Fleetstar; the low-level pipe for this application being much the same but with a more acute 'S' bend.

BSA SERVICE SHEET

Changes 20523/20700/20701/20772
Models A and B Groups 1970

On Home and Overseas models excluding USA to comply with noise level regulations.

Old No	New No	Description	Model
70-9724	*71-1815	Exhaust pipe complete	B25
70-9652	*71-2000	Silencer complete	B25, B44SS
02-0204	14-0101	Bolt)Bracket to	B25, B44SS
82-9020	cancelled	S/Washer)Silencer	B25, B44SS
02-2395	14-1301	Nut)	B25, B44SS
24-8784	cancelled	S/Washer) Bracket to	B25, B44SS
14-0302	14-1303	Nut) frame	B25, B44SS
70-9725	*71-1813	Exhaust pipe complete	B44SS
70-9127	71-1839	Exhaust pipe L/H)	A65 L, T
70-9130	71-1837	Exhaust pipe R/H)	
68-2789	71-1933	Exhaust pipe L/H)	A50R
68-2791	71-1935	Exhaust pipe R/H)	
71-1319	71-1710	Silencer)	
68-2781	71-1842	Silencer bracket L/H)	A50R, A65L, A65T
68-2780	71-1841	Silencer bracket R/H)	

B Group models must use new type exhaust pipe and silencer together. A Group models may use new type silencer with old pipes providing correct silencer brackets are also used.

Fig 7.22. The original BSA information detailing the introduction of the megaphone silencer, again to meet USA noise level regulations but without the power-sapping effect as with the previous cigar-shaped item.

Fig 7.23. How the megaphone silencer looks on the late '70 B25S; not bad on the eye?

Fig 7.24. B40 Military silencer type as supplied from '70. This is a fibreglass filled 'absorption' silencer, also supplied in bright chrome for military use on escort machines which required its improved silencing capabilities.

Exhaust system finishes

All Unit Single exhaust systems carry a chrome plate finish, usually 'bright' chrome except for WDB40 and Roughrider models which used 'dull' chrome, and the OIF high pipe models which featured 'black' chrome to match the matt black lozenge silencer. Occasionally the model for which the pipe is intended will be found stamped at the outlet end of the genuine item.

Fitting your exhaust system

All Unit Single pipes carry a front fixing strap to the front engine to frame bolt. This may need persuasion to position it correctly and the majority which fit to the offside require a ⅛" spacer on the bolt between the strap and the frame lug – to avoid the step on the frame lug.

The commonest problem with the Unit Single low level pipes is their frequent contact with the head of the bottom engine to frame bolt – the long one under the engine. This contact can be the source of an annoying rattle and if left alone it will put a nice dent in the pipe, although you won't see it until you remove the pipe. This bolt was specially made with a thin rounded head (with only two flats) by BSA to try and provide sufficient clearance with the pipe. Omission of the spacer under the front mounting strap of the pipe (as described above) will move the pipe inward and make the problem worse hence fitting a thicker spacer at this position to get clearance is worth trying. This is also worthwhile to cure the occasional '69/70 problem of the pipe contacting the frame tube just forward of the lower engine bolt, and similarly contacting the outer timing cover of sidepoints engines just below the kickstart.

Don't go mad with the thickness of the front spacer though, positioning the pipe too far outboard will bring it into contact with the inner surface of the footpeg (if it isn't already), risk it fouling the kickstart lever and spoil alignment with the silencer. If you have a pipe which isn't touching something it shouldn't, somewhere along its length; consider yourself lucky!

A similar state of affairs afflicts the R/H high level pipes of models with the Welded/Duplex frame (not the C15S Swan-Neck competition frames thankfully as these have an 'outside-frame' pipe) where they pass between the frame tubes immediately forward of the silencer. Original pipes don't foul here, but pattern pipes can be an absolute nightmare in this region. After you have got over the tantrum resulting from trying a fifth different pattern pipe and finding that just like the other four it won't line up with the silencer 'cos it's hitting the frame, consider sawing the end off, welding bits of pipe back on with the right bend and leaving it at that – its hard to see the bit hidden under the oil tank.

A semi-frequent problem with the low level exhaust systems is a drooping silencer. Being supported only at and near its front end, the rear end of the silencer can adopt a downward attitude in use, particularly if it is one of the longer, heavier types - notably the restrictive '69/70 B25/B44 item. The easiest solution is to elongate the two ³⁄₈" mounting holes in the silencer bracket; ie the angled ⅛" thick bracket which fits between the silencer and the pillion footrest hanger. This will allow you to slacken the pipe-to-silencer clamp, hoist the silencer rear end upward, and then tighten the two ³⁄₈" bolts and the clamp.

Fig 7.25. Silencer bracket for '67 to '70 B25/B44 with low-level exhaust. It comes new with slightly elongated ³⁄₈' bolt holes; elongate them more if you need to hitch your silencer upward to prevent it visually seeming to droop.

C15 and B40 road models have a flat triangular plate which mounts the silencer to the pillion foot peg bolt.

In mid-1970, again seemingly to comply with US noise regulations, UK B25 and all B44SS models adopted the A65 megaphone silencer which had similarly just been introduced on those models. This required a new downpipe, of the same bend as previously but with the outlet end enlarged to 1½" to suit the silencer *(figs 7.21-7.23)*.

The OIF silencer

The large black painted 'lozenge' silencer *(fig 7.26)* fitted to OIF SS and T models has its own set of problems which stem from age and use. Namely these relate to rust and vibration problems; the former attacking the back and the latter the welded-on mounting brackets. As such it behaves much as the usual Japanese trail bike silencer, at least welding it back together followed by a lick of matt black paint is simple enough. B25 and B50 versions of this silencer are identical other than the size of inlet to suit the 1³⁄₈" or 1½" exhaust pipe. Late production examples have an angled tail pipe to direct exhaust gases away from the indicator.

The OIF B25 Fleetstar is theoretically alone of the '71 onward models to be fitted with a low level exhaust system as standard. I say 'theoretically' because the '72 B50 parts book gives part numbers for a low level system for the UK B50 SS model. Whether any machines were supplied to this spec remains conjecture. Certainly, a B50 low level exhaust pipe is listed by at least one pattern exhaust system supplier but this does not follow the same run as the original BSA item which would go above the footpeg as does the OIF Fleetstar item, rather than below it as do the pattern pipes. The low level OIF Fleetstar pipe is therefore similar to

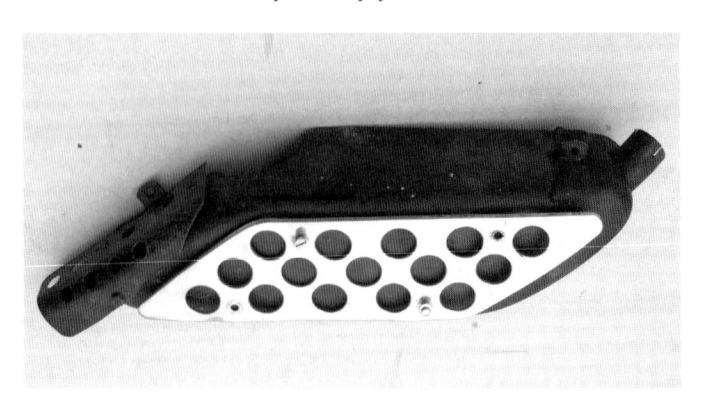

Fig 7.26. Silencer fitted to OIF models showing the two separate heat shields in position

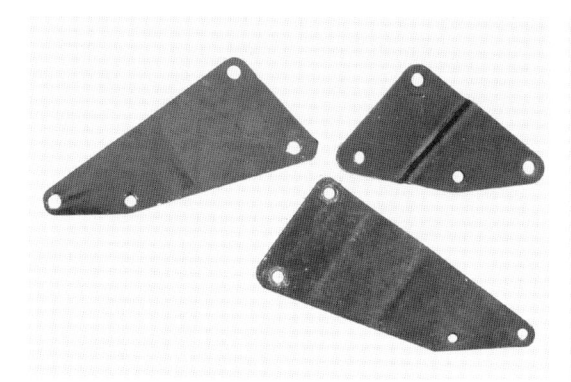

Fig 7.27. High level silencer brackets for B25, TR25w, B44VS. Left, B44VS and '69 TR25w. Right top, '69 USA B25. Right bottom, '70 TR25w and USA B25

Fig 7.28. Low level silencer brackets. Top, first used on C15E Trials Pastoral and subsequently B25, B44 '67 - '68 and all B40 Military. Middle '69 - '70 B25, B44. Bottom '72 B25 Fleetstar. Not shown are the simple small triangular plate for all C15, B40 Star and the elongated version for the SS models

the previous Starfire low level pipe, but the staggered bend below the kickstart is more severe and the outlet end is enlarged to $1^1/_2$" diameter to suit the A65 megaphone silencer to which it is married. Other changes required by the fitment of this low level system are: a stepped spacer behind the o/s footpeg to create space for the pipe to run above it, a much-extended o/s rear engine plate which now also forms the silencer bracket, and a kickstart lever with more severe angle of bend to prevent it fouling the pipe. Use of this system is one way to make your OIF single sound more like a British Bike than the lozenge silencer does. Alternatively the 'peanut' silencer from the earlier trail models is often seen fitted to OIF models, and to good effect.

The B50 MX 'silencer' is a development of the earlier scrambles reverse-cone mega but more severely convoluted in shape to fit between the o/s shock absorber and rear wheel and should be modified (with a vice!) as shown in *fig 7.30* if still in original condition.

The '73 B50MX and '74 TR5MX fitted eye catching twin right hand high level silencers in an attempt to combat exhaust noise to meet USA regulations without sacrificing power output. These were also capable of accepting spark arrestors in the outer ends, again to suit the yanks and their dry countryside. The 1-into-2 manifold for this system still turns up from time to time, but the silencers themselves are now hard to find.

Fig 7.29. The real thing; '71/'72 B50MX silencer, well tucked-in

JULY 1971
No. 24/71

BSA

SERVICE SHEET

EXHAUST SYSTEM
B50 MX

A limited number of the first B50 MX models to be despatched had a condition whereby on full compression of the rear suspension the megaphone silencer fouled the rear wheel spoke.

To rectify, deform the outlet end of the megaphone cone by compressing in a clamp or vice to make the outlet oval and measure $1\frac{1}{4}''$ across. Secondly, fit a $\frac{1}{4}''$ distance piece between the megaphone bracket and its fixing point on the frame.

END VIEW

Top view of megaphone silencer

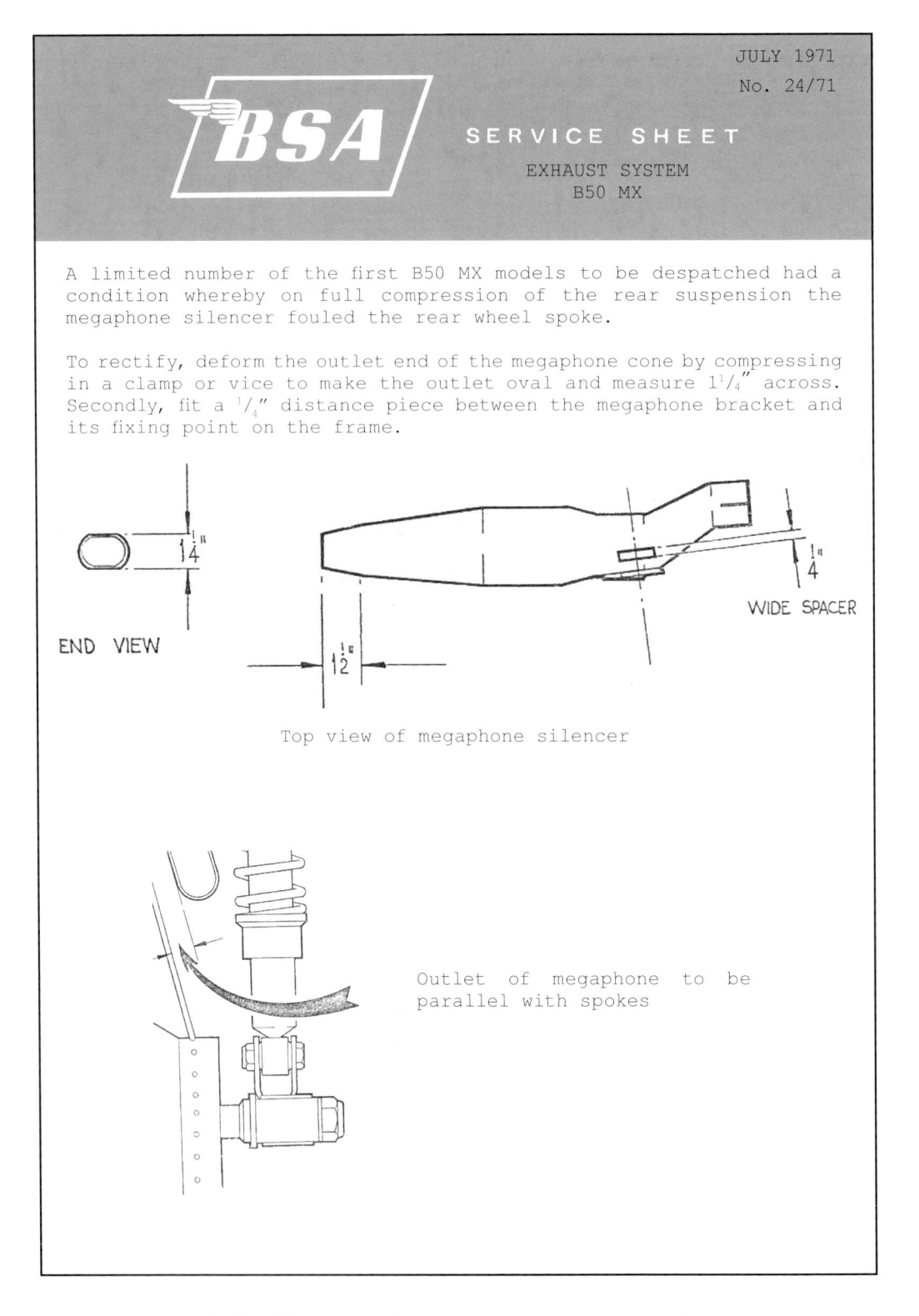

WIDE SPACER

Outlet of megaphone to be parallel with spokes

Fig 7.30. BSA's suggested modifications to the B50MX megaphone.

Exhaust Systems

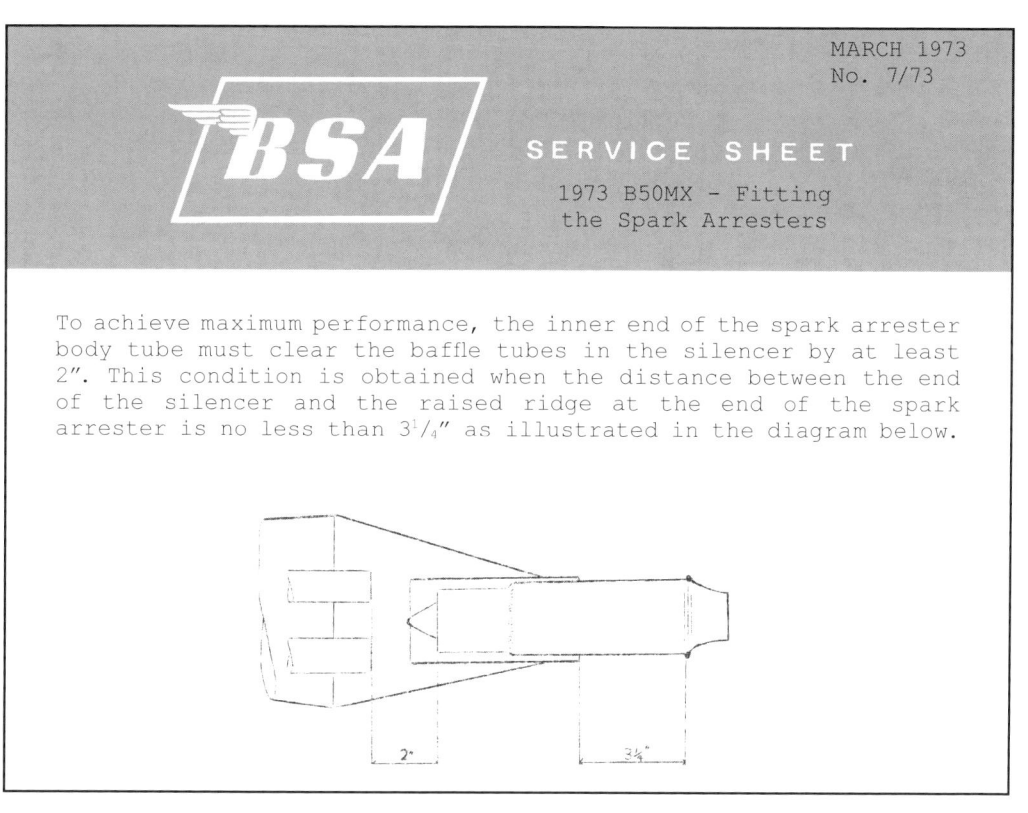

> MARCH 1973
> No. 7/73
>
> **BSA** SERVICE SHEET
> 1973 B50MX - Fitting
> the Spark Arresters
>
> To achieve maximum performance, the inner end of the spark arrester body tube must clear the baffle tubes in the silencer by at least 2". This condition is obtained when the distance between the end of the silencer and the raised ridge at the end of the spark arrester is no less than $3\frac{1}{4}$" as illustrated in the diagram below.

Fig 7.31. BSA service sheet describing the fitting of the spark arresters

Fig 7.32. '73 B50MX and TR5MX twin silencers with spark arrestors. The black chrome finished high level pipe to suit this system and the 'Y' manifold has a modified outlet bend compared to the '71/72 system.

8. STANDS

Side Stands '59 to '70

All models fitted a side stand except the '68 to '70 Fleetstar. The basic design (*see fig 8.1*) is a steel casting with a welded-on foot up to the end of '69, with a one-piece item with its end angled outward for '70. Why they bothered changing it I haven't yet fathomed (although the '70 type is easier to find with your left toe to flip it down. The upper end of the stand is forked to fit onto the lug provided on the frame to which it is connected by the same shouldered and hardened pivot bolt used for all of these stands. This bolt is retained by a tab washer which should not be omitted as the bolt will definitely unscrew without it.

Should you need to source a replacement (because they do wear away), the welded-on foot is the same item as the grooved pad used on the relatively common Bantam foot brake pedal.

C15 T and S Swan Neck framed competition models are alone in carrying the side stand on the offside rather than the nearside, which is already too congested with the foot peg and brake pedal in the normal nearside stand position. The stand used on these models differs by having the foot welded on at a different angle and by the addition of a second lug opposite the first for the spring to hook onto. The spring is carried outboard of the stand, which is also different to usual practice.

Leaving aside the one-piece '70 item and the offside competition version, the standard item comes in two different lengths which are fully interchangeable – except that they alter the angle of lean when the bike is resting on the side stand. This is something often overlooked if/when alterations are made to tyre or wheel sizes and the result can be rather precarious regarding the stability of the bike on its stand.

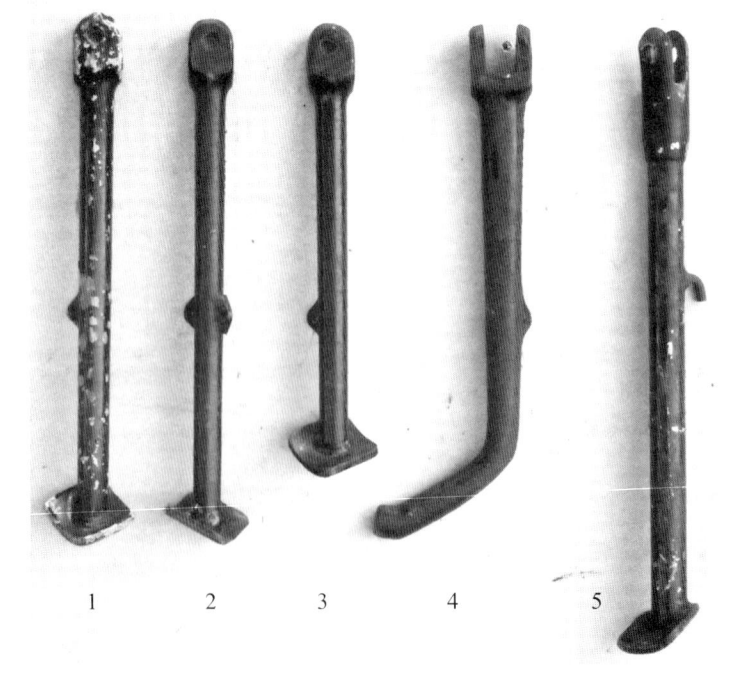

Fig 8.1. Side stands all years

1. For Swan-Neck frame C15/B40 road models
2. R/H item for competition machines to '62 with 2nd welded-on spring lug and foot reversed
3. For most Welded/Duplex frames to '69 (some models in off-road form seem to have fitted the earlier C15 item to compensate for larger wheel/tyre sizes);
4. For all models '70 only but fully interchangeable with earlier types. Often mistaken for the contemporary A65 stand, which is substantially longer;
5. The stand for '71 onward OIF models.

The shorter of these two stands at $8^1/_4$" from pivot centre to foot centre is used on all B25, B44, TR25w and B40 military models '67 to '69; it seems able to cope with the slight changes in wheel and tyre sizes used on these models. The longer version at $9^1/_2$" long over these distances is fitted to C15 and B40 road models for all years and '63 onward competition models with the Welded/Duplex frame. Again, it seems able to cope with the different size wheels of these models.

Side stand problems

Other than the foot, wear usually takes place around the pivot area on all of these stands. To minimise this, avoid kick-starting the bike while it is leaning on this stand as this will accelerate wear and damage to the bolt, lug sides, lug hole and insides of the stand's forked end which will also spread if you persist in this abuse. In severe cases, the frame tubing carrying the lug can also distort and destroy the correct geometry of the stand. If you can wobble the end of your stand up and down by more than 1" then wear at the pivot point has reached a point where attention is needed; the first thing to try is a new pivot bolt before resorting to surgery.

The B40 military models have a pivot bolt with an extended thread to accept a lock nut instead of the lock-washer under the bolt head. This extended bolt now seems unavailable, fitment of the standard bolt with lock-washer seems to be the sensible alternative. If the lock-washer is omitted the pivot bolt will unscrew in use - potentially dangerous.

Sloppiness of fit at the pivot will also result in the stand folding up too far. On C15 and B40 road models this will result in the foot of the stand coming into contact with the rear brake anchor strap - a potentially dangerous condition if allowed to persist - I have seen examples of this strap significantly worn away and hence weakened by the hammering action of the stand.

The stand itself doesn't usually bend but if it does, heating it to red-hot will allow it to be persuaded straight and this remedy can also be applied if the forked end has become distorted.

OIF Side Stand '71 On

The OIF side stand is something of a problem area. Not only does it bend, especially if the bike is habitually started whilst resting on it, but the frame plate on which it pivots readily breaks off around the pivot point. Basically these failures are due to this arrangement being too flimsy. The stand itself is tubular with a solid brazed-on clevis fork at its upper end; the bending usually occurs on the tube just below the join with the solid forked end - the tube is clearly too weak for the stresses at this point. The forked end will also spread apart in use as wear occurs. The pivot arrangement of the stand on the frame lug is by a pivot bolt and locknut, this bolt passes through a hardened sleeve in the frame which must not be omitted.

Unlike most of the OIF cycle parts, the side stand was not a new design having previously been used on Bantam Bushman models for which it was perfectly adequate. Once you have heated and straightened your stand, avoid anything more than the weight of the bike being carefully applied to it. The foot and its wear and replacement if necessary, is the same as the pre '70 side stands.

The original frame plate on which the stand swivelled was a fabrication of two layers of steel plate. Replacement of any missing areas can be satisfactorily achieved by welding-in a single piece of the correct thickness to match the remaining piece.

Centre Stand

In keeping with the main frame types, there are three basic designs of centre stand, for Swan Neck Frames, Welded/Duplex frames (two distinct types), and OIF models, as shown in *fig 8.2*. None of the these centre stands are interchangeable due to the different fixing methods on the frame.

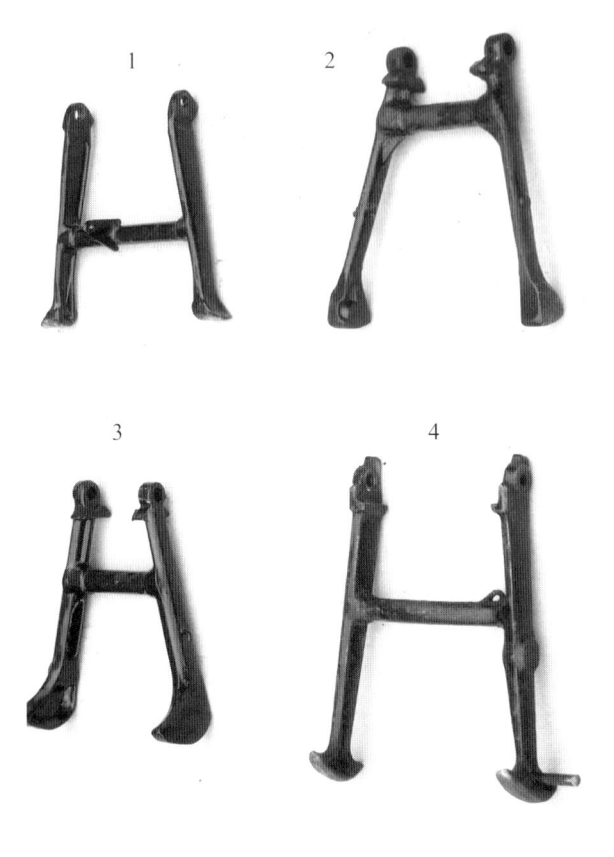

Fig 8.2. The four centre stands.

1 For C15/B40 Swan-Neck frame, the B40 item being approximately 1" longer below the cross-tube (see Fig 8.3).

2 Welded/Duplex framed models to mid '68 and all B40 Military. The C15E version has full rather than flat-sided feet.

3 Welded/Duplex framed models mid '68 to '70. Similar versions with detail differences are used on larger BSA models.

4: '71 onward OIF

C15 and B40 Swan Neck frame stands

The centre stand for C15 and B40 road models, comprises a malleable iron casting for each leg, these being connected by a welded-on centre tube. Originally, this design of stand was available in two different lengths to suit B40 or C15 models, the longer was fitted to the B40 as required by its larger wheels and therefore slightly increased ground clearance. This design of stand differs from the later Unit Single stands by dint of its method of attachment to the frame; each leg pivots on a clevis pin between a pair of lugs on the frame, the shape of each leg around the pivot point being such that it limits the extent of travel of the stand. These frame lugs are very robust and well up to the job; unlike the welded-on plates of the later frames which can distort in use.

In use the feet of the stand, which are rather modest in area, tend to wear quite quickly, likewise the pivot pins and pivot holes meaning that the stand travels beyond the correct 'down' position. The usual worn condition of these stands is therefore one where both wheels remain in contact with the ground when the stand is down. Refurbishment should therefore commence with returning the worn pivot holes back to size – drill out and braze-in steel sleeves – to restore the correct geometry of the stand when down. This should be followed by brazing or welding steel pads under the feet to hold the rear wheel 1" clear of the ground. In this way the C15 item can even be modified to suit the 18" B40 size wheels.

Also check that the frame and anything else such as the silencer, do not connect with the stand when it is up. It should be held clear by the edges of the legs around the pivot holes bottoming in the mounting slots first before contact is made elsewhere.

When the pivot holes are worn the C15/B40 centre stand is also prone to make contact with the rear brake anchor strap when folded up; it shouldn't when in 'as new' condition.

In common with some Bantam models, the C15/B40 item is sprung via a swivelling 'C' bracket. Ensure that this is free to swivel on the shouldered bolt which connects it to the frame.

The C15 and B40 competition models do not have provision for a centre stand except for the two versions of the C15 Trials Pastoral; the C15A framed version can fit the B40 stand *(fig 8.3)*, the '64 and '65 C15E Duplex/Welded framed version fitted a new stand, much the same as that fitted to the Welded/Duplex framed models of '67, this being used on C/B25, B44 and B40 military models.

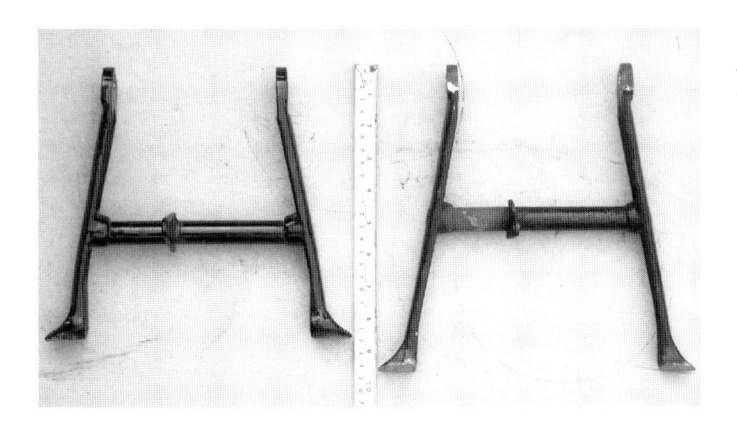

Fig 8.3. C15 and B40 centre stands, approximately 1" difference in overall height. These can be identified by the part number cast inside the legs; C15 has the '40' part number, B40 the '41' number.

Centre stands for the Welded/Duplex framed models

This design comprises two cast steel legs with a welded-on cross tube. It pivots on a ½" diameter bar which passes through two lugs on the frame, shaped to provide the 'stops' for both positions of the stand. Grease nipples are provided on the stand at the pivot points and the pin (which carries a Thackeray spring washer to limit side play of the stand) has a sleeve fitted over its centre portion to resist bending of the frame lugs. All B44 competition and off-road models omit the centre stand, no lugs are provided for one, likewise the TR25w. The legs of this stand are rather slender which often results in bending near the feet if abuse is received. As with any of the solid cast parts of your bike, heating locally to red hot will allow the offending area to be put straight.

From mid '68 this stand was superseded on B25 and B44 models by a similar design but featuring legs of heavier section. For this stand the frame lugs and hence the pivot points are spaced closer together, the two stands are therefore not interchangeable. This stand is sometimes found to be questionable regarding its positioning due possibly to variations in the machining of the stops; when 'down' it sometimes goes too far forward, even when new. Addition of metal to the two (make sure they are identically dealt with) stops on the stand - preferable to altering the frame stops – is the best course of action. This should result in the stand adopting a 7 o'clock position when viewed from the n/s rather than its more usual, and suspect, 8 o'clock. Whilst examining the position of this centre stand, have a look at its 'up' position, you may wish to consider removal of metal from the appropriate stops to allow it to rest higher.

OIF centre stand

The '71 onward OIF centre stand was originally available only as an optional extra, which explains its scarcity then and now. It was of a new design to suit the new frame for '71 and is therefore not interchangeable with any of the previous Unit Single centre stands. Other than this it follows the usual arrangement of two cast legs with a welded on cross-tube connecting these, the whole pivoting on two shouldered bolts at the frame lugs. It also follows the usual pattern of wear and distortion of the feet, pivot holes and stop-pegs; although this is a robust design which copes well in use.

The OIF centre stand does not seem to suffer from the inadequacies of the side stand but, as usual, don't habitually start the bike while it is on the stand.

Alternative Stands

Should you be desperate for a centre stand, the contemporary stand from the twin cylinder models, both BSA and Triumph, will often be found to fit the '67 onward Unit Singles. The only difference often seems to be the additional peg sticking out from the nearside leg of the twin cylinder item (which needs this for your toe to hook onto due to the n/s exhaust pipe being in the way). This unwanted extra is easily rectified by application of a hacksaw.

The less often seen o/s of the '70 USA B25 Starfire. The only B25 model not to have provision for a centre stand. This is an early '70 model, as indicated by the badly fitting front guard. Modification of the mounting brackets to correct this were introduced during the '70 season.

9. CONTROLS

Handlebars

This is probably the part of the bike most likely to be changed by the owner to suit their personal taste and comfort. Other than the C15 and B40 Star models which originally had handlebars with welded-on clutch and brake lever brackets, all Unit Singles have handlebars which can be swapped and changed with ease.

For the purists amongst us who require handlebars exactly matching the originals, the best plan is to refurbish a genuine bar by re-chroming it after any necessary straightening. To avoid possible problems of lack of rotational clearance at the twist grip, original BSA handlebars were sometimes left un-chromed in this area.

For those requiring a close approximation, the BSA parts book for the model in question will provide a very good illustration of the shape and style of bars you need. Beyond this it is purely a matter of personal taste for the owner to decide what handlebars they prefer to fit. The limiting factors regarding choice of handlebar are:

> *Cable length.* Fitting higher than standard bars may necessitate longer control cables; depending on how much slack you have in these to start with and how much higher

Fig 9.1. 1971 T25T - neat 'n' tidy.

you want to go. Lowering the bars may result in excessive slack in the cables and an untidy layout.

Restricted steering travel. Handlebars which are insufficiently high to clear the petrol tank; including leaving sufficient space for the fingers between any of the controls and the tank, are a no-no for reasons of safety.

Handlebar straightening

If the bike has been dropped at any time it is likely that the handlebar end will have hit the ground with some force meaning that the bars may no longer be true. It must be stated that the risk of weakening the handlebar by straightening it after it has been bent should be considered carefully by the owner and preferably a new replacement should be obtained. Any such steps to straighten the handlebars are undertaken entirely at the owner's risk. As such, any severe kinks or indentations which are visible in the surface of the handlebar, eg at the clamp position where this has bitten-in when the bar bent at this point, render it scrap. Only slightly out-of-true handlebars should be considered suitable for straightening.

To check the symmetry of handlebars a flat surface is required on which ten or so parallel lines are drawn an inch or so apart and long enough to span the bars. The handlebars should be placed with the straight centre portion (where the clamps fit) parallel with the uppermost line. The tips of the bars should then rest on the flat surface on the area where the other lines are drawn. With a perfectly straight pair of bars two things should be apparent:

> The whole length of the straight centre portion and both ends should contact the surface at the same time.

> Both ends should be level and parallel in relation to the lines on the surface.

Performing this check will make it obvious which side of a handlebar has been bent up and back; the usual direction of damage. Straightening can be done cold – at the owners risk as explained above – or hot using a welding torch or similar to get the offending area red hot. If this is your preferred method do not quench the hot metal, allow it to cool slowly.

If you are forced to attempt the straightening cold your main problem may be to hold the bars securely enough to apply sufficient force without them slipping around. Leaving them attached to the bike is one solution; another is to fit them to a slave top yoke which can then be held in a vice. Both of these methods avoid vice marks on the chrome. Applying sufficient leverage will be the next issue; a solid steel extension bar such as from socket set, slipped inside the bar end may be enough alone or will allow further extension with another piece of tube slipped over it.

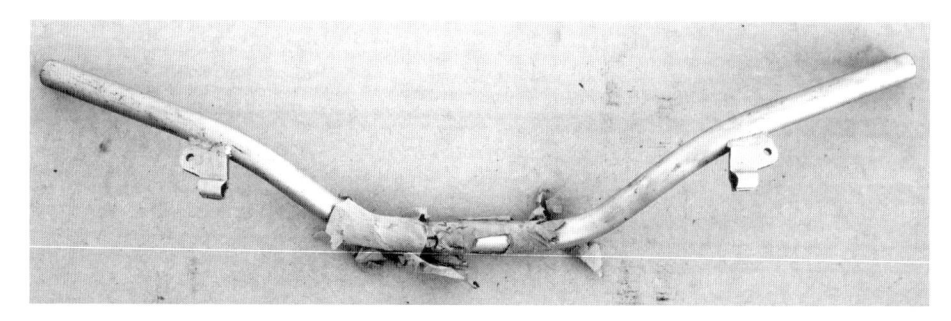

Fig 9.2. Original BSA handlebars, still with traces of the brown paper wrapping – lovely!

The bars shown in *fig 9.2* have the welded-on lever brackets as per C15 and B40 Star, or, as in this case, due to the dull chrome finish B40 Military Mk1; the shape is identical for these models. Note the gracefulness of the bends; not always replicated on pattern bars.

Clutch and Brake Levers

All clutch and brake lever assemblies and blades are interchangeable on all Unit Single models prior to the OIF T and SS models introduced for the '71 season (the OIF B50MX models used the earlier pre-OIF type handlebar levers - specifically the '70 pattern as shown in *fig 9.3*).

These levers are 7/8" between the centres of the pivot bolt and cable nipple holes and this is a common feature of BSA models in general. Other manufacturers used levers of 1" for this dimension and these should not be fitted in error.

The levers used on C15 and B40 Star models were 'plain' blades; all other Unit Single models used ball-ended levers; the ball being a safety feature as it reduces the likelihood of the rider or anyone else being stabbed by the lever in an accident - especially relevant in competition.

The mounting brackets for these levers are brass castings, chrome plated to match the levers and originals are 'handed' in that the clamp arrangement to the handlebar is almost horizontal; hence fitting a clutch lever bracket in the brake lever position would result in it being upside down, and vice-versa. Pattern copies of clutch and brake lever assemblies often have the clamp arrangement vertical so they can be used on both sides of the handlebar (one casting required rather than two different ones, hence cheaper).

For '70 the cast bracket was enlarged to provide enough metal for a hole to be drilled through it to mount a rear view mirror; this was applied on both brake and clutch lever brackets. The exception to the clamp-on brackets is found on C15 and B40 Star models and also B40 Military Mk.1, which have steel lever brackets welded to the handlebar. This is an economy measure and whilst being perfectly serviceable it does restrict the range of handlebar positioning. For example, reversing this handlebar to permit adoption of a 'racing crouch' (well, we can all dream), would result in the levers facing backward.

Fig. 9.3. The modified lever bracket with additional hole to mount a rear view mirror (clutch lever same modification) introduced for '70 on all Unit Singles in current production and subsequently fitted to all B50MX machines. Simple elegance!

A common mistake is to confuse the C15/B40 handlebar with the equivalent handlebar with welded-on brackets, as fitted to BSA bantam models which can be distinguished as the brackets have circular cable abutment holes, the cable holes on Unit Single lever brackets have two internal flats, above and below to suit the 'cam type' of cable adjuster used which fits into these holes.

All Unit Single lever brackets accept this adjuster on both clutch and brake cables which is of the same type throughout, the threaded portion has two flats to suit the hole in the lever bracket and these stop it rotating as the adjuster nut is turned. The adjuster nut has a face cam arrangement on its end which bears against the bracket. This provides ¼ turn adjustment for the cable and prevents the adjuster nut unscrewing. This arrangement and these levers as a whole are known as 'cam type' levers/adjusters. Rather than the knurled ring cam-adjuster, '67/'68 models featured cables with four-pointed star adjuster – it works just the same. OIF cables generally have a flatter, wider knurled ring for cable adjustment. It really is a good idea to stick to the original type of clutch and brake lever assemblies if obtaining replacements; if you don't then clutch and front brake cables will have to be specially made as the standard off-the-shelf items won't fit into levers with different types of adjusters.

Clutch and brake lever wear and repair

Problems with these levers stem from damage and wear causing separate specific troubles. Damage caused by an impact from an unexpected angle will often bend the cast brass

Fig 9.4. Clutch lever brackets (pre '70 type) left; pivot screw hole worn oval, right; equivalent item after bushing of the pivot screw hole

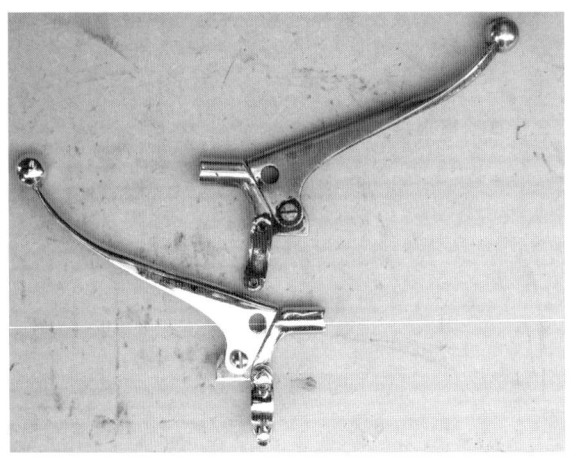

Fig 9.5. Handlebar levers, clamp on type as fitted prior to '70. Top, lever with a bent bracket, shabby and in need of attention. Below; the equivalent lever after receiving attention (thread inserts, straightening and bushing of pivot hole) and a re-chrome.

bracket; this will show itself by the integral rib which projects inwards along the handle bar not being fully in contact with this item. A gap such as this between rib and handle bar means that the clamp is bent. It is worthwhile attempting to straighten a bent clamp by holding the curved clamp in a vice (protection for the brass clamp is required) and pushing the rest of the bracket back into position relative to it. Also check for a twisted bracket and correct it in the same way.

Wear usually confines itself to the area around the pivot pin, the hole for this will wear oval, particularly on the clutch lever as this sees much more action than the brake lever. The remedy for a pivot hole which has worn oval in the bracket is to carefully enlarge it – in the direction of the lever, ie opposite the direction of wear – with a small round file. Don't drill it out as the new hole will be concentric with the old worn one, ie out of position. This needs to be done to allow the pivot hole to be bushed with a ¼" hollow steel dowel as used on the joint faces of the engine casings. Aim for a press fit and then cut off flush any excess dowel which protrudes from the bracket. Having been pressed into place by squeezing in a vice, the dowel may need its inside easing with a round file or reamer to allow a new pivot screw to fit nicely. Avoid re-using the old ¼" diameter pivot screw as a step will have worn on it corresponding to the worn hole in the bracket.

The horizontal surfaces around the pivot hole can also wear under the action of the lever blade over a high mileage but, unless severe, this wear can be ignored as it can be compensated for by tightening the pivot screw to close-up the blade.

Stripped threads in the brass lever brackets for the clamp screws can be fitted with a thread repair insert, the original Amal items use a 1BA thread for which thread inserts are available.

If trying to put a lever assembly together from a box of mixed parts it will be found that the clamp strap is peculiar to these original Amal items; correct straps from other levers will often be found to have screw holes spaced too widely. The 1BA clamp screws are also peculiar to the original levers having a narrow 'fillister' head.

Straightening bent clutch and brake levers

A bent lever blade, which will often have curled up if the bike has been dropped on it, can usually be persuaded back into shape by applying a mallet to the outside of the bend while the lever is supported on a block of wood. Nil by hammer and vice in this operation, please, if surface damage to the lever is to be avoided. After any or all of the above work a re-chrome will probably be in order.

When setting up the lever assembly, up and down wobble and sloppiness of the lever blade on the bracket is controlled by the pivot screw. This is threaded into the lower surface of the blade, thus tightening the screw closes up the top and bottom surfaces of the blade to pinch on the bracket between them. In practise, slacken the locknut underneath, adjust the screw to allow free lever movement with minimal clearance and tighten the locknut.

OIF brake and clutch levers

All OIF T and SS brake and clutch lever assemblies (*see fig 9.6*) are of a new different design in die-cast Aluminium, parts of which are not interchangeable with the earlier pre-'71 version.

The lever blades, either steel for SS models or light alloy (with a steel-bushed pivot hole) for T models, move on the ¼" UNF pivot screw which is located in the lever body. The lever body is now much enlarged from previous practice to contain switchgear for the lights, indicators and horn.

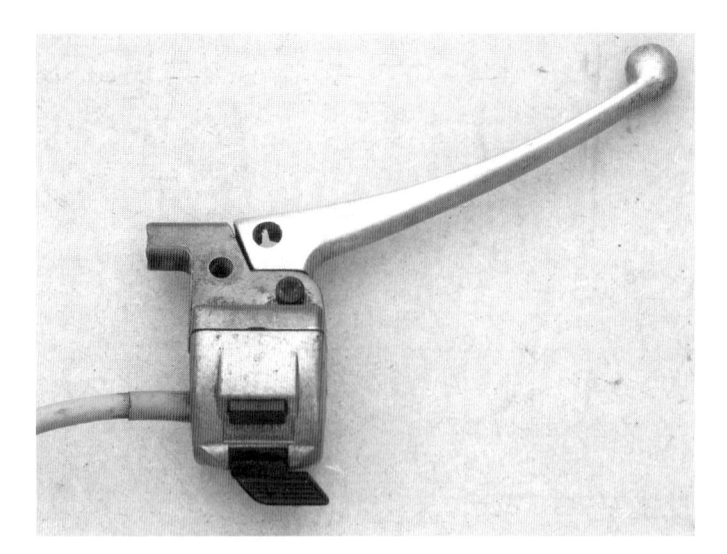

Fig 9.6. OIF Roadster '71 on brake and clutch lever. Alloy lever (shown) for 'T' models, 'SS' models have a pressed steel lever blade

B50MX models use the '70 pattern handed brackets and steel ball-ended levers to suit this earlier design; this being much simpler and more practical for off-road use. Wear of the OIF roadster levers now centres on the hole in the lever and the pivot pin, replacement of both of these items being the simplest option with bushing of the levers being a possibility as described previously for the bracket.

Damage from impact, if severe enough, will result in the bracket/switch housing breaking. Being a die-cast Aluminium component, replacement is an easier proposition than repair. Bent levers can be brought back to their original shape as explained above for the earlier type of steel blades. The alloy ones, being aluminium alloy will need to be softened before force is applied. This is done by smearing soap on them and then heating them until the soap turns black. This colour change acts as an indicator of the correct temperature having been reached at which the aluminium will have softened (correctly called 'annealing'). As the bent lever is persuaded back towards its correct shape it will rapidly, almost instantly be felt to work harden. Don't force it further without again annealing it: forcing it to bend in its hardened state will break it. The annealing process can be repeated as many times as required with no harm - so long as the correct temperature, as indicated by the soap, is reached but not exceeded - if this is omitted the first thing you will notice to indicate temperature is that your lever has melted.

Control Cables

Assuming that you have more or less standard rise handlebars you should expect off-the-shelf new cables to fit, even these days!

Alterations to cables

It's not possible to lengthen a cable but, should the need arise, the cable inner, outer or both can be shortened; useful if you can start with a longer cable from another model to make the one you need.

A cable inner can be shortened by snipping through it with sharp, heavy duty pliers or similar. Alternatively, sawing through it will fray the strands unless the cable is sandwiched inside two pieces of wood. The nipple can easily be removed from the discarded end of inner cable by heating it with a blow torch. In doing this you see the 'fisted' end of the inner cable and how it fits in the counter-bored hole in the nipple. This will need to be replicated when you put the nipple back on the end of the shortened inner cable. This is done by holding the inner cable vertically in a vice with the nipple sitting on the jaws with the cable through it, and protruding by about 1/8". The protruding strands of cable can be gently tapped down into the counter-bore of the nipple with a hammer and then finished off tight in there with a small punch.

The nipple should be soldered back on with a blowtorch, plumbers solder and passive flux. The solder should be seen to penetrate through the nipple onto the cable and to fill the counter bore. Shortening an outer needs the ferrule to be pulled off the end first and the outer alone to

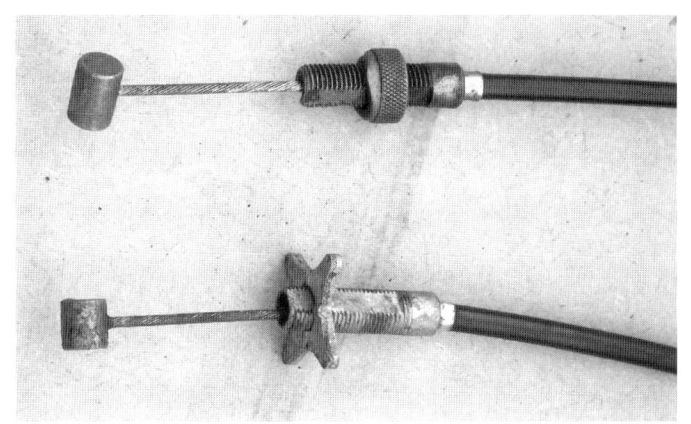

Fig 9.8 This adjuster is commonly found on the TR25w and from '71 onward on OIF machines. It is often not supplied with the cable and with UNF thread rather than Cycle. The three types are interchangeable.

Fig 9.7. Cable adjuster types for the 'cam type' levers – the commonly found knurled adjuster, top, used for all years of Unit Single production and, below, the Star adjuster mostly used in '67/'68.

be cut through in the required position. Under the plastic cover the outer is actually a coil spring; cutting through one coil is all you need to do. To avoid the risk of accidentally cutting the inner, a few strokes of the saw blade will weaken the outer sufficiently to enable it to snap if bent to and fro.

If the nipple hasn't been removed from the inner, the unwanted piece of outer can be removed by unravelling it. To do this hold the nipple on the inner in a vice and get your assistant to pull the inner tight. You then need a good pair of thin nose pliers to grip the end coil of the outer and pull it hard – it will unwind from the inner. Do this as close to the nipple in the vice as possible to reduce distortion of the inner.

Twistgrip and throttle cable

The twistgrip is made up of a rotor (to which the throttle cable is attached) and a body which separates into top and bottom halves. The twistgrip assembly used on the Unit Singles is common to most British bikes from the '50s onward. The only original fitment twistgrip on Unit Singles which is an exception to this is the plastic bodied 'quick action' item used on C15 Scramblers, B44GP and B50MX models. In design this follows the basic arrangement of the metal bodied item.

Two sizes of the metal twistgrip assembly were used and fitted, and to widen the scope of the picture, these were applied across the BSA range (and to most other contemporary British bike marques) with some semblance of standard practice to determine which was used, relating to the size of carburettor it was connected to.

Fig 9.9. Small, (left), and large (right) standard twist grips. The large item is commonly used with Monobloc 389 and Concentric 900 series carbs. All smaller carbs commonly used the smaller twistgrip

The general rule from Unit Single days is that the small bodied twistgrip is used with Monobloc carburettors 375 and 376, and Concentric 600 series. The larger bodied twistgrip was standard fitment with Monobloc 389 and Concentric 900 series carbs as these carburettors need a faster action twistgrip to compensate for the greater travel of the throttle slide which they have. The three main parts of the two sizes of twistgrip are not interchangeable.

Fitting a twistgrip and carburettor other than as described above is fairly straightforward (BSA did it themselves occasionally eg early A65 Star models used a 389 carb with a small twistgrip) but doing so will speed up or slow down the action of the throttle. A small twistgrip with a 389 or 900 series carb will result in a throttle action which requires a lot of wrist action to go from throttle closed to fully open - possibly useful on a trials bike? The throttle cable from the aforementioned A65 Star is the off-the shelf part to go for if this set-up is required.

The problem of obtaining a suitable cable for a non-standard twistgrip to carburettor combination is due to different size nipples being used on the end of the cable which fits into the twistgrip rotor (of course – you didn't expect 'joined-up thinking' and standardisation did you?). Making a one-off cable to suit whatever set-up you have is sometimes the only option. If doing this it is worth sticking to the usual set-up of a mid-adjuster on the cables for the larger carbs and no adjuster – other than at the carburettor top – on cables for the smaller instruments.

The abutment for the cable outer at the twistgrip body is a split ferrule. Of course there are two sizes of this item, large or small to suit the twistgrip size.

Other differences relating to the twistgrip size are the two clamp screws joining the two halves of the body and the friction damper for the rotor. The screws for the larger assembly are 1BA size with slotted 'fillister' heads and dull chrome plated finish (same as the clutch and brake lever clamp screws). Those for the smaller twistgrip size are the same as used on the monobloc carburettor float bowl – 2BA with countersunk fillister head.

The friction damper situated in the lower half of the twistgrip is essentially the same item on each size of twistgrip although the adjusting screw (slotted cheese head on the larger item, slotted grub screw on the smaller) size isn't. It is 1BA with the larger and 2BA with the smaller item with a locknut on each to suit.

Today there are many pattern twistgrip assemblies in circulation as these have seemingly always been available through accessory shops and spares suppliers. Mostly these are perfectly serviceable as replacements for the original Amal manufactured items to the extent that originals now seem to be in the minority on today's vintage machines. An instant give-

Controls 173

Fig 9.10. The B40 Military Mk1 control layout. Any metal bits not painted green are finished in dull chrome. These original-pattern rubber grips are difficult to find nowadays. The combined horn/dip switch was originally a cast-aluminium 'Clear-Hooters' item, superseded by this CEV item shown. The twistgrip is the 'small' item, connected to a 626 Concentric carb.

away for a pattern item is the small cast-in badge on the top of 'Doherty' (a long standing pattern parts supplier) twistgrips; all Amal items were fully plain in this period.

Originally all three main parts of the roadster twistgrip were made from die-cast zinc (later pattern items have a plastic rotor). On Unit Singles, the two halves of the twistgrip were chrome plated (dull chrome on WDB40), other makes, and some BSA models used a cheaper painted finish or no finish at all on the zinc.

Re-chroming the halves of the body is straightforward for those in the business but don't expect a perfect result if the zinc has corroded and blistered through the original chrome; the pits in the metal underlying these blisters are invariably deep.

Correct throttle cable operation
Setting up of the twistgrip in use comes down to the cable adjuster being set to provide minimal free play of the twist grip rotor (at all handlebar positions) so that the throttle slide at all times rests on the carburettor throttle stop screw with the throttle closed.

This will be aided by lubrication of the cable and twistgrip internals, particularly of the rotor on the handlebar. Packing the inside of the twistgrip with grease is a good idea as it helps keep water out which can otherwise penetrate easily through the join between the two halves.

Careful routing of the cable is a key factor in obtaining correct throttle operation. There are two main options for throttle cable route from the twist grip; the standard arrangement being

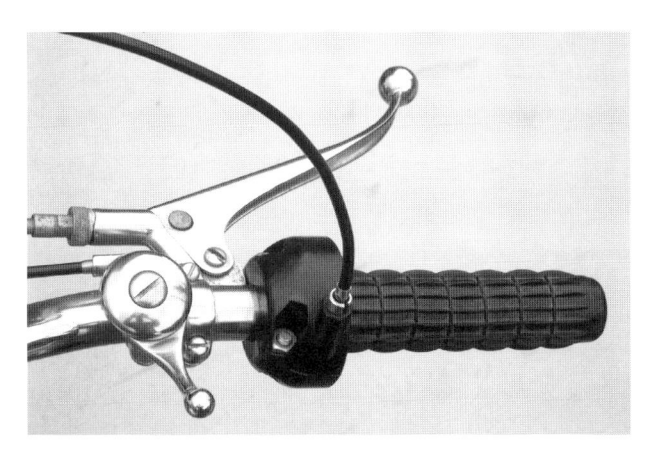

Fig 9.11. Quick-action plastic twistgrip as found on C15 Scrambler, B44GP and B50MX. Cable routing is the up-over option.

down-under to disappear under the offside front of the petrol tank; the other, a favourite for off-roaders as it gets the cable out of harm's way, being up-over, the cable similarly disappearing under the front of the tank. The thinking behind the up-over method is to avoid contact between the cable and passing obstructions during steering. Because of the movement involved in the rotation of the forks, don't attempt to clip the cable in any way which restricts its movement, one clip to the frame top tube under the tank should suffice.

If the twistgrip is removed or dismantled, check the condition of the cable inner where it wraps around the rotor – this is where it will snap due to metal fatigue resulting from it repeatedly being bent and straightened as the grip is rotated. Replace it if any strands of the cable inner have broken and become separate.

Getting home with a snapped throttle cable is quite feasible by pulling manually on the cable inner; alternatively taping a spare cable alongside the one in use – ISDT fashion – can't be faulted and is a worthwhile precaution if you do serious distances. Seal the ends of the spare cables with electricians tape if you adopt this measure.

Handlebar Grips

The handlebar rubbers originally fitted are clearly shown in the various Unit Single parts books but basically three types were commonly fitted.

Fig 9.12. Handlebar robber grips: left is the 'balloon' grip commonly fitted from '67 onward; centre is the Scrambles, MX and Military grip; right is the standard C15/B40 roadster and trials grip. Often changed to suit the riders preferences, the 'balloon' grip seems to be a popular choice.

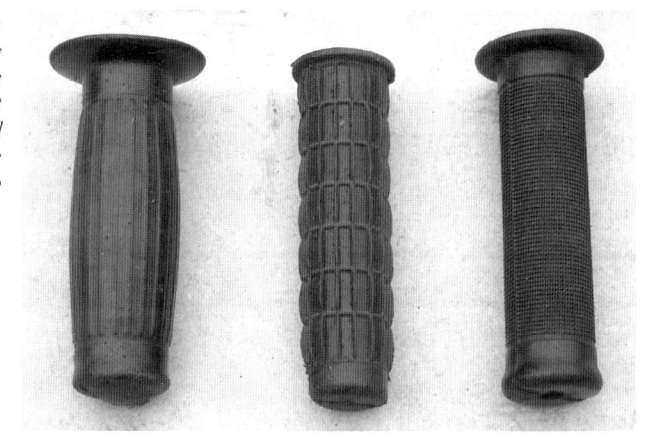

The rubber should be a tight fit on the handlebar or twistgrip although some after-market grips were supplied with glue; the fashionable 'Gran Tourismo' balloon grips, for example, which originally came with a glass phial of adhesive. If attempting to glue a rubber in place, thoroughly de-greasing first is a must. When fitting the twistgrip rubber avoid pushing it fully home as this would cause its inner end to come into contact with the twistgrip body and act as a friction damper in use. Removing an unwanted but firmly fixed rubber is easily done with a sharp knife. Warming and softening a handlebar rubber by pouring boiling water over it will usually aid fitting/removal.

Valve Lifter

Standard fitment on all C15 competition models, all B40, B44 and B50 models, and B25 models for '67 and '68 only. At the handlebar, the same design of valve lifter lever assembly was used on all of the above models. This is visually a miniature version of the clutch or brake lever and this design seems peculiar to BSA models. The correct design is not now available as a pattern or after-market part and none of those available seem to fit the nipple of the standard Unit Single valve lifter cable – which has a ¼" barrel nipple.

The original valve lifter lever has a pressed steel blade mounted on a die-cast zinc bracket with 1BA pivot screw with locknut and 2BA clamp screws (again as per monobloc float bowl), the whole being chrome plated (dull chrome on B40 military models). Correct positioning of the lever on the left handlebar depends to some extent on other considerations; original factory pictures show it as being fitted either above or below the handlebar depending on the model.

The lower position, allowing the lever to be operated by the index finger is most comfortable and allows the lever to 'fall easily to hand' but this may not be practical if it fouls the petrol tank with the steering on full left lock. This can easily be the case with the larger types of standard tank used in conjunction with low handlebars. In the UK at least, if fork travel is restricted by anything contacting the tank – including your fingers if these are trapped against it by the handlebar – it is an MOT failure as well as being downright dangerous.

Unless either tank or bars can be changed 'plan B' is to mount the lever on top of the bars as it originally was on some C15 competition models. In this position it is less comfortable to operate as it doesn't fall readily to hand. Correct setting up of the free travel at the lever when it is operated can alleviate the discomfort a bit; the adjustment is done at the cable end on the rocker box by loosening the locknut and turning the adjuster back or forth as required. Aim for ⅔ of lever travel being free play with the exhaust valve being lifted for the last ⅓ of lever travel.

Two types of valve lifter cable were used, the difference being due to the lever on the rocker box changing from '62. The first type followed pre-unit practice with the cable terminating in a clevis at the rocker box lever, these being connected by a small nut and bolt. This cable does a 'U-turn' above the engine and approaches the head steady bracket from the rear.

The subsequent type approaches the engine from the front along the head steady stay and the cable outer locates on the end of the rocker box lever, now twisted at 90 degrees to form the outer cable abutment. With this design the cable outer moves with the rocker box lever so avoid clipping the cable firmly to the head steady stay.

Fig 9.13. OIF left hand handlebar controls; with valve-lifter lever means B50.

The two cable types are interchangeable but are determined by which valve lifter lever you have on the rocker box.

Because it is a die-cast zinc item the valve lifter lever bracket is somewhat prone to damage – the socket for the cable outer is quite susceptible – and it also suffers from wear at the pivot hole. Bushing a worn hole along the lines of the method described earlier for the clutch lever is a cure. It would also help to obtain a pivot screw with a plain shank to act as a bearing surface against the inside of the pivot hole. The original pivot screw was fully threaded which means the thread bears directly on the zinc casting – cheap, but not good practice.

Choke Lever

A small number of Unit Single models feature an air control (choke) lever connected to the air slide in the carburettor (if fitted) whether your bike should have one or not will be clearly shown in the parts book. This lever is mounted on top of the right hand handlebar and can be either a separate unit clamped inboard of the brake lever, or to save space, mounted on top of the brake lever bracket instead of the clamp strap. If the latter is the case the brake lever clamp screws will be fitted upward from underneath through clearance holes in the bracket then to thread into the air control body. Converting from threaded bracket to un-threaded or vice-versa is straightforward with either a drill or 1BA thread insert kit.

The air control lever assembly is an easy to obtain pattern part being common to many British bikes. In use the large slotted central screw acts on a damper assembly for the lever and needs to be tightened down just sufficiently to allow the lever to move freely but not return to its closed position on its own. Just to confirm, the normal running position is with the lever fully open (clockwise), full choke is obtained with the lever closed. Early C15 competition models fitted with the choke operate this directly on top of the carburettor; the choke knob is pushed downward until it locks on, and is rotated to unlock it.

There is no harm in fitting or removing an air control in contradiction to the parts book. It is there to help starting with a cold engine and to provide clean carburation until the engine warms up. In practice a good flooding of the carb without recourse to the air lever may be sufficient to help you get going. On the other hand, the need for copious flooding and the resulting petrol wastage may suggest that an air lever would be a good idea: it is a case of 'know thy beast' and doing what works best.

For the remaining handlebar controls, ie the horn push with or without dip switch see *Chapter 17 Electrics*.

Foot Controls

The other 'controls' on your bike are those operated by the feet. On the o/s, on the engine are the gear change lever and kickstart lever.

Gear change

The gear change lever is tightened on the splines of the gear change shaft by a ¼" BSCy pinch bolt (fitted from underneath). This bolt needs to be fully tightened as a loose fit of the lever on the splines will hasten stripping of these. This bolt was supplied in high-tensile material originally, and in lieu of the correct bolt, consider fitting a ¼" BSF (same thread) Allen cap screw instead; These are similarly high tensile material.

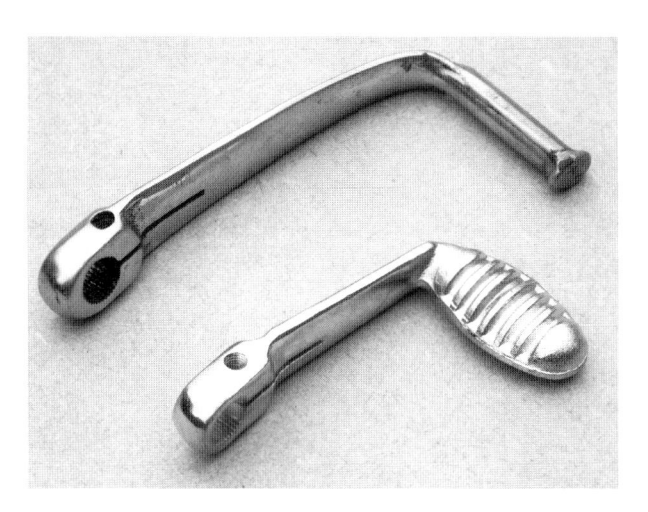

Fig. 9.14. The two Unit Single gear levers. The standard item (top) is fitted with an 'acorn' rubber. The short 'competition' pedal (below) is only used with the short competition footpegs.

Two designs of gear lever *(fig 9.14)* can be found for Unit Singles; the larger, standard lever is common to A50/65 models and is used on all except C15 competition models and B44GP. These instead used a short stubby lever with an integral ridged foot instead of the usual 'acorn' rubber.

A damaged standard lever is probably easiest to cure by buying a new replacement; these are commonly available. The more scarce competition lever can be heated to red hot and straightened if bent. If it is suffering from stripped splines, this end can be cut off and replaced by welding on a serviceable end from a standard lever. Re-plating after such surgery will no doubt be required, bright chrome being the requirement on all gear levers, except for the dull chrome finish of B40 military models.

Kickstart Lever

The kickstart lever is of the folding type for all Unit Single applications. This aside, there are several different designs to be found, some of common application and some particular to certain models *(fig 9.15)*.

The folding pedal used for most of these levers is common and interchangeable. Sloppiness of this pedal can often be cured by fitting a new pivot bolt, ball and spring and in severe cases a new pedal. The lever can however be built-up with weld and re-shaped in most cases. When folded out the pedal should be at exactly 90 degrees to the bike; if it swivels too far to the rear, replace the worn parts.

Kickstart lever types

All Unit Single kickstart levers to the end of '67 fit onto a ⅝" diameter spindle, regardless of model. From the start of the '68 season, the shaft diameter was enlarged to ¾" which brought the Unit Singles into line with the larger BSA models. As a result, the standard BSA kickstart lever from these larger and earlier models was then adopted with few exceptions to the end of Unit Single production.

The two exceptions to the fitting of the ¾"spindle standard kickstart lever which have so far come to light are: the slightly shorter version used on '73 B50MX machines *(fig 9.16)*, and the '72 OIF B25 Fleetstar lever which is cranked further out to clear the low level exhaust system used on this model. Should an equivalent exhaust system be fitted to '72

B50SS machines (as shown in the BSA Parts Book), this modified kickstart lever would similarly be required.

The earlier ⅝" kickstart levers fall into two categories, those for road use and those for competition/off-road models; there being two types of each. The two alternatives for road use are of the same design and differ only in length, the shorter at 6¾" overall is used on all C15 models. The longer at 7⅛" overall is applied to all B40, B25 and B44 models to the end of the '67 season. A third, even shorter version was fitted to Triumph Tiger Cubs which can be fitted if you are desperate. Other than considerations of length (longer means less pressure is needed at the pedal) these levers are fully interchangeable.

Which competition kickstart is fitted depends on the frame type: the Swan-Neck competition frame to the end of '62 used a 'U' shaped kickstart lever which curls around and under the foot peg. This design of lever is a nightmare to use as its downward travel is limited by the footpeg painfully contacting your lower shin, unless you ineffectually jab at it with your toes rather than your instep. Hence, you cannot get a good swing on this lever to start the engine, which probably contributed significantly to the legend of the supposedly difficult to start energy-transfer equipped models, which initially used this design of kickstart. Due to this design of kickstart lever being practically useless, BSA advised the fitment of a standard (B40 length) lever used in conjunction with folding footpegs.

Competition models from '63 onward, built around the Welded/Duplex frame, and the B44GP feature a kickstart lever which not only folds from its lower end but is fitted to the spindle by being pinched onto splines rather than by the usual cotter pin and nut. This design is hard to find nowadays but is a joy to use should you manage to obtain one with the necessary splined kickstart spindle for distributor or side-points engine. This type of kickstart was also used on Tiger Cub off-road machines which doesn't improve the supply problem and unfortunately generates more demand for it. The leaf springs which locate the folding arm may be found to foul the timing cover of side points engines and require 'adjustment' to provide clearance.

Fig. 9.15. Kickstart levers.

1. Early 'U' bend competition kickstart
2. Later competition kickstart
3. C15
4. The ¾" longer version for B40 and all other road models to '67,
5. The '68 onward kickstart for ¾" spindle as used on most larger BSA's for many years,
6. '72 B25 Fleetstar lever.

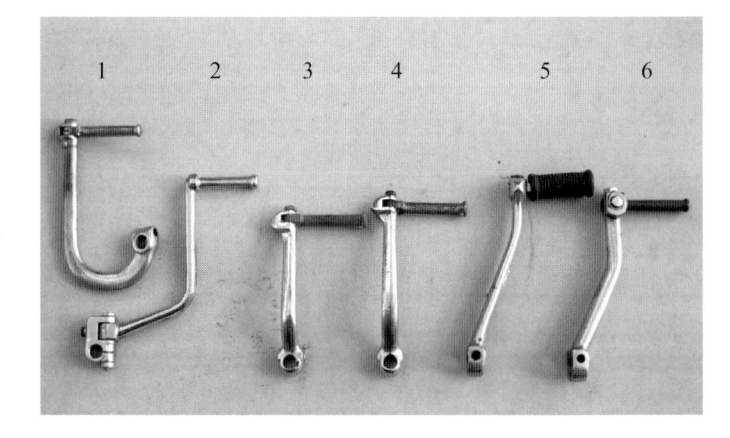

Controls *179*

Fig. 9.16. The shortened '73 B50 MX kickstart lever, about 1" under-length compared to the standard lever.

Brake Pedals

Expect second-hand examples of this part to be bent to some degree. Re-alignment is however straightforward if you are able to get the offending area red-hot. Wear at both the pivot hole and at the brake-rod clevis hole may be noticeable if lubrication has been neglected. Unless severe, wear here is of little consequence until perhaps the pedal can wobble enough to foul the engine chaincase: boring out and bushing being the standard remedy if the pedal is one of the harder-to-find examples.

Brake pedal types

As expected by now, there were a number of variations in brake pedal design and these are illustrated in *figs 9.17 to 9.21* below.

Fig. 9.17. C15 and B40 Swan Neck framed models. Roadster version shown above, competition version below. If in doubt, the giveaway is the position of the stop-bolt boss; inside or outside as can be seen.

Fig 9.18. (Right) Welded/Duplex frame brake pedals.

Top, the short pedal fitted to the competition models '63 to '65

Fig 9.19. Centre and bottom are variations of the '67 to '70 pedal used on all B25, TR25w, B44 and B40 military

The two lower brake pedals in *fig 9.18* are marked with part number 47-7001 or 47-7014; the lower number being the earlier version with the straighter arm. The bottom example permits a higher at-rest position. Both of these carry two tapped holes for stop-bolt and brake light switch actuating bolt, and are interchangeable.

The '66 and '67 B44VE and VS parts books are misleading about which brake pedal is fitted to these models. The under-lying logic here is that brake pedal length should depend on the type of foot pegs used – to give correct foot to brake-pedal position. The short competition pegs require the short competition brake pedal (shown in *fig 9.18*, top)

Fig 9.20. The longer Enduro type foot pegs used on the '66 and '67 B44VE/VS require a longer brake pedal. As this pre-dated the military/roadster item (shown above) the pre-unit pedal shown below marked 42-7025 was fitted (see footpegs section p186).

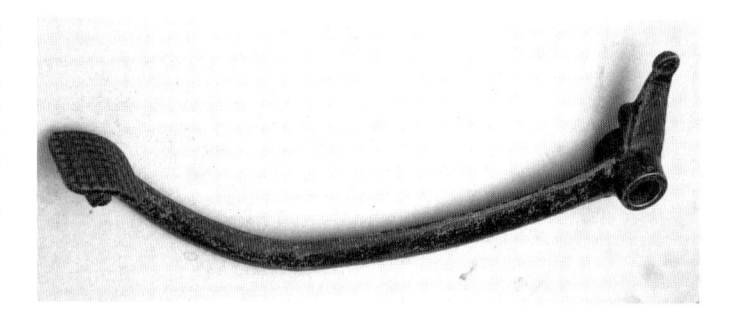

This long Enduro type brake pedal (*fig 9.20*) has one tapped hole which allows it to use the stop bolt and peg subsequently used on the '67 to '70 models (with the Welded/Duplex frame) for adjustments to the at-rest position.

All brake pedals without the stop-bolt feature usually rest against the underside of the foot peg which became standard practice on all of the OIF models (the n/s peg for these having a cast-in boss for this purpose).

The B44GP brake pedal is of the longer length to suit its forward positioned foot pegs but is specific to this model with the pivot end resembling the short competition item and the pedal end having a triangular pad as was later used on the OIF item.

Controls   *181*

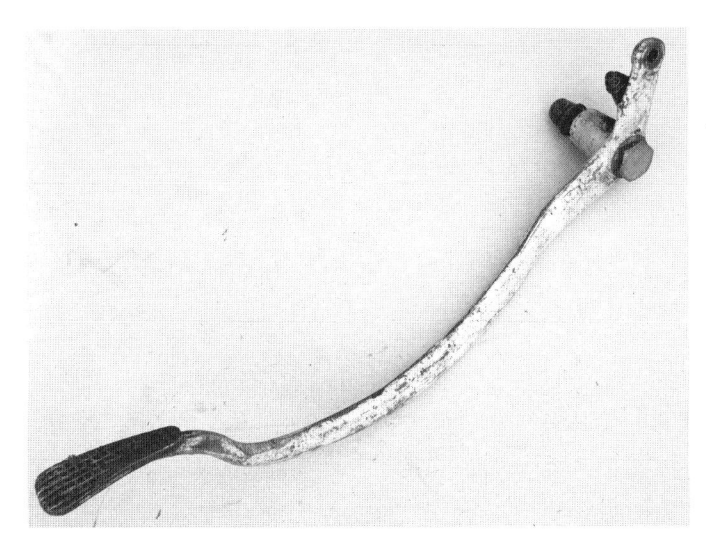

Fig 9.21. OIF rear brake pedal used on all models '71 to '73. The triangular pad is a carry over from the much earlier B44GP pedal

Brake pedal – correct operation

In use, the pedal needs at most 1" of free travel before the brake is applied; less than this if you can get away with it without the brake binding. Changes in the amount of weight being carried can affect the biting point of the rear brake. If you are in the habit of running with minimal free play at the pedal consider enlarging this before riding two-up, otherwise a tactful explanation to your passenger as to why smoke is coming from your rear brake may be needed. The rear brake linkage geometry is found to alter slightly on most models with rear suspension movement. This undesirable condition would be eradicated if the pedal to brake rod connection remained always in perfect alignment with the swinging arm spindle axis, but it doesn't as it has to move with brake pedal travel. This is one advantage of cable operated or hydraulic rear brake control.

Fig. 9.22. Brake pedal set-up '59 to '62 competition models.

Rear brake rod

Brake rod lengths. Other than the clevis end having plain holes to accept a pin, or one half threaded to accept a screw and locknut, the brake rods prior to '71 are all interchangeable but some variations in length are found.

If you are trying to make a brake rod from scratch, replicating the original part will be difficult if an exact copy is required; although something that will do the job is easily possible. The original brake rod will have a rolled rather than cut thread for strength, and the clevis end will have the front end of the rod both screwed into it and locked in place by an off-centre cross-drilling and cotter pin. This is necessary to prevent the rod unscrewing from the clevis by the rotation of the knurled rear brake adjuster at the other end.

Introduced in January '67, the shorter length brake rod is suitable for earlier C15 and B40 road models, the longer replacement is suitable for all models prior to OIF. In practice, the rod simply needs to be long enough to ensure that it protrudes fully through the adjuster nut, for safety reasons.

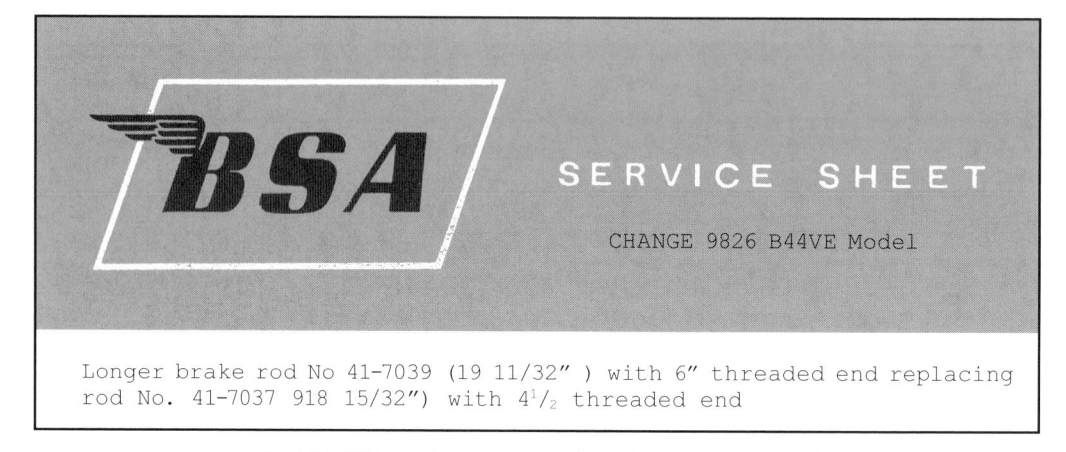

```
                  BSA           SERVICE SHEET

                                CHANGE 9826 B44VE Model

Longer brake rod No 41-7039 (19 11/32" ) with 6" threaded end replacing
rod No. 41-7037 918 15/32") with 4½ threaded end
```

Fig 9.23. BSA service sheet specifying the longer brake rod

The OIF brake rod has its forward end bent at 90 degrees to connect to the brake pedal (common practice on all Bantam models) and is alone in being threaded ¼" UNF rather than the previous ¼" BSF. Check for wear on the inside of the bend where the rod fits through the hole in the pedal; if a step has worn in the rod replace it.

All brake rods should be straight to avoid adding a spongy feel to the rear brake action. Used items are frequently bent to some extent and should be straightened with care to avoid manipulating them too much in an effort to straighten them, particularly the threaded portion. The problem is metal fatigue leading to a fracture, ie snapping, which you don't want to happen just when you require to stop in a hurry. To be on the safe side reject any rod which has suffered serious damage, particularly cuts or worn areas and avoid trusting one which has been welded back together.

At the rear end of the brake rod should be the adjuster nut for rear brake clearance which will be the same circular steel item with knurled rim on all but B40 miliary and OIF models; these having a cylindrical die-cast zinc item with two or four ears to provide finger grips and threaded BSF or UNF to suit the rod.

The adjuster is prone to seizure on the rod. Lubrication is needed for the adjacent moving parts but this will gather road filth which will gum-up the thread. If this area is left dry it will sieze up quicker due to rust.

The adjuster should rotate easily on the rod by finger pressure only. If it needs pliers or similar to turn it then it will soon chew-up from the effect of these. If lubrication doesn't free it then remove the whole brake pedal and lever assembly with the rod and nut, then protect the nut in a vice while the rod is unscrewed from it. The thread will need to be cleaned/tidied with a tap inside the adjuster and a die or die nut used on the rod.

Forward of the adjuster on the brake rod is the rear brake lever which is connected to the rod by the cylindrical 'swivel' which passes through it. The adjuster bears against the outside of this barrel-shaped item and has a face-cam profile on its end so that it will lock in position against the swivel with every 180 degree turn as it is adjusted.

The two lobes of the cam profile will wear away over years of adjustment and should be restored with a file – without them it is possible for the adjuster nut to unscrew in use.

On the rod forward of the brake lever and its swivel are a spring and nut. The purpose of these being to keep the adjuster and swivel in contact with each other at all times. Thus the nut should be adjusted to compress the spring by about ¼ of its free length and this will need to be maintained whenever the adjuster is moved.

Footpegs

Although not exactly 'controls' the relationship of the riders footpegs to the brake pedal as explained above, suggests that this is as good a place as any in this book to deal with them. The choice of footpegs for the competition models also determines to some extent whether the short competition gear pedal is appropriate rather than the longer standard item.

Footpeg fitting

There are, as usual, issues and foibles which relate to the various Unit Single foot pegs *(fig 9.24)*. Most models except competition machines prior to '71 use a taper fit for the riders foot pegs. If the male and female tapers of frame and peg are in good condition then this method can work well. Freeing the peg should require a thump from a heavy mallet to free the taper fit after loosening the fixing bolt. Too often the taper fit is not found to be secure and is simply a nuisance and results in a peg which insists on moving in use.

Fig 9.24. Correct footpeg to brake pedal set-up for most roadster models prior to '71 (B44SS shown, other models similar in principle) the main point being that the footpeg is clear of the brake pedal.

Fig 9.25. Wrong - the footpeg has rotated on its taper and is in contact with, or applying pressure on the brake pedal.

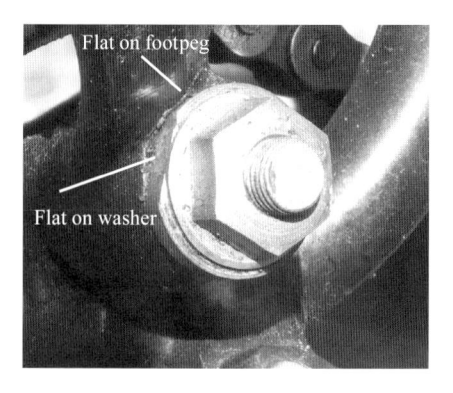

Fig 9.26. The reason for the problem; insufficient engagement between the flat on the washer which is incorrectly positioned for the machined shoulder on the footpeg. The shoulder on the footpeg is often insufficiently deep - as in this picture - to provide positive engagement. The remedy is to build up this area of the footpeg with weld and re-cut the shoulder.

BSA used a left-hand thread for the fixing of the taper fit n/s footpeg prior to '70 (stud and nut) and the o/s peg (nut and bolt) on all C15 and B40 road models because of the resulting tightening effect gained with any foot peg rotation caused by the riders foot pressure. Such foot peg rotation with a right-hand thread in these positions would result in them loosening even more. The o/s riders peg of the Welded/Duplex frame will rotate clockwise if loose, and is therefore fitted with a r/h thread which then tightens as a result of peg rotation.

The roadster l/h stud and nut method prior to '70 is not really a satisfactory method of firmly fixing the n/s peg and is basically a headache. On the Welded/Duplex frame – where the tapered boss is of the smaller diameter rather than the larger size used here on the C15/B40 Swan-neck frame – the footpeg is particularly prone to rotation in use: until it contacts the brake pedal and you realise this is the reason the rear brake is binding. In part this is due to a less than accurate location between the milled flat on the peg and the flat on the splined washer *(see fig 9.26)*.

The only sure-fire solution to a continually slipping foot peg is to drill out the tapered boss to accept a $^3/_8$ bolt as per the o/s example and fit pegs of the '70 pattern with the locating extension. Welding an extension onto the pre-'70 pegs is of course an option rather than sourcing replacements. If doing this, give consideration to the correct position required for each extension; they are handed. I am not sure why it took BSA so long to introduce this necessity; the only advantage of the tapered pegs being the small achievable range of foot peg position.

Fitting and removal of the l/h stud to/from the frame is best done by putting the lock-plate onto its splines which then allows an adjustable spanner to be applied with one jaw tightened on the flat. Expect and ensure that the stud is fully tight in the frame. If the '67 -'69 $^3/_8$" l/h thread inside the frame boss has stripped then recourse to the '70 foot peg fixing as explained above is necessary. (*See fig 9.27*)

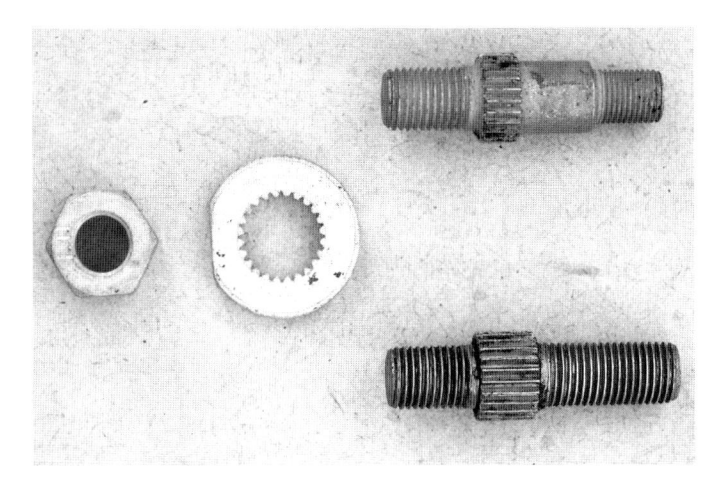

Fig. 9.27. The left-hand threaded stud, splined lock-washer and nut. This fixing arrangement for the left hand footpeg was used on all models prior to '70 on all but the off-road models. The last of these, the B44VS adopted this method for '68. The lower example of the two studs shown (⁷⁄₁₆" 20tpi L/H both ends) is as fitted to C15 and B40 Swan-Neck frame models, the upper example (reduced to ³⁄₈" 26tpi L/H in the frame) is for the Welded/Duplex framed B25, TR25w, B44 and B40 Military '67 -'69

The OIF models wisely do away with the questionable tapered foot peg bosses and rely on milled flats on both peg and frame to provide positive location. This method, in principle the same as the earlier competition method (which uses a differently machined locating flat) is pretty much foolproof except that no adjustment of foot peg position is possible.

Illustrated below *(figs 9.28 to 9.33)* are most of the different types of Unit Single footpeg. The same foot peg rubbers were fitted to all of the fixed footpegs (see *fig 9.28*) with a change for '65 from oval to round cross-section.

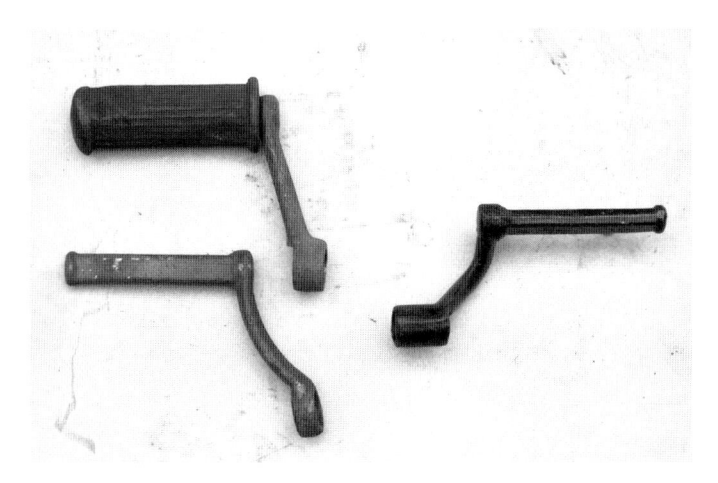

Fig 9.28. C15 and B40 road models all years, n/s and o/s as seen from riders eye view. There were two versions of the n/s, the early type (below) and late (above) are shown, the later, heavier section item has a pronounced step to better locate the splined lock-plate with its left hand nut and was introduced to combat the bending visible in the lower example. The n/s tapered boss for the footpeg is of larger diameter than the o/s.

C15A Trials Pastoral uses pegs of equivalent shape to the roadster items above but adapted for folding (using the standard pillion peg arrangement of bolted-on swivel boss).

C15 Competition foot pegs are shown in *fig 9.29*. The fixed type were produced in one, two and three ring versions; these all being made from the same casting but cut to different lengths (at the factory – honest!).

The three ring version was fitted to the C15S frame, same peg both sides; the two ring version to the C15C frame and the one ring version is as yet an 'unknown', it has the machined shoulder positioned slightly higher than the other two types. The parts book for the '65 C15 competition models shows the two-ring peg with different numbers for n/s and o/s. Examination of an

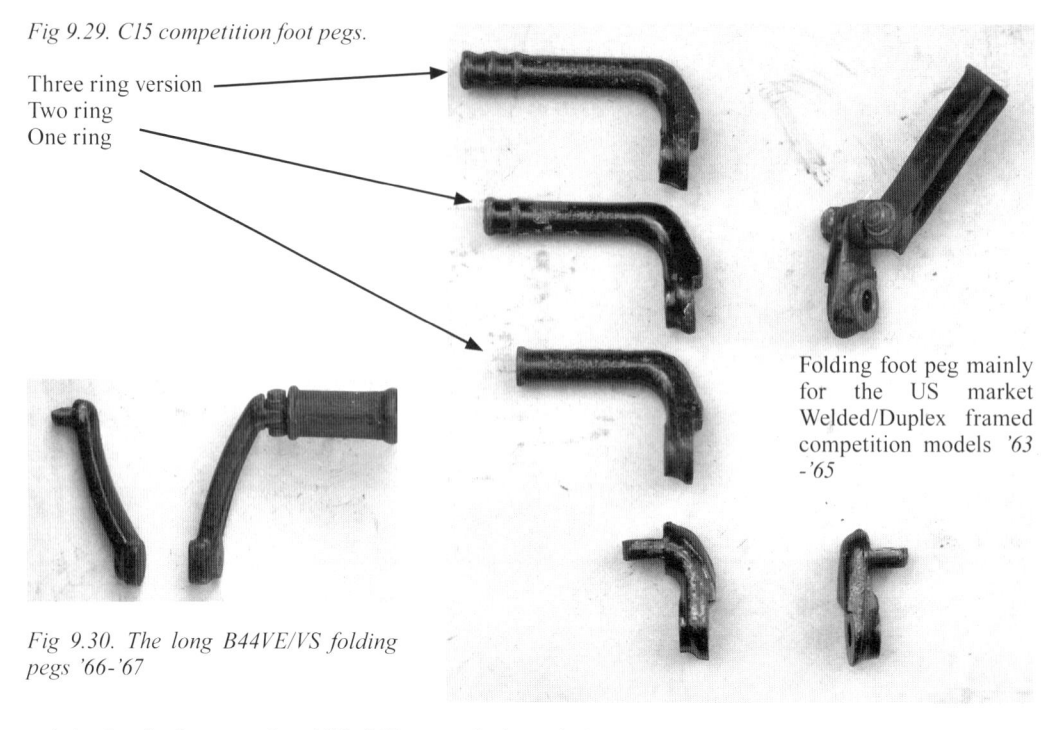

Fig 9.29. C15 competition foot pegs.

Three ring version
Two ring
One ring

Folding foot peg mainly for the US market Welded/Duplex framed competition models '63 -'65

Fig 9.30. The long B44VE/VS folding pegs '66-'67

original pair shows only a $^1/_8$" difference in length from machined mounting face to the peg-end between the two otherwise interchangeable pegs, the n/s item being longer at $4^1/_{16}$".

Also shown are the equivalent competition folding footpegs, mainly for the USA market. At the bottom of *fig 9.29* are the handed items for the C15S frame with integral swivel, the '63 to '65 item *(fig 9.29 top right)* is not handed and is fitted on both sides of the C15C frame.

The C15E Trials Pastoral fits mirror-image long footpegs which are peculiar to this model; the tapered mounting bosses for these on this frame are positioned directly opposite each other rather than staggered which is the norm for this type of fitting on the Welded/Duplex frame and are as per the B40 Military prototype C15CA front footpeg position.

Fig 9.30 shows the handed '66/'67 long B44VE and VS folding pegs with integral swivel. These use the same mounting method as the C15 competition riders pegs shown in *fig 9.29* and are therefore interchangeable with them.

All of the competition pegs are fixed by nuts on the ends of a long through-stud, the ends of which are prone to distortion after arduous use.

Fig 9.32 shows the fixed and folding pegs '67 to '70. Prior to '70, the same part is fitted both sides. Below *(figs 9.32)* are the '70 types with locating extension - these being handed due to the positioning of the extension. The fixed foot pegs were used on B25 and B44 road models for home market and general export and B40 military. Folding footpegs were used on all other models and for the USA market. All are interchangeable but the '70 type is recommended if you plan to spend a lot of time standing on them. As may be noticed, not all of these examples are in perfect condition, heating to red-hot for straightening is easy enough, welding is suitable for more severe damage.

Fig 9.31. B44GP n/s footpeg (o/s is the mirror image) with additional stiffening bracket which bolts to the engine lower mounting stud.

The '71 onward OIF riders foot pegs (*fig 9.33*) are fixed for UK 'SS' models, or folding for all other models. These are handed due to the brake pedal stop boss on the n/s item and would otherwise be interchangeable were it not for the offset of the n/s peg required to clear the primary chaincase. The $1^{1}/_{32}$" spacing block shown above left is fitted behind the o/s peg if a low level exhaust pipe is used. The folding pegs can be fitted with plain, or for MX, serrated arms as shown, plus these are normally sprung downward by the components shown. The standard short folding arm is carried over from the pre-OIF models.

Fig 9.32. Top, fixed and folding footpegs '67 to '69. Below, '70s type foot pegs with locating extensions. The earlier versions are not 'handed' as are the '70 types

Fig 9.33. OIF footpeg '71 on. The rectangular spacer shown is required to allow a low level exhaust pipe to pass inside the footpeg as per the 'B25 Fleetstar

Below are the folding pegs for T and MX models, the latter use the gripped peg

All of the above riders foot pegs are interchangeable with others having the same type of frame fitting, with the exception of the n/s C15/B40 roadster peg which has a larger diameter taper. Footpegs from other BSA models can be used: A65 pegs have the same size taper as C15/B40 n/s and pegs using a the smaller size taper were fitted to some pre-unit models.

Pillion foot pegs.

Fig 9.34 shows on the left the folding arms. The folding arm at the bottom is found on the B40 military and, most commonly, as the folding riders footpeg used on export Unit Singles. as explained above. Middle and top are early and late full length folding arms, the later version, with welded-on reinforcement, was introduced from about '67 and used to the end of OIF production.

On the right are the swivel bosses used with the folding footpegs, the middle two being the most widely used types from '58 to '70 with the longer of these being found on the nearside to allow the footpeg to clear the rear brake rod. Top is the extended example from the '69 and '70 B25 with l/h high-level exhaust. Bottom is the OIF type with milled flat to prevent rotation and UNF rather than BSCy thread.

All of the folding footpegs do this by pivoting on a 5/16" bolt. The fixing nut for this bolt should be of the self-locking type or be fitted with a spring washer. Thus, the stiffness of the pedal movement can be adjusted by tightening or loosening the pivot bolt and nut. Both the bolt heads and the nut are thin prior to '71 to produce a discrete appearance.

In the 'down' position, the pedal should be horizontal; if it 'droops' below this fit a new pivot bolt, and if still unsatisfactory build up the ends of the pedal fork with weld and re-shape these to stop the pedal at the right position.

The pillion foot peg rubbers have a larger square hole along with a tendency to split at the corners of the square. Two lengths are still commonly available to suit the short and long folding foot peg arms shown below *(fig 9.34)*. Original rubbers were generally marked 'BSA' on two opposite sides.

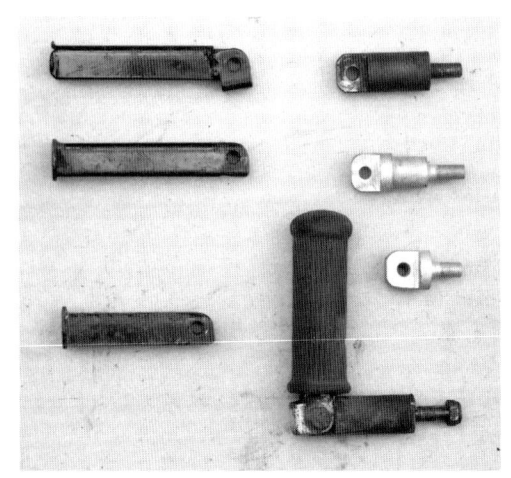

Fig 9.34. Pillion foot pegs and bosses.

Left Top. Late full length folding arm

Left Middle. Early full length folding arm

Left Bottom. B40 Military and also used as the folding riders footpeg on many Unit Singles

Right. Alternative swivel bosses (see text above)

10. SEATS

'Motoplas' were a subsidiary of BSA (note the address see *fig 10.2*) who supplied them with all of the seats fitted to BSA models at this time, along with many other components and accessories such as leg shields, for example. The original Motoplas information shown in *figs 10.1 to 10.2* dates from late '65 (illustrated, for '66 season) and '72, and clearly outlines how the same seats were sometimes applied to different models across the BSA range, although it is a bit vague and contradictory in some areas.

MOTOR CYCLE DUALSEATS
2. (BSA)

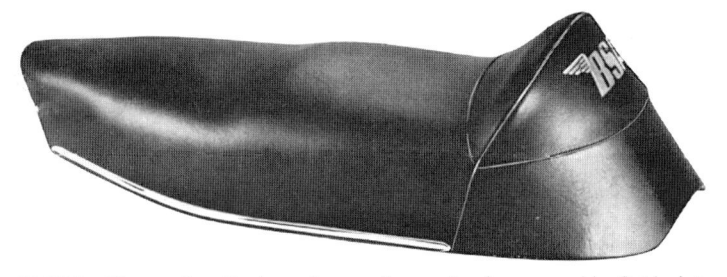

68-9330. The perfect Dualseat for comfort and safety, superbly finished in elasticated leather cloth—styled on the lines of a racing seat. Fitted with stainless steel embellishers, and embossed in gold with B.S.A. Trade Mark. Suitable for all B.S.A. A50 and A65 machines.

40-9120. A similar safety styled Dualseat is also available for C15 and B40 models.

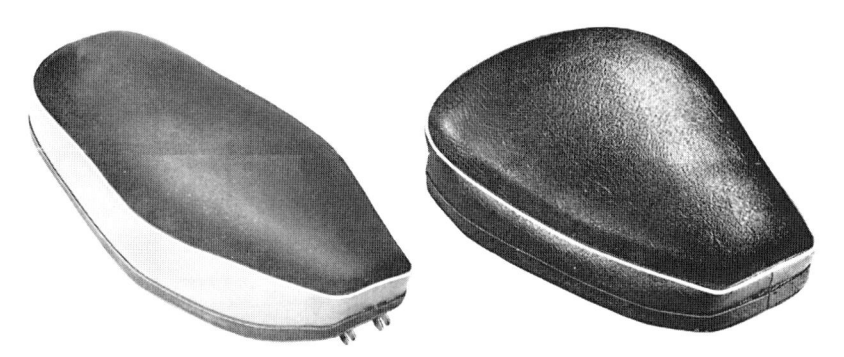

90-9312. Comfortable Dualseat, finished in hard-wearing PVC. As fitted to D7 1962. Also available with alternative fittings (40-9080), as fitted to C15, B40 1962.

40-9056. Short Competition Seat, finished in tough, durable PVC. Also available in extra hard-wearing PVC XX.

Fig 10.1 Motoplas seats as fitted to Unit Singles

MOTOPLAS

PART NO.	DESCRIPTION	SUITABLE FOR	Manufacturer's Recommended Retail Price
	Colour Codings (please quote when ordering):		
	(a) Black (g) Two-tone Grey		
40-9056 PVC	Short Competition Seat in PVC (a)	B.S.A. Motor Cycles C15S, C15T	75/-
40-9056 PVC XX	Short Competition Seat in PVC XX (a)	C15S, C15T	87/-
90-9312	Standard Dualseat (a, g)	D7 1962, 1963, 1964, 1953-64	88 -
40-9080	Standard Dualseat (a, g)	C15 and B40 1958-64	88 -
68-9056	Standard Dualseat (a, g)	A50 and A65, 1964, 1962-64	107/6
68-9183	Standard Dualseat (a)	A50 and A65, 1935-66	107/6
68-9330	Safety Styled Dualseat (a)	A50 and A65	150 -
68-9168	Clubmans Single Seat (glass fibre base) (a)	A50 and A65	P.O.A.
40-9120	Safety Styled Dualseat (a)	C15 Sportsman and B40	135/-
41-9085	Single Seat (glass fibre base) (a)	Victor	P.O.A.
90-9341	Standard Dualseat (a)	D7 De Luxe with strap	98 -
90-9345	Standard Dualseat (a)	D7 Silver Bantam, less strap	88 -
40-9082	Standard Dualseat (a)	C15 and B40, 1965-66	88/-

BSA MOTORCYCLE DUALSEATS

Colour Codings (please quote when ordering): (a) Black (g) Two-tone Grey

82-9777	Singleseat	Fleetstar C25	£4.50
90-9308	Singleseat	D7, D10 and D14	£4.50
90-9372	Standard Dualseat (a) with Strap	D7, C10 and D14 1962-68	£5.10
40-9080	Standard Dualseat (a, g)	C15 and B40 1958-66	£5.10
68-9330	Safety styled Dualseat (a)	A50 and A65 1965-69	£8.70
90-9374	Safety styled Dualseat	D10/14 Sports 1966-68	£6.90
82-9732	Safety styled Dualseat	C25, B25 and B44 1967-70	£7.50
82-9916	Dualseat	D7, D10 and D14 1959-71	£5.00
83-2621	Dualseat	250/500 Singles, 1971-72	£8.70
83-3866	Dualseat	250/500 Singles, 1971-72	£8.70
83-4427	Dualseat	A65 Twins, 1971	£8.95
83-4287	Dualseat	A65 Twins, 1972	£8.95
83-3653	Dualseat	A75 Triple with small tank, 1971-72	£8.95
83-3853	Dualseat	A75 Triple with large tank, 1971-72	£8.95
83-2746	Dualseat	500 Victor MX, 1971-72	£7.60

DUALSEAT REPLACEMENT COVERS — B.S.A.

8-9091	Pointed Nose	D1, D3, C11, B31, B33, C10, C10L, M20, M21, M33, A7, A10, Gold Star (rigid and plunger) 1949-57	£1.76
8-9092	Round Nose	C11G, C12, B31, B33, A7, A10, Gold Star (all swinging arm) 1954-58	£1.76
8-9094	Short Competition	C15S and C15T, Police single-seat	£1.30
8-9101	Standard Dualseat	D7 (swinging arm) 1958-61; C15 (swinging arm) 1958-60	£1.76
8-9103	(ditto)	D7, C15 and B40 1962-67	£1.76
8-9118	(ditto)	A65 1964-66	£1.76
8-9262	(ditto)	A65 Safety Style 1965-69	£2.25
8-9267	Dualseat	D10 Supreme and D14 1966-69	£1.7
8-9279	(ditto)	D7 and D10 Silver 1965-67	£1.7
8-9283	(ditto)	D10 Sports, B44 Victor Enduro and C25, B25 1966-68	£2.07
8-9350	(ditto)	C25, B25 and B44 1969	£2.07
83-3349	Dualseat Cover	1971-72 B25 and B50SS	£2.25
83-4323	Dualseat Cover		£2.25
83-3339	Dualseat Cover	1971-72 B50MX	£1.85
83-4290	Dualseat Cover	1971 A65 Twins	£2.60
83-4290	Dualseat Cover	1972 A65 Twins	£2.60
83-3657	Dualseat Cover	1971-72 Triple for small tank model	£2.60
83-3857	Dualseat Cover	1971-72 Triple for large tank model	£2.60

MOTOPLAS CO. LIMITED
Armoury Road, Birmingham 11. (Telephone: Birmingham **VICTORIA** 1008)

Fig 10.2 Seats and replacement covers for Unit Singles and other BSA models

'Safety' as mentioned by Motoplas means it has a racing hump, no doubt to stop you slipping off the back when pulling a wheelie.

These lists also provide other useful facts regarding original specifications; eg the two-tone grey seat-cover for C15 and B40 models. Clearly this was original fitment for most machines up to the end of the '65 season. My limited understanding is that black was reserved for SS80 and SS90 models, grey for the basic Star models to the end of the '65 season, thereafter they reverted back to black until the end of production for the C15 and B40 Star with the new style 'one piece' black cover, part no 40-9082, introduced for '66 (with white piping at front and rear end seams). This new seat is based on a parallel sided pan as subsequently used on the later Bantams.

'66/'67 Sportsman models fitted the humped 'safety' seat, similar to the B25/B44 item but initially lacking the stainless trim strips which were introduced in November. '66 and subsequently used on B25/B44 to '70.

Incidentally, the colour of the petrol tank centre bung and knee-grip rubbers should match the grey or black seat colour on C15 and B40 models. The grey tank rubbers and hence the seat cover were discontinued in October. '65.

As ever, expect exceptions to what should be 'original fitment' as indicated in *fig 10.2*. If the correct seat colour was temporarily unavailable, then an alternative would have been used if it was on the shelf at Armoury Road.

The change below refers to the introduction of the 'one piece cover' on C15 and B40 models (seat 40-9082); it isn't really one piece, it has separate bits for the front and rear ends but the sides were now integral with the top and not formed from a separate strip of material.

```
CHANGE 9049 OCTOBER '65
Dual seat with one piece cover and white piping front and rear
only No. 40-9082 to replace 40-9080 (See Fig 10.3)

Black knee grips 40-8029/30 and tank grommet 40-8017 replace
grey grips and grommet 40-8012/13 and 40-8108.
```

The grey seat cover issue rears its head again with the '69/70 B25/B44 models (listed as 8-9350 above). In this case the colour shade of medium grey is applied to a textured 'basket weave' surface pattern of PVC which nowadays seems to be unavailable as a raw material

Fig 10.3. Black seat with white piping on a '66 C15 Star

from which new replacements could be made. The best reasonable solution is therefore to use the readily available black version as fitted to '67/'68 models if an original BSA grey cover cannot be located.

As can be interpreted from the above Motoplas data, some commonality occurs between seats for different models. Seat covers are shared between models, which means that foams, and to some extent seat pans, are common between different models.

This commonality mainly applies between Unit Singles and contemporary Bantam seats (D7 onward). The standard C15/B40 seat pan (40-9080) is the same as the standard D7 Bantam pan, the only differences is the front mounting bracket which protrudes further forward for the Bantam, and the position of the rear bracket from seat to shock-top bolts. Although the two mounting studs for this are captive, welded on the pan, original pans have three alternative positions for these, depending on which model the common pan was intended for. Similarly, as already mentioned, the later parallel sided C15/B40 seat (40-9082) was pressed into service on the later Bantams, as well as being the basis for the '67 -'70 B25/B44 humped seat.

The early type C15/B40 seat pan 40-9080 *(see fig 10.4)* is widest under the riders bum, becoming narrower from this point backwards. This example is actually taken from a Bantam as indicated by the position of the two ragged holes where the rear bracket captive bolts have torn out – a common problem. The two undamaged holes just to the rear of these are the correct positions for the rear mounting bolts for C15/B40. Later parallel sided seats gained a third pair of holes between the original two pairs so that this pan could, in modified form, be fitted to the Welded/Duplex frames.

Fig 10.4. C15/B40 early type seat pan 40-9080

If the earlier wide seat pan is fitted to a '66/'67 C15/B40 which should have an oil tank with the additional breather tower, then it may result in the edge of the seat fouling the tower. The narrower seat which was originally fitted for these years misses the tower.

For comparison *fig 10.5* shows the later seat pan with parallel sides as used in flat form on C15 and 40 roadsters from '65. Shown here is the '69/'70 B25/B44 version with the turned-up rear end to support the hump. The rear mounting bracket is offset by $^3/_8$" to the n/s. The perforations near the front are due to corrosion and require new metal to be let-in.

Sharing of seats continues with the humped 'safety' seat found on C15 Sportsman and B25/B44 models to '70 is the same pan as the humped Bantam Sports item, with the same mounting bracket differences. The humped seat pan is modified from the flat parallel-sided Bantam pan introduced from late D7

Fig 10.5. The later seat pan with parallel sides

Seats 193

onward for all Bantams excepting the sports models; this is the seat with the central hand strap on Bantam models.

The '66 to'68 humped seat pans have their front ends simply cut off to length whereas '68 to '70 have the front edge folded downward as a continuation of the seat pan sides; they are otherwise interchangeable.

Fig 10.6. The '69 to '70 humped seat as used on all B25/B44 models at this time with grey cover and Stainless Steel side trims.

The WDB40 uses the earlier, Bantam, C15/B40 Star seat pan and foam, but modified by having shallower sides, a centrally pressed hollow to clear the rear mudguard and the rear quarter angled slightly upward (the sides are cut, with a welded-on stiffening plate added to each side after bending). The mounting points are repositioned as the seat is mounted lower than usual (to make the bike suitable for 'private Shorthouse') so it bolts directly to the frame loop at the rear, has the front mount positioned further back to locate on a cross bar between the sub-frame tubes, and rests on rubber buffers by the shock tops. All in all a much sturdier arrangement than usual and well able to cope with short but possibly portly squaddies. The cover on the WDB40 seat is similar to the black C15/B40 Star cover but has shallower sides.

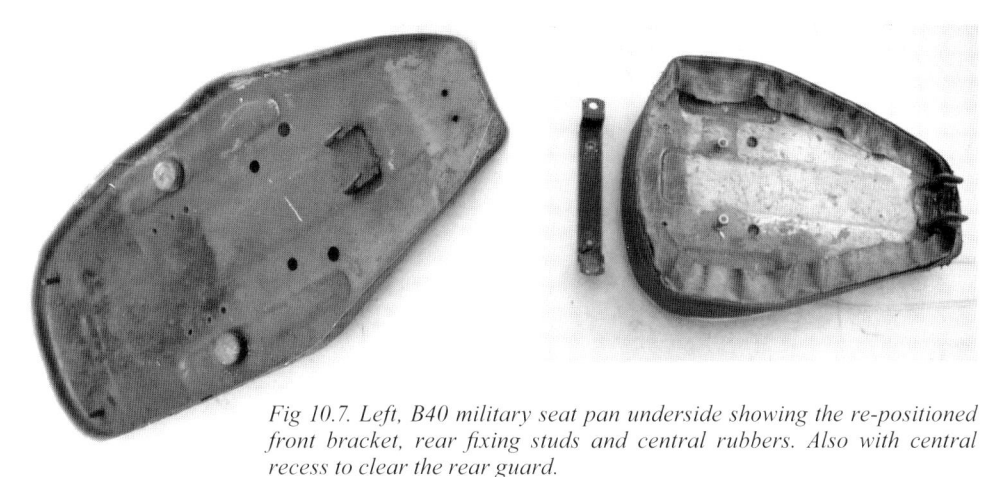

Fig 10.7. Left, B40 military seat pan underside showing the re-positioned front bracket, rear fixing studs and central rubbers. Also with central recess to clear the rear guard.

Right, the short competition dual seat. The additional bracket is required to mount it on the welded/Duplex frame.

This habit of re-using existing parts continues in that the '68 to '70 TR25w uses the (almost) flat WDB40 seat pan, further modified to allow the front standard type mounting bracket to be recessed into the underside of the pan *(see Fig 10.8)*. The rear mounting bracket is also

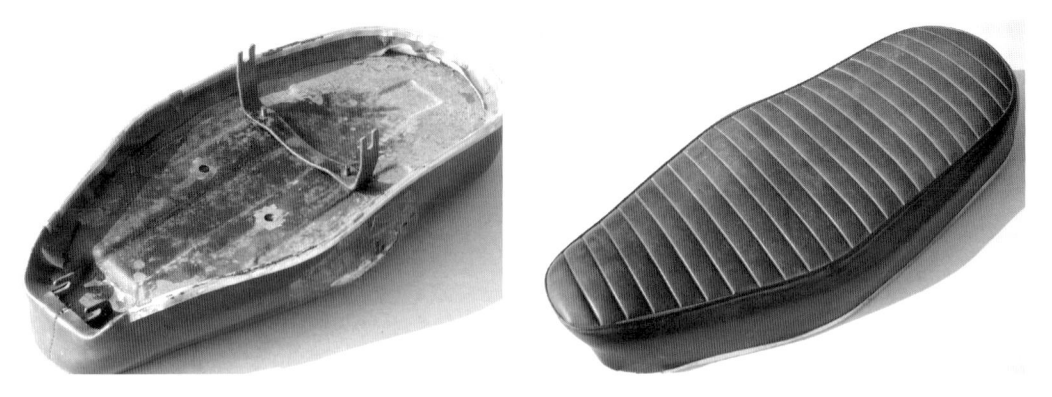

Fig 10.8. TR25w seat pan (left) and cover (right)

shorter than the BSA version; these measures result in a lower seat height to counteract the Triumph's larger rear tyre/larger front wheel. The TR25w conceals all of this under the traditional ribbed top Triumph seat cover with a silver lower edge trim-strip as per the contemporary Triumph twin models. This seat, and those from the contemporary B25 and B44 models are fully interchangeable.

Seat Brackets

The rear dual seat bracket – a 1" by ⅛" steel strap – is, for all of the non-military models prior to '71, not symmetrical; it kicks out further on the nearside to suit the nearside shock–top mounting which are further outboard than the offside one. The TR25w bracket is similar but specific to this model, it is shorter in height and also curved to clear the top of the rear guard *(fig 10.8)*.

On the Welded/Duplex frames the fork ends of the seat bracket are wider apart than the space between the sub-frame tubes, hence the dual seat for these models will not simply lift on and off. To prevent the bracket scraping the paint off the frame when removing the seat, withdraw the shock top bolts sufficiently to clear the bracket ends, nudge the seat backward to free the front mount and rotate the seat before lifting clear. This situation is also likely to be found on swan-neck B40 and C15S frames.

It is quite common for the underside of seat pans fitted to the Welded/Duplex frames to foul the top of the rear guard, regardless of the rider's girth. The easiest solution is to raise the seat pan slightly by inserting spacing washers as necessary on the two captive bolts between the seat pan and bracket.

Competition Seats and Brackets to '70

The 'short competition seat' *(fig 10.7)* is of one basic type throughout its production period and was used on all C15S and C15C framed models, the '66 B44 Victor Special/Enduro, and was optional on the C15 trials pastoral. It was also used on the C15/B25/A65 police, B40 Military and GPO Bantam models D7 onward. Variations focus on the mounting brackets which depend on the frame on which the seat is mounted. For the Unit Singles, Swan-neck frames require the front bracket to project further forward than for the duplex/welded frame. The rear bracket for Swan Neck frames is of conventional type being a strap which extends down to the top shock bolts.

Seats 195

The rear bracket to suit the Welded/Duplex frame bolts on to the same two captive bolts provided by the rear edge of the pan, but is a stepped strip which connects to the two specially provided mounting tubes welded to the inside of the subframe. On WDB40 models these tubes accept the two seat rubber support pads; these can easily be removed to fit the single seat to these machines as was originally specified for one batch.

The short competition seat pan is not simply a cut off version of a standard pan, it is an individual pressing. It is therefore not easy to produce an authentic short trials seat from a roadster seat with a hacksaw, though you can of course produce something that 'will do' as it is the same shape as the front half of the early C15/B40 and WDB40 pan.

The heavy duty alternative cover originally available (*see fig 10.2*) for the competition machine is a thicker type of leather cloth with a coarser texture leather effect. Equivalent materials for this are still available.

OIF Seats and Brackets

The OIF dual seats all use a common pan, foam and cover, the latter with the ribbed top on the Triumph models. The introduction of the larger tank for some home market models in '72 necessitated the front end of the seat – pan, foam and cover - being cut short at the front to provide clearance (*see fig 10.2 No. 83-4323*). Therefore the front edge of the standard seat pan (to suit the small petrol tank) is lipped downward whereas the shorter '72 seat for use on home market models with the larger petrol tank (B50 Gold Star and similarly the B25 Fleetstar

Fig 10.9. Above. The OIF B25 Fleetstar seat

Fig 10.10. Right. The '71/'72 OIF seat underside showing the two-bolt fixing in the centre, rubber buffers to the rear

single seat) is simply the standard item cut shorter at the front, with no downward lip.
The OIF B25 Fleetstar seat (*see fig 10.9 and 10.10*) is basically the same seat as used on the contemporary 650cc Triumph 'Saint' police models, the single seat for these machines being modified to hinge in usual Triumph twin manner.

With regard to the OIF dual seats (commonly known as the 'banana' seat because they are curved when viewed side-on rather than flat), the only difference between the BSA and Triumph versions is the cover; plain for BSA, ribbed for Triumph. The B50MX uses its own particular single seat, subsequently fitted to the Triumph TR5MX.

The OIF seats all have a bolted-on front bracket and also bolt directly to the frame seat loop, with additional rubber buffers, much the same arrangement as the earlier WDB40. With all these fittings correctly in place the OIF seat is well supported to avoid stress damage, the main enemy being the usual rust.

Below, as good a place as any to put some nice B50 factory shots - ostensibly to illustrate the seats used at this time. Being factory publicity shots (generally taken prior to quantity production), there are several discrepancies to be seen between these shots and the subsequent production machines. The '72 Gold Star for example, tank knee grips and screwed-on badges are not found on production machines. Also the short USA front guard but on this home market model as denoted by the large petrol tank. All of this is 'par for the course' in terms of OIF build spec.

1971 Gold Star SS

1972 MX

1972 Gold Star

1972 CCM

1973 MX

Fig 10.11 Factory publicity shots of B50 models showing the seats used

Fig 10.12. B50MX seat, a bit square but well padded

Seat Restoration

It is still sometimes possible to happen upon an original seat which is in good, usable condition, but in reality expect the opposite. Even a seat which looks OK from above is likely to be seriously deteriorated once you look underneath.

As such, some form of replacement seat is often in order. The pattern seats currently available are of variable quality, the main shortcoming often being the pan. If possible choose one which replicates the original in terms of metal thickness (18 gauge originally), formed by pressing rather than fabrication and with pressed-in stiffening ribs. Buying an off-the-shelf replacement is the easiest solution but for those pursuing perfection, restoring your original seat can give a more authentic result.

Dismantling the seat simply requires the edge of the cover to be unclipped or unhooked from under the pan. Seats with the stainless steel trim strips along the sides additionally require their 2BA retaining nuts to be removed (three each side) to release the trim and free the cover. Be prepared to cut these nuts off as they are prone to seizing.

Problems with an ageing, original seat

If used in a damp climate the seat foam will have harboured moisture and helped the pan to rust, often right through. In use the pan, even under a modestly girthed rider, will fatigue and crack around the mounting points. All damage of this nature can be repaired by welding or brazing, the question is whether it is worth repairing or is too far gone.

BSA didn't really give their seat pans much defence against the ravages of rust in the first place, just one thin coat of black cellulose paint – out of sight, out of mind. It is worthwhile applying a more durable finish after the necessary repairing and blast-cleaning, such as powder coating.

The foam itself is far from indestructible as it can become distorted in shape and also hard and crumbly if exposed to the air and ultra-violet light when the cover splits. Replacement requires a piece of high-density foam rubber as used for upholstery. This is less squashy than ordinary foam rubber and is made from small pieces of the ordinary variety glued back together. It comes in various thicknesses and densities and can be identified by its motley appearance and is generally known as 'recon'.

To replicate the shape of the original foam (which was specially moulded) will need the upper surface of the new foam to be rounded on the corners, and to some extent sculpted rather than simply cutting around the seat base and leaving the foam flat with square sides. This is an obvious shortcoming with many pattern seats as they lack the correctly rounded foam rubber, and produce a very square-looking seat as a result. The best way I have found to cut the foam is to use a bandsaw, but sharp knives and fine tooth saw blades can be equally useful.

Any resulting imperfections in the upper surface of the foam can be smoothed over if necessary with the addition of a thin layer of soft ordinary foam ¼" thick or less. This is attached with contact adhesive and should result in the foam being a fraction bigger than the base all around. Tightening down the cover will compress the foam slightly to match the seat pan size. If desired, and possibly recommended if you are trying to persuade distorted foam back into shape, the foam can be glued to the pan with contact adhesive.

The seat cover is probably the most durable of the three main components, but being on the outside it is the most likely to suffer accidental damage. The only perishable part is the stitching holding the separate pieces of PVC together, although the PVC will tend to harden with age and split.

If the cover is otherwise sound apart from rotted stitching it is possible to hand stitch through the original holes in the PVC to render it intact.

Buying a new replacement cover should be an easy enough exercise for most Unit Singles but if you are prepared to master the art of the sewing machine, a new cover can be made from PVC leather-cloth. As a pattern, use the old cover by carefully un-picking the stitching and open the separate pieces out flat to draw around them. After cutting out the new pieces draw a line around them on the back, near the edge, to mark the position of the line of stitching as per the old pieces; this will usually be about $5/16$" in from the edge.

If piping is required, it can be bought, or made from a strip of leather-cloth $5/8$" wide. On the back of this glue a length of string along its middle (use contact adhesive) and fold the leather-cloth over to trap the string.

Sewing the pieces of seat cover together is done inside-out with all the layers of PVC pinned or tacked together along the joins. You will need quite a heavy-duty sewing machine for this (by today's standards) and something such as an old hand-cranked Singer is ideal for going through several layers of leather-cloth. By hand-cranking, the rate of progress is very easy to control so it can't run away with itself and sew your fingers to the cover. Use heavy-duty nylon button-hole thread with a needle to suit as you follow the stitch line. After sewing, turn it the right way out and feel smug. Indeed, most would feel justified in broadcasting our new-found abilities with the sewing machine but beware doing this as a stream of requests for alterations to skirts etc may ensue. With this in mind, plan 'B' is to buy a large bunch of flowers prior to sweet-talking someone more skilled than yourself in the black art of sewing.

The BSA logo on the rear of the seat can be applied by cutting a stencil from sticky backed plastic, applying this to the seat and then dabbing through onto the cover with a cloth bearing gold paint. Alternatively a gold pen (usually available at Christmas) can be used, the quality of the result being dependant on the steadiness of the hand.

If you are considering using leather for the cover rather than PVC you will need to seal the foam with plastic sheet of some sort to keep the water out and prevent the seat becoming an enormous sponge: leather alone won't do this.

Attaching the edge of the seat cover to the base was done in one of two ways by BSA depending on the age and model of the seat:

1. If your cover has a 1" wide band of leather-cloth around its lower edge as a 'trim', as per early C15, WDB40 and others, then the cover is folded around the lower edge of the seat pan and fixed there by 'U' shaped spring clips. These are then hidden by the band of leather cloth.

2. If your cover lacks the band of leather-cloth as described above (late C15, most B25, B44 and TR25w machines) the cover will wrap around the lower edge of the seat pan and hook onto sharp triangular teeth stamped inward from the sides of the pan. These teeth were originally then squashed flat to secure the cover which had been hooked on. This method requires a thin rubber 'edge protection strip', 'U' shaped in cross-section, to be fitted around the potentially sharp lower edge of the pan under the cover to prevent the cover being cut.

   Typically, refurbishing this type of seat is likely to result in these triangular teeth breaking off when the old cover is removed hence attaching the new cover is a bit of a problem with few of the original teeth remaining.

   The best solution is to remove the teeth, have the seat pan blast-cleaned, powder coated and then scuff the inner sides with abrasive paper to provide a key for the new cover to be attached with contact adhesive. Clamping to aid adhesion may be needed.

   '67 C15 Sportsman, B25 and B44 seats of this type have the additional stainless steel trim strips along the lower seat edges as shown above by Motoplas. These are fixed with three special 2BA bolts each which are captive in the strips and which protrude inward through the sides of the pan to be retained there by nuts. This arrangement also helps to stop the cover coming loose. These trim strips are becoming difficult to find in good condition, but can be straightened and re-polished if the damage is slight.

OIF models use the triangular teeth method with an additional protective plastic beading strip over the cover along the edge of the pan. This in turn is retained by metal clips which are screwed to the seat base.

Fitting a new cover

On all seats, a good way to fix a new cover in the correct position over the foam and base while attaching the lower edge to the pan, is to cut a piece of 20mm plywood or similar, to the shape of the pan and use a couple of large 'G' clamps to sandwich the whole lot together (*see fig 10.13*). This allows the foam to be slightly squashed down as the clamps are tightened so as to produce a nicely taut cover when the clamps and board are removed. Grappling with a cover, foam and pan without the aid of clamps may well result in a major tantrum as you simply don't have enough hands to cope with it. Turning it upside down and kneeling to force it to submit may help, but go for the clamp method if possible. The clamping method is a bit harder to apply to the OIF 'banana' seats because they aren't flat, but clamping smaller areas one at a time should result in success or try clamping with 6mm ply or similar which should be flexible enough to follow the seat curvature if more clamps are used.

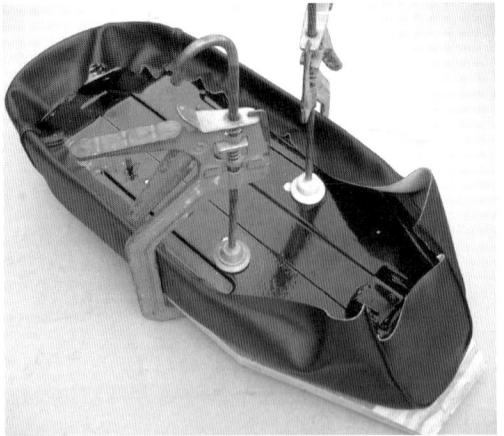

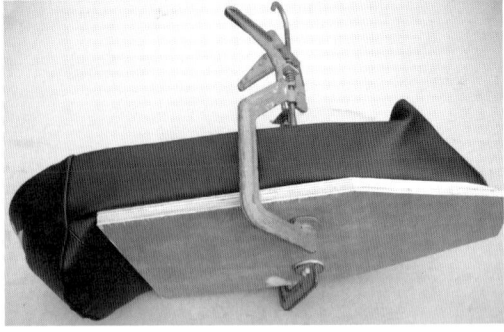

Fig 10.13 Left and above, fitting a new cover using the clamping method.

Small tears in an otherwise good cover can usually be repaired to a reasonable standard with 'vinyl weld' solvent. If the cover is removed from the seat it is a good idea to patch behind the tear as well: using an inner tube patch from your puncture repair kit works well. This won't show through to the outside as an obvious lump of something stuck inside the cover.

Hopefully the above suggestions will result in a seat at least as good as new in appearance and which will provide an acceptable level of comfort for your rear end.

Fig 10.14. B40 Military seat, an original example - thinner than most, firmer than most!

11. PETROL TANKS

Petrol Tank Mounting

At last, the petrol tank; the crowning glory. No matter what state the rest of the bike is in, if the tank looks good you are half way there.

All BSA Unit Single tanks are rubber mounted with a single fixing bolt, the famous BSA 'centre bolt fixing' *(see figs 11.3-11.5)*, used throughout most of the BSA range from pre-Unit days. Apart from necessitating a hole through the middle of the tank this is a very good arrangement, essentially being 'quick release', and resulting in a tank which is fully rubber mounted and pretty much fool-proof if you have all the right bits. The potentially troublesome bits in question are the mounting rubbers and the centre-bolt spacing tubes; you have to have the right ones to suit the tank and frame and there are several differing versions needed to marry up between different frames and tanks.

Tank mounting rubbers
C15 and B40 Swan Neck frames
These are the simplest of the lot, just three rubber buffers plugged into holes in the frame top tube and front tank mounting bracket (see *fig 11.1*). The tank simply sits on these and is held down onto them by the centre bolt. The front mounting bracket rubbers on C15 competition models differ by being specially shaped to help the tank resist side pressure from your knee.

Fig 11.1. C15 tank mounting rubber (3 off). Also used as the n/s side panel rubber '67 - '70 on B25

Welded/Duplex frames
These consist of two horseshoe shaped saddle rubbers between the frame top tube and the tank and two anti-roll rubber buffers fitted in holes on each side of the headstock on the gusset plates *(fig 11.2)*

The saddle rubbers differ between tank types and also between front and rear positions in some cases. There are at least six different examples of this rubber for the Welded/Duplex frame, plus versions from other BSA models to cause further confusion. If you cannot obtain replacements corresponding to the originals the simplest plan is to start with a larger, thicker and more easily available example (such as that for an A65) and modify it. The two critical sizes to work to in this exercise are the diameter of the frame top-tube and of the channel in the underside of the petrol tank - this varies considerably.

The saddle rubbers sometimes move in use and are also easy to dislodge when fitting the tank unless taped or glued to the underside of the tank or the frame tube. Either of these alternatives is a good idea and they should be positioned as far forward and rearward as is practicable.

The anti-roll rubbers also vary in thickness to suit the different tanks. They need to provide some resistance when pushing the tank over them to ensure there is no free movement of the tank when fitted, so obtaining the correct thickness does matter. Thicker than required rubbers can be reduced to the correct thickness and thinner than required can be built-up by the addition of extra glued-on layers cut from an old inner-tube or similar.

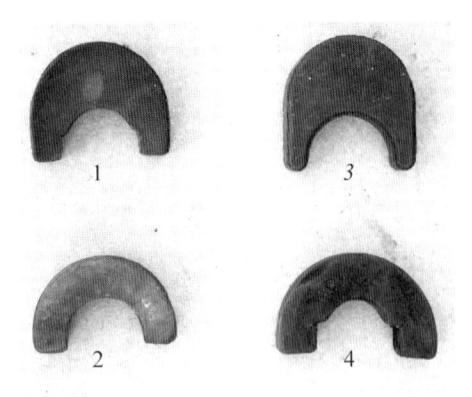

Fig 11.2. Left, saddle rubbers for the petrol tank on Welded/Duplex frame models. Above, anti-roll rubbers for the Welded/Duplex framed models

Fig 11.2 (left) shows the saddle rubbers for the Welded/Duplex framed models. 1 and 2 are the pair for the '67/'68 GRP tanks. 3 is the B40 military rear (front is ½" less in height), 4 is the '69/'70 front rubber for the large metal tank (rear lacks the cut-outs). Be prepared to make your own as few types of these rubbers are available today. The front rubber needs the internal cut-aways to clear the headstock gusset plates.

Three of the many thicknesses of petrol tank anti-roll rubber are shown in *fig 11.2 (right)*. Be prepared to modify them to obtain the exact thickness you need. The best tools I have found for reducing these rubbers are a band-saw and a belt sander.

OIF frames
The '71 onward models follow the Welded/Duplex arrangement with two horseshoe and two anti-roll rubbers (*fig 11.3*). The horseshoe rubbers are peculiar to OIF models to suit the larger diameter top tube and are again different front and rear, but at least one pair serves all models. As a starting point for manufacturing your own, the more common items from the OIF Twin cylinder machines – both BSA and Triumph – offer the best starting point.

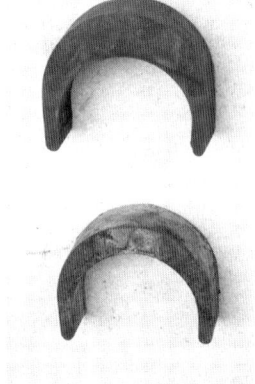

Petrol tank centre bolt fixing and rubber
The centre bolt rubber comes in only two types across the whole Unit Single range and which one you need depends on whether your tank has a plain 1¼" hole right through it, or if it has a welded-in cup with a ½" hole (or separate fitted chrome cup on most B25/B44/B50 steel tanks which also secures the tank trim strip), The C15/B40 can be found with either type of centre bolt fixing. The later tanks mostly feature a plain centre bolt hole. But it is wise to consult the spares manual to determine the exact mix of centre bolt parts for each tank.

Fig 11.3. OIF petrol tank saddle rubbers. Top is the front rubber.

Each of the two centre bolt rubbers is designed to grip the tank in a different way:

Tanks with a plain hole
These accept a large chamfered rubber which expands in diameter as the centre-bolt nut is tightened, thus griping on the inside of the tube. *Fig 11.4* shows BSA's original info pertaining to the centre bolt fixing of the C15 and B40 tanks which can be found with either of the two centre-bolt designs.

Petrol Tanks

NOVEMBER 1961

BSA

SERVICE SHEET
No. 64

PETROL TANK MOUNTING
MODELS C15 STAR, C15 SPORTS STAR & B40

An improved method of mounting the petrol tank is employed on machines now leaving the works. The new tank and fixing components will be supplied against all future replacement orders.

Mounting

To mount the tank, assemble the bolt, distance tubes, washers and rubber, as shown in the illustration, and before tightening the top nut, slide the tank over the assembly and on to its mounting pads. Do not press down before tightening.

Spares numbers of the new tanks and mountings are as follows:

SPARES NO.	DESCRIPTION	MODEL
17540-8086	Petrol tank	C15 Star
18641-8021	" "	B40 Star
18640-8078	" "	C15 Sports Star
11140-8073	Mounting bolt	All models
11640-8088	Distance tube (long)	" "
11640-8089	" " (short)	" "
10940-8085	Mounting rubber	" "
40524-5160	Nut	" "

NOTE: C15 Star and B40 models already have bolt 11140-8073 fitted, but the C15 Sports Star has a longer bolt No. 11140-8075, this bolt must therefore be changed.

Fig 11.4. BSA's information sheet on centre bolt fixing

With this expanding-rubber method the critical part is the spacer tube inside the rubber, which must be of the correct length to permit the rubber to be compressed by the right amount as the centre nut is tightened. This tube is approximately ¼" shorter than the top surface of the rubber.

Tanks with a small cup
Tanks with the small cup within the centre-bolt tube in the tank accept a small cylindrical rubber which is simply compressed until the nut is tightened against the top of the spacer tube *(See fig 11.5)*. This shows a cross-section through the simpler rubber-in-a-cup centre-bolt design. The part labelled 42-8017 is the rubber.

Both of these methods rely on the correct pressure from the nut to sufficiently compress the rubber. This is achieved by fitting the correct length of steel spacer tube inside it. The tube is shorter than the rubber which allows this to compress by the correct amount and no more, until the nut (with washer) tightens against the tube end. Both centre bolt fixing arrangements are compared in *fig 11.6*.

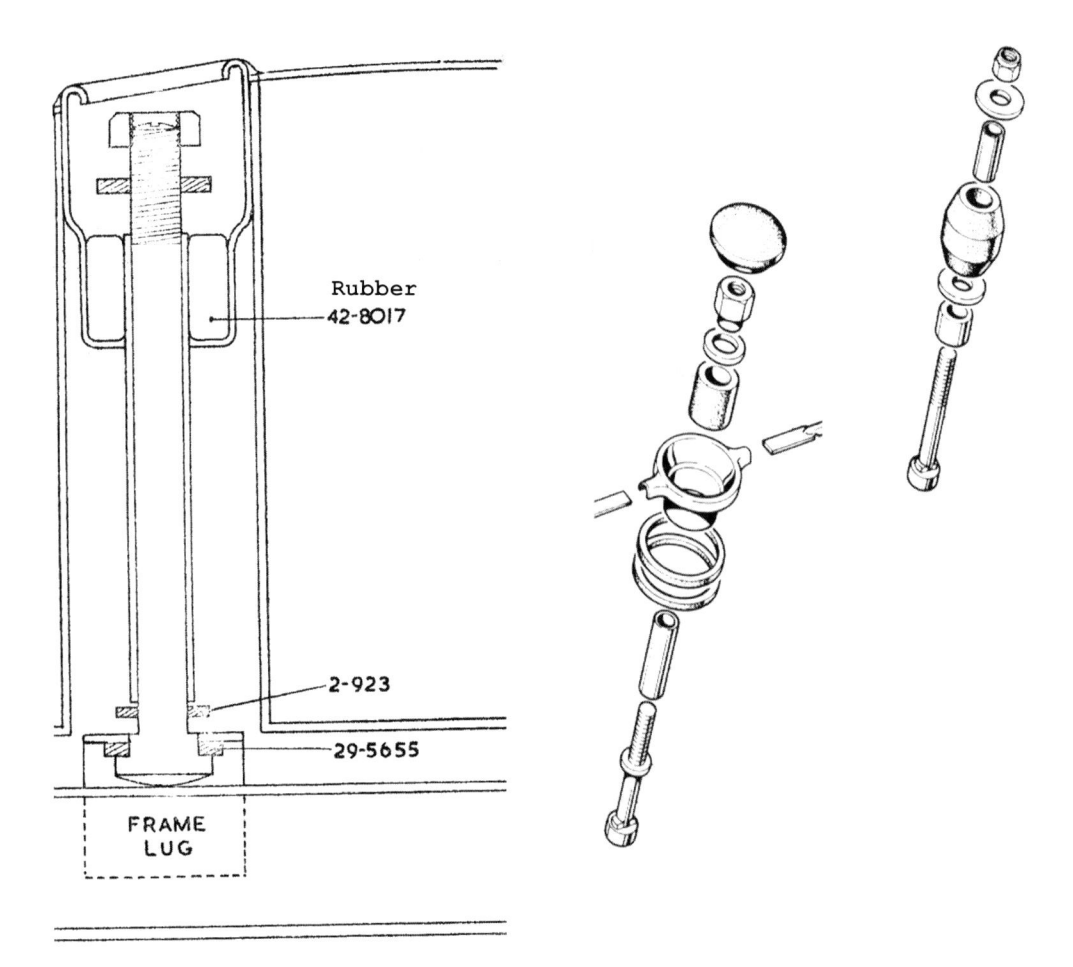

Fig 11.5. The centre bolt fixing design of the tanks with small cup and rubber

Fig 11.6. Both centre bolt fixing arrangements shown side-by-side for comparison.

Tanks for C15 and B40 Road Models '59 to '67.

Basically, for these models there are three different tanks: the 'eyebrow', 'round badge' and 'pear shaped badge' tanks

Eyebrow tank

C15 Star, '59 to '63. 2.5 UK gals. Pear shaped plastic badges. *(See fig 11.7)*

Called the 'eyebrow' tank because the raised ridge sweeping back from the top of the badge resembles an eyebrow.

Fig 11.7. The C15 eyebrow tank as fitted to '62

Round badge tank

B40 Star/SS90/C15SS80 models '61 to '63. 3 UK gals. $3^{1}/_{2}$" round plastic badges. Chrome plated *(see fig 11.8)*. Being rather bulbous to the eye, this tank is not the most stylish example but is worth considering as an option if you require more fuel capacity.

As the name implies, this tank has round badges which are alone in being retained by a spring clip rather than by screws. It carries the same knee-grips mounted on brackets screwed to the tank sides as the eyebrow and pear shaped badge tanks.

Pear shaped badge tank

C15 Star, '62 to '67 and other C15 and B40 road models from '64 on (see *fig 11.9* and BSA Service Sheet, *fig 11.11*). 2.625 UK gals.

The tank has pear shaped plastic badges and tapped holes for knee grip brackets, usually chromed for civilian customers, fully painted otherwise. Variations on this tank include one used for police models with four pummels - tapped holes - on the upper surface for a radio rack, and also the 'civil defence' B40 tank with a flat area replacing the badge recesses to permit the Home Office transfer to be fitted instead of the usual plastic items.

Fig 11.8. Left, early B40 and SS80 round badge tank

Fig 11.9. Right, the commonly found pear shaped badge tank which replaced the C15 eyebrow tank from '62 and which was subsequently fitted to almost all C15 and B40 road models to '67. These tanks and the '59 -'62 steel competition tank (fig 11.11) are interchangeable on all versions of the Swan-Neck frame.

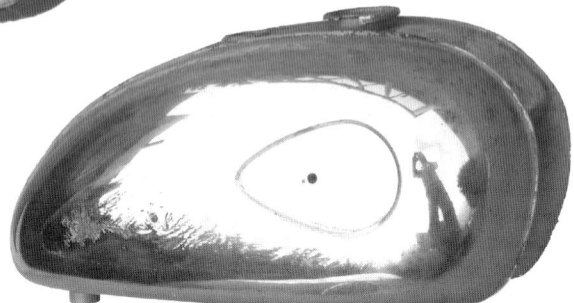

```
                                          AUGUST 1963

                                    SERVICE SHEET
                                       No. G.25.
                      PETROL TANK, Models C15, C15 SS80,
                         B40, B40 SS90, C15 & B40 Police

In the interests of standardisation a new petrol tank No. 40-8079
has been introduced to replace the tanks previously used on the
above models.

When using the latest type tank as a replacement the following
parts are also necessary:-

For C15 model, No. 175 40-8086 tank.
     Use 118 41-8012/3 beading and 109 40-8108 grommet.

For B40 model, No. 186 41-8021 tank
     Use badges 137 40-8014/5 and 109 40-8108 grommet, and
     screw 102 40-8016 (2).

For SS80 & SS90 models, No. 186 40-8078 tank
     Use 109 40-8108 grommet

For C15 & B440 Police models. No. 40-8093 tank
     40-8095 tank and 109 40-8108 grommet.
```

Fig 11.10. Introduction of the same common petrol tank for all C15 and B40 road model. This tank was usually chrome plated with pear-shaped tank badges. The Police version merits a different part number due to its four pummels to mount the radio rack.

Tanks for the C15 competition models '59 to '65

Competition steel tank for Swan Neck frames,
Fig 11.11 shows the small steel competition petrol tank fitted to Trials/Scrambles/USA Starfire models '59 to '62 and C15A Trials Pastoral '62/'63. 2 UK gals. Chrome plated, pear shaped plastic badges and filler cap on the right. Similar to the pear shaped badge tank but smaller.

Fig 11.11. The small steel C15 competition tank fitted as standard to the off-road models from '59 to '62. This tank is interchangeable on all other types of the Swan-neck frame.

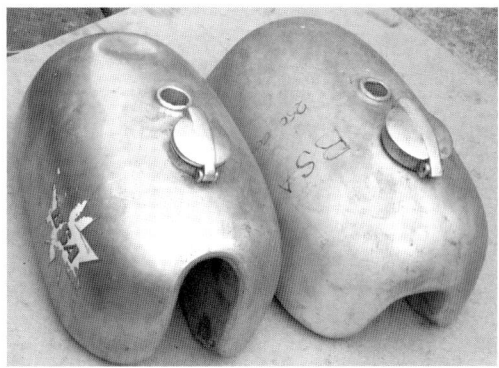

Fig 11.12. C15 competition aluminium tanks for:

Right, '62 T and S special models (previously an option).

Left. The subsequent version with the deeper frame tube channel is for the Welded/Duplex competition models '63 onwards. It can be fitted to the Swan Neck frame with appropriate rubbers. From '66 - '70 this same tank was fitted to the B44VS.

Competition aluminium tank for Swan Neck frames.
This is a shortened version of the earlier Gold Star Trials/Scrambles tank (*see fig 11.12, right*). It was first fitted as standard on the '62 Trials/Scrambles Special (previously optional for earlier competition models). 2 UK gallons (when new). Again on all versions of the Swan Neck frame this tank is interchangeable with the four steel tanks previously shown. Unlike the small steel competition tank, it rests on three standard rubber buffers.

Swan Neck frame steel tank construction and fitting

The steel C15 and B40 roadster tanks are electric-resistance welded along their two raised seams on the tank top. Partial separation of this weld is the most likely source of leaks on this tank type for which the cure is welding or brazing along the seam externally or tank sealant internally. All of the above steel roadster tanks, but not the competition tank, carry chrome beading along the upper two weld seams which hook on at the rear end and attach with a 4BA screw at the front. All these tanks are mounted on the frame in the same way with centre bolt fixing and three rubber buffers beneath. This means that these tanks are fully interchangeable, and also that they are not prone to the splitting by vibration as most other centre-bolt BSA tanks as they are supported beneath the front of each half.

Both types of centre bolt mounting rubber arrangement can be found on most of these C15 and B40 tanks, just check you have compatible tank and centre-bolt rubber as explained on *p204*.

Tanks for C15/B40 competition models '63 to '65

Aluminium tank

Basically, this is the aluminium tank from the previous Swan Neck frame competition models, but modified for the Welded/Duplex frame fitted to '63 to '65 C15 Trials/Scrambles/USA Starfire models and B40 Enduro Star '64/'65. 1.75 UK gals.

This differs from the earlier Swan Neck aluminium tank in that the frame tube channel is much deeper to suit the higher Welded/Duplex frame top tube (*see fig 11.12, left*). The mounting rubber arrangement is the same as all tanks for this frame - centre bolt fixing, two horse shoe shaped saddle rubbers between the tank and top tube and an anti-roll rubber on each headstock gusset plate. This same tank was subsequently used on all B44 Victor special machines with the yellow painted area added from '67.

The boss to accept the aluminium 'Monza' cap is welded onto all of these aluminium tanks. Both sizes of Monza cap, commonly called 'big' and 'small' were used, the big Monza, generally up to about '62, and the small introduced prior to this. As such, both sizes of cap can be found on original Swan Neck frame aluminium tanks with either size occasionally found later, although the small cap predominates.

All of these aluminium tanks were made for BSA by 'LYTA' of London. To some extent they were hand-made and so they vary slightly in shape and capacity. LYTA unfortunately no longer trade but various modern copies are available with quality ie metal thickness and faithfulness to the original design, largely depending on the price you pay.

Steel tank

C15E Trials pastoral steel tank '64 to '65.
A bit of a rarity this one *(fig 11.13)*, this model being very limited in production and only intended for Australia. The tank is the C15 competition steel tank (from the Swan Neck frame) but modified with a deeper channel for the frame top tube to allow it to be fitted to the Welded/Duplex frame. This tank is of 1.75 UK gals, chromed with indents for pear shaped plastic badges and is outwardly similar to the steel C15 competition tank. The main difference is the filler cap which is central and positioned close to the centre bolt on the Pastoral tank.

Fig 11.13. One of the very few examples of the C15E tank which now remain in captivity

Both small steel competition tanks are based on the contemporary D7 Bantam tank; the basic pressing for the sides are the same. Conversion of the bantam tank to C15 competition spec is possible but a lot of detail work is involved. The Bantam tank is often confused with the C15 competition version; the main easy-spot difference is the fixing method, the bantam item having brackets front and rear rather than the centre-bolt fixing hole.

Petrol Tanks

Tanks for Welded/Duplex frame B25/B44/WDB40 '67-'70

All of these use the same mounting arrangement as the '63 on C15 Competition models described above but the horseshoe rubbers and anti-roll rubbers vary in size and thickness to suit the tank being fitted. All of the tanks intended for the Welded/duplex frame are fully interchangeable with the correct rubbers.

GRP petrol tank
C25/B25/B44 '67 to '68 GRP petrol tank: 1.75 UK gals.
Styled to suit the super sports image of the new models (with side panels to match), the new GRP (glass reinforced plastic commonly called fibreglass) tanks for '67 models have indents for pear shaped plastic badges with one fixing screw hole tapped 3BA *(fig 11.14)* and are in the following colour schemes:

UK	C25 Barracuda	Bushfire Orange/Ivory or Nutley Blue/Ivory
USA	B25 Starfire -	Nutley Blue/Ivory
UK	B44 Victor Roadster	Royal Red/Ivory or Peony Red/Ivory
USA	B44 Shooting Star	Peony Red/Ivory

The subsequent '68 GRP tanks are the same shape and size as the '67 item but have larger indents for metal pear shaped badges (*fig 11.14*) with two screw holes tapped 1/8" BSW and are finished in:

B25	Starfire	Nutley Blue/Ivory
B44	Shooting Star	Peony Red/Ivory

GRP was a good material in which to produce the sharp edged outline and detailed surface relief of the new racy-looking tank but in this application GRP has safety shortcomings. In an impact, a GRP tank will split and leak the highly flammable contents whereas a steel tank will tend to dent rather than split and not leak the contents.

Concerns regarding this and the small capacity of these tanks led to them being phased out by BSA towards the end of the '68 season and to replace them with close equivalents in steel with a similar 'sculpted' look. This applied to the GRP oil tank as well, which was replaced by a steel tank with GRP cover at the same time.

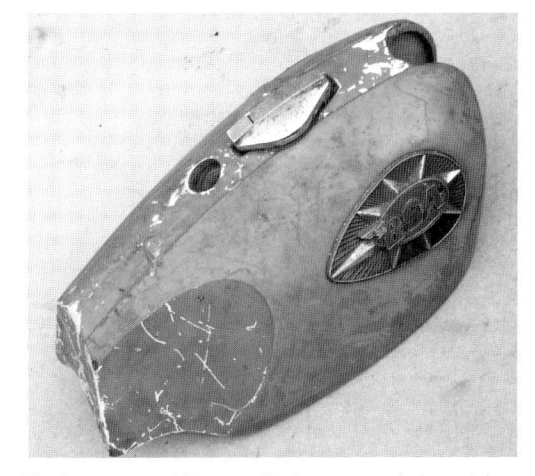

Fig 11.14. Left, GRP tank with plastic pear-shaped badges means '67 spec. Right same style but with large metal badges, '68 spec.

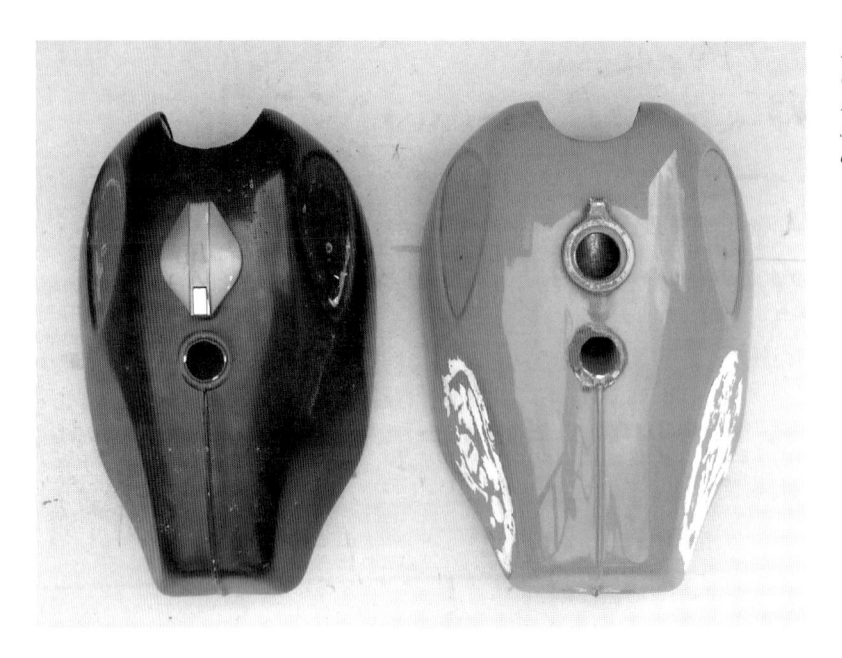

Fig 11.15. Small (left) and large B25/B44 steel tanks seen together for comparison

Steel tanks

'69 and '70 B25/B44 steel tanks.

The steel replacement for the GRP petrol tank *(fig 11.15)* soon after became standard fitment on the USA B25 Starfire for the '69 season, in Bushfire Orange and Gold finish. The general shape and appearance of the steel tank mirrored that of the GRP version it replaced with large metal badges screwed on as before and with added stick-on knee grip rubbers. This 'small steel' Starfire tank as it is now known also produced a capacity increase to 2.5 UK gals.

In keeping with the general trend at the time for UK models to have larger capacity tanks than their USA equivalents[*], the '69 UK Starfire had a tank of the same style but wider, to hold 3.25 gals. The '69 B44 used this larger steel tank for all markets – as did some A65 Lightning and Firebird models at this time with chrome finished knee-grip panels. It is sometimes difficult to tell which of the two sizes of steel tank you might be looking at unless they are next to each other. Measured across the underneath at the widest point the larger tank is 13¼" wide, the small steel tank is 12" wide. The small steel version is relatively rare compared to the larger one.

The steel B25/B44 'sculpted' tanks have a plain, unobstructed centre bolt mounting hole. They could therefore be fitted with the larger expanding type of centre bolt mounting rubber.

---

[*]This view, true or not came down to how bikes were thought to be used at the time ie A motorcycle was thought to be bought in the USA primarily as an item of leisure equipment, much as a set of golf clubs, for a bit of fun at the weekend. Plus, a small tank enhances sexy looks (the bike, not the rider), very important when parked outside Joe's diner.

The rest of the world was deemed still to use bikes largely for day to day transport ie serious riding, hence if this is the case you don't want to be stopping for petrol every day, hence fit a bigger tank. This supposition has been verified in the metal in the UK by the large numbers of BSA's and other marques returned to these shores from the USA; these machines often show signs of damage and neglect but are generally low mileage whereas the equivalent UK machine is likely to have a long history of use and repair with consequent high mileage. Nothing judgemental is intended by this, it just seems to be the way it is.

Fig 11.16. Steel tank beading holder and associated centre bolt fixing components. Specifically, this collection is from the '72 Fleetstar with large petrol tank - the only Unit Single to use a beading strip fore and aft of the centre bolt (despite what the OIF parts books may show). The tabs on the ends of the beading strips hook through the apertures in the beading holder. The trim strips are specific to each different tank.

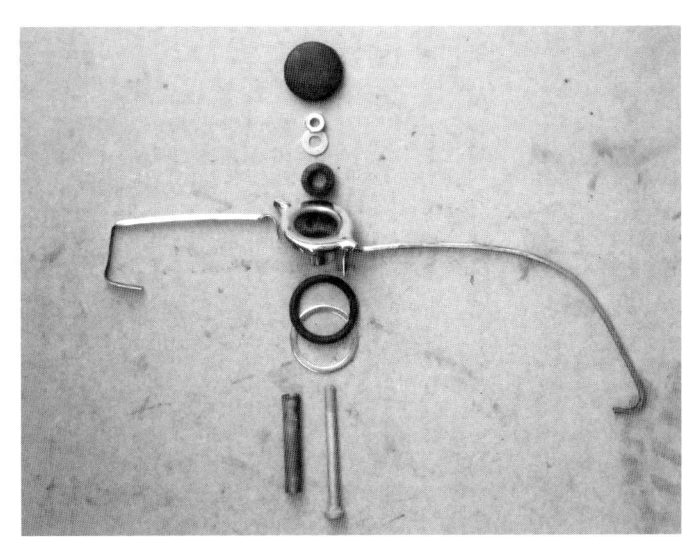

In actuality they are fitted by inserting the chrome 'beading holder' (which traps the end of the chrome trim strip) into the centre-bolt hole *(see fig 11.16)*. This then accepts the smaller type of mounting rubber. With this arrangement, do not omit the large 'O' ring which fits in the groove on the tank around the centre-bolt hole, under the beading holder. Without the 'O' ring the paintwork on the tank will suffer. Even with the 'O' ring in place, check that the edge of the chrome beading holder does not contact the surface of the petrol tank when the centre-bolt is tightened. The 'O' ring should also be fitted with a steel spacing ring to prevent this unwanted contact; position this above the 'O' ring under the beading holder.

'70 saw the continued usage of the large steel tank on the UK B25 Starfire and UK and USA B44 shooting Star. The small steel tank on the USA B25 Starfire was replaced by the smallish (2.75 UK gals) and teardrop shaped steel B25 Fleetstar tank in a new colour scheme of flamboyant aircraft blue with white stripes *(fig 11.17)*. This tank being standard fitment on the Fleetstar from '68 to '70, both with or without tank-top pummels and radio rack depending on customer requirements.

Fig 11.17. Tatty but original '70 USA B25 Starfire tank; an old BSA favourite also found on the B25 Fleetstar at this time.

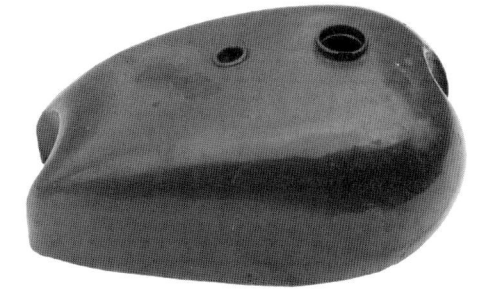

Fig 11.18. The B40 Military tank which has no badges or indents and which is based on the pre-unit tanks for the Goldstar and A10.

Fleetstar petrol tank
B25 '68 to '70 (and USA B25 1970). Steel, 2.75 UK gals, chromed with black or white colour scheme for Fleetstar use. (Same tank as that shown in *fig 11.17*, but a different finish.)

An old favourite with BSA, this tank had been fitted in various incarnations since the early 1950's, mainly to USA models from the Pre-Unit A and B ranges. It now differed for its new application to the Fleetstar by having a push and turn filler cap (rather than hinged butterfly) and no indents for plastic tank badges.

The two Fleetstar versions intended for 'Police' and 'other fleet users' affected the tank in that the former required four tapped holes (pummels) on the upper surface to mount a grid very much in the Triumph style. Other fleet users had a plain tank without this feature. The Fleetstar version of this tank carried a chrome finish with painted areas whereas the '70 USA Starfire version did not, being painted all over.

Military
B40 military models '67 to '70 petrol tank. Steel, 3.5 UK gals, no badge indents *(see fig 11.18)*.

Another old favourite for BSA, this tank is a slightly modified version of the Pre-Unit A and B model's UK tank, the main difference being the lack of badge indents. Unfortunately, in the UK at least, this has resulted in many WDB40 tanks being robbed from their noble steed for conversion to BSA Goldstar tanks (sacrilege I say, I await the day when two-a-penny Goldie tanks are converted for use on the much more practical WDB40). It is just as well that new Goldie tanks are now being remanufactured.

This tank is standard fitment for all Military B40s for all markets from '67 onward, Mk1, Mk2, and Roughrider. The only change was the repositioning of the filler cap to the offside from late '70 onward to help get the fuel in easier.

The small steel Fleetstar tank (in deep Bronze Green) is occasionally seen fitted to military B40 machines. It is shown as such in some BSA literature, and it does look the part, but as yet there is no evidence that machines were originally supplied as such. Fitting this smaller tank to the WDB40 is not straightforward on standard Mk1 machines but is easy on the Mk2/Roughrider version due to the difference in Zener heat sink position (now under the bottom yoke rather than under the tank).

B44 Victor Enduro/Victor special '66 to '70.
Aluminium, small Monza filler cap, 1.75 UK gals. Please see notes above for C15 Competition models aluminium tank '63 to '65 – it's the same tank! *(see fig 11.12)*

B44 Victor GP '65 to '67.
Aluminium, 1.375 UK gals, small Monza cap.
Similar at a glance to the contemporary Victor Special tank due to the paint job, but actually a totally different item due to the larger channel for the frame top tube, and top, front cutaway to clear the oil filler cap by the headstock on the frame tube. Later production versions of this tank appear to have been fitted with a plastic 'bung' in place of the usual Monza cap *(see figs 11.19 -11.21)*

Around the lower edge of the tank, the weld between the side and base is left as a raised seam. Originally made by LYTA, there are good quality replicas of this tank available now.

Fig 11.19. B44GP petrol tank; original but having lost most of its paint.

Fig 11.20. The push-in plastic bung with breather pipe and O-rings.

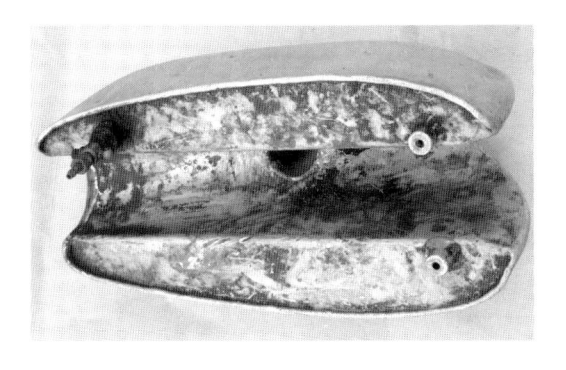

Fig 11.21. The underside of the B44GP tank (shown in fig 11.16), altogether different from the B44VS item (fig 11.12).

TR25w '68 to '70.
This uses its own style of tank of 3¼ gallons capacity.
Individual in appearance *(see fig 11.22)*, if to some eyes unattractive due to its flat top and square sides, it seems not to have any foibles other than those which afflict most Unit Single tanks; namely splits at the front due to vibration and rust. It carries a central polished aluminium trim strip and large die cast and chromed Triumph style tank badges. It is fully interchangeable with all of the BSA tanks used on the Welded/Duplex frame which the triumph model uses.

Fig 11.22. TR25w tank '68 - '70. Odd styling, it actually looks better on the bike than when seen in isolation. The tank badges are in keeping with the contemporary Triumph range

Other tank options - swaps from other models.
In principle any other BSA tank with a centre-bolt fixing is a possibility but in reality some will go straight on and some not. If you cannot find the tank you should have (or don't want it) then the tank from another Unit Single of the same frame type is the best bet. The resulting bike/tank combination should then at least look like the two are compatible. Due to the changes to the frame top-tube, Welded/Duplex tanks will fit on a Swan Neck frame but not vice-versa. Similarly, OIF tanks will fit on Swan Neck frames but not vice-versa. The OIF tank will not readily fit the Welded/Duplex frame without altering the tank lower rear to clear the duplex 'seat-tubes', and/or repositioning the centre fixing bolt. Specially made mounting rubbers are likely to be needed for any of these tank swaps.

The same compatibility problems affect the chances of tanks from larger models in the BSA range; both Unit and pre-Unit, fitting straight onto the Unit Single frames. The least fraught permutations are fitting the swinging-arm pre-Unit tanks onto the Swan Neck frame.

Tank splitting due to vibration
Steel tanks fitted to the Welded/Duplex frame B25/WDB40/B44 models from '67 onward should be found to have either two $5/16$" Cycle tapped holes or threaded studs on the underside, one on each half, near the front. These are to mount a tie-strap which helps reduce vibration of the tank. Left unchecked, this vibration will result in the tank splitting, usually along the front top edge by the frame headstock. Therefore, do not omit the tie strap if your tank has provision to fit one. If it is missing, make one from a piece of mild steel strip (no more than

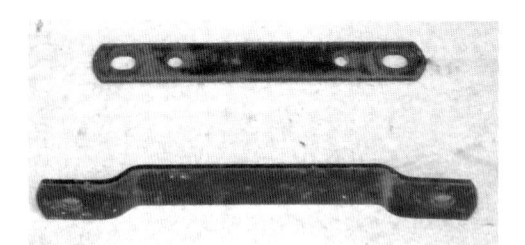

Fig 11.23. Tie straps for the B25 and B44 steel petrol tanks '68 to '70. The longer stepped strap is used with the two sizes of 'sculpted' tank. The shorter, straight strap is used on the B25 Fleestar teardrop tank (and USA '70 B25 Starfire). The '72 onward OIF tank tie strap is much as the smaller strap shown here.

1" by $1/8$" cross section is required). The boffins at Umberslade Hall did not include provision for this feature when they designed the '71 onward OIF models but subsequently re-thought this in response to split tanks – perhaps they should have taken more notice of the in-house experience and wisdom at Small Heath rather than trying to 're-invent the wheel'.

Unfortunately the modification to include two brackets *(fig 11.23)* on the underside of both sizes of steel tank to enable the fitment of a tie strap was implemented close to the end of production. Hence such improved tanks were mainly offered as spare parts/replacements rather than as original fitment. The arrangement for the OIF tie strap comprises a small welded-on bracket on each half of the tank to hold a short captive bolt. The holes in the ends of the stay- a flat strip of steel - fit onto the exposed bolt thread and are secured by nuts.

An additional area to check for fractures is around the central bolt fixing of the B25/B44 steel tanks. Any metal to metal contact here between chrome beading holder and the tank will lead to leaks in this area as indicated by bubbling paint. Check that the 'O' ring and seating ring *(fig 11.16)* are sufficient to create clearance between the beading holder and tank.

Tanks for OIF models '71 Onward

Whilst visually similar, the four slim, 2 gallon tanks introduced for the new style '71 T and SS models have subtle differences *(figs 11.24 and 11.25)*. Firstly, materials, which were steel or aluminium for road or trail use, respectively; secondly, shape, rounded front for Triumph and squarer front end for BSA. Additionally, the steel tanks have a bayonet filler cap offset to the right; the Trail models a central Monza alloy cap *(figs 11.26 and 11.27)*.

The B50MX fitted a slimmer 1 gallon tank of the same style as the BSA 'T' models for '71 and '72, adopting the BSA 'T' two gallon tank for '73. The '73 Triumph TR5MX adopted the 1971 Trail Blazer alloy tank but with a heavier duty Monza cap.

Late '71 saw the appearance of the 3 gallon steel tank on the home market B50SS and this continued into '72 on this model, export models continuing to use the 2 gallon item *(fig 11.28)*. This larger tank required the front end of the seat to be shortened to accommodate

Fig 11.24. Left, '71/'72 slim B50MX tank, '72 colours shown here.

Fig 11.25. Below, the polished aluminium version, with Flambordeau and white stripes paintwork.

Fig 11.26. Square front end means BSA (aluminium Trail version '71 shown).

Fig 11.27. Rounded front end means Triumph (Steel version shown) despite what the badge says!

Fig 11.28. The '72 home market large tank; difficult to find an angle from which it looks good. Here the '72 B25 Fleetstar version is shown with threaded pummels for the radio rack.

it but other than this, all of these tanks are interchangeable. The large tank was standard fitment on the '72 B25 Fleetstar but in this application it gained four tapped holes on its upper surface to mount a radio rack – much as the previous Fleetstar and C15 Police models. '72 modifications on all tanks current at that time was the repositioning of the fuel tap bosses further to the rear and later the tie strap assembly explained above.

The alloy tanks often display slight blistering of the paint around the filler cap. This is possibly due to residue under the paint remaining from the welding-on of the filler neck. If re-painting these tanks, clean this area thoroughly.

B50 models also sometimes suffered from a lack of clearance between the tank and rockerbox. Please note the BSA Service Sheet shown below *(fig 11.29)* about the omission of a rubber pad.

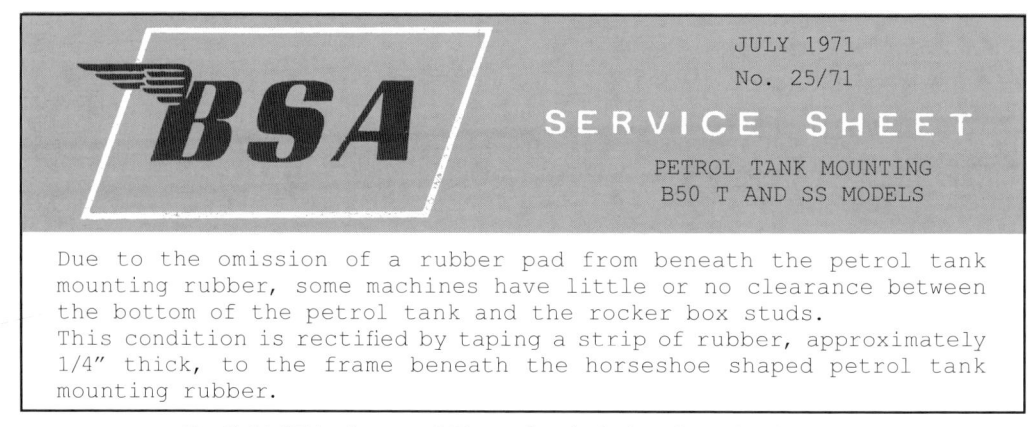

```
                                              JULY 1971
                                              No. 25/71
  BSA                    S E R V I C E   S H E E T
                                        PETROL TANK MOUNTING
                                        B50 T AND SS MODELS

  Due to the omission of a rubber pad from beneath the petrol tank
  mounting rubber, some machines have little or no clearance between
  the bottom of the petrol tank and the rocker box studs.
  This condition is rectified by taping a strip of rubber, approximately
  1/4" thick, to the frame beneath the horseshoe shaped petrol tank
  mounting rubber.
```

Fig 11.26. BSA solution to B50 petrol tanks fouling the rocker box studs

Unit Singles and the Ethanol Problem

At the time of writing the predominant issue relating to these petrol tanks in general, and the GRP tanks specifically, is the increasing use of ethanol in petrol and its detrimental effect on GRP and some earlier types of internal tank sealant - it dissolves both.

Steel tanks are not immune to the effects of ethanol either. Ethanol, if allowed to, will absorb water from the atmosphere, left inside your steel tank this contaminated mixture will corrode the inside. Without wishing to rely on the crystal ball to foretell what future developments may transpire, it is simple common sense that owners should protect their investments and take unprotected tanks and associated equipment out of use until remedial action - application of ethylene proof sealant - has been taken.

Tank Repairs

In addition to dealing with ethanol problems, our now aging tank may require attention in other areas depending on the sort of damage it is displaying – splits, perforation due to rust (usually underneath after water has got inside) and dents. Wherever possible, the first two types of defect should be repaired by welding or brazing in preference to internal sealants which are an obstacle to future options of applying heat to affect a repair.

Dents require a different approach, the first thing to decide being whether to fill it and paint over or to remove the dent. The latter solution has to be done if chrome plate is the intended finish in the dented area.

Dent removal

The accepted method of dent removal is to get behind the dent with a specially shaped steel tool and push it out. If you feel like attempting this remedy, the main thing you will need is time; firstly to fashion an appropriately shaped steel bar, $\frac{1}{2}$" to $\frac{3}{4}$" diameter will do and made with a rounded end which is placed at the point of contact behind the dent to knock the dent out.

Reaching behind the dent can be done through the filler neck or through a hole cut in the underside of the tank with a large hole-saw or jigsaw. Obviously this will need to be welded up later.

The knocking is done by fixing the free end of the bar in a vice and hitting the bar between the vice and the tank. The book says that hitting it downwards causes it to rebound upwards and strike the back of the dent. In this form it is known as a 'snarling iron'. In practice it may be found to work better to strike the iron upwards from below against the dent. Additionally, pressing the inside of the dent downwards onto the tool and malleting the tank around the dented area (not directly on it) may be found to work. Be prepared to experiment as exactly which method works best depends on the shape, size, severity and position of the dent.

Moving the metal back to its original position should be done gradually with many small blows rather than a few heavy handed blows. These small blows each produce a small shallow protrusion in the dented area as a witness to the impact of the tool. Indeed, the outward protrusion produced by each blow of the iron tells you where it is and where it may need moving to as it is being done 'blind' that is to say you are looking from the outside and can't see it where the tool is positioned directly. An additional aid to aiming the blows can be rigged up in the form of a fixed pointer which indicates the position of the tip of the tool.

Smoothing off the perhaps rippled or pimpled surface of the dent after it has been restored to its original position may need the head of the iron to be re-shaped so that it matches more closely the contour of the tank in the area being worked on. It can then be struck against the inside of the tank as before but now with a flat lump of steel in opposition to it outside the tank. Alternatively, the area being worked on can be held firmly against the iron whilst a hammer is used carefully from the outside to smooth the surface. Expect to finish the job to a perfectly level surface with a little filing or linishing.

Centre bolt problems

Whilst being an excellent and simple design, the centre bolt fixing arrangement can create problems if water is allowed to enter and lie there undisturbed. The rubber grommet covering the hole needs to capable of providing a seal to exclude water and should be replaced if perished. Rust damage which can result from this is difficult to repair other than by cutting out the complete central tube and welding in a purpose made replacement. A replacement tank is usually the easier option.

Tanks which have a hinged filler cap will need this to be removed before much of the above renovation work is carried out. The cap hinges on a roll-pin which will need to be driven out; I do this by using the blunt end of a drill bit – of correct diameter to fit closely in the hole in the cap where the roll-pin hides – with a copper mallet to hit the pointed end. Padded protection of the nearby paintwork is recommended along with an obliging assistant to hold the tank whilst you do the necessary. Re-fitting the Monza cap is effected in much the same way.

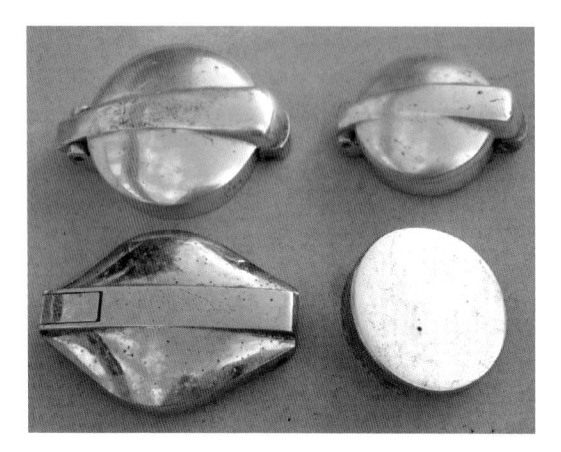

Fig. 11.27. Petrol tank caps. Top, large and small Monza caps for aluminium tanks. Bottom left, '67 -'70 B25 and B44 roadster Monza cap. Bottom right, bayonet cap used on most other unit single petrol tanks

Fig 11.28. Petrol tank taps. Top left, '58 -'62. Top right, '62 -'66. Bottom left, '67 -'68 (with adaptor for GRP tanks). Bottom right, '69 onwards.

To some extent the above dates are approximate, and at times the thread size is the determining factor in deciding which tap will fit your tank. It should be remembered that the BSP ('gas') threads used are measured according to the BORE size of the pipe and not the o/d. The three sizes of thread seen on these taps are $1/8$", $3/16$" and $1/4$"

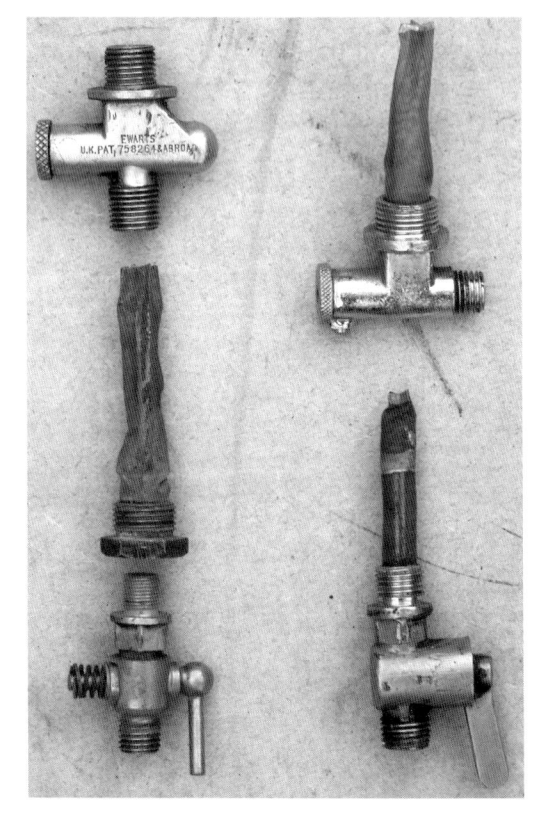

12. OIL TANKS AND LUBRICATION

In terms of what to put in the tank, take your pick, I am not qualified to say that one oil is better than another. I can say what I prefer to use - a good quality 'straight' 40 oil which is most similar to BSA's original recommendation *(see Rupert Ratio Unit Single Manual Volume 1 The Engine)*.

The separate oil tank found on machines made before '71 (except B44GP) will be one of three basic types, with detail differences found within each type: oil tanks for Swan Neck frame, the Welded/Duplex frame of '63 -'67 and '67 -'70 (B25/B44).

C15 and B40 Swan Neck Frame Oil Tanks

C15/B40 models using the Swan Neck frame (not '63 onward competition models and WDB40 which use the Welded/Duplex frame) all used an oil tank mounted on the o/s to match the style of the n/s side panel. All were mounted on brackets from the frame by two $^5/_{16}$" BSCy tapped-hole fixings on their inner surface and a welded-on rear bracket to the sub-frame to mudguard boss. The roadster version of this tank changed to captive nuts ($^5/_{16}$" BSCy) on flat brackets instead of the tapped holes for '65 and gained a froth tower/breather on the top surface, rearward of the filler cap from '66, to replace the earlier arrangement of pipe-stub breather on the back of the tank.

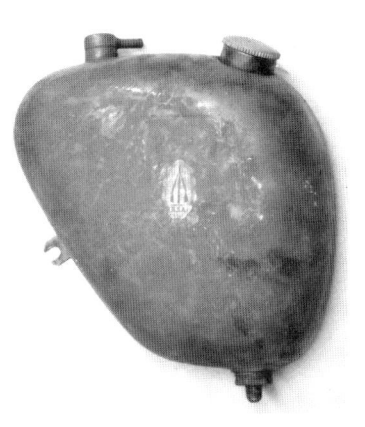

The competition example of this tank used on the C15S Swan Neck frame up to '62 is visually similar (same pressings for the two main parts) but is immediately identifiable by the

Fig 12.1. C15/B40 roadster oil tank, '66/'67 version.

froth tower/breather which angles upward from the back of the tank *(fig 12.2)*. Original fixing was by two tapped holes and a longer rear bracket similar to the roadster. During '60 this changed to three tapped holes on the rear of the tank and a separate mounting plate.

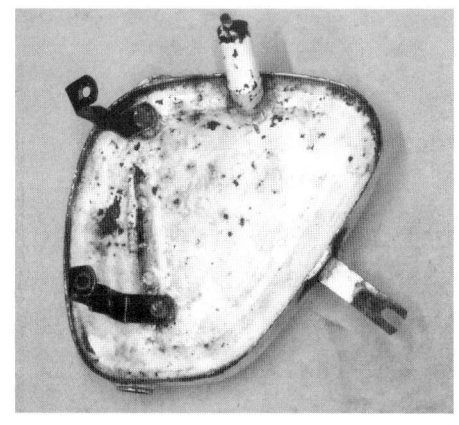

Fig 12.2. Front and back of the '59 to mid '60 C15 competition oil tank showing the angled froth tower/ breather on the rear of the tank.

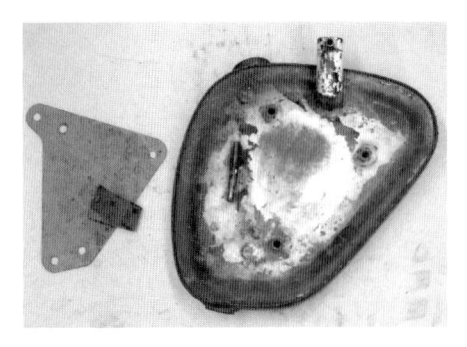

Fig. 12.3. The '60 onward C15 competition oil tank with revised mounting arrangement.

As with the roadster version, the rear bracket on the competition tank is prone to vibration fractures. This led to changes to the mounting arrangement shown in *fig 12.3*.

The two versions of this competition tank and their specific mounting brackets cannot be mixed. The later versions of the front two mounting brackets from the frame are as per the earlier two except for being $^1/_8$" shorter on the offside to accommodate the thickness of the new tank mounting plate.

Similarly, none of the roadster oil tank mounting components can be mixed with the competition versions, moreover, the roadster tank and side panel when fitted are parallel to each other and the axis of the bike; the competition items converge inwards at the front resulting in the whole central tinware being narrower between the rider's legs.

The changes to the competition oil tank were to overcome vibration cracks around the mounting points, particularly the rear bracket to the subframe, this bracket is also prone to falling off the roadster tank after springing a leak as the tank starts to crack around it.

Whilst none of the above three versions of this tank are interchangeable, conversion from one to another is a case of applying basic fabrication techniques, the two main pressings which form the tank are identical throughout.

Oil Tanks for Welded/Duplex Frames

Central oil tank
A new design of tank, fitted to the first off-road models using the Welded/Duplex frame from '63 onward, is usually known as the central oil tank (albeit with a bias to the o/s) and was borrowed from the A50/A65 with minor changes *(see fig. 12.4)*. These amounted to a screw cap with a shorter filler neck and alterations to the return pipe arrangement. This tank was fitted to '63 onward C15/B40 competition models, B44VS to '67 and all B40 military models. The latter model's tank fitted a bayonet cap and additional return pipe/rocker feed changes may prevent straightforward swapping of these otherwise identical tanks.

This type of tank was therefore original fitment on the earliest versions of the Welded/Duplex frame. It cannot be fitted to the later versions of this frame (C/B25 and B44VR/SS '67 on, B44VS '68 on) as a replacement for their intended oil tank as the top mounting points on the frame are different. The frame is the same at the bottom tank mounting area except for the addition on the later frame version of a short length of steel tube in the offside rubber bush hole. Removal of this and reversion to the original design is easy in this instance; this bit of tube has a tendency to detach itself anyway.

The central tank is fully rubber mounted on three rubber buffers with only one fixing bolt at the top-rear bracket, which undoubtedly helps it not shake itself to bits. Unfortunately the top rear mount connecting the tank to the frame - although fitted with a top-hat rubber bush - is clearly not rubbery enough as this bracket commonly detaches itself from the tank due to stress in use. Other than that, this tank is a trouble-free design.

The Welded/Duplex frame oil tank '63 to '67 with short screw-cap filler neck was also subsequently used on the B40 military with detail differences. The example in *fig 12.4* is undergoing repair to the top-rear mounting bracket.

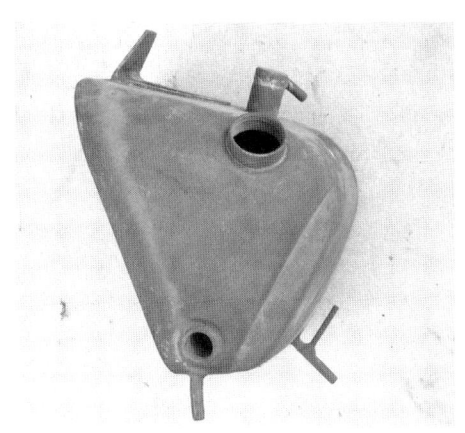

Fig 12.4. Welded/Duplex frame oil tank '63 to '67 with short screw-cap filler neck.

B25/B44 oil tank, '67 to '70

The final oil tank design fitted to the later Welded/Duplex-framed models on the o/s of the machine was firstly moulded in GRP with the stylish new side panel integrally moulded with it. This was fitted to C25, B25 and B44 road machines for '67/'68, with replacement by a steel tank with separate GRP cover before the end of the '68 season. Top mounting was by two top-hat rubber bushes, the single bottom mount being a captive peg on the GRP tank which locates in a small rubber top-hat bush in the tubular addition to the frame as detailed above. Other than the choice of material which usually renders this tank scrap if fractured, this is a trouble free design.

The somewhat angular steel tank which replaced the GRP item and is fully interchangeable with it, can be found in four guises which amount to detail differences to suit the exact model of B25, TR25w or B44 for which it was intended (*fig 12.5*).

The Triumph item for '68 -'69 will have two brackets with spring clips for the two GRP side panel Dzus fasteners - the push to fit, quarter turn to release type fastener - and a vertical filler neck.

The B25 Starfire and B44 SS '69 item will have the two side panel brackets as above and a slightly angled filler neck. The '70 version for these models has no side panel brackets and a shorter filler neck (still angled) to now leave a smaller bruise on the inside of the rider's right thigh (*fig 12.6*). This was also fitted to the '70 TR25w.

The B25 Fleetstar item always has a bare tank without the brackets for a cover, and with the long angled neck for '68 and '69, becoming short neck for '70.

B44VS follows Fleetstar practice for '69 and '70 having started with a similar tank but with more rounded corners in '68.

The steel oil tank uses the same two top rubber mounts as the GRP item, the brackets on the tank now being welded rather than bolted as on the GRP item. The bottom mount for the steel tank changed to a $^5/_{16}$" UNF tapped-hole in the tank instead of the GRP tank's peg arrangement.

Fig 12.5. A long filler neck indicates that this tank is of '69 manufacture. Welded-on side panel brackets indicate B25/B44SS/TR25w use. The TR25w version has a vertical filler neck, rather than angled and was carried over from '68.

Fig 12.6. Short, angled filler neck identifies this as '70 oil tank for all B25/B44/TR25w models.

Oil tank mounting problems

The mounting bolt for the new '69 arrangement passes up through the same small tubular fitting on the frame, but I think the design of this arrangement must have been thought up by a newly engaged apprentice at BSA.

The tapped hole in the tank underside for the mounting bolt is invariably out of alignment with the frame tube through which the bolts passes. The bolt should be fitted with a rubber sleeve on its free length to act as a bush between itself and the fixing tube on the frame. The original rubber sleeve is actually a short length of $^5/_{16}$" bore herringbone oil pipe. This is a push fit both on the bolt and in the frame which means that it usually doesn't allow the bolt to align with the tapped hole in the tank. It is usually necessary to reduce the o/d of the rubber just enough for it to tilt and engage with the threaded hole. This bolt tightens in place by 'bottoming' in the tapped hole in the tank; not best engineering practice! Possibly as a result of the above issues, the steel tank can crack around the bottom tapped hole and also around the welded-on top brackets.

Oil Tank Repairs

Being hollow, all of the steel oil tanks can suffer from dents, especially the tank on C15/B40 Swan Necked frame models as it is more prominent in position.

Dent removal from the inside follows the same practise as described in Chapter 11 Petrol Tanks *(p217)* although the return pipe inside the tank filler neck may make access difficult. It may well be easier to take the tank apart to allow easy dent removal. This is easily done on the two types of tank for the Welded/Duplex frame by grinding off the weld bead along the seam joining the two halves.

The C15/B40 tank can be dealt with by making a cut with a hacksaw or a thin cutting disc around the tank alongside the resistance welded join around its inner edge. The aim is to cut only through the top/outer layer of steel to allow it to separate from the flat back of the tank. Pushing dents out of the outer surface is now a piece of cake with suitable mallets and hammers, and the welding required for rejoining the two halves is straightforward for a competent welder.

Alternately, you could just source a replacement tank as all but the competition tanks are relatively plentiful. However, one benefit of separating the two tank halves to aid repair is that this allows the inside to be properly cleaned out.

Cleaning the oil tank

Even after a thorough flushing out, the amount of crap inside these tanks often has to be seen to be believed; it makes the exercise of oil changing a complete fallacy when the clean (and expensive) oil is immediately contaminated by the residue inside the tank. As such, just draining the old oil out before putting the new in is just not good enough. As well as repeated flushing with paraffin or petrol, try a rag fastened on to the end of a stick to allow mopping around the insides of the tank. Replace this rag with a new bit repeatedly until it comes out of the tank as clean as it went in and then give the tank a final flush.

Fig 12.7. As good a place as any for a nice '73 B50MX. Not that it can be seen here, but one modification for this year was to the oil tank breather. The oil tank is the main frame on OIF models and the breather pipe which is situated near the filler cap was bent to point rearward. The plastic pipe connected to it was routed to a 'T' piece on the chaincase breather pipe.

Filler Caps and Dipsticks

All C15 and B40 models other than military, and B44VS to '67, use the standard BSA screw cap (widely used on earlier models) which has the suitable oil grades shown on it in relief. The same item, without the writing as fitted to the primary chaincase of pre-unit models, will fit equally well, as will a B25 rocker box cap.

B40 Military, B25, TR25w and B44 models '67 to '70 all use a chrome plated bayonet cap; the military version being finished in dull chrome.

This design of cap is widely used across the BSA range and can be found with or without an integral dipstick. These come in different lengths to suit the tank for which the cap is intended (*see fig. 12.8*) If in doubt, a good rule of thumb to the correct oil level in the tank is that it should be filled to about 1½" below the return pipe aperture inside the tank. This is so that a stream of return oil can clearly be seen exiting the return pipe inside the tank.

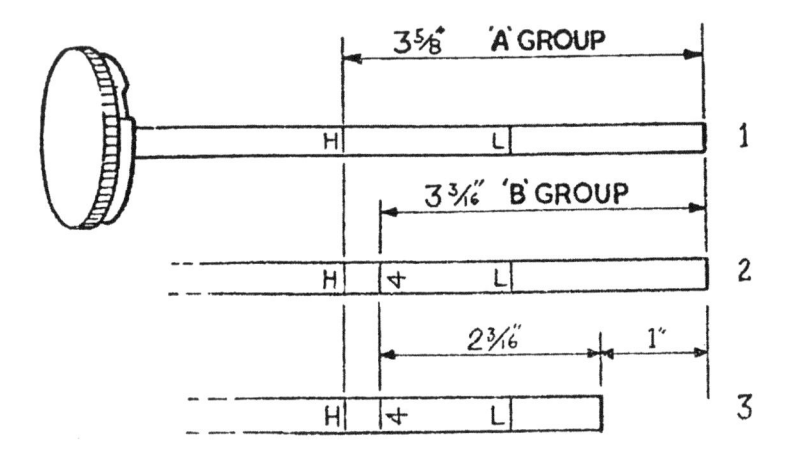

Fig 12.8. Oil tank dipsticks
1. A Group models. The 'H' mark on all dipsticks is intended for the 'A' series oil tanks only.
2. B Group models. Dipsticks fitted to all 'B' models use the mark labelled 4 in the diagram. indicating the maximum level of 4 pints. On the long dipsticks this is 3³⁄₁₆" from the bottom of the dipstick.
3. The later short dipsticks are 1" shorter than the earlier dipsticks but carry the same marks.

The '71 onward OIF models have a screw cap with crossed screwdriver slots and an integral dipstick to suit the oil filler neck on the frame, just behind the headstock. This cap is particular to these models.

Similarly, the B44GP has a screw cap in this location, (*fig 12.9*) for this model a standard unvented chaincase cap is used.

Fig 12.9. The B44GP oil filler neck with breather pipe, the cap for this is a chaincase screw-cap.

Lubrication

Overview

The Unit Single carries its lubricating oil for the engine either in a purpose made tank on the offside of the machine, or inside its frame tubes. This latter system was used on the B44 Victor GP and subsequently all '71 onwards models and as a result led to the name 'Oil-in-Frame' or OIF for short.

Regardless of the type of container (and in the following, all references to the oil tank refer equally to the frame of all OIF models) the oil is circulated from the tank to the engine by the oil pump inside the engine via the 'feed' pipe and then back via the 'return' pipe.

At the outlet from the tank a metal gauze filter is fitted to prevent unwanted debris in the oil being fed to the engine. A similar gauze filter is fitted in the engine sump where the oil is collected prior to returning to the tank return.

In addition to the feed and return pipes there is a smaller rocker feed pipe to the top of the engine. The take-off point for this pipe will be either from a branch on the return pipe stub on the oil tank or from a branch on the oil pipe union under the engine. Original pipes are rubber with a moulded herring-bone pattern on the outside. Pipe sizes are :

> Early feed and all return pipes ¼" bore.
>
> Later feed pipe is $^5/_{16}$" bore; 'later' being for all end-fed engines which were provided with an enlarged feed pipe stub on the oil pipe union under the engine. The corresponding feed pipe stub on the banjo or feed from the oil tank was similarly enlarged to match.
>
> Rocker feed – $^1/_8$" bore.

Original rubber pipe used for these applications was predominantly reinforced by nylon inside the tube walls. It may be a case of using whatever replacement rubber pipe is available these days but if possible select carefully: the tubing needs to be stiff enough not to collapse when bent. It should also be a firm push-fit onto the relevant metal pipe stubs with external pipe clips providing belt-and-braces security. A little oil inside the pipe and on the metal stub will help a new pipe slip into place.

If making new pipes avoid cutting them to the shortest possible length to get from A-to-B, cut to allow generous sweeping curves so they are not pulled tight to fret against frame or engine. On models with a high level exhaust pipe, ensure that the exhaust pipe does not contact the oil pipes. On C15C framed models, and early B44s, these two are in very close proximity so BSA fitted a coil spring as protection along the outside of the oil feed pipe just below the tank. If you are forced to re-use old oil pipes ensure they are clean internally before re-fitting and the same goes for the tank.

The OIF models are at a bit of a disadvantage when it comes to cleaning inside the 'tank'. The best suggestion is to flush out through both the front down tube and also the top tube via the drain plug under the seat tube. Preferably use paraffin for this. The lack of an area for unwanted particles in the oil to collect is solved - at least on B25/T25 models - by the external oil filter on the return line. This in itself is an excellent reason for fitting an external filter to B50 models which did not normally have one as standard. This just requires the B25 rear engine plate to accommodate the filter.

One design fault on the '71 on OIF frame is that the circulation of the oil largely bypasses the whole of the top tube. This can be rectified by taking a feed line from the drain plug on the underside of the seat tube which is explained in more detail in *The Rupert Ratio Unit Single Manual Vol 1 The Engine*.

In use, keep an eye on the oil in the tank by taking the cap off occasionally as per the hand book. Reassure yourself that there is a clear return of good, clean oil with sufficient in the tank and enjoy a carefree ride.

B25 and B44 models with the GRP oil tank seem rather prone to ejecting oil as described in the BSA service sheet in *fig 12.10*.

User tips for models to '70
It is worthwhile fitting a length of plastic or rubber tubing from the breather pipe on the oil tank to a safe discharge point; this is fitted as standard to the breather pipe from the frame of B44GP and OIF models. If the above happens and excess oil is blown out of the breather; or if the bike rolls off its side stand, ends up in a heap and the tank contents pour through the breather, the tubing will prevent the spilt oil coating everything you don't want it to.

The OIF oiling system has a few foibles as described in *Fig 12.11* but it is actually a simplified arrangement compared to the previous B44GP system.

Changing the filter - external filters
The 'British Filters' oil filter shown in *Fig 12.12* with paper element was first fitted to B40 military models from '69 onward. The element is also used on '70s Triumph twins and is readily available. Earlier B40 military models fitted a similar unit made by Vokes and use a now hard to obtain gauze filter element. It is possible to wash the Vokes element in petrol and re-use it if it is otherwise sound.

In addition to the original BSA external filters there are several after market types now available which can be fitted in the return line to the tank. All are a good idea providing that they do not restrict the return flow. An oil pump which is not fully efficient may be overwhelmed by such a filter, resulting in a poor oil return and a smoky exhaust.

Internal filters
The filter normally found in the oil tank is a wire mesh 'strainer' and is only effective at stopping large particles in the oil. Damage, tears or holes in the mesh means replacement, otherwise it can be washed and re-used. The mesh is soft soldered in place and replacement is possible. Three types were used:-

> The Swan-Neck framed and OIF models use the same filter

> Welded/Duplex framed models using the 'central' oil tank have their own filter shared with the Unit Twins

> B25 and B44 models '67 -'70 and B44GP share a third design originally used on pre-unit models.

Oil Tanks And Lubrication

BSA

APRIL 1967

SERVICE SHEET
No. 158
C25, B25, B44 ROADSTER &
SHOOTING STAR MODELS - OIL TANK

It is essential that the oil tank on the above models is not <u>overfilled</u>. When replenishing the oil in the tank the machine must be on the centre stand <u>not</u> on the prop stand, otherwise the air space above the oil which is needed for normal breathing, is reduced, and oil is liable to be blown out of the breather pipe.

Fig 12.10. Don't overfill the oil tank!

BSA

MAY 1971

SERVICE SHEET
<u>OIL CHANGE</u>

When changing the oil on the 1971 B25T/B25SS, it is necessary to remove both the filter screen (C) and drain plug (B) to insure that all of the used oil is removed from the frame. Also remove and clean all filters per Owners Manual

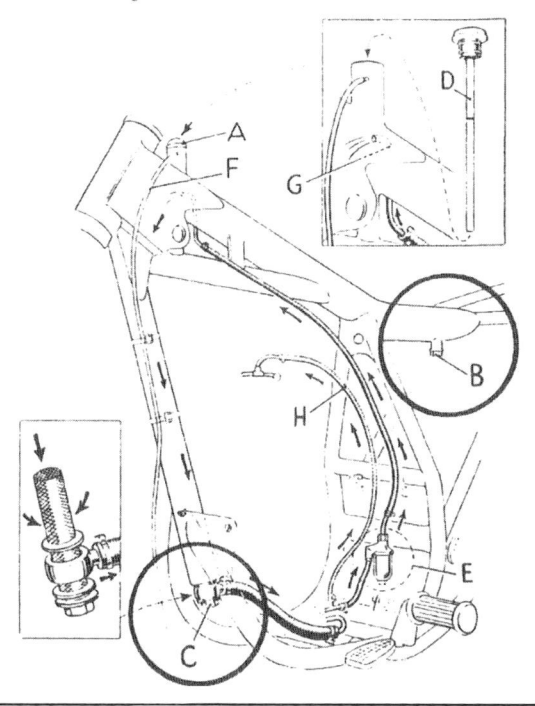

Fig 12.11. Some foibles of the OIF lubrication system

MAY 1971

BSA SERVICE SHEET

OIL FILTER
The external oil filter, which is connected into the oil return pipe, must be fitted with a new element every 4,000 miles. This element change (along with oil change at 1500 mile intervals) will insure that the engine is operating with clean oil.

CHANGING THE OIL FILTER
The filter is located between the rear engine mounting plates. Unscrew the centre bolt and withdraw the filter bowl. Extract the filter element, clean the filter bowl, and install a new element making sure that the sealing rings are in position.

Oil Filter Assembly

Fig 12.12. Changing the oil filter on late B40 Military and OIF 250cc machines

Fig 12.13. The '67 - '68 Vokes oil filter (top) and the 69 onward British Filters unit which replaced it (bottom). Doing this on a B40 Military Mk. 1 requires an adapter plate. The same filter saw service on the OIF 250cc models and is a suitable way to improve filtration on all unit singles

13. SIDE PANELS, CENTRAL TINWARE AND AIR FILTERS

C15 and B40 Side Panel Mounting

All C15/B40 road models and competition models to '62 carry a nearside side panel to match the oil tank on the offside *(fig 13.1)*. At a glance, this panel looks the same as that fitted to contemporary Bantam models but in reality is not: it is wider and flatter along its lower edge. Fixing of the side panel to the flat inner panel which lies inboard is simply done by screwing two chromed sleeve nuts through the cover onto the studs provided. If necessary, these two mounting studs can be persuaded one way or t'other to ensure they line up perfectly with the holes in the outer cover. The two sleeve nuts should be captive on the outer cover by dint of a small circlip fitted in the external groove near the inner end.

The other requirement for correct side panel fixing is to have the correct spacer tubes on the studs to provide a positive stop for the fixing screws. These are held captive on the studs by the small piece of rubber tubing inside the tube which grip on the stud. The correct length of the spacer tubes is $1^5/_8$" and $^1/_2$" o/d. Other lengths are suitable for other BSA models but not the Unit Single. These allow the fixing nuts to be fully tightened without distortion to the outer cover which would happen were the spacing tubes omitted.

Fig 13.1. C15 side panel, front, left and back, right.

C15 central tinware

On C15 and B40 road models the key component for the fixing of all the central tinware is the battery carrier. This bolts to the frame tube and also carries the lower fixing bracket for both the oil tank and inner side panel. The top mounting bracket for these bolts directly to the frame tube.

In the example shown (fig 13.2) the lack of the integral circular air filter inside the centre panel (just a large hole there instead) indicates B40 components rather than C15. Additionally, the details of the oil tank - breather tower and reinforced mounting points identify that component as being of '66 date.

Fig 13.2. C15 and B40 roadster central tinware arrangement showing the battery carrier and the two studs which accept the chromed sleeve nuts. The spacer tubes are omitted from the studs in this picture.

The C15 and B40 Swan-Necked frame models alone carry a central strip of tinware to cover the gap between the oil tank front and the n/s side panel. The C15 roadster version of this panel is of equal width throughout and carries the ignition switch and air filter. The latter item is contained in a circular housing which is attached to the back of the panel – or it should be, they have a tendency to come adrift and require welding back on – and which protrudes through to the front as a short tube onto which the carb-to-filter rubber tube pushes.

The B40 version is the same central panel but without the integral filter housing. Instead it has a plain hole, $1^7/_8$" or on later models 2" diameter, for an adapter tube, which screws onto the carb to poke through. The same circular filter housing, but now as an independent part, is a push-fit into the end of the carburettor adapter. C15 and B40 Police models use the same circular air filter housing but modified with a threaded insert to allow it to screw directly onto the carburettor.

Fig 13.3. C15 and B40 roadster central tinware to frame top brackets; B40 above, identical to the C15 item below except for the slightly larger radius of the curved portion which fits around the frame tube. the two mounting bolts and nuts show are $^5/_{16}$" Cycle with reduced heads.

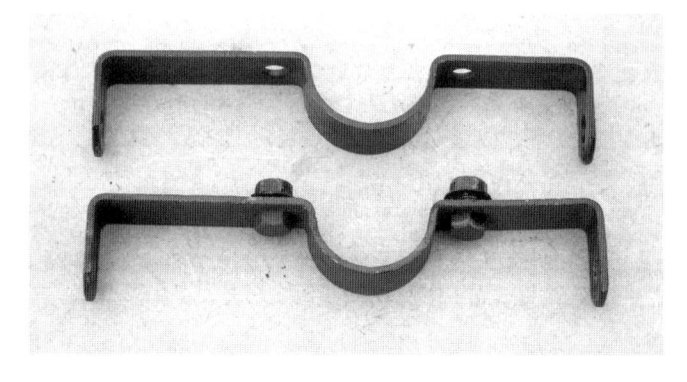

Fig 13.4 shows the B40 air-filter housing, easy to obtain if you separate this part from the C15 centre panel to which it is normally brazed. The now hard-to-obtain circular air filter element for C15 and B40 roadsters is a steel mesh and gauze sandwich which is covered by a domed perforated steel sheet disc. All is retained in the housing by a large wire circlip which can be fabricated from coat-hanger wire.

Fig 13.4. The B40 air-filter housing

The C15 competition side panel as used on the models with Swan-Necked frame is a modified standard cover with a 'D' shaped cut-away for the carb to air filter hose, and a small rectangular one for the inner panel bracket *(see fig 13.5)*. The parts book which shows this same part for the '62 C15 Trials pastoral does not accurately depict this cover.

The competition version of the centre panel of the tinware is much slimmer than the roadster version and narrows in the middle, with one large central hole in which the AC horn is fitted. If no horn was required - usually on scramblers - this hole was covered by a circular blanking plate, just visible in *fig 13.6*.

Fig 13.5. Competition side panel for Swan Neck models until '62 - in essence a modified roadster part. The larger cutaway at the front is for the air filter hose, the smaller cutaway at the rear is for the inner panel bracket.

Fig 13.6. The air filter hidden by the competition side panel shown in Fig 13.5. Circular blanking plate can be seen on the left of central tinware. The side panel spacer tubes are shown in position on the two studs.

Welded/Duplex Framed Models

The first competition models using the Welded/Duplex frame, C15C/B44E&EA, do not have a side cover as such but have an air box lid initially to suit the small coffin-shaped filter box *(fig 13.7)* and, on B44 models, a larger triangular GRP assembly *(see fig 13.8)*. The side panels are shown in *fig 13.10* and filter elements are shown in *fig 13.9*.

The B44VE and VS for '66 to '67 had a GRP air filter box. The enlarged mounting holes shown in *fig 13.8* carry rubber grommets for the mounting bolt (front) and spacing studs (top).

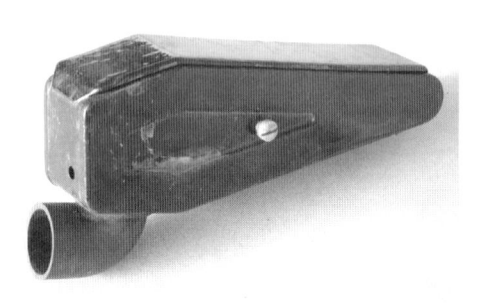

Fig 13.7. Left, the '63 to '65 competition air filter box, the holes are for 'P' clip mounting to the frame, front and rear, and, right shows the competition air box mounted on the frame - the air filter element for this design is unfortunately not available at this time.

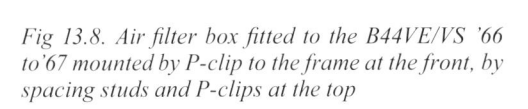

Fig 13.8. Air filter box fitted to the B44VE/VS '66 to '67 mounted by P-clip to the frame at the front, by spacing studs and P-clips at the top

Fig 13.9 Air filters, right is the OIF box and filter element for road and trail models, bottom left is the C15/B40 pncake filter, middle left the B40 Enduro Star Vokes item, top left the '67 -'70 B25/TR25w/ B44 'pillbox' filter

Fig 13.10. B44GP o/s and n/s GRP side panels, attached by Dzus fasteners to the GRP airbox

B40 Military airbox

The B40 Military has its air filter in the usual position on the n/s of which the hinged lid forms the side panel. The military airbox is prone to vibration splits around the rear mounting bracket, but other than this it is a robust component which is generally found in battle-scarred, but victorious, condition as shown in *fig 13.11*. The small tube by the front mounting bolt connects to the original type 'butterfly' carburetter by a rubber pipe - ignore this if you have changed to a better carb. The small cylindrical boss by the lower corner contains a small porous plug retained by a circlip. This allows any moisture which has collected within to drain out without allowing air inward.

Fig 13.12 shows the air filter and associated components. With a suitable spacer underneath it, the similar, and more easily available filter element from the '67 to '70 B25/B44 can be fitted.

Fig 13.11. The B40 Military airbox (above left) and (right), the internal components.

B25 and B44 side panels, '67 to '70

B25 and B44 road models '67 to '69 use GRP for the n/s side panel, of stylish and individual shape, unlike any of the rather functional earlier offerings. The GRP oil tank on the o/s initially had its outer surface moulded as a mirror image of the n/s panel. From late '68 a plain steel oil tank was introduced with a GRP cover moulded in the previous stylish design. The pair of GRP side panels was dropped for '70 to be replaced on the n/s by a plain steel panel to match the bare steel tank on the o/s.

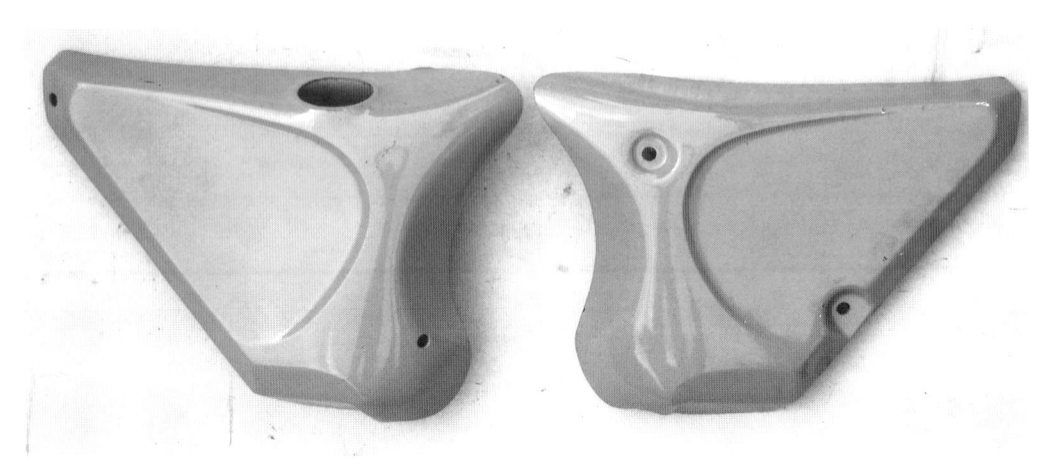

Fig 13.13. B25/B44 GRP side panels '67 to '69. The o/s panel (left) is fitted for '69 only over the steel oil tank introduced for that year. The n/s panel (seen right) is fitted to B25/B44 models (excluding Fleetstar and Victor Special) '67 to '69 before being superseded by the bare steel oil tank and steel side panel for '70. Fleetstar and B44VS fit the steel parts for '68 to '70. The steel side panel in fig 13.15 was fitted to all models for '70 (and Fleetstar/B44 prior to this).

The 68 to '70 B25 Fleetstar and B44VS use the same steel n/s panel which would be applied throughout the range in '70, excepting the Police spec Fleetstar which used this cover but deepened by $1^{1}/_{4}$" to accommodate a larger battery. The steel n/s panel is always matched by the bare steel oil tank on the o/s on those models which fit it.

The TR25w has its own style of GRP side panels for '68 and '69 (*fig 13.14*). These are square sided to match the look of the petrol tank on this model. For '70 the TR25w adopted the BSA parts for that year ie the smooth steel n/s panel matched by bare oil tank on the o/s.

Fig 13.14. TR25w side panel with square-ish styling which in some ways matches the tank. The '68 - '69 Triumph panels use the same mounting points as the BSA items and are therefore interchangeable.

B25/B44 side panels, correct fitting

Each of these panels, regardless of side or material, is fixed by two Dzus fasteners which push-on to attach the cover and take a quarter turn to undo. The positions of these fasteners are the same throughout which means that the GRP and steel n/s panels are fully interchangeable.

Firm fixing of the nearside panel is achieved by it being pulled up tight (in theory) against two rubber buffers as the Dzus fasteners are pushed home. The buffers are positioned behind the cover at 2 and 7 o'clock (to the Dzus fasteners 10 and 4 o'clock) on the toolbox and beneath the battery tray. The '69 GRP cover for the oil tank is made firm by the rubber collar between itself and the tank filler neck in addition to the two Dzus fasteners.

Don't expect these panels to fit correctly without adjustment to the mounting brackets, rubber buffers and possibly the length of Dzus fasteners used. A typical situation when attempting to fit the nearside GRP cover (the steel version generally fits better but can suffer the same problems) may present the following:

1. Front of cover too low allowing the top front corner of the cover to rest on the frame tube by the ignition switch.

2. Rear of cover too high causing the top rear corner of the cover to foul the lower edge of the seat and/or the frame tube under the seat.

3. Cover not in full contact with both rubber buffers resulting in it rattling; usually against the frame tubes which it should not be in contact with.

4. Dzus fastener heads not sitting flat and true against the GRP when fitted.

I hate saying it as it smacks of heresy, but twisting the top/front mounting bracket anti-clockwise, and bending its outer surface outward will cure 1 and 4. To lower the rear of the cover and thus curing 2 above,, remove the ¼" spacer which was originally fitted at the toolbox lower mounting point between it and the frame rail to allow this, and the side cover mounting clip it carries, to drop slightly. To solve 3 above requires an additional thickness of rubber to be glued onto the standard rubbers to allow both to contact the cover.

Further to all of this, each Dzus fastener carries a rubber spacer on its narrow shank to hold it captive on the cover and also to act as a buffer for the cover when fitted. These can be cut from ¼" bore rubber tubing of approx ½" OD cut to length to fit exactly the length of Dzus fastener shank (the narrow portion) visible on the inside of the cover. These are simply pushed into place over the point of the Dzus fastener.

Fig 13.15. The standard n/s steel side panel first applied to B25 Fleetstar and B44VS from '68 and used across the range for '70.

Dzus fasteners are given as being 'short' or 'long' in the '69 and '70 parts books but don't expect them to fit as described if the brackets have been adjusted to get the cover to sit right. I have found the nearside cover top left mount to require a long (1^1/$_2$") stud with lower right being short (1^1/$_8$") regardless of what the parts books may say.

The equivalent steel nearside cover fitted to '68 on Victor Special, Fleetstar and all other models for '70 seems generally to fit better than the GRP item, usually without 'adjustments' being necessary. For the steel panel, BSA also listed a thin rubber strip which was held around the frame tube by the ignition switch to prevent the edge of the cover fretting against it.

B25 Police models
B25 Fleetstar Police models have a modified version of the steel panel by dint of the widening of the welded-on upper surface by 1^1/$_4$" (*fig 13.16*). This extra width then extends as a strip all the way around the edges of the panel. The reasoning behind this stems from the larger battery used for Police models (two 6v batteries connected in series) necessitating a larger battery tray. This in turn requires the side panel to be positioned outboard to provide space. The resulting gap between panel and frame is then filled by the 1,^{1}/$_4$" wide edge strip. Dzus studs, the top rubber and bottom buffer brackets are extended to suit for this panel.

The offside GRP side panel over the steel oil tank fitted only to '69 B25 Starfire and B44 Shooting Star models suffers problems in fitting much as the nearside GRP panel. Adjustments to the two mounting brackets, which in this case are welded to the oil tank, may well be necessary. A short front Dzus fastener and a long rear one may be the best choice to give optimum positioning. Instead of rubber buffers, a rubber collar between the panel and the neck of the oil tank prevents the cover rattling. Due to unevenness of the inner surface of the GRP panel (and resulting variations in thickness) it is not uncommon for the cover to foul the tank on the bulge below the filler neck and for the end of the rear mounting bracket to contact the cover and prevent alignment of the rear Dzus fastener. Faced with this situation 'something will have to give' and either steel or GRP will require further 'adjustment'. Take care though, if the GRP is forced to 'give' too far it will crack.

Fig 13.16. Fleetstar Police n/s panel '68-'70

Refurbishment of the GRP side panels is problematic if anything more than a rub-down and re-spray is needed. If the GRP has cracked or split, affecting a repair will be difficult as chopping out the damage and filling will not remain invisible; cracks will invariably reappear through any paint applied over them. Digging out any crack and filling with epoxy resin stands as good a chance as any other approach.

Thankfully, quite acceptable replica GRP side panels are available in most of the original colours and replacement of a damaged panel is the best solution. However, these replacements also replicate the original fitting problems!

All of the steel panels are straightforward to refurbish. Dents can be pushed out, splits can be welded and blasting and repainting are the norm.

OIF Side Panels

'71 onward OIF models, other than B50 MX, fit steel side panels of simple design (*fig 13.17*), the fitting being relatively straightforward. On the forward face of the sloping frame tubes to the rear of the side panels are two studs. These correspond with two holes in the rear surface of each side panel which thus locate over the pegs. The top front corner of each panel is then attached to the frame bracket beneath the seat nose by a short Dzus fastener.

These panels are not as shown in the original BSA publicity material and parts books. Instead the parts books for these models display a prototype design of panel which is larger, more angular and differing at the front mounting point. These prototype panels share the front fixing method with the larger GRP panels fitted to the B50 MX, and the different frame bracket mounting the Dzus fastener clips.

Fig 13.17. OIF SS/T side panels (with a non-standard colour scheme). See also fig 13.18 for a top view).

Legend has it that problems in successfully pressing the detail around the front fastener of the steel prototype necessitated several hasty redesigns before the final simple arrangement was put into production.

The two rear holes in each panel which fit over the pegs on the frame were initially just punched through with a top-hat rubber bush fitted over each peg to prevent metal-to-metal contact. Subsequently, the rather ragged punched holes in the panels were improved by the addition of a small steel ring around each hole and with the top-hat rubber replaced by a grommet - the same grommet as used on the alternator cable where it exits the engine as it happens.

Modern replicas of the OIF side panels are thankfully available from some outlets and this has overcome the shortage of offside panels which originated from BSA themselves. Picture the scene at Small Heath: two presses, one stamping out near side panels, the other, stamping out offside panels. For some reason, the offside panel press malfunctions and production of offside panels is halted. The press producing nearside panels is kept running. In the increasingly troubled circumstances prevailing at BSA at this time, the discrepancy in the number of panels produced was never redressed (a similar situation exists with the offside OIF headlamp bracket).

The same design of side panel was subsequently fitted to the Triumph Adventurer which shared many OIF Unit Single parts. The only difference being the provision of a hole near the top rear corner of the offside panel for fitment here of an ignition switch.

Whilst they generally fit as intended, the OIF side panels assume a somewhat unusual angle when in position; there are no horizontal edges and hence the transfers can only be correctly applied truly horizontally whilst the panel is fitted to the bike. Actually, this is good advice for the application of transfers to all of the Unit Single side panels.

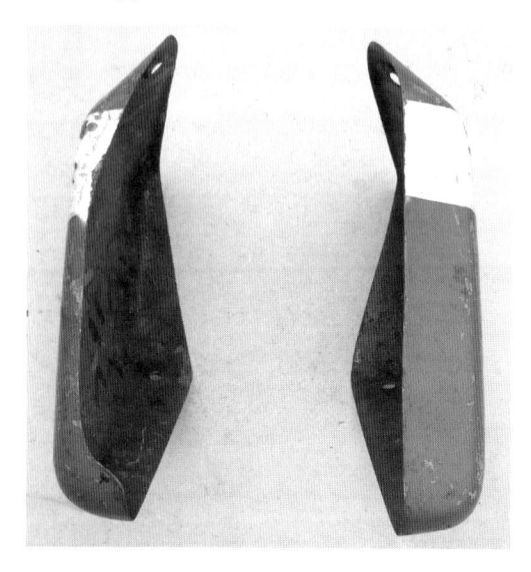

Fig 13.18. OIF SS/T side panels seen from above to illustrate that they are not an identical pair.

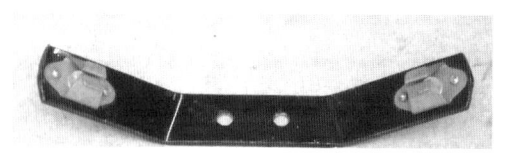

Fig 13.19. Side panel front mounting bracket. This type is not shown in the '71/'72 parts books despite it always being used on the T and SS models. The version shown in the parts books was fitted to MX models only.

Being a simple sheet steel pressing, any dents can easily be pushed out and damage repaired prior to painting. The most susceptible parts are the rear mounting holes which will fret away against the frame mounting pegs if the rubbers have deteriorated.

Damage here is best repaired by brazing or silver soldering a small steel reinforcing ring on the inside around the ragged hole-edge - much as the last examples of these panels had from new.

B50MX

As previously mentioned, B50MX models fitted larger GRP panels to enable the racing number to be affixed (*see figs 13.20-13.22*). Rear edge fitment is peg, hole and grommet as per the roadsters.

Fig 13.20. '72 B50MX square side panel square, in white GRP and painted surround,

Fig 13.21. (below left), B50 MX oval, in white or yellow GRP.

Fig 13.22. (below right) B50MX oval.

No hard-and-fast rules seem to have been applied with regard to shapes and colours and the intended country of sale.

14. MUDGUARDS

Rear Mudguards and Associated Parts

C15 and B40 Star and Sports Star models to '63

All share rear guards of the same profile, with the Sports Star models being chromed, and have a rounded outer section with flat valanced sides (*see fig 14.1*). Whilst being similar in appearance to the rear guards fitted to larger BSA models at that time, those for the C15 and B40 are identified by their shape at the lower front end – indented to clear the swinging arm and with a riveted-on mounting strap from the end of the guard which bolts to the frame. Whilst being visually simpler, he guard for the B40 is slightly enlarged overall from the C15 item and is actually much the same as the A65 Star item except for the front-end mounting method described above.

Fig 14.1 '63 C15SS 80 250 Sport Star (top) and B40 SS90 350 Sport Star - still using the standard guards but with chrome finish. These were to be replaced next year by slimmer blades

Sport Star models '64 onward

In 1964 the Sports Star models changed to chromed 'blade' guards (ie no valances) of rounded cross-section (*fig 14.2*). These do not have the front mounting arrangement as described above and terminate slightly above the swinging arm. They have a riveted-on strap which is bolted to the threaded bosses on each inner side of the subframe. If fitted, the flat valanced side of the standard mudguard also bolts directly to these bosses.

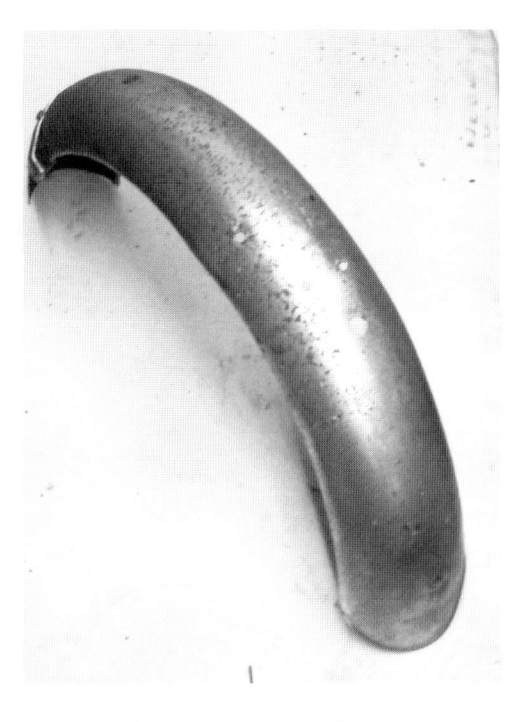

Fig 14.2. Round profile blade rear guard as used on '64 onward C15/B40 SS and Sportsman models. The riveted-on bracket to connect to the subframe bosses can just be seen at the top left.

Competition guards '59 -'62
The competition rear guard in chromed steel has a similar front strap arrangement to connect the guard to the subframe and is physically very much as the B40 Sports Star item, 6" wide and with a round profile. Unlike most other Unit Single rear guards the competition item for the swan-neck frame has a flared rear end with no bead. The C15 Trials and Scrambles 'Special' models of '62 differ in material – aluminium – but not design.

'63 onward C15, B40 and subsequently B44VS models '66 (Welded/Duplex frame)
These continue with the rounded section chromed steel item, now with mounting points to suit the new frame and a rear end beaded edge. The B44GP fitted an aluminium guard, much shortened at the front and mounted from four points on the frame seat-loop.

B25 and B44 models '67 on
The version employed on all '67 onward B25 and B44 models, changed to a 'D' shaped cross section but are otherwise interchangeable. This guard was employed to the end of the '70 season with alterations to the holes for the rear light assembly and number plate for '69 *(see fig 14.3)*. *Fig 14.4* shows the additional pressing featured on this guard only when fitted to '68 -'70 Fleetstar police models - this detail was necessitated by the larger battery. TR25w follows B25 practice although the 'D' shaped grab rail requires extra holes and the rear guard is always painted.

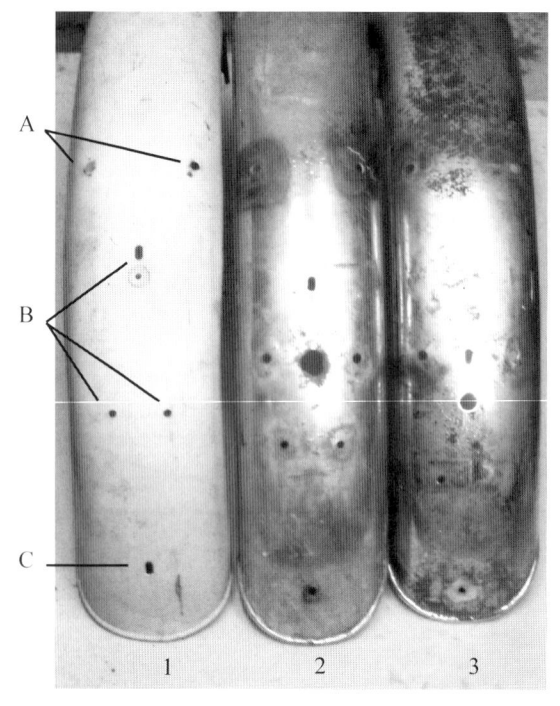

Fig 14.3. '66 to '70 rear guards.
1   B40 Military Mk1.
2   B25/B44 '66 to '68
3   B25/B44 '69 to '70

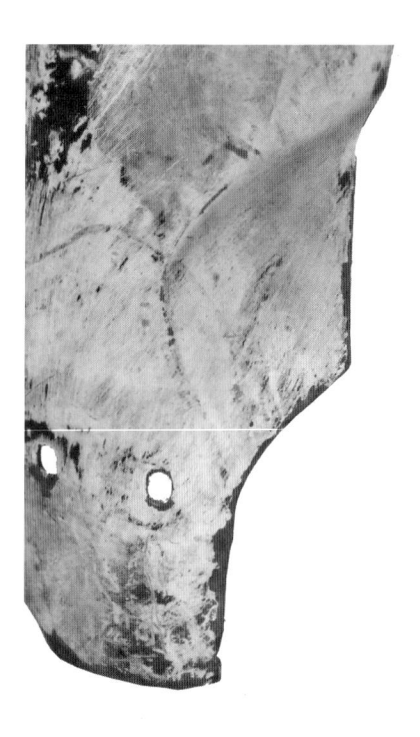

Fig 14.4. '68 to '70 Police Fleetstar rear guard, showing additional pressing to provide clearance for the enlarged battery.

In *fig 14.3* ('66 -'70 rear guards), note that the top pair of holes 'A' for attaching to the subframe are level on each guard. 'B', the single elongated hole and pair of holes arrowed are the mounting points for the aluminium rear light housing and its pressed steel lamp backing plate. On mudguards 2 and 3 this trio of holes is seen positioned closer to the mudguard rear end. 'C' is the lower number plate mounting hole. The distance between this and the trio of holes 'B' is reduced on guard 3. The number plate is therefore not interchangeable between guard 3 and guards 1 and 2.

USA models do not have the lower number plate mounting hole as they mount the USA regulation plate from the top bracket only.

Mudguard defects and repairs

There are two main enemies for the mudguards - rust, and metal fatigue due to vibration. The rear end of the rear guard is the area most likely to suffer from vibration splits. Rust can attack anywhere but principally from the inside due to moisture. The rear guard is particularly susceptible to rust damage due to additional items having been spot welded on the inside, such as squares of sheet metal reinforcement at the mounting holes, and guide loops to thread the rear light wires through. If rust has built up between these items and the guard itself the best plan is to remove them by grinding before removing the rust on the guard by blasting.

To replace the metal ground off, the repaired guard will need 'penny' washers on the mounting bolts to act as a strengthener. The rear light wires can be retained by dabs of silicon rubber. Standard tin bashing skills, welding, filing etc will be required to complete things before repainting the finished guard.

Mudguards

In the case of a rusty chrome plated guard only a really good example stands a chance of a visually acceptable new layer of chrome. The alternatives are to use paint or purchase a pattern replacement in chrome or stainless steel if one of the correct profile can be sourced.

Rear mudguard support rails

Welded/Duplex framed models '67 -'70 except B40 Military Mk1

These models fitted a rear mudguard support rail. Four versions were produced –

   The standard item fitted to B25/44 models *(fig 14.5)*

   The modified type fitted to B40 Military Mk2 *(fig 14.6)*

   The 68 TR25w *(see fig 14.10)* with integral grab-rail and chrome finish *(see p248)*

   The '69/'70 TR25w type plain bracket (for use with separate 'D' shaped grab rail, bolted directly to the mudguard *(see fig 14.11))* which lacks the four upstanding lugs.

The pair of mounting holes for these rails can be seen at 'A' in *fig 14.3*

Fig 14.5. '67 to '70 rear guard loop stay for B25 and B44 models. The TR25w equivalent is chromed with an integral grab-rail for '68 and black with no grab-rail mounting points for '69 and '70.

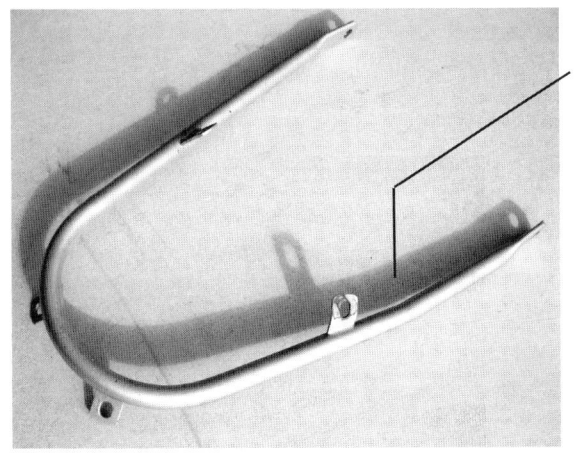

Fig 14.6. B40 Military Mk2 rear guard stay. The o/s kink is to allow clearance for the pannier support rail to pass inside. The n/s is already offset by ³/₈" at its front end

OIF rear mudguard

In effect, one size fits all for the '71 to '73 models *(fig 14.7)*, the differences lie in the materials and finishes listed below which match the front mudguard (notwithstanding the usual possibilities for the fitting of parts from the other OIF models at this time).

SS models   mild steel painted finish.

T models   mild steel, painted for '71, chrome plated for '72.

MX models   stainless steel. This item also differs from the roadster guards in having no holes provided for any of the rear light components, and no dimple for the wiring to pass under the seat loop.

B50   differs from that on the 250cc models by having an additional hole for the breather pipe clip.

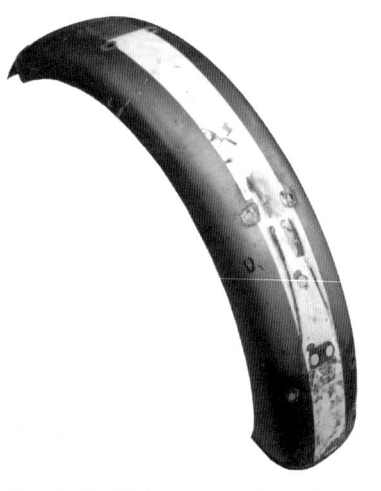

No shortcomings are specific to the OIF rear mudguard though it shares, to some extent, the weaknesses in the face of rust and vibration which afflict the earlier guards. However split rear ends are not as common as on the previous efforts.

Fig 14.7. OIF rear mudguard. The colour scheme identifies it as a '71 B50 though the mounting holes are the same for all other models/years except the MX.

Whilst not specifically the fault of the mudguard, looking directly at examples of the OIF singles from the rear will often show the rear guard and tail light assembly to be set to the n/s slightly in relation to the rear wheel.

Grab rails

Prior to '71, this item was standard fitment on all road machines destined for the USA and an optional extra everywhere else. For '71 the grab rail became integral with the rear guard loop stay on road and trail machines and therefore became a standard item for all markets. OIF models which varied from this spec were the B50MX (no loop stay) and the '72 B25 Fleetstar which had a plain loop with no chrome rail protruding upward to interfere with the fitting of police equipment.

C15 and B40 grab rail '59 to '67.

This is mounted directly to the vertical sides of the valanced rear mudguard of the road machines; the extra holes for this are standard on the guards for the USA Star models. The example shown *(fig 14.8)* has gained a couple of non-standard holes through the tubing which will require filling prior to re-plating. The general shape of this item is much as the equivalent part for the pre-unit models.

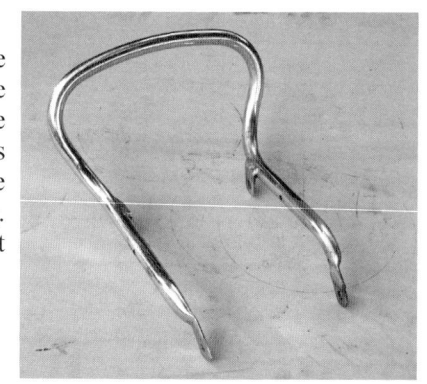

Fig 14.8. C15 and B40 grab rail

B25 and B44 grab rail '67 to '70.
Shown in *fig 14.9*, this grab rail is similar to, but not to be confused with the A65 item. The two are not interchangeable.

TR25w '68 and '69 combined grab rail/rear mudguard loop stay,
This is interchangeable with the B25/B44 loop stay but lacks the lugs for the small connecting straps to the frame seat loop *(see fig 14.10)*.

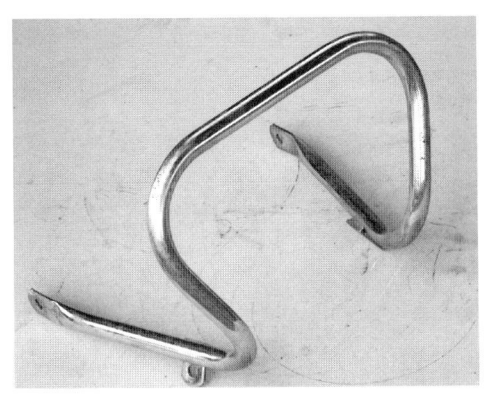

Fig 14.9. '67 to '70 B25 and B44 grab rail

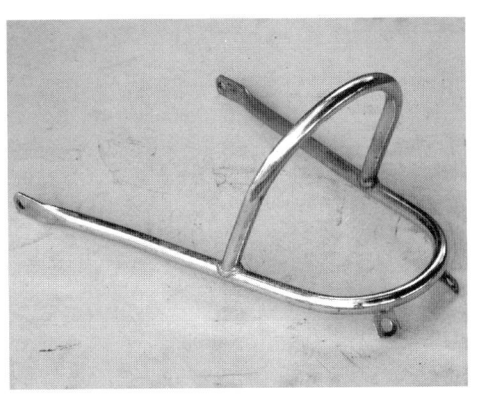

Fig 14.10 '68 and '69 TR25w grab rail.

TR25w grab rail '70
The '70 TR25w grab rail seen from the front in *fig 14.11*. Its central mounting lug (mostly hidden in this shot) bolts directly to the rear mudguard. Used with a plain loop stay for the rear guard which is identical to the BSA item but lacking the grab rail mounting lugs.

OIF models grab rail '71 on.
The '71 onward loop stay and grab rail for OIF models (*fig 14.12*). The chrome plated part is pop-riveted into the sockets on the loop stay and is therefore easy to separate for refurbishment and to re-attach. Similar at a glance to the equivalent part for the '71 onward OIF twins, easy differentiation depends on the forward mounting lugs at the top of the shock absorber position: straight as in this case for the singles, cranked inward for the twins.

The '72 B25 Fleetstar item is a plain loop without the grab rail.

Fig 14.11 TR25w grab rail for '70

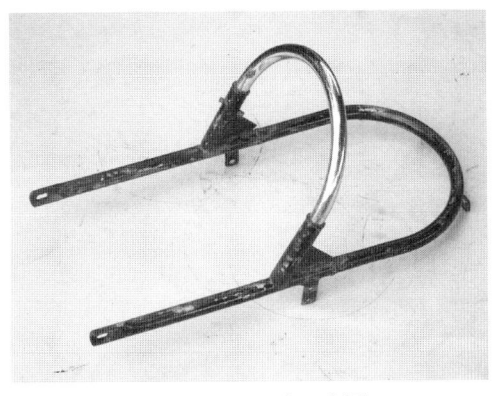

Fig 15.12. OIF grab rail '71 on

Rear Number Plates and Light Housings

The C15 and B40 Star models used the boxed-in assembly similar to that used on A10 and other contemporary BSA models (*fig 14.13*). Sports and Competition models (and B44VE '66) used the open sided assembly as used on Bantams. On both of these types the shape of the number plate itself changed for the '65 season from the short rectangle suitable for displaying 6 digit registration numbers to a longer 'shield' shape for 7 digit numbers. This was necessitated by the addition of the date letter suffix ('C' for '65) to the registration number in all parts of the UK (the previous 'A' and 'B' for '63 and '64 were only used in areas where the 6 digit sequences had been exhausted).

Fig. 14.13 Number plates
Right, the '58 to '64 six digit rear number plate, open sided for competition models, the equivalent boxed-in version being used on the roadsters.

Left, the long, 7 digit plate used from '65. This is the boxed in version for roadster C15 and B40 models, the open sided equivalent were used on the competition models.

B25 and B44 models from '67 adopted the cast aluminium light housing (fig 14.14) with a separate number plate common throughout the BSA range at this time, though with detail differences. B25 and B44 models feature this housing with a cutaway for the rear guard loop stay to pass through. B40 Military Mk1 (all years) use the same housing without the cutaway as also used on Bantam sports models. Mk2 and B40 Roughrider use the version with cutaways.

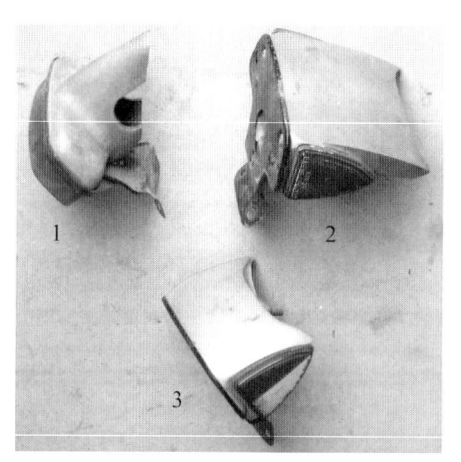

Fig 14.14. Aluminium light housings
1. '67 and all B40 Military
2. '68 B25/B44/TR25w
3. '69 - '70 B25/B44/TR25w

Fig 14.15 The '63 onward rear light adaptor housing to allow use of the 679 rear light on some of the USA models.

For B25 and B44 this housing was changed for '68 and again for '69 although the '68 type continued to be used on the B25 Fleetstar well into '69. The change for '68 was to meet USA requirements for side reflectors by allowing fitment of red 'church window' reflectors to the sides of the rear light casting. From this time the circular amber reflectors mounted on the headstock gusset beneath the tank nose also became standard on USA models, until superseded on all '71 B25/T25 by rectangular reflectors (on the electric box), which were in turn superseded by large round amber reflectors for B50 and B25FS in 1972.

The separate rear number plate used with the three different designs of cast aluminium rear light housings ('67 to '70) is more confusing than the parts books suggest. US owners are spared this area of confusion as machines for this market were supplied without number plates and mudguards were not drilled for them at the rear single mounting point.

Across the whole B25 and B44 range for the UK market from '67 to '70 two shapes of rear number plate appear:

> The shield   carried over from previous years but now no longer integral with the rear light and supporting bracket. This plate has two ¼" mounting holes in its upper corners and one integral lower bracket and stud below the middle rear. *(Fig 14.16)*
>
> The oven tray   rectangular in shape and mounted horizontally, this carries the same attachment points as described for the 'shield'. *Fig 14.16 and 14.17*

The two different shapes of rear number plate which were used as original equipment seemingly without any hard and fast rules despite what the parts books show, between '67 and '70. Both of these shapes of plate - oven tray and shield - are found with the two alternative mounting point spacings *(see p242)*.

Selection by BSA of which shape to fit seems to be quite random when parts books for these models are compared and adherence by BSA to the illustrated part seems to have been minimal. More confusion stems from the fact that each number plate shape has two versions, the difference being in the vertical distance between the upper and lower mounting

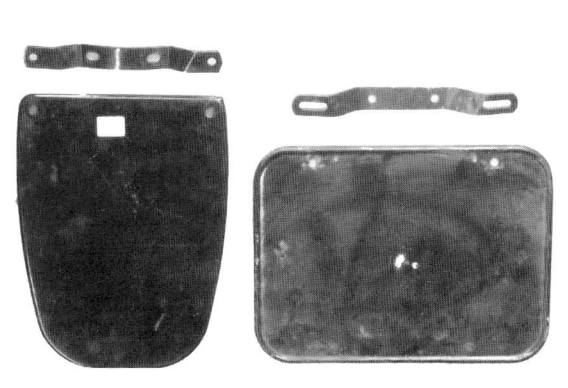

Fig 14.16. The '67 to '70 'oven tray' and 'shield' rear number plates. These, with their respective top bracket are interchangeable but both are to be found with two alternative distances between the top and bottom mounting points to suit the '67/'68 or '69/'70 rear mudguard.

Fig 14.17. '71 onward OIF 'oven tray' rear number plate for Home models; As per the pre-OIF item but lacking the lower fixing point and now with 4 holes to accept the new mounting brackets

points, and this can be irksome to say the least when trying to bolt these parts in place if you have collected a mixture of incompatible parts. The determining factor in this is the rear mudguard; the guard used for '67 and '68 has a distance of approximately 6" between the upper and lower holes for the mounting of the number plate; the guard for '69 and '70 has this distance at 5".

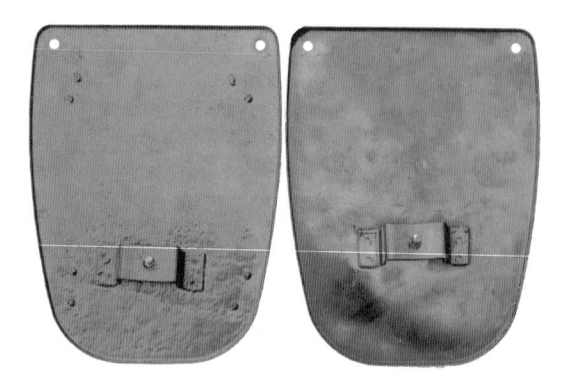

Fig 14.18. Rear number plate; left '67 to '68, right '69 to '70. Rust can be a problem.

Whichever number plate you have, its holes and its upper mounting bracket, need to match the holes on the mudguard. Even with all of the correct parts, it is a good job that the lower central mounting hole on the guard for the number plate stud is often slotted – it needs to be, and be prepared to extend it to get the plate and its upper bracket to connect to the guard. The upper bracket itself is another variable in the equation. Short ones go with the 'shield' plate, long ones with slotted outer holes are for the 'oven tray' but additionally different depths of bend are found with these brackets: good luck!

As can be seen from these used number plates in *fig 14.18* surface rust can become a problem if cleaning is neglected, particularly around the mounting holes.

As seen in *fig. 143,* identifying the guard, and hence the number plate type required is visually easy, the give-away being the upper mounting hole for the alloy housing; the '67/'68 guard has the slotted ¼" hole for this on its own some 3" above the two $5/_{16}$" loop stay holes. The '69/'70 guard has the slotted ¼" hole directly between the $5/_{16}$" loop stay holes.

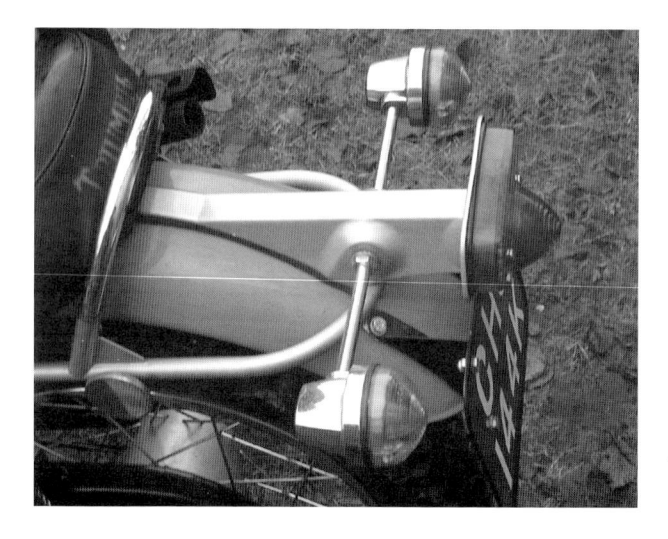

Fig 14.19. OIF rear light housing for '71'72. The otherwise identical item for the twins at this time lacks the-tilted up front end which on the singles hides the cables to the rear light.

Contemporary B40 Military models from this period all used the earlier set-up. Visually on the bike the effect of all this is that the '69/'70 arrangement has the rear light/number plate assembly positioned nearer the end of the guard, resulting in the number plate end overhanging the guard (and the plate being closer to vertical to suit USA regulations), the previous set-up doesn't overhang.

OIF models used a new, pressed steel housing for the rear light, which now also mounted the indicators *(fig 14.19*. The number plate was mounted separately to the guard on two handed brackets and was the previous 'oven tray' but now with four mounting holes. The only variations found in this set-up relate to the pressed steel housing on which detail alterations were made during production. The pressed steel housing for the Unit Singles has a tilted-up forward end which hides the wires to the rear light which here pass outside the mudguard. The otherwise identical housing for the twin cylinder models is shorter, lacking the tilted-up fore-end.

Front Mudguards

C15 Star

The C15 Star front mudguard for all years is easily confused with the much more common Bantam guard of the same era, but is deeper and slightly wider. The easiest way to tell the two apart is the mounting brackets; the C15 item has a pair of brackets each side next to the fork legs (*fig 14.20*), the Bantam has only one single bracket each side,to the rear of the forks.

The same guard was chromed for the SS80 when this was introduced until it was replaced by a chrome blade without valances from 1964. This new guard is effectively the same shape as the later front chrome roadster guard fitted until 1970 on the B25 etc except for the six fixing points as per the standard C15 guard.

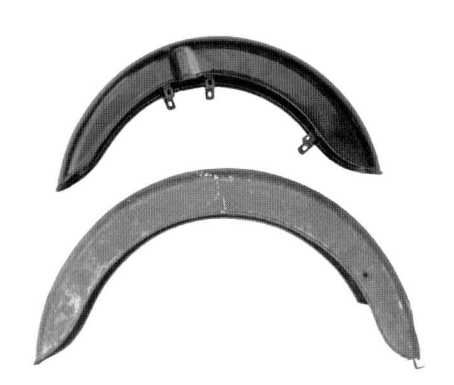

Fig 14.20. C15 front (top) and rear (below) guards. All of the projecting mounting brackets are likely to fall off due to age, vibration and metal fatigue.

All C15 and B40 road models mounted the front mudguard from a 'Y' bracket (*fig 14.21*) bolted to the two studs on the inner side of each fork slider, and by a straight tubular stay on each side at the lower rear end of the guard. The length between hole centres for the straight stay is 7⅞" for C15, 8⅝" for B40 and 11⅛" for '64 onward SS models with the blade guards.

Making these tubular mudguard stays yourself (and other similar items such as the engine head steady tube used on Welded/Duplex framed models), requires tube of the correct diameter (usually ½" o/d) prior to flattening and drilling the ends. Flattening the end is best done by squeezing the tube-end in a vice with an open-ended spanner positioned each side

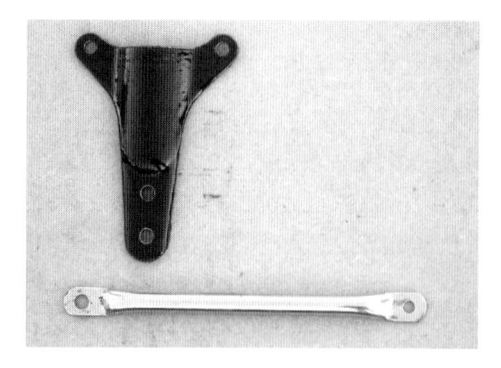

Fig 14.21. Front mudguard 'Y' bracket for C15 and B40 road models and straight tubular bottom stay: SS80 version shown (to '63) which is identical to the C15 star but chrome plated; $^5/_{16}$" hole at forks, ¼" at guard.

so that the curved edge between the spanner jaws imprints at the edge of the required flat section. This replicates the original press-tool very well and promotes strength in this area.

C15/B44 Competition Models

C15 competition models fitted chrome steel blades except for the Trials and Scrambles 'Special' models of '62 which used aluminium instead. The front competition guard has no bead at either end and has a slight flare at the front.

Chrome plated steel mudguards with beaded ends were introduced for '63 and the B44 Competition models continued using the '63 on front competition steel guard until the end of '66, the B44GP having an equivalent in aluminium. The steel competition front guard is of the same profile as the B40 Military front guard, hence this item offers a good starting point to replicate the now unobtainable competition item for models from 'a'63 onward it will fit straight on.

B40 Star

The B40 Star front guard is visually similar to the C15 item but is slightly deeper and wider and is effectively the same as the early A65 Star front guard. The SS90 version is the same item chromed prior to '64 and afterwards being a blade with six mounting points much as the C15 item. The same B40 guard with revised mounting points reappeared on the '68 -'70 B25 Fleetstar.

B25 Fleetstar

The B25 Fleetstar mudguard (*fig 14.22*) for '68 to 70 is the same shape and size as the B40 Star front guard but lacking the second pair of mounting lugs for the 'Y' brackets from the forks. The hole shown in *fig 14.22* just behind the o/s fork leg indent is for the front brake cable guide rubber. *Fig 14.23* shows the n/s mounting brackets for the Fleetstar front guard, '69/'70 version of the lower stay shown, the '68 version is straight.

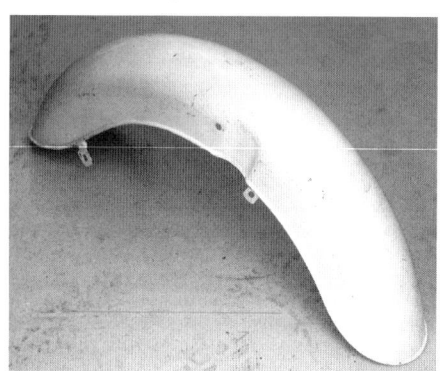

Left, Fig 14.22. The B25 Fleetstar front mudguard.

Above, Fig 14.23. n/s mounting brackets for the '69/'70 Fleetstar. The '68 model has a straight bottom stay.

B25/B44

The '66 to '70 B44VS (*fig 14.24* top) has a slightly larger radius and two pairs of mounting holes behind the forks for inside stays. B40 Military Mk1 is physically the same but with an extra pair of holes at the leading end.

The '67 to '70 B25/B44 roadster front guard (*fig 14.24* bottom). The mounting holes consist of two pairs forward of the forks plus one single hole at the rear end, all for fixing stays outside the guard as shown in *fig 14.26*.

Fig14.24. Front mudguards for (top) the B44VS '66 to '70 and below the B25/B44 for '67 to '70. TR25w is as the lower example but has a painted finish.

These front mudguards stand up well to normal use with vibration fractures around the mounting lugs and rust (at least in the UK) is the main enemy. If dirt and moisture is allowed to accumulate on the underside the guard will eventually rot through: the same applies to the rear guards.

Mudguard stays

The '59 to '62 C15 competition front guard stay main loop is shown in *fig 14.25*. For '62 this gained an additional pair of holes to accept the new vertical stay which improved mudguard stability.

The B25 and B44 road models '67 to '70 front mudguard stays and their arrangement are shown in *fig 14.26*. The front stay (left of the pair), is the '67 item with tilted-up front end; this bolts to the top hole on the bottom of the centre stay as shown. The '68 to '70 replacement for this front stay is flat and bolts to the lower of the two holes.

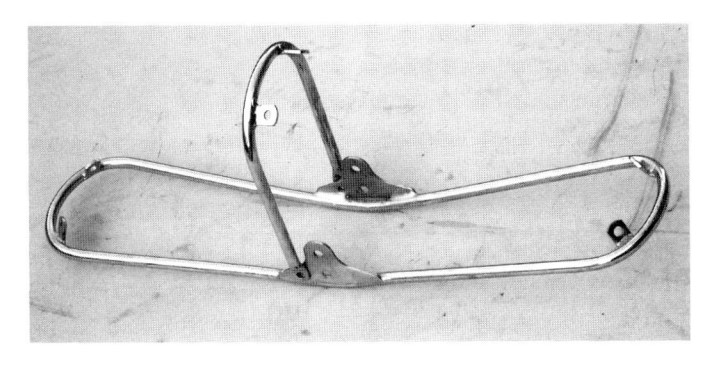

Fig 14.25. The '59 to '62 C15 competition front guard stay main loop

Fig 14.26. 67 to '70 B25 and B44 mudguard stays for the front mudguard showing their arrangement

Fig 14.27. B40 Military Mk1 front guard stay arrangement. The same arrangement is used on all competition and off-road models '62 -'70. The '67 onward B44VS models omitted the front stay

The front mudguard rear stay shown here on the right in *fig 14.26* is the '67 to '68 item; the '69 to '70 version has the front lugs tilted upwards to curl up under the TLS brake mechanism used for these years. The stay arrangement for the B40 Mil Mk1, competition and off-road models and the '67 on B44VS is shown in fig 14.27.

OIF front mudguard

OIF front guards are shown in *fig 14.28*, on the left is a '72 B50SS item (modified with 3rd stay kit explained in the BSA service sheet in *fig 14.29*, and alternatively found with a third wire stay in this position) of 'Home and General Export' length but lacking front number plate mounting holes, hence intended for export to anywhere but the USA! USA version is approximately 6" shorter at the front. The equivalent front mudguard for the OIF twins is to all intents and purposes the same and is interchangeable but is of a slightly larger radius to suit the 19" front wheel of these models.

The mudguard on the right in *fig 14.28* is '71 B25T distinguishable by the black stripe (white usually being B50 which was finished in chrome plate for '72). This has just two central mounting holes to attach it to the bottom yoke bracket and is also used on the MX models (in stainless steel). The holes carry rubber grommets for the mounting bolts and this arrangement avoids all of the vibration fracture issues of the SS item.

Fig 14.28 OIF front mudguards. Left '72 B50SS, right '71 B25T

The 1971 Triumph models T25T and T25SS are as the BSA models except for the colour schemes.

Mudguards

MAY 1972
No 11/72

BSA SERVICE SHEET

'A' GROUP TWINS AND 'B' GROUP MODELS
FRONT MUDGUARD STAYS

The front mudguard currently fitted on 'A' Group Twins and 'B' Group models have two additional stays, one each side, connecting the mudguard to the existing stay.

Should owners of 1971 and early 1972 machines wish to update their models, a bolt on stay kit is available from the factory Service Department, as follows:-

    'A' Group Twins   97-4403 (2 off)
    'B' Group   97-4436 (2 off)

Due to manufacturing tolerances, there may be slight variation in the position of the stay and hence, when assembling, it will be advisable first to fit the stay to the fork leg. Mark the position of the hole using the stay as a pilot. Remove mudguard for drilling with a 0.440 in. diameter hole to accept the rubber grommet.

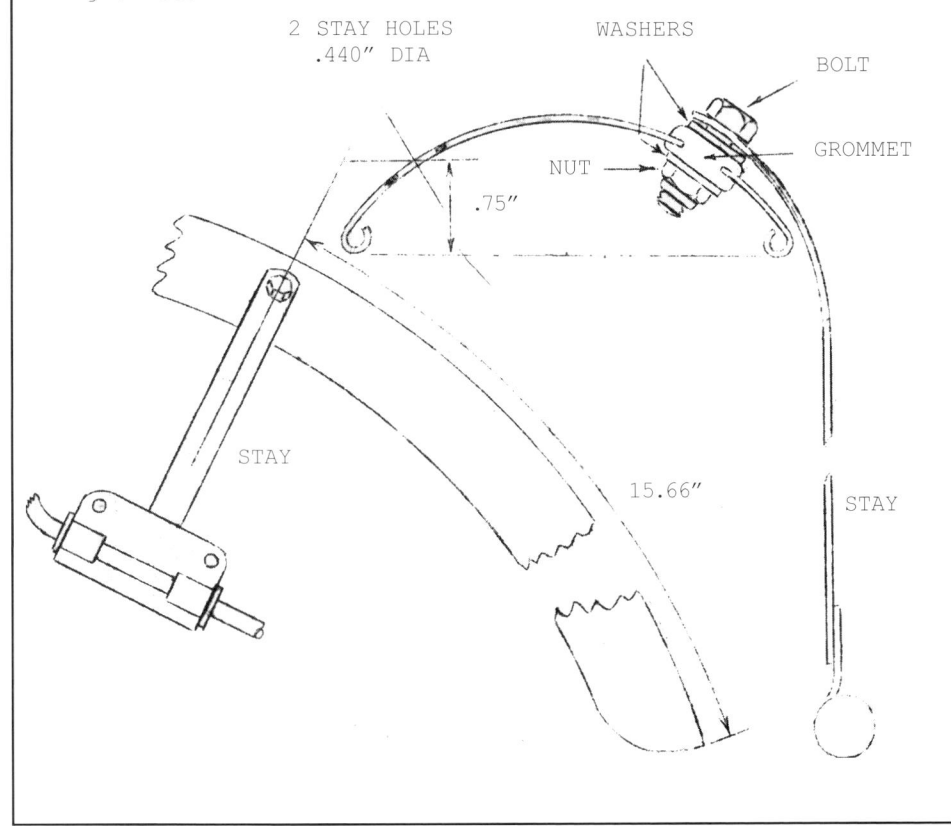

Fig 14.29. BSA Service Sheet detailing the third stay kit modification

Fitting the correct stays should also result in the front guard being positioned centrally between the fork legs. If you have the 'fog slicer' fitted on the front guard (the number plate) it is nice on the eye to see this lining up perfectly with the centre rib on the front tyre. If the front guard looks wonky try slackening all the mounting bolts between the guard and the forks and pull it into position as they are tightened. If this doesn't work suspect distorted mounting brackets meaning removal and individual attention.

Front number plate

A front number plate (*fig 14.30*) was standard fitting on home market models only, export models did not carry a front mudguard as standard. Front mudguards of the export models do not carry mounting holes for the number plates.

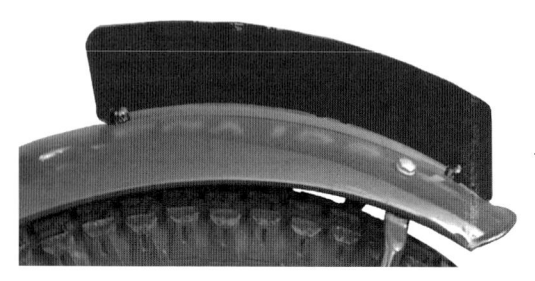

Fig 14.30. The standard curved front number plate, seen here on a B40 Military, and as fitted to all home market Unit Single road models from '58 to '72. Injection molded plastic replaced steel from '71. This item is smaller and slimmer than the equivalent part for the pre-unit models and can be fitted either way around - leaning forwards or backwards - original factory shots show no hard-and-fast rule.

Fig 14.31. The '67 to '70 modified version with cutaway for the mudguard stay. Easy to modify from the standard item.

If a curved number plate is carried on the front mudguard it will be steel to early '71, this was then superseded by an injection-moulded plastic item. The hole centres are the same spacing for all years for the two fixing studs which means full inter-changeability, except that the '67 to '70 plate requires a semi-circular cut-away to clear the mudguard stay on the B25 and B44 roadsters (*fig 14.31*).

The metal plate carries a flat-bottomed rubber beading strip on its lower edge to fill the space between the plate and the mudguard.

Competition Number Plate

The '59 to '65 front competition number plate (*fig 14.32*) attaches to the bottom yoke pinch bolts by the brackets on the rear of the competition number plate. The 'with lights' version is shown; the 'without lights' version has the brackets positioned $3/_8$" lower to raise the plate. The plate is $10^3/_4$" by $2^1/_2$".

Fig 14.32 Competition front number plate used until '65

15. PAINTS AND FINISHES

Any BSA these days, Unit Single or otherwise, which is still resplendent in its original paintwork and plating is a rare bird indeed. As such, the main aim of this chapter is to assist the restorer who wishes to apply an original looking finish to their motorcycle, to obtain the correct shade of paint or type of plating. This sounds simple enough, but the exercise is actually far from straightforward. Matching an old shade of paint by eye is not an exact science and plated finishes available now are not necessarily the same as those originally applied.

Paintwork

The problem starts with the question, what did BSA actually put on a bike when a particular colour was quoted in factory literature? The answer is probably anything that looked something like it was supposed to. The reality was that distinct variations in any colour could occur, particularly with the metallic or 'flamboyant' colours. Reasons for this are many: BSA obtained their paints locally, latterly from Carrs of Birmingham, in batches. Due to human error variations in shade could easily occur between batches (still a problem today if you watch the semi-trained monkey operating the paint mixing machine at your local DIY store).

BSA's relative lack of quality control was no worse than the rest of the automotive industry at the time in tolerating varying paint batches; this was then compounded by variations in application: the next problem area. Consistency of finish relied on different workers applying the same amount of paint to different BSA parts over time – and expecting them to match?

The flamboyant colours can vary greatly as they were a two-part finish; a metallic base coat (usually silver) with a tinted lacquer over this, these days known as 'candy' finish. The thickness of tinted lacquer applied over the base coat subsequently affects the resulting shade, more tinted lacquer equals a darker shade and it is very difficult to produce exactly the same shade with these relatively inconsistent methods (see *fig 15.1*). The story goes of how Jack Harper, the then service manager at BSA, was questioned as to why the paint shade of a spare part supplied did not match when offered up to the bike: "Oh, you want a Friday part, that one's a Monday part" was the reply.

Additionally by now, the fading caused by sunlight will have had a marked effect on any old examples of BSA paint except for those hidden in the darkest recesses of a machine, or still in the tin.

Faced with this situation today neither I nor anyone else can look at a BSA and categorically say that its colour is right or wrong. If it approximates to one which is known and can be recognised then that should be good enough. The arguments tend to start when two supposedly identical machines are parked side by side and the colours don't quite match - they could both be right.

Within these limitations, to help the Unit Single restorer, the best I can offer is a modern day paint match equivalent which I have obtained by my own matching of an original, unfaded BSA paint sample to a modern colour chart. These are listed towards the end of this chapter on p269.

> **DECEMBER 1971**
> **No. 44/71**
> **SERVICE SHEET**
> All Models
> AEROSOL PAINTS COLOUR FINISHES
>
> It would seem that some difficulty has been experienced in matching colours with the aerosol cans of paint, available from Spares Department, for touching up or even respraying.
>
> The final colour of many paints, especially Flamboyant, Hi-Fi and Polychromatic finishes, depends to a great extent on the colour of primer. Detailed below are the routines used at the factory and if these are followed satisfactory results will be achieved.
>
> 1. Coat the bare metal with a light grey oxide primer. In the case of a chromed component, such as a fuel tank, the first coat must be yellow etching primer, to provide a key for the light grey oxide primer.
>
> 2. Spray a silver base coat on all parts to be finished in Hi-Fi or Flamboyant colours. The component is now ready to receive Hi-Fi or Flamboyant lacquer.
>
> 3. Polychromatic paint is applied straight on to the light grey oxide primer.
>
>   In the case of a two tone fuel tank, apply the lightest colour first over the entire tank then follow with a Polychromatic finish.
>
> The above procedures are unimportant in the case of ordinary flat colours.

Fig 15.1. BSA Service Sheet describing procedure for painting Flamboyant, Hi-Fi and Polychromatic paints

Model colours and years

BSA's list of finishes shown below is much more than just a colour chart for paints, it also covers combinations of these colours and includes tank badges and plated finishes. To identify the finish for a machine, this list should be referred to from the code numbers given for each model and year which can be found in the BSA spare parts books, or other original BSA literature. These code numbers for the Unit Single models are listed on p262-268. Just for the sake of clarity, 'flamboyant' colours comprise a tinted lacquer over a Silver base, 'polychromatic' and 'metallic' are equivalent to modern day metallic ie a tinted metallic base under clear lacquer.

USA specification models in the BSA range often displayed particularly garish styling and finishes to appeal to tastes prevalent over the pond. Shown in *fig 15.2* and *15.3* is the USA B25 Starfire for 1969, one of the thousand or so produced with matt black engine cases. Tank and side panels of this machine are Bushfire Orange. The tank is the 'small steel' item with the Moss Gold centre stripe (the stripe is the same width as the tank cutaway for the headstock) bordered by single black pinstripes. Note also the black pinstripe bordering the scooped area of the side panel. The high level exhaust doesn't aid side panel removal; a good example of the eye-catching but less practical features of the USA models.

Paint, Finishes And Transfers

Fig 15.2. Left, '69 USA spec B25 with black crankcases, barrel, head and rockerbox and Bushfire Orange colour scheme, which is not seen to best effect in black and white!

Fig 15.3. Below. The same bike, n/s detail

Suffix numbers for various finishes

BSA listed most cycle parts with part number followed by a suffix which specified the colour and the finish, such as blue centre with white lining and chrome side panels - suffix of /268. Listed below are the suffix numbers for the various motorcycle finishes. The suffix should always be added to the part number when ordering replacement parts - those were the days!.

However, in keeping with the BSA's 'rule of thumb' approach to colour shades, the actual publicised colours for any model/year should not be regarded as categorical. Colour changes were not always publicised and changeovers sometimes happened mid-season, sometimes with considerable overlap from new to old. Additionally, non-standard colours were applied as required by the customer; any shade desired could be applied – at a premium of course.

Suffix	Colour and/or finish	Suffix	Colour and/or finish
/1	Cadmium	/27	Royal Red (Post Office)
/2	Dull Chrome	/28	Indonesia Khaki
/3	Bright Chrome	/29	Beige & Blue
/4	Dull Green (Dutch)	/30	Silver & Blue
/5	Matt Khaki (Egyptian)	/31	Silver
/6	Rust Proof Black	/32	French Army Green
/7	Black Enamel	/33	Blue (BSS.104)
/9	Green Enamel	/34	Devon Red (BSS.540)
/12	Chrome Plate Devon Red, Lined Gold	/35	AA Yellow
/13	Chrome Plate & Matt Silver, Lined Black	/36	BSA Maroon & Chrome, Lined Gold
		/37	BSA Maroon
/17	Chrome Plate, Black, Lined Gold	/38	Metallic Green, Chrome Plate, Lined Dark Green
/18	Mist Green (Pastel)		
/19	Chrome Plate, Matt Silver, Lined Red	/39	Metallic Green (Shade D)
/21	Polished Aluminium	/40	Dark Green
/23	Polychromatic Grey	/41	Chrome Rim, Maroon Hub
/24	Polychromatic Silver Beige	/42	Chrome Rim, Dark Green Hub
/25	Swedish Army Grey	/43	Chrome Rim, Beige Hub
/26	Chrome Plate, Silver Beige, Lined Red	/44	Chrome Rim, Black Hub

/45	Chrome Rim, Mist Green Hub	/108	Royal Red, Cream Panels, Double White Lining
/47	Black & Cream (Tank Badge)		
/48	Maroon & Cream (Tank Badge)	/109	Royal Red, Chrome Panels, Double Gold Lining
/49	Blue & Cream (Tank Badge)		
/50	Green & Cream (Tank Badge)	/110	Nutley Blue, Chrome Panels, Single Gold Lining
/51	Maroon & Silver Lined Gold (Chaincase)		
/52	Light Grey (India) (BSS.631)	/111	Ivory, Blue & Red Lining
/54	Black, Red Panel, Lined Gold	/112	Nutley Blue, Double Gold Lining
/55	Black, Lined Gold	/113	Mist Green, Cream Panels, Maroon & Gold Lining
/56	Alloy Rim, Black Hub		
/57	Bronze Green (W.D.) (BSS.224)	/114	Black, Cream Panels, Maroon & Gold Lining
/58	Dark Green, Mist Green, Lined Gold		
/59	Bantam Major Grey	/115	Royal Red, Single White Lining
/60	Scamic Green (Indian Army)	/116	Metallic Almond Green, Chrome Panels, Double Gold Lining
/61	Grey Hub, Chrome Rim		
/63	Sapphire Blue	/117	Metallic Gunmetal Grey, Chrome Panels Double Gold Lining
/64	Bantam Tank Cream		
/65	Light Stone (Arab Legion)	/118	Metallic Princess Grey, Chrome Panels, Double Red Lining
/66	Burma Police Grey		
/67	Libyan Ochre	/119	Black With Silver Star (Tank Badge)
/68	Guayaquil Blue (Ecuador)	/120	Black, Chrome Panels, Double Gold Lining
/69	White		
/70	Chrome Rim, Guayaquil Blue Hub	/121	Balck, Double Gold Lining
/71	White & Chrome Lined Blue (Tank) (Ecuador Police)	/122	Royal Red, Double Gold Lining
		/123	Royal Red, Chrome Panels, Single Gold Lining
/72	Maroon & Cream Panel, Lined Gold & Black	/127	Metallic Princess Grey, Chrome Panels, Double Gold Lining
/73	Hammer Finish Silver		
/74	Dark Green Chrome Panel Lined Gold	/128	Chrome Rim, Honey Beige Hub
/79	Columbian Dark Blue	/129	Chrome Rim, Dark Lavender, Grey Hub
/80	Columbian Deep Yellow		
/81	Navy Blue	/130	Chrome Rim, Devon Red Hub
/82	Gpo Green (BSS.223)	/131	Red With Gold Star (Tank Badge)
/83	Lebanon Khaki	/132	Blue Surround, Silver Trade Mark, Cream Centre (Tank Badge)
/84	Dark Lavender Grey		
/85	Honey Beige	/134	Red Surround, Gold Star, Silver Centre (Tank Badge)
/88	Nutley Blue		
/89	Mid. Grey	/135	Brilliant Red Surround, Gold Star, Silver Centre (Tank Badge)
/90	Polychromatic Green & Chrome Petrol Tank		
		/136	Black Surround, Silver Star, Silver Centre, (Tank Badge)
/91	Polychromatic Blue & Chrome Petrol Tank	/137	Royal Red, Ivory Panels, Single Gold Lining
/92	Portuguese Grey		
/93	Indonesian Grey	/139	Olive Drab (Burma Army)
/94	Indonesian Green	/140	Polychromatic Shell Blue Sheen
/95	Formosa Green	/141	Polychromatic Zircon Green
/97	Gold With Maroon Centre (Tank Badge)	/142	Devon Red, Chrome Panels, Double Gold Lining
/98	Gold With Black Centre (Tank Badge)		
/99	Bayard Crimson, Ivory Panels, Gold Lining	/143	Devon Red, Ivory Panels, Lined Gold & Black
/100	Metallic Almond Green	/144	Chrome Rim, Nutley Blue Hub
/101	Metallic Gunmetal Grey	/145	Nutley Blue, Ivory Panels, Single Gold Lining
/102	Metallic Princess Grey		
/103	Gold With Brilliant Red Centre (Tank Badge)	/146	Nutley Blue, Chrome Panels, Double Gold Lining
/104	Ivory	/147	Mist Green, Ivory Panels, Maroon & Gold Lining
/105	Bayard Crimson		
/106	Deep Blue	/148	Black, Ivory Panels, Maroon & Gold Lining
/107	Syrian Green		

Paint, Finishes And Transfers 259

/149	Royal Red, Ivory Panels, Double White Lining	/194	Admiralty Light Grey (Ariel)
/150	Chinese Red	/195	Glamour Red (Ariel)
/151	Chinese Red, Chrome Panels, Double Gold Lining	/196	Deep Claret (Ariel)
/152	Royal Dutch Blue	/197	Chrome White (Ariel)
/153	Wedgewood Blue	/198	Chrome Admiralty Grey (Ariel)
/154	Wedgewood Blue, Chrome Panels, Double Gold	/199	Semi-Bright Chrome
/155	Chrome Rim, Wedgewood Blue Hub	/200	Mist Green, Ivory Tank Recess, Single Gold Line
/156	Bronze Green, Chrome Panels, Double Gold Lining	/201	Mandarin Red (USA Gold Star)
/157	Israeli Army Brown	/202	Mandarin Red, Chrome Panels, Single White Lining
/158	Admiral Blue	/203	Royal Red, Ivory Panels, Double Gold Lining
/159	Admiral Blue, Chrome Panels, Double Gold Lining	/206	Port Dickson Green
/160	Venezuela Grey	/207	Silver Beige, Chrome Panels, Double Gold Lines
/161	Venezuela Grey, Chrome Panels, Double Gold Lining	/208	Red & Black With White Lining (Side Panels)
/162	Black, Chrome, Single Gold Lining	/209	Crystal Grey
/163	Mimosa Yellow	/210	Crystal Grey, Chrome Panels, Double Gold Lining
/164	Scooter Grey	/211	Dark Chrome Green (Ariel)
/165	Heat Resiting Silver	/212	Aircraft Blue (Ariel)
/166	Israeli Army Dark Sand Semi-Gloss	/213	Gold, Chrome Panels, Single Red Lining
/167	Flamboyant Blue	/214	Black Centre Red Wings, Gold Letters (Side Cover Badge)
/168	Flamboyant Blue, Chrome Panels, Double Gold Lining	/215	Saudi Arabian Dark Grey
/169	Nutley Blue, Ivory Panels, Double Gold Lining	/216	Gold, Single Red Line (Side Panel)
/170	Flamboyant Red	217	White & Chrome Double Gold Line
/171	Flamboyant Red, Chrome Panels, Double Gold Lining	/218	Yellow On Polished Alloy, Single White Line
/172	Flamboyant Blue, Chrome Panels, Single Gold Lining	/219	White & Chrome Panels, Double Black Line
/173	Flamboyant Red, Chrome Panels, Single Gold Lining	/220	White & Chrome Panels, Single Black Line
/174	Flamboyant Blue, Chrome Panels, Single White Lining	/221	Sapphire Blue, Silver Panels, Single Gold Line
/175	Flamboyant Blue, Single White Line	/222	Formosa Green, Chrome Panels, Double Gold Line
/176	Flamboyant Red, Chrome Panels, Single White Line	/223	Peony Red, Ivory Panels, Single Gold Line
/177	Flamboyant Red, Single White Line	/226	Peony Red
/178	Porter Fleck, Gold Star, White Centre (Tank Badge)	/227	Flamboyant Aircraft Blue
/179	Porter Fleck, Gold Star, White Centre (Tank Badge)	/228	Flamboyant Aircraft Blue, Chrome Panels, White Lines
/180	Dark Metallic Blue	/229	Flamboyant Aircraft Blue, Single White Line
/181	Grey Primer Undercoat		
/183	Two Tone Grey (Dual Seat)	/230	Brilliant Red, Chrome Panels, Single White Line
/184	Dark Metallic Blue, Chrome Panels, Double Gold Lining	/231	Orange
/185	High Gloss Olive Green BS 1220	/233	Black, Chrome Panels, Single White Line
/187	Light Grey (U.N.C.F.)	/234	Black, White Line
/188	Light Grey, Chrome, Double Gold Lining	/235	Flamboyant Electric Blue
/189	Cherokee Red (Ariel)	/236	Flamboyant Electric Blue, Chrome Panel, Single White Line. Top Section White/Blue Line
/190	Oriental Blue (Ariel)		
/191	Seal Grey (Ariel)		
/192	White (Ariel)	/237	Flamboyant Electric Blue, Single White Line
/193	Gold (Ariel)		

/238	Flamboyant Aircraft Blue, Chrome, Single White Line	/274	Grey (Carrs. C5685)
/239	Grenadier Red	/275	Chrome Side Panels, White Centre Plus 1 Blue & 2 Red Centre Stripes, Gold Lining
/240	Grenadier Red, & White, Single Black Line		
/241	Grenadier Red & Silver, Single Black Line	/276	Flamboyant Red, White Lining
		/277	Flamboyant Red, White Lining, Chrome Knee Grip
/242	Nutley Blue, Silver, Single Gold Line	/278	White, Blue Lining
/243	Black, Ivory Panel, Double Gold Line	/279	Flamboyant Red, Gold Lining
/244	Bushfire (Orange)	/280	Flamboyant Aircraft Blue, White Stripes, Red Lining
/245	Bushfire & White, Gold Lines		
/246	Firecracker Red	/281	Polychromatic Etruscan Bronze
/247	Firecracker Red, Chrome Panels	/282	Crystal Grey
/248	Nutley Blue Lined Gold	/283	Crystal Grey, Chrome Panels, Single Black Line
/249	Bushfire & Ivory Lined Black		
/250	Peony Red Lined Gold	/284	Flamboyant Red, Black centre stripe, Black side stripe, Red lining.
/251	Firecracker Red, Single Gold Line		
/252	Danish Khaki	/285	Polished Alloy sides, Black centre stripe, Black side stripe, Red lining.
/253	Raf Blue BS.633		
/254	Hi-Fi Red.	/286	Flamboyant Blue, White centre stripe.
/255	Hi-Fi Red, Silver centre stripe, lined Gold.	/287	Flamboyant Red, White centre stripe.
		/288	Grey.
/256	Greek Dark Grey	/289	Everglade.
/257	Starfire Orange, Moss Gree Centre Stripe, Single Black Line	/291	Polished Alloy sides, Black centre stripe, Red lining.
/258	Starfire Orange, Single Black Line	/294	Pacific.
/259	Peony Red & Ivory	/295	Bronze, White bottom.
/260	Peony Red, Single White Line	/296	Bronze.
/261	Firebird Red	/297	Stirling Moss, White Bottom.
/262	High Bodied Self Etch Black (Starfire USA)	/298	Stirling Moss.
		/305	White.
/263	Bushfire, Moss Gold Centre Stripe Single Black Line	/306	Black Instrument finish.
		/307	Silver Sheen.
/264	Bushfire, Single Black Line	/309	Firecracker Red top, Grey bottom.
/265	Bushfire Orange And White, Lined Black	/310	Chromed tank, Firecracker Red, Gold lining.
/266	Polychromatic Aircraft Blue	/314	Polished Aluminium, White centre stripe, Flambordeaux side stripes.
/267	Polychromatic Aircraft Blue, Chrome Panels, White Lined.		
		/315	Hi-violet.
/268	Blue Centre, (Carrs. C5663) White Lining, Chrome Side Panels	/322	Etruscan Bronze.
		/330	Chromed tank, Firebird Red, White lining.
/269	Blue Centre, (Carrs. C5666) White Lining, Chrome Side Panels		
		/357	Chromed tank, burgundy sides, Gold lining.
/270	Grey Centre, White Lining, Chrome Side Panels		
		/358	Burgundy.
/271	Blue (Carrs. C5663)	/359	Burgundy top, Black bottom.
/272	Blue (Carrs. C5666)		
/273	Polished Alloy & Yellow With Polished Cap		

Unit Single Colours by Model

The following list has been compiled from advertised specifications in original parts books for these machines and additionally the factory despatch books which show what was actually produced.

To make the best use of the following information, first determine which code numbers apply to your machine from the options given, colour names can then be found on the BSA list of suffixes, colours and finishes (above). The modern paint match can be found on p269.

Any painted parts not specifically mentioned can be assumed to be black. The numbers shown below, eg '34', '27' etc are the colour suffix numbers given in the table of suffixes, colours and finishes above.

'UK' in the following listings represents 'Home market and general export', BSA speak for everywhere except the USA. 'USA' means just that. As the USA was BSA's largest market in the '60's, a different specification for machines sent there in terms of both parts and finishes was the norm.

Pinstriping, originally applied by skilled hand and horsetail brush, can be expected to vary slightly in appearance. The specified thickness of the pinstripe line is not given in the finish codes but is generally $^1/_8$". This, and other known dimensions are given in the listings below.

Other painted stripes applied to tanks such as those on USA B25 and OIF models are of the dimensions given below by the relevant model.

C15 Star models '59 to '67.

The colours below apply to the petrol tank, oil tank and all central tinware, mudguards, front mudguard lower stays and the rear light housing. All other painted parts are black.

The C15 petrol tank; the 'eyebrow' tank originally fitted from '59 to '63 was not chromed. Subsequent tanks, without eyebrows, fitted from '62 onward were usually chromed for the civilian market. The changeover between the two types of tank was gradual and with protracted overlap; the old style eyebrow tank (and associated colour options) continued to be fitted to machines destined for the general export market long after the new shaped tank with revamped finishes was introduced for the home and USA markets.

C15 Star models offered the widest range of finishes found on Unit Singles with several foibles:

Red (34)	Fuschia Red/Devon Red was applied only to the eyebrow tank.
Red (27)	Royal Red was applied only to the later chromed tanks.
Nutley Blue (88)	When applied to the eyebrow tank Ivory (145) panels were used. This was intended primarily for the USA market until '62.

Hubs with associated brake and nave plate centres finished in Black (7) from '59 to '62, thereafter Silver (31). Competition models continued to use black.

C15 Star	Market	Colours
59	UK	Devon Red (34) or Polychromatic Green 133 changed to Metallic Almond Green (100) mid-year (see note 2, p269)
	USA	Nutley Blue (88) (tank 145, guards 112)
60	UK	Devon Red (34) Metallic Almond Green (100)
	USA	As 1959
61	UK	Devon Red (34) or Metallic Almond Green 100
	USA	As 1959
62	UK	Nutley Blue (88) (eyebrow tank 169) or Devon Red (34) or Black (7)
	USA	Nutley Blue (88) (chrome tank 110, mudguards 112)
63	All	Eyebrow tank colour as '62 or Pear shaped badge/chrome tank: Nutley blue (88), tank (110) or Royal Red (27), tank (173) or Black (7), tank (120).
64	All	As '63 except double gold lines applied to petrol tank around the chrome panels ($^3/_{16}$" inner, $^1/_8$" gap, $^1/_8$" outer) or Royal Red (109) or Black (120) or Nutley Blue (146).
65	All	As '64
66	All	As '64
67	All	As '64 except reversion to single gold line in keeping with new pattern of painted/chrome areas on petrol tank. Black (120) or Royal Red (173) or Nutley Blue (110)

C15 Competition models '60 to '65, all variants and markets.

Colour was applied only to the steel petrol tank with chrome panels (110) and with the option of painted guards to match if these were not chromed (alloy for '62 Trials/Scrambles Special). All models used Nutley Blue (88) except USA '62 C15 Starfire Roadster models which used Flamboyant Blue (172). All other parts were Black (7) or chrome plate. (Evidence in the metal indicates that the oil tank and central tinware for the '62 model was also finished in Flamboyant Blue (167) rather than the usual Black.)
Hubs, brake plate and nave plate centres Black (7).

The Trials Pastoral models intended for the Australian market ('63 C15A frame prefix and '64/'65 C15E prefix) invariably carried Nutley blue (88) on the petrol tank and mudguards. The petrol tank of the C15E version was painted blue all over without chrome or painted panels.

C15SS80 and Sportsman '61 to '67

The application of colour follows the same pattern as C15 Star models with the stated colour being applied to the petrol tank (with chrome panels), oil tank, side panel and all central tinware. Mudguards and lower front stays being chrome plated with option of Black (7) in '62.

C15SS80 & Sportsman	Market	Colours
61 SS80	UK	Black (7), tank (120).
	USA	As UK
62 SS80	UK	Flamboyant Blue (167), tank (168) or Black (7), tank (120).
	USA	Flamboyant Red (170) tank (173)
63 SS80	UK	As 62
	USA	As 62
64 SS80	UK	As 62
	USA	As 62 Flamboyant Blue (167), tank (168).
65 SS80	UK	As 62
	USA	Flamboyant Blue (167), tank (168).
66 Sportsman	UK	Flamboyant Blue (167), tank (168)
	USA	As UK.
67 Sportsman	UK	As '66 (new style tank paintwork)
	USA	As UK.

B40 Star '61 to '67.

This model followed contemporary C15 practice regarding the parts receiving colours other than Black as detailed above.

B40 Star	Market	Colours
61 to 66	UK	Royal Red (27), tank (109) or Black (7), tank (162)
61 to 66	USA	As UK.
62 on B40 B	USA	Flamboyant Blue (168) as SS90 ???)
67	UK	At the start of the '67 season a small number of B40 Star models with the new 'G' engine were produced and supplied to the 'General Export' market (another example of a superseded model still being supplied to minor markets whilst the USA and UK took priority for the new models). Due to the rarity of these machines and lack of hard data from BSA it can not yet be categorically stated whether the painted area of the tank followed the previous pattern or the new style as per the '67 C15G. Colours used continued as before: Royal Red (27) or Black (7).

SS90

62 to 66 SS90	UK	Flamboyant Red (170), tank (173)
Super Star, Sportsman	USA	Flamboyant Blue (167), tank (168).

Non-standard colours
Other significant non-standard colours periodically applied to C15 and B40 Star machines to special order by fleet users were as follows:

Light Grey (187)	Bronze Green (Civil Defence) (57)
Light Stone (65)	Port Dickson Green (206)
Dark Sand (166)	White (305)

B25 '67 to '70

B25 Colours '67 to '70 were applied to the petrol tank and on some models (up to '69) matching GRP oil tanks and side covers were fitted. The occasional application of pinstripes on both petrol tanks and GRP side panels necessitates a new BSA code number for these items different to that of the base colour. Mudguards were chromed as standard except on Fleetstar models.

B25 Fleetstar models carried the same colour, white (usually for Police) or black (usually for other users) over the tanks, nearside steel side panel and both mudguards. The black version carried a white pinstripe around both guards (234), the exception to this being the 1970 only Nutley Blue and chrome Fleetstar option (discontinued during the season).

Full width front wheel hubs of B25/B44 machines '68 to '70 were usually finished in silver. An undocumented exception to this appears to be the twin-leading-shoe hub of late '69 production which was finished in translucent red lacquer of the same type and shade as used on the contemporary large metal tank badges.

B25	Market	Colours
67 UK Barracuda:	UK	Tank: Bushfire Orange/Ivory (249) or Nutley Blue/Ivory (145) Oil tank and side panel to match, Orange (264) or Nutley Blue(248)
67 USA Starfire	USA	Tank: Nutley Blue/Ivory (145). Oil tank and side panel Nutley Blue (248).

Production of the Barracuda continued well into the '68 season as the introduction of the catalogued '68 B25 was delayed. Machines featuring the Orange and White colour scheme are less common than the Blue and White models and were made in two small batches; one at the start of the '67 season and one at the start of the '68 season. The Bushfire Orange colour is sometimes referred to as 'Tangerine' by BSA but it is not to be confused with '71 Triumph 'Tangerine'.

B25	Market	Colours
68 Starfire	UK	Tank - Nutley Blue/Ivory (145) matching oil tank and side panel (248).
68 Fleetstar Police	All	Front forks and guard stays, oil tank, steel side panel, mudguards White (69). Tank (220).
68 Fleetstar (other)	All	Black (7), tank 233, guards 234 (white pinstripe 1" from edge.

69 Starfire:	UK	Tank and GRP side panels - Flamboyant Aircraft Blue (227) Although not advertised by BSA, Black GRP side panels seem in reality to be the norm for UK models in '69. This probably follows from problems in applying the painted flamboyant finish to the GRP: GRP being best coloured by the required colour pigment being mixed in with the GRP resin. This is not easy with the complex and more expensive flamboyant recipe.
69 Starfire	USA	Tank - Bushfire Orange/Gold (263), GRP side panels Bushfire Orange with Gold pinstripe (264).
		The Gold is applied in a stripe along the tank top and rear, the stripe being equal in width to the top front frame-tube cutaway in the tank. 1,038 of these machines were supplied with Black engine parts (262) ie crankcases, rockerbox, head and barrel (these last two with polished fin edges). Getting the paint to stay on the Aluminium is a problem. Try having the parts chemically degreased then vapour bead blasted to provide a key, followed by etch primer and matt black (after extensive masking-off; don't paint the insides and joint faces). The ease with which this finish on an engine is damaged in use is probably why it was soon dropped.
69 Fleetstar	All	as '68.
70 Starfire	UK	Tank: Flamboyant Aircraft Blue (227), Oil tank and steel side panel Black (7).
70 B25 Woodsman	UK	Petrol tank as USA B25, oil tank and steel side panel Black (7). Mudguards chrome or Flamboyant Aircraft Blue (227).
70 Starfire:	USA	Tank Flamboyant Aircraft Blue, White lines (280), Oil tank and steel side panel White (69). Petrol tank white lines, the top being equal in width to the top, front frame tube cutaway. Along the sides (measured from bottom edge of the tank) – $7/8$" gap, $1/8$" pinstripe (red), $7/8$" white stripe, $1/8$" pinstripe.
70 Fleetstar	All	As 1969 plus Nutley Blue/chrome option (tank 110, oil tank and steel side panel 88 with chrome guards).

B44 '65 to '70

B44 models fall into two camps as regards the colour schemes; the roadster models ('67 to '70 Victor Roadster and Shooting Star) which follow the same styling as contemporary B25 UK models but in different colours, and the off-roaders ('67 to '70 Victor Enduro/Special and '65 to '67 Victor GP) which only have colour, yellow, applied to part of the aluminium tank; the remainder of the machine being black or chrome.

B44 65 to 70	Market	Colours
65 - 67 Victor GP	All	Tank Yellow on polished alloy (218). All other parts Black (7), Polished Aluminium (21) or Chrome (3).
66 Victor Enduro/Special	All	Tank polished aluminium (21), all other parts Black (7) or Chrome (3).
67-70 Victor Enduro/Special	All	Tank Yellow on polished Alloy (218). All other parts Black (7) or Chrome (3).
67 Victor Roadster	UK	GRP petrol tank in Royal Red and Ivory (137) or Peony Red and Ivory (223). GRP oil tank and side panel to match petrol tank in Royal Red (27) or Peony Red (250).
67 Shooting Star	USA	GRP petrol tank in Peony Red and Ivory (223), GRP oil tank and side panel to match (250).
68 B44 Shooting Star	All	GRP petrol tank in Peony Red and Ivory (223), GRP oil tank and side panel to match in Peony Red. Later 1968 models: steel petrol tank in Peony Red (226), steel oil tank Black (7) with both GRP side panels Peony Red (250)
69 Shooting Star	All	Steel petrol tank in peony Red (226), GRP side panels Peony Red (250).
70 Shooting Star	All	Steel petrol tank in Flamboyant Red (170). Oil tank and nearside steel side panel Black (7).

OIF models '71 on

'71 onward OIF models introduced some new colours and additionally the new style applications of colours were not particularly simple: stripes etc were now a common feature. The colour stated was applied to the petrol tank, side panels and mudguards, the latter with additional centre stripes in black or white. The frame and most of the painted cycle parts of BSA models were in BS Dove grey (288) until May '71 and thereafter Black (7) which continued until the end of Unit Single production; Triumph models were always Black. Additionally, Silver (165) was applied to wheel hubs, the lower portion of the grab rail and the rear light housing on both BSA and Triumph models

Considering the production problems faced by BSA at this time, variations in build state and quality of the finished product were surprisingly not much worse than usual to begin with. But the rate of changes and notification of these, increasingly led to deteriorating consistency, particularly for the '72 season. Significant numbers of the OIF machines are listed as 'N/S' in the despatch books; ie non-standard, which primarily relates to the fitment of wheels, mudguards or tank from the other models rather than colour variations, but these also are not unknown. For example the black or white mudguard stripes of '71 were not an accurate indicator of 250cc or 500cc; the black or silver finish of front brake plates seems to adhere to no specification, with black prevalent in '72.

Paint, Finishes And Transfers

Thus the number of unspecified oddities found on these late-production machines is perhaps not surprising as BSA fought their losing battle to stay afloat - this applies to the finishes used as much as the rest of the machine. As such the following information regarding finishes results from detective work in the metal, in addition to BSA's published data.

All OIF petrol tank top stripes are the same width as the top, front cutaway in the tank (for the oil filler cap on the frame). Side stripes are 4½" wide measured squarely across them. The black or white mudguard stripes on OIF B25/B50 follow the following dimensions:

Front: 1¼" wide terminating ½" from front and rear ends of guards.
Rear: 2⅛" wide terminating ⅜" from rear end of guard.

OIF models 71	Market	Colours
B25 Goldstar (pre 4/2/71)	UK	Tank and side panels Flamboyant Blue (227), Mudguards Flamboyant Blue, White centre stripe (286).
B25 Goldstar (post 4/2/71)	UK	Tank Flamboyant Red with Black stripes (284). Side panels Flamboyant Red (170). Mudguards Flamboyant Red, Black centre stripe (293).
B25 Goldstar	USA	as UK post 4/2/71
B25 Victor Trail	All	Tank Polished Aluminium with Black stripes (291). Side panels Flamboyant Red (170). Mudguards Flamboyant Red, Black centre stripe (293).

Other than pre-production and demonstration models, the B50 was not produced in quantity until late in the '71 season (May '71). The small number produced prior to this date had the frame and associated cycle parts finished in Dove Grey. All '71 production from 5/71 onward, ie none of the '71 B25 machines but the vast majority of B50 machines, had these parts finished in black.

It must be stated again that whilst this information is reproduced from original BSA literature, the lack of adherence to the given specifications for these machines is a significant factor; the transition from '71 to '72 for the B50 models being particularly vague. With regard to the B50MX, the colour and shape of the side panels seems to be, in effect, random rather than linked to any intended market. The only constant in these is hopefully the fact that the n/s panel matches that on the o/s!

B50 71-73	Market	Colours
71 B50 Gold Star	UK	Tank Flamboyant Red with Black stripes (284). Side panels Flamboyant Red (170). Mudguards Flamboyant Red with White stripe (287) or black stripe (293)
71 B50 Gold Star SS	USA	As UK
71 B50 Victor Trail	All	Tank Polished Alloy sides, Black centre stripe, Black side stripe Red lining (291). Side panels Flamboyant Red (170). Mudguards Flamboyant Red, Black centre stripe (293).
72 B25 Fleetstar	UK	Petrol tank, mudguards, side panels White (69) remaining parts Black (7). (Black as an option to White also offered)
72 B50 Gold Star	All	Tank, side panels and mudguards Hi-violet (315).

72 B50 Victor Trail	All	Tank Polished Aluminium, White centre stripe, Flambordeau side stripes (314). Although not listed, the alloy tank with Hi-Violet (315) centre and side stripes, white lining was also produced. Side panels White (69). Mudguards Bright Chrome (3).
71 B50 MX	UK	Tank as T models, side panels Black (GRP) with painted White oval panel. Mudguards Stainless Steel.
	USA	Tank as T models, side panels Black (GRP) with painted Yellow square panel. Mudguards Stainless Steel.
72 B50 MX	UK	As 71 except side panels option in Hi-violet (315) with White panels
72 B50 MX	US	As 71 except side panels option in Hi-violet (315)
73 B50 MX	All	Tank Yellow (218) side and centre stripes lined black, side panels/guards as 71 for UK and USA respectively

Triumph models

Triumph	Market	Colours
68-70 TR25w	All	The TR25w used the same basic scheme for all years where colour was applied to the petrol tank and mudguards, all other parts were either black or chrome with black GRP side panels. Tank Hi-Fi Scarlet (254). Tinted lacquer sprayed over Silver base. Mudguards Hi-Fi Red, Silver centre stripe (7/8" wide), lined Gold. The Silver stripe is actually the Silver base coat left uncovered by the scarlet lacquer.
71 T25T and T25SS	All	Tank Tangerine. Mudguards Tangerine, Black centre stripe (dimensions as per BSA equivalents), lined White. Side panels Black.
74 TR5MX	All	Tank Polished Aluminium with Argosy Blue panels lined Gold, side panels black (GRP), Stainless Steel guards.

B40 Military

Painted finish usually applied to all parts except handlebars, exhaust system, lamp rim and tank cap which were normally dull chrome finish. The paint shade used is dependant on the customer.

British Army	Bronze Green (57)
RAF	RAF Blue (253)
Royal Navy	Unknown at present possibly (81)
Australian Army	Bronze Green (57)
Danish Army	Danish Khaki (252)
Jordanian Army	Dark Sand (166)
Israeli Army	Light Stone (65)

Paint Matches for BSA Unit Single Original Colours

These paints relate to those available in the UK at the time of going to press. Unfortunately, the availability of these matches in every corner of the world cannot be guaranteed, nor their continued availability in the future.

Suffix	**Colour**	**Modern Equivalent**
34	Devon Red/Fuschia Red	BS 540
88	Nutley Blue[1]	Skoda Medium Blue 4456
133	Polychromatic Green[2]	Mitsubishi G53
244	Bushfire Orange[3]	RAL 2010 Signal Orange
100	Metallic Almond Green	Volkswagen Zederngren Metallic K6Y
27	Royal Red (Post Office Red)	Rover CMC
227	Flamboyant Aircraft blue[4]	RAL 5022
57	Bronze Green	BS Deep Bronze Green 224
252	Danish Khaki	RAL 7022
65	Light Stone	Rover 452 Unable to differentiate this from 166 Dark Sand.
166	Dark Sand	Rover 452
167	Flamboyant Blue	Honda 7006M
170	Flamboyant Red	Suzuki 5014M
226	Peony Red	BS 1-025
288	Dove Grey	BS 627
315	Hi-Violet[5]	Harley Davidson 5017M
314	Flambordeau[5]	
218	Yellow	RAL 1023
7	Black	OK, take your pick!
69	White	Max Meyer 1.1700 or 1.1860. Not just any white!
31	Silver	RAL 9006 (satin).
104	Ivory	Rover Pale Ivory.
254	Hi-Fi Scarlet	Kymko 5002M
	Tangerine (1971 T25T and SS)	BS 593 Rail Red.
	Argosy Blue	Honda 7006M blue

Notes to the paints
'BS'   Stands for British Standard.
'RAL' A standard colour numbering system for paints..

1   Nutley Blue (88) is these days regarded as being the same as Sapphire Blue (63) despite originally being listed separately by BSA. They themselves referred to 'Sapphire Blue (88)' just to confuse things and support the contention that any difference isn't worth bothering about.

2   Polychromatic Green 133 (also listed as 'Turquoise' in the despatch books) originally specified in the early '59 parts book for the C15 Star is not included in the master list of colours subsequently compiled by BSA in the late '60's. It is believed that this is due to it being the same shade as that used on the contemporary Sunbeam Scooter ie Polychromatic Zircon Green 141 which superseded it in the listing, 133 being deleted to avoid duplication. On the '59 C15 Star the Polychromatic Green 133 was replaced as an option mid season by the more restrained Metallic Almond Green 100.

3   Also referred to as 'Starfire Red', 'Starfire Orange' and 'Tangerine' by BSA in '67/'68. As far as can be determined these are all the same shade as also used on the Bantam 'Bushman' models and not to be confused with the darker '71 Triumph T25 'Tangerine' shade. Bushfire Orange was originally developed by BSA (using the time honoured 'rule of thumb' method) by mixing equal amounts of Royal (Post Office) Red and AA Yellow. No doubt there were plenty of half empty tins of both these colours lying around at Small Heath! This method can of course be replicated by the modern day owner to obtain this colour.

4   Whilst being 'flamboyant' in that this dark blue shade is applied over Silver base, the resulting effect is opaque to the extent that it gives the appearance of a solid, flat colour. The match given is therefore to be applied over silver until this is obscured as per original. Alternatively use opaque Aircraft Blue BS 381 alone.

5   A 'flamboyant' finish of tinted lacquer applied over silver. Not listed as a separate colour but as a component of the petrol tank finish with White top stripe. Flambordeau differs in that the tinted lacquer (known as the 'ink') is applied directly to the polished Aluminium tank rather than over yellow Chromate etch primer and silver base coat as are the other flamboyant colours. It is the same tinted lacquer as the Hi-Violet colour but applied in only one thin layer to maximise the visibility of the polished Aluminium beneath. This gives the Flambordeau colour a distinctive lustre but unfortunately doesn't help its adhesion.

Beneath all of these colours you will need to apply the appropriate primers and undercoats to suit the underlying metal or fibreglass and the type of paint being used. Consult your supplier regarding issues of paint compatibility.

The modern equivalents listed to match the BSA Flamboyant colours are of the same composition as the original ie Silver base under tinted lacquer. These days this is commonly known as 'candy'. In comparison, a metallic finish will give a slightly more grainy appearance and is much cheaper as an alternative if an acceptable shade can be obtained.

Paint Compatibility

If you are doing your own painting and varnishing then please note that not all paints are compatible and can blister or craze when applied to a surface having an incompatible finish. Always do a test first. Otherwise it may mean having to start again…

Plated Finishes

On BSA Unit Singles you may find the following plated finishes applied for the sake of appearance and to keep corrosion at bay.

>   Bright Chrome plate
>   Dull Chrome plate (military models)
>   White Cadmium plate

Additionally other applied chemical finishes such as 'bonderising' and black phosphate could be applied unseen for reasons of engineering such as to help paint adhesion or inhibit corrosion or wear. The B40 Military, for example, specified 'bonderising' of steel parts, followed by a red oxide primer then a grey undercoat beneath the top colour coat.

An important plated finish in this category is the Hard Chrome plating applied to fork stanchions of all Unit Singles '70 onward and also shock absorber piston rods. Hard chrome is an engineering material which is wear resistant, rather than a decorative finish, and must not be replaced in such applications by Bright Chrome, which isn't.

The three plated finishes, normally high on the list of priorities for the restorer, all require the work to be farmed-out to one of the many specialists who advertise these services in the classic press.

Bright chrome plating is easy to commission in this way; dull chrome is more difficult to obtain, and expensive. Two versions of the dull chrome finish appear to have been applied on the military machines. Some parts, such as handlebars and exhaust pipes, have a pitted surface texture which suggests shot blasting before the chrome is applied. Others, such as levers for example, do not have such a pitted surface and are simply smooth and dull in appearance.

A short cut to an authentic looking dull chrome finish (with or without prior shot blasting) is to apply bright chrome and then vapour bead blast this at low pressure to dull-down the bright chrome. If your chrome has been applied properly the low pressure blasting should not lift it.

White cadmium (cadmium plating), originally applied to the various fasteners, spindles etc is difficult to obtain these days having largely been outlawed due to the toxic nature of the plating process. The substitute is BZP, Bright Zinc Plate which is equally (in)effective at keeping corrosion at bay in ideal conditions but is brighter with a slightly bluish tint.

If sending any parts to be plated do as much cleaning, re-shaping and preparation yourself as is possible. The plating will not hide defects and the plater is not likely to make any assumptions about how you want things to look.

Tank Badges

As a finishing touch for any BSA, and also as an item which in itself has a finish and range of colour options, this part deserves separate consideration.

Separate screwed-on badges on the petrol tank were a common feature on most Unit Singles and other post war BSA's, the alternative usually being a decal (transfer). On Unit Singles, the separate screwed-on badges were used up to the end of the 1970 season; the OIF models all have tank decals despite what the BSA publicity shows for the large tank '72 B50 Gold Star.

Two materials were used for the badges themselves, plastic (acrylic) beginning with the C15 and subsequently, from 1968 onward, metal (die-cast Zinc).

Plastic tank badges

Two shapes were fitted to the Unit Singles, the 3¼" diameter 'small round' badge (the 'large round' 4" diameter badge was used by BSA on various pre-unit models) was fitted to the B40 Star and SS90 up to '62 and also the C15SS80 to '62. All these models shared the same large capacity 'round badge' tank. Except for the above, all other C15 and B40 variants with the smaller capacity steel petrol tanks, fitted the pear-shaped plastic badge.

The design of the plastic badges comprised a clear acrylic moulding, the reverse surface of which (against the tank) is in relief with decorative paint finishes applied which show through to the outside.

Only one version of the small round badge was fitted, which was mainly silver in colour and subsequently fitted to '65 onward Bantam models. These attach to the tank by means of a spring clip on the back of the badge which hooks into a loop welded in the badge recesses of the tank.

The pear shaped badges can be found in several different colour schemes to suit the full range of BSA models to which they were fitted. They are also 'handed' unlike the round badges.

The colour variants refer to the background colour surrounding the central metallic 'BSA' with its eight star points; these are most commonly Red, which was used on all C15 and B40 models and '67 C25/B25 machines with blue GRP tanks. Originally these were in an opaque royal red with a Silver BSA and star. The pattern items available today are a bit gaudy by comparison, with gold BSA and star and a translucent, rather flamboyant background red. However they don't look out of place.

The other commonly available colour variant is black, which on Unit Singles was used on '67 441cc road models and some of the relatively few Barracudas which were orange rather than blue. Alternatives to the black badges on these two models for '67 were pear shaped badges with a flecked Oatmeal background colour – now very hard to find. It cannot categorically be said whether any particular '67 machine was fitted with black or oatmeal badges, choice of which by BSA seems to be rather random and depended, as usual, on which was in stock at the time. This flecked or speckly background paint finish was also employed on the blue or green pear shaped badges fitted to early A50/65 models.

Should you be in need of some of the pear shaped badges in the harder to find colours they can be replicated. Mask off the BSA and star with blue-tack or similar and then remove the surrounding unwanted paint by low pressure vapour bead blasting. This area can then be repainted as you wish.

The pear shaped plastic badges are held in place by a single 3BA screw. If this screw is over tightened the badge will crack even with the moulded rubber backing (fitted from '65) in place to act as a cushion. BSA tried to counteract the tendency to crack by changing from countersunk screws - badges part number 40-8014/15 irrespective of colour – to cheesehead screws – badges part number 40-8122/3.

Metal tank badges '68 to '70 B25 Starfire (not USA '70) and B44 Shooting Star.

As previously stated these are die-cast zinc items, handed, and with a decorative shiny gold anodised finish (which fades over time) applied to the base metal. Today's replacements for these badges are pleasingly made using the original dies by the original manufacturer. Over this, colours were added to selective areas.

Die-cast pear shaped tank badge colour schemes '68 to '70.

'68 B25 and B44	Red outer background and outer rim, White inner oval background, Red BSA letters.
'69 UK B25	Red outer background and outer rim, Red inner oval background, White BSA letters.
'69 USA B25, '70 UK B25, & '69/'70 B44 Shooting Star	Slate Grey BS 633 (gloss) inner oval with Off White BS 4-046 and (matt) inside White BSA letters as above

33% reduction

Transfer	Model	Applied to
1	B44 Shooting Star '67 / '68 USA	Petrol tank top rear of centre bolt
2	C25 250 Shooting Star '67 / '68	As above
3	B44GP and B44VS '67 to '70	Petrol tank sides
4	B44GP	Petrol tank top, rear of centre bolt
5	B44SS USA '67, all markets '68	Side panels both sides
6	B44 VS '67'69	Petrol tank rear of centre bolt. The '67/'68 version with crossed flags can be made by 'borrowing' the flags from transfer 6. There was no tank top transfer for '70
7	B44VR '67	Side panel and oil tank

25% reduction

Transfer	Model	Applied to
1	C15 Sportsman '66 / '67	Oil tank and side panel
2, 3	C15 and B40 '58 to '67 All road and competition models with lights	Top of rear number plate bracket
4	C15 Starfire competition models (USA only) '59 to '62 with steel petrol tank	Top of petrol tank opposite filler cap
5	All C15 and B40 models and B44 VE/VS 66/67	Oil tank level indicator
6	C15 SS80 (not shown) and B40 SS90 '64/'65	Oil tank and side panel. The previous version of this transfer ('60 to '63) with 6-point stars is now unavailable
7	C15 and B40 competition models with an aluminium tank '65	Petrol tank both sides. These models in previous years used a black BSA logo
8	B44 VE/VS '66	Petrol tank sides
9	C15/B40 '62 to '64 competition models with aluminium tank, B25 Fleetstar '69 to '70 ('68 white), B40 Military	Petrol tank sides
10	All models to 1970	Side panel and oil tank if no other transfer is specified

33% reduction

Transfer	Model	Applied to
1	C25 Barracuda '67 home market	Oil tank and side panel
2	B25 Starfire '68/'69	Oil tank and side panel(s)
3	B44 Victor Special '69/'70	Oil tank and side panel
4	B44 Shooting Star '69/'70	Oil Tank and side panel(s)
5	B25 Starfire USA '67	Oil tank and side panel
6	B25 Fleetstar and Police Fleetstar '70	Oil tank and side panel
7	B25 Starfire USA '69	Petrol tank top forward of filler cap
8	TR25w '68/'69	Side panels

33% reduction

Transfer	Model	Applied to
1	B25, B44 '67 on, export market	O/S top of front down tube
2	B25 Starfire '70 USA only	Oil tank
3	B25 Starfire '70 USA only	Side panel
4	TR25w '70	Oil tank and steel side panel
5	B25 Starfire '70 home market	Oil tank and steel side panel
6	B25 Fleetstar (not police) '70	Oil tank and steel side panel

33% reduction

Transfer	Model	Applied to
1	B25SS '71 (silver outline to red letters)	Petrol tank both sides. Not listed in the parts book. This transfer is believed to have been fitted to the flamboyant blue machines
2	B25 and B50 '71, B50 '72	Petrol tank both sides on the black stripe
3, 4	B25SS and B50SS '71 respectively	Both side panels. The same transfers lacking the 'SS' are also available but have not yet been confirmed as original fitment
5	B50MX '72	Petrol tank both sides at top of the side stripe
6	B50SS '72	Both side panels
7, 8	B50T '72	Both side panels alternate colours. Although not specified, 7 is appropriately coloured to suit the machines with tank finish in flambordeau and 8 the high violet machines

50% reduction

Transfer	Model	Applied to
1, 2	B25T and B50 '71 respectively	Both side panels
3	B50MX '71	Petrol tank top between filler cap and centre bolt
4	B50MX '73	Petrol tank both sides (chrome outline to red letters)

50% reduction

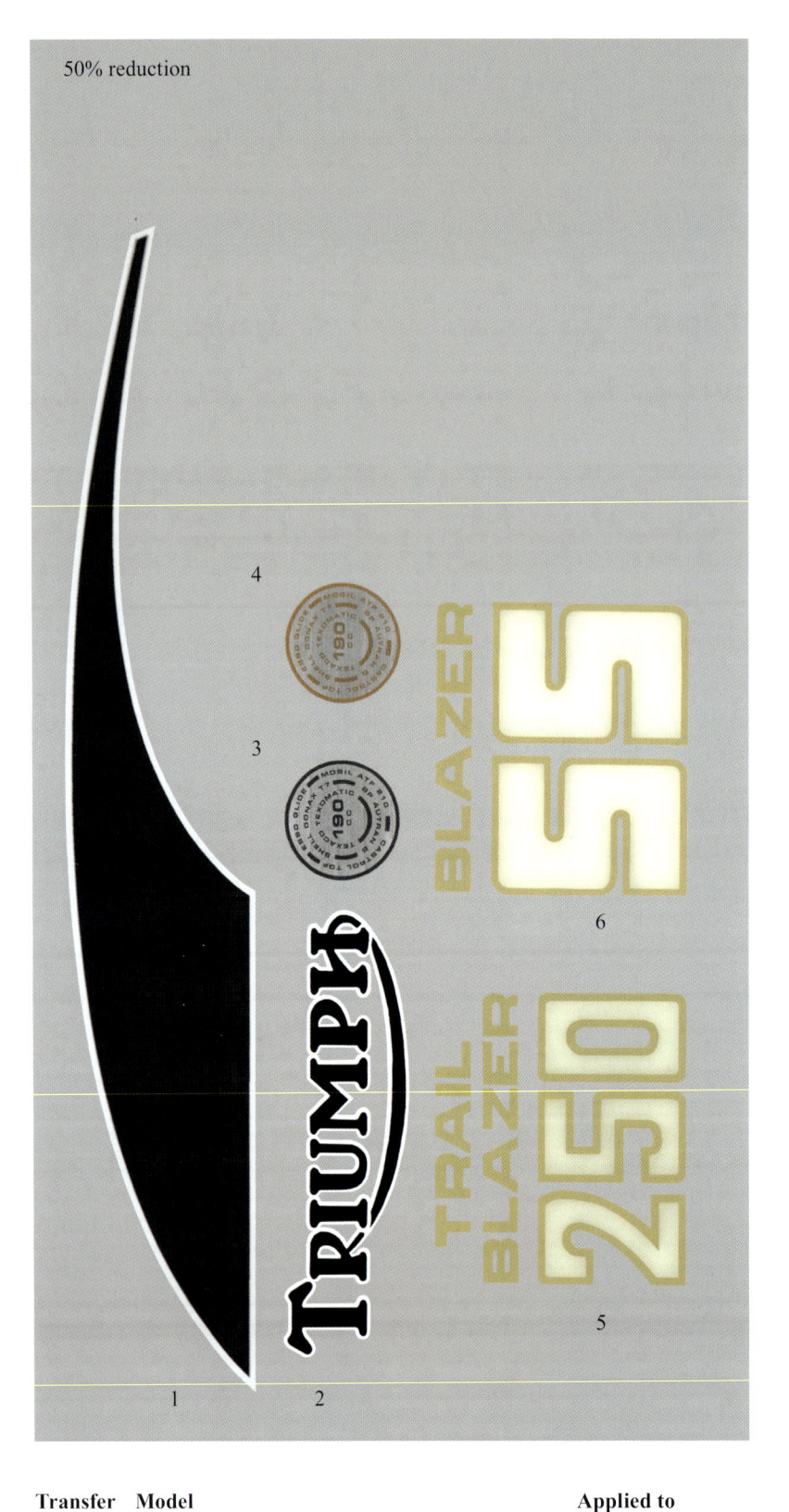

Transfer	Model	Applied to
1	Triumph T25T and SS '71	Petrol tank sides
2	Triumph T25T and SS '71, '73 TR5MX	Petrol tank sides
3, 4	All models '72	Fork stanchion top nut. Commonly applied in black. Gold alternative not specific to any model
5	T25T '71	Side panels
6	T25SS '71	Side panels

Of these colours, the slate grey/off white version appears to use normal opaque paint but the red/white version uses translucent colours to allow the underlying Gold anodised finish to shine through.

Reproducing this translucent appearance on the unpainted replacement badges now available cannot be achieved with ordinary gloss paint. Instead, pay a visit to your local chemist and select a suitable rich, translucent red nail varnish (accompanied, if possible by an obliging female, who, by her mere presence will greatly reduce the likelihood of funny looks from other customers, and on the fingernails of whom the trial splodges of shades of red will look less out of place). Likewise the translucent white.

The metal tank badges are each retained by two $1/8$" BSW fillister-headed screws. Grease or similar anti-seize compound on the threads of these will ease future removal as drilling out the remains of such a small screw is a fiddly headache after it has seized and sheared off. Similarly the 3BA screw used to fix the pear shaped plastic badges.

Transfers (Decals)

The momentous event of affixing the transfers usually signifies the end of any restoration work and is usually associated with feelings of satisfaction and conclusion. Best not cock it up then, eh?

With this in mind, always apply transfers to the complete assembled machine, preferably whilst on its centre stand and with the wheels chocked to keep it level and horizontal. This should help you put them on straight.

Most of the transfers available today come as either 'waterslide' (same as the transfers for your old Airfix models) or as self-adhesive with sticky on the back. Both of these types are easy to apply but both have limitations in use regarding durability. The self-adhesive type will last as long as the glue on the back stays viable and after a time this will degrade and the transfers will start to let-go and disintegrate around the edges. The waterslide type, have no adhesion to the side panel and are therefore fragile and brittle in use. Varnishing or lacquering over both of these types of transfer will make them a little more durable but will not address the problem of their method of adhesion.

The best solution I have found is to revert to the time-honoured 'gold-size' method whereby a better type of adhesive is used to attach the transfer. Some transfers continue to be available today for fixing by this method but it is not common as it is a more involved process.

In short, 'gold size' is traditionally a type of varnish which is painted onto the back of the transfer and allowed to partially dry and go tacky before the transfer is applied - result, it sticks good and proper. It gets its name from its original use which was to attach gold leaf.

This process can be replicated with the self-adhesive transfers by firstly removing the sticky backing by carefully wiping off with white spirit on a clean rag. The transfer can then be treated as a waterslide type and the paper backing removed by soaking in water.

The 'size' can either be polyurethane varnish or acrylic lacquer applied as a complete overall coat to the area of bike receiving the transfer, usually the side panel. This is then left to become almost completely dry before the transfer – without its paper backing, dried, and carefully offered up is pressed into place and rubbed down.

One potential worry in all of this is the use of acrylic lacquer either as 'size' or over the transfer as a varnish. While liquid the solvent it contains will react with the transfer and effectively dissolve it. Therefore don't use it as a finishing lacquer over a transfer, and as 'size' don't apply the transfer until it is very nearly dry.

Selection of transfers

Illustrations of the original transfers for Unit Singles are shown in the colour section. Original replacement transfers are these days rather scarce and if you do get lucky the chances are that their condition will have deteriorated with age. Unit Single owners are therefore fortunate that Classic Transfers and the BSA Owners club of Great Britain has had reproduced the vast majority of transfers required, with more in the pipeline as originals emerge for copying. These transfers can also be obtained from the stockists of classic bike transfers in the UK as can those for the Triumph badged models.

APPLYING TRANSFERS (DECALS)

It should be noted that two types of transfers (decals) have been used on our models. These are the traditional varnish applied type and the self-adhesive type.

Applying the self-adhesive type is merely a matter of removing the backing paper and pressing downwards onto the painted surface.

Applying the varnish type is slightly more difficult but with care a perfect finish will be achieved.

Firstly cut away the paper edging as close as possible to the transfer. Remove the tissue from the face of the transfer and separate one edge of the backing from the actual transfer to facilitate removal at a later stage. Varnish the face of the transfer and allow to dry for five minutes. Then place the tacky side of the transfer on to the part to which the transfer is to be fixed and carefully remove the thick backing paper.

Allow to dry for half an hour or so and then moisten the remaining backing paper with a wet rag or sponge. It can then be removed and the transfer must be varnished to preserve it.

Fig 15.4. Triumph's own advice for successful application of transfers is reproduced above

Those transfers as yet unobtainable can be substituted with others from similar models/years or, these days thanks to the wizardry of computer technology, artwork matching the original designs can be created and produced in the form of cut vinyl graphics to stick on your machine. This is a fairly basic process for the modern day automotive sign writer should you want to commission one.

At the time of writing a handful or so of Unit Single transfers are currently unavailable. If anyone has original examples of the following I would urge them to contact Classic Transfers or the BSA Owners Club who can arrange for them to be copied –

Side panel six-point star for SS80 and 90 prior to '64.

AFS tank transfer for B40 'Civil Defence'

Side panel transfer for USA B40 Sportsman '64 to '65

Fig 15.5. B50MX tank logo from '73. Not transfers but individual chrome and red stick-on letters. Similar in appearance to the '71 red with silver outline BSA logo transfer but in reality a different beast; and no, the photo isn't wonky, straightness was lacking at the factory.

Transfers

These have been included to show the designs and general colour scheme of the transfers. Printed colours can never be an exact match with the actual colour specified by BSA so these are approximate only. The transfers have been reduced in size to fit on a page. All transfers on a singe page have been reduced by the same amount so the relative size is correct. Reductions vary between 25% and 50% as indicated on each page.

Fig 15.6. '68 -'70 large metal tank badge. This colour scheme (grey oval and white letters) identifies it as a '69 -'70 B44SS and '70 UK B25

16. NUTS AND BOLTS

Screwthreads

The screwthread, in my humble opinion the second most important invention ever (after the wheel of course). On your Unit Single the job they do is vital – holding all the bits together in the right places. This is of the utmost importance but is too often taken for granted or subject to ignorance on a grand scale. I hope to alleviate this ignorance, or at least persuade you that any old bolt will just not do for your BSA.

Some background first. The Imperial (British) system of screwthreads is superior to other systems in engineering terms and has been carefully and thoughtfully applied to your BSA Unit Single. Having been invented in times BC (see Archimedes and Hanging gardens of Babylon etc) the helix, spiral or screwthread was widely applied to the solving of problems requiring linear movement to be easily created by rotary movement; ie you turn it and something moves along. Use of the screwthread in the form of nuts and bolts for fasteners and machinery mushroomed as the industrial revolution got under way. But there was a problem: standardisation. Your skilled engineer of the time or village blacksmith may well have been able to craft some excellent nuts and bolts for your Newcomen steam engine, but they would be unlikely to fit with the equally good nuts and bolts made by the blacksmith in the next village. This is an over-simplification of the true picture but I hope you get the gist.

Enter Joseph Whitworth, later Sir, and a true hero of the industrial revolution. His 'Whitworth' standard screwthread was the first to be widely accepted because it was a good general purpose thread and a 1" Whitworth bolt made by blacksmith A would now fit the 1" Whitworth nut made by blacksmith B. Standardisation achieved.

The Whitworth thread is very good for some things, for screwthreads into aluminium castings for example, but it also has its drawbacks caused by its coarse thread. A coarse thread means that it has relatively big teeth in relation to the diameter of any given bolt, and also few of them per inch of length of the bolt. This last factor is called the TPI - Teeth (or Turns) per Inch - and is important terminology to know.

Disadvantages of a coarse thread
The solid metal remaining in the middle of a Whitworth bolt is thinner than the solid metal in the middle of a bolt with a finer thread. Thus the coarse thread bolt is relatively weak.

The coarse thread with few TPI necessitates a steep angle of helix as it spirals around the bolt. The result is that a nut on such a bolt will tend to come loose more easily under the influence of vibration when compared with a nut and bolt with a fine thread.

Clearly, applications exist where such things as increased strength and resistance to vibration are important (eg on your BSA) and hence there was a need for other different, but standardised screwthreads each to suit a particular area of application. Following the Whitworth thread others were introduced - British Standard Fine (BSF), British Standard Brass (BSB), British Association (BA), British Standard Pipe (BSP) (also known as 'gas thread' and also available as BSPT – Tapered Pipe thread), British Standard Cycle (BSCy) in both 26 TPI and 20 TPI series.

Other specialised threads were also introduced; the above list simply represents those specified by BSA somewhere on most, if not all Unit Singles. The key point being that each thread is the optimum solution to a particular fixing/fastening job and BSA put it there to do that job for good reason. This is why you will not find a wheel spindle with a Whitworth thread – wrong application – but even today some bicycle wheel spindles still use the now long obsolete 26 TPI BSCy thread because it is the right one for the job; strong and resistant to vibration.

So, whilst the wide range of threads used on your Unit Single may be confusing until you get the hang of it, and expensive compared with the wider use of fewer thread types, it is undoubtedly good engineering, or, quality.

BSCy, or Cycle threads as they are commonly known, was widely applied to products of all British bicycle and motorcycle makers because it is relatively strong and vibration resistant, and therefore spot-on for vibratory machines rattling along bumpy roads.

It is however rather a complex thread. Unlike most of the other thread series' listed above, the TPI does not decrease (from the usual 26 or 20) as thread diameter increases. Hence large diameter threads can have the same 26 TPI fine thread as the smallest bolts. Good engineering it may be but this definitely does complicate things and leads to the use of 'specials' with uncommon thread sizes and TPI's. For example, the thread on the Duplex/Welded frame swinging arm spindle, $^{13}/_{16}$" 20 TPI Cycle thread, is not used anywhere else on the machine. With so many possible variants with this system the wheel has almost, but not quite, come full circle back to the time of blacksmiths A and B designing their own threads.

This takes the Unit Single nut and bolt story up to 1969: confusing but with underlying logic. Now it really does take a turn for the worse. This stems from the metric system. In Europe screwthread development and standardisation took place in a similar parallel manner to our Imperial efforts but evolved into a different and simpler system, the ISO-metric screw thread system, eventually with two common versions, isometric coarse and isometric fine. I personally regard the metric screwthread system as the 'jack of all trades and master of none' in comparison to the imperial system, but, definitely a cheaper and easier system as evidenced by the shelves in any of today's home improvements megastores.

Anyway, back to the plot. The Americans, being staunchly imperial (feet and inches, gallons etc) but liking the simplicity of the coarse or fine metric system, decided to go their own way and combined the two. They applied the metric threadform (the shape of the tooth) to imperial sizes and thus unified the two systems in a third, the 'Unified' system, available in coarse (UNC) and fine (UNF). In the Americas often called NC and NF. Following World War Two, the Unified system was increasingly adopted by the British automotive industry in preference to the original Whitworth derived threads, now increasingly regarded as non-preferred.

Returning to BSA. By the mid '60s it was reasonably concluded that on grounds of cost and economies of scale, they would adopt the increasingly available and therefore cheaper Unified threads. Hence, for the '69 season/range BSA replaced many of the Cycle threads on any given machine with UNC or UNF – but not all. Hence the confusion multiplies. BSA chose to hang on to many of the special application Cycle threads and change only the ordinary nuts, bolts and screws and studs. Also newly introduced threaded parts tended to feature Unified threads – the Triumph forks fitted for '69 for example. It may well have been intended that further UNC/UNF introductions would happen when redesigns of engines or cycle parts occurred. Hence, mainshaft threads, various spindle threads, petrol tap threads, oil filter, inspection cap, yoke stem threads and many more remained unchanged.

A further big step towards full use of unified threads came with the introduction of the revamped '71 Oil in Frame range. Here the completely new cycle parts featured unified threads throughout, whereas some unchanged engine parts remained Cycle. In terms of convenience and simplicity this is quite a mess really, because for the owners of '69 onward machines a new set of A/F spanners would be required as the old Whitworth spanners (still needed for many of the fasteners) did not fit the new Unified nuts and bolts.

Spanners

Which brings us on to the spanners (also sockets) you need for your Unit Single. Whitworth spanners, needed for all of the fasteners on your BSA up to '68, have sizes written on them which relate to the diameter of the screwthread, not the size of the head. Whitworth spanners fit the hexagon sizes of all the Imperial thread series - Cycle, Gas, BSF etc although the BA series of thread sizes, all being smaller than 1/4" have their own BA spanners to suit.

Originally, Whitworth bolts had a larger size hexagon head than BSF bolts of the same thread diameter; hence Whitworth spanners will have two alternative sizes written on each end of them. BSA in particular often chose a smaller than standard hexagon head size for their bolts – handlebar clamp bolts for example, 5/16" Cycle with a head size normally found on a 1/4" bolt, known as a reduced head.

In effect for the whole range of Whitworth, BSF and Cycle screwthreads there is quite a limited range of hexagon head sizes applied to several different thread sizes. The whole range of spanner jobs on your pre-'68 Unit Single will require only about six spanner sizes (excepting a couple of larger oddities).

Unified threads followed metric practice and measured their spanners by the size across flats of the hexagon head they fit. Hence a 1/2" AF spanner fits a 1/4" UNF or UNC bolt and nothing else. Here I think the Whitworth system has the edge in terms of simplicity, fewer spanners are needed as the range of head sizes is smaller.

So, to distil all of the above down to the essentials - If you have a BSA Unit Single made prior to '71 you need a set of Whitworth spanners in sizes ranging from 3/16" to 7/16". Also get socket spanners in these sizes. If you have a BSA made in '69 or later, (therefore '69 -'70 machines need both Whitworth and AF spanners) obtain the equivalent size range in AF tools ie 3/8" to 3/4". A spanner and socket to fit the 2BA hexagon head is also needed as well as one or two larger odd spanner sizes depending on the model you have.

My main message underlying all of the above is to stick to the original BSA specification regarding what fasteners/screwthreads to use on your bike and get the correct tools to fit them, it is simply good practice. Only in this way will you know exactly where you stand.

Where you stand was greatly helped by BSA for '69 onward models by the additional information about nuts and bolts included in the parts books for each model. From now on length, diameter and thread of each bolt were specified. No coincidence that this bonus happened when the Unified threads and potential nut and bolt chaos was introduced: thank you BSA.

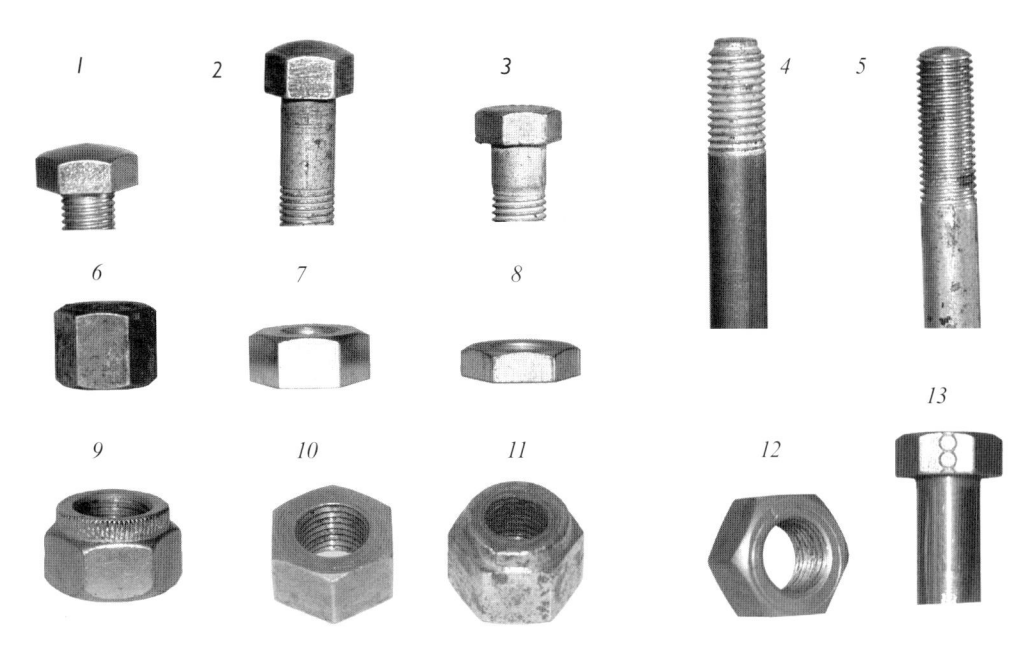

Fig 16.1. Nuts and bolts.

1. ⁵/₁₆ BSCy bolt referred to as a setscrew ie it has a thread running the length of the bolt. This is a standard fitment '58 to '70 and has a domed head.
2. Reduced head AF bolt (handlebar clamp bolt)
3. Reduced and thin head AF bolt (eg C15 central tinware to frame)
   Rubery Owen found written on the bolt heads indicates the original manufacturer
4. UNF stud (spigot end)
5. BSCy stud (domed end)
6. Reduced size AF nut
7. Plain, full nut, single chamfer
8. Half nut
9. Clevelock nut, widely applied '71 on (and previously used on '69 -'70 forks)
10. Plain single chamfer nut equivalent size to the Nyloc nut (11)
11. Nyloc nut, increasingly used from '67
12. UNF plain nut showing the circle on one end indicating it has a Unified thread
13. UNF bolt head - the row of circles indicates Unified thread

A few useful facts about your Unit Single screwthreads: ¼" BSF is identical to ¼" Cycle. Although the tooth form is slightly different, ¼" UNC is interchangeable with ¼" Whitworth.

Unified nuts and bolts are marked for easy identification by circles - a chain of small circles marked along the side of bolt heads and one circular groove around the hole on one end of the nuts shown in *fig 16.1*. Unified studs are identified by the solid core projecting visibly beyond the thread on each end, whereas the equivalent Whitworth/Cycle/BSF studs have slightly domed ends as seen in *fig 16.1*.

The original ¼" engine screws in either 26 TPI Cycle pre '69 or ¼" UNC subsequently, originally had Phillips, 'raised cheese-head' heads. Hard to find these days, the originals tend to chew-up easily if the wrong size Phillips screwdriver is used. These days most have been replaced with Allen bolts or screws. These are easy to obtain and don't chew-up but can be tightened with the key way beyond the level originally intended – so beware stripped threads in the aluminium casings, likewise the smaller 2BA screws used in some places.

Self-locking 'Simmons' or 'Phillidas' nuts were introduced from the mid '60s onward starting with the B40 military, in many but not all applications on the bike. These are generally referred to as 'Nyloc' nuts (with the plastic insert) and were in common usage on civilian models by '68.

The self-locking UNF nuts introduced from '69 and used throughout the OIF cycle parts from '71 are known as 'Clevelock' nuts. These lack the plastic insert and instead have the extended portion of the nut squeezed inward to grip onto the bolt thread. These are difficult to find nowadays but originals can be re-plated if in good enough condition. After several fittings/removals, all of the above self-locking nuts will lose their ability to grip the male thread and should be replaced.

Finishes Used on Fasteners

Only inside the engine were fasteners often left 'self colour' ie unplated bare steel. In all external applications all fasteners were plated to inhibit corrosion and improve appearance. This was either with White Cadmium or sometimes chrome plate in high visibility positions, the fork top nuts for example. The former, due to its highly toxic plating process has almost entirely been replaced by Bright Zinc Plate, BZP, on fasteners. The problem with the plating of these fasteners is keeping it there; Cadmium and Zinc will both corrode through quickly in damp/salty conditions if not protected by oil or grease. Likewise Chrome, being porous, will permit rusting of the underlying steel if unprotected and additionally may flake off when spanner pressure is applied. The only way to maintain the original appearance of your nuts and bolts is care and protective maintenance - same as the rest of the bike.

The alternative is to fit stainless steel fasteners. These are relatively expensive but without the above shortcomings - definitely fit and forget and excellent on a bike which will see foul weather. If you are fussy, the problems may lie in finding stainless Cycle thread fasteners with slightly domed hexagon heads as per the many originals, and/or reduced heads. Additionally many of the special or non-standard fasteners are likely to be unobtainable in stainless unless you have a lathe and the raw materials when you can make them yourself.

Nuts

Like the bolts, nuts were all originally turned from solid hexagonal bar; a process wasteful of material and expensive, this method produces a stronger nut than the modern 'cold forming' (squashing it into shape) method. Original spec. BSA nuts are invariably 'single chamfer' being flat on the side which contacts the washer or part being fixed. Cold formed nuts are invariably chamfered both sides.

Washers

In general BSA fitted what are now called Imperial 'table three, heavy' washers although like the nuts and bolts, the range of specials for specific applications is extensive. In short, try to avoid fitting the easily obtainable metric equivalents if possible and apply a modicum of common sense regarding the outside diameter and other variables for any particular application. The eye can be a good judge in this case, 'if it looks right, it is right'. Try to avoid re-using old distorted washers as these will not perform their load-spreading function well.

When assembling parts of your Unit Single using nuts and bolts the correct spanners may be less convenient than your favourite adjustable spanner but they will save you pain in the long run. The key to this is their length; which is proportional to the size of nut they fit and is designed to permit the correct tightening torque to be applied with normal hand pressure. An over-length spanner ie your favourite adjustable on a ¼" bolt, is asking for a stripped thread.

All parts which screw together should do this by finger pressure alone with final tightening being the job for the spanners. If the spanner is needed prior to this the parts should be separated and each thread cleaned/tidied with a tap or die. This is particularly necessary with tapped holes in fixtures such as the frame where paint or powder coating may be causing an obstruction. All screwing together jobs should therefore be approached with a 'dry run' first and only fully tightened if no problem is encountered.

The amount of pressure necessary for tightening the various size nuts and bolts is simply down to experience. If in doubt, intentionally over-tighten a spare ¼" nut and bolt and feel how much force is needed to shear it; you now know not to push this hard on the real thing.

Undoing a seized nut and bolt may also cause it to shear. This in itself is probably a good thing; it had to come out and you can now replace it with new components in better condition and with a smear of grease or 'copperslip' on the thread to prevent future seizing.

Few torque wrench settings were provided by BSA for the nuts and bolts used on the Unit Single cycle parts. References to those I have found are as follows:

Fork stanchion top nuts	50-55 ft.lbs
Bottom yoke pinch bolts	20-25 ft.lbs
Front wheel spindle clamp bolts	15 ft.lbs

Looking After Your Threads

Be prepared to obtain a small range of taps and dies to suit the thread sizes commonly used on your bike. The OIF models are easiest: UNF in ¼", $5/16$" and $3/8$" will be most useful along with UNC in ¼" and $5/16$". Other, larger sizes are also found, the wise approach to any screw thread problem is to buy the correct tap or die and deal with it properly rather than risk the creation of more damage.

Earlier models with Swan-Neck and Welded/Duplex frames require the above sizes in 26 TPI Cycle thread with various larger one-offs in 20TPI as the need arises, with the '69/'70 models additionally requiring the UNF threads eg n/s foot peg boss $7/16$" 20 TPI L/H, front wheel screw-in spindle $9/16$" 20 TPI L/H, Brake pedal spindle $7/16$" 20 TPI (R/H).

17. ELECTRICS

Rewiring Your Unit Single

This chapter begins with help for those brave enough to tackle a full or partial rewire from scratch, rather than adopting the easy approach of replacing a tatty and suspect loom (also called the wiring harness) with a complete new replacement bought from your spares supplier. So, for those not scared by the invisible (electricity), arm yourselves with the following:

    Wire strippers/cutters/crimpers.

    Soldering iron, solder and flux (passive paste flux).

    Wire of the correct colours and Amp rating
        See the wiring diagram for the correct colours and try to avoid using any old wire/colours you have to hand as this will simply lead to confusion and frustration later. The colours used in original looms (made by Lucas in the case of Unit Singles) are not random but actually follow a Lucas code widely used in the automotive trade at the time wherein specific colours of wire always do the same job eg. Red is always for Earth connections. Cables should be 14 strands each of 0.3mm with a total of 1sq.mm rated at 8.75 amps minimum. With a 12v supply this is capable of carrying 105 watts. Similarly but infuriatingly, Wipac had their own different colour code for wires doing the same jobs, as found on most Bantams for example.

    The connectors required
        6mm ¼" female spades and shrouds (8mm for Zener diode connection if fitted) and male/female bullets for soldering rather than crimping.

    Ring lugs in 5, 6 and 8mm sizes.

    Loom tape, and electricians insulating tape,

    Sleeving and shrink wrap tube
        In a variety of small sizes. All of these being black in colour.

Purchasing all of the above in the quantities available, boxes of fifty etc is bound to cost more than a new replacement loom off the shelf, but does, of course, work out cheaper if you envisage making several looms over a period of time.

Making your own loom

If you have the remains of the old loom to copy as a starting point, stretch this out fully on a large board and pin it down in an approximate layout to the position it takes on the bike. Directly alongside it you can then draw a diagram of the routes taken by all the different colours of wire in the harness. Any missing wires will require the wiring diagram in the manual to be consulted. The correct colours of wire can then be pinned in place on the board as required after the old loom has been removed.

If you do not have a loom to copy the first thing to do is to consult the wiring diagram and tape the correct colours of wire in place on the bike itself so the lengths required can be found from the positions of the components being connected.

Another aid if starting from scratch is the illustration in the BSA spare parts book for your bike, this will be found to be an accurate representation of the original loom and will clearly show where the loom branches and what sort of connectors are used.

Any wiring being done by following only a wiring diagram must bear in mind that the red earth wires are not normally shown but must be included in the loom. As a general rule Unit Singles do not use the frame as the earth. Even if components such as the rectifier are bolted directly to the cycle parts, earth wires are usually found to be connected as well.

Earth connections

The general arrangement of earth wires is shown in *fig 17.1* regardless of the fact that some components may vary in position or not be present depending on the model of Unit Single.

Earlier models particularly have much the same earth wire arrangement but without the Zener diode. OIF models have most of these components inside the electric box, which has an earth wire connection from the box to the external components.

There are only a few parts of the electrical circuit which conduct electrically through the cycle parts; one such is the return connection from the rear light and OIF rear indicators) through the rear mudguard which is earthed at one of the forward mudguard mounting points.

Similarly another is the headlamp and associated lights which conduct through the headlamp shell to its earth connection through the female bullet connector riveted to the inside of the shell, or on the bulb holder and thence to the earth wire in the loom. Included in this is the earth connection for the speedo illumination bulb which earths via its fixing bracket to the headlamp shell or top yoke if mounted here. If the speedo bulb is mounted in a rubber cup or bezel, a return earth wire will be needed either from the speedo body to the steel mounting bracket (B25 etc '67 to '70) or via an earth wire connection on the bulb holder itself (OIF '71 onward) to the main loom. The speedo cable itself is not used to make the electrical earth connection.

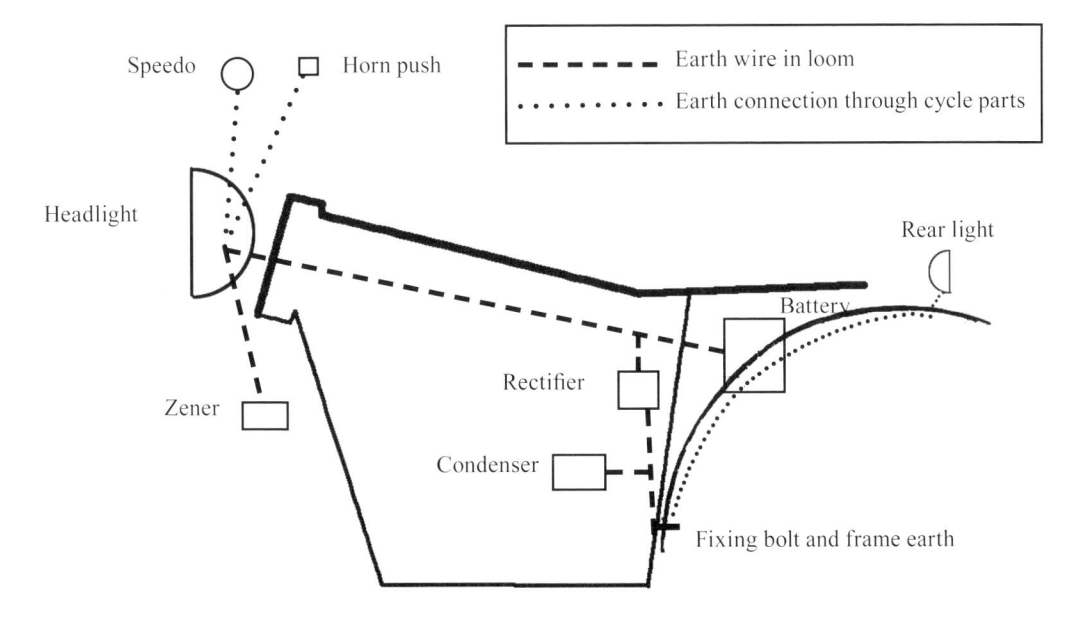

Fig 17.1. Earth connections - schematic diagram

> **OCTOBER 1971**
> **No. 36/71**
>
> # BSA
> ## SERVICE SHEET
> **B GROUP**
> **ELECTRICAL BOX**
>
> When conducting the pre-delivery checks and after servicing 1971/2 'B' Group machines be sure that all cables running to and from the electrical box are firmly secured keeping them clear of engine and exhaust. Check that all snap connectors are pressed fully home and that the metal insert is fully covered by the insulating sheath.
>
> **CHANGES 8948/9/50. Introduced August 1965**
> To improve the wiring harness and include the three charge rate, new electrical equipment is now being fitted.
> MODELS C15, SS80, B40, SS90.
> 19-876 switch and cable assembly (54937650) - for cowl type headlamp MCF575P (19-738) used on the above models except for U.S.A. is replaced by:-
> 19-892 switch and cable assembly (54937919)
> 19-580 headlamp (54052559B) with harness 19-876 (54937650) used on C15, SS80, SS90 U.S.A. models is replaced by:-
> 19-588 headlamp (54052559D) with harness
> 19-895 (54937920).
> 19-1670 battery (54028263) used on all models is replaced by:-
> 19-1772 (54028459).
> The battery and headlamps only are interchangeable, the harness is not.

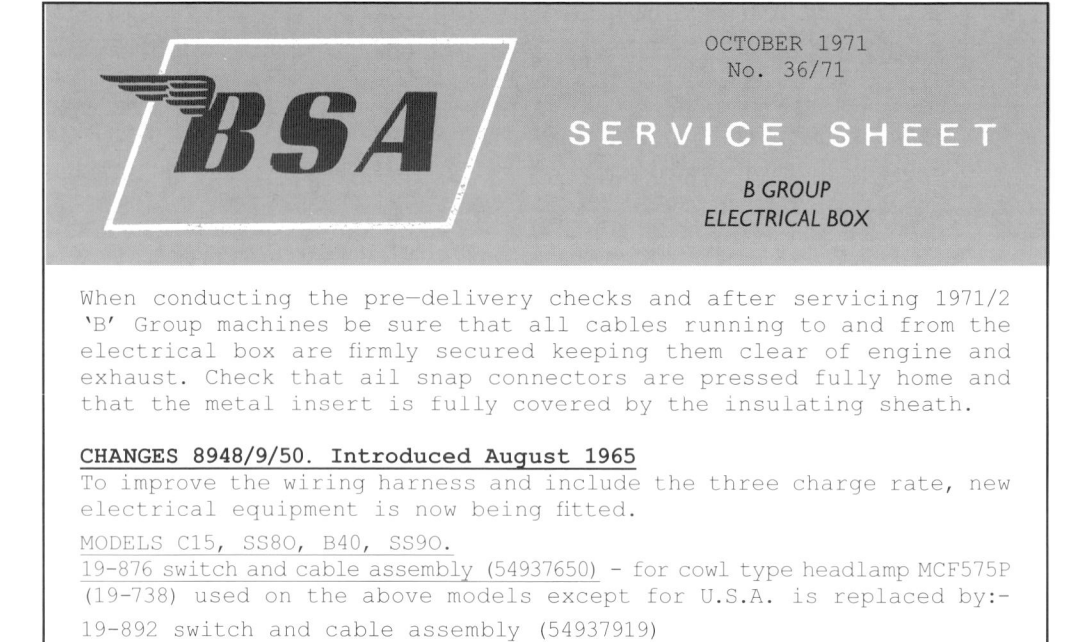

Fig 17.2. BSA Service Sheets advising on checking and securing electrical connectors and new equipment (see also fig 17.42)

A third earth connection not provided with a separate wire is the earth side of the ignition system which conducts from the engine through one of its several points of contact with the frame, which then connects to any of the earthed components bolted to it. It is worth bearing this fact in mind if modern paints such as powder coating are applied to the frame as these are excellent electrical insulators. As a minimum, remove this coating from the insides of the engine mounting lugs to restore metal to metal contact and thus electrical continuity or run a separate earth wire from the engine to the loom, from one of the rocker box studs for example, to guarantee that this is not the underlying reason behind a poor or absent spark.

The frame is therefore part of the earth system but it is not relied upon primarily to conduct the earth side of the circuit for most of the components bolted to it.

Returning to making a loom, after all the wires including the earth wires are taped in place on the board or frame (leave a couple of inches extra length at the wire ends to be on the safe side) they need to be gathered together wherever necessary with short pieces of electricians tape so the loom can be lifted intact without falling apart.

The loom tape (self amalgamating tape) which is not sticky but is able to bond to itself) can then be wound around and along the entire loom leaving the ends of the wires exposed for connectors to be fitted. Sealing the ends of the loom tape to prevent unravelling can be done with short lengths of heat shrink tubing. The extremities of the loom having fewer cables can easily be sleeved with suitably sized tubing. For example the single black and white lead to the points should be sleeved along its full length after exiting the end of the loom to cover its whole distance to the points. The inner ends of these sleeves should be sealed into the main loom by binding with the loom tape as you progress along the wires from which the branch separates.

The portion of the loom which wraps around the headstock between frame and headlamp is subject to abrasion as the forks move, so it should be protected by additional 1" diameter sleeving in this area and into the headlamp. The aim of all the binding and sleeving is to protect the cable from abrasion and to prevent water getting in - not that water in itself will damage the wiring, but rather to prevent it travelling along the wires to the attached components which may be damaged by water.

The ends of the wires can now be trimmed to the exact length to match the original loom or to reach the components they will connect to.

Connectors
The modern colour coded crimp-on items are questionable on two counts. Firstly they can be prone to not gripping securely onto the end of the wire resulting in poor electrical connection and secondly, their bright red or blue insulation is going to stick out like a sore thumb on your bike, yuk.

Do try to use the same type of connectors as originally used by BSA, which were bullets and spades (shrouded) with ring lugs for the ammeter and other nut and bolt connections. I would recommend soldering all terminals and lugs onto the wires, in addition to any crimping required. Successful soldering of these components to the loom wires relies on clean, uncorroded surfaces to be joined and more importantly, flux applied to the joint prior to heat.

Attaching the loom to the bike
When attaching the loom to the bike, experiment to find the best routing before finally clipping it in place. Modern black cable ties are fine for this and should help produce a finished, fitted loom which is unobtrusive, functional and discrete; you are not meant to notice it!

Within the headlamp the loom should be anchored under the clip on the inside of the shell. Do this after making sure there is enough slack in the loom around the headstock to permit unrestricted movement of the forks. On modern replacement headlamp shells this clip may be lacking. If necessary pop-rivet a 2" x ¾" strip of aluminium sheet in the bottom of the shell next to the loom hole - which must be fitted with a grommet. The piece of sheet metal is bent around the loom to grip and secure it.

At this stage (if not before) it would be wise to put some power through the loom to check everything works. Do this by connecting either a battery or battery charger to the battery leads on the loom and verify (ignition on) that all the lights and horn work and the sparking plug sparks when the bike is kicked over.

Electrical Fault Finding

Electrical faults are one of the principle areas of British Bike ownership which are likely to generate tantrums, frustration and high blood pressure.
If something doesn't work there are just three possible reasons:

> No power getting to it.
> No earth (return) connection.
> Defective component

These conditions are generally blamed on 'gremlins'; mythical beings who inhabit the world of electricity and whose aim in life is to undermine ones confidence in, and understanding of electrical workings. These creatures can however be banished by the application of logic and patience to electrical problems.

The first step is a visual check with careful examination by touch (to feel for loose connectors etc) of the easy to access parts of the electrics. Disconnecting and reconnecting a suspect component will often pin-point a bad contact, which you can then deal with. A loose spade connector for example can cause troublesome intermittent contact but can easily be cured by gently squeezing it in some pliers. All connections should be felt to grip together and require pulling force to separate them.

Testing

To undertake more thorough testing you will need a small multi-meter to fault-find and a power supply to put some electric into the wires - the battery on the bike connected as normal or a battery charger in its place will do. (But make sure the battery is charged up first!)

When faced with an apparently non-functioning component, first test that power (6v or 12v) is reaching it by identifying and removing –ve feed wire from the component. On the wiring diagram this will be the wire which comes from the battery, usually through a switch, not the red earth wire if one is fitted here. Set the meter to DC volts and connect its –ve lead to the end of the feed wire and its +ve lead to the positive power supply (battery or charger) connection. It should register the expected 6v or 12v when switched on. If it doesn't, trace the offending wire back, testing at every connection until the break in the supply is found by finding where the power does reach to. It is likely that this will lead you to a switch. If so, treat this in the same way by identifying the power supply wire and checking that this is supplying power to the switch. Obviously put right any bad connection identified in this way.

If power is found to be successfully reaching the non-working component, next test its earth connection. This will need the meter to be set to a resistance setting. Connect one of the meter leads to the end of the positive earth wire which would be connected to the battery +ve terminal, and the other to the earth connection for the component ie the red earth wire or the frame earth point where it is bolted on. If you are dealing with a switch this will be the feed wire to the component being switched on (eg the wire to the stop light from the brake light switch). The meter should respond just as if the two ends of its test leads are touched together; this shows there is 'continuity' which means a good connection. No response from the meter means no continuity which implies there is no earth connection along this route. You should now fault-find along the earth route to find the break as you did the feed route.

A good power feed and a good earth connection at a non-working component means the component itself is duff. Verify this by substitution and swap it for a known working component (usually a new one). Sorted! Now put the kettle on.

I know I have made this testing sound ridiculously simple and in reality it may be much more time consuming and confusing as each different component will require the brain in gear to work out exactly where to poke the probes of the test meter, but the underlying logical method is the key to success. Those who favour the alternative method of randomly poking, pushing or swapping-in alternative components may of course get lucky and solve the problem. On the other hand this may not work, the price being extra frustration and wasted time.

Of the electrical components on the bike, the rectifier, ignition coil and Zener diode (if fitted), are sophisticated enough to have their own foibles when upset.

Rectifier testing
Both the original 'plate' type and the modern replacement encapsulated type can be tested as per BSA's own instructions. This requires a test meter set to resistance and a methodical approach. Connect the probes to one of the two AC terminals (from the alternator) and one DC terminal (+ve or –ve). Swapping the probes over on these two terminals should show that it only conducts one way. Repeat this for both pairs of AC and DC terminals (8 permutations are possible). In all cases, any suspect readings of conduction where it shouldn't or no conduction when it should simply means fit a new replacement.

Ignition coil testing
Between the low tension +ve and –ve terminals there should be electrical continuity and for 12v coils a resistance of 3.3 - 3.8 ohms, 6v in the region of 1.7 - 1.9 ohms. There should also be NO continuity between both of the low tension terminals and the HT lead socket. There should be no connection between any of these terminals and the metal casing.

An ignition coil which runs hot in use is not normal and should be replaced. Have a look to see that the casing hasn't been pinched and distorted by the mounting clamp as this may have damaged the internals even if it still works, for the time being. A spark plug with too wide a gap can cause the coil to work too hard and become hot.

Zener Diode (12v models only) testing
The Zener diode cannot be fully tested for correct operation at home without some high spec. testing equipment which most owners are unlikely to possess. Other than by direct replacement, there is still some checking that can be done with a meter. In both directions with the usual pocket multi-meter no continuity should be found. This simple check will show if the Zener is displaying the most common manner in which they go wrong: conducting to earth when it shouldn't. If working properly it should start conducting when the voltage in the bikes electrical system reaches 13v. Checking for this and that the Diode hasn't ceased to conduct at all (its other favourite way of going u/s) requires the aforementioned sophisticated test equipment.

Of these two possible Zener problems the former shows itself on the bike as a repeatedly flat battery and difficult starting due to lack of sparks. Basically it is providing a short to earth which can be temporarily solved by disconnecting the white/brown wire from the Zener, then running with all the lights on to get you home. The latter malady of not leaking to earth above 13v shows itself by blown bulbs, a boiled battery and a misfiring engine. Putting all the lights on may effect a temporary get-you-home improvement.

Problems with the Zener can often be avoided by correct fitting in the first place. Most important is that it must be mounted on a heat sink with something in the region of 70 square inches of total surface area to dissipate the heat which is generated as the diode allows current to leak to earth as per the original BSA or Triumph designs (*fig 17.3*). Next, a clean,

Fig 17.3. Left, Triumph Zener diode and heatsink and on the right, the more usual BSA triangular heatsink. Both types are used from '67 -'70 and are mounted on the bottom yoke (except B40 Military Mk1 which places it under the petrol tank

flat area of contact to permit heat conduction between the base of the Zener and the heat sink is vital otherwise it will fry itself.

Lastly the fixing nut must not be over tightened as this risks shearing off the fixing stud which is made of brass. In response to the hamfisted owner, BSA repeatedly revised downwards the specified torque figure for this nut ending up with only 2 ft/lb's which is not much more than finger tight, or just enough to prevent the Zener rotating in use.

Capacitors testing
The points capacitor (condenser), and the 2MC ignition capacitor, if fitted on later models in lieu of the battery, can both be checked for correct operation with a multi-meter. Basically a capacitor acts as a rechargeable battery and will soak up electricity until full. They will then release this stored electricity as required. This happens many times per second at normal engine speeds in the ignition capacitor.

The test firstly requires discharge of the capacitor by briefly connecting its negative terminal (on the end of the points condenser, small spade on the 2MC) to its positive terminal (the metal case of the points condenser) with a spare bit of wire. Connecting the test meter (set to a resistance setting) across these terminals should see the reading indicate conductivity momentarily and then reduce as resistance increases due to the power from the meter charging the capacitor momentarily. Further testing requires the capacitor to firstly be discharged, as described, each time.

The original 2MC capacitor is nowadays hard to find as a genuine Lucas new spare, the capacitor usually supplied instead is a general purpose electronic component. This means that it is easily and cheaply obtained from electronics suppliers as a 22000uf electrolytic capacitor rated at 16 watts. Values higher than these can also be used but will be more expensive. These capacitors will require wires to be soldered onto their terminal pins to permit connection to the loom; the –ve pin being indicated by the row of '-' symbols marked along the side of the capacitor adjacent to it. The physical size of the capacitor (they vary) may well be smaller than the original 2MC so a mounting spring may need to be fashioned from a wire coat hanger or similar.

Electrics 289

Main Electrical Components

The electrical components fitted to the Unit Single are shown in Fig 17.4 -17.6. In order to aid identification the BSA part numbers are also shown.

Ammeters

1 2 3

1 B25, B44, B40 Military '68 -'70. Display -12 +12
2 C15, B40 road models all years. Display - +
3 B25, B44, B40 military '67. Display -8 +8

36403
36421

36084

36296

Rectifiers

Rectifier '58 -'64

Zener diode
All 12v models

Ignition

Standard coil 6v and 12v

47111

49345

Energy transfer coil

Points condenser '68 -'72 for 6CA points

45152
45110 (12v)

45149
45150

54441582

Horns

C15, B40 road models '58 -'62

C15 competition '59 -'62

All 12v models '67 -'72 (B25, B44, B40 Mil, B50)

C15, B40 Road models '63 - '67

C15, B40 competition models, '63 -'65

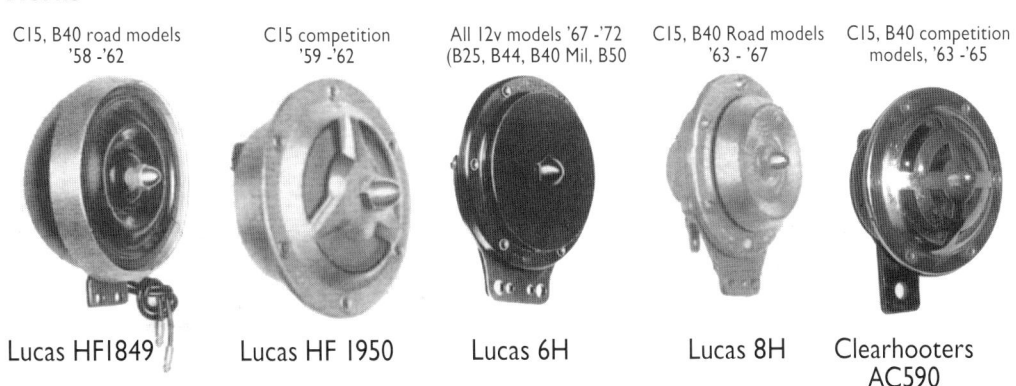

Lucas HF1849

Lucas HF 1950

Lucas 6H

Lucas 8H

Clearhooters AC590

Fig 17.4. Ammeters, rectifiers, ignition components and horns

Switches

Horn Push
C15, B40 comp, B44VS, TR25w
'59 - '68

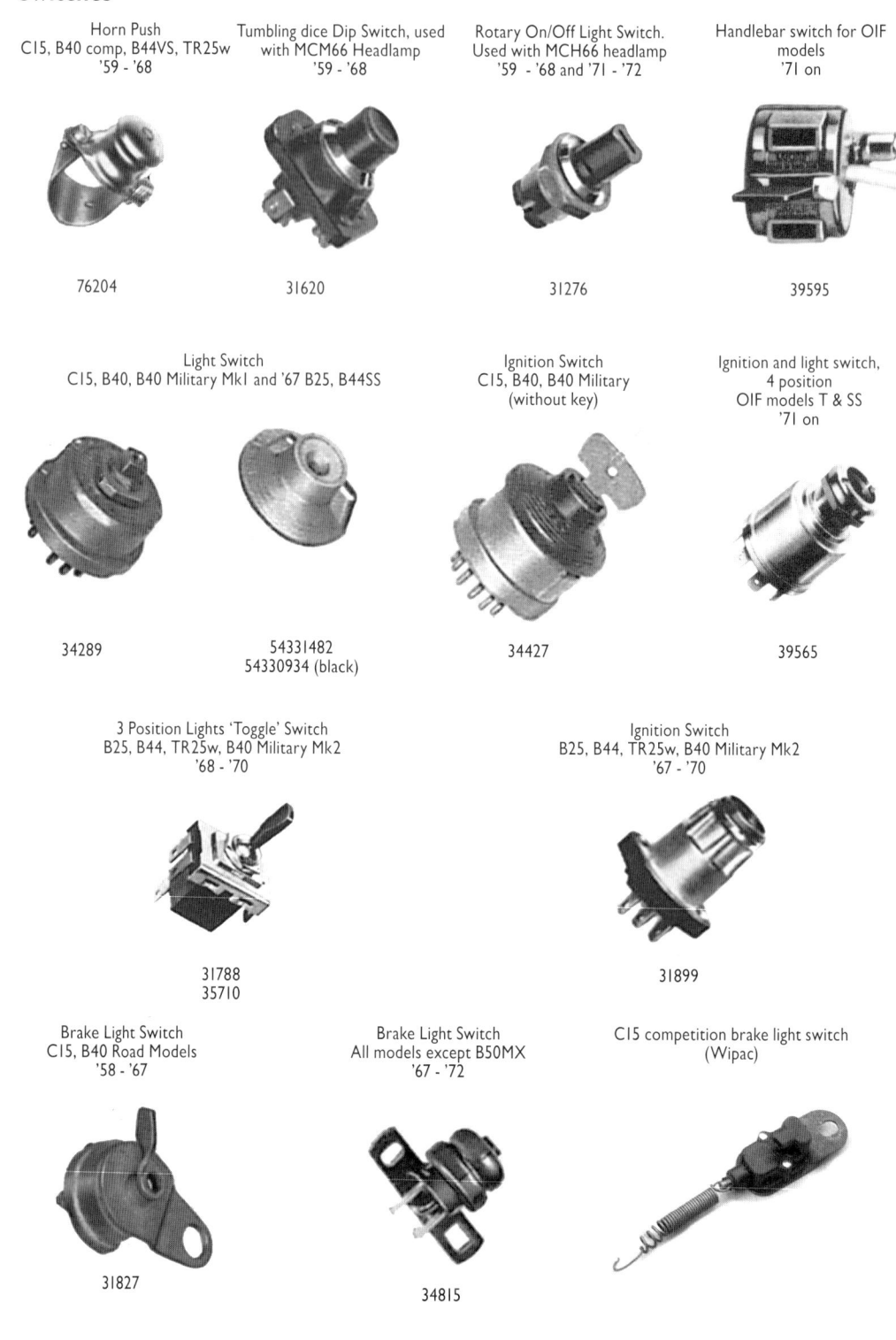

76204

Tumbling dice Dip Switch, used
with MCM66 Headlamp
'59 - '68

31620

Rotary On/Off Light Switch.
Used with MCH66 headlamp
'59 - '68 and '71 - '72

31276

Handlebar switch for OIF
models
'71 on

39595

Light Switch
C15, B40, B40 Military Mk1 and '67 B25, B44SS

34289

54331482
54330934 (black)

Ignition Switch
C15, B40, B40 Military
(without key)

34427

Ignition and light switch,
4 position
OIF models T & SS
'71 on

39565

3 Position Lights 'Toggle' Switch
B25, B44, TR25w, B40 Military Mk2
'68 - '70

31788
35710

Ignition Switch
B25, B44, TR25w, B40 Military Mk2
'67 - '70

31899

Brake Light Switch
C15, B40 Road Models
'58 - '67

31827

Brake Light Switch
All models except B50MX
'67 - '72

34815

C15 competition brake light switch
(Wipac)

Fig 17.5. Switches

Electrics

Headlights

C15, B40 road models
6" headlamp with backing ring
'58 - '67

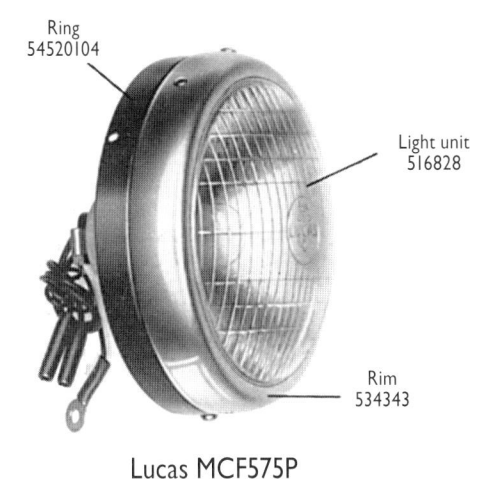

Ring 54520104
Light unit 516828
Rim 534343

Lucas MCF575P

C15, B40 competition, B44VS, TR25, OIF B25 and B50
6" headlamp. Switch configuration specific to model
All years

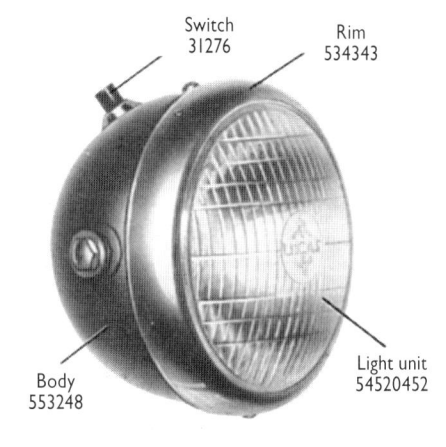

Switch 31276
Rim 534343
Body 553248
Light unit 54520452

Lucas MCH66

B25, B44 Road models
7" headlamp
'67

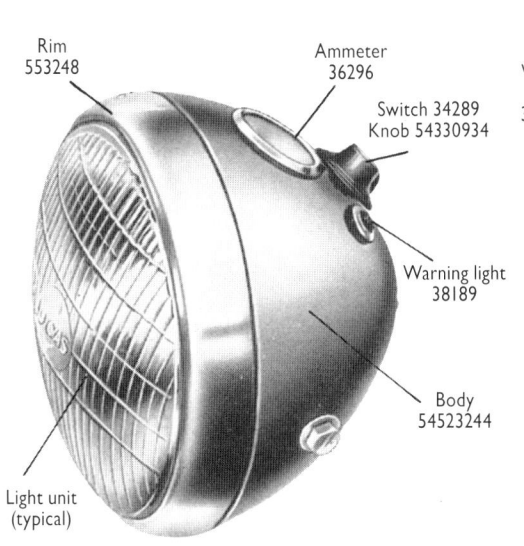

Rim 553248
Ammeter 36296
Switch 34289 Knob 54330934
Warning light 38189
Body 54523244
Light unit (typical)

Lucas SS700P

B25, B44 Road models
7" headlamp
'68 - '70

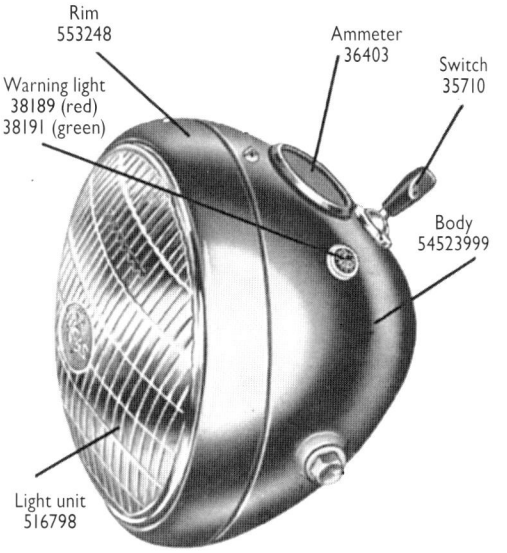

Rim 553248
Warning light 38189 (red) 38191 (green)
Ammeter 36403
Switch 35710
Body 54523999
Light unit 516798

Lucas SS700P

Fig 17.6. Headlight assemblies

B40 Military MkI
'67-'70

- Light switch 34289
- Ammeter 36296
- Ignition switch 34427
- Rim 553248
- Light unit 516798

Lucas MCH61

C15 and B40 Sportsman Models
'66 - '67

- Switch 34289
- Knob 54330934
- Body 54523202
- Ammeter 36084
- Rim 534343

Lucas MCH56

OIF Unit Singles
'71 -'72

- Switch 31356
- Shield 54525212
- Rim 434343
- Light unit 54525272

Lucas MCH66

Indicator fitted to OIF models
'71 -'72

- Stanchion 54581641
- Shell, bulbholder 554548
- Lens assembly 54581638

Lucas Model 874

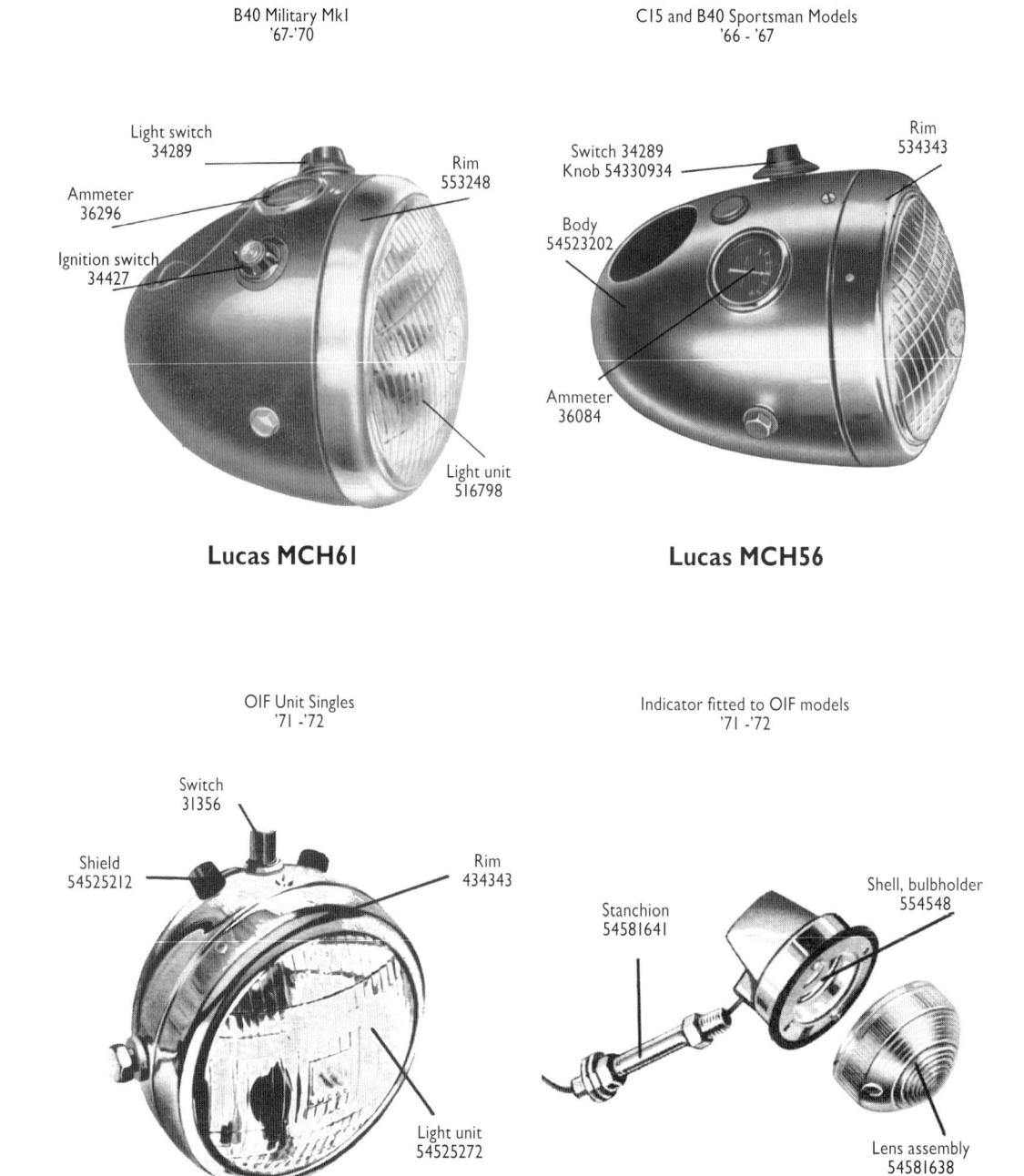

Fig 17.6 (cont.). Headlight assemblies and indicator

Electric box

The OIF electric box as found on SS and T models is shown in *figs 17.7* and *17.8*. Here is where the ignition coil and switch, Zener diode, 2MC capacitor, points condenser and flasher unit all live. This example is post April '71 when this type of top mounting for the box was introduced. Despite what the parts books may say, the rectangular reflector changed to circular for the first B50 models then reverted to rectangular with no hard-and-fast rule being applied to the end of production.

Fig 17.7. Electric box, post April '71 for SS and T models

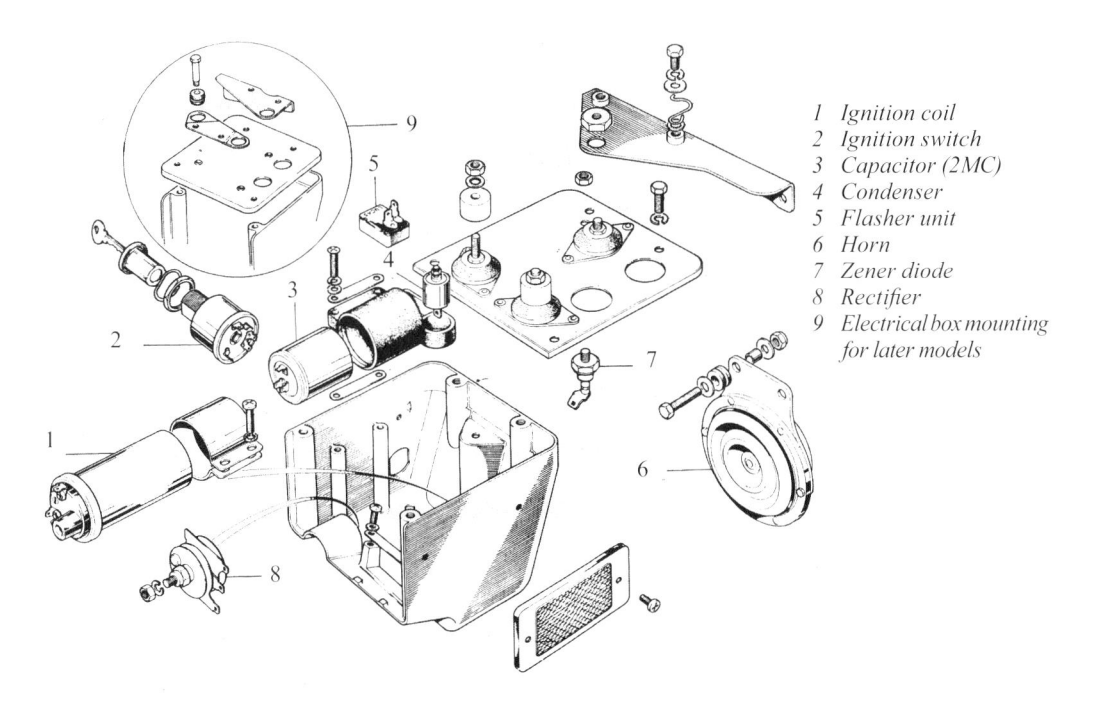

1 Ignition coil
2 Ignition switch
3 Capacitor (2MC)
4 Condenser
5 Flasher unit
6 Horn
7 Zener diode
8 Rectifier
9 Electrical box mounting for later models

Fig 17.8. Electrical box internal components. The inset (9) shows the later mounting method

Rectifier

Whilst the job it does has not changed over the years – converting AC electric to DC – the performance and design of this item has undergone improvements. Yes, you can probably locate an old original selenium plate rectifier as fitted to the first C15 models if you try, but don't put your trust in one to still work reliably today. If you desire one of these for reasons of cosmetic originality, fine; just connect in the modern replacement somewhere out of sight and have dummy wires going to the original.

The modern equivalent – an encapsulated bridge rectifier, containing four diodes and providing full-wave rectification as per the original, is also much cheaper today than an original. This item is easily sourced through the BSA parts suppliers but can be found even cheaper at the usual electronic components suppliers as found on most retail parks. What you need is one rated at 8 Amps, 200 Volts and which is preferably in a metal case with a central mounting hole. These are sometimes described as 'solid state' rectifiers to differentiate them from the original type; they are, but so were the originals, solid state simply means no moving parts.

The original plate rectifier usually included a captive bolt for its attachment to the bike. On this bolt there should also be an earth wire connection from the wiring harness, usually by ring-lug, so as to earth both the rectifier and frame at this point. Fitting the modern encapsulated type will require an additional earth wire connection from the +ve spade terminal to the wiring harness earth lug as its metal case is not the earth connection.

The rectifier case should also be marked for the –ve lug and with a wiggly line symbol for the two AC connections from the alternator which are usually diagonally opposite each other.

C15 and B40 road models
These mount their rectifier under the cross-brace of the sub-frame under the seat in one of the two holes provided for the energy transfer ignition coil if that system is used instead. The third hole in this channel-shaped bar is where the horn usually hangs from on these models.

B25 and B44 models '67 to '70
The rectifier is mounted on the back of the triangular tool box under the n/s side panel where a ¼" hole is provided near the top. The B40 Military Mk1 mounts the rectifier on the near side of the rear mudguard, by the top, rear corner of the airbox.

OIF models
OIF models mount their rectifier inside the electric box under the tank excepting MX models which, if not fitted with Energy Transfer electrics, mount theirs on a plate fitted to the frame under the seat.

Horn
As with the rectifier an original horn *(figs 17.9-10)* which is still in working condition may now be something of a rarity. Substituting a modern replacement, which doesn't look the same, for the non-working original is the easy solution.

However, despair not; unless there is actual physical damage which renders the horn u/s it may simply be in need of having its points cleaned or adjusted. If your horn has any form of adjustment screw on the back, unscrew it anti-clockwise until it becomes loose then screw it back in with the power connected. If you are lucky the horn may start making a noise at some point and then simply require the screw to be adjusted until maximum noise is obtained. If your horn has a large centre screw on the back avoid disturbing this until you have the horn making some noise, you can then adjust the centre screw to affect the note and noise to some extent; but it should be left where the maker put it unless you know it has been disturbed.

If however, your horn remains as dead as the proverbial Dodo, you will need to dismantle it to clean the points; this is easily done by removing the six screws or rivets (drill the latter out) around the rim. Cleaning the points with emery paper or similar should suffice to restore electrical continuity, but before reassembling, have a look for any other signs which would

Electrics *295*

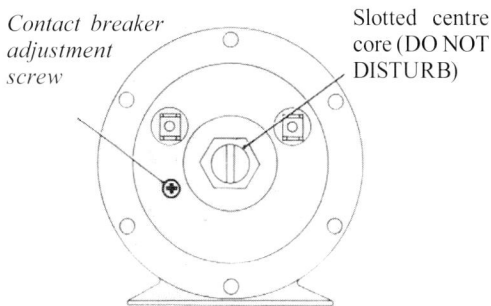

Fig 17.9 Lucas 6H horn in halves

Fig 17.10 Adjustment screw on 9H horn (this screw is similarly positioned on the 6H and 8H models).

render the horn terminally dead, such as burning or broken wires. Reassembly is easiest to do with pop-rivets or small screws and nuts, perhaps just fit a couple of these to start with and then test the horn to see that it works before finishing the job – if it doesn't and you want another look inside, you won't have wasted so much time! The following horns were fitted to the Unit Singles.

Model	**Year**	**Horn**
C15, B40 road models	up to '62	Lucas HF1849
C15 and B40 road models	'63 on	Lucas 8H
C15 Comp. models	up to '62	Lucas HF1950
C15, B40 Comp. models	'63 to '65	Clearhooters AC590
B44VE, VS	'66	Bulb horn (how quaint!).
B44VS	'67	Clearhooters AC590
B44	'68 on	Lucas 6H
B25, B40 mil, B50	all years	Lucas 6H

Note C15, B44 and B50MX/Scrambles models do not fit a horn

All of the above can be seen in *fig. 17.4* but realistically, if your bike is not being shown in concours events, and you aren't fixated on originality, then it may be easiest to buy a cheap modern replacement.

Fig 17.11. C15 roadster and competition horns up to '62

BSA SERVICE SHEET

Adjustment of Model HF1849.

Service experience with this horn shows that a small amount of adjustment may be needed at infrequent intervals to ensure that the horn continues to give its best performance.

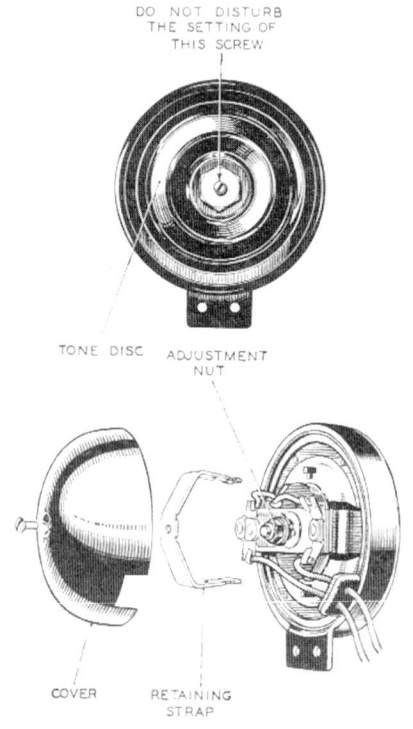

Fig. 25. Model HF1849 Horn with Rear Cover removed for Contact Breaker adjustment.

To make this adjustment, first remove the cover and retaining strap from the rear of the horn. Then, with the horn operating and using a 2BA spanner, turn the adjustment nut slowly in an anti-clockwise direction until the best performance is obtained. Usually, only a very small amount of movement will be necessary.

Important : The slotted screw in the centre of the tone disc on the front of the horn is accurately set during manufacture, and is secured in position by a locknut. This setting must not be disturbed.

Fig 17.12. The joys of British bike ownership: along with all the other maintenance jobs you are also expected to adjust your C15 horn to maintain peak performance, the term 'fit and forget' being not yet invented.

Horn position

C15 and B40 road models
Horn mounted below the cross-bar of the sub-frame under the seat.

Competition models to '62 with the Swan-Neck frame
Mount the horn facing forward on the central tinware between the oil tank and n/s side panel. From 1963 (Welded/Duplex frame) onward the replacement horn has a small bracket on the back by which it stands upward from the $^5/_{16}$" hole in the o/s rear engine plate.

'67 B25 and B44 models and the B40 military Mk2
The 12v Lucas 6H horn commonly used from '67 onward was something of a vagrant as it never stayed put in one place for long but moved around the area in front of the engine. This was probably due to the usual vibration problem causing it to drop off, and also it tended to block access to the exhaust tappet for adjustment. '67 models have the horn hanging via a small triangular plate from the hole in the bottom of the o/s headstock gusset plate.

Fig. 17.13. Left, the usual position for the horn for '68 to '70 mounted from the head steady tube. Not much room to spare around the horn on the B44SS, and right, the '67 - '68 horn mounting position

Although parts books show additional positions for '68 to '70 B25/B44 models, I have only found two alternatives in the metal where the horn was mounted from a tab added to the head-steady tube; either centrally positioned or close to the front end.

B40 Military Mk1
The horn is mounted on a triangular bracket upward from the n/s of the front engine mount, or, if crash bars are fitted, from the bracket provided on the top of the n/s bar.

OIF models
These continue the homeless theme for the horn. Despite the two mounting holes of the integral horn bracket now carrying rubber bushes to help counter vibration, the horn moved from the bottom of the electric box, to the n/s front electric box bracket, to the o/s front electric box bracket. Take your pick; regardless of model, I don't think anyone is in a position to argue that where you put it is categorically wrong.

Fig 17.14. OIF horn mounting on the electric box bracket nearside, earlier production models mount the horn on the offside

The OIF horn mounting is shown on the n/s extended front electric box bracket (*fig 17.14*). This is the final type of electric box mounting dating from April '71 onward.

Previous to this the horn was fitted on the o/s with the isolastic rubber bush method of electric box mounting. Pre-production models show the horn bolted directly to the lower edge of the electric box - guaranteed to fall off.

AC horns

The electric horn used on competition models with energy transfer electrics is AC powered, meaning that it is fed directly from the alternator. As a result, the noise it produces will get louder and higher in pitch as engine revs and alternator output increase. Conversely, at tick-over speeds it will sound like a bee in a jam-jar whose buzz is drowned by engine noise. This uselessness explains the fitment of a bulb horn instead on the '66 and '67 Victor Special models.

Capacitor (2MC)

Fig 17.15 shows the frame bracket provided for the 2MC capacitor on '68 to '70 B44VS and TR25w machines on which this component was standard fitment. B25 and B44SS models gained this feature for '70. Fitting this capacitor (or a cheaper modern equivalent) as a replacement for the battery to any 12v Unit Single is a worthwhile expedient. If the rest of the electrics are in good order – particularly the alternator output – this set-up should produce good lights and reliable starting. This has the advantage of side stepping the costs and problems associated with battery maintenance and condition on machines which these days may be used infrequently.

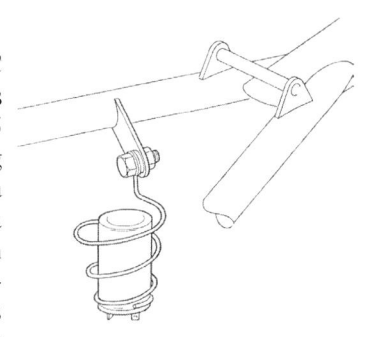

Fig 17.15. The frame bracket for the 2MC capacitor '69 -'70, B25/B44/TR25w

Indicators

Should you wish to fit indicators to a pre '71 machine the wiring diagram in *fig. 17.16* should be followed. Some '70 machines, B44VS for example had wires for fitment of indicators included in the main loom. The indicator is illustrated in *fig 17.6 (p292)*.

The Lucas indicators fitted as standard to the '71 onward OIF models are generally up to the job once the limitations and fragility of the chrome finish plastic body is taken into consideration. This is locked into position on the hollow indicator stem by a nut which alone is often inadequate to prevent the indicator head rotating in use. Loctite is a recommended cure for this. The other shortcomings relating to these plastic components are stripped threads and cracking, which can respond to gluing but replacement may be a better solution.

On the OIF models the indicator stem length is:

Indicator	Year	Length
Rear	All	$4^{1}/_{4}$" plain portion, $6^{1}/_{4}$" overall
Front	'71	$1^{1}/_{2}$" plain portion, $3^{1}/_{2}$" overall
	'72	increased by $^{1}/_{2}$" inside the headlamp shell to accommodate the stiffening strip and fixing nut.

Other lengths were produced for other contemporary BSA and Triumph models.

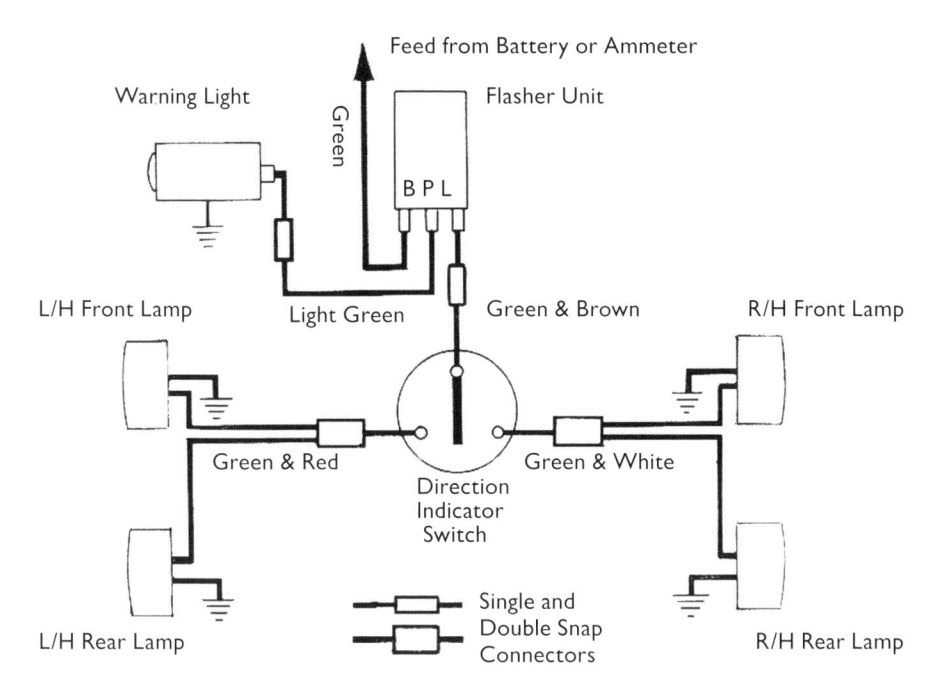

Fig. 17.16. Wiring diagram for the flasher unit for fitting indicators to pre-'71 models

Headlamp Shells

Table 17.1 shows the types of headlamp shells used on the Unit Singles. Illustrations of these shells is shown in *fig 17.6*.

Table 17.1 Headlamp shell identification

Shell	Model	Year	
BSA part	C15/B40 Star	'58 - '67	headlamp mounted on the forks nacelle.
No. 41-4061	SS80/90	to '65	headlamp mounted on the forks nacelle.
MCH66*	C15T	all years	
	C15 Starfire (USA)	all years	
	B40 Enduro Star	all years	
	B44VE/VS	all years	
	TR25w	all years	
	B25/B50 OIF, T & SS	all years	
MCH56	C15 Sportsman	'66 - '67	
MCH61	B40 military MK1	'67 - '70	
700P	B25/B44VS/SS	'67 - '70	

* The MCH66 is found with six different formats of switches and warning lights for unit single applications, dependant on year/model. See *figs 17.19* to *17.23*

Two sizes of headlamp light unit were fitted as standard, 6" (actually closer to 5¾") fitted to everything but the '67 to '70 road models which instead have a 7" unit. All carry a British Pre-Focus headlamp bulb with main and dip beam filaments of either 6 or 12 volt depending on the model. All carry a pilot bulb except the competition/off-road models prior to '68.

C15 and B40
C15 and B40 Star and early SS models for all years used an open backed headlamp shell which bolts directly to the front of the fork trouser assembly; the shell was identical for both

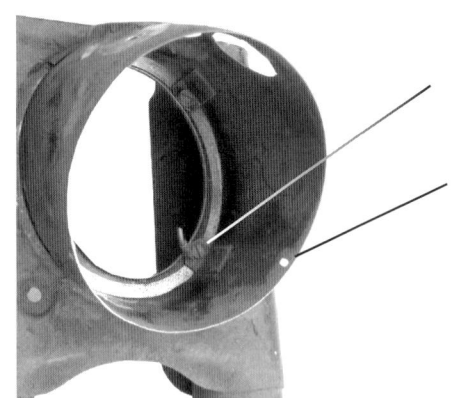

Fig 17.17. C15/B40 headlamp shell fixing detail; 2BA screws at rear connect to the trouser assembly (one of which carries the earth wire connection).

Also visible is one of the two 4BA slotted holes at the leading edge to provide an adjustable connection to the headlamp backing ring.

models *(fig 17.17)*. This is the same basic design as used across the BSA range in the early '60's, on Bantam, unit and pre-unit twin models with detail differences for each. However, the twin cylinder models are 7" diameter rather than the Unit Single 6".

The shell for the C15 and B40 models features an ammeter hole on the left and lighting switch (small 'D' shaped hole) on the right with central 60mm speedo hole. The C15/B40 shell can be produced from a 'two switch' Bantam shell by opening out the left hand switch position to accept the ammeter.

Sandwiched between the shell and the trouser assembly is the chrome backing plate which provides a chrome bezel along the join; again this is standard BSA practice with this design of headlamp mounting. No doubt as a cost cutting exercise, the very last '67 C15 Star 'G' models lost the chrome plate and instead fitted a silvered plastic edge protection strip to the rear edge of the shell.

The front edge of the shell carries the painted headlamp backing ring to which the chrome lamp rim fits, and is mounted on the shell by 4BA nuts and bolts. The holes for these near the front edge of the shell are slotted to permit some adjustment to the direction of the headlamp beam. One of the four 2BA nuts and bolts which mount the shell at the rear to the trouser assembly must carry an earth connection wire to the wiring loom to ensure that everything electrical forward of the headstock functions correctly.

MCH 56 headlamp: C15 and B40 Sportsman

'66 -'67 C15 Sportsman and '65 USA B40 Sportsman models carry a separate chromed headlamp shell, the Lucas MCH56 item as shown in *fig 17.18*. The layout of instrumentation on this is the same as for the basic Star models except the ammeter and switch positions are reversed. This headlamp shell is similar to but slightly deeper than the equivalent (and slightly cheaper) Wipac item fitted to contemporary Bantam sports models. '65 onward versions of the MCH56 shell carry a red main beam warming light between the switch and ammeter.

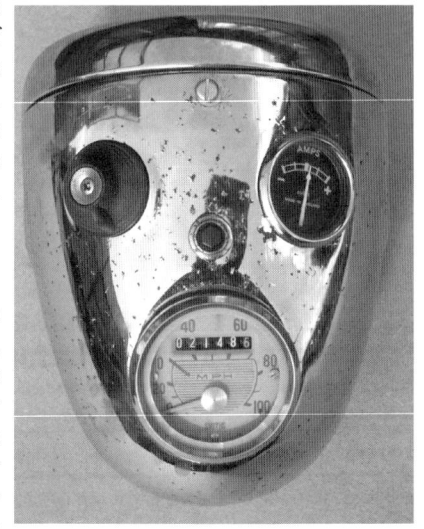

Fig 17.18. '66/'67 C15 Sportsman separate chrome headlamp (MCH56 shell) also previously fitted to the '65 USA B40 Sportsman

Electrics 301

MCH 66 headlamp: C15 Competition, B44VS, TR25w and OIF models

C15 competition models (except UK Scramblers), B40ES, B44VE/VS, TR25w and all OIF models all carry the 6", hemispherical MCH 66 shell. Detail differences of this shell in terms of switch holes and layout are extensive over the range of models and years for which it was used with additional variants for off road models of other marques, Triumph for example being most notable in this. When fitted to the TR25w and OIF models this shell was chrome plated, all those fitted to the BSA Unit Singles are painted black up to '70.

The illustrations below (*figs 17.19 - 17.23*) show five of the six variants of this shell as applied to Unit Single models. The parts books for these models prior to OIF give little or no information regarding layout details of the headlamp components and the books for the B44VS and TR25w, although better, are unclear and to some extent contradictory.

The correlation to bear in mind when considering these permutations of switches is that the fitment of a pilot bulb in the headlamp requires a three position lighting switch; 'off', 'on, pilot and rear' and 'on, headlamp and rear'. A simpler on/off lighting switch on the headlamp means no pilot light unless, as with OIF models, additional switches can be mounted elsewhere such as on the handlebar.

Fig 17.19. '59 to '64 C15 competition headlamp; on/off turn switch on right, tumbling-dice dip/main beam push switch on left. Used with handlebar mounted horn push button.

Fig 17.20. '65 to '67 C15 competition and '66 to '67 B44VS headlamp; now with main beam warning light.

Fig 17.21 (Below). '68 (and early '69 TR25wC and B44VSC), TR25w, B44VS same but painted black. Still used with single horn push button switch on the handlebar. The three position toggle switch on the right allows fitment of a pilot light. This version continued to be used on '69 models to 12/68 and was then superseded by the headlamp with central three-position toggle switch and main beam indicator on the left (not illustrated). This necessitated the use of a new wiring harness usually supplied with the headlamp, along with the Ducon handlebar switch (see fig 17.29) as indicated below in the Parts Service Bulletin.

```
         Service Sheet   G.54, 12/1968
            Change 11853 B44VS 1969
Old No.  New No.  Description
19-984   19-1192  Headlight with harness
19-1472  19-214   Horn push (Ducon)
```

Fig 17.22. '70 B44VS headlamp, as '69 but now with 2nd warning light. TR25w same but chrome plated. Used with the Ducon horn/dip switch.

Fig 17.23. OIF headlamp, all models, '71 onward excepting MX which lacked lights.

700P headlamp: B25, B44 road models

The 7" parabolic shell Lucas 700P (*fig 17..6*) was used in three versions on the B25 and B44 road models from '67 to '70. As usual, other versions exist, as were fitted to other marques and BSA models. This shell was equipped as follow:

1967	central ammeter, red main beam warning light to left, central rotary lighting switch (as C15) rear of the ammeter requiring a small 'D' shaped hole.
1968/69	as '67 except larger 'D' hole for toggle lighting switch.
1970	as '69 except green main beam warning light to left and red oil pressure warning light to right of ammeter. All have 5/16" BSCy threaded mounting holes.

The '67 rotary light switch is as previously used on C15 models and requires a small ½" diameter 'D' shaped hole in the shell. The ammeter for '67 only is an 8-0-8 item.

The following version for '68 and'69 is identical other than that the 'D' shaped lighting switch hole is enlarged to ⅝" to accept the three position toggle switch which replaced the rotary switch. The ammeter from '68 on became a 12-0-12 item. The '70 shell is as previously with the addition of a second warning light to the right of the ammeter. This was red for the oil pressure warning light, the main beam indicator now became green.

MCH 61 headlamp: B40 Military Mk1
The B40 Military Mk1 uses a 7" MCH61 shell *(fig 17.6)* (usually painted green) which is deeper to accommodate the speedo, central ammeter and rotary lighting and ignition switches on left and right. This shell with detail differences was used on the first A65 Rockets and also some Norton models.

B40 Military Mk2 and Roughrider
The B40 military Mk 2 and Roughrider models use the '68 – '69 version of the 700P shell with painted rather than chrome finish.

Headlamp shell repair
Any damage to the thin metal of the headlamp shell requires the application of straightforward but rather delicate sheet metal skills. Dents are easy to push out of a shell which has suffered impact and the most common problem, the captive mounting nuts coming loose, is easy enough to repair if the nut (or a replacement) is brazed or silver-soldered back on prior to re-plating or painting. Welding the nut on is less likely to result in a neat, tidy repair but perhaps you are happy to live with visible blobs of weld and holes burnt through the thin shell?

The OIF headlamp shell has larger, $^7/_{16}$" mounting holes as these also carry the front indicator stems. '72 models were originally fitted with a curved reinforcing bar from one nut to the other inside the shell to reduce the likelihood of the nuts detaching from the shell – it is worthwhile fitting this bar to '71 models.

If repair is beyond question, some good replica shells are available, but only for the more common variants. One of these can of course be the starting point for one of the less common versions if you are armed with drills and round files. If contemplating this first cover the delicate chrome of the new shell with a couple of layers of masking tape or similar before marking out the apertures required. Anything but the smallest holes should be made by chain-drilling with a 1/8" drill or similar and finished by filing to shape. Larger drills will distort the metal around the hole and risk flaking off of the chrome: as I said, 'delicate sheet metal skills' are required.

Inside most genuine Lucas headlamp shells will be found a strip of metal, riveted to the inside of the shell, for the purpose of anchoring the wiring harness. This strip of metal is simply bent around the thick end of the harness to accomplish this.

Do take the trouble to obtain correctly fitting rubber grommets for the wiring access holes in the underside of the shell; without these there is a risk of the sharp edge of these holes chafing the wiring in use leading to short circuits. Additionally the harness should carry a tough outer sleeve (black plastic) in this location and around the headstock for additional protection. *(see p285)*

Fitting the light unit to the rim shouldn't raise issues and it should be obvious to see which way around it goes as the two prongs inside the rim locate on the boss or lug provided on the light. This should result in any writing on the glass being the right way up and the beam pointing in the right direction when you switch it on. Securing the light to the rim should be done with at least three 'W' clips (five is good) equally spaced around the rim. These clips are also sometimes used for retaining the glass of Aluminium greenhouses, should you need an alternative supply.

If you are painting a headlamp shell avoid building up a thick layer which will stop the close fitting rim pushing onto the front edge of the shell. Powder coating for example is a thick enough layer to make this a distinct and frustrating possibility which can only be overcome by local removal of the finish.

Final connection of wiring to the headlight should include earth connections wherever provision is made for these; often on the main headlight bulb holder for example. Occasionally a headlamp shell will be found to have a female bullet connector riveted inside it, usually on shells which contain the speedo. Always make an earth connection to such a socket; no such connection means: no speedo illumination. Reliance on any cycle parts of the bike, in this case the headlamp shell and its mounting bolts to provide an earth connection, is to be avoided as it is tempting the gremlins to interfere with the normal workings of the electrics.

Pilot Light

Unit Singles have a headlamp pilot bulb on all machines except C15/B40 competition models and the B44VS prior to '68. The correlation between pilot bulb and switch gear means that a three position lighting switch is needed for a pilot bulb to be fitted (rotary, toggle or handlebar see Chapter 18 Instrumentation) to give 'off', 'pilot' and 'head'. The C15/B40 and B44 competition machines have only an on-off lighting switch.

Rear Light

The Lucas rear light should be either the 564 item or the 679 'tit' item *(fig 17.24)*. The former was used on all C15 and B40 models except '63 onward competition variants for the USA and UK B40 Military Mk 1 and Mk 2. These used the 'tit' as did all B25, B44 and B50 models. Both of these designs use a staggered pin, dual filament stop/tail bulb in either 6v or 12v. The copper braid earth wire needs to be intact - an often overlooked cause of the rear light not working.

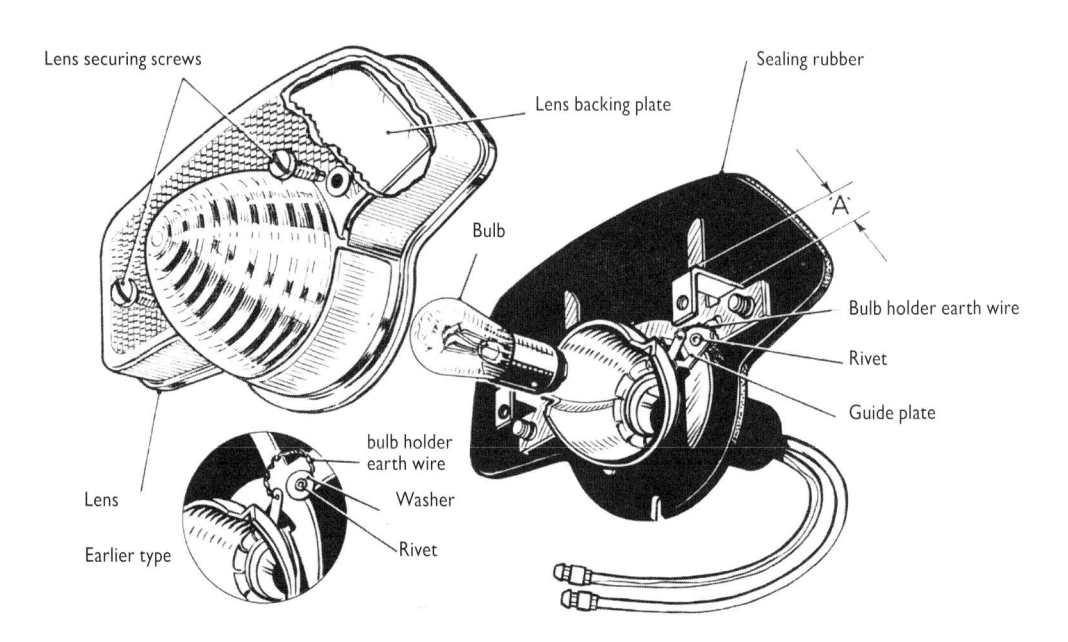

Fig 17.24 Rear light assembly Lucas 679

Ignition Switches

On C15 and B40 road models the ignition switch *(fig 17.25)* is fitted on the central tinware adjacent to the oil tank. This three position rotary switch has an 'off' centre position, 'ignition' rotate clockwise, and 'emergency' rotate anti-clockwise (these are marked on the rubber cap as 'emg - off - ign'.

From '62 this switch gained a centre slot for a rudimentary ignition key, the 'emg' position (flat battery) requiring the key to be pushed inward before turning from 'off'. This switch has an array of pins on its rear which requires the correct socket to connect it to the loom. From '62, this socket became a separate component and was no longer integral with the loom. Connection to the loom was now via bullet connectors on short wires from the socket.

Should you use the emergency ignition position to allow starting with a flat battery, you should continue with the ignition in the 'emg' setting until the engine begins to misfire. This indicates that the battery has received sufficient charge to allow the engine to run normally on the 'ign' setting. The B40 Military Mk1 uses the same rotary ignition switch (without the key) and is wired to give on-off-on positions.

OIF models
OIF models had their ignition switch fitted on the electric box on the nearside. This is a four position switch as shown in *fig 17.25*. Connections and key positions are shown in *fig 17.26*.

Competition models
C15, B40 and B44 off-road machines up to '67 and B50MX do not have an ignition switch and are therefore always 'on'. The engine is stopped by means of a small horn-push type switch mounted centrally on the handlebars.

Lighting Switches

C15, B40 road models all years, B40 Military Mk1 and '67 B25 and B44 excluding B44VS
This is the same design as the ignition switch *(fig 17.25)* with rotary switch positions of 'off', 'pilot/rear' and 'headlamp/rear' being obtained by turning clockwise once and again respectively.

Fig 17.25. Ignition switches. Top, C15, B40 road models from '62 with rudimentary key, prior to this and also for the B40 Military Mk1 the switch was similar but without the key. Middle, '67 -'70 B25, TR25w, B44 and B40 Military Mk2. Bottom, 4 position, '71 onward, for all road and trail models

LIGHTS ONLY
1-3

OFF
2-3

IGNITION ONLY
1-2

IGNITION AND LIGHT
1-2-3

Fig 17.26. Internal connections for the OIF model's ignition lighting switch relative to the four key positions

The rotary lighting and ignition switches are very similar in construction and appearance but can be distinguished by counting the pins on the rear, or corresponding socket holes. On

Fig 17.27. Left, 3 position toggle switch used for all B25, B44, and TR25w '68 -'70. The two position toggle switch on the righ may be found on '68 TR25w as a replacement for the rotary on-off switch

the ignition switch these are grouped as 6 and 4; on the lighting switch these are grouped as 7 and 3. Due to this the two types of switch are not interchangeable.

Horn and Dip Switch (Combined)

The Wipac Ducon switch *(fig 17.28 and 17.29)* was widely used on Unit Singles until the advent of the OIF models. The earlier type used on the C15 and B40 Star to '66 has its body made from chrome plated die-cast zinc. The second version used subsequently has this body moulded from black plastic. In either case a chrome plated cover forms most of the visible outer surface. Visually this is an elegant design, compactly mirroring the appearance of the twist grip on the right. The downside is its fragility, particularly the plastic version, and all are prone to the plastic dip lever snapping off if knocked. The internals of each are small, fiddly and difficult to work on after removing the chrome cover which is necessary to remove or connect the wires. Delving deeper into this switch, for example to access the horn push or dip/main beam switch knob, requires the circular Tufnol disc to be prised off of its fixing studs. Carry this out with the switch contained in a plastic tub or similar to catch the sundry small components which will make a bid for freedom. Refitting these parts and the Tufnol disc is best carried out by someone who has eight fingers on each hand.

Cover removal is done by first withdrawing the small slotted grub screw from the underside, which is also the means by which the switch is secured on the handlebar. The grub screw is pointed to bite into the bar and hopefully grip it to prevent the switch rotating. In practice it is difficult to tighten the screw with sufficient force to guarantee this, especially with the plastic

Fig 17.28. Ducon switch with cover removed; this is the later type with the black plastic body. Removal of the brown Tufnol disc allows access to the horn push and dip switch.

Fig 17.29 Ducon handlebar switch in position on the left hand bar.

Electrics

bodied type. The solution is to centre punch the underside of the handlebar to provide a location for the screw-point. If you have a slim enough punch then do this through the screw hole itself to avoid having to punch separately, and then having to locate the screw-point in the punch mark blind. This also makes it easier to get the punch mark in the right place.

C15 competition models, B40 Enduro Star, B44VE and VS to '68

When fitted with lights, these models house most of their switch gear on the MCH66 headlight shell. The lack of a pilot light in the headlamp means that head and rear lights are controlled by a simple rotary on-off switch on the left with a push button 'tumbling dice' dip switch on the right in *fig 17.30*. The handlebar therefore mounts a horn push-button on the left if the electric AC horn (used with energy transfer systems) is fitted. Some competition models replaced this by a more effective bulb horn (the AC horn sounds like a bee in a jam jar and can be difficult to hear above the exhaust note). On these competition models a push-button kill switch is normally mounted centrally on the handlebar, although this is often not shown in the BSA parts books.

Fig 17.30. Left, rotary on off switch and right, tumbling dice dip-switch fitted to the MCH66 headlight shell

B40 Military

the B40 military models were fitted with a more conventional combined horn/dip switch on the left handlebar, this was initially a cast aluminium 'Clearhooters' item *(fig. 17.31)*, subsequently replaced by a cheaper CEV plastic switch with chrome cover *(fig 9.10)*.

OIF handlebar switch

The OIF models have a handlebar switch, fitted on the left side of the bars, *(see fig 17.31)*. This controls headlight dipping on the central lever, headlamp flash on the upper push button, and horn on the lower push button, see below for wiring on both left and right switches.

OIF MODELS LEFT SWITCH

	Action	Cables
Horn	Push	W-PB
Headlamp flash	Push	W-UW
Dip	Lever Up	U-UR
Main	Lever Down	U-UW

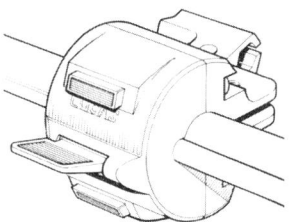

OIF MODELS RIGHT SWITCH

	Action	Cables
Indicators	lever left	LGN-GR
	Central off	
	Lever Right	LGN-GW
Starer	Push (not used)	W-WR
Kill	Push disconnects	W&WY

Fig 17.32. Handlebar switch for OIF models controlling headlight dip and flash (R/H side switch shown the L/H switch is the mirror image). Switch action and cable wiring are shown for both left and right switches.

Fig 17.31. The Clearhooters combined horn and dip switch fitted to the first B40 military models.

Stop Light Switches

C15 and B40 road models
C15 and B40 used the 'D' shaped Lucas item with an operating lever actuated by the peg on the brake pedal *(fig 17.33)*. The switch has an integral mounting bracket with $^7/_{16}$" hole for the nearside swinging arm bolt and a rubber boot covers the inner side with the bullet connectors to the loom. This is a robust and reliable design; adjustment of the switch by rotating it on the swinging arm bolt is easily affected. The same design of switch but with differing mounting plates and operating levers was fitted to a variety of contemporary BSA models - adaption is possible.

C15, B40 and B44 competition and off-road models
C15 competition models along with B40 and B44 off-roaders to '66 used the rectangular Wipac stop switch as found on Bantams with a spring and clamp connection to the brake rod to actuate it. If fitted, this switch is mounted on the swinging arm at the rear brake anchor strap bolt.

All models '67 on
These all use the Lucas button switch as standard which is a cheap and cheerful type. The plastic body will not withstand undue pressure from the brake pedal if incorrectly positioned *(see fig 17.35, 17.36)*, or from the 2BA mounting screws if these are over tightened. On used examples a common problem is loosening of the spade terminals in the plastic body. These also form the internal switch contacts and may need repositioning to restore correct operation.

'70 models (except B44VS) and OIF models (except MX) featured a stop light switch on the front brake cable *(fig 17.34)*. This is to some extent superfluous if normal rules of good riding are adhered to and both brakes are applied together to retard progress.

Additionally, the effect of this switch on the front brake is to give a spongy feel to the handlebar lever and render it harder to set up and achieve a nice feel to its action. The simple answer from the rider's point of view is to fit a cable without a switch and tape up the ends of the wires which connect to it.

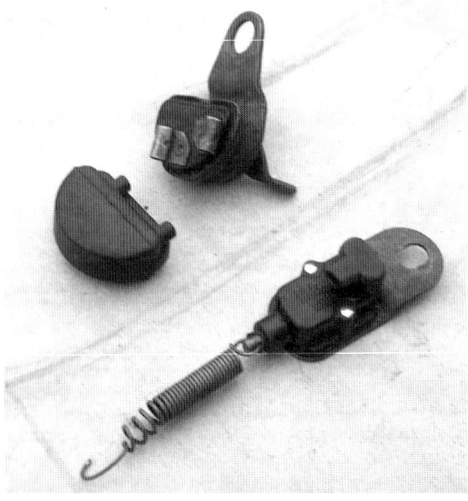

Fig 17.33. Top, C15 and B40 roadster Lucas brake light switch with rubber cover. Below, the Wipac item for competition models fitted with lights.

Fig. 17.34 Front brake cable with brake light switch, commonly found from '70 onward

Electrics

> November 1968
> No 189
>
> # BSA SERVICE SHEET
>
> Models B25, B44 and A75
> Rear Brake Stop Light Switch
>
> Stop Light switch No. 19-916 type 118 SA Lucas no. 34815
>
> Mechanical Adjustment
>
> If the 118 SA switch is out of alignment after the brake has been adjusted, there may be excessive pressure on the switch, which would damage the fixing base.
>
> To ensure the maximum service life for the switch, the following procedure should be adopted, after the rear brake has been adjusted.
>
> 1. Slacken the two fixing bolts of the stop lamp switch.
> 2. With the brake in the fully off position (brake lever against frame stop), insert a 1/32" (0.793 mm) spacer between the contacting brake mechanism and the switch plunger. Adjust switch so that the switch plunger is fully depressed (see sketch).
> 3. Lock the fixing bolts in this position.
> 4. Remove spacer (switch plunger will now extend under spring pressure to press against the contacting brake mechanism)
> 5. Ensure that the switch is operating correctly.

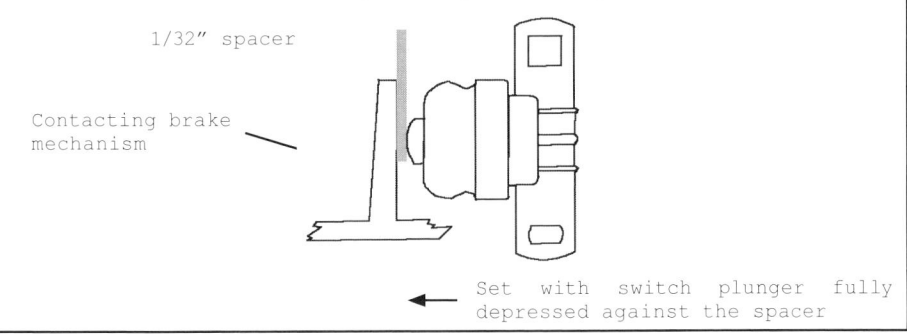

Fig 17.35. BSA information for all B25/B44/B50 and B40 Military '67 -'72 switch shown in fig 17.35

Below, Fig 17.36. OIF brake light switch arrangement.

Battery

The traditional lead/acid battery fitted to the Unit Single road models is in itself a robust and efficient item which, under original conditions of use and maintenance, could be expected to last at least a couple of UK winters. The issue these days is that usage as originally intended for Unit Singles is rarely the case; a battery which is neglected and possibly rarely called upon will die young.

Given that the limited leisure usage of these machines is probably unlikely to change, there are two alternatives to frequently buying a replacement battery:

Replace the battery with a capacitor

Install one of the battery chargers and status monitors commonly available today which remain hooked up to the battery during periods when the machine is laid-up.

The only other normal maintenance a battery will require is to keep the electrolyte up to the required level by topping up with distilled water if the level drops due to evaporation.

OIF models use a battery of the same physical size as that fitted to B25, B44 and B40 Military from '67 onward at $3^{1}/_{4}$" wide, $5^{1}/_{2}$" long and 5" high. The C15 and B40 roadster battery (6v) is $2^{1}/_{4}$" wide, $4^{1}/_{2}$" long and $5^{1}/_{2}$" high. Within these size limitations it is worth obtaining the battery with the highest available Amp Hour rating regardless of the rating originally specified by BSA. When installing a battery on OIF models be careful that the -ve lead does not contact battery carrier.

A battery which is known to be in good condition but which repeatedly loses its charge on the bike means that it is connected via the wiring harness to a defective component. The most likely suspects in this situation are the rectifier and the Zener diode (if fitted) which should be checked as per the fault-finding procedure explained earlier in this chapter. Leaving the ignition switched on will drain the battery if the engine stops with the points closed. This condition should produce an ignition coil which is warm to the touch as a tell-tale.

You can also buy sealed batteries which tend to stay charged up for longer and which are largely maintenance free, but are somewhat more expensive.

Battery box

This is not so much a box, more of a tray with a few brackets etc welded on, the exact design being dependant on year and model.

C15, B40 road models

These all used the same battery box for all years *(fig 17.37)*. This takes the form of a tray with one folded-up side which bolts to the brackets on the near-vertical frame tube behind the engine. To the battery tray is welded the stepped bracket which provides the lower front mounting point for the oil tank and n/s inner side panel. The battery box assembly is therefore an integral part of the collection of central tinware which these models use.

The battery is retained in the box by wire loops with a flip-over clip to tighten them *(fig 17.38)*. This wire is the same thickness as a common-or-garden wire coat hanger (should yours be missing) and the clip, which effects tightening of the wires by having its holes for these positioned to produce an 'over-centre' mechanism, is the same as on the Bantam D7 and onward. Under the battery should be found a rectangular rubber mat, $^{1}/_{16}$" thick.

Electrics 311

Fig 17.37. The convoluted bracketry of the C15 and B40 road models' battery tray for all years. As usual, here missing the wires and catch to retain the battery; these can be seen on the example shown in fig 13.3, p230 and below

C15 Competition, B44 pre'68

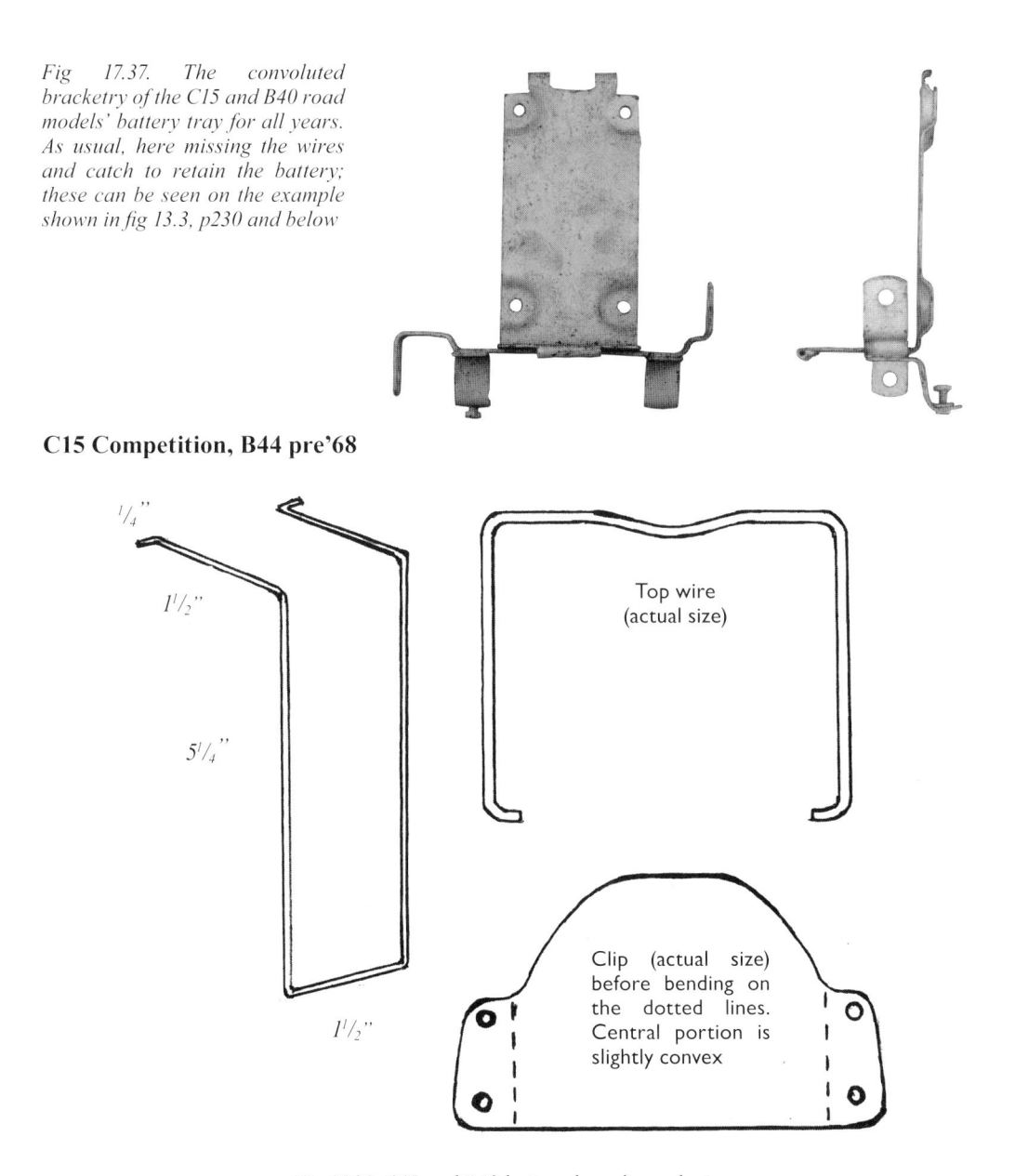

1/4"
1 1/2"
5 1/4"
1 1/2"

Top wire (actual size)

Clip (actual size) before bending on the dotted lines. Central portion is slightly convex

Fig 17.38. C15 and B40 battery box clip and wires

All C15 competition models omit the battery and lack any provision for one as they use AC electrics and Energy Transfer ignition. They, and the B44 models prior to '68 which subsequently carried the off-road baton, cannot easily be made to accept a battery – there is no physical space in which to put the normal 12v item - should you choose to rewire to the common and user-friendly 12v positive earth system. The optimum way forward in this situation is to convert to 12v and fit the 2MC (or modern equivalent) instead of the battery as this is small enough to be easily secreted away. Fitting this device should and will provide easy starting and running (with lights) without a battery if the Alternator, rectifier, Zener Diode and wiring in general are in top form. Any shortcomings in the rest of the electrics will adversely affect starting and necessitate the fitting of a battery to overcome them - should you not wish to find out where the weakness lies in your system. In this situation, it is a case of finding a suitable position, behind the engine or behind the air filter depending on the model, and making a bracket to accept the biggest battery which will fit the limited space available.

The Welded/Duplex competition framed models did not have need of a battery (ie 12v +ve earth electrics) or a place to put it, until the arrival of the C/B25, B44 road models and B40 Military in '67. The oil tank and the air filter were redesigned to make space for a battery on these road models.

B25, TR25w and B44 (excluding GP, VE, VS '66 -'67)
These models feature a battery tray *(fig 17.39)*, rubber mounted on three bolts which was used until the end of the '70 season with the advent of the OIF models. This tray gained an extra bracket on its front lower edge for '68 which has a ¼" hole in it for the attachment of the point's condenser. This was necessitated by the change from the 4CA points assembly – which has the condenser mounted on the point's plate – to the 6CA type which doesn't, the condenser has to be mounted remote from the points somewhere else on the bike and bunging a bracket for it on the front of the battery tray was probably as good a solution as any.

The B40 Military Mk.1 is alone in fitting two condensers ('belt and braces'), one on the 4CA points plate and a second, of the type used with the 6CA points but mounted by the ignition coil on the frame top tube.

Bracket for Dzus fastener

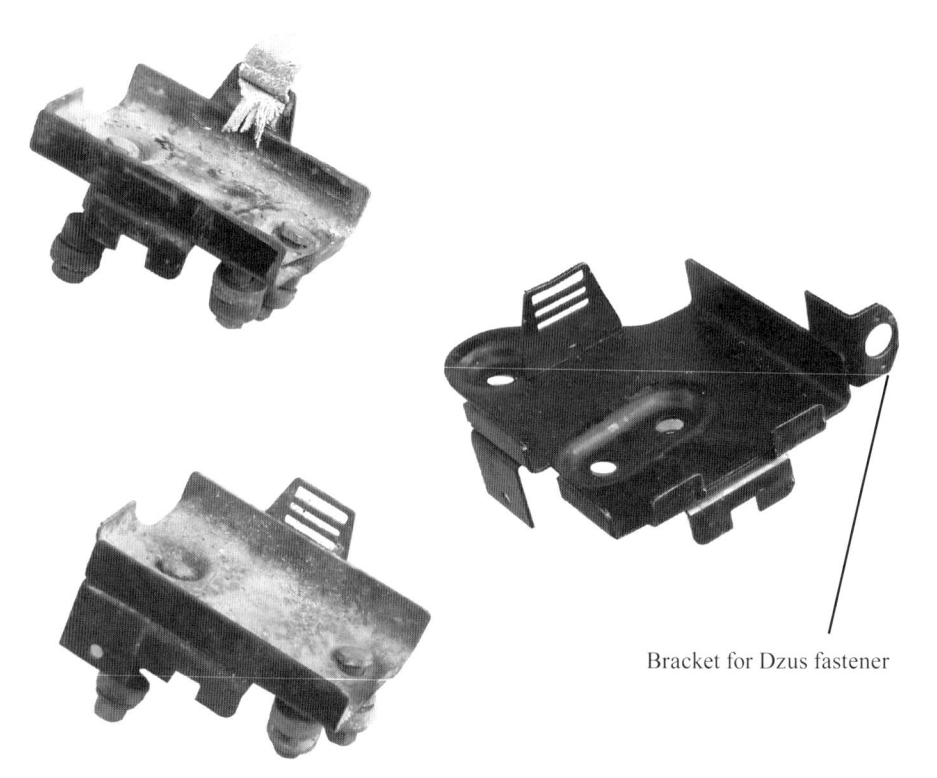

Fig 17.39. Top, '67 battery tray, below '68 to '70 tray with additional mounting bracket for external condenser necessitated by adoption of the 6CA points assembly, and right, enlarged Fleetstar version; note that this carries the bracket for the side panel rear Dzus fastener usually carried on the tool box - not fitted on the Fleetstar. The 6CA points assembly with remote capacitor was introduced during the '68 season. Early models retaining the 4CA points are indicated by a 'Y' stamped by the engine number.

The rubber mounting of the B25/B44 battery tray only works properly if all of the right bits are present and in the right order, not, as usually shown in the parts books and with all of the rubber spacers being 1" O/D by $^7/_{16}$" thick. The correct mounting is described below.

> One 3" long $^3/_8$" cycle thread bolt with under the tray and from the top; $^3/_8$" thin washer, steel spacer 1$^5/_{16}$" long (which is actually the same part as the pillion footpeg plate spacer on Bantams), $^3/_8$" thin washer, rubber spacer, frame, rubber spacer, thin $^3/_8$" washer and nut, nyloc from '68 onward.

> Two short shouldered bolts 1$^1/_2$" long, with a plain shank $^3/_8$" diameter by $^7/_8$" long, reducing to $^5/_{16}$" cycle thread for the remaining $^5/_8$". These shouldered bolts have thinner than standard heads. Two rubbers are fitted to each of these bolts with the frame bracket sandwiched between them, the whole lot being retained by a 1" O/D $^5/_{16}$" washer and nut, again nyloc from '68.

The small bracket which carries the side panel rubber buffer slots onto the forward of these two bolts between the upper rubber and the frame rail. B25 Fleetstar Police models use an enlarged version of this tray to accommodate two 6v batteries (connected in series) to cope with the power demands of the radio, flashing blue lights, sirens etc. This tray uses the same mounting arrangements as the standard item.

The B40 Military models have their own design of battery tray *(fig 17.40)* which is repositioned on the frame tubes to the offside rear of the engine – having been evicted from the usual position under the seat by the need to accommodate both the oil tank and a large air cleaner box there.

The resulting tray with sundry welded-on brackets to attach it to the frame (at four points) has all the hallmarks of an apprentice job and suffers in use from bits fatigue-fracturing until they drop off. Second hand battery trays of this type are therefore hard to find in pristine condition. Most suffer in addition from the ravages of battery acid which is more of a problem for the military item as the tray is made of thinner metal than the roadster version.

In its exposed position the battery of military machines is hidden under a GRP cover which is held in place by the rubber battery strap. Cherish this now rare item if you have one, especially if it is moulded in the GRP of one of the less common colours – they were not all green.

The '71 onward OIF battery tray is of one design for all years and models except the B50 MX which didn't fit it; this tray hung on two steel straps from rubber mounts on the n/s of the seat tube, with an integral peg under the leading edge of the tray which locates in a rubber bush on the frame. Simple and straightforward, no problems in use are exhibited by this design.

Fig 17.40. B40 Military battery tray

OIF battery tray
OIF battery tray with associated mounting bolts *(fig 17.41)* which also mount the tool tray on the other side of the frame tube.

All of the above trays for Welded/Duplex and OIF models carry the same rectangular rubber pad under the battery. This is 1/8" thick with turned-up edges. Fleetstar Police models to '70 use an enlarged version to suit their battery tray, the '72 B25 Fleetstar used the same arrangement as the other OIF models.

Fig 17.41. The OIF battery and tool tray mounted from the main frame tube under the seat

Battery charging changes
Fig 17.42 (i and ii) explains BSA's reasons behind the change of wiring harness design for '65 C15 and B40 road models to avoid the overcharging problems sometimes experienced with these models.

January 1965

SERVICE SHEET
No 115

ALTERNATOR MODELS BATTERY CHARGING

On some machines manufactured before the 1965 Season there has been a tendency for the battery to be overcharged when running without lights. For the 1965 Season this condition has been overcome by a new wiring arrangement.

Earlier models can be converted quite simply by fitting an extra wire to connect the green and white generator lead to the number 4 terminal on the lighting switch, as sketch overleaf. Obtain a length of suitable cable approximately 36" long, locate the green and white generator lead single snap connector and exchange it for a double snap connector Lucas No. 850641. Connect the extra lead to the outlet side of the double snap connector and then to number 4 terminal of the lighting switch.

This arrangement will reduce the charge to the battery when running without lights but will not affect the charge in other switch positions.

Fig 17.42 (i). BSA Service Sheet detailing the wiring changes on 1965 C15 and B40 models

Electrics 315

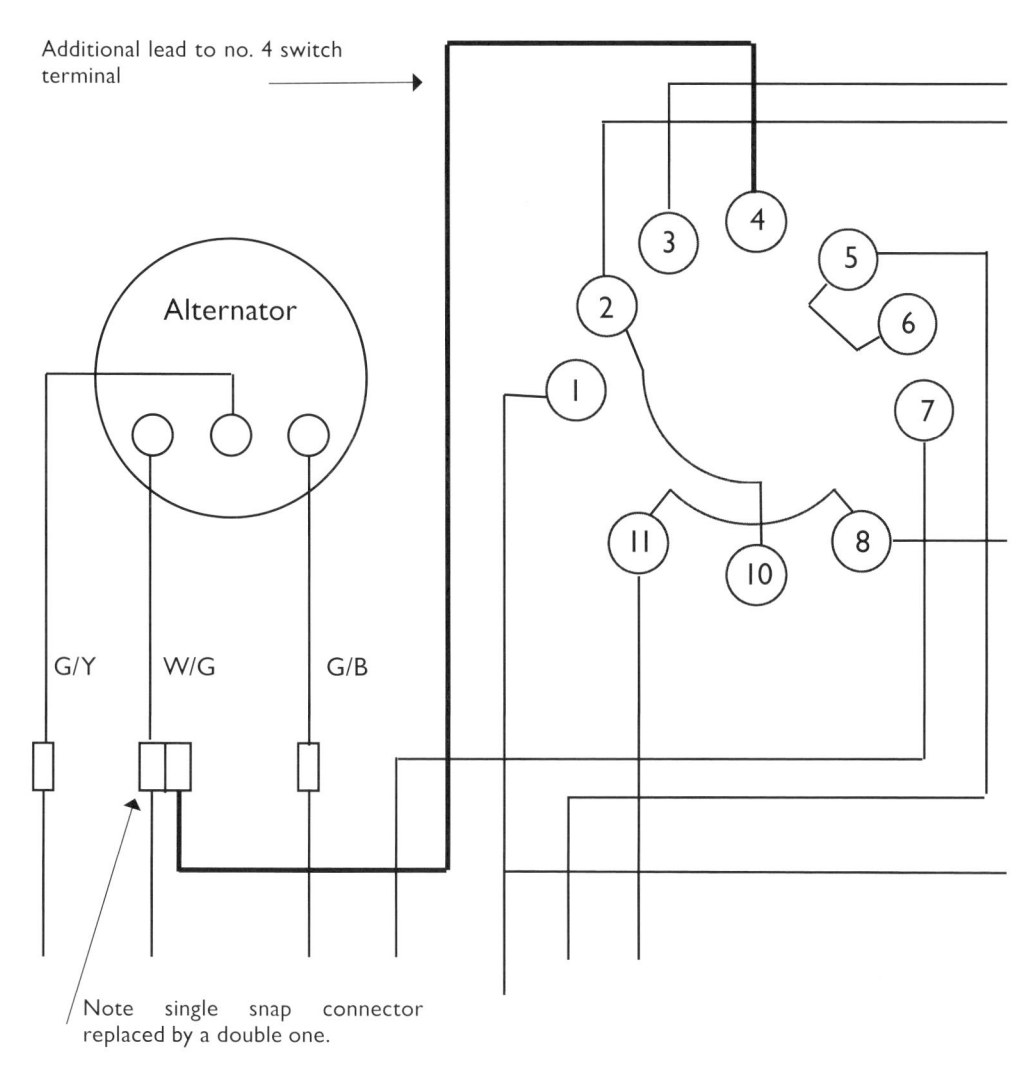

Fig 17.42 (ii) Wiring diagram for the additional lead described in fig 17.42 (i) for '58 -'64 C15 and B40 road models

18. INSTRUMENTATION

Speedometer

Originally produced by Smiths Industries, the 'clock' on your Unit Single should be a thing of beauty with an impressively optimistic dial displaying a potential top speed way above that at which your mount would self-destruct. Along with this blatant deceitfulness, don't expect this delicate instrument to work reliably or for long; if yours does then truly the gods have smiled upon you. For us in the UK, it is fortunate that the annual MOT test requires only that a speedo be fitted – it doesn't have to work.

Premature death of the speedo is most often caused by vibration when the bike is used; hence BSA increasing the amount of rubber to mount the instrument on later Unit Single models is a good idea. This offers some improvement but cannot totally solve the vibration problem which may well result in the needle coming loose and dancing around to its own tune rather than reflecting the rate of progress. Other malfunctions can stem from the drive cable which should terminate squarely at the 'clock' and not force the rubber mounted innards of the later magnetic speedos to bend or twist out of position, and from which grease should not spread into the instrument.

Replacement

Should you desire to replace a defunct speedo with a (temporarily) working one, the chance of finding a genuine new spare is now slim. Reconditioning by one of the specialists in this black art is a more realistic proposition as good, working second hand examples are now few and far between. Speedo repair is beyond the scope of this book other then that which can be achieved by accessing the dial on the Chronometric instruments. These do at least permit removal of spider's webs etc from under the glass by removing the small slotted screws under the base of the 'D' shaped instruments. Beyond this don't be tempted to fiddle unless your other hobby is watch repairs. It is more than likely that you will do damage unless you are in possession of both experience and the right equipment. Avoid touching the dial itself with your fingers or indeed, anything else; in particular the white letters on the Chronometric dials can smudge very easily.

The magnetic instruments have a crimped-on bezel which cannot be removed without destroying it. A new bezel is required to be crimped in place when reconditioning these units. As such, the only maintenance easily possible on these instruments is to check that the internals are secure in the case by checking the tightness of the two or three screws underneath as these can vibrate loose.

Lastly for those trying to source an instrument, reasonable pattern copies of some of the larger 80mm instruments are now available for consideration. Sadly the scarcity, value and wide inter-changeability of these speedos means that it is the part most likely to be missing from the box-of-bits project you have just acquired and replacement is not likely to be cheap. Unless you have a machine known to be original with respect to the speedo, the next question, should you want to rebuild to standard spec. is which one should your bike be fitted with, to enable the search to begin? If you are not interested in originality then any similar Smiths instrument of the right size and shape to physically fit will do, but don't expect it to read accurately.

Speedometer types and identification

Two different designs of speedo, Chronometric and magnetic, were used between '59 and '73 on the Unit Single with many detail variations within each.

Chronometric speedometers

Clockwork in design, Chronometrics were used until '62. On Unit Singles, these are black faced and 'D' shaped on C15 competition models except for the 80mm circular clock used on the USA C15 Starfire models in '62 only. The various types of Chronometric speedometer fitted are shown in Table 18.1.

Table 18.1 Chronometric Speedometers

Models	Years	Diam/Shape	Face colour	Speed range	Code No.	Revs/mile
C15T	'59 – '62	'D' shape	Black	0 – 75mph	SC1102/07	1600
C15T European spec.	'59 – '62	'D' shape	Black	0 – 120kph	SC1102/08	1600
C15 Starfire Roadster/Scrambler	'60	'D' shape	Black	0 – 100mph	SC1101/14	1600
	'61	'D' shape	Black	0 – 100mph	40868A	1600
	'62	80mm	Black	0 – 120mph	SC5301/03	1600
Fleetstar police	'68 – '72	80mm	Black	0 – 120mph	SC5301/41	1600

'Clockwork' means that it has gears inside to move the needle. The spindle on which the needle is located is rotated by a gear from an adjacent shaft which itself both rotates and oscillates in and out of mesh with the needle spindle gear. This thereby creates an intermittent drive to the needle spindle, the speed of the drive and rate of meshing increasing and decreasing with road speed. This intermittent drive also results in the apparent jerkiness of the needle on the dial. When not being driven, ie out of mesh with the oscillating drive the needle is pulled back towards zero by a return spring.

Fig 18.1. C15T 'D' shaped Chronometric speedo. SC 1102/07 seen on the dial is as listed in the parts book for this model.

Magnetic speedometers

'Magnetic' simply means that there is no physical contact between the needle spindle and the drive from the rear wheel. On the lower end of the needle spindle is an aluminium disc. Whilst aluminium is not regarded as a magnetic material it reacts to the magnetic flux created by a closely positioned magnet which is rotated by the drive cable. This drags the aluminium disc and needle spindle around with it, causing the needle to move on the dial against the pull of a return spring.

Based on the above descriptions of 'the works' for the two types of instrument the simpler magnetic type with fewer moving parts is understandably cheaper; hence the change to this type by BSA from '63.

Of the two types the Chronometric instrument is more likely to give an accurate and reliable indication of speed and for this reason later C15 Police and B25 Fleetstar Police models were generally fitted with a Chronometric instrument (and specifically an instrument which was calibrated by the maker and therefore guaranteed to give an accurate reading when supplied, m'lud).

Table 18.2 shows the variations of colour, size and gearing for the magnetic instruments. Road models were fitted with a 60mm diameter instrument with a black face to '62, then with a re-style to a grey face which was used on all C15 and B40 road models to '67 and TR25w for '68. The introduction of the grey face instrument on the C15 Star coincides with the minor styling change of new petrol tank shape and colour options which happened at this time (see Chapters 11 Petrol Tanks and 15 Paints and Finishes)

C15/B40/B44 off-road models from '63 to '66 use the circular 80mm diameter darker grey face instrument as later used on B25, B44 and '69 TR25w models to the end of '69 (with matching tacho, if fitted, from '69 onward). Before '67 the speedometer was mounted in a metal cup with rubber rim similar to the contemporary A65 arrangement; the Unit Single version has an integral steel stiffening bracket underneath to allow it to be bolted directly to the top yoke.

The '67 to '70 speedo cup is made wholly of rubber and it is important when fixing this to its mounting plate not to omit the four ¼" x ¼" steel bushes through which the screws pass.

The B40 Military Mk2 also used the same grey face speedo in the rubber cup mounting but with a dull chrome bezel. The much commoner B40 Military Mk1 used a grey face speedo identical to the above but with longer mounting studs to suit its fitment to the headlamp shell via a clamping bracket similar to the original C15 arrangement. This is the same speedometer as used on early A50/65 Star models except for the dull chrome military bezel, and additionally features a bottom, rather than a side 'trip' knob.

Fig 18.2. Speedometer used on '68 TR25w, mounted in the metal cup peculiar to that year and model.

18.3. Above, the '63 to '66 C15 competition and B44VE metal speedo cup with rubber rim.

Fig 18.4. The '67 to '70 rubber cup, here shown on the '67 only B44VS pressed steel mounting plate.

Table 18.2 Magnetic Speedometers and rev counters

Model	Date	Diam.	Face colour	Speedo range	Code No	Revs per mile
C15 Star	'58 - '60	60mm	Black	0 - 80mph	SN3103/67	1680
				0 - 130kph	SN3103/68	1680
	'61 - '62	60mm	Black	0 - 80mph	SN3170/11	1680
				0 - 130kph	SN3170/12	1680
C15SS80,	'61 - '62	60mm	Black	0 - 100mph	SN3170/36	1680
				0 - 160kph	SN3170/37	1680
B40 Star/SS90	'61 - '62	60mm	Black	0 - 100mph	SN3153/85	1568
				0 - 160kph	SN3153/86	1568
C15 Star	'63 on	60mm	Light grey	0 - 80mph	SSM2001/00	1600.
				0 - 130kph	SSM2001/01	1600
C15SS80, B40 Star/SS90	'63 on	60mm	Light grey	0 - 100mph	SSM2001/02	1600.
				0 - 160kph	SSM2001/03	1600
C15 Trials, Starfire Roadster B40 Enduro Star, B40 Mil Mk2	'63 on	80mm	Grey	0 - 120mph	SSM5001/03	1600.
				0 - 190kph	SSM5001/04	1600
TR25w	'68	60mm	Grey	0 - 100mph	SSM2001/02	1600
				0 - 160kph	SSM2001/03	1600
TR25w	'69	80mm	Grey	0 - 120mph	SSM5001/03	1600
				0 - 190kph	SSM5001/04	1600
TR25w	'70	80mm	Black	0 - 120mph	SSM5007/02	1600
				0 - 190kph	SSM5007/03	1600
B25/B44SS	'67 - '69	80mm	Grey	0 - 120mph	SSM5001/03	1600
				0 - 190kph	SSM5001/04	1600
B44VS	'67 – '69	80mm,	Grey	0 - 150mph	SSM5001/05	1000
				0 - 250kph	SSM5001/06	1000
Tacho to match above (B44VS)		80mm	Grey	0 - 10,000rpm	RSM 3001/03	4:1
B40 military Mk I*	'67 to '70	80mm	Grey	0 - 120mph	SSM4001/02A	1600
B25/B44SS	'70	80mm	Black	0 - 120mph	SSM5007/02	1600
				0 - 190kph	SSM5007/03	1600
B44VS	'70	80mm	Black	0 - 150mph	SSM5007/00	1000
				0 - 250kph	SSM5007/01	1000
B25T/B50T OIF	'71-'72	80mm	Black	0 - 120mph	SSM5007/02	1600
				0 - 190kph	SSM5007/03	1600
Tacho to match above (B25, B44SS, B25T and B50T)				0 - 10,000rpm	RSM 3003/13	4:1
B25SS, T25SS, B50SS OIF	'71-'72	60mm	Black	0 - 120mph	SSM2001/07	1600
				0 - 190kph	SSM2001/08	1600
Tacho to match above (B25SS, T25SS, B50SS)				0 – 12,000rpm	RSM2001/02	4:1

* Longer casing studs for headlamp mounting bracket and bottom rather than side trip shaft, usually with dull chrome bezel

Fig 18.5. The OIF 60mm black faced instruments, from a 250cc SS model.

For the '70 season (ie not yet OIF) these clocks, other than the B40 Military, changed to black faced instruments which are otherwise the same as previously. These 80mm black faced instruments were also available in the smaller 60mm size for the B25SS and T25SS '71 onward OIF range. The OIF black faced instruments, 60mm diameter items shown here (*fig 18.5*) mount directly under the fork stanchion top-nuts.

All of the 80mm magnetic speedos fitted to Unit Singles feature two odometers, the normal odometer showing the total miles travelled which cannot be reset, and the other is the 'trip' meter which can be reset to zero by means of the trip shaft. The 60mm magnetic instruments lack the second re-settable trip odometer.

Which speedo for your bike?

The above overview outlining which speedo your Unit Single should have is made confusing by the fact that many more variations were produced for fitment to other models. Each speedo type; Chronometric or magnetic, and size; 60mm, 80mm, or 'D' shape, was available with several possible dial ranges eg 0-70mph or 0-100mph and the equivalents in kph for the continent. The relevant ones for the Unit Single are shown in *Tables 18.1 and 18.2*

Determining exactly which speedo your bike should have is done by looking it up in the BSA parts book where its code number can be found. This number, typically beginning 'SN' or 'SC' for a pre '62 instrument and 'SSM' for the later types will be found on the dial. Tacho's for the later models are coded beginning 'RSM'.

This number will categorically decide which clock you should have on the bike, but, if finding the right one is a problem you could possibly use a slightly different one to do the job. The main issue with this is whether it will read accurately or not. The key to determining this is the revs-per-mile figure which unfortunately, is not provided in the parts books. On the 'D' shaped dial shown in *fig 18.1* the revs-per-mile figure is shown as '1600'. To find out which revs-per-mile figure will give you an accurate speedo, read on...

Fig 18.6. '58 to '62 60mm C15 black face magnetic speedo. The 100mph version of this clock was fitted to SS and B40 models during this period.

Finding the revs-per-mile figure, pre '63
Several variants of the magnetic black-face 60mm and Chronometric 'D' shaped speedos were produced and fitted to the early C15 and B40 models. The alternatives vary depending on the mph/kph range displayed eg 0 - 80mph, and the rear tyre size fitted as standard.

The relationship between the 'clock' and the rear wheel is indicated on the dial in small print as a four digit number eg '1350'. This represents the number of rotations of the rear wheel per mile multiplied by two (this 'two' stems from the 2:1 speedo drive unit on the rear wheel fitted as standard with the speedos fitted to '62; the speedo drive multiplies the wheel rotations by the ratio given). For example, an 18" wheel fitted with a 3.50" tyre has a nominal diameter at the road surface of 25" (18 + 3.5 + 3.5). This wheel has a circumference (25 multiplied by 3.14) of 78.5". This wheel will rotate 807 times in a mile (63360 inches in a mile, divided by 78.5 = 807). Then 807 multiplied by 2 (the speedo drive ratio) gives 1614 rotations of the speedo drive cable per mile. This figure would therefore be seen on the dial of a speedo which would read accurately for this tyre size.

This is the revs-per-mile figure of the drive to the speedo and this number is one of the main variables in the speedo saga due to the wide range of tyre sizes fitted. Otherwise identical speedos can display several different versions of this number: up to '62, the only way to compensate for variations in tyre size was to fit a different speedo.

Using the above formula the correct speedo revs-per-mile figure can be found which will read accurately for your tyre size. In practise, expect some variations from this ideal figure for purposes of standardisation so 1600, for example is commonly found rather than 1614 as calculated above. Pre-unit models which used a speedo driven from the engine gearbox were not restricted to the 2:1 drive from the rear wheel. Hence Chronometric speedos with a revs-per-mile figure around 1000, or other numbers, can be found but these are not suitable for Unit Single applications.

Doing the maths for 17" wheels shows that to read correctly, C15 Star models to '62 should be fitted with a 60mm, black face speedo with a 0 to 80mph dial and a revs-per-mile figure closer to 1700. These figures are shown in *Tables 18.1 and 18.2*

Finding the revs-per-mile figure for magnetic speedos - '63 onward
As mentioned above, all of the C15 and B40 black face speedos (to '62)are used with a 2:1 speedo drive unit on the rear wheel. This was in effect a constant in the equation with rear wheel size and the clock internal gearing being the variables. The grey face magnetic speedos which replaced the earlier instruments involved a re-think of this approach to reduce costs.

In practice the reason behind this change taken by BSA (and other manufacturers) was to reduce the wide and potentially confusing range of speedos (expensive) and instead introduce a small range of alternative speedo drives. In this way the speedo drive now became the main variable in the equation with alternatives over or under the normal 2:1 ratio to compensate for different sizes of rear tyre. The speedo head became much more of a constant in the equation with two alternative revs-per-mile figures - 1600 and 1000

It must be stated that BSA's selection of drive unit/speedo head combination for any given rear tyre was not always consistent and was subject to a rule-of-thumb approach: this margin of error tended to increase with the magnetic instruments.

Speedo Drive Units

Fitted on the o/s of the rear wheel spindle, speedo drive units from '62 have a more rounded outside shape than the rather square cornered previous design (but the two types are fully interchangeable) and were made with ratios of 2:1 for a 3.50" x 18" rear tyre, 19:10 for a smaller 3.00" x 18" or 3.50" x 17" tyre, and 21:10 for a larger 4.00" x 18" tyre (as on OIF 'T' models).

These three speedo drive ratios are compatible with the larger 80mm diameter 120mph grey or black face instruments and the 60mm light grey or black face items which all have a revs-per-mile figure of 1600 shown on the dial.

The similar speedo head but reading to 150mph fitted to the B44VS (also common on the A65) has a different internal ratio and is used with a drive unit having a ratio of 15:12, often referred to as 1.25:1 which is the same thing, for use with a 4.00" x 18" rear tyre. The 150mph speedometer has a revs-per-mile figure of 1000 and should only be used with the 1.25:1 drive unit.

Due to the 17" wheels of the C15, the later road models fitted with the 60mm light grey, 80mph instrument used the 19:10 drive unit (as on contemporary Bantams), whereas the B40 road models kept to a 2:1 drive unit to suit the 3.50" x 18" rear tyre.

Speedo drive maintenance and user tips

The speedo gearbox wears out if not greased, hence the provision of the grease nipple, although early production units had a blanking screw instead. A badly routed cable will create friction, putting undue load on the drive gears in the unit which will then grind themselves away. Usually the teeth on the drive ring will let go first rather than those on the spindle which connects to the cable.

With the single centrally mounted speedo fitted as standard to B25 and B44SS models from '67 to '70, the speedo cable will tend to foul the rear point of the 700P headlamp shell. There is no easy solution to this, the easiest way around the problem is to put a slight but permanent kink in the cable just below the speedo head and fit the headlight at the front of its mounting slots.

Dismantling
To access the speedo drive gears requires a fairly simple strip-down procedure to be followed. The felt seal in its steel housing on the inner side can be flipped out by twisting a flat screwdriver between its inner washer and the drive ring. The drive ring is released by pushing out the four small rivets holding its retaining plate (around the wheel spindle hole). The drive spindle is removed after releasing the domed brass end cap; to do this select a small drill bit which will just fit (its plain end) into the square cable drive socket. Tapping the protruding end of the drill bit with a copper hammer will drift out the brass end cap and spindle. Take care not to lose the small thrust washers from the drive spindle. It will be seen that the brass end cap, and opposite it the threaded brass union for the cable, are simply a press-fit in the die-cast zinc body, if loose, use Loctite when re-fitting. The threaded union can be released in the same way using a suitable drift from behind it inside the body.

The main reason for removal of both of these brass fittings is to convert an under-slung drive to overhead or vice-versa, the norm for Unit Singles being under-slung; the two fittings are simply swapped and pressed back in using a vice. Making this change will not effect the direction of rotation of the cable drive which for Unit Singles should appear to turn clockwise when the square drive in the threaded brass union is viewed head-on, and the drive ring is rotated in the direction of wheel rotation by the fingers. If jumbling for a speedo drive check for this rotation as anti-clockwise drives were produced for other makes; they are otherwise identical if you can't read the part number on the inner face around the steel felt seal housing. Later parts books specify this part number – eg BG5330/31 which is a 2:1 unit used on B25/B44 models – and the ratio. An otherwise identical drive unit but with a different part number stamped on it will do fine. The difference may be something minor such as a different size of hole for the wheel spindle. Don't be surprised if these numbers have been obliterated; they shouldn't be, but an incorrectly fitted drive which rubs against the back wheel hub as it rotates will lose metal in this area, then it's anyone's guess - unless you do a little test:

Bend a matchstick 90 degrees in the middle and poke one end in the cable socket of the drive so the free end points outward like one of the hands on a clock. Rotating the drive ring exactly ½ a revolution (check the drive-dogs position) will rotate the match pointer 1 revolution for a 2:1 drive. If it is a 19:10 or 21:10 unit the difference will be clearly visible from the match-stick position.

Late production drive units have the two internal dogs on the drive ring drilled to render them a weak-link between the rear wheel and speedo. Thus should any seizure occur from drive to clock the dogs will shear off to prevent more expensive damage elsewhere.

Fitting the speedo drive
Correct fitting of the drive unit on the rear wheel should render it fixed and unable to spin on the spindle when all spindle nuts securing the rear wheel to the swinging arm are fully tightened. Achieving this should of course not affect the ability of the rear wheel to spin freely and if it doesn't, investigation is required; don't run it in the expectation that it will soon free-off, which would be tempting fate in the form of costly damage. The two types of Unit Single speedo drives are shown in *fig 18.7.*

Repeated and excessive tightening of the rear spindle or associated nuts will distort the metal of the drive body (die cast zinc) around the centre hole. This will be squashed between the spindle spacer under the drive and the nut or spacer outboard of it causing it to pinch on the spindle. If necessary, open out the hole to restore a close sliding fit on the spindle and if the metal of the drive around the hole has been squashed thin then consider adding a shim washer to restore it to the correct thickness.

When tightening the offside of the rear wheel spindle, rotate the drive to give an angle of cable exit from the drive to be at about 10 degrees to the swinging arm. This will give the cable an easy life. Always pack the drive unit with grease before fitting and additionally via the nipple during servicing until grease can be seen to start to emerge between drive unit and wheel; this will help keep water out. Originally the later type speedo drive units were painted

Above, Fig 18.7. Speedo drive gearboxes: left, the square profile '59 to '62 item, right, the rounded body type, '62 onward..

Left, Fig 18.8. The pressed steel cover which replaces the speedo drive on C15 Scrambles models.

> December 1966
>
> # BSA
>
> ## SERVICE SHEET
>
> No 147
>
> WHEEL DRIVEN SPEEDOMETER GEARBOXES
>
> Speedometer gearboxes driven from the rear wheel are fitted with a grease nipple for lubrication purposes.
>
> The gearbox should be given two shots from a hand gun every 5,000 miles using Esso Aviation General Purpose Grease No.1, or similar.
>
> To make the gearbox 'fail safe', in the event of inadequate lubrication, both driving dogs are drilled and will break off should the gearbox seize up.
>
> To prevent loss of the domed end cap, due to thrust, the cap and cable connector are locked in position by 'Stake' indentations into annular grooves in addition to the outer torque re-action tabs.
>
> If the speedometer stops recording, disconnect the drive cable at the gearbox end and check that the gearbox is functioning by revolving the rear wheel. If the gearbox is satisfactory then the trouble lies in the cable or the speedometer head. This can be checked by reconnecting at the head, and again revolving the rear wheel.

Fig 18.9. BSA service sheet describing servicing the speedometer gearbox

Fig 18.10. Top, the '69 -'70 double base plate for speedo and (optional extra) tacho. Bottom left, the single, centrally mounted steel bracket for the rubber cup. Bottom right, the '67 -'70 rubber cup for the 80mm speedo and tacho

silver with a lubrication advice sticker (now available for restorers) on the flat oval surface next to the cable connection.

C15 Scrambles models. B44GP and B50 MX models are not provided with a speedo drive on the rear wheel. The GP uses the pre-unit type of crinkle hub and plain hub cover and the MX hub has a pressed-in dust cover and extended wheel spindle spacer.

Speedo Cable

Following on from the previous tip regarding cable angle to the drive, the routing of the cable from drive to clock should be as smooth as possible. The maker's recommendation is that no bend in the cable should have a radius of less than 6", not that I've ever fitted a speedo cable with a ruler in my hand to check; simply looking at the run of the cable should tell you that there are no sharp bends. The main factor in achieving this lies in obtaining the correct length of cable for your machine in the first place. These are :

C15 Star	4'8"	
SS80 and B40	4'10½"	
C15 competition '63 on	5'2"	
B25, B44 to '70	5'2"	
B40 Military Mk 1	4'10½"	
B40 Military Mk 2	5'2"	
B25/B50 OIF '71	5'3"	(1971 OIF BSA models featured grey rather than black speedo and tacho cables)

Second to this comes consideration of the best places to clip the cable to the frame: these being, once to the swinging arm, once or twice to the offside frame tube under the engine and once or twice to the front down tube but with no clip within 6" of the bottom yoke to allow free movement of the forks. Check also that the cable is not likely to be trapped between the bottom yoke and the steering stop on the frame. Routing the speedo cable along the frame top tube is not the best pathway.

The 2'9" tacho cable which may be found on '69 onward models is difficult to fit without a tight bend from its drive unit on the front of the engine, particularly so on OIF machines if the tacho drive unit isn't of the modified ('72) type; the previous type of drive unit causes the cable to foul the '71 onward frames. Basically the fault lies with BSA, just allow the cable as much latitude as your eye will permit before clipping it once to the front down tube.

At the speedo or tacho head, the drive cable inner will be seen to have a crimped-on brass ferrule and washer; these should be in contact with their seating inside the end of the outer cable when in use so the inner is supported and hangs from here. If this is not the case and the inner cable stands too proud of the outer it will put upward pressure on the internal mechanism of the clock when the cable is screwed on.

Shortening a speedo cable, for instance to make a hard-to-find tacho cable, is fairly easy to do and should be carried out at the drive unit end. First, note the difference in length between the inner and the outer so this can be reproduced later.

Next, the crimped-on aluminium ferrule on the outer should pull off fairly easily if the outer next to it is gripped in a vice and the ferrule is gripped under the flange on its end with pliers. These can then be tapped to persuade it to move. While dealing with this ferrule prepare it

Fig 18.11. Twin clocks on a '69 B44 Shooting Star; speedo on the left, tacho on the right on their purpose made mounting bracket: nice.

for re-fitting by spreading the hexagonal crimped portion (unless you have access to a new ferrule and the correct crimping tool). Do this by tapping inside it the plain end of a drill bit which is exactly the same diameter as the cable outer.

After sawing off the outer and inner cables to the correct respective lengths the end 1" of the inner will need to be squared-off so it can again fit into the speedo drive. It cannot simply be filed square as it is as this will break through some of the separate wire strands causing it to disintegrate. This can be overcome by solidifying the end 1" with soft solder before filing. However, the cable will be reluctant to allow the solder to fully penetrate its strands; to overcome this it should be degreased, and repeatedly dipped in paste flux as it is carefully heated with a small blowtorch and the solder applied to it until it can be seen to have completely tinned. After cutting the cable outer to length with a junior hacksaw, the ferrule can be pushed back on and fixed by firmly centre-punching twice, opposite each other, half way along that part of the ferrule containing the cable.

With the inner cable effectively hanging from its brass ferrule, both ends should be short enough not to 'bottom-out' in either the speedo head or drive unit. Otherwise, expect expensive damage to the clock due to upward pressure from the cable inner on its internals. It is worth checking modern replacement speedo/tacho cables for this shortcoming. Cables with an external reinforcing spring around the top 6" should not be used with magnetic instruments as this lack of flexibility just puts more pressure on the rubber mounted speedo innards.

Tachos

Provision for this optional extra was introduced for the start of the '69 season on all B25, TR25w and B44 models and continued thus on the subsequent OIF B25, T25 and B50 models. All tachos for Unit Single use should match the speedo in diameter and dial colour: they are of 4:1 ratio. This will be seen marked near the centre of the dial. The 60mm black face tacho as used on some OIF models is still quite easy to obtain in the UK. This tacho was produced in quantity for the still-born Bandit/Fury 350cc twin and these therefore became surplus stock, subsequently made available to dealers at knock-down prices in the late '70's. Code numbers marked on the dials of the '62 onward magnetic clocks are shown in *Table 18.2*.

Ammeter

This is a standard fitment in the headlamp shell on all of the road models from '59 to '70. These are all of the same size; 1½" diameter, black faced and of Lucas manufacture. All of the 6v models, ie C15 and B40 Star and Sports Star to '67 have ammeters with a scale on the dial simply marked + or – to indicate the battery being charged or discharged. 12v models ie B25, B40 Military and B44 from '67 used firstly a dial marked +8 and -8 for this year only (known as an 8-8 ammeter) and from '68 to '70 a 12-12 item. *(see Chapter 17 Electrics, fig 17.4 p289)*

In use, don't expect the ammeter to give an accurate or steady reading with the engine running, be satisfied with a general trend of the needle towards + or – depending on whether the engine is running and what else may be switched on. At rest the needle should be somewhere near the middle. A +ve indication means the battery is being charged, -ve that it is being discharged.

As with the speedo and tacho, the ammeter can succumb to vibration. This usually results in the needle coming loose, for which there is no easy cure. In addition the 'glass' being plastic, has a tendency to fog with age. The outside can be improved by rubbing with metal polish on a rag which removes the fogging. Similarly the inside of the glass, if this can first be accessed by carefully cutting through the plastic body near the base with a junior hacksaw – try to cut through the two glued areas (often coloured pink) which connect the body of the ammeter to the base. If trying this, make sure you don't cut too deep and damage the internals. After cleaning up the inside of the face glue the two halves back together with polystyrene cement or super-glue.

Attaching the electrical connections, ring lugs on the two loom wires, to the 2BA studs requires a bit of care so as to avoid over-tightening the nuts which will simply break the plastic casing.

Should it be suspect in any way, the ammeter can easily be by-passed electrically by putting both wires on to one stud. If the needle seems to be working the wrong way, simply swap the wires over.

The ammeter's chrome bezel can also be a bit of a problem; firstly it is crimped onto the rim of the plastic body and the grip of this can loosen resulting in the ammeter rattling in the headlamp, secondly the four tabs which secure the bezel to the headlamp shell are fine if undisturbed but these can break off if the ammeter is removed and replaced by causing them to be bent to and fro. Careful application of silicon rubber around the ammeter inside the headlamp will cure both of these problems and also prevent ingress of water here should your bike ever be subject to inclement weather.

Warning Lights

Count the number of idiot (warning) lights on the handlebar controls of today's motorcycles and two questions may come to mind; firstly, how did we manage without them; secondly, do we really need them? I am happy to be considered old-fashioned by answering these questions with - people managed, and no, we don't need them, they don't tell you anything which you shouldn't already be aware of. But then motorcycles are made to be sold to all sorts of people including those who like to see Christmas decorations all year round.

BSA were therefore merely and lamentably following fashion by introducing the main beam warning light (red) to the headlamp shell of some models from '65; the Americans were responsible for this due to their regulations. '70 saw the addition of the oil pressure warning light (red) and the main beam warning light was now green, and '71 the amber indicator repeater.

These warning lights were a standard Lucas item fitted to many British motorcycles and cars in the '60s and '70's. Those used up to '70 have a raised hexagonal lens of the appropriate colour, those from '71 onwards have a flat grid-pattern coloured lens. All are simply a push-fit in their hole in the headlamp, as is the bulb holder with the wire connections into the back of the plastic lamp housing. All of these lights should have a rubber washer or shroud ('71 on) fitted between the chrome bezel and the headlamp shell to prevent water entering, check the parts book to see which you should have.

The plastic body of the light is an interference fit in the headlamp hole, and will 'give' if it has been in and out a few times, resulting in an insecure fit. This is not easy to remedy without recourse to modern day glue or silicon sealant added inside the headlamp shell. The push-in bulb holder for these lights should carry two wires; one centrally to the bulb as the feed wire and the other to the bulb holder which is the earth/return.

Fig 18.12. As good a place as any for a nice B44 Victor Special shot. This is an early '69 model, just one warning light (main beam) on the headlight centre top.

19. TOOLS

BSA produced a list of tools specifically for the '68 B44 models (figs 19.1). BSA did not produce such lists for the majority of models, however, these B44 tools will serve as a guide to the equivalent tool requirements for other Unit Singles, many being common across this range of models. I particularly like the sentence 'the owner will decide if his individual skills are suitable'. Pictures of the front fork tools, the most needed special tools, are shown in *fig 4.11, p59*.

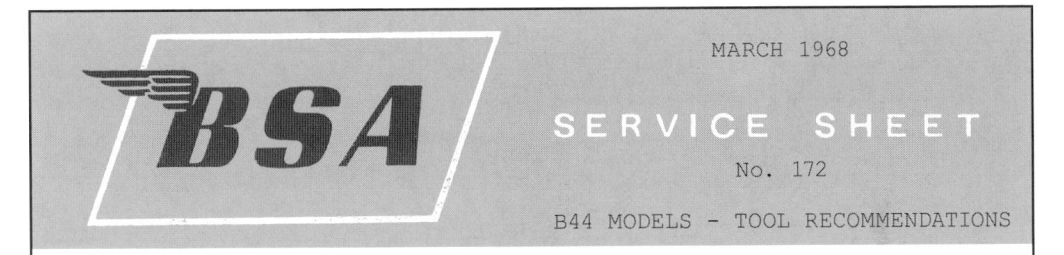

MARCH 1968

BSA

SERVICE SHEET

No. 172

B44 MODELS - TOOL RECOMMENDATIONS

This bulletin sets out the tools which permit the owner and the dealer, to carry out work on the B44 group of machines with ease and confidence.

LIST 1.
The kit contained with the machine is referred to as 'Road Kit' and makes possible the following adjustments and replacements:-

  Change sparking plugs.
  Change bulbs
  Adjust rear suspension units
  Remove and refit tyres
  Adjust rear chain

DRAWING NO	DESCRIPTION
60-767	Screwdriver set
29-9252	Double ended tyre lever
68-9463	Tyre lever - tommy bar
68-9464	Plug spanner - tubular
40-9017	Double ended box spanner ($1/2$" x $9/16$" BSF)
68-9462	'C' spanner
67-9026	Double ended ring spanner ($1/4$" x $5/16$" BSF)
19-8301	Lucas screwdriver with .015" feeler
68-9467	Tyre valve key

LIST 2
We recommend the enthusiastic owner to study the list of tools below because, with them, a great variety of adjustments routine and exceptional maintenance plus such work as de-coke, top overhaul, clutch repairs etc, etc, may be carried out. Of course, the Workshop Manual is an essential guide to the correct methods to be employed and having looked at this manual and the tool list, the owner will decide if his individual skills are suitable.

Fig 19.1. BSA Service Sheet specifying tools for the road, in the workshop and for the dealers

Service Sheet 172 continued...

DRAWING NO	**DESCRIPTION**
(BSA Tools only)	
	Set of three double ended spanners
	$^3/_{16}"$ x $^1/_4"$ BSF
	$^1/_4"$ x $^5/_{16}"$ BSF
	$^5/_{16}"$ x $^3/_8"$ BSF
	Double open ended 2 BA - 3BA spanner
	Set of three socket heads
	$^1/_4"$, $^5/_{16}"$, $^3/_8"$ BSF
	Ratchet handle for sockets
	4" extension for sockets
40-9010	Double ended ring spanner $^1/_4"$ x $^3/_8"$ BSF
	Tubular spanner $^9/_{16}"$ AF
	Tubular spanner $^5/_8"$ BSF
	Tubular spanner 1" BSF
	Phillips screwdriver 8"
	Rubber headed mallet
	Allen key $^3/_{32}"$ AF for $^5/_{32}"$ screw
61-3340	Valve spring compressor
61-5035	Valve grinding tool
61-3700	Clutch nut key
61-3583	Clutch sleeve puller
61-3761	Contact breaker extractor bolt
	Set of feeler gauges
65-9133	Tappet spanner

Plus the tools in List No.1

LIST 3

This bulletin also hopes to assist the dealer by listing tools which will make adjustment, repair and replacement so much easier and quicker.

Where the Workshop Manual lists tools these are contained in Lists 2, 3 and 4 where appropriate. Broadly, this List 3 helps the dealer to execute most dis-assembly and assembly procedures associated with pure parts replacement and the usual top overhaul plus day-to-day service to the owner.

DPAWING NO	**DESCRIPTION**
	TOP OVERHAUL TOOLS
61-3340	Valve spring compressor
61-5035	Valve grinding tool
61-3293)	
61-3290)	Valve seat cutting tool
61-3300)	
61-3382	Valve guide drift
65-9153	Tappet spanner
61-3707	Piston ring slipper
	TRANSMISSION TOOLS
61-3700	Clutch nut key
61-3774	Clutch locking tool
61-3583	Clutch sleeve extractor
	Double ended box spanner
	9/16" Whit. (Rotor and clutch nuts)
	Box spanner 15/16" Whit. (Gearbox sprocket nut)

```
    Service Sheet No. 172 continued...
                        FRONT FORK REMOVAL TOOlS
    61-3350             Fork leg puller tool
    61-3001             Fork cap nut spanner
                        Cranked ring spanner ⁹/₁₆" AF
    61-3765             Damper rod recovery tool

                        OTHER TOOLS
    61-3761             Contact breaker cam extractor
                        Allen key ³/₃₂" AF for ⁵/₃₂" screw
    61-3773             Universal pinion extractor
                        Torque wrench
    00-5177             Stroboscope and timing disc

    LIST 4.
    The hand tools and equipment brought together in the listing
    below recognise that the dealer is always prepared to
    consider and, if possible, will carry out major repairs to
    engine and frame.

    The Workshop Manual is the guide to procedures at all times,
    the list below giving a clearer and possibly a more convenient
    approach to determine a dealer's requirements.

    DRAWING NO          DESCRIPTION
                        CRANKSHAFT BALANCING TOOLS
    61-3770             Crankpin nut socket
    61-3771             Flywheel bolster
                        Drilling machine (to balance flywheels)
                        'V' blocks (for trueing flywheels)

                        FRONT FORK STRIPPING TOOLS
    61-3005             Oil seal holder fitting and removal tool
    61-3006             Oil seal extractor punch
    61-3007             Oil seal assembly tool
    61-3063             Steering head cup extractor

                        REAR SUSPENSION.
    61-3503             Dismantling and assembly tool

                        BEARING AND BUSH REPLACEMENT
    61-3653             Small end bush extractor
    61-3778             Main bearing inner race extractor
```

At the risk of 'preaching to the converted,' anyone who has a relationship with a British motorcycle expects to do more than simply ride it. The laying on of spanners is a necessity which is at least tolerated, and at best relished enthusiastically by those who expect their mount to have a measure of reliability. Those British bike owners who are exceptions to this are possibly seeking some sort of quasi-religious experience, by enduring a life of suffering in the face of continual mechanical misadventure, or are perhaps happy to continually buy the beer for their circle of mechanically competent friends.

Those who like tools and their uses are, perhaps, more likely to be tempted by owning a classic bike, which in turn will encourage the acquisition and use of more tools. As such I don't expect these lists to be fully useful except to the few readers who are starting from scratch: as most of us probably have serviceable equivalents for at least some of the items listed.

Personally when riding I like to carry insurance in my jacket pocket in the form of basic tools which equate to BSA's suggested 'road kit'. These have been carefully selected to include tools which fit the various screws, nuts and bolts etc on the bike, and which are as small as possible; 'stubby' screwdrivers for example rather than full length ones. They also seem to act as a talisman; if I carry them I tend not to need them.

Acquisition of the tools from the additional BSA lists may or may not be a priority depending on the extent to which you see your role as mechanic. On the other hand, don't be tempted to take on the more involved jobs without the necessary tools, either pukka BSA, modern equivalents or home-made.

Whilst I don't intend to be too evangelical in extolling the virtues of practical work as a form of therapy or relaxation (other authors have already done plenty of this), part of British bike ownership can have exactly this effect once you accept and come to terms with it being a necessity and begin to see it as a pleasure.

Other than your pockets, space for carrying the toolkit supplied with the bike (standard provision on all of road models and clearly illustrated in the relevant BSA parts book) is provided under the n/s side panel. On C15 and B40 models a steel clip is provided inside the cover to retain the tool pouch *(fig 19.2)*. On B25, TR25w and B44 road models (and VS '68 -'70) a triangular toolbox is provided adjacent to the battery. On OIF models excluding the MX, a tray is provided *(see fig 17.41)*

Fig 19.2. The only toolbox as such found on the Unit Singles, specifically the '67 -'70 B25, TR25w and B44 next to the battery under the n/s side panel. The side panel of C15 and B40 road models carries a clip on its inner side to retain a tool pouch

OIF models have a tool tray under the seat behind the nearside panel (fig 17.41).

The toolkit originally supplied with your bike when new is clearly illustrated in the Parts book for your model (personally I have never yet acquired a second hand machine with an intact toolkit!) A typical example is shown in fig 19.4.

Maintenance – checking and adjusting.

In terms of time allocation maintenance is hopefully 99% checking and 1% wielding the spanners. This may seem disproportionate but if you consider that all the time you are riding the bike you can be checking/monitoring it by sight, sound and feel then those proportions may not be far wrong. Therefore maintenance should start and continue whenever you use the bike and not just be a static exercise of topping up the oil or putting air in the tyres.

One of the factors which attract people to older machinery in general may be the level of interaction and intimacy required. Compared to any modern motorcycle, a BSA Unit Single requires attention to a degree which will either suit you - or not. With the right maintenance the Unit Single owner should feel confident that his bike can be relied upon to deliver as expected. What he cannot do is ignore it and still expect it to perform. Those who prefer such one-sided deals are more suited to modern machinery.

Following this basic approach to Unit Single maintenance there is actually very little to do on a routine basis in terms of jobs which haven't already announced their desire for attention. Check oil levels, tyre pressures and condition, clean and adjust the points, lubricate exposed controls, adjust the chains and so on, ie the basic stuff contained in the hand book for your model should be carried out periodically depending on the mileage you do, along with the lovingly applied oily rag.

For those without the luxury of a handbook for their machine here is a typical example *(fig 19.3)*, other machines will vary slightly in terms of filter positions etc, but the basic jobs are much the same.

ROUTINE MAINTENANCE

Weekly
Check tyre pressures and check for stones and other sharp objects
Oil brake pedal pivot and other all exposed controls and cables
Check electrolyte level in the battery and top up if with distilled water if required. More frequent checks may be necessary in a hot climate.

250 Miles
Check oil level in the tank, and top up as required

500 Miles
Grease the swinging arm pivot

1,000 Miles
Clean the air filter

2,000 Miles
Change the engine oil and clean the oil filters
Check rear and primary chain tightness and adjust if required
Check all nuts and bolts for tightness
Check contact breaker adjustment
Grease brake cam spindles, and speedometer drive
Oil the central stand pivot
Check oil levels in gearbox, and primary chain case, and top up if necessary

6,000 Miles
Change oil in gearbox
Clean contact breaker

12,000 Miles
Drain and refill front forks

Fig 19.3. Maintenance schedule for the Unit Singles

The more involved and time consuming of jobs all seem to stem from the bike telling you something needs doing: a change in performance, a rattle, an abnormal vibration or oil leak should all mean investigate and fix rather than ignore and carry on.

I think I personally manage to avoid a lot of mechanical misfortune because I spend time looking at and touching my bikes (perverse I know!); in effect carrying out static maintenance checks. I don't want to find that I need new petrol pipes because there is petrol dripping on the floor; I need to see the pipe first starting to crack and perish and change it then. I don't want something to drop off on the road to tell me a nut and bolt needed tightening; I need to have felt around the bike, to have nudged various parts with the heel of my hand, to have reacted to the rattle I could hear and tightened the loose bolt I found.

There may be a fine line though between the above precautionary measures and fiddling for the sake of fiddling. Going around tightening all the nuts and bolts just one more time to make sure; and shearing one off in the process, is a sure sign that you are overdoing things. 'If it ain't broke, don't fix it' and knowing where to draw the line between picking up the spanners or not is something which can only be learnt by experience.

Successful repair and maintenance of your Unit Single also depends on applying your efforts at the right 'pitch', mainly in terms of the force to use and care to apply. If you are in the habit of working with agricultural machinery then application of your favourite 2ft Stilsons to your C15 will end in disaster. At the other end of the scale is the clock repairer, who's related mechanical techniques are equally inappropriate for the Unit Single because they are, in practise, far too delicate.

With this overview in mind, your bike is definitely on the delicate side of your car for instance, when it comes to fitting or removing parts and the amounts of force and care to be applied in doing so. Applying yourself in this judicious way should save a lot of grief and is generally known as 'having a feel for it'.

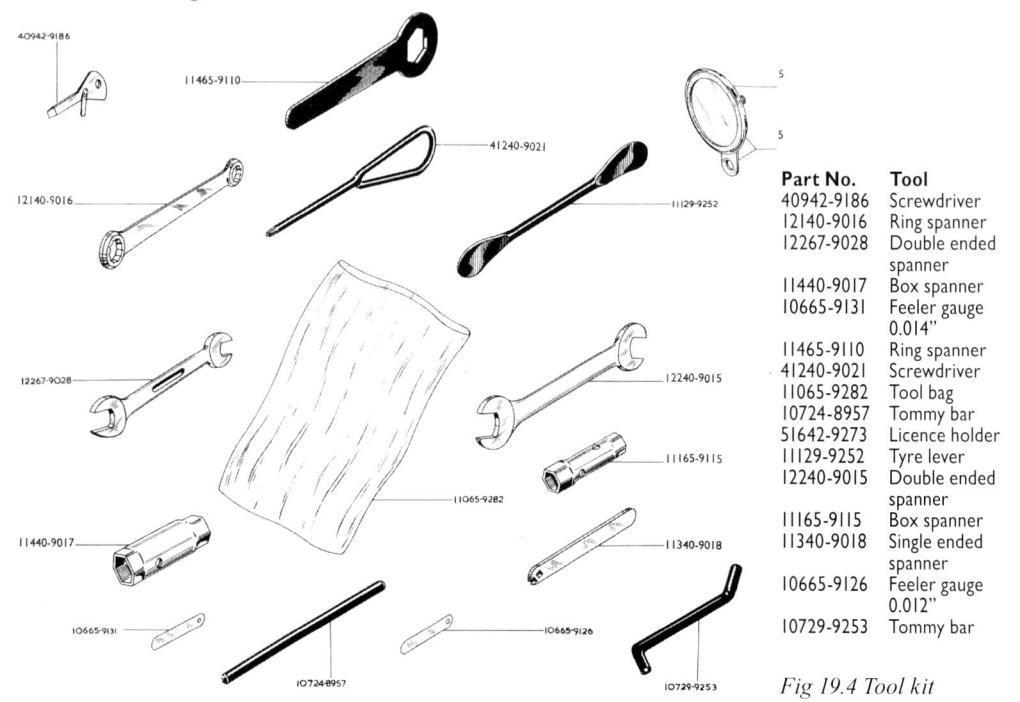

Part No.	Tool
40942-9186	Screwdriver
12140-9016	Ring spanner
12267-9028	Double ended spanner
11440-9017	Box spanner
10665-9131	Feeler gauge 0.014"
11465-9110	Ring spanner
41240-9021	Screwdriver
11065-9282	Tool bag
10724-8957	Tommy bar
51642-9273	Licence holder
11129-9252	Tyre lever
12240-9015	Double ended spanner
11165-9115	Box spanner
11340-9018	Single ended spanner
10665-9126	Feeler gauge 0.012"
10729-9253	Tommy bar

Fig 19.4 Tool kit

A popular and effective riposte to the Royal Enfield Crusader which had set the standard in the move towards light weight and unit construction. Seen here is a prototype C15 (registered 2/58), much as the production model although it appears to be fitted with a Bantam centre stand. The James Dean lookalike below is no doubt considering exactly what he is rebelling against with such a sensible machine.

20. INDEX

Air filter and housing
    Competition 232
    Filter elements 232
    Gauze 144. 151
    Housings 231-233
    Military, B40 233
    Service interval 333
Ammeter 285, 289, 291, 292, 299, 300, 302, 303, 327

Bashplate 40
Battery 310
    Box C15/B40 310, 311
    Charging C15/B40 314
    Tray '67 – '70 312
        B40 Military 313
        OIF 314
Brakes
    Adjustment
        Front 99, 100
        Rear 182
    Anchor 104, 115
    Brake rod, rear 181
    Burnishing 101
    Improvements 109, 110
    Lever, front 167
    Linings 105, 106
    Operation 103-105
    OIF Rear brake 102
    Pedal, rear 179, 181
    Plates 105, 124
    Re-lining and refitting 107-109
    Shoes 97, 107, 108
    Twin leading shoes 99, 100, 109

Capacitor
    Ignition 2MC 25, 288, 293, 298, 311
    Points 288
Centre stand 162
    C15/B40 162
    OIF 164
    Welded/Duplex frame 163
Chain 134, 135
    Wear and adjustment 136
Chainguard 140, 143
Choke lever 176
Clutch lever 167
Control cables 170
Cylinder head steady 41

Date codes 5
Decals *see* Transfers

Diode *see* Zener diode
Dip switch 306
Dip stick *see* Oil tanks

Earth wires 283
Electric box 293
Electrical components
    Illustrations 289-290
    Testing 286-288
Electrical connectors 285
Electrical fault finding 286
Ethanol fuel 216
Exhaust systems 144-159
    B50MX silencer 157-159
    Competition silencer 148
    Fitting 155
    High level 149, 150, 151
    Silencer 144-146
    Silencer bracket 156, 157

Filler cap *see* Oil tanks
Footpegs 183-188
    Competition 186
    L/H stud 184
    OIF 187
    Pillion 188
Forks, front
    Checking 57
    Forks, overhaul 58
    Interchangeability 96
    Modifications 61, 62
    Oil seal holders 80
    Removal 63
    Sliders 52, 53, 55
    Springs 87
    Stanchions 80, 81, 82
    Nuts 88-89
    Tools 59
    Trousers, C15/B40 92
    Types, identification 50
        C15 64, 65, 66
        Heavyweight 50, 52, 53, 60, 61, 66-68, 79, 92, 93
        OIF 50, 55, 60, 62, 63, 73-74, 78, 96
        Rod Damper 43, 50-55, 60-62, 66-69, 79-84, 87-89, 93
        Shuttle valve 50, 51, 54, 55, 69, 60, 63, 65, 71, 72, 81-83, 87-89
    Yokes 83-87
    Fitting 78, 79

Index

Frames *See also* Swan Neck, Welded/Duplex & OIF frames	
Checking	26
Dating	5
Numbers	2, 6
Repair	29
Types	10
Gear change lever	176
Grab rails	244, 245
Handlebars	165-166
Grips	174
Levers	103, 105, 167-168, 308
Repair	168
Straightening	166
Switches	307
Headlamps	
Brackets	92-95
Spacers	95
Shells	299-303
Repair	303, 304
Headlights	291-299
Headrace bearings	57, 76-78, 96
Horns	173, 283, 289, 290, 294-298, 307
Button	307
Mounting	297
Repair and adjustment	295
Hubs	
Front	116-120
6" full width	116, 117
7" half width	116, 117
7" full width	116, 118
7" full width TLS	116, 119
8" full width	116, 119
8" half width	116, 118
6" conical	119, 120
8" conical	119, 120
Rear	111-115
Full width	111-113
Crinkle	111, 113-114
Conical	111, 115
Ignition coil	287, 293, 310
Ignition switch	290, 292, 293, 305
Indicators	169, 2458, 249, 298-299, 307
Kickstart lever	177-179
Lights *see* Headlight, Pilot Light, Rear Light	
Light switches	290, 292, 302, 305-307
Stop light	286, 290, 308-309
Dip switch	173, 290, 302, 306, 307
Maintenance	31, 46, 115, 280, 310, 316, 322, 332-334
Model identification	3
Mudguards	
Front	249-252
Brackets	250
Mounting	91, 253
Stays	251-254
Rear	240-246
B25/B44/TR25w	241
C15/B40	240, 241
OIF models	244
Support rail	243
Number plates	
Front	254
Rear	246-248
Nuts and bolts	276-281
Finishes	280
Threads	276
Repair	281
OIF frame	25, 26
Problems	25
OIF front hub *see* Hubs	
OIF front mudguard *see* Mudguards	
Oil filters	226, 227, 228, 333
External	226
Internal	226
Oil pipes	222, 225
Oil tanks	
B25/B44/TR25w	221, 222
C15/B40	219
Central	220, 221
Cleaning	223
Filler cap/dipstick	224
Mounting	222
Repairs	222, 223
Paints	
B25	264-267
B40	263, 268
B44	266
B50 (OIF)	267, 268
C15	261-263
Compatibility	270
Modern matches	269, 270
Original colours	256-260
Triumph models	268
Paintwork	255
Part numbering	1
Petrol tanks	
B25/B44/B40 military	209-213
C15/B40	205-208
Caps	218
Mounting	201-204
Centre bolt fixing	202, 204
Rubbers	201, 202
OIF models	215
Repairs	217
Splitting	214
Triumph TR25w	213
Types	
Eyebrow	205, 261, 262
Round Badge	205, 206, 271
Pear shaped badge	205, 207, 262
Pillion footpegs *see* Footpegs	188

Pilot light	301, 304	Swinging arms	
Plated finishes (*see also* Paints)	270	Swan Neck frame	31-33
		Bushes	32
Rear hubs *see* Hubs	111	Spindle	33
Rear light	304	Welded/Duplex frame	33-37
Housing	246, 248	B44	34
Rectifier	287, 293	Bushes, Silentbloc	35
Rewiring (*see also* Wiring)	282	OIF frame	37-39
Screwthreads *see* Nuts and Bolts			
Seats	189-200	Tachometer	318, 319, 320, 324, 325, 326
B25/B44/TR25w	193	Tank badges	213, 271-273
Brackets	194	Throttle cable	171, 172, 173
C15/B40	190	Tool box B25/B44/TR25w	235, 332
Competition models	194	Tools	329-332
Cover fitting	199	Transfers (decals)	273-275
OIF models	195-197	Illustrations (colour)	*colour section*
Restoration	197	Twistgrip	171-174
Servicing *see* maintenance		Tyre inflator	41
Shock absorbers	42-49	Tyre pressures	133, 333
Application lists	48, 49	Tyres	126, 333
Assembly	45		
Bushes	45, 46	Valve lifter	174-176
Dampers	42-47		
Dismantling and checking	43, 45	Warning lights	299, 327-328
Removal	42	Welded/Duplex frame	17-23
Shrouds	47	B44 frame	19-21
Springs	46	B40 Military	21
Shuttle valve forks *see* Forks		Identification	17
Side panels	220-222, 229-240	Problems	25
B25/B44/TR25w	234-236	Wheels	
B50MX	239	Alignment	132,133
C15/B40	229	Bearings	120-122
C15 competition	231	Building	128-130
Colour (*see* paints)		Refurbishing	126
OIF models	237-238	Rims	125
Side stand	15, 25, 26, 28, 32, 160-161	Spindle spacers	113, 122, 123
Silentbloc *see* Swinging arm	35	Spokes	127,128
Spanners	278	Spoke pattern	131
Speedometer		Wiring	282-286
Cable	325-326	Earth connections	283
Chronometric	317	Connectors	285
Drive	321-325		
Magnetic	317-320	Yokes *see* Forks	
Mounting	318, 324		
Replacement	316	Zener diode	287-289, 293, 310
Revs-per-mile	319-321	Heatsink	288
Spokes *see* Wheels		Testing	287
Sprockets	137-140		
Stop light *see* Rear light, Light switches			
Swan Neck frame	10-15		
Identification	10-15		
Problems	15		
Subframe	15		